FOR Dummies
BESTSELLING BOOK SERIES

Taxes 2007 For Dummies®

Cheat Sheet

Important IRS Information

W9-DEU-922

$ **IRS Tax Forms and Publications.** Only the most commonly used forms come with your annual IRS 1040 booklet. For anything more obscure (and with the IRS, that covers a lot of ground) call **800-829-3676.** Everything (and we mean everything) is also available on the IRS Web site at www.irs.gov. In one of the niftier inventions, many of these Internet forms are available in a (secure) fill-in format. If you're in a pinch for time, hate using computers and printers, and can't wait for some oddball form by mail, you can also usually obtain forms at your local library, bank, and state and local government offices.

$ **Recorded tax information.** TeleTax, **800-829-4477** (TTY/TDD) **800-829-4059,** is a free service that provides prerecorded answers to commonly asked tax questions and can answer specific questions about what's happened to your refund. It's often quicker and more accurate than trying to find an IRS employee who knows the answer. The TeleTax service can't answer every question, but chances are good that you can find at least some of the information you're looking for there. TeleTax is available 24 hours a day, 7 days a week, 365 days a year. Your Form 1040 booklet has a complete listing of topics, or you can access the directory over the phone when you call TeleTax. Remember, you need a touch-tone phone to use TeleTax.

$ **TeleTax automated refund information.** Before you call to check on your refund, make sure that you have a copy of your tax return handy. In order to get refund information, you need to know the first Social Security number shown on your return, your filing status, and the exact whole-dollar amount of your refund. Simply phone the TeleTax number and follow the cheerful recorded instructions. The IRS updates refund information every seven days. If you call to find out about the status of your refund and don't receive a refund mailing date, wait a few days before calling back.

$ **Toll-free tax help.** The IRS prefers that you contact a local IRS office to rap about your tax questions, but help is also available at **800-829-1040.** Remember to have the necessary information at your fingertips to help you get to the root of your question or problem. Be sure to obtain the person's name and record the date (as well as the time of the call) just in case.

$ **IRS Problem Resolution Program.** Any problems you have that can't be resolved through normal channels, as we discuss in Chapter 18, may qualify for the IRS Problem Resolution Program. Begin this journey by calling **800-829-1040.** Explain your problem to a specially trained representative who will try to fix it. If the representative can't fix it, he or she will evaluate your case to see whether it meets the necessary criteria for the Problem Resolution Program. The IRS representative will then assign you to a caseworker at your local district service center. This process may take some time on the phone, but it's generally better than corresponding by mail. The process could take months if you send your letter to the wrong address (or sometimes even if you send it to the correct address).

Last-Minute Tax Tips

$ **Double-check your return for mistakes that can cost you money, time, and audits.**

Put your name and Social Security number on every page, check the arithmetic, attach W-2s and any 1099s where federal tax was withheld, and sign and date the return. Verify what you've transferred over from last year's return items that you need for this year's return.

$ **Scavenge for overlooked deductions, especially if you're self-employed.**

Determine whether you can save money by electing the filing status of married filing separately or head of household.

$ **Make sure the data is correct on the forms that you receive from financial institutions and your employer(s).**

These forms sometimes contain mistakes. Follow up promptly with the document's issuer to get errors corrected.

$ **File your extension (Form 4868), if necessary, to allow yourself enough time to fill in the forms correctly and ensure that you take all the deductions to which you're legally entitled.**

Don't make the mistake of waiting until you have the money to pay before filing. The penalty for doing so can be as much as 25 percent of the tax that you still owe. Ouch!

$ **Keep copies of everything that you file with the IRS and your state and obtain a mailing receipt if you file at the last minute and a lot of money (or a big issue) is at stake.**

You'll need documentation if you ever get audited. You may need copies of your return for other purposes, and the data on your tax returns can provide valuable insights.

Our Time-Tested Strategies for Tax-Wise Living

$ **Use tax laws to reduce your taxes.** If you educate yourself about the tax laws and incentives, you can dramatically and permanently reduce the taxes that you pay over your lifetime. Now more than ever, with the recent major tax law changes, it pays to understand tax-reduction strategies.

$ **Use retirement accounts as a simple but powerful way to reduce your income taxes.** The new tax laws dramatically increase the amount you can contribute to these accounts. Lower income earners also can get free government matching money from contributions (see Chapter 20).

$ **Take control of your taxes.** Find out enough about the tax laws by reading the relevant sections of this book so that you can prepare your own return or intelligently hire a good tax preparer. Don't forget to review your return when someone else prepares it.

$ **Try preparing your own return.** If your situation hasn't changed since last year, you're probably wasting your hard-earned dollars paying a tax preparer to plug your new numbers into this year's return. Unless your finances are complicated or the tax laws have dramatically changed in an area that affects you, try preparing your own return. If you get stuck or want another opinion, you can always go to a preparer at that point.

$ **Get, and stay, organized.** Try keeping your tax and financial documents organized year-round. This practice saves many hours not only when you prepare your tax return but also when you make important financial decisions.

$ **Remember that the IRS isn't always right.** Whether providing advice over the phone or challenging taxpayers' returns, the IRS makes mistakes, so don't panic if you get a call from Uncle Sam. If you haven't knowingly cheated or defrauded the IRS, you have little to fear from audit notices or other IRS letters. Calmly organize your supporting documents to prove your case.

$ **Learn from your return.** After you've gone to all the time and trouble of preparing your tax return, don't let that effort go to waste. Use the information to identify areas for better financial management in the coming year. Especially helpful is Part V of this book, which helps you plan ahead to take advantage of the recently passed tax law changes.

$ **The more you consume, the more you pay in taxes.** As you earn and spend your income, you not only must pay income tax on your earnings, but you also incur sales tax and other taxes on your purchases. Moreover, many of the best tax breaks available for people at all income levels are accessible only if you're able to save money to invest.

$ **Invest tax-wisely.** Don't overlook tax implications when investing your money. Remember, it isn't what you make, it's what you get to keep that matters.

$ **Don't buy real estate only for tax purposes.** Owning your own home and other real estate can be an investment that helps reduce your taxes. But don't purchase real estate just because of the tax benefits — these benefits are already reflected in the price that you pay for a property.

$ **Know when estate planning matters.** The recent tax law changes significantly increase amounts that you can pass on to your heirs and reduce the estate tax rate. Read up on this issue (see Chapter 25) so that you know when and what you need to do to arrange your financial affairs.

$ **Keep taxes in perspective.** Life has so much more to offer than just working and making money. If you do such a good job reducing your taxes that you gain great wealth, don't forget to enjoy it and share it with others.

For Dummies: Bestselling Book Series for Beginners

More Bestselling For Dummies Titles by Eric Tyson

Investing For Dummies®

The complete guide to building wealth in stocks, real estate, mutual funds, and small business. With updated coverage on everything from Internet brokerages to information sources, this friendly guide shows you how to assess your situation, gauge risks and returns, and make sound investments. Also check out the latest edition of Eric's *Mutual Funds For Dummies*!

Personal Finance For Dummies®

Discover the best ways to establish and achieve your financial goals, reduce your spending and taxes, and make wise personal finance decisions. *Wall Street Journal* bestseller with more than 1 million copies sold in all editions and winner of the Benjamin Franklin best business book award.

Home Buying For Dummies®

America's #1 real estate book includes coverage of online resources in addition to sound financial advice from Eric Tyson and frontline real estate insights from industry veteran Ray Brown. Also available from America's best-selling real estate team of Tyson and Brown — *House Selling For Dummies* and *Mortgages For Dummies*.

Real Estate Investing For Dummies®

Real estate is a proven wealth building investment but many people don't know how to go about making and managing rental property investments. Real estate and property management expert Robert Griswold and Eric Tyson cover the gamut of property investment options, strategies, and techniques.

Small Business For Dummies®

Take control of your future and make the leap from employee to entrepreneur with this enterprising guide. From drafting a business plan to managing costs, you'll profit from expert advice and real-world examples that cover every aspect of building your own business.

Taxes 2007

FOR

DUMMIES®

Taxes 2007 FOR DUMMIES®

by Eric Tyson, MBA

Financial consultant and bestselling author

Margaret Atkins Munro, EA

Tax advisor

David J. Silverman, EA

Tax advisor

Wiley Publishing, Inc.

Taxes 2007 For Dummies®

Published by
Wiley Publishing, Inc.
111 River St.
Hoboken, NJ 07030-5774
www.wiley.com

Copyright © 2007 by Eric Tyson, David J. Silverman, and Margaret Atkins Munro

Published by Wiley Publishing, Inc., Indianapolis, Indiana

Published simultaneously in Canada

For general information on our other products and services, please contact our Customer Care Department within the U.S. at 800-762-2974, outside the U.S. at 317-572-3993, or fax 317-572-4002.

For technical support, please visit www.wiley.com/techsupport.

Wiley also publishes its books in a variety of electronic formats. Some content that appears in print may not be available in electronic books.

Library of Congress Control Number: 2006934809

ISBN: 978-0-470-07901-0

Manufactured in the United States of America

10 9 8 7 6 5 4 3 2 1

1B/TQ/RR/QW/IN

About the Authors

Eric Tyson, MBA, is a bestselling author, syndicated columnist, and lecturer. He works with and teaches people from myriad income levels and backgrounds, so he knows the financial and tax questions and concerns of real folks.

After toiling away for too many years as a management consultant to behemoth financial-service firms, Eric decided to take his knowledge of the industry and commit himself to making personal financial management accessible to all of us. Despite being handicapped by a joint B.S. in Economics and Biology from Yale and an MBA from Stanford, Eric remains a master at "keeping it simple."

An accomplished freelance personal-finance writer, Eric is the author of other *For Dummies* national bestsellers on Personal Finance, Investing, Real Estate Investing, and Home Buying. His work has been critically acclaimed in hundreds of publications and programs including *Newsweek, The Los Angeles Times, Chicago Tribune, Kiplinger's Personal Finance Magazine, The Wall Street Journal,* and NBC's *Today Show,* ABC, CNBC, PBS's *Nightly Business Report,* CNN, FOX-TV, CBS national radio, Bloomberg Business Radio, and Business Radio Network.

Margaret Atkins Munro, EA, (who answers to Peggy) is a tax advisor, writer, and lecturer with more than 30 years' experience in various areas of taxation and finance with a mission in life to make taxes understandable to anyone willing to learn. Her practice is concentrated in the areas of family tax, small business, trusts, estates, and charitable foundations.

She is a graduate of The Johns Hopkins University and has also attended University College Cork (Ireland) and the Pontifical Institute of Mediaeval Studies in Toronto, and she feels that her ability to decipher the language in the Internal Revenue Code derives completely from her familiarity with a variety of obscure medieval languages.

Peggy is the author of *529 & Other College Savings Plans For Dummies*. She lectures for the IRS annually for its volunteer tax preparer programs and speaks on a variety of tax-related topics.

David J. Silverman, EA, has served on the Advisory Group to the Commissioner of Internal Revenue. David has a Certificate in Taxation from New York University and has been in private practice in Manhattan for more than 25 years.

He regularly testifies on tax issues before both the Senate Finance Committee and the House of Representatives Committee on Ways and Means. As the result of his suggestions regarding penalty reform that he made while testifying before these committees, legislation was enacted that reduced the amount of penalties that may be assessed in a number of key areas.

David is the author of *Battling the IRS,* which has received critical acclaim in *The New York Times, Money, The Wall Street Journal,* and numerous other publications. David has been a contributing editor and wrote a monthly column for *Smart Money* magazine and is frequently interviewed on national TV and radio as an expert on tax issues.

Dedication

My deepest and sincerest thanks to my family, friends, clients, and students for their enthusiastic support and encouragement. My wife, Judy, as always, gets special mention for inspiring my love of books and writing.

—Eric Tyson

None of this is worthwhile without the love of my immediate family — my husband Colin, my son Jacob, my parents-in-law MIL and FIL, and especially my parents, Cynthia and Harvey, who are proud of, but never surprised at, my achievements. To all of you, this book is a testament to your belief in me.

—Margaret Atkins Munro

To my wife, Betsy, who provided the inspiration; my late father, Louis, whose writing skills I hope I inherited; and my daughters, Joanna and Lisa, who assisted with the essential research and editing.

—David J. Silverman

Authors' Acknowledgments

Special thanks to the people at CCH, a Wolters Kluwer business — especially Glenn Borst, JD, LLM; Geralyn Jover-Ledesma, LLB, CPA; and Kenneth L. Swanson, JD, LLM, who provided the technical review. Every chapter in this book was improved by their knowledge, insights, and experience.

We also want to thank all the good people at Wiley Publishing, Inc. Special recognition goes to Mike Baker and Chad Sievers.

Publisher's Acknowledgments

We're proud of this book; please send us your comments through our Dummies online registration form located at www.dummies.com/register/.

Some of the people who helped bring this book to market include the following:

Acquisitions, Editorial, and Media Development

Project Editor: Chad R. Sievers

(Previous Edition: Chrissy Guthrie)

Acquisitions Editor: Mike Baker

Technical Editor: CCH, a Wolters Kluwer business: Glenn Borst, JD, LLM; Geralyn Jover-Ledesma, LLB, CPA; and Kenneth L. Swanson, JD, LLM

Editorial Manager: Michelle Hacker

Editorial Assistants: Erin Calligan, Joe Niesen, David Lutton

Cartoons: Rich Tennant (www.the5thwave.com)

Composition Services

Project Coordinator: Kristie Rees

Layout and Graphics: Denny Hager, Stephanie D. Jumper, Barry Offringa, Ronald Terry, Erin Zeltner

Anniversary Logo Design: Richard Pacifico

Proofreaders: Betty Kish, Jessica Kramer, Dwight Ramsey

Indexer: Anne Leach

Special Help
Vicki Adang

Publishing and Editorial for Consumer Dummies

Diane Graves Steele, Vice President and Publisher, Consumer Dummies

Joyce Pepple, Acquisitions Director, Consumer Dummies

Kristin A. Cocks, Product Development Director, Consumer Dummies

Michael Spring, Vice President and Publisher, Travel

Kelly Regan, Editorial Director, Travel

Publishing for Technology Dummies

Andy Cummings, Vice President and Publisher, Dummies Technology/General User

Composition Services

Gerry Fahey, Vice President of Production Services

Debbie Stailey, Director of Composition Services

Contents at a Glance

Contents

Introduction

*W*elcome to *Taxes 2007 For Dummies* — the up-to-date revision of our annual best-selling book by your humble authors — Eric Tyson, Margaret Atkins Munro, and David J. Silverman. We can hardly believe this book has now been in print for more than a decade! These pages answer both your tax-preparation and tax-planning questions in plain English and with a touch of humor. Our book can help you make sense of the newest tax laws. We also promise to help relieve your pain and misery (at least the tax-related portion), legally reduce your income tax bill, and get you through your tax return with little discomfort.

We also help you keep your mind on your taxes while you plan your finances for the upcoming year. As you probably know, Congress and political candidates engage in what seem like never-ending discussions about ways to tinker with the nation's tax laws. Where appropriate throughout the book, we highlight how any resulting changes may affect important decisions you'll need to make in the years ahead.

In addition to helping you understand how to deal with federal income taxes, we explain how to handle and reduce some of those pesky and not-so-insignificant taxes slapped on by states and other tax-collecting bodies.

We also show you how to steer clear of running afoul of tax laws. The fact that Congress keeps changing the tax rules makes it easy for honest and well-intentioned people to unknowingly break those laws. We explain how to clear the necessary hurdles to keep the taxing authorities from sending threatening notices and bills. But, if you do get a nasty letter from the tax police, we explain how to deal with that frightful situation in a calm, levelheaded manner so that you get the IRS off your back.

What's New in This Edition

Hardly a year goes by when there isn't some change to the nation's income tax laws. On May 17, 2006, President George W. Bush signed the *Tax Reconciliation Bill* into law. Although this bill wasn't a major tax bill from the standpoint of most individual taxpayers, some of the bill's provisions may affect your tax return for 2006 and beyond. Among some of the more significant elements of this bill that we cover in this book include

- **Alternative Minimum Tax (AMT) relief:** Increasing numbers of nonwealthy Americans are getting whacked by the AMT, but Congress provided some small relief, at least for tax year 2006. (See Chapter 8.)

- **Long-term capital gains and stock dividends tax rates:** The lower tax rates that apply to assets sold at a profit after more than one year and to dividends paid on stock holdings have been extended for a couple more years. (See Chapter 22.)

- **Roth Individual Retirement Account (IRA) conversions:** The income limits on who can convert a regular IRA will be eliminated after 2009.

- **Changed age limits for the Kiddie Tax:** Now, for tax purposes, kids get to be treated, well, like kids, for even more years. (See Chapter 24.)

We also explain how you can earn more income subject to lower income tax rates and sock more money into tax-advantaged retirement accounts. You may also be able to reduce your tax bill through the significantly lower tax rates on stock dividends and long-term capital gains, higher exemptions, credit and deductions, greater retirement plan contribution limits, and dramatically increased small business write-offs for equipment purchases.

Throughout this book, we highlight new tax provisions with this icon. Although searching for and reading passages marked with this icon quickly tells you what's new, don't overlook the many tax-reducing strategies and recommendations throughout the rest of the book.

Why Buy This Tax Book?

At their worst, some annual tax-preparation books are as dreadful as the IRS instruction booklets themselves — bulky, bureaucratic, and jargon-filled. In particular cases, preparation books simply reproduce dozens of pages of IRS instructions! At their best, these books tell you information you won't find in the IRS instructions — but the golden nuggets of tax information often are buried in massive piles of granite. *Taxes 2007 For Dummies* lays out those golden nuggets in nice, clean, display cases so that you won't miss a single one. There's still plenty of granite, but we don't use it to bury you — or key insights!

Among the three of us, we have more than seven decades of experience providing personal financial and tax advice to real people just like you. We understand your tax and financial concerns and know how to help solve your quandaries!

Most people's tax concerns fall into three categories: filling out their forms properly, legally minimizing their taxes, and avoiding interest and penalties. *Taxes 2007 For Dummies* addresses these concerns and helps take some of the pain and agony out of dealing with taxes. Here are the various practical ways that you can use this book to complete your forms, legally reduce your taxes, and avoid penalties:

- **As a reference:** For example, maybe you know a fair amount about your taxes, but you don't know where and how to report the dividends you received from some of your investments. Simply use the Table of Contents or Index to find the right spot in the book with the answers to your questions. On the other hand, if you lack investments — in part, because you pay so much in taxes — this book also explains legal strategies for slashing your taxes and boosting your savings. Use this book before and after April 15.

- **As a trusted advisor:** Maybe you're self-employed, and you know that you need to be salting money away so that you can someday cut back on those long workdays. Turn to Chapter 20 and find out about the different types of retirement accounts, which one may be right for you, how it can slash your taxes, and even where to set it up.

- **As a textbook:** If you have the time, desire, and discipline, by all means go for it and read the whole shebang. And please drop us a note and let us know of your achievement!

Your Tax Road Map

If you've already peeked at the Table of Contents, you know this book is divided into parts. Here's a brief description of what you can find in each of the six major parts.

Part I: Getting Ready to File

This part helps you understand how and why taxes work the way they do in the United States of America. You can explore how to fit taxes into your personal financial life. Here, you can also master time-tested and tax advisor–approved ways of getting organized and ready to file your tax returns. We also help you figure out what taxes you have to pay and what other tedious tax forms you're required to complete at other times of the year.

Part II: Tackling the Various Forms

In this part, we walk you through the process of completing the multiple versions of Form 1040 and confronting the typical challenges that taxpayers face. We promise not to reprint pages from the incomprehensible IRS manuals, and we try to make the process of filling out your Form 1040 as painless as possible. (*Note:* We've tried to use the final versions of forms when possible, but because the IRS doesn't take our publishing schedule into account when posting forms, we've had to use draft versions for certain ones.)

Part III: Filling Out Schedules and Other Forms

Schedules A, B, and C. No, this isn't an elementary school class! In this part, we show you, line by line, how to complete the common Form 1040 schedules — such as the ones for itemized deductions, interest and dividend income, profit and loss from a business, capital gains and losses, and so on. You'll also be happy to know that we give you a brief primer on other useful forms, such as the ones that self-employed and retired people must complete to make estimated tax payments throughout the year.

Part IV: Audits and Errors: Dealing with the IRS

No matter how hard you try to ward off nasty letters from the IRS, sooner or later you may receive that dreaded thin envelope from the friendly tax folks with a message challenging your return. The operative word here is *challenge*. As long as you think of this situation as an opportunity to play show and tell, you'll do fine.

So you'll be tickled to know that *Taxes For Dummies* goes beyond dealing with the annual ritual of filing your tax return by offering tips, counsel, and a shoulder to cry on. You find out how to sweep the IRS off your doorstep swiftly, deftly, and without breaking a sweat. And you can keep those pesky IRS agents out of your bank account while you keep yourself (and your loved ones) out of jail.

Part V: Year-Round Tax Planning

Because taxes are a year-round obligation and an important piece of your personal finance puzzle, this part provides tons of practical planning advice that you can use in May, July, October, and any other month of the year. We show you how to accomplish common financial goals, such as purchasing a home or squirreling away enough loot so you don't have to work into your 80s — all in a tax-wise manner.

You may be tempted to skip this section after you make it past April 15, but don't make that mistake. Part V can pay off in tens or even hundreds of thousands of dollars someday, saving you headaches and heartaches when you file returns each and every year.

Part VI: The Part of Tens

These top-ten lists often cover big-picture issues that cry out for top billing in their very own section. You may also enjoy plowing through these short (but highly useful) chapters.

Glossary

The pages near the back of a book about taxes usually include horrible little technical details that are best avoided by normal readers. However, here you can find a helpful glossary.

Icons Used in This Book

This target marks recommendations for making the most of your taxes and money (for example, paying off your nontax-deductible credit-card debt with your lottery winnings).

The info by this friendly sign is useful if you want to discover ways to reduce your taxes — and all the suggestions are strictly legit.

This icon is a friendly reminder of stuff we discuss elsewhere in the book or of points we really want you to remember.

This alert denotes common, costly mistakes people make with their taxes.

Don't become shark bait. This icon alerts you to scoundrels, bad advice, and scams that prey on the unsuspecting taxpayer.

This nerdy guy appears beside discussions that aren't critical if you just want to know the basic concepts and get answers to your tax questions. However, reading these gems can deepen and enhance your tax knowledge. And you never know when you'll be invited to go to a town meeting and talk tax reform with a bunch of politicians!

Tax laws keep changing — Congress continues to enact new tax laws, provisions expire, and the IRS keeps tinkering with the tax code. This icon alerts you to the new changes.

The *Military Family Relief Act* contained many provisions designed to ease the tax burden on military members. This icon shows you places where you may be able to save.

Some tax problems are too complex to be handled in any one book. If you're one of the unlucky ones who's in a tax situation that can spell big trouble if you get it wrong, consult a tax advisor to be on the safe side. We tell you how to select one in Chapter 2.

Part I
Getting Ready to File

In this part . . .

Do you feel disorganized? Do you not know where to turn for tax help? Are you in a bad mood about all the forms you must complete and the taxes you have to pay? We can't eliminate all those forms and taxes, but we can help you to think about your taxes in the context of your overall financial situation and what our great politicians do with all the money you send them. But maybe you already know that! Although complaining about government waste isn't nearly as fun, you also can find out how to get organized — and stay organized — throughout the year. And we explain how to find competent tax help, should you be at your wits' end.

Chapter 1

Understanding the U.S. Tax System

*M*ost everyone — including your humble authors — finds taxes to be a pain. First, everyone faces the chore of gathering various complicated-looking documents to complete the annual ritual of filling out IRS Form 1040 and whatever form your state may require. You may need to become acquainted with some forms that are new to you. Perhaps you need to figure out how to submit a quarterly tax payment when you no longer work for a company and now receive self-employment income from independent contract work. Maybe you sold some investments (such as stocks, mutual funds, or real estate) at a profit (or loss), and you must calculate how much tax you owe (or loss you can write off).

Whenever money passes through your hands, it seems that you pay some kind of tax. Consider the following:

✔ When you work and get paid, you pay federal, state, and local taxes (on top of having to deal with the migraines your bosses and difficult customers give you).

✔ After paying taxes on your earnings and then spending money on things you need and want (and paying more taxes in the process), you may have some money left over for investing. Guess what? Your reward for being a saver is that you also pay tax on some of the earnings on your savings.

Even if your financial life is stagnant, tax law changes during the past year may require you to complete some new forms and calculations. And, if you're like most people, you're currently missing out on some legal tax reduction tactics.

Unfortunately, too many people think of taxes only in spring, when it comes time to file that dreadful annual return. Throughout this book, you can find all sorts of tips, suggestions, and warnings that help you discover the important role that your taxes play in your entire personal financial situation year-round. In fact, we devote Part V of the book to showing you how to accomplish important financial goals while legally reducing your taxes.

A brief history of U.S. income taxes

Federal income taxes haven't always been a certainty. In the early 20th century, people lived without being bothered by the federal income tax — or by televisions, microwaves, computers, voice mail, and all those other complications. Beginning in 1913, Congress set up a system of graduated tax rates, starting with a rate of only 1 percent and going up to 7 percent.

This tax system was enacted through the 16th Amendment to the Constitution, which was suggested by President Teddy Roosevelt (a Republican), and pushed through by his successor, President William H. Taft (another Republican), and ultimately ratified by two-thirds of the states. (Sorry, Mr. Forbes, Mr. Bush, and Mr. Limbaugh — not all Republicans have been anti-tax-and-spend!) Note that we, your good authors, are independents, which means that we happily take swipes at Republicans, Democrats, and other political pundits throughout our book.

In fairness, we must tell you that the 1913 federal income tax wasn't the first U.S. income tax. President Abraham Lincoln (Republican) signed a Civil War income tax in 1861, which was abandoned a decade later.

Prior to 1913, the vast majority of tax dollars collected by the federal government came from taxes levied on goods, such as liquor, tobacco, and imports. Today, personal income taxes, including Social Security taxes, account for about 85 percent of federal government revenue.

In 1913, the forms, instructions, and clarifications for the entire federal tax system would have filled just one small, three-ring binder! (And we're not even sure that three-ring binders existed back then.) Those were, indeed, the good old days. Since then, thanks to endless revisions, enhancements, and simplifications, the federal tax laws — along with the IRS and court clarifications of those laws — can (and should) fill several dump trucks. Since World War II, the size of the federal tax code has swelled by more than 400 percent! And, according to the Tax Foundation — a nonprofit, nonpartisan policy research organization — complying with the tax laws costs everyone more than $200 billion annually.

Figuring Out the U.S. Tax System

You'll pay more in taxes than you need to if you don't understand the tax system. Who wants to pay more when you already feel like you're paying plenty and you work hard for what money you do earn?

When you try to read and make sense of the tax laws, you quickly realize that you're more likely to win the lottery than figure out some parts of the tax code! That's one of the reasons that tax attorneys and accountants are paid so much — to compensate them for their intense and prolonged agony of deciphering the tax code!

But here's a little secret to make you feel much better: You don't need to read the dreadful tax laws. Most tax advisors don't read them themselves. Instead, they rely upon summaries prepared by organizations and people who have more of a knack for explaining things clearly and concisely than the IRS does. CCH Inc. — the organization responsible for technically reviewing this fine book — has compiled a *Federal Tax Reporter* publication that details all federal tax laws. This publication now has in excess of 55,000 pages!

We hope that you include our book as a comprehensible resource you can count on. *Taxes 2007 For Dummies* helps you discover how the tax system works and how to legally make the system work for *you*. You'll quite possibly be bothered by some of the things this book shows you that don't seem fair. But getting angry enough to make the veins in your neck bulge definitely won't help your financial situation or your blood pressure. (We don't want to see your medical deductions increase!) Even if you don't agree with the entire tax system, you still have to play by the rules.

You can reduce your taxes

The tax system, like other public policies, is built around incentives to encourage desirable behavior and activity. Home ownership, for example, is considered good because it encourages people to take more responsibility for maintaining properties and neighborhoods. Therefore, the government offers all sorts of tax benefits (*allowable deductions*) to encourage people to own homes (see Chapter 23). But if you don't understand these tax benefits, you probably don't know how to take full advantage of them, either.

Even when you're an honest, earnest, well-intentioned, and law-abiding citizen, odds are that you don't completely understand the tax system. This ignorance wreaks havoc with your personal finances because you end up paying more in taxes than you need to.

Adding insult to injury, you may step on a tax land mine. Like millions of taxpayers before you, you can unwittingly be in noncompliance with the ever-changing tax laws at the federal, state, and local levels. Your tax ignorance can cause mistakes that may be costly if the IRS and your state government catch your errors. With the proliferation of computerized data tracking, discovering errors has never been easier for the tax cops at the IRS. And when they uncover your boo-boos, you have to pay the tax you originally owed *and* interest *and*, possibly, penalties. Ouch!

So don't feel dumb when it comes to understanding the tax system. You're not the problem — the complexity of the income tax system is. Making sense of the tax jungle is more daunting than hacking your way out of a triple-canopy rain forest with a dinner knife. That's why, throughout this book, we help you understand the tax system, and we promise not to make you read the actual tax laws.

You should be able to keep much more of your money by applying the tax-reducing strategies we present in this book.

- ✔ You may be able to tax shelter your employment earnings into various retirement accounts such as 401(k) and Keogh plans. This strategy slashes your current income taxes, enables your money to grow tax-free, and helps you save toward the goal of retirement.

- ✔ The less you buy, the less sales tax you pay. You can buy a less expensive, more fuel-efficient car, for example. (You'll spend less on gasoline, including gasoline taxes, as well.)

- ✔ When you invest, you can invest in a way that fits your tax situation. This strategy can make you happier and wealthier come tax time. For example, you can choose tax-friendly investments (such as tax-free bonds) that reduce your tax bill and increase your after-tax investment returns.

Beyond April 15: What you don't know can cost you

Every spring, more than 100 million tax returns (and several million extension requests) are filed with the IRS. The byproduct of this effort is guaranteed employment for the nation's more than 1 million accountants and auditors, and 2 million bookkeeping and accounting clerks (not to mention more than a few tax-book authors and their editors). Accounting firms rake in more than $30 billion annually, helping bewildered and desperately confused taxpayers figure out all those tax laws. So that you can feel okay about this situation, keep in mind that at least some of the money you pay in income taxes actually winds up in the government coffers for some useful purposes.

Given all the hours that you work each year just to pay your taxes and the time you spend actually completing the dreaded return, on April 16, you may feel like tossing the whole tax topic into a drawer or closet until next year. Such avoidance, however, is a costly mistake.

During the tax year, you can take steps to ensure that you're not only in compliance with the ever-changing tax laws, but also that you're minimizing your tax burden. If your income — like that of nearly everyone we know — is limited, you need to understand the tax code to make it work for you and help you accomplish your financial goals. The following case studies demonstrate the importance of keeping in mind the tax implications of your financial decisions throughout the year.

The costs of procrastination

Consider the case of Sheila and Peter, the proud owners of a successful and rapidly growing small business. They became so busy running the business and taking care of their children that they hardly had time to call a tax advisor. In fact, not only did they fail to file for an extension by April 15, but they also didn't pay any federal or state income taxes.

By August, Peter and Sheila finally had time to focus on the prior year's income taxes, but by then they had gotten themselves into some problems and incurred these costs:

- ✔ **A penalty for failure to file,** which is 5 percent per month of the amount due, up to a maximum of 25 percent (for five months).

- ✔ **Interest on the amount due,** which at that time was running about 9 percent per year. (*Note:* This rate is adjusted over time based on current interest rate levels.)

- ✔ **A larger tax bill** (also caused by lack of planning), which turned out to be far more expensive than the first two expenses. Because they had incorporated their business, Peter and Sheila were on the payroll for salary during the year. Despite the high level of profitability of their business, they had set their pay at too low a level.

  A low salary wouldn't seem to be a problem for the owner and only employee of a company. The worst that you'd think could happen to Peter and Sheila is that they might have to eat more peanut butter and jelly sandwiches during the year. But because they received small salaries, the contributions they could make to tax-deductible retirement accounts were based on a percentage of only their small salaries.

  The rest of the business profits, however, had to be taken by Sheila and Peter as taxable income, because they had their company set up as an S Corporation. (We explain the different types of corporations and their tax consequences in Chapter 21.) This gaffe caused Sheila and Peter to pay thousands in additional taxes, which they could've legally — and easily — avoided.

- ✔ **Loss of future investment earnings,** which means that over time Sheila and Peter actually lose more than the additional taxes. Not only did Peter and Sheila miss out on an opportunity to reduce their taxes by making larger deductible contributions to their tax-sheltered retirement accounts, but they also lost the chance for the money to compound (tax-deferred) over time.

The consequences of poor advice

Getting bad advice, especially from someone with a vested interest in your decisions, is another leading cause of tax mistakes. Consider the case of George, who wanted advice about investing and other financial matters. When he received a solicitation from a financial advisor at a well-known firm, he bit. The polished, well-dressed advisor, who was actually a *broker* (someone who earns commissions from the financial products that he or she peddles), prepared a voluminous report complete with scads of retirement projections for George.

Part of the advice in this report was for George to purchase some cash-value life insurance and various investments from the broker. The broker pitched the insurance as a great way to save, invest, and reduce George's tax burden.

Through his employer, George could invest in a retirement account on a tax-deductible basis. However, the broker conveniently overlooked this avenue — after all, the broker couldn't earn fat commissions by telling people like George to fund their employers' retirement accounts. As a result, George paid thousands of dollars more in taxes annually than he needed to.

Funding the life insurance policy was a terrible decision for George, in large part because doing so offered no upfront tax breaks. When you contribute money to tax-deductible retirement accounts, such as 401(k) plans, you get to keep and invest money you normally would've owed in federal and state income taxes. (See Chapter 20 to find out more about retirement accounts and check out Chapter 22 for the other reasons why life insurance generally shouldn't be used as an investment.)

Understanding Your Income Tax Rates

Many people remember only whether they received tax refunds or owed money on their tax returns. But you *should* care how much you pay in taxes, and you need to understand the total and the *marginal* taxes that you pay, so you can make financial decisions that lessen your tax load.

Although some people feel happy or fortunate when they get refunds, you shouldn't feel so good. All a refund really indicates is that you overpaid your taxes during the prior year. When you file your income tax return, all you do is balance your tax checkbook, so to speak, against the federal and state governments' versions of your tax checkbook. You settle up with tax authorities regarding the amount of taxes you paid during the past year versus the total tax that you actually are required to pay, based on your income and deductions.

Last year, the IRS issued more than $200 billion in individual income tax refunds. If you figure just a 5 percent interest rate from a money market fund, taxpayers threw away more than $10 billion in interest on money that they could've invested.

Total taxes

The only way to determine the total amount of income taxes you pay is to get out your federal and state tax returns. On each of those returns is a line that shows the *total tax* (line 62 on Form 1040 returns). Add the totals from your federal and state tax returns, and you probably have one of the largest expenses of your financial life (unless you have an expensive home or a huge gambling habit).

You need to note that your taxable income is different from the amount of money you earned during the tax year from employment and investments. *Taxable income* is defined as the amount of income on which you actually pay income taxes. You don't pay taxes on your total income for the following two reasons. First, not all income is taxable. For example, you pay federal income tax on the interest that you earn on a bank savings account but not on the interest from municipal bonds (which are essentially loans that you, as a bond buyer, make to state and local governments).

A second reason that you don't pay taxes on all your income is that you get to subtract deductions from your income. Some deductions are available just for being a living, breathing human being. For tax year 2006, single people receive an automatic $5,150 *standard deduction,* and married couples filing jointly get $10,300. (People older than 65 and those who are blind get slightly higher deductions.) Other expenses, such as mortgage interest and property taxes, are deductible to the extent that your total itemized deductions exceed the standard deductions.

A personal budget or spending plan that doesn't address, contain, and reduce your income taxes may be doomed to failure. Taxes are such a major portion of most people's expenditures that throughout this book we highlight strategies for reducing your taxable income and income taxes right now and in the future. Doing so is vital to your ability to save and invest money to accomplish important financial and personal goals.

Your marginal income tax rate

"What's marginal about my taxes?" we hear you asking. "They're huge! They aren't marginal at all!" *Marginal* is a word that people often use when they mean small or barely acceptable. Sort of like getting a C– on a school report card (or "just" an A– if you're from an overachieving family).

But when we're talking about taxes, *marginal* has a different meaning. The government charges you different income tax rates for different parts of your annual income. So your *marginal tax rate* is the rate that you pay on the last dollars you earn. You generally pay less tax on your *first,* or lowest, dollars of earnings and more tax on your *last,* or highest, dollars of earnings. This system is known as a graduated income tax. Graduated tax brackets are recorded in Greece as far back as 2400 B.C.

Our advice is to keep an open mind, listen to all sides, and remember the big picture. Back in the 1950s (an economic boom time), for example, the highest federal income tax rate was a whopping 90 percent, more than double its current level. And whereas during most of the past century the highest income earners paid a marginal rate that was double to triple the rate paid by moderate income earners of the time, that gap was greatly reduced during the past generation. Still, the highest income earners continue to pay the lion's share of taxes. In fact, the Congressional Budget Office recently found the top 1 percent of all income earners pay about 20 percent of all federal taxes. The top 20 percent pay slightly less than two-thirds of the total individual income taxes collected.

Are your income tax rates fair? You be the judge

Like most Americans, you probably think you pay too much in taxes. It may not be much comfort to you, but the average total taxes that citizens in the United States pay are low when compared with what citizens of other industrialized countries in Europe and Asia pay. However, low and moderate income earners in the United States pay higher income taxes than their overseas friends, and high-income earners generally pay less.

A tremendous debate rages, and much gnashing of teeth is heard, about how much high-income earners and the wealthy (relative to other taxpayers) should pay in taxes. On the far right of the political spectrum, politicians and commentators argue that burdening the people who work hard and generate jobs (that is, the high-income earners) with oppressive taxes is unfair and economically harmful. At the other end of the spectrum, you hear diehard liberals pleading that the well-heeled don't pay their fair share and need to face higher taxes to help pay for deserving programs for the poor and disadvantaged.

As with many disagreements, the people at the polar extremes think they're right (intellectually, not politically speaking) and that the other side is wrong. The politically liberal have a tendency to idealize how well government solves problems, and they therefore advocate more taxes for more programs. On the other hand, the politically conservative have a tendency to idealize how well the private sector meets the needs of society at large in the absence of government oversight and programs.

Although we can agree that easy access to tax revenue encourages some wasteful government spending and pork-laden programs, we also know that taxes must come from somewhere. The questions are how much and from whom? Equity, fairness, and stimulation of economic growth are concerns in the design of a tax system. You rarely hear blustery commentators or news programs thoughtfully discuss these issues.

The fact that *not all income is treated equally* under the current tax system isn't evident to most people. When you work for an employer and have a reasonably constant salary during the course of a year, a stable amount of federal and state taxes is deducted from each of your paychecks. Therefore, you may have the false impression that all your earned income is being taxed equally.

Table 1-1 gives the 2006 federal income tax rates for singles and for married people filing jointly.

Table 1-1	2006 Federal Income Tax Brackets and Rates	
Singles Taxable Income	*Married-Filing-Jointly Taxable Income*	*Federal Tax Rate*
Less than $7,550	Less than $15,100	10%
$7,550 to $30,650	$15,100 to $61,300	15%
$30,650 to $74,200	$61,300 to $123,700	25%
$74,200 to $154,800	$123,700 to $188,450	28%
$154,800 to $336,550	$188,450 to $336,550	33%
More than $336,550	More than $336,550	35%

Remember that your marginal tax rate is the rate of tax that you pay on your last, or so-called highest, dollars of taxable income. So, according to Table 1-1, if you're single and your taxable income during 2006 totals $36,000, for example, you pay federal income tax at the rate of 10 percent on the first $7,550 of taxable income. You then pay 15 percent on the amount from $7,550 to $30,650 and 25 percent on income from $30,650 up to $36,000. In other words, you effectively pay a marginal federal tax rate of 25 percent on your last dollars of income — those dollars in excess of $30,650.

After you understand the powerful concept of marginal tax rates, you can begin to see the value of the many financial strategies that affect the amount of taxes you pay. Because you pay taxes on your employment income and on the earnings from your investments other than retirement accounts, many of your personal financial decisions need to be made with your marginal tax rate in mind. For example, when you have the opportunity to moonlight and earn some extra money, how much of that extra compensation you get to keep depends on your marginal tax rate. Your marginal income tax rate enables you to quickly calculate the additional taxes you'd pay on the additional income.

Conversely, you quantify the amount of taxes that you save by reducing your taxable income, either by decreasing your income — for example, with pretax contributions to retirement accounts — or by increasing your deductions.

Actually, you can make even more of your marginal taxes. In the next section, we detail the painful realities of income taxes levied by most states that add to your federal income burden. If you're a middle-to-higher income earner, pay close attention to the section later in this chapter where we discuss the *Alternative Minimum Tax*. And as we discuss elsewhere in this book, some tax breaks are reduced when your income exceeds a particular level — here are some examples:

✔ Itemized deductions, which we discuss in Chapter 9 and record on Schedule A, are reduced for tax year 2006 when your *adjusted gross income* (AGI — total income before subtracting deductions) exceeds $150,500 ($75,250 for married persons filing separately).

✔ Personal exemptions are a freebie — they're a write-off of $3,300 in tax year 2006 just because you're a living, breathing, human being. However, personal exemptions are whittled away for single-income earners with AGIs of more than $150,500, married people filing jointly with AGIs of more than $225,750, and married persons filing separately with AGIs of more than $112,875.

✔ If you own rental real estate, you may normally take up to a $25,000 annual loss when your expenses exceed your rental income. Your ability to deduct this loss begins to be limited when your AGI exceeds $100,000.

✔ Your eligibility to fully contribute to *Roth Individual Retirement Accounts* (see Chapter 20) depends on your AGI being less than or equal to $95,000 if you're a single taxpayer or $150,000 if you're married. Beyond these amounts, allowable contributions are phased out.

Your marginal income tax rate — the rate of tax you pay on your last dollars of income — should be higher than your average tax rate — the rate you pay, on average, on all your earnings. The reason your marginal tax rate is more important for you to know is that it tells you the value of legally reducing your taxable income. So, for example, if you're in the federal 28 percent tax bracket, for every $1,000 that you can reduce your taxable income, you shave $280 off your federal income tax bill.

State income taxes

Note that your *total marginal rate* includes your federal and state income tax rates. As you may already be painfully aware, you don't pay only federal income taxes. You also get hit with state income taxes — that is, unless you live in Alaska, Florida, Nevada, South Dakota, Texas, Washington, or Wyoming. Those states have no state income taxes. As is true with federal income taxes, state income taxes have been around since the early 1900s.

You can look up your state tax rate by getting out your most recent year's state income tax preparation booklet. Alternatively, we've been crazy — but kind — enough to prepare a helpful little (okay, not so little) table that can give you a rough idea of your state tax rates (see Table 1-2). This table reflects state individual income taxes. Some states impose other taxes, such as local, county, or city taxes, special taxes for nonresidents, or capital gains taxes, which aren't included in this table.

Table 1-2	State Marginal Tax Rates					
State	**Filing Status***	**Taxable Income**			
		$25,000+	**$50,000+**	**$100,000+**	**$250,000+**
Alabama	All	5%	5%	5%	5%
Alaska		(No personal income tax)			
Arizona	Singles	3.74%	4.72%	4.72%	5.04%
	Marrieds	3.2%	3.2%	3.74%	4.72%
Arkansas	All	6%	7%	7%	7%
California	Singles	6%	9.3%	9.3%	9.3%
	Marrieds	2%	6%	9.3%	9.3%
Colorado	All	4.63%	4.63%	4.63%	4.63%

State	Filing Status*	Taxable Income			
		$25,000+	**$50,000+**	**$100,000+**	**$250,000+**
Connecticut	All	5%	5%	5%	5%
Delaware	All	5.2%	5.55%	5.95%	5.95%
District of Columbia	All	7%	8.7%	8.73%	8.7%
Florida		(No personal income tax)			
Georgia	All	6%	6%	6%	6%
Hawaii	Singles	7.60%	8.25%	8.25%	8.25%
	Marrieds	6.80%	7.60%	8.25%	8.25%
Idaho	Singles	7.8%	7.8%	7.8%	7.8%
	Marrieds	7.8%	7.8%	7.8%	7.8%
Illinois	All	3%	3%	3%	3%
Indiana	All	3.4%	3.4%	3.4%	3.4%
Iowa	All	6.8%	8.98%	8.98%	8.98%
Kansas	Singles	6.25%	6.45%	6.45%	6.45%
	Marrieds	3.5%	6.25%	6.45%	6.45%
Kentucky	All	5.8%	5.8%	6%	6%
Louisiana	Singles	6%	6%	6%	6%
	Marrieds	4%	6%	6%	6%
Maine	Singles	8.5%	8.5%	8.5%	8.5%
	Marrieds	7.0%	8.5%	8.5%	8.5%
Maryland	All	4.75%	4.75%	4.75%	4.75%
Massachusetts	All	5.3%	5.3%	5.3%	5.3%
Michigan	All	3.9%	3.9%	3.9%	3.9%
Minnesota	Singles	7.05%	7.05%	7.85%	7.85%
	Marrieds	5.35%	7.05%	7.05%	7.85%
Mississippi	All	5%	5%	5%	5%
Missouri	All	6%	6%	6%	6%
Montana	All	6.9%	6.9%	6.9%	6.9%
Nebraska	Singles	5.12%	6.84%	6.84%	6.84%
	Marrieds	3.57%	6.84%	6.84%	6.84%
Nevada		(No broad-based income tax)			
New Hampshire	All	–5% only on dividend and interest income on stocks and bonds			

(continued)

Table 1-2 (continued)

State	Filing Status*	Taxable Income			
		$25,000+	$50,000+	$100,000+	$250,000+
New Jersey	Singles	1.75%	5.525%	6.37%	6.37%
	Marrieds	1.75%	2.45%	5.525%	6.37%
New Mexico	All	6%	6%	6%	6%
New York	Singles	6.85%	6.85%	7.25%	7.25%
	Marrieds	5.25%	6.85%	6.85%	7.25%
North Carolina	All	7%	7%	7.75%	8.25%
North Dakota	Singles	2.10%	3.92%	4.34%	5.04%
	Marrieds	2.10%	3.92%	3.92%	5.04%
Ohio	All	4.27%	4.983%	6.61%	7.185%
Oklahoma	All	6.65%	6.65%	6.65%	6.65%
Oregon	All	9%	9%	9%	9%
Pennsylvania	All	3.07%	3.07%	3.07%	3.07%
Rhode Island	All	Flat rate of 25% of federal income tax liability			
South Carolina	All	7%	7%	7%	7%
South Dakota		(No personal income tax)			
Tennessee	All	–6% on interest and dividends from stocks and bonds			
Texas		(No personal income tax)			
Utah	All	7%	7%	7%	7%
Vermont	Singles	3.6%	7.2%	8.5%	9%
	Marrieds	3.6%	7.2%	7.2%	9%
Virginia	All	5.75%	5.75%	5.75%	5.75%
Washington		(No personal income tax)			
West Virginia	All	4.5%	6%	6.5%	6.5%
Wisconsin	All	6.5%	6.5%	6.5%	6.75%
Wyoming		(No personal income tax)			

* Filing status "married" refers only to married couples who file jointly.

The second tax system: Alternative Minimum Tax

You may find this hard to believe, but there's actually a second federal income tax system (yes, we groan with you as we struggle to understand even the first complicated tax system). This second system may raise your income taxes higher than they'd otherwise be.

Through the years, as the government has grown hungrier for revenue, taxpayers who slash their taxes by claiming many deductions have come under greater scrutiny. So the government created a second tax system — the *Alternative Minimum Tax (AMT)* — to ensure that higher income earners with relatively high amounts of itemized deductions pay at least a minimum amount of taxes on their incomes.

If you have a bunch of deductions from state income taxes, real estate taxes, certain types of mortgage interest, or passive investments (such as limited partnerships or rental real estate), you may fall prey to the AMT. The AMT is a classic case of the increasing complexity of our tax code. As incentives were placed in the tax code, people took advantage of them. Then the government said, "Whoa, Nelly! We can't have people taking *that* many write-offs." Rather than doing the sensible thing and limiting some of those deductions, Congress created the AMT instead.

The AMT restricts you from claiming certain deductions and requires you to increase your taxable income. So you must figure the tax you owe under the AMT system *and* under the other system and then pay whichever amount is *higher* (ouch!). Unfortunately, the only way to know for certain whether you're ensnared by this second tax system is by completing — you guessed it — another tax form (see Chapter 8).

Chapter 2

Tax Return Preparation Options and Tools

*B*y the time you actually get around to filing your annual income tax return, it's too late to take advantage of many tax-reduction strategies for that tax year. And what can be more aggravating than, late in the evening on April 14 when you're already stressed out and unhappily working on your return, finding a golden nugget of tax advice that works great — if only you'd known about it last December!

Be sure to review Part V, which covers the important tax-planning issues that you need to take advantage of in future years. In the event that you've waited until the last minute to complete your return this year, be sure to read Part V thoroughly after you file your return so you don't miss out next year.

If you're now faced with the daunting task of preparing your return, you're probably trying to decide how to do it with a minimum of pain and taxes owed. You have several options for completing your return. The best choice for you depends on how complex your tax situation is, how much you know about taxes, and how much time you're willing to invest.

Preparing Your Own Return

You already do many things for yourself. Maybe you cook for yourself, do home repairs, or even change your car's oil. You may do these tasks because you enjoy them, because you save money by doing them, or because you want to develop a particular skill.

Sometimes, however, you hire others to help you do the job. Occasionally, you may buy a meal out or hire someone to make a home improvement. And so it can be with your annual income tax return — you may want to hire help, but you may end up, like most people, preparing your own return.

Doing your own income tax return is an especially good option if your financial situation doesn't change much from year to year. You can use last year's return as a guide, filling in the new numbers, doing the required mathematical operations on the new return, making a copy of your completed return (you always need to keep a copy of your tax return for your files), and mailing it.

You may need to do some reading to keep up with the small number of changes in the tax system and laws that affect your situation (this book can help). Given the constant changes to various parts of the tax laws, you simply can't assume that the tax laws that apply to your situation are the same from one year to the next just because your situation is the same.

Another benefit of preparing your own return includes the better financial decisions that you make in the future by using the tax knowledge you gain from learning about the tax system. Most tax preparers are so busy preparing returns that you probably won't get much of their time to discuss tax laws and how they may apply to your future financial decisions. Even if you can schedule time with the preparer, you may end up sitting in his or her office thinking about how much more your bill will reflect when he or she adds the cost of the personal tutorial you're sitting through.

Last, but not least, doing your own return should be your lowest-cost tax-return-preparation option. Of course, we're assuming that you don't make costly mistakes and oversights and that the leisure time you forego when preparing your return isn't too valuable!

You bought this book, which was a smart move. You're confident enough to tackle the tax forms yourself, and you're savvy enough to know you need expert guidance through the thicket of annual tax law changes. Give our advice a try before throwing in the towel and paying hundreds (perhaps thousands) of dollars in tax-preparation fees. And if you stay alert while preparing your return, reading the list of deductions that don't apply to you may motivate you to make changes in your personal and financial habits so that you *can* take some of those deductions next year.

Using IRS Publications

In addition to the instructions that come with the annual tax forms that the good old Internal Revenue Service mails to you every year, the IRS also produces hundreds of publications that explain how to complete the myriad tax forms various taxpayers must tackle. These booklets are available in printed form or through the IRS's Web site (www.irs.gov; see the section "Internal Revenue Service" later in this chapter for more on what the site has to offer) or by mail if you simply call and order them from the IRS (800-829-3676). Additionally, the IRS provides answers to common questions through its automated phone system and through live representatives. If you have a simple, straightforward tax return, completing it on your own using only the IRS instructions may be fine. This approach is as cheap as you can get, costing only your time, patience, photocopying expenses, and postage to mail the completed tax return.

Unfortunately (for you), IRS publications and employees don't generally offer the direct, helpful advice that we provide in this book. For example, here's something you don't see in an IRS publication:

> STOP! One of the most commonly overlooked deductions is . . . You still have time to . . . and whack off hundreds — maybe thousands — of dollars from your tax bill! HURRY!

Another danger in relying on the IRS for assistance is that it has been known to give wrong information and answers. When you call the IRS with a question, be sure to take notes about your phone conversation, thus protecting yourself in the event of an audit. Date your notes and include the name of the IRS employee (and office location and employee number) with whom you spoke, what you asked, and the employee's responses. File your notes in a folder with a copy of your completed return.

In addition to the standard instructions that come with your tax return, the IRS offers some pamphlets that you can request by phone such as:

- ✓ **Publication 17:** Your Federal Income Tax is designed for individual tax-return preparation.
- ✓ **Publication 334:** Tax Guide for Small Business (For Individuals Who Use Schedule C or C-EZ) is for (you guessed it) small-business tax-return preparation.

These guides provide more detail than the basic IRS publications. Call 800-TAX-FORM (800-829-3676 for those who hate searching for letters on phone keypads) to request these free guides. (Actually, nothing is free. You've already paid for IRS guides with your tax dollars!)

The IRS also offers more in-depth booklets focusing on specific tax issues. However, if your tax situation is so complex that this book (and Publications 17 and 334) can't address it, you need to think long and hard about getting help from a tax advisor or from one of the other sources recommended in the "Hiring Help" section later in this chapter.

IRS publications present plenty of rules and facts, but they don't make it easy for you to find the information and advice you really need. The best way to use IRS publications is to *confirm facts* that you already think you know or to check the little details. Don't expect IRS publications and representatives to show you how to cut your tax bill.

Perusing Tax-Preparation and Advice Guides

Privately published tax-preparation and advice books are invaluable when they highlight tax-reduction strategies and possible pitfalls — in clear, simple English. We hope you agree with the reviewer comments in the front of this guide that say *Taxes For Dummies* is top of the line in this category. Such books help you complete your return accurately and save you as much money as possible. The amount of money invested in a book or two is significantly smaller than the annual cost of a tax expert.

Taxes For Dummies covers the important tax-preparation and planning issues that affect the vast majority of taxpayers. A minority of taxpayers may run into some nitpicky tax issues caused by unusual events in their lives or extraordinary changes in their incomes or assets. This book may not be enough for those folks. In such cases, you need to consider hiring a tax advisor, which we explain how to do later in this chapter (see the section, "Hiring Help").

Buying Software

If you don't want to slog through dozens of pages of tedious IRS instructions or pay a tax preparer hundreds of dollars to complete your annual return, you may be interested in computer software that can help you finish off your IRS **Form 1040** and supplemental schedules. If you have access to a computer and printer, tax-preparation software can be a helpful tool.

Tax-preparation software also gives you the advantage of automatically recalculating all the appropriate numbers on your return if one number changes — no more painting out math errors with a little white brush or recalculating a whole page of figures because your dog was sleeping on some of the receipts. (Just don't let your cat walk on your keyboard or another family member use the computer before saving and printing out your return!) The best tax-preparation software is easy to install and use on your computer, provides help when you get stuck, and highlights deductions you may overlook.

Before plunking down your hard-earned cash for some tax-preparation software, know that it has potential drawbacks. Here are the big ones:

✔ **Garbage in, garbage out.** A tax return prepared by a software program is only as good as the quality of the data you enter into it. Of course, this drawback exists no matter who actually fills out the forms; some human tax preparers don't probe and clarify to make sure that you've provided all the right stuff, either. Tax software programs also may contain glitches that can lead to incorrect calculating or reporting of some aspect of your tax return.

✔ **Where's the beef?** Some tax software packages give little in the way of background help, advice, and warnings. This lack of assistance can lull you into a false sense of security about the completeness and accuracy of the return you prepare.

✔ **Think, computer, think!** Computers are good at helping you access and process information. Remember that your computer is great at crunching numbers but has a far lower IQ than you have!

TaxCut and *TurboTax* are the leading programs, and they do a reasonable job of helping you through the federal tax forms. One way to break a tie between good software options is considering price — you may be able to get a better deal on one software package. (*TurboTax* carries a higher suggested retail price.) Procrastinating also offers some benefits, because the longer you wait to buy the software, the cheaper it generally gets — especially when you buy it after filing for an extension. (You may also want to examine whether the tax software you buy can import the data from the checkbook software you've been using to track your tax-deductible expenses throughout the year.)

Accessing Internet Tax Resources

In addition to using your computer to prepare your income tax return, you can do an increasing number of other tax activities via the Internet. The better online tax resources are geared more to tax practitioners and tax-savvy taxpayers. But in your battle to legally minimize your taxes, you may want all the help you can get! Use the Internet for what it's best at doing — possibly saving you time tracking down factual information or other stuff.

On the Internet, many Web sites provide information and discussions about tax issues. Take advice and counsel from other Net users at your peril. We don't recommend that you depend on the accuracy of the answers to tax questions that you ask in online forums. The problem: In many cases you can't be sure of the background, expertise, or identity of the person with whom you're trading messages. However, if you want to liven up your life — and taxes make you mad — a number of political forums enable you to converse and debate with others. You can complain about recent tax hikes or explain why you think that the wealthy still don't pay enough taxes!

The following sections describe some of the better sites out there.

Internal Revenue Service

When you think of the Internal Revenue Service — the U.S. Treasury Department office charged with overseeing the collection of federal income taxes — you probably think of the following adjectives: bureaucratic, humorless, and stodgy. Difficult as it is to believe, the IRS Web site (www.irs.gov) offers fun graphics and some mildly amusing writing. For example, one headline article on the IRS's homepage was "Teenager Tanya Taylor Tries to Tackle

Taxation Training Interactively." The article was about a then high school junior Tanya Taylor of Tyler, Texas, taking home her first paycheck. "Many of my friends thought they got to keep *all* of their pay," Tanya chuckled, adding, "Boy, were they shocked to see all of the deductions! Fortunately, my boss gave me a heads-up of what to expect." The article goes on to explain how Tanya's employer had Tanya visit the IRS Web site so she could find out about the taxes that are deducted from her paycheck and where that money goes.

The IRS site also has links to state tax organizations, convenient access to IRS forms (including those from prior tax years), and instructions. To be able to read and print the forms, you need a software program like Adobe Acrobat Reader, which you can download for free from many Internet sites, including the IRS site or the Adobe Web site at `www.adobe.com`. To download forms from the IRS site, start browsing at `www.irs.gov/formspubs/index.html`.

You can complete your tax forms online at the IRS site using Adobe Acrobat Reader. The IRS site even features a place for you to submit comments on proposed tax regulations, with a promise that the "comments are fully considered." Is this the IRS we know and love?

Directories

A number of sites on the Web claim to be *directories*. Be forewarned that some sites marketing themselves as providing collections of all the best tax stuff on the Internet may not be nearly as objective as they lead you to believe. Some sites may simply provide links to other sites that pay them a referral fee.

Dennis Schmidt's Tax and Accounting Sites Directory (`www.taxsites.com`) is organized into various categories, such as state taxes, tax forms, software, and law. This site is a comprehensive collection of tax Web sites. There are no frills, graphics, reviews, or even commentary. Schmidt is a professor of accounting at the University of Northern Iowa.

Research

For true tax junkies, the U.S. Tax Code Online (`www.fourmilab.ch/ustax/ustax.html`) is a search engine that enables you to check out the complete text of the IRS. Hyperlinks embedded in the text provide cross-references between sections at the click of a mouse. (We know we promised not to subject you to the tax code, but if you're interested, it's all laid out for you.) And, if you really have nothing better to do with your time, check out the government sites with updated information on tax bills in Congress (`www.house.gov/jct/` and `http://waysandmeans.house.gov/`).

CCH Inc.'s site (`www.cch.com`) is geared toward tax and legal professionals who need to keep up with and research the tax laws. Access to most of the site's resources is granted by subscription only.

Tax preparation sites

A number of Web sites enable you to prepare federal and state tax forms and then file them electronically. Many of these sites allow you to prepare and file your federal forms for free if you access their site through the IRS Web site. Just go to `www.irs.gov`, and click on any link for "Free File" to see if you qualify. If you access a tax preparation site directly instead, you may have to pay a fee for a service that would be free through the Free File program.

For example, at H&R Block's site (www.hrblock.com), you enter your data on interview forms that are provided, and the necessary calculations are performed. Although using the Web site to perform your calculations is free of charge, H&R Block charges you $9.95 if you want to print your filled-out IRS forms (requires using Adobe Acrobat Reader software) or file them electronically through the site. Preparing and filing state forms (most, but not all, state forms are available on the site) costs extra ($14.95).

If you don't want to use "Free File," a reasonable priced alternative worth your consideration can be found at CCH Inc.'s Complete Tax Web site (www.completetax.com), where you enter data on interview forms and calculate your tax. For only $34.90, you can print your completed return and electronically file your tax return with the IRS and any state that accepts electronic returns.

Unless you're using a speedy modem connection on your computer (such as a cable modem or DSL connection), preparing tax forms online can be painfully slow compared to having a software program on your hard drive. Remember that if you're simply after the tax forms, plenty of the sites mentioned in this section offer such documents for free as do public libraries and post offices.

Hiring Help

Because they lack the time, interest, energy, or skill to do it themselves, some people hire a contractor to handle a home-remodeling project. And most people who hire a contractor do so because they think that they can afford to hire a contractor. (Although sometimes this last part isn't true, and they wind up with more debt than they can afford!)

For some of the same reasons, some people choose to hire a tax preparer and advisor. By identifying tax-reduction strategies that you may overlook, competent tax practitioners can save you money — sometimes more than enough to pay their fees. They may also reduce the likelihood of an audit, which can be triggered by blunders that you may make. Like some building contractors, however, some tax preparers take longer, charging you more and not delivering the high-quality work you expect.

Deciding whether you really need a preparer

Odds are quite good that you can successfully prepare your own return. Most people's returns don't vary that much from year to year, so you have a head start and can hit the ground running if you get out last year's return — which, of course, you copied and filed!

Preparing your own return may not work as well whenever your situation has changed in some way — if you bought or sold a house, started your own business, or retired, for example. In such an event, start by focusing on the sections of this book in Parts II and III that deal with those preparation issues. If you want more planning background, check out the relevant chapters in Part V.

Don't give up and hire a preparer just because you can't bear to open your tax-preparation booklet and get your background data organized. Even if you hire a tax preparer, you still need to get your stuff organized before a consultation.

As hard and as painful as it is, confront preparing your return as far in advance of April 15 as you can so that if you feel uncomfortable with your level of knowledge, you have enough time to seek help. The more organizing you can do before hiring a preparer, the less having your return prepared should cost you. Avoid waiting until the 11th hour to hire an advisor — you won't do as thorough a job of selecting a competent person, and you'll probably pay more for the rush job. If you get stuck preparing the return, you can get a second opinion from other preparation resources we discuss in this chapter.

If you decide to seek out the services of a tax preparer/advisor, know that tax practitioners come with various backgrounds, training, and credentials. One type of professional isn't necessarily better than another. Think of them as different types of specialists who are appropriate for different circumstances. The four main types of tax practitioners are preparers, enrolled agents, certified public accountants, and tax attorneys.

Preparers

Among all the tax practitioners, *preparers* generally have the least amount of training, and more of them work part time. H&R Block is the largest and most well-known tax-preparation firm in the country. In addition, other national firms and plenty of mom-and-pop shops are in the tax-preparation business.

The appeal of preparers is that they're relatively inexpensive — they can do basic returns for $100 or so. The drawback is that you may hire a preparer who doesn't know much more than you do! As with financial planners, no national regulations apply to tax-return preparers, and no licensing is required. In most states, almost anybody can hang out a tax-preparation shingle and start preparing. Most preparers, however, complete some sort of training program before working with clients.

Preparers make the most sense for folks who don't have complicated financial lives, who are budget-minded, and who dislike doing their own taxes. If you aren't good about hanging onto receipts or don't want to keep your own files with background details about your taxes, you definitely need to shop around for a tax preparer who's going to be around for a few years. You may need all that paperwork stuff someday for an audit, and some tax preparers keep and organize their clients' documentation rather than return everything each year. (Can you blame them for keeping your records after they go through the tedious task of sorting them all out of the shopping bags?) Going with a firm that's open year-round may also be safer, in case tax questions or problems arise (some small shops are open only during tax season).

Enrolled agents (EAs)

A person must pass IRS scrutiny to be called an *enrolled agent (EA)*. This license enables the agent to represent you before the IRS in the event of an audit. The training to become an EA generally is longer and more sophisticated than that of a typical preparer. Continuing education also is required; EAs must complete at least 24 hours of continuing education each year to maintain their licenses.

Enrolled agents' prices tend to fall between those of a preparer and a certified public accountant (we discuss CPAs in the next section). Tax returns with a few of the more common schedules (such as Schedule A for deductions and Schedule B for interest and dividends) shouldn't cost more than a couple hundred dollars to prepare. If you live in an area with a relatively high cost of living, expect to pay more.

The main difference between enrolled agents and CPAs and attorneys is that EAs work exclusively in the field of taxation, which makes them more likely to stay attuned to the latest tax developments. Not all CPAs and attorneys do. In addition to preparing your return (including simple to complex forms), good EAs can help with tax planning, represent you at audits, and keep the IRS off your back. You can find names and telephone numbers of EAs in your area by contacting the National Association of Enrolled Agents (202-822-6232; www.naea.org).

Certified public accountants (CPAs)

Certified public accountants (CPAs) go through significant training and examination to receive the CPA credential. To maintain this designation, a CPA must complete at least 40 hours worth of continuing education classes every year.

CPA fees vary tremendously. Most charge around $100 per hour, but CPAs at large accounting firms and in high-cost-of-living areas tend to charge somewhat more. Some CPAs charge $300-plus per hour.

Competent CPAs are of greatest value to people completing some of the more unusual and less user-friendly schedules, such as K-1 for partnerships. CPAs also are helpful for people who had a major or first-time tax event during the year, such as the childcare tax-credit determination. (Good EAs and other preparers can handle these issues as well.)

Whenever your return is uncomplicated and your financial situation is stable, hiring a high-priced CPA year after year to fill in the blanks on your tax returns is a waste of money. A CPA once bragged to Eric (your humble coauthor of this book) that he was effectively making more than $500 per hour from some of his clients' returns that required only 20 minutes of an assistant's time to complete.

Paying for the additional cost of a CPA on an ongoing basis makes sense if you can afford it and if your financial situation is reasonably complex or dynamic. If you're self-employed and/or file many other schedules, hiring a CPA may be worth it. But you needn't do so year after year. If your situation grows more complex one year and then stabilizes, consider getting help for the perplexing year and then using other preparation resources discussed in this chapter or a lower-cost preparer or enrolled agent in the future.

If you desire more information about CPAs in your area, we suggest that you contact the local organization of CPAs in your state. To locate your state's group, call toll-free directory assistance at 800-555-1212 and ask for the number for your state's "Society" or "Association" of CPAs. You can also visit the American Institute of Certified Public Accountants listing of state CPA associations and useful state tax links at `www.aicpa.org/states/info/index.htm`. If you're considering hiring a CPA, be sure to ask how much of his or her time is spent preparing individual income tax returns and returns like yours.

Who's best qualified — EA, CPA, or preparer?

Who is best qualified to prepare your return? That really depends on the individual you want to hire. The CPA credential is just that, a credential. Some people who have the credential will try to persuade you not to hire someone without it, but don't always believe this advice.

Some tax-preparation books perpetuate the myth that only a CPA can do your taxes. In one such book, in a chapter about choosing a tax preparer, entitled "How to Prepare for Your Accountant," the authors say, "Choosing an accountant isn't something that should be done casually. There are more than 300,000 certified public accountants." These authors then recommend that you ask a potential preparer, "Are you a certified public accountant?" (As you may have guessed, the firm behind the book is a large CPA company.)

What about all the non-CPAs, such as EAs, who do a terrific job helping prepare their clients' returns and tax plans throughout the year?

If you can afford to and want to pay hundreds of dollars per hour, hiring a large CPA firm can make sense. But for the vast majority of taxpayers, spending that kind of money is unnecessary and wasteful. Many EAs and other tax preparers are out there doing outstanding work for less.

Tax attorneys

Unless you're a super-high-income earner with a complex financial life, hiring a *tax attorney* to prepare your annual return is prohibitively expensive. In fact, many tax attorneys don't prepare returns as a normal practice. Because of their level of specialization and training, tax attorneys tend to have high hourly billing rates — $200 to $400-plus per hour isn't unusual.

Tax attorneys sometimes become involved in court cases dealing with tax problems, disagreements, or other complicated matters, such as the purchase or sale of a business. Other good tax advisors also can help with these issues.

The more training and specialization a tax practitioner has (and the more affluent the clients), the higher the hourly fee. Select the one that best meets your needs. Fees and competence at all levels of the profession vary significantly. If you aren't sure of the quality of work performed and the soundness of the advice, get a second opinion.

Finding Tax Preparers and Advisors

The challenge for you is to locate a tax advisor who does terrific work, charges reasonable fees, and thus is too busy to bother calling to solicit you! Here are some resources to find those publicity-shy, competent, and affordable tax advisors:

- ✔ **Friends and family:** Some of your friends and family members probably use tax advisors and can steer you to a decent one or two for an interview.

- ✔ **Coworkers:** Ask people in your field what tax advisors they use. This strategy can be especially useful if you're self-employed.

- ✔ **Other advisors:** Financial and legal advisors also can be helpful referral sources, but don't assume that they know more about the competence of a tax person than you do. Beware of a common problem: Financial or legal advisors may simply refer you to tax preparers who send them clients.

- ✔ **Associations:** EAs and CPAs maintain professional associations that can refer you to members in your local area. See the relevant sections earlier in this chapter.

Never decide to hire a tax preparer or advisor solely on the basis of someone else's recommendation. To ensure that you're hiring someone who is competent and with whom you will work well, please take the time to interview at least two or three prospective candidates. In Chapter 29, we list key questions that you need to ask prospective tax advisors before hiring them. Because you've gone to the trouble and expense of tracking down this book, please make use of it — you've got many more chapters to check out. The more you know before you seek a tax advisor's services, the better able you'll be to make an informed decision and reduce your expenditures on tax preparers.

Chapter 3

Getting and Staying Organized

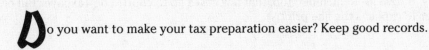

Do you want to make your tax preparation easier? Keep good records.

Do you want to make sure you claim every deduction you're entitled to? Keep good records.

Do you want to survive an IRS audit and not pay additional tax, interest, or penalties? Keep good records.

Do you want to save money by not paying tax preparers $50 to $200 or more an hour to organize your stuff? Keep good records.

If you're like most people, you probably aren't a good bookkeeper. But without good records, you may be in trouble, especially if you're ever audited. Furthermore, some tax preparers and accountants love to see you walk into their offices with shoeboxes full of receipts. Knowing that they can charge you a hefty hourly fee and then turn around and pay someone else $20 an hour to organize your receipts brightens their day.

Life is filled with many challenges, and compiling your tax records is certainly one of them. Look at this step as an opportunity to connect with your past — you may not find only tax records for the most recent year, but you may also find old report cards or to-do lists from five years ago (that still have unfinished business). Taking the time to rummage is often worth it. You may finally be able to itemize your deductions this year, but you first need to be able to produce those charitable receipts, medical bills, and mortgage and real estate tax bills.

A recent General Accounting Office report revealed that more than one million taxpayers overpaid the IRS more than half a billion dollars by using the standard deduction rather than itemizing their deductions on Schedule A. We tell you how to avoid this disaster in Chapter 9. What is disturbing about this report is that half of these taxpayers used tax preparers to do their returns.

Finally, perhaps you can easily imagine yourself the night before an IRS audit wondering how you're going to support your claim for all those business entertainment costs. Do you know what happens when you're audited and you can't document your claims? First, you get socked with additional tax and interest. Then come the penalties — and the IRS has a lengthy list of them.

But enough horror stories! You know that you must take some steps now to avoid the misery associated with not keeping good records. Although resurrecting your records for this current tax return may be impossible, it isn't too late to establish good habits for next year. In this chapter, you discover a few tried and proven ways of keeping track of everything you need to survive — not only this tax-preparation season, but also in future tax situations.

To deal effectively with the IRS, you need documentation, because the tax laws place the burden of proof primarily on the taxpayer. Do you think this policy means that you're guilty until proven innocent? Unfortunately, the answer is *yes*. But don't let that depress you. Remember that you need to produce documentation only if you're audited. Even if you're not being audited, you still need to organize your records now. If you *are* audited and lack the tax records that you need to support your case, don't throw in the towel. This chapter shows you how to overcome such a problem — just in case you failed Recordkeeping 101.

As a result of the IRS horror stories broadcasted on TV, Congress shifted the burden of proof for when taxpayers and the IRS end up in court. But don't get too excited over this provision. The fine print is murder. You still have to present credible evidence and be cooperative (Boy Scouts to the head of the line), and the provision applies only to tax audits that began after July 22, 1998. Shifting the burden of proof doesn't mean that you can sit back and say, "Prove it." Remember, too, that few cases go to court. The Taxpayer Bill of Rights in Chapter 18 explains the fine print.

Keeping Good Records

Tax records pose a problem for many people because the IRS doesn't require any particular form of recordkeeping. In fact, the IRS recommends, in general terms, that you keep records only to file a "complete and accurate" return. Need a bit more detail? Read on.

Ensuring a complete and accurate tax return

"Hey, my return is complete and accurate," you say. "All the numbers are within the lines and neatly written without any math errors. And when I e-filed, the IRS didn't spit it out!" In case you don't feel like flipping through countless pages of government instructions on what constitutes a "complete and accurate" return, we thought you may want to check out several common problem areas at a glance and the types of records normally required.

✔ **Itemized deductions:** Receipts, receipts, who's got the receipts? If you're planning on itemizing your deductions on Schedule A (see Chapter 9 for more information), you need the numbers to calculate your deductions and to prove your claims in case you're audited. Here's a list of expenses you'll want to have proof that you paid in the order you'll find them on Schedule A (see Chapter 9):

- **Medical expenses:** Keep all your receipts, and make sure you get receipts for all services that you receive during the year, including cab fares to and from the doctor's office. The list of allowable medical deductions is long and fairly inclusive, and as healthcare costs continue to rise faster than most people's salaries, more and more people will find they can take a medical deduction.

- **Mortgage interest payments:** You should receive these payments, which are documented on Form 1098, from the bank that holds your mortgage.

- **Real estate taxes:** Keep a copy of your real estate tax bill, and either the canceled checks, a receipt from your city or town, or a line item on your Form 1098 (if your mortgage company pays your taxes for you).

- **Personal property taxes:** Keep a receipt for your excise tax bill.

- **State and local income taxes:** Hang on to copies of your canceled checks if your bank still gives you back your checks. Otherwise, when the IRS wants proof, you'll have to pay for copies from your bank.

- **Charitable deductions:** For donations in excess of $250 (per donation), keep a written receipt or letter from the charity that states the amount and nature of your donation.

- **Casualty or theft losses:** You just never know when your number will come up in the burglar lottery, or you drop your diamond ring down the garbage disposal. If you don't have your receipts, don't despair, though; you have other ways to prove this deduction. Check out "Casualty losses" section, later in this chapter.

- **Unreimbursed job expenses, safe deposit box fees, tax preparation fees, and other miscellaneous itemized deductions:** Once again, keeping your receipts makes these deductions easy to prove.

You may be rejoicing to find that you don't have enough deductions to itemize in 2006, so you can trash all your receipts now. And, you may also be assuming that the same will be true in 2007. Keep in mind, though, that your finances, and your tax situation, can do funny things from year to year; be sure to hang on to your 2007 receipts so that you keep all your deduction options open down the road.

✔ **Dependent expenses:** If you plan to claim someone other than your qualifying child as a dependent, you need to be able to prove (if you're audited) that you provided more than 50 percent of that person's total support. The length of time that you provide the support doesn't mean anything — it's the total cost that matters. So be ready to show how much you paid for your dependent's lodging, food, clothes, healthcare, transportation, and any other essential support stuff. (See Chapter 4 for the rules for claiming dependents and the definition of a qualifying child.)

✔ **Car expenses:** If, for the business use of your car, you choose to deduct the actual expenses rather than the standard mileage rate (which is 44.5 cents per mile for 2006), you need to be able to show the cost of the car and when you started using it for business. You also must record your business miles, your total miles, and your expenses, such as insurance, gas, and maintenance. You need a combination of a log and written receipts, of course!

✔ **Home expenses:** If you own your home, you not only need to keep track of your mortgage and real estate tax payments, but you also need to keep precise records of your purchase price and purchase expenses, plus the cost of all the improvements and additions you make over time (save your receipts, please!). Although you may not be selling your house this year, when you do, you'll be thankful you have all your receipts in a neat little file. (Chapter 12 discusses house sales in detail.) If you rent a portion of your house, or you run a business from it, you'll also need your utility bills, general repair bills, and housecleaning and lawn-mowing costs in order to calculate your net rental income or your home office expense. (See Chapter 11 for more information on the home office deduction and Chapter 13 for how to calculate net rental income.)

✔ **Business expenses:** The IRS is especially watchful in this area, so be sure to keep detailed proof of any expenses that you claim. This proof can consist of many items, such as receipts of income, expense account statements, and so on. Remember that the IRS doesn't always accept canceled checks as the only method of substantiation, so make sure that you hang on to the bill or receipt for every expense you incur. (See Chapter 11 if you're self-employed and Chapter 9 if you're an employee.)

Setting up a recordkeeping system

The tax year is a long time for keeping track of records that you'll need (and where you put them) when the filing season arrives. So here are some easy things you can do to make your tax-preparation burden a little lighter:

✔ **Invest in an accordion file.** You can buy one with slots already labeled by month, by category, or by letters of the alphabet, or you can make your own filing system with the extra labels — all this can be yours for less than $10.

✔ If $10 is too much, you can purchase a dozen or so of those manila file folders for about $5 (or less). Decide on the organizational method that best fits your needs, and get into the habit of saving all bills, receipts, and records that you think you can use someday for your tax purposes and for things that affect your overall financial planning. This basic advice is good for any taxpayer, whether you file a simple tax return on **Form 1040EZ** or a complicated **Form 1040** with several supplemental schedules. Remember that this plan is only minimal, but nevertheless is much better than the shoebox approach to recordkeeping.

✔ If your financial life is uncomplicated, then each new year you can set up one file folder that has the year on it (so in January 2007 you establish your 2007 file). During the year, as you receive documentation that you think you'll use in preparing your return, stash it in the folder. In January 2008, when you receive your dreaded Form 1040 booklet, or the address label they sometimes send instead, toss that in the file, too. Come springtime 2008, when you finally force yourself to sit down and work on your return, you have everything you need in one bulging file.

✔ If you're a 1040 user and a real perfectionist, you can arrange your records in a file according to the schedules and forms on which you'll report them. For example, you can set up folders such as these:

- **Schedule A:** Deductible items (such as mortgage interest, property taxes, charitable contributions, and job-related expenses)

- **Schedule B:** Interest and dividend income stuff

- **Schedule D:** Documents related to buying, selling, and improving your home, and the sale and purchase of investments such as stocks and bonds

You 1040 filers have so many options that you truly need to take the time to figure out about your return — we can help you there — so that you can anticipate your future tax needs.

Tracking tax information on your computer

A number of financial software packages enable you to keep track of your spending for tax purposes. Just don't expect to reap the benefits without a fair amount of upfront and continuing work. You need to figure out how to use the software, and you need to enter a great deal of data for it to be useful to you come tax time. Don't forget, though, that you still need your receipts to back up your claims; in an audit, the IRS may not accept your computer records without verifying them against your receipts.

Watch out for state differences

Although the IRS requires that you keep your records for only three years, your state may have a longer statute of limitations with regard to state income tax audits. Some of your tax-related records may also be important to keep for other reasons. For example, suppose that you throw out your receipts after three years. Then the fellow who built your garage four years ago sues you, asserting that you didn't fully pay the bill. You may be out of luck in court if you don't have the canceled check showing that you paid.

The moral is: Hang on to records that may be important (such as home improvement receipts) for longer than three years — especially if a dispute is possible. Check with a legal advisor whenever you have a concern, because statutes of limitations vary from state to state.

If you're interested in software, consider personal finance packages such as Quicken (from Intuit) or Microsoft Money. With these packages, you can keep track of your stock portfolio, pay your bills, balance your checking account, and best of all, get help with tabulating your tax information. Just remember that the package tabulates only what you enter. So if you use the software to write your monthly checks but neglect to enter data for things you pay for with cash, for example, you won't have the whole picture.

Deciding when to stash and when to trash

One of the most frequently asked questions is how long a taxpayer needs to keep tax records. The answer is easy — a minimum of three years. That's because the statute of limitations for tax audits and assessments is three years. If the IRS doesn't adjust or audit your 2003 tax return by April 15, 2007 (the three years starts running on April 15, 2004), it missed its chance. On April 15, 2007, feel free to celebrate another auditless year with a "Shredding the 2003 Tax Year" party. (If you filed after April 15 because you obtained an extension of time to file, you must wait until three years after the extension due date rather than the April 15 tax date. The same is true when you file late — the three-year period doesn't start until you actually file your return.)

However, we must add one point to the general three-year rule: Save all records for the assets that you continue to own. These records can include purchase slips for stocks and bonds, automobiles, your home (along with its improvements), and expensive personal property, such as jewelry, video cameras, or computers. Keep these records in a safe-deposit box in case you suffer a (deductible casualty) loss, such as a fire. You don't want these records going up in smoke! Some taxpayers take the practical step of videotaping their home and its contents, but if you do, make sure that you keep that record outside your home. You can save money on safe-deposit box fees by leaving your video with relatives who may enjoy watching it because they don't see you often enough. (Of course, your relatives may also suffer a fire or an earthquake.)

In situations where the IRS suspects that income wasn't reported, IRS agents can go back as far as six years. And if possible tax fraud is involved, forget all time restraints!

Reconstructing Missing Tax Records

The inscription above the entrance to the national office of the Internal Revenue Service reads:

> *Taxes are what we pay for civilized society.*

But any taxpayer who has ever had a tax return examined would probably enjoy a little less civilization.

Our experience shows that the number-one reason why taxpayers must cough up additional tax when they're audited is lousy recordkeeping. They don't get themselves into this situation by fabricating deductions, but rather because most taxpayers aren't very good bookkeepers and they fail to produce the records that properly substantiate the deductions they have a right to claim.

When taxpayers misplace tax records or simply don't save the ones that they need to be able to claim the deductions they're allowed under the law, all is not lost. Other ways exist for gathering the evidence that establishes what was actually spent — but obtaining the necessary evidence may prove time-consuming. And yet, when you consider the other option — paying additional tax, interest, and penalties on disallowed deductions from an audit where you couldn't prove what you spent — your time and energy will be amply rewarded. The following sections describe some ways to reconstruct lost or forgotten records. (You may also want to look at Chapters 16 and 17, which tell you how to fight back against an IRS audit when it comes to tax records.)

Property received by inheritance or gift

The starting point for determining whether you made or lost money on a sale of a property is the property's tax basis. (Remember, to the IRS, *property* can be more than just real estate; it also includes stocks, bonds, cars, boats, and computers.) *Tax basis* is an IRS term for cost. Your basis usually is what you paid for something.

However, the rules for determining the tax basis for property you inherited or received as a gift is different. Because you don't know the cost of the inheritance, the tax basis for determining the taxable gain or loss of the property you inherited is the *fair market value* of the property on the date of the titleholder's death. For property received as a gift, the tax basis is either the donor's cost or the fair market value on the date you received the gift (see Chapter 12).

The best time for determining your basis in either a gift or an inheritance is when you receive that gift or inheritance, not years later after people who may have that information have long since forgotten or even died. If you know the basis of the property you've received, either through a gift or an inheritance, because you have access to either the Gift Tax Return (Form 709), the Estate Tax Return (Form 706), or because your Uncle Don told you upfront what your basis is in this property, great! When you sell the property, you're all set with your initial basis information, and calculating your gain or loss will be a matter of simple math.

If, on the other hand, Uncle Don hasn't been so accommodating, and the relevant Estate or Gift Tax Returns aren't available, you're not out of luck, but you'll need to do some research on your own.

If there has been no estate tax return prepared for an estate, you're responsible for establishing the date-of-death value for your inheritance. You can use four methods to compute your tax basis: newspaper ads, local real estate board and broker records, the property's assessed value, and the *Consumer Price Index* (CPI). (You know the CPI: It tells you that what cost $10 last month costs $50 this month. Seriously, it probably costs $10.02, and the CPI is an official government measure that tells how much prices increase over time.)

Challenging the established values

When you inherit something, don't automatically assume that its fair market value as reported on the estate tax return is correct, especially where real estate and art are concerned. The IRS constantly challenges the value placed on an item for estate tax purposes, and so can you. If, using a reasonable method for valuation, you arrive at a value different than on the estate tax return, chances are good that the IRS will accept your valuation. Remember, though, that your "reasonable method" needs to be just that, and you need to be able to provide substantiation, in the event of an audit, for how you arrived at your value.

If an estate tax return has been filed for the estate and you decide to challenge the value placed on your inheritance,

beware! The estate's executor has likely placed as low a value on the property as possible in order to minimize the estate taxes, and you probably want as high a value as possible in order to minimize your capital gain when you sell the property. When you successfully argue for an increased value, you'll lower your income taxes, but you may raise the amount of estate tax the estate pays. Generally speaking, estate tax rates are substantially higher than income tax rates, so your success on the income tax side of this equation will only cost you (and your family) more on the estate tax side. Think twice before you challenge an estate tax valuation!

Researching newspaper ads

Start at your local library or your local newspaper office to find a copy of the newspaper printed on the date for which you're trying to establish the value. The classified ads in the real estate section may reveal the price of similar property offered at that same time. Back issues often are kept on microfilm, so you can look backward or forward for six or so months in case you can't find any values for a particular date. The Internet is also a wonderful resource for current and prior values. More and more newspapers now allow you to access their archives online.

If a piece of real estate exactly like yours wasn't offered for sale at that time, you may have to find an ad for one as close as possible in description to yours and simply estimate the price. For example, suppose that you're trying to figure out how much Uncle Jesse's farm was worth when he left it to you in 1980. You now want to sell the 100-acre farm and farmhouse, and you're searching for its value in 1980. You check out some 1980 ads from *The Daily Bugle* and find

- ✔ An ad showing a house and 50 acres for $75,000
- ✔ An ad showing a house and 60 acres for $85,000

Because the farm with ten more acres was selling for $10,000 more, assume that an acre was worth around $1,000. The IRS will find your assumption reasonable. Therefore, Uncle Jesse's farm has 40 more acres than the one selling for $85,000, so you can figure that the value of the farm in 1980 was $125,000 ($85,000 + $40,000).

The IRS won't simply accept the statement that you looked up this information. Remember, all IRS agents act as if they come from Missouri (the "Show Me" state — in case you were absent from school the day your fifth-grade teacher lectured on state mottoes). If you go to all the trouble to visit the library, make sure you come away with a photocopy of the paper's real estate section. The IRS requires documentation, especially when you use an alternative method to establish something's value.

Consulting local real estate board and broker records

If your trip to the library or local newspaper office comes up short, try the local real estate board or a real estate broker (one may owe you a favor or want your business). Individual brokers or local real estate boards usually keep historical data on property sold in their respective areas. Again, you may have to estimate selling prices if you don't find a property exactly like yours.

Obtaining assessed values

The assessed-value method may uncover the most accurate estimate of a property's value. Because property taxes are collected on the basis of assessed values, try to obtain the property's assessed value on the date you're interested in. With that information and the percentage of the fair market value that the tax assessor used in determining assessed values, divide the percentage into the assessed value to come up with the market value.

You can obtain assessed values for property (and the percentage of the fair market value of property assessed in its vicinity) from the government office that receives or collects property taxes, which you can usually find in the courthouse of the county where the property is located. Don't forget to get a copy of this information. For example, if the assessed value was $2,700 and the percentage of the fair market value at which the property was assessed was 30 percent, the fair market value was $9,000 ($2,700 ÷ 30 percent).

Using the Consumer Price Index (CPI)

Unlike baseball, when you're assessing the value of real estate, you're not out on three strikes. When all else fails, use the CPI method. Because you already know the amount for which you sold the property, another trip or call to the library enables you to determine the increase in the CPI between the acquisition date and the sale date. For example, say you sold a tract of land for $300,000. If the CPI has tripled since you inherited it, your tax basis is $100,000.

Determining the property's acquisition date depends on how you acquired the property. If you inherited it, the acquisition date is the date of the previous owner's death. If the property was a gift, the acquisition date is the date the property originally was purchased by the person who gave you the gift.

If your local library doesn't have CPI data, you can obtain it by writing to the U.S. Department of Labor, 200 Constitution Ave. NW, Washington, DC 20210. This information also is available on the Internet at the Consumer Price Index home page (`www.bls.gov/cpi/home.htm`). Click on "Tables Created by BLS" *(Bureau of Labor Statistics)*.

If you use the CPI to value real estate, don't be surprised if the IRS doesn't accept your valuation. Notwithstanding the recent slowdown, real estate prices in past years have risen at much higher rates than the CPI in many major metropolitan areas, and the IRS knows it.

Securities received by inheritance or gift

Establishing a stock or a bond's price on a particular date is much easier than coming up with the value of other property, especially if the stock or bond is traded on a major securities exchange.

When you inherit a stock or bond, your tax basis usually is the value of the stock or bond on the deceased's date of death. Sometimes an estate — to save taxes — uses a valuation date that is six months after the date of death. If you receive the security as a gift, you often have the added task of establishing the date when the donor acquired the security, because you normally must use the value on that date (including any commission expense). Not to confuse you, but sometimes you must use the value on the date you received the gift. We explain all this information in Chapter 12. You can write to the transfer agent to find out when the stock was acquired. The transfer agent is the company that keeps track of the shares of stock that a company issues. Your stockbroker can tell you how to locate the *transfer agent*, or you can consult the *Value Line Investment Survey* at your local library.

After you determine the acquisition date, either the back issue of a newspaper or a securities pricing service can provide the value of the security you're looking for on any particular day. A back issue of a newspaper won't reveal whether any stock dividends or splits (affecting the share price) occurred since the acquisition date. A good pricing service can provide that information.

One service that we recommend for determining the value of stocks and bonds (plus any stock splits or stock dividends) is Prudential-American Securities Inc., 921 E. Green St., Pasadena, CA 91106; phone 626-795-5831; `www.securities-pricing.com`. This company charges $4 to determine the value of a stock or bond on a given day, with a minimum fee of $10.

Also, consider checking with the investment firm where the securities were (or are still) held. The firm may be able to research this information — maybe even for free.

Improvements to a residence

How many homeowners save any of the records regarding improvements that they make, even when those expenditures are substantial? Not nearly enough. Why? Because improvements to a home quite often are made during a 30- to 40-year span, and saving records for that many years is a lot to ask of anyone. For example, landscaping expenditures — one tree or bush at a time — can really add up.

The point of counting every tree and bush and other improvement to home sweet home is to raise the *basis,* or total investment, that you have in your residence so that you can reduce your taxable profit when you sell. (See Chapter 12 for details.)

Although the 1997 law eliminated the fiendish recordkeeping requirements for sales in which a profit of $500,000 or less for couples filing jointly and $250,000 for singles is realized, for sales above these amounts you still need records to prove, for example, that you didn't make more than these threshold amounts ($500,000/$250,000). And if you buy a house today, say for $350,000, you don't know what the sales price will be in 10, 20, 30, or more years when you finally sell it. Here's hoping it's $1 million. So tax records are still important.

Before you estimate how much you spent on residential improvements, you first have to determine what improvements you spent the money on. This step is necessary because if you can't document the amount spent, you at least can establish that an improvement was made. Your family photo album (which may contain before and after pictures) is probably the best source for obtaining such information.

Obtaining a Certificate of Occupancy

If you can't get a receipt from the contractor who made improvements to your home, hike down to the county clerk's office to obtain a copy of the Certificate of Occupancy (the house's birth certificate, so to speak), which shows what your house consisted of when it was built. Records at the county clerk's office also reveal any changes in the house's assessed value as the result of improvements you made, along with any building permits issued. Any of these documents can clearly establish whether improvements were made (assuming, of course, that you did obtain the proper permits for these improvements).

Getting an estimate

When original invoices, duplicate invoices, or canceled checks aren't available, obtain an estimate of what the improvement would cost now, and then subtract the increase according to the CPI (as explained in "Using the Consumer Price Index" earlier in this chapter). This procedure can help establish a reasonable estimate of what the improvement originally cost.

Casualty losses

A casualty loss is probably the most difficult deduction to establish. Few people consistently save receipts on the purchase of personal items, such as jewelry, clothing, furniture, and so on. If the casualty loss occurred because of a fire or hurricane, any receipts that you may have had were probably destroyed along with your property. Although a police, fire, or insurance company report establishes that a casualty loss was sustained, how do you establish the cost of what was stolen or destroyed? The answer: with a little bit of luck and hard work.

For example, the value of an expensive necklace that was stolen was once established by using a photograph that showed the taxpayer wearing the necklace. The taxpayer then obtained an appraisal from a jeweler of the cost of a similar necklace. Because jewelry is a popular gift, receipts sometimes don't exist.

Although you can prove to the IRS that you have enough money to afford the lost or stolen item, the IRS also needs proof that you had the item in your possession. For example, suppose that your $10,000 Rolex watch is stolen (we feel for you). To make the IRS folks happy, you must prove two things:

 ✔ That you can afford the Rolex, which your total income from your tax return can prove.

 ✔ That you had the Rolex, which can be established by a statement from a friend, a relative, or an acquaintance asserting that you actually owned the item. If the Rolex was a gift, a statement from the giver also helps.

You can use an appraisal from the Federal Emergency Management Agency (FEMA) if you obtained a disaster loan as evidence for tax purposes to claim a casualty loss.

Business records

If business records have been lost or destroyed, you can often obtain duplicate bills from major vendors. You shouldn't have a great deal of trouble getting copies of the original telephone, utility, rent, credit card, oil company, and other bills. Reconstructing a typical month of automobile use can help you make a reasonable determination of the business use of your automobile. If that month's use approximates an average month's business use of an auto, the IRS usually accepts such reconstructed records as adequate substantiation.

Using duplicate bank statements

If all your business income was deposited in a checking or savings account, you can reconstruct that income from duplicate bank statements. Although banks usually don't charge for copies of bank statements, they do charge for copies of canceled checks. These charges can be quite expensive — about $4 to $5 per check — so do some legwork before ordering copies of all your checks. For example, obtain a copy of your lease and a statement from your landlord saying that all rent was paid on time before you request duplicate copies of rent checks.

Ordering copies of past returns

By ordering copies of past returns with **Form 4506, Request for Copy or Transcript of Tax Form,** you can have a point of reference for determining whether you have accounted for typical business expenses. Past returns reveal not only gross profit percentages or margins of profit, but also the amounts of recurring expenses.

Requesting Copies of Lost Tax Returns

Last year's tax return is the starting point for filling out this year's tax return. It serves as a guide to make sure you don't forget anything. But what if you can't locate your 2005 return? Or suppose you need a return from a previous year but can't find it?

You can request a copy of your previous returns and all attachments (including Form W-2) by using Form 4506. You must pay a $39 charge when you file the form. If you don't need a photocopy of your return, but only the information that was included on it, you can order a *Tax Return Transcript,* which shows the data entered for all the lines from your submitted return. You can order your Tax Return Transcript by using a Form 4506-T. File both the Form 4506 and the Form 4506-T with the Internal Revenue Service Center where you filed your return. There is no charge for a transcript (as opposed to $39 for an actual photocopy), which most banks accept in lieu of your income tax return when you're applying for a loan. It can take up to 60 days to receive a copy of a tax return. Transcripts, however, don't take as long. Returns and transcripts are generally available for the current year and the three previous years.

Returns filed six or more years ago may or may not be available for making copies, but tax account information generally still is available for those years.

If you need a record of the changes the IRS made to your original return showing any penalties, interest, and payments made subsequent to filing your return or showing if an amended return was filed, you need a *Record of Tax Account Information*. You must order this printout by phone.

Ordering a Tax Return Transcript or a Record of Tax Account Information by phone is quick. Simply call 800-829-1040 and follow the voice prompts. You may be put on hold before you speak with a live person who can process your request. The Tax Return Transcript or Record of Tax Account Information should arrive by mail in about ten business days.

Understanding the Cohan Rule

Before we end this discussion about undocumented claims, we must tell you about the case of George M. Cohan and the resulting *Cohan Rule*. It's the story of one person's victory over the IRS, and it may inspire you to defend your own rights as a taxpayer. Even if some of the rights that taxpayers earned because of his victory have been eroded over the years, Cohan's battle for the right to estimate deductions still has repercussions today.

In 1921 and 1922, George M. Cohan deducted $55,000 in business-related travel and entertainment expenses. The IRS refused to allow him any part of these entertainment and travel deductions on the grounds that it was impossible to tell how much Cohan spent because he didn't have any receipts to support the deductions he claimed.

Cohan appealed to the Second Circuit Court of Appeals, and the court established the *rule of approximation*. The court instructed the IRS to "make as close an approximation as it can, bearing heavily, if it chooses, upon the taxpayer whose inexactitude is of his own making." (Isn't "inexactitude" a lovely way of saying "no records"?)

For more than 30 years, the *Cohan Rule* enabled taxpayers to deduct travel and entertainment expenses without having to substantiate what they spent. Taxpayers had only to establish that it was reasonable for them to have incurred travel and entertainment expenses in the amount they claimed they spent.

Congress changed the law regarding travel, use of a car, and entertainment expenses in the early 1960s. Since that change, taxpayers no longer can deduct travel or entertainment expenses without adequate substantiation.

The *Cohan Rule* still applies, however, to other expenses whose records aren't available. Under the *Cohan Rule,* the Tax Court routinely allows deductions based on estimates for the following deductions:

- Petty cash and office expenses
- Delivery and freight charges
- Tips and business gifts
- Cleaning and maintenance expenses
- Small tools and supplies
- Taxi fares
- Casualty losses (fire, flood, and theft losses)

For some expenses, obtaining receipts for what you spend is impractical, if not downright impossible. Petty cash and tips are just two examples of such expenses.

The *Cohan Rule* doesn't mean that you can stop keeping receipts and simply use estimates. You must have a valid reason for relying on the *Cohan Rule,* such as impracticability or lost or destroyed records. In fact, taxpayers have had penalties assessed against them for not attempting to obtain duplicate records that were lost when they moved, and for periodically destroying all business records immediately upon the filing of their tax returns. One court held that the unexplained loss of corporate records carries a strong presumption that the records would have prejudiced the taxpayer's position.

In case you're scratching the back of your head and wondering if any of this will work, the question you have to ask yourself is, if you were sitting on a jury and saw this evidence, would you believe it? If the answer to this question is yes, guess what? You're most likely going to prevail.

Chapter 4

No Form Fits All (Or, What Kind of Taxpayer Are You?)

You have to make some key decisions before grabbing those good ol' tax forms and marking them up. Even though you're anxious to begin, read the relevant portions of this chapter first. We explain some important issues you must resolve each tax year before you knuckle down to complete your return.

What Rendition of 1040 Shall We Play?

If you could get across town by taking one bus rather than having to transfer and take two, you'd do it, right? That is, unless you enjoy riding city buses, sightseeing, or wasting time and money by transferring.

Like your transportation options, you have a few choices of tax forms — three, to be exact. In order, from mind-challenging (read *simplest* in IRS jargon) to mind-numbing (read *complex*), they are **Form 1040EZ, Form 1040A,** and **Form 1040.**

The simpler forms are easier to finish because they have fewer lines to complete and far fewer instructions to read. They may even save you a bit of time and maybe a headache or two, but — and this *but* is important— the simpler forms offer you far fewer opportunities and options to take deductions to which you may be entitled. Thus, in a rush to save yourself a little work and time, you can cost yourself hundreds, maybe thousands, in additional tax dollars.

How can you tell if you should take the easier route, and just use the standard deduction, or if you should itemize and dig for all the deductions you can possibly, and legally, find? Check out Chapter 9, which explains all of your deduction options to you, before you choose which version of the Form 1040 to fill out. Remember, you can only itemize your deductions if you file Form 1040.

Form 1040EZ

Here's the lowdown on this *EZ-est* of tax forms. (They actually test-marketed this form before they started using it — very much like Procter & Gamble does before they try something new, like a purple-colored toothpaste. Unfortunately, the IRS has a bit of an advantage over Procter & Gamble — if you don't like the forms, you can't switch to Brand X.)

The easiest form to fill out and file is the 1040EZ. All you need to do is insert your name, address, occupation, Social Security number, wages, unemployment compensation, and taxable interest. Your refund can be deposited directly into your bank account. To find out whether you can use this form, see Chapter 5. Form 1040EZ is a breeze. You don't have to make any computations if you don't want to. Just plug in the numbers and skip the math, if you want. If you owe, the IRS bills you. And if you're due a refund, the IRS sends you a check. How EZ! (Just don't forget to attach your W-2s.)

Form 1040A (the short form)

For those of you whose economic or personal lives are a bit more complicated, congratulations! You've just graduated from Form 1040EZ. Your reward may be Form 1040A. But there's something you need to know: The best way to be certain that you need to use Form 1040A is to review Form 1040 before reaching for Form 1040A. Check to make sure there isn't any deduction or tax credit you can use on Form 1040. To find out whether you qualify for Form 1040A, see Chapter 5.

Can I itemize? Should I itemize? And what the heck are itemized deductions?

Deductions are just that: You subtract them from your income before you calculate the tax you owe. (Deductions are good things!) To make everything more complicated, the IRS gives you two methods for determining the total of your deductions: itemized and standardized deductions. The good news is that you get to pick the method that leads to the best solution for you — whichever way offers greater deductions. If you can itemize, you should, because it saves you tax dollars. The bad news is that if you choose to itemize your deductions, you must use Form 1040.

The first method — taking the standard deduction — requires no thinking or calculations. If you have a relatively uncomplicated financial life, taking the standard deduction is generally the better option. Symptoms of a simple tax life are: not earning a high income, renting your house or apartment, and lacking unusually large expenses, such as medical bills or losses from theft or catastrophe. Single folks qualify for a $5,150 standard deduction, heads of household receive a $7,550 standard deduction, and married couples filing jointly get a $10,300

standard deduction in tax year 2006. If you're age 65 or older, or blind, your standard deduction is increased by $1,250 if single and not a surviving spouse, and by $1,000 each if married.

Some deductions — moving expenses, the penalty for early withdrawal from savings, and so on — are available even if you don't itemize your deductions. The bad news: You have to file Form 1040 to claim them. The good news: We tell you how to do this in Chapter 7.

The other method of determining the total of your allowable deductions is itemizing them on your tax return. This method is definitely more of a hassle, but if you can tally up more than the standard deduction amounts, itemizing saves you money. If you have large unreimbursed medical expenses, have a mortgage on your home, give a lot to charity, or pay a lot in state and local taxes, you probably want to add these amounts up, just in case. Use Schedule A of IRS Form 1040 to total your itemized deductions. (See Chapter 9 for more about using Schedule A to itemize deductions.)

Form 1040 (the long form)

Because Forms 1040A and 1040EZ are easier to complete than Form 1040, you should use one of them unless Form 1040 allows you to pay less tax. But if you don't qualify for filing Form 1040A or 1040EZ, you must use Form 1040.

This form is the one that everybody loves to hate. *The Wall Street Journal* believes that tax professionals invented the form — the newspaper's editors even refer to the tax laws as the "Accountants and Lawyers Full Employment Act." We think that complicated tax laws should be called the "IRS Guaranteed Lifetime Employment Act."

If you itemize your deductions, claim a host of tax credits, own rental property, are self-employed, or sell a stock or bond, you're stuck — welcome to the world of the 1040.

If you think the only factor that might prevent you from using a Form 1040A is that you've always itemized your deductions in the past, do Schedule A, Itemized Deductions, first (see Chapter 9). It's a reasonably easy form to complete, and if your deductions don't add up to your standard deduction, you're off the 1040 hook.

If you're depressed because you have to use the simpler forms for your 2006 return and you want to be able to deduct more and have more favorable adjustments to your income in the future, all is not lost. At a minimum, you can make things better for 2007 by planning ahead. (Be sure to read Part V.) You may be able to do some last-minute maneuvering before you file your 2006 return. We direct you to these maneuvers as we walk you through the line-by-line completion of your return.

Choosing a Filing Status

When filing your return, you must choose the appropriate filing status from the five filing statuses available for 1040A and 1040 users. (Users of Form 1040EZ must file as *single* or as *married filing jointly,* with no dependents.) You select a status by checking the appropriate box directly below your name on page 1 of Form 1040 or Form 1040A, where it says "Filing Status":

- ✔ Single
- ✔ Married filing jointly
- ✔ Married filing separately
- ✔ Head of household
- ✔ Qualifying widow(er) with dependent child

Each filing status has its own tax rates. As a general rule, you pay the lowest tax if you're able to file jointly or as a qualifying widow(er). Those individuals who are married filing separately pay tax at the highest rate. However, like every rule, a few circumstances exist in which married filing separately saves couples money, as we explain later in this section. In addition, you can select a different filing status every year. For example, because you filed jointly last tax year doesn't mean you automatically have to file that way this tax year.

Single

Most people who aren't married file as *single.* The IRS doesn't recognize couples living together, regardless of sexual orientation or state law, as being married for filing purposes.

However, if you were widowed, divorced, or legally separated by the end of the tax year (December 31, 2006) and provided support to dependents, such as children or an elderly parent, you may be able to save yourself some tax dollars by filing as *head of household* or as a *qualifying widow(er)*. You can find out more in the upcoming section, "Head of household."

State laws sometimes differ from federal laws regarding filing status. If you live in a state that recognizes civil unions and same-sex marriage and you have legally entered into one of these unions, although you're still required to use the *single* or *head-of-household* filing status for your federal return, you must use either the *married filing jointly* or *married filing separately* status for your state income tax return.

Married filing jointly

If you're married, you probably share many things with your spouse. One of the more treasured tasks you get to share is the preparation of your annual tax return. In fact, this may be the one time during the year that you jointly examine and combine your financial information. Let the fireworks begin!

For your 2006 return, you're considered married if you got married by or were still married as of the end of the tax year — December 31, 2006. In some rare instances, married folks can save money by filing their taxes as *married filing separately*. This somewhat oddball status can be useful for couples who have large differences between their two incomes and can claim more itemized deductions by filing separately. See the section "Married filing separately," later in this chapter, to determine whether you can save money by filing separately.

If you file a joint return for 2006, you may not, after the due date for filing, amend that return to change to a married filing separately filing status. You're "jointly" stuck!

You can file jointly if you meet any of the following criteria:

- ✔ You were married as of December 31, 2006, even if you didn't live with your spouse at the end of the year.
- ✔ Your spouse died in 2006, and you didn't remarry in 2006.

  If your spouse died during the year, you're considered married for the entire year, providing you didn't remarry. You report all your income for the year and your spouse's income up to the date of his or her death.

- ✔ Your spouse died in 2007 before you filed a 2006 return. If you're filing jointly in 2006, but your spouse died in either 2006 or before you managed to file your return in 2007, you're exempt from the "both must sign" rule. Only you are required to sign the return. After your name, write the words, "surviving spouse."

You and your spouse may file jointly even if only one of you had income or if you didn't live together all year. However, you both must sign the return, and you're both responsible for seeing that all taxes are paid. That means if your spouse doesn't pay the tax due, you may have to.

If you've signed that joint return, but are either unaware of what's on it, or someone (your spouse) has exerted pressure on you to sign that return, you may be a candidate for the *Innocent Spouse Rule* (see Chapter 18). This rule can, in some instances, relieve a spouse who was unaware of his or her spouse's shenanigans from sharing joint responsibility for what is owed.

Spouses who are nonresident aliens or dual-status aliens

If one spouse is a nonresident alien and doesn't pay U.S. income taxes on all his or her income, regardless of the country (or countries) in which it is earned, then the couple may not take the married filing jointly tax status.

The same is true when your spouse is a dual-status alien — that is, if during the year, your spouse is a non-resident as well as a resident. You may file jointly if:

✔ You were married as of December 31, 2006, even if you didn't live with your spouse at the end of 2006.

✔ If your spouse is a nonresident alien, or if either of you are dual-status aliens, you can make a special election to file jointly. IRS Publication 519 (U.S. Tax Guide For Aliens) explains how to make this election.

A couple legally separated under a divorce decree may not file jointly. On the other hand, if one spouse lived away from the home during the entire last six months of the tax year (July 1, 2006, through December 31, 2006), the remaining spouse, if taking care of dependents, may be able to file under the more favorable head of household status (see "Head of household," later in this chapter).

Although this suggestion is decidedly unromantic, if you're considering a late-in-the-year wedding, especially in December, you may want to consider the tax impact of tying the knot so soon. A considerable number of couples pay higher total taxes when they're married versus when they were single. On the other hand, what spells commitment more than sending money together with the one you love to the IRS?

Some couples have been known to postpone their weddings until January and use the tax savings to pay for the cost of their honeymoons! Others choose not to marry, and they cohabit instead. Although we don't want to criticize or condone such decisions, it's unfortunate that such a high tax cost of getting married exists for a sizable minority of couples (see "The marriage penalty" sidebar, later in this chapter).

Married filing separately

The vast majority of married couples would pay more taxes if they chose to file separate returns. The IRS won't stand in the way of your filing separate returns. However, by filing separately, you may be able to avoid the marriage penalty and save on your combined tax bill. To determine whether filing separately is to your benefit, figure your tax both ways (married filing jointly and married filing separately).

Besides saving money, another reason you may choose to file separately is to avoid being responsible for your spouse's share of the joint tax bill whenever you suspect some kind of monkey business (for example, your spouse is underreporting taxable income or inflating deductions).

If your marriage is on the rocks, married filing separately may be the way to go. Remember, if you both sign that tax return, you're both on the hook for any amounts due. Even if the tax owed may be solely due to your soon-to-be ex-spouse's income, if he or she refuses to pay the bill, you may have to. This is a case where paying a little more upfront can save you a whole lot down the road.

Even though married filing separately on your federal return may work out to be the same as filing jointly, don't overlook the possibility that by filing that way you may save state taxes.

If you file separately, be aware that the following restrictions may apply:

- You can't take the standard deduction if your spouse itemizes deductions. Both spouses must itemize their deductions, or both must claim the standard deduction.

- You can't claim the credit for child and dependent care expenses in most cases. The amount of income you can exclude under an employer dependent care assistance program is limited to $2,500 instead of the $5,000 by filing jointly.

- You can't claim a credit for qualified adoption expenses.

- You can't take the earned income credit.

- You can't exclude from your taxable income the interest you earned from series EE U.S. Savings Bonds issued after 1989, even if you paid higher education expenses in 2006.

- You can't take the credit for being elderly or disabled unless you lived apart from your spouse for all of 2006.

- You may have to pay more tax on the Social Security benefits you received in 2006.

- You usually report only your own income, exemptions, deductions, and credits. Different rules apply to people who live in community property states (see the sidebar "Filing separately in community property states," later in this chapter).

- You can't deduct interest paid on your student loan.

- You may have a lower Child Tax Credit than you would have if you filed jointly. The Child Tax Credit is a $1,000 tax credit for every "qualifying child" (see "Defining Who Is a Qualifying Child" later in this chapter for specific information) under the age of 17 at the end of the year (see Chapter 5).

- If you own and actively manage real estate, you can't claim the passive loss exception (see the particulars in Chapter 13).

- You can't claim the Hope Scholarship and Lifetime Learning credits.

- You can't claim the $4,000 IRA deduction for a nonworking spouse. And you may not be able to deduct all or part of your own $4,000 IRA contribution if your spouse is covered by a retirement plan.

- You can't transfer funds from a traditional IRA to a Roth IRA.

- Your capital loss limit is $1,500 instead of $3,000.

- Income levels at which personal exemptions and itemized deductions start being reduced are half the amount for joint filers.

Instead of filing separately, you may be able to file as a head of household if you had a child living with you, and you lived apart from your spouse during the last six months of 2006. See the "Head of household" section later in this chapter for more information.

Emotional estrangement doesn't qualify as living apart for head of household status. In a recent Tax Court case, a couple became estranged but continued to reside in the same dwelling. The court rejected the idea that *emotional estrangement* equated to actual separation. *Living apart* requires geographical separation and living in separate residences.

For many, the choice between filing jointly and filing separately comes down to a simple matter of dollars and cents — which leads you to pay the least tax? For many married couples, the fact that you're married means that you're paying higher taxes than if you and your spouse shacked up and filed as single taxpayers. Welcome to the so-called *Marriage Penalty,* which is the annual tax you pay for being married.

If you and your beloved fall into the Marriage Penalty category, you may be able to limit the amount of your penalty by filing as married filing separately. Take the time to prepare three returns — two separate and one joint and see which filing status produces a lower tax bill for you and your honey. We know it's a time sink, so you may want to spend $50 and spring for a computerized tax program that does the number crunching for you. (See Chapter 2 for our software recommendations.)

Married couples most likely to save tax dollars filing separately are those who meet both of the following criteria:

✔ Couples who have two incomes

✔ Couples who have hefty deductions for medical expenses, miscellaneous itemized deductions, or casualty losses

If you fall under this umbrella, by all means complete the three tax returns to determine which filing status works best for you.

Table 4-1 shows an example of how the same income and the same deductions can be used to obtain a very different result when you compare a joint return with two separate returns. In this example, you earn $75,000, your spouse earns $65,000, and your spouse has a casualty loss (see Chapter 9) of $13,000. If you file a joint return, the two of you lose that deduction because casualty losses can't be deducted until they exceed 10 percent of your income, in this case $14,000. But if you and your spouse file separate returns, your spouse is entitled to a $6,500 deduction, because the loss is $6,500 greater than 10 percent of your spouse's income ($13,000 – $6,500 = $6,500). For the purpose of this illustration, the $100 nondeductible portion of casualty loss and the rate reduction credit isn't being considered.

Table 4-1	Filing Jointly versus Separately: A Sample Couple		
	Jointly	*Husband*	*Wife*
Gross income	$140,000	$75,000	$65,000
Casualty loss	$13,000	$0	$13,000
Less 10 percent of income	($14,000)	($0)	($6,500)
Deductible casualty loss	$0	$0	$6,500
Taxes (state, local, real estate, personal property, and so forth)	$5,000	$3,000	$2,000
Mortgage interest	$9,500	$9,500	$0
Total itemized deductions	$14,500	$12,500	$8,500
Personal exemptions	$6,600	$3,300	$3,300
Taxable income	$118,900	$59,200	$53,200
Tax	$22,840	$11,358	$9,858

Amounts may vary slightly depending on whether you use the tax tables or the rate schedules.

Filling out both joint and separate returns and comparing them is worth doing the numbers. For example, in Table 4-1, the sample couple saves a total of $1,624 by filing separately. Their combined separate tax bill comes to only $21,216 instead of $22,840.

Filing separately in community property states

Community property states are Arizona, California, Idaho, Louisiana, Nevada, New Mexico, Texas, Washington, and Wisconsin. If you and your spouse live in one of these states, you have to follow your state's law in determining what is community income and what is separate income, if you want to file separately.

In a community property state, each spouse, as a general rule, must report one-half of the joint income. However, this step isn't necessary if:

✔ You and your spouse lived apart for the entire year

✔ You and your spouse filed separately

To qualify, at least one of you must have salary, wages, or business income — none of which was transferred between you and your spouse. Child support isn't considered a transfer. You can also disregard the community property rules and file a separate return without having to report any portion of the community property income where your spouse fails to inform you of the income and acted as if the income was exclusively his or hers. Nor does the IRS require you to include an item of community property income on your separate return where you didn't know of the income, had no reason to know of it, or where it would be unfair to make you pay tax on income. This is an area where you should either read IRS Publication 555 (Federal Tax Information on Community Property) or consult a tax advisor.

The potential for savings doesn't stop there. Say your combined income is $225,750 or more, congratulations! But as a reward for your financial success, a portion of all your personal exemptions starts getting whittled away. (Personal exemptions are those $3,300 deductions you get for yourself and each of your dependents.) When one spouse's income is less than half that amount, you may be better off filing separately and piling your dependents' personal exemptions onto that spouse's return, if that person is otherwise entitled to the dependency exemption.

If you think you could have saved money in a previous year by filing separately, sorry. There's nothing you can do about it now. After you file a joint return, you can't turn back the clock and change it to separate returns. On the other hand, if you and your spouse filed separately, you can (within three years from the due date of your return or two years from the date the tax was paid) file an amended return and switch to filing jointly. You may want to do this if, when audited, some of the deductions you and your spouse claimed were disallowed, or if you get an insurance recovery greater than you expected, reducing the amount of the casualty loss. If you're making estimated tax payments during the year, it doesn't matter whether you make joint or separate payments. You can still file your actual return however you choose and divide the estimated tax payments in accordance with the rule for joint refunds in Chapter 18.

Head of household

Beginning in 2005, simpler rules govern whether you may file as head of household. Under these rules, you may file as head of household if you were unmarried, or separated and considered unmarried at the end of the year, and you paid more than half of the cost of a maintaining a home that:

✔ Was your parent's main home for the entire year, provided you can claim them as your dependent (see Table 4-2 to compute that figure). Your parent didn't have to live with you in your home, or

✔ You lived in for more than half of the year (temporary absences, such as for school, vacation, or medical care, count as time lived in your home) with any or more of the following:

- Your qualifying child (which we explain in "Defining Who Is a Qualifying Child" later in this chapter).

- Any other person you can claim as your dependent.

- Your qualifying married child, but only if he or she doesn't file a joint income tax return with his or her spouse, and only if that child is a U.S. citizen, U.S. national, or a resident of the United States, Mexico, or Canada (an exception is made for certain adopted children).

  You can't claim head of household status on the basis of a person who is your dependent only because he or she lived with you for the entire year, or because you're entitled to claim that person as a dependent under a multiple support agreement. (Check out "Dependent Exemptions" later in this chapter for more information.)

Table 4-2	How to Compute the Cost of Maintaining a Home	
	Amount You Paid	**Total Cost**
Property taxes	$_____	$_____
Mortgage interest expense	$_____	$_____
Rent	$_____	$_____
Utility charges	$_____	$_____
Upkeep and repairs	$_____	$_____
Property insurance	$_____	$_____
Food consumed on the premises	$_____	$_____
Other household expenses	$_____	$_____
Totals	$(a)_____	$(b)_____
Subtract Total (a) from Total (b) and enter here		($_____)

Note: If you paid more than half of the total cost, you qualify for head of household status.

In the case of a birth or death of a dependent, you must have provided more than half the cost of keeping up a home that was that person's home for more than half the year, or if he or she wasn't alive that long, then he or she must have been a member of your household during the period of the tax year that he or she was alive.

The cost of keeping up a home doesn't include clothing, education, medical expenses, vacations, life insurance, or transportation. These are personal support items that are taken into account to determine if you're entitled to claim a $3,300 personal exemption deduction for the support of a dependent. See the section "Figuring Personal and Dependent Exemptions," later in this chapter, for more on when and how to claim these deductions.

Qualifying widow(er) with dependent child

If you meet all five of the following tests, you can use the tax table for married filing jointly.

- ✔ Your spouse died in 2004 or 2005, and you didn't remarry in 2006.

- ✔ You have a child, stepchild, adopted child, or foster child whom you can claim as a dependent.

- ✔ This child lived in your home for all of 2006. Temporary absences, such as for vacation or school, count as time lived in your home.

- ✔ You paid more than half the cost of keeping up your home for this child.

- ✔ You could have filed a joint return with your spouse the year he or she died, even if you didn't actually do so. (But you can't claim an exemption for your deceased spouse.)

The marriage penalty

Some couples' first year of marriage brings surprises. Others find that the song remains the same. But of all the many things that newlyweds discover about being married, one of the most annoying is the *marriage penalty*, a tax-law inequity that forces millions of married couples to pay more tax than they would if they were single and living together.

Briefly, the penalty occurs for this reason: When two people get married, the second person's income is effectively added on top of the first person's income, which can push more of the couple's income into higher tax brackets. Not only that, but the couple may also lose some itemized deductions and personal exemptions with a higher combined income.

You should know, however, that not all couples pay higher taxes. In fact, in most cases couples find that their joint tax bill is less. Another situation occurs with couples in which one spouse doesn't earn any income or has a low income. Those couples sometimes receive a marriage bonus.

Yet, according to *The Wall Street Journal,* a study by the Congressional Budget Office determined that 21 million couples paid an average of $1,400 more in taxes per couple than they would've paid on the same income had they remained single.

The tax law changes enacted in 1993 made the marriage penalty even worse because the tax rates were raised for higher-income earners. And many of the tax benefits enacted in 1997 are phased out for higher-income couples.

Couples more likely to be hit with the marriage penalty are two-income-earning households, especially spouses who have similar individual incomes and/or are higher-income earners. Why? Because U.S. tax brackets are graduated, which simply means that you pay a higher tax rate at higher-income levels (see the discussion in Chapter 1).

Can you do anything about it? In a small number of cases, married couples can cut their tax bills simply by filing separately.

Some people opt for another approach — not marrying, or getting a divorce. By living together as unmarrieds, you and your significant other each pay taxes at the individual rate. We're not advising this course, but it's simply what we hear and see. You also need to know that you can't divorce in December just to save on your taxes and then remarry the next year. Taxpayers who've tried this scam in the past have been slapped with penalties in addition to the extra taxes they would've owed if they'd stayed away from divorce court.

If you decide not to stay married for the long haul just to save on income taxes, be warned that unmarried couples aren't eligible for any of the significant survivor's Social Security benefits if one partner passes away or splits. A person who doesn't work is particularly vulnerable; if he's married and his spouse passes away or divorces him, the nonworking spouse qualifies for Social Security benefits based on the working partner's income history and Social Security taxes paid. If you aren't married and you don't work, you aren't entitled to Social Security benefits if your partner leaves you.

Congress has tried recently to address the inequities of the marriage penalty, and it has had some limited success. Standard deductions for married couples are now double what they are for individuals, and the amount of income eligible for the 10 and 15 percent tax brackets are now exactly twice as large as they are for singles. There is still more work to be done, however. It remains to be seen if, in these days of large federal deficits, Congress will continue to whittle away at this penalty, or if it will just assume that paying more tax never really figured into your reasons for marrying in the first place.

If your spouse died in 2006, you may not file as a qualifying widow(er) with a dependent child. But see whether you qualify for filing jointly and refer to the "Filing a Return for a Deceased Taxpayer" section near the end of this chapter. And if you can't file as a qualifying widow(er) with a dependent child, see whether you can qualify as a head of household. If you don't meet the rules for a qualifying widow(er) with a dependent child, married filing a joint return, or head of household, you must file as a single.

For example, suppose that a mother with children died in 2004, and the husband hasn't remarried. In 2005 and 2006, he kept up a home for himself and his dependent children. For 2004, he was entitled to file a joint return for himself and his deceased wife. For 2005 and 2006, he may file as a qualifying widow(er) with dependent children. After 2006, he may file as head of household, if he qualifies. If he doesn't qualify, he files as single.

Figuring Personal and Dependent Exemptions

You 1040A and 1040 filers have another hurdle to jump: Lines 6a–6d of these forms ask you to figure your total number of exemptions. (You 1040EZ filers have line 5 to contend with, but it's a breeze. See Chapter 5.)

Whether or not you pay any income tax, you as a taxpayer are entitled to an exemption amount of $3,300 in 2006, which is used to decrease taxable income. What you need to figure out is whether you get to claim your exemption on your income tax return, or if someone else can claim your exemption on his or her return.

The following two sections explain how you decide who gets to claim your exemption.

Personal exemptions

You can take one personal exemption for yourself and one for your spouse. Here are the details.

- ✔ **Your own:** You may take one exemption for yourself unless someone else can claim you as a dependent. For example, if your parents can claim you as a dependent but they choose not to, you still can't claim an exemption for yourself. This situation usually applies to teenagers with part-time jobs. If that is the case, check the Yes box on line 5 of Form 1040EZ; don't check box 6a on Form 1040 or 1040A.

- ✔ **Your spouse:** If filing jointly, you can take one exemption for your spouse, provided that your spouse can't be claimed on someone else's return.

  If you file a separate return, you can claim your spouse as a dependent only if your spouse isn't filing a return, had no income, and can't be claimed as a dependent on another person's return.

  If, by the end of the year, you obtain a final decree of divorce or separate maintenance, you can't take an exemption for your former spouse even if you provided all of his or her support.

  If your spouse died and you didn't remarry, you can claim an exemption for your spouse only if you file jointly. For example, Mr. Jones died on August 1. Because the Joneses were married as of the date of Mr. Jones's death, Mrs. Jones can file a joint return and claim an exemption for her husband. Mrs. Jones reports all her income for 2006 and all of Mr. Jones's income up to August 1.

  On a separate return, you can take an exemption for your deceased spouse only if this person had no income and couldn't be claimed as someone else's dependent.

Dependent exemptions

You can claim an exemption for a dependent if he or she is your qualifying child (see the section "Defining Who Is a Qualifying Child" later in this chapter). You're also allowed to claim a dependency exemption for your qualifying relative if you provide more than half of his or her support, if this person can't be claimed as a dependent on anyone else's tax return, and if he or she passes the five dependency tests. (Don't forget that if you claim someone, that person can't claim a personal exemption on his or her own tax return.)

Okay, you may open your booklets and begin the tests now. In order for a person, other than your qualifying child, to be your dependent, he or she must meet all five of the following tests:

Test 1: Member of your household or relative

Your dependent must either live with you for the entire year as a member of your household or must be related to you by blood or marriage. The required relationships are very specific, so that your parents' siblings qualify on the relationship part of this test, but their children, your cousins, need to live with you for the entire year.

If you file a joint return, you don't need to show that a dependent is related to both you and your spouse. The dependent only needs to be related to one of you.

Temporary absences are ignored. If a person is placed in a nursing home for constant medical care, the absence is also considered temporary.

Here are some more details you may need to consider:

- **Death or birth:** A person who died during the year but was a member of your household until death meets the member of your household test. The same is true for a child who was born during the year and was a member of your household for the rest of the year. A child who was born and died in the same year qualifies, but a stillborn child doesn't. The child must have been born alive — even if for just a moment — to qualify as an exemption.

- **Violation of local law:** A person doesn't meet the member of your household test if your relationship violates local law.

- **Adoption:** Before the adoption is legal, a child is considered to be your child if he or she was placed with you for adoption by an authorized adoption agency (and the child must have been a member of your household). Otherwise, the child must be a member of your household for the entire tax year to satisfy this test.

- **Foster care:** A foster child or adult must live with you as a member of your household for the entire year to qualify as your dependent. However, if a government agency makes payments to you as a foster parent, you may not list the child as your dependent.

- **Employees:** Your nanny or live-in housekeeper doesn't qualify for this test. Living with you may be a requirement of their job, but it doesn't meet the member of the household test.

Test 2: Married person

If your dependent is married and files a joint return, you can't take this person as an exemption.

Personal and dependency exemption phaseout

Depending on your filing status, each $3,300 exemption to which you are entitled is whittled away in $66 increments ($132 for married filing separately) as your income rises above these limits:

Married filing separately	$112,875
Single	$150,500
Head of household	$188,150
Married filing jointly or qualifying widow(er)	$225,750

Here's how it works: For every $2,500 or part of $2,500 of income above these amounts, you have to reduce every $3,300 exemption by 2 percent. For example, if your income is $161,700 and you're single, your personal exemption is reduced to $2,970

Here's the math:

Your exemption	$3,300
Your income	$161,700
Phaseout amount	$150,500
Difference	$11,200
$11,200 ÷ $2,500 (4.48 rounded up to 5)	5
5 × 0.02	10%
$3,300 × 0.10	$330
Exemption allowed ($3,300 − $330)	$2,970

To do the calculation using your numbers, you can find the necessary worksheet in the Form 1040 instruction booklet, which you can obtain at your local post office or bank, on the Internet at www.irs.gov, or by calling 1-800-829-3676.

Test 3: Citizen or resident

The dependent must be one of the following:

- ✔ A U.S. citizen or U.S. resident alien
- ✔ A resident of Canada or Mexico
- ✔ Your adopted child who isn't a U.S. citizen but who lived with you all year in a foreign country

You can't claim a person who isn't a U.S. citizen or resident and lives abroad (in a country other than Canada or Mexico) as a dependent.

Test 4: Income

The dependent's gross income must be less than $3,300. Gross income counts all taxable income, but doesn't include nontaxable income, such as welfare benefits or nontaxable Social Security benefits. Income earned by a permanently and totally disabled person for services performed at a sheltered workshop school generally isn't included for purposes of the income test.

Of course, there are exceptions. Your qualifying relative can have a gross income of $3,300 or more under one of the following conditions:

- ✔ He or she was under the age of 19 at the end of 2006.
- ✔ He or she was under the age of 24 at the end of 2006 and was also a student.

Your qualifying relative is considered a student if he or she is enrolled as a full-time student at a school during any five months of 2006. A school includes technical, trade, and mechanical schools. It doesn't include on-the-job training courses or correspondence schools.

Test 5: Support

You must have provided more than half of your qualifying relative's total support in 2006 in order to claim him or her as your dependent. If you file a joint return, support can come from either spouse. If you remarried, the support provided by your new spouse is treated as support coming from you. For exceptions to the support test, see the sidebar "Children of divorced or separated parents and persons supported by two or more taxpayers." (You can't miss it with a title like that!)

Support includes food, a place to live, clothing, medical and dental care, and education. It also includes items such as a car and furniture, but only if they're for the dependent's own use or benefit. In figuring total support, use the actual cost of these items, but figure the cost of a place to live at its fair rental value. Include money the person used for his or her own support, even if this money wasn't taxable. Examples are gifts, savings, Social Security and welfare benefits, and other public assistance payments. This support is treated as not coming from you.

Total support doesn't include items such as income tax and Social Security taxes, life insurance premiums, or funeral expenses. A person's own funds aren't considered support unless they're actually spent for support. For example, your mother received $2,400 in Social Security and $400 in interest. She paid $2,000 for rent and $400 for recreation. Even though her income was $2,800, she spent only $2,400 for her own support. If you spent more than $2,400 for her support, you can claim her as a dependent because you provided more than half her support.

Children of divorced or separated parents and persons supported by two or more taxpayers

The parent who had custody of the child for most of the year is the one entitled to claim the child as a dependent — provided that both parents together paid more than half of the child's support.

A noncustodial parent can claim the child if any of the following apply:

✔ The custodial parent gives up the right to claim the child as a dependent by signing **Form 8332, Release of Claim to Exemption for Child of Divorced or Separated Parents.** The form allows for the release of an exemption for a single year, a number of years, or all future years. The noncustodial parent must attach this form to the return.

✔ A decree or separation agreement signed after 1984 provides that the noncustodial parent is unconditionally entitled to the exemption and the custodial parent isn't. You must list the child's name, Social Security number, and the number of months the child lived in your home. You also must attach a copy of the cover page of the decree or agreement with the custodial parent's Social Security number written next to his or her name, along with the page that unconditionally states that you can claim the child as a dependent. Don't forget to attach a copy of the signature page of the decree or agreement.

✔ A decree or separation agreement signed before 1985 provides that the noncustodial parent is entitled to the exemption, and that this parent provided $600 or more toward the child's support.

✔ In the extreme right column on line 6 of your 1040 where you list your total exemptions, you must list the number of dependents who didn't live with you separately from the number who did.

Note: If you fail to pay child support in the year it's due, but pay it in a later year, it isn't considered paid for the support of your child in either year.

Even if you can't claim a child because your ex-spouse is claiming the child, you still can claim the child's medical expenses, and you're entitled to the Child and Dependent Care Credit if you're the custodial parent. When the child reaches his or her majority, the custodial parent rules no longer apply. The parent who provides more than 50 percent of the child's support is entitled to the exemption.

Note: The special rules for divorced or separated parents don't apply to parents who never married each other. In such situations, you either have to provide more than half the support of the child or enter into a multiple support agreement (Form 2120).

Even if you didn't pay more than half of a dependent's support, you may still be able to claim this person as a dependent if all five of the following apply:

✔ You and one or more eligible persons paid more than half of the dependent's support. An eligible person is someone who could have claimed the dependent but didn't pay more than half of the dependent's support.

✔ You paid more than 10 percent of the dependent's support.

✔ No individual paid more than half of the dependent's support.

✔ Dependency tests 1 through 4 are met.

✔ Each eligible person who paid more than 10 percent of support completes Form 2120, **Multiple Support Declaration,** and you attach this form to your return. The form states that only you will claim the person as a dependent for 2006.

Securing Social Security Numbers for Dependents

You must list a Social Security number on line 6c column (2), Form 1040 and 1040A, for every dependent. If your dependent was born and died in 2006 and didn't have a Social Security number, write "Died" in column (2). No Social Security number, no deduction, and no right to claim head of household status. Check out Chapter 24 for the ins and outs of how you get one.

If you're in the process of adopting a child who is a U.S. citizen or resident and can't get a Social Security number until the adoption is final, you can apply for an adoption taxpayer number that you can use instead of a Social Security number. To get one, file **Form W-7A, Application for Taxpayer Identification Number for Pending U.S. Adoptions.**

Filing for children and other dependents

Even if you're able to claim someone else (your child, your grandchild, and so on) as a dependent on your return, that person may have to file his or her own income tax return in the following circumstances:

✔ The dependent had unearned income (generally, income other than wages, income from self-employment and tips), and the total of that income plus earned income exceeds $850.

✔ The dependent had earned income in 2006 on which income tax has been withheld.

✔ The dependent had no unearned income but had earned income that exceeds $5,150.

✔ The dependent had gross income that exceeds the larger of (a) $850 or (b) the earned income up to $4,900 plus $300.

For example, suppose that your teenager has interest income of $200 and salary from a summer job of $450. This dependent doesn't need to file because the total income was less than $850. If your teenager had no unearned income but earned $2,000 from a summer job, he or she wouldn't have to file either because the earned income was under $5,150, unless income tax was withheld, and he or she wanted to request a refund.

But here's an important point: Your dependent, who isn't going to have a tax liability in the first place, doesn't need to have income tax withheld from his or her paycheck. Instead, have that dependent claim an exemption from income tax when completing his or her Form W-4. If the dependent didn't claim an exemption on his or her Form W-4, he or she must file to get back the tax that was withheld from his or her paychecks. Remember, though, when he or she reaches $5,150 in income, withholding will have to start, and a new W-4 must be filed with the employer.

You may encounter another wrinkle in the IRS rules for this exemption from withholding to apply — the teenager's investment income (interest) can't exceed $300. If it does, he or she can't claim an exemption from withholding if his or her total income exceeds $850. There's no such thing as being too young when introducing your kid to convoluted tax laws.

A child under the age of 18 (up from 14 prior to 2006) with more than $1,700 in investment income is subject to the *Kiddie Tax*. This income is considered earned by the child's parents at the parents' tax rate (see Chapter 8 for more details on this wonderful tax law nuance).

Defining Who Is a Qualifying Child

In 2005, the IRS finally decided to make a uniform definition for who, exactly, is a qualifying child for the following tax benefits:

- Dependency exemptions
- Head of household filing status
- The earned income credit (EIC)
- The child tax credit
- The credit for child and dependent care expenses

In order for your child to qualify for any of these benefits, he or she needs to meet the age test, the relationship test, the residency test, and the support test. If he or she doesn't meet the requirements of all of these tests, unfortunately he or she isn't your qualifying child in the eyes of the IRS.

Age test

For your child to qualify under the age test for dependency exemptions, head of household filing status, and the earned income credit, he or she must be under the age of 19 at the end of the year or under the age of 24 if a full-time student for some part of each of five months during the year (not necessarily consecutive). No age test applies for a child who is permanently and totally disabled.

To qualify for the child tax credit, your child must be under age 17 by the end of the tax year.

To be eligible for the child and dependent care credit, your child must be under age 13, or permanently and totally disabled. For the purpose of this credit only, expenses you pay for that child in the year of his or her 13th birthday before that birthday can be used to claim the credit; expenses incurred and paid after that birthday can't.

Relationship test

The child must either be your child, adopted child (even if the adoption isn't yet final), stepchild, or eligible foster child (any child placed with you by an authorized placement agency, or by a judgment, decree, or any other court order), your brother, sister, stepbrother, stepsister, or the descendent of one of these relatives.

Residency test

Your qualifying child has to live with you for more than half of the year. Although the days don't have to be consecutive, they do need to add to at least 183. Temporary absences for school, vacation, military service, medical reasons, or for detention in a juvenile detention center, don't count as time away from you.

An exception is made for children who are born during the tax year, provided that they lived with you for the entire period they were alive. So a child who is born on December 30, 2006 is your qualifying child, even though he or she may not make it home from the hospital until January 1, 2007. An exception is also made for a child who dies during the year and for a child kidnapped, provided that his or her kidnapper isn't related.

Finally, the children of divorced or separated parents qualify under the rules set out in the sidebar in this chapter entitled "Children of divorced or separated parents and persons supported by two or more taxpayers."

Support test

Your child must not have provided at least half of his or her own support in order to meet the standards of this test. Calculate how much he or she spent on his or her share of housing costs (including rent, utilities, furnishings and repairs, but not mortgage interest, insurance, or real estate taxes), on clothing, on food, on education, and on medical and dental bills not reimbursed by insurance. Also add vacations and travel, and any other miscellaneous expenses that he or she paid for his or her benefit, and then compare this number against the total cost of that child's share of these items. If the amount he or she paid is less than 50 percent, you meet this test.

If you're having some difficulty in figuring out whether or not your child qualifies under the support test, use the nifty worksheet in **IRS Publication 501, Exemptions, Standard Deduction, and Filing Information.**

Filing a Return for a Deceased Taxpayer

When someone dies, a separate taxpaying entity is created — the decedent's estate. If the estate has more than $600 in income or has a beneficiary who is a nonresident alien, the executor or administrator for the estate (the person responsible for winding up the decedent's financial affairs) must file **Form 1041, U.S. Income Tax Return for Estates and Trusts.** This filing is in addition to the decedent's final tax return.

Suppose the decedent died before April 15. The executor must file a tax return for that individual for the prior year and for the current year. For example, if someone died on April 1, 2007, a return must be filed for 2006, and a final return for 2007 must be filed by April 15, 2008, reporting all the deceased's income and deductions for the period January 1, 2007, through April 1, 2007.

If a decedent died in 2006, you must allocate his or her income based on what was earned and received prior to and including the date of death, and what was received after the date of death. Income received prior to death is reported and taxed on the decedent's final Form 1040; after the date of death, all income received is reported on the Form 1041 for the estate. The good news is that even though you report only part of the year's income on the Form 1040, you get to deduct the full amount of the decedent's personal exemption ($3,300) and the standard deduction, if you're not itemizing.

If the surviving spouse didn't remarry in the same year as the death, a joint return can be filed. The surviving spouse reports his or her income and deductions for the entire year and the deceased's up to the date of death. If you remarry in the same year that your spouse dies, you can file jointly with your new spouse, but not with your deceased spouse.

Medical expenses paid within one year of the decedent's death must be deducted on the decedent's final return; an estate can't take this type of deduction on its Form 1041. If you've already filed that last return, and then you pay more bills (within the one year time limit), you may amend that final return (by filing IRS Form 1040X), take the larger medical deduction, and receive a refund.

If the deceased owned E or EE Savings Bonds and chose not to report the interest during his or her lifetime, the tax on the interest has to be paid by the survivor, unless an election is made to report the interest on the decedent's final return. Doing so may make sense if the deceased died early in the year and had little income and large deductions.

Either the surviving spouse or the executor can sign the deceased's final personal income tax return. Write "DECEASED," the decedent's name, and the date of death at the top of page 1 of the 1040.

If the deceased's final Form 1040 isn't joint with his or her surviving spouse and a refund is due, the person who is receiving the refund must also file a Form 1310, aptly named "Statement of Person Claiming Refund Due a Deceased Taxpayer." Who said the IRS wasn't any good with words?

Must I File?

Yes, you must file a tax return when your income exceeds the amounts for your age and filing status, as shown in Table 4-3.

Table 4-3	When You Must File		
Marital Status	*Filing Status*	*Age**	*Filing Required When Gross Income Exceeds*
Single, divorced, legally separated	Single	Under 65	$8,450
		65 or older	$9,700
	Head of household	Under 65	$10,850
		65 or older	$12,100

Marital Status	Filing Status	Age*	Filing Required When Gross Income Exceeds
Married with a child and living apart from spouse during last 6 months of 2006	Head of household	65 or older	$12,100
Married and living with spouse at end of 2006 (or on date of spouse's death)	Married (joint return)	Under 65	$16,900
		65 or older (one spouse)	$17,900
		65 or older (both spouses)	$18,900
	Married (separate return)	Any age	$3,300
Married and not living with spouse at end of 2006 (or on date of spouse's death)	Married (joint or separate return)	Any age	$3,300
Widowed before 2006 and not remarried in 2006	Single	Under 65	$8,450
		65 or older	$9,700
	Head of household	Under 65	$10,850
		65 or older	$12,100
Qualifying widow(er) with dependent child		Under 65	$13,600
		65 or older	$14,600

*If you turn 65 on January 1, 2007, you're considered to be age 65 at the end of 2006.

When to file

If you don't file by April 16, 2007, you'll have to pay penalties and interest. If you live or work outside the United States, you have an automatic extension of time to file until August 15, 2007.

If you know that you can't file by April 16, you can get an automatic six-month extension of time to file — until October 15, 2007 — by filing **Form 4868, Application for Automatic Extension of Time to File U.S. Individual Income Tax Return.** Keep in mind that you must file this form by April 16, 2007. If you use a credit card to pay the balance owed for 2006, you don't have to separately file **Form 4868;** it's done automatically for you. We explain how to pay by credit card in Chapter 5. You can also obtain extensions of time to file by calling 888-796-1074 or by using your personal computer and a tax software program. The choices are endless, so don't blow the April 16 filing date.

If you're living outside the country, **Form 4868** only automatically extends the due date of your return until August 15, 2007. Form 4868 doesn't, however, extend the time to pay. You'll be charged interest and a late payment penalty of 0.5 percent a month on your unpaid balance if you don't pay at least 90 percent of your tax by April 16, 2007.

If you don't file

You can end up crushing rocks. Remember, Al Capone didn't go to prison for running rackets; he went to the big house for tax evasion. Realistically, though, it's more likely that you'll be assessed penalties that make crushing rocks seem like a stroll in the park. Annually, the IRS prosecutes only 5,000 individuals (you can't call them taxpayers) for tax evasion. Some 80 percent are members of organized crime or drug dealers, and the balance is made up of high-profile individuals and others. You don't want to be one of the others. Even though the government currently is interested in high-profile CEOs, you never know who the IRS may decide to take an interest in. The IRS moves in mysterious ways.

If you don't file, based on the information reported to the IRS by your employers, the IRS either prepares a substitute return and assesses a late filing penalty of 25 percent, a late payment penalty of 0.5 percent a month to a maximum of 25 percent plus interest (and possibly a 75 percent fraud penalty), or issues a summons for you to appear with your tax records so that the IRS can use those records to prepare a more accurate return. Interest and penalties are charged whichever way the IRS decides to proceed.

Where to file

The IRS Web site (www.irs.gov) lists all the addresses to which you can send your forms. So does your instruction booklet. Just look for the "Where To File" link in the "Resources" section.

How to file

Okay, so this whole book is supposed to be about this subject. But what we mean in this short section is that you have a couple ways to get the forms — and the check, if necessary — to IRS Central: You can file the old-fashioned way through the U.S. Postal Service, or you can file electronically.

Electronic filing

Although electronic filing became the most popular form of tax filing for the first time in 2005, we still need to define it. You or the company that offers this service files your return either over a telephone line or one of those faster cable connections. All you need is a computer and a modem.

Through a link on the IRS Web page (www.irs.gov), a group of software companies are offering free online tax filing. Why are they doing this? To ensure that the IRS doesn't jump into the online tax filing market with a competitive product. If free electronic filing sounds too good to be true, you're probably right. We have experienced that when someone offers something for nothing, usually a gimmick is involved. Some companies may have something up their sleeves and try to solicit you for their financial services or products. Others only offer a stripped-down version of their regular software for free — if your taxes are more complicated, they're happy to sell you the necessary software to prepare your return (the electronic filing remains free). Another catch we noticed is that, although they'll file the federal return for free, you need to pay a fee to file your state return.

Each participating software company has set its own eligibility requirements for free filing. Generally, those requirements are based on age, adjusted gross income (AGI), eligibility to file Form 1040EZ, eligibility to claim the Earned Income Credit, state residency, and active duty military status (if applicable). Each company has a description of the criteria for using its free service.

The advantage of electronic filing is that you get your hands on your hard-earned refund in about 10 days, which is approximately three weeks faster than by mail. Also, you can have your refund deposited directly into your bank account. Your state return gets filed along with your federal return at the same time. One transmission does it all.

Some tax preparation firms not only prepare and electronically file your return, but they also loan you money based on the projected amount of the refund. These clever loans are called *refund anticipation loans*.

Our principal objection to these refund anticipation loans is that they're too pricey. Here's why: According to the IRS, the average refund taxpayers received in 2004 was $2,063. Some tax preparation firms can arrange for an on-the-spot loan for the amount of your refund. According to the Consumer Federation of America and the National Consumer Law Center, the typical loan for the average refund of $2,063 bears a 222.5 percent annual percentage rate. This is the result of the loan being repaid within 10 days when the refund is deposited into a special account set up by the lender. A class action suit was once settled against H&R Block involving deceptive business practices concerning their refund loans. This tax filing season, you may notice a number of car dealerships offering tax preparation services. They're hoping that by offering this service together with refund anticipation loans, they can seduce more people into driving off the lot with one of their latest models. How's that for one-stop shopping?

Filing by mail or other private delivery service

Face it, many taxpayers (nearly half) still do it the old-fashioned way, with a trip to the post office late on the night of April 16. If you're one of those taxpayers who feels the job isn't done right without that postmark on the upper right-hand corner of the envelope, you need to consider the following.

✔ Make sure you have proof of mailing. For the post office, that means a Certified Mail receipt.

✔ If you choose to use a private delivery service, you need to know that only certain types of deliveries (such as Airborne, DHL, FedEx, and UPS) provide you with adequate proof (in the form of dated receipts) should the IRS question whether you have timely filed.

A Final Bit of Advice

Here's an old saying from a wise man — the father of one of us. He said, "Son, there are two kinds of payments in the world you should avoid: too early and too late." That kind of advice also applies to filing your taxes. Filing taxes late leads to IRS interest and penalties; paying your taxes too early, or withholding too much, is simply an interest-free loan to the federal government. Thanks for the advice, Dad.

Part II
Tackling the Various Forms

The 5th Wave — By Rich Tennant

And this is Bud Mellnick who writes all of our tax publications.

GLORSPITZ.

Overheard at the IRS

In this part . . .

Rituals make the world go 'round. And what ritual is quite so enjoyable as completing one's tax return? Visiting your local department of motor vehicles to renew your driver's license? Waiting in line at the post office to buy some stamps? Cleaning up an overflowing toilet? Figuring out who to call when you lock your car keys in the trunk?

It all starts with Form 1040 in its three guises: 1040EZ, 1040-A, and plain old 1040. After you get the form right, you have the challenge of finding the tax documentation needed to plug answers into those small lines. And just when you're ready to start (after pulling out your hair), you find yourself wading knee-deep through those dreadful IRS instructions.

Thanks to the *For Dummies* translation of jargon into plain English, here is what you need to know to get an A+ on tax return preparation. And we show you some tricks along the way to make it easier on yourself next time around.

Chapter 5

Easy Filing: 1040EZ and 1040A

In This Chapter
▶ Living the really EZ life: Using the 1040EZ
▶ Living the semi-easy life: Using the 1040A
▶ Letting the IRS do the math for you

*I*t's best to begin a challenging part of the book with something EZ. Trust us, things get much more complicated in a hurry. However, if you can file a simplified tax form, you'll be able to bypass much of what's in the rest of Part II of this book. For now, though, take a look at the easier forms (1040EZ and 1040A). They're easier because you don't have as many lines to fill out, as many schedules to complete and attach, or as many receipts and records to dig out.

The most difficult decision to make is whether to choose the 1040EZ or the 1040A (the infamous *Short Form*). From then on, it's downhill. In fact, the forms are so simple that the IRS computes the tax for you.

Who Can File a 1040EZ?

With the 1040EZ (see Figure 5-1), all you have to do is fill in the numbers — a snap with this short form. The IRS likes this form because an optical scanner can process it. You'll like this form, too, because you don't have to do the math. The nice folks at the IRS can do it for you (see the sidebar "Let the IRS figure your tax," later in this chapter). You may use the 1040EZ if you meet the following criteria:

✔ You're single or married filing jointly and don't claim any dependents.

✔ You (and your spouse, if married filing jointly) are younger than age 65 on December 31, 2006, and aren't blind, which otherwise entitles you to increase your standard deduction.

✔ You have income only from wages, salaries, tips, taxable scholarships or fellowship grants, unemployment compensation, dividends from the Alaska Permanent Fund, and qualified state tuition program earnings — and not more than $1,500 of taxable interest income.

✔ Your taxable income (line 6) is less than $100,000. That's taxable income after deducting $8,450 if single or $16,900 if married.

✔ You aren't receiving any advance earned income credit (EIC) payments. You can find out whether you received any advance EIC payments by referring to box 9 of your W-2. (See Chapter 6 for more on advance EICs.)

✔ You aren't itemizing deductions (on Schedule A) or claiming any adjustments to income (for example, an IRA or student loan interest deduction) or tax credits (such as childcare expenses).

Department of the Treasury—Internal Revenue Service

| Form **1040EZ** | **Income Tax Return for Single and Joint Filers With No Dependents** (99) **2006** | | OMB No. 1545-0074 |

Label (See page 11.)
Use the IRS label. Otherwise, please print or type.

L A B E L H E R E	Your first name and initial	Last name		Your social security number
	If a joint return, spouse's first name and initial	Last name		Spouse's social security number
	Home address (number and street). If you have a P.O. box, see page 11.		Apt. no.	▲ You **must** enter your SSN(s) above. ▲
	City, town or post office, state, and ZIP code. If you have a foreign address, see page 11.			Checking a box below will not change your tax or refund.

Presidential Election Campaign (page 12) ▶

Check here if you, or your spouse if a joint return, want $3 to go to this fund? . . ▶ ☐ **You**   ☐ **Spouse**

Income

Attach **Form(s) W-2** here.

Enclose, but do not attach, any payment.

1 Wages, salaries, and tips. This should be shown in box 1 of your Form(s) W-2. Attach your Form(s) W-2. — **1**

2 Taxable interest. If the total is over $1,500, you cannot use Form 1040EZ. — **2**

3 Unemployment compensation and Alaska Permanent Fund dividends (see page 13). — **3**

4 Add lines 1, 2, and 3. This is your **adjusted gross income.** — **4**

5 If someone can claim you (or your spouse if a joint return) as a dependent, check the applicable box(es) below and enter the amount from the worksheet on back.
   ☐ **You**   ☐ **Spouse**
   If no one can claim you (or your spouse if a joint return), enter $8,450 if **single;** $16,900 if **married filing jointly.** See back for explanation. — **5**

6 Subtract line 5 from line 4. If line 5 is larger than line 4, enter -0-. This is your **taxable income.** ▶ **6**

Payments and tax

7 Federal income tax withheld from box 2 of your Form(s) W-2. — **7**

8a **Earned income credit (EIC).** — **8a**

b Nontaxable combat pay election.   **8b**

9 Credit for federal telephone excise tax paid. Attach Form 8913 if required. — **9**

10 Add lines 7, 8a, and 9. These are your **total payments.** ▶ **10**

11 **Tax.** Use the amount on **line 6 above** to find your tax in the tax table on pages 24–32 of the booklet. Then, enter the tax from the table on this line. — **11**

Refund

Have it directly deposited! See page 18 and fill in 12b, 12c, and 12d or Form 8888.

12a If line 10 is larger than line 11, subtract line 11 from line 10. This is your **refund.** If Form 8888 is attached, check here ▶ ☐ — **12a**

▶ **b** Routing number   ▶ **c** Type: ☐ Checking ☐ Savings

▶ **d** Account number

Amount you owe

13 If line 11 is larger than line 10, subtract line 10 from line 11. This is the **amount you owe.** For details on how to pay, see page 19. ▶ **13**

Third party designee

Do you want to allow another person to discuss this return with the IRS (see page 19)? ☐ **Yes.** Complete the following. ☐ **No**

Designee's name ▶   Phone no. ▶ (   )   Personal identification number (PIN) ▶

Sign here

Under penalties of perjury, I declare that I have examined this return, and to the best of my knowledge and belief, it is true, correct, and accurately lists all amounts and sources of income I received during the tax year. Declaration of preparer (other than the taxpayer) is based on all information of which the preparer has any knowledge.

Joint return? See page 11.
Keep a copy for your records.

| Your signature | Date | Your occupation | Daytime phone number |
| Spouse's signature. If a joint return, **both** must sign. | Date | Spouse's occupation | (   ) |

Paid preparer's use only

| Preparer's signature ▶ | Date | Check if self-employed ☐ | Preparer's SSN or PTIN |
| Firm's name (or yours if self-employed), address, and ZIP code | | EIN | Phone no. (   ) |

For Disclosure, Privacy Act, and Paperwork Reduction Act Notice, see page 23.   Cat. No. 11329W   Form **1040EZ** (2006)

Figure 5-1: Form 1040EZ, Page 1.

If you can't file Form 1040EZ, all is not lost. You may be able to use another simplified form: 1040A (see "Who Can File a 1040A?" later in this chapter).

Filling Out a 1040EZ

The IRS has provided nice little boxes where you can put your numbers (but please leave off the dollar signs). What a considerate organization!

Line 1: Total wages, salaries, and tips

Enter your wages (from box 1 of your W-2 form). If your employer hasn't provided you with this form by January 31, 2007, go squawk at your payroll and benefits department. If you still don't have that W-2 in hand by February 15, phone the IRS and let them know. If you're interested in what all those boxes on your W-2 mean, see Chapter 6, line 7.

Line 2: Taxable interest income of $1,500 or less

Enter your interest income on line 2. You can locate this amount in boxes 1 and 3 of your 1099-INTs, which your bank and other investment companies should provide. If this amount is more than $1,500, you can't use the 1040EZ. Sorry!

Line 3: Unemployment compensation and Alaska Permanent Fund dividends

Once upon a time, unemployment compensation wasn't taxable. But that was before "tax reform." To report your unemployment compensation received during the tax year, enter on line 3 the amount from box 1 of Form 1099-G that your state sends you.

Although you can elect to have tax withheld at the rate of 10 percent on your unemployment, so you won't be caught short next April 15, this offer is one that most people are likely to refuse. Form W-4 V, Voluntary Withholding Request is used to request this election. To turn on the withholding faucet, check box 5 of the form and submit it to the unemployment office where you file for benefits. After you voluntarily elect to have 10 percent withheld, you can change your mind — just file a new Form W-4V with your unemployment office and check box 7.

To get the lowdown on Alaska Permanent Fund dividends, skip ahead to line 13 in the 1040A section of this chapter. Please don't be annoyed when we ask you to refer to different sections. We're asking you to do it because we don't want to bore you by constantly having to repeat the same instructions all over the place.

Line 4: Adjusted gross income

Add the amounts of lines 1, 2, and 3 together and enter the total here. The figure on line 4 is your adjusted gross income (AGI).

Line 5: Deductions and exemptions

From your AGI, you have to subtract your standard deduction and personal exemption. The amount you can deduct is indicated to the left of the boxes, but you first have to take the IRS *yes-or-no test*. The question asks if someone can claim you (or your spouse if a joint return) as a dependent. If you can answer "no," then enter either $8,450 if you're single, or $16,900 if you're filing a joint return with your spouse, and move on.

If your answer is yes to yourself (and/or your spouse, if married filing joint), check the appropriate box on line 5, and then complete the worksheet on the back of Form 1040EZ to find the amount you can deduct from your income. That's because if someone else is entitled to claim you as a dependent, you aren't entitled to a personal exemption for yourself.

As an example, pretend that you're preparing the return of a teenage dependent who earned $3,300 last summer. Because we know that at first glance this worksheet (on page 2 of the form) looks intimidating, we help you wade through it.

Line A.	Enter the amount of her wages	A.	$3,300
	Additional amount allowed by law		$250
			$3,550
Line B.	Minimum standard deduction	B.	$ 850
Line C.	The larger of A or B	C.	$3,550
Line D.	Maximum standard deduction if single	D.	$5,150
Line E.	The smaller of C or D	E.	$3,550
Line F.	Exemption amount (because you claim her, enter 0)	F.	0
Line G.	Add lines E and F and enter that amount on line 5 on Form 1040EZ	G.	$3,550

Whether you're able to take the full amount of the deduction or are limited because you (or your spouse) is someone else's dependent, you should feel good about this number that you're deducting from your taxable income. The IRS is effectively saying that this amount of income is tax-free to you.

Line 6: Taxable income

Subtract the amount that you entered on line 5 from line 4, and enter the remainder here. Line 6 is your taxable income. If line 5 is larger than line 4, enter zero (-0-).

Line 7: Federal income tax withheld

Enter your federal tax withheld (shown in box 2 of your W-2) here. Your federal income tax withheld is the amount of tax that you already paid during the tax year. Your employer withholds this money from your paycheck and sends it to the IRS. Don't overlook any withholding from box 4 of Forms 1099-INT or 1099-G, the forms where interest income and unemployment compensation are reported.

Line 8a: Earned income credit (EIC)

Single filers whose adjusted gross income (from line 4) is less than $12,120 may be eligible for the EIC (see Chapter 14 for more details about this credit). The credit can be as high as $412 for a single filer with no kids and is subtracted from your tax. For joint filers with no kids, the income limit is $14,120. If you don't owe tax, the credit is refunded to you. You don't have to compute the credit. Just look up the credit for your income in your instruction booklet and enter that amount here.

A number of studies show that almost a third of the people who claim the EIC have no right to do so. So here's what happens to people who get caught. In addition to all the penalties the IRS can impose, anyone who fraudulently claims this credit is ineligible to claim it for ten years. For taxpayers who are merely careless or intentionally disregard the rules, the penalty is two years.

Rounding off dollars

No pennies please, even though the form has a column for cents. You're supposed to round to the nearest dollar when filling out your 1040, 1040A or 1040EZ. Drop amounts under 50 cents and increase amounts from 50 to 99 cents to the next dollar. If you have one W-2 for 5,000.55 and another for 18,500.73, enter 23,501 ($5,000.55 + $18,000.73 = $23,501.28) not $23,502 ($5,001 + $18,501).

Line 8b: Nontaxable combat pay election

Income you earn while performing military service in a designated combat zone is exempt from income tax, and generally speaking, it's also excluded from the definition of earned income for the purpose of calculating the EIC. This exclusion is good, if the amount of that income, including your Basic Allowance for Housing (BAH) and your Basic Allowance for Subsistence (BAS), would otherwise push you over the limit to claim the EIC. For some people, though, excluding this income eliminates all earned income from your return. In this case, you may elect to include your nontaxable combat pay for the purpose of calculating the EIC. If you make this election, fill in the amount of your nontaxable combat pay in line 8b, add it to any other earned income you have, and then proceed with calculating your credit.

Line 9: Credit for federal telephone excise tax paid

In one of the odder tax twists this year, and as a result of several tax court cases that didn't go the IRS's way, the IRS has agreed to stop collecting federal excise tax on long distance phone calls. The IRS also has agreed to refund the tax collected, retroactive to services that were billed after February 28, 2003.

The IRS will allow you to claim either the actual amount of tax you paid in the period from February 28, 2003, through May 25, 2006, as a credit, or will allow you to claim a *safe-harbor* amount. Check out Chapter 14 to find out more about how to claim this credit.

Line 10: Total payments

Add the amounts on lines 7, 8, and 9, and put the sum here.

Line 11: Tax

To figure your total federal income tax for the year, look up the amount on line 6 in the tax tables (available at www.irs.gov) for your income bracket and filing status. For example, if you're single and your taxable income (on line 6) is $32,100, find the row for $32,100 to $32,150 and read across to the "Single" column. In this example, your tax is $4,589.

When you've found the appropriate row and column for your taxable income and filing status — and while you have your finger in the right place — enter the amount here on line 11.

Line 12a: Refund time!

The last computation that you have to make is quite simple. Look at lines 10 and 11. If the amount on line 10 is larger than line 11, you're going to get a refund. Just subtract line 11 from line 10 and enter the amount on line 12a. The amount on 12a is your refund!

You can have your refund deposited directly into your bank account, which should speed up your refund by more than three weeks. However, a number of people we know are reluctant to take the IRS up on this offer. Their reason: "The IRS knows too much about me already."

If we haven't scared you away, the sample check in Figure 5-2 shows you how to get the information that the IRS needs to wire the money to your account from your check. Your routing number referred to on line 12b is the nine-digit number at the bottom left in Figure 5-2. On line 12c, check the type of account and then enter your account number on line 12d, which is the number to the right of the routing number in Figure 5-2.

If you can't decide which of your accounts you want your refund deposited to, you can now choose to have your refund split between as many as three accounts, including your IRA or Health Savings Account (HSA). If you want your refund deposited to more than one account, fill out **Form 8888, Direct Deposit of Refund,** and attach it to the back of your return. Check out Chapter 8 to find out more about this new option.

If the numbers on the bottom of your check are confusing or you have only a savings account, don't hesitate to call your bank. Anyone answering the phone should be able to tell you the bank's routing number over the phone. You can lift your account number right off your bank statement. It's that EZ!

```
PAUL MAPLE                                                      1234
LILIAN MAPLE
123 Main Street                                            15-0000/0000
Anyplace, NY 10000  _____ 20 _____

PAY TO THE
ORDER OF_____  | $ |_____|

                                                          DOLLARS

ANYPLACE BANK      (Routing      (Account
Anyplace, NY 10000  Number        Number
                    (line 11b)    (line 11d)
For _____

|:250000005|  |:200000··86·              1234
```

Figure 5-2: A sample check.

Line 13: Amount you owe

Yes, you guessed it. When the amount on line 11 is larger than that on line 10, you still owe because you didn't have enough tax withheld during the year. Subtract line 10 from line 11 and enter the amount on line 13. Fess up and pay up.

Plastic anyone? Whether you file your return electronically or by mail, you can charge the balance due with a toll-free call or Web site visit. Official Payments Corp. (888-2-PAY-TAX, that's 888-272-9829 or www.officialpayments.com) and Link2Gov Corp. (888-PAY-1040, that's 888-729-1040, or www.PAY1040.com) accept Visa, MasterCard, American Express, and

Discover payments, and partial payments are allowed. You can pay the balance on your 2006 return, make estimated tax payments (Form 1040ES), and make a payment when you request an extension of time to file.

The four reasons why paying with plastic isn't especially attractive are

- ✔ Credit-card companies often charge an obscene rate of interest of 20 percent or higher.

- ✔ Resolving billing disputes can prove to be a nightmare. After you make a payment, you can't cancel it. You can place a stop payment on a check.

- ✔ Credit-card companies may potentially release confidential information when they sell the mailing list of their customers, which most of them do.

- ✔ Credit-card holders (that's you) pay a "convenience fee" of about 2.49 percent on top of their interest charges, because the IRS doesn't pay the fee that credit-card companies normally collect from merchants. You'll be advised of the "convenience fee" right upfront. If it's too high, hang up.

We can think of better ways to earn frequent-flier miles.

The new and friendlier IRS has become quite ingenious! It constantly is coming up with more convenient (convenient for whom?) direct payment methods such as:

- ✔ **Paying by telephone.** The IRS has your bank deduct your payment directly from your account. You can make balance due, estimated tax (Form 1040ES), and extension of time to file payments (Form 4868) this way. To sign up for this marvelous option, dial 800-555-4477.

- ✔ **Paying electronically.** Electronic filers will be prompted to a payment option that allows for the direct payment from your account by your bank. You can file early and direct your bank to send what you owe on April 16, 2007. That's the last day this delayed payment option is available.

Finishing up

If you're filing a paper return, don't forget to attach your W-2s (and any other tax forms that you may have received that show amounts of tax withheld, such as a 1099-INT) to your return. Staples are just great! (And staples are preferable to tape and paper clips. You don't want your W-2s going one way at IRS Central and your tax return going another.)

If you owe money, make your check payable to the "United States Treasury," and write your Social Security number in the lower-left corner of the front of your check, along with the notation "2006 Form 1040EZ income tax" — just in case the folks at the IRS think you're trying to make a payment on your new boat but sent them the check by mistake.

Finally, sign your return and mail it, together with your check (but don't staple your check to your return — just leave it loose in your return envelope, together with your stapled return) to the IRS Service Center for your area. Normally, an addressed envelope is provided with your tax form. If you don't have the address, see the addresses provided on the back cover of your tax instruction booklet, which is also available on the Internet at www.irs.gov.

If you're filing electronically just keep your W-2's (and 1099-INTs, if you have them) in a safe place so you'll have them to show the IRS if the IRS comes calling. Any money you owe can be deducted directly from your bank account by filling in the correct routing information (see Chapter 4 for specific details). The computer program you use guides you through all the finishing steps, including providing your electronic signature. The final step is to click the button and send your return. What could be E-Zer?

With electronic filing, you can prepare and file your taxes on one date, and arrange to make the payment on another. Through the wonders of modern technology (and the IRS's willingness to be somewhat flexible), you can instruct the IRS not to take the money for your 2006 taxes from your account until April 16, 2007 (remember that April 15, 2007, is a Sunday) even though you may have filed your return in February or March. And who said the IRS wasn't flexible?

Who Can File a 1040A?

If you don't meet the requirements to file a Form 1040EZ, but you really don't think your situation is that complicated, you may be able to file a Form 1040A (the so-called "Short Form"). You may file a Form 1040A if you meet all the following requirements:

✔ You have income only from wages, salaries, tips, taxable scholarships, fellowship grants, pensions or annuities, taxable Social Security benefits, withdrawals from your individual retirement account (IRA), unemployment compensation, interest, and dividends.

✔ Your taxable income (line 27, page 2) is less than $100,000. That's not your total income. That's your income after all allowable deductions.

✔ You aren't itemizing your deductions.

When you meet all the criteria for filing Form 1040A, be sure to check the section "Who Can File a 1040EZ?" earlier in this chapter to determine whether you can file the even easier Form 1040EZ.

You can also use Form 1040A (see Figure 5-3) and claim the EIC (including making the nontaxable combat pay election), the deduction for contributions to an IRA, nondeductible contributions to an IRA, the credit for child and dependent care expenses, the credit for the elderly or the disabled, child tax credits, education credits, or the student loan interest deduction. You may use the 1040A even if you made estimated tax payments for 2006, or if you can take the exclusion of interest from series EE U.S. Savings Bonds issued after 1989.

You can't use 1040A if you received a capital gain distribution on Form 1099-DIV that includes entries in boxes 2b, 2c, or 2d. Why? Drop down to line 10 to find out.

Completing Form 1040A

We hope you've already figured out your filing status and exemptions. If you need help, see Chapter 4. You can round off to the nearest dollar so you don't have to fiddle with pennies. See the sidebar "Rounding off dollars," earlier in this chapter.

Line 6: Exemptions through line 9b: Qualified dividends

Amazingly enough (because the IRS rarely does anything that makes much sense), the first part of Form 1040A and Form 1040 are identical. So check out the Form 1040 instructions in Chapter 6 to find out how to complete Lines 6 through 9b of your 1040A.

Form **1040A**	Department of the Treasury—Internal Revenue Service		
	U.S. Individual Income Tax Return (99) **2006**		IRS Use Only—Do not write or staple in this space.

Label
(See page 18.)

Use the IRS label. Otherwise, please print or type.

Presidential Election Campaign ▶

L A B E L   H E R E

Your first name and initial | Last name | OMB No. 1545-0074

Your social security number

If a joint return, spouse's first name and initial | Last name

Spouse's social security number

Home address (number and street). If you have a P.O. box, see page 18. | Apt. no.

▲ You **must** enter your SSN(s) above. ▲

City, town or post office, state, and ZIP code. If you have a foreign address, see page 18.

Checking a box below will not change your tax or refund.

Check here if you, or your spouse if filing jointly, want $3 to go to this fund (see page 18) ▶ ☐ You ☐ Spouse

Filing status
Check only one box.

1 ☐ Single
2 ☐ Married filing jointly (even if only one had income)
3 ☐ Married filing separately. Enter spouse's SSN above and full name here. ▶
4 ☐ Head of household (with qualifying person). (See page 19.) If the qualifying person is a child but not your dependent, enter this child's name here. ▶
5 ☐ Qualifying widow(er) with dependent child (see page 19)

Exemptions

6a ☐ **Yourself.** If someone can claim you as a dependent, **do not** check box 6a.
b ☐ **Spouse**
c Dependents:

(1) First name Last name	(2) Dependent's social security number	(3) Dependent's relationship to you	(4) ✓ if qualifying child for child tax credit (see page 21)
			☐
			☐
			☐
			☐

If more than six dependents, see page 21.

Boxes checked on 6a and 6b
No. of children on 6c who:
• lived with you
• did not live with you due to divorce or separation (see page 22)
Dependents on 6c not entered above
Add numbers on lines above ▶

d Total number of exemptions claimed.

Income

Attach Form(s) W-2 here. Also attach Form(s) 1099-R if tax was withheld.

If you did not get a W-2, see page 24.

Enclose, but do not attach, any payment.

7 Wages, salaries, tips, etc. Attach Form(s) W-2. | 7
8a **Taxable** interest. Attach Schedule 1 if required. | 8a
b Tax-exempt interest. **Do not** include on line 8a. | 8b
9a Ordinary dividends. Attach Schedule 1 if required. | 9a
b Qualified dividends (see page 25). | 9b
10 Capital gain distributions (see page 25). | 10
11a IRA distributions. 11a | 11b Taxable amount (see page 25). | 11b
12a Pensions and annuities. 12a | 12b Taxable amount (see page 26). | 12b
13 Unemployment compensation, Alaska Permanent Fund dividends, and jury duty fees. | 13
14a Social security benefits. 14a | 14b Taxable amount (see page 28). | 14b
15 Add lines 7 through 14b (far right column). This is your **total income.** ▶ | 15

Adjusted gross income

16 Penalty on early withdrawal of savings (see page XX). | 16
17 IRA deduction (see page 28). | 17
18 Student loan interest deduction (see page 31). | 18
19 Jury duty pay you gave your employer (see page XX). | 19
20 Add lines 16 through 19. These are your **total adjustments.** | 20
21 Subtract line 20 from line 15. This is your **adjusted gross income.** ▶ | 21

For Disclosure, Privacy Act, and Paperwork Reduction Act Notice, see page 58. | Cat. No. 11327A | Form **1040A** (2006)

Figure 5-3: Form 1040A, Page 1.

Line 10: Capital gain distributions

If you own mutual funds, you may be the recipient of capital gain distributions. How can you tell? If you receive a Form 1099-DIV and box 2a has a number in it, you've received a capital gain distribution on which you're going to owe some tax.

Normally, you'd include your capital gain distributions with your other capital gains on Schedule D (see Chapter 12), which would mean, of course, that you couldn't file a Form 1040A. However, if your only capital gain income comes in the form of distributions from mutual funds (box 2a only of the 1099-DIV, mind you), and if you fit the profile of a Form 1040A filer in all other regards, you're off the hook. Just fill in the total amount from box 2a of your 1099-DIV into line 10 of your 1040A.

Before leaving line 10, remember that if you want the reduced capital gain rates to apply, you must use the capital gain worksheet in your instruction booklet when you get to line 28. That's the line where you compute your tax. We supply you with a worksheet in Chapter 8 so you can make this tax-saving computation.

Lines 11a and 11b: Total IRA distributions

The custodian of your IRA, bank, or investment company should send you a Form 1099-R, Distributions from Pensions, Annuities, Retirement or Profit-Sharing Plans, IRAs, Insurance Contracts, etc., by January 31 for the prior tax year if you withdrew money from your IRA. The amount in box 1 of this form is entered on line 11a, and the amount in box 2a is entered on line 11b. Because this is an IRA, the amounts in boxes 1 and 2a are usually the same.

But if you made nondeductible contributions to your IRA, not all the money you withdraw is taxable. To compute what's taxable in such instances, you're going to have to fill out **Form 8606, Nondeductible IRAs** (see Chapter 6 for the lowdown on IRA distributions). If you elected to have tax withheld on your IRA payments, don't forget to enter the tax withheld (from box 4 of your 1099-R) on line 39, together with the tax withheld from your paychecks as reported on your Form W-2.

Lines 12a and 12b: Total pensions and annuities

If you received income from a pension or an annuity during 2006, the payer will provide you with a 1099-R showing the amount you received in box 1 and the taxable amount in box 2a. (See Chapter 6 to find out whether the pension plan computed the correct amount.) Enter the amount from box 1 on line 12a and the amount from box 2a on line 12b. If income tax was withheld, enter the amount from box 4 on line 39, along with the tax withheld from your salary as indicated on your W-2. To understand what all those boxes on your 1099-R mean, flip to Chapter 6.

Line 13: Unemployment compensation, Alaska Permanent Fund dividends, and jury duty fees

If you received unemployment compensation in 2006, you'll receive a **Form 1099-G, Certain Government and Qualified State Tuition Program Payments** from your state early in 2007. Enter the amount you find on box 1 of that form on line 13 of your 1040A (see Chapter 6 to find out more about this issue).

If you were forward thinking enough when you put in your unemployment claim, you may have had 10 percent income tax withheld from your payments. Be sure to include any amounts you find in box 4, Tax Withheld, on line 39 of your 1040A.

As for Alaska Permanent Fund dividends, when you think of Alaska, you may picture open spaces, clean air, and plenty of snow. All true, but you also need to think of all that oil hiding underneath the tundra. And thanks to the oil, every year residents receive a small cash dividend, ranging in value from between $500 and $2,000, depending on the year. Although normal dividends and distributions are reported on Form 1099-DIV, distributions from the Alaska Permanent Fund aren't; the state sends a notice of payment instead.

Let the IRS figure your tax

Instead of you struggling with the math that's part of every income tax form, you may want the IRS to figure your tax for you. For 1040EZ and 1040A filers who don't want the hassle, letting the IRS compute your tax after you enter your basic information on the forms is headache-free. If you're entitled to a refund, the IRS will send you a check. If you owe money, the IRS will bill you. And if you're entitled to the earned income credit or credit for the elderly or disabled, you don't have to spend hours filling out the forms.

Be careful, though: Even the IRS makes mistakes (no kidding!). If you're entitled to one of the credits, check the IRS computation (the credits will be itemized on it) when you receive your bill or refund check.

Here's how 1040EZ filers do it: On lines 1 through 8, fill in the lines that apply to you. If your income is less than $12,120, you may be entitled to the earned income credit. So print "EIC" on line 8, in the blank space to the right of the text, "Earned income credit (EIC)." By doing this, you alert the IRS that you're entitled to the earned income credit.

Attach your W-2s. Sign your return and send it to the IRS Service Center for your area. Ignore all the "subtract this line from that and enter it here" on Form 1040EZ. The IRS does all that fun stuff.

For 1040A filers, fill in any of lines 1 through 26 that apply. If you're entitled to a credit for child and dependent care

expenses, you must complete Schedule 2 (the child and dependent care form) and attach it to your return. Enter the amount of credit on line 29.

If you're entitled to claim a credit for the elderly or the disabled, attach Schedule 3, and, on lines 1 through 9 of Schedule 3, check the box for your filing status (single, married, and so on). On Form 1040A, line 30, in the space to the right of the words "Schedule 3," print "CFE." You won't have to tackle this nightmarish form. The IRS will prepare it for you.

If you're entitled to the earned income credit, the IRS will fill in the credit for you. Print "EIC" in the blank space on line 41. Fill in page 1 of Schedule EIC and attach it to your 1040A.

Fill in lines, 31, 32, 33, 34, and 37 if they apply.

Sign your return. Attach your W-2s and make sure that your Schedule 2 or 3 is attached if you're claiming any childcare or elderly and disabled credits. If you're claiming a child, adoption, or education credit, attach the appropriate schedules. Mail your return to the IRS Service Center for your area.

Here's a warning, however: Although this method sounds EZ, it may lead to a false sense of security because you may overlook something like an important deduction that can work to your tax advantage. Also, the IRS isn't infallible and may make an error.

For folks in Alaska, if you're filing Form 1040EZ, enter your distribution from the Permanent Fund on line 3. For 1040 filers, it goes on line 21. In case you're asking who makes up these rules, aliens from outer space wouldn't be a wild guess.

For those individuals lucky enough to sit on a jury in 2006 who received payment from the court for the experience, line 13 is also where you need to include your jury pay. You need to declare this income, even if you have to give it to your employer because they continued to pay you during your jury service. If you fall into this category, put the full amount of your jury duty fees on line 13, and then deduct them on line 19.

Lines 14a and 14b: Social Security benefits

Sad to say, but for many of you who have diligently saved for your retirement years, or for those of you who continue to work even after you've begun collecting Social Security benefits, you may owe some income tax on those benefits. If you have any income other than your Social Security, you probably want to check out Chapter 6 to see if a portion of your benefits is taxable.

If, after you've completed the worksheets, you find you have some taxable Social Security income, enter the total amount of your Social Security (box 5 of your Form SSA-1099) on line 14a and the taxable portion on line 14b. If on the other hand you don't need to include any part of your Social Security benefits in your taxable income, don't even bother filling out line 14a. The IRS doesn't want to know this information unless there's some tax involved.

To make paying your taxes easier, Congress passed a law that enables you to have tax withheld on your Social Security at rates of 7 percent, 10 percent, 15 percent, or 25 percent, so that you won't owe a bundle next April 15. Send **Form W-4V, Voluntary Withholding Request,** to the Social Security folks when you want tax withheld.

Line 15: Total income

Here you put the total of lines 7 through 14b. All those numbers to add!

Line 16: Penalty on early withdrawal of savings

If you cash a Certificate of Deposit before its maturity date, chances are good that you'll have to pay a penalty. Line 16 is where you can deduct the amount of that penalty. You can find the correct amount on your Form 1099-INT in box 2, which your bank has to mail to you by January 31, 2007.

Line 17: Your (and your spouse's) IRA deduction

If you think the government wants you to save for your retirement, you're right! IRA rules have become much more flexible in the last few years. You're now entitled to deduct up to $4,000 ($5,000 if you're age 50 or older) for yourself, and another $4,000 for your spouse ($5,000 if age 50 or older), even if he or she isn't working at a paid job. All you need is enough earned income (wages) to cover the total amount of IRA contributions you're making. And, of course, nothing in this life comes without a price. Your contributions may be limited if you, or your spouse, is eligible to participate in a retirement plan at work. Check out Chapter 7 and 20 for more about IRAs and IRA phaseout amounts.

Tax-deductible and nondeductible IRAs, along with Roth IRAs, now are somewhat more flexible savings vehicles with more people eligible to contribute to them. See Chapter 20 for details.

Line 18: Student loan interest deduction

You can deduct up to $2,500 of interest that you paid on a loan used to pay for higher education (what comes after high school) and certain vocational school expenses. Ask the vocational school whether it qualifies for this deduction if you have to borrow to pay the tab. The interest you paid is reported on **Form 1098-E, Student Loan Interest Statement.**

You must meet a host of rules before you can nail down this deduction. The main rule is that if you're single, the deduction quickly gets whittled away after your income hits $50,000 and disappears altogether at $65,000. For joint filers, it starts to shrink at $105,000 of income, with the deduction getting wiped out at $135,000. In Chapter 7, we explain who's entitled to the deduction, for how many years it can be claimed, and what loans and education expenses qualify. You can deduct interest for the full term of the loan rather than merely for 60 months, which was the case prior to 2002.

The beauty of the student loan interest deduction is that you don't have to itemize your deductions to claim it. You can still claim the standard deduction (see "Line 24: Standard deduction") if you also have this deduction. As with any loan, where the amount still owed decreases over time, you pay the most interest at the beginning of the payback period and the least at the end. So, if you're just starting to repay your student loans, you're in luck. If you're close to the end, the deduction's not worth much, but congratulations! Your education is almost all paid off!

Line 19: Jury duty pay you gave your employer

If your employer continued to pay you while you sat on a jury, you probably had to hand over any check you received from the court to your boss. No problem! Even though you have to declare the amount you received from the court on line 13, you can deduct any amounts you gave to your employer here, on line 19.

Line 20: Total adjustments

Add lines 16 through 19. What could be easier?

Line 21: Adjusted gross income

Now you get to subtract the total of the deductions that you claimed on lines 16 through 19 and entered on line 20 from your total income (line 15). Do the subtraction and enter that amount here.

You may be entitled to claim the EIC, and now is the time to check out Chapter 14 to see if you qualify.

Line 22: Successful transcription of adjusted gross income to back of Form 1040A

You enter your adjusted gross income on line 22 (which you already totaled on line 21). Be careful; don't transpose numbers!

Lines 23a and 23b: Standard deduction questions

Check the appropriate box(es). If you or your spouse is 65 or older (born before January 2, 1942) or either of you is blind, you're entitled to an increased standard deduction. To figure the increased amount, refer to Chapter 9. Enter that amount on line 24.

If you're married filing separately and your spouse itemizes deductions, check box 23b and enter zero (-0-) on line 24. You aren't entitled to any standard deduction because both you and your spouse must use the same method. Unless you want to claim a zero standard deduction because your spouse is itemizing his or her deductions, you must abandon using Form 1040A to be able to itemize your deductions on the regular 1040.

Line 24: Standard deduction

So many choices! Find your filing status and enter the number here.

- ✔ Single: $5,150
- ✔ Head of household: $7,550
- ✔ Married filing jointly or qualifying widow(er): $10,300
- ✔ Married filing separately: $5,150

If you checked the first box on line 23a because you're older than 65, you're entitled to increase your standard deduction by $1,000 if married, and by $1,250 if single. If you checked box 23b, enter zero (-0-) on this line. For someone who is single, blind, and older than 65, the standard deduction is increased by $2,500 for a total of $7,650. If you and your spouse both are older than 65, your standard deduction of $10,300 increases by $2,000 for a total of $12,300. If all the boxes on line 23a are checked (older than 65 and blind), the increase in the standard deduction is $4,000, for a total of $14,300.

If your parent or someone else can claim you as a dependent, go to Chapter 9 to compute your standard deduction. Enter that amount (instead of the standard deduction to which all others are entitled).

If you think that you can get a higher deduction by itemizing your deductions on Schedule A, you can't file with Form 1040A. The standard deduction versus itemized deduction option is available only when filing Form 1040.

Line 25: IRS subtraction quiz

Go ahead and subtract the amount you have on line 24 from your adjusted gross income on line 22. Put the result of this mathematical computation here. If you ended up with a number on line 24 that was larger than the one on line 22 (and you started to wonder how you can subtract a larger number from a smaller number), you have to start over from the beginning. No! Just kidding! If line 24 is larger than line 22, you enter (-0-) on line 25.

Line 26: Total number of exemptions times $3,300

If the amount on line 25 is $112,875 or less, multiply the number of exemptions you claimed on line 6d by $3,300 and enter the total here. If you housed someone displaced by Hurricane Katrina, you may be entitled to an additional exemption amount of $500 per person (up to four people) if they stayed with you for at least 60 days, and if they are unrelated to you.

After the amount on line 25 is more than $112,875, your personal exemptions begin to phase out. If you fall into this category, Chapter 4 helps you calculate your limited exemption amount.

Line 27: Taxable income

Now subtract the amount on line 26 from line 25, and carefully place that number here. Well done! You've arrived at your taxable income.

Line 28: Find your tax

Using the tax tables (available at www.irs.gov) to find your tax means that you don't have to make a mathematical computation to figure your tax. For example, if you're single and your taxable income is $43,610, look up the bracket between $43,600 and $43,650 and read across to the single column. The appropriate tax is $7,464.

If you have entries on your Form1040A on lines 9b or 10, stop! Don't use the tax tables, or you'll pay more than you have to. Use the tax computation worksheet that we provide at line 44 in Chapter 8 or the qualified dividends and capital gain worksheet in the Form 1040A Instruction Booklet.

We hate to be negative, but more and more taxpayers are finding themselves snagged by the Alternative Minimum Tax (AMT). Fortunately, if you're otherwise able to file a Form 1040A, your chances of falling into this category are small; however, if you have a large family and are claiming many dependents, the AMT may just catch you. If your filing status is single or head of household and your taxable income on line 27 is $42,500 ($62,550 for married filing joint, and $31,275 for married filing separately), check out the worksheet in your Form 1040A instruction booklet and do the calculations.

If you're subject to the AMT, add the amount from line 25 of the worksheet in your instruction booklet to the amount from the tax tables (or from your qualified dividends and capital gain tax worksheet), and then place the total on line 28 of Form 1040A. To the right of the amount, place "AMT" so the IRS knows you're not giving them extra money out of the goodness of your heart.

Line 29: Credit for child and dependent care expenses

Use Schedule 2 to figure this amount. Chapter 14 explains exactly who qualifies, and how to fill out this form.

Line 30: Credit for the elderly or the disabled

Use Schedule 3 to compute this credit. Schedule 3 is substantially the same as Schedule R of the Form 1040, and we show you how to fill out both of these forms in Chapter 14.

Line 31: Education credits

"The more you learn, the more you earn." The government likes it when you further your education because it can collect more tax.

If you, your spouse, or one or more of your dependents, attended a post-secondary school during 2006, you may qualify for the Hope Scholarship Credit, the Lifetime Learning Credit, or both. In order to get the credits, though, you need to fill out **Form 8863, Education Credits (Hope and Lifetime Learning Credits).** We explain the credit and show you how to complete the form in Chapter 14.

Line 32: Retirement contributions credit

This credit is designed to encourage joint filers with incomes below $50,000 ($37,500 for heads of households and $25,000 for single filers) to save for retirement. Once again, there are all sorts of rules and regulations surrounding who may use this credit and under what circumstances. We tell you if you're entitled to this credit in Chapter 14 and, if so, how to complete the **Form 8880, Credit for Qualified Retirement Savings Contributions.**

Line 33: Child tax credit

If you have dependent children, you can cut your income tax bill by up to $1,000 per child. Welcome to the child tax credit. Of course, not every taxpayer qualifies due to income limits on the credit (although if you're filing a Form 1040A, you most likely do qualify). And not every dependent child qualifies. Chapter 4 explains which children qualify and which don't. Remember, to be eligible for this credit, a child must be a U.S. citizen or resident and under age 17 on December 31, 2006.

To compute the child tax credit, the IRS directs you to a worksheet in your instruction booklet. We lay out a plain English version in Chapter 14.

There are two types of child tax credit available to you:

- ✔ **Child tax credit:** Most people who are eligible to claim this credit will find it easy to compute. This credit is nonrefundable, so you actually have to have some tax showing on line 28 in order for it to be valuable.

- ✔ **Additional child tax credit:** This credit is refundable (you may get more tax back than you actually paid in), so it comes into play only when the regular child tax credit exceeds your tax. People with three or more kids get to compute the refundable credit two ways and then choose the method that produces the largest refund. If you have fewer than three kids, you can use only one method, which — if nothing else — makes your tax return less complicated. You compute whether you're entitled to the additional credit on **Form 8812, Additional Child Tax Credit.** Enter the amount from line 13 of Form 8812 on line 41.

Line 34: Total credits

To compute your total credits, add the amounts from lines 29 through 33, and enter them here.

Line 35: Another IRS subtraction problem

Gee whiz, it never ends, does it? Now subtract your total credits (line 34) from the amount on line 28. Enter that remainder here. However, if your total credits are more than the amount on line 28, you get the easy way out and can enter zero (-0-).

Line 36: Advance earned income payments

This amount is in box 9 of your W-2s, which your employer provides for you.

By filing Form W-5, EIC Advance Payment Certificate, with your employer, you don't have to wait until you file your return to claim this credit. Depending on the amount of your wages and your filing status, up to $1,648 (the 2006 maximum amount — it increases every year) can be added to your paycheck throughout the year. This advance payment is available only when you have at least one qualifying child — see line 6 in Chapter 8.

Line 37: Total tax

Add lines 35 and 36 to arrive at your total tax.

Line 38: Total federal income tax withheld

Add together the amounts from box 2 of all your W-2s and W-2Gs, plus any amounts that are listed in box 4 on your 1099-INT, 1099-G, 1099-R, and 1099-DIVs. These amounts have been withheld from payments you have received or amounts that you have already paid to the U.S. Treasury during 2006. Be careful not to miss any payments — you want to get credit for what you've already paid!

Line 39: 2006 estimated tax payments and amount applied from 2005 return

The U.S. income tax system is based on a "pay-as-you-go" system — you're supposed to pay your tax on income as you earn it, not at the end of the year after you've figured out how much you've earned. Accordingly, if you don't have taxes withheld from your income, you need to make periodic payments to the IRS in order to pay as you go. Chapter 15 goes into great detail about how you go about making these payments. What you need to know here is that if you've made estimated income tax payments throughout the year, fill in the amount of those payments here on line 39.

If you have overpaid your current year's tax, you may elect to apply that overpayment against your next year's tax liability. This is a reasonably common practice, especially if you're a taxpayer who must make estimated tax payments (as opposed to withholdings). If you elected to apply your 2005 overpayment to your 2006 tax liability, you should add that amount to your estimated tax payments and put the total on line 39 of your Form 1040A.

Line 40a and 40b: Earned income credit and nontaxable combat pay election

Just as with the Form 1040EZ, if your adjusted gross income (AGI) falls below certain levels, you may be entitled to the earned income credit (EIC). Check out Chapter 14 for the income limits for this credit as well instructions for how to fill out Schedule EIC. Whether you're filing a Form 1040A or a Form 1040, you need to complete and attach this form to your return in order to get the credit.

In order to qualify for the 2006 EIC, your income needs to fall below the following amounts: Married filing joint with no children — $14,120, with one child — $34,001, with two or more children — $38,348; Single with no children — $12,120, with one child — $32,001, and with two or more children — $36,348. Unfortunately, even if your income is within the allowed limits, if you have investment income from interest, dividends, and capital gains of more than $2,800, you're just out of luck. This credit is intended to benefit people whose income is almost entirely from working.

The credit can be as high as $4,536 for someone with two kids. The exact amount of the credit is based on your income, filing status (married or single), and whether you have one, two, or no children. If the credit exceeds your tax, the difference is refundable. Not bad!

Anyone who fraudulently claims the EIC is declared ineligible to claim it for ten years. For people who are reckless or intentionally disregard the rules, the penalty is two years. The IRS initiated a program in 2004 where 25,000 filers had to precertify that their children lived with them for more than six months to be eligible for the credit. The IRS actually wanted to contact twice as many filers, but Congress wouldn't let them.

If you served in a military combat zone in 2006, and you want to include a portion of your nontaxable combat income in order to get the most advantage from EIC, you can. Check out line 8b of the 1040EZ earlier in this chapter to see how you make the election.

Line 41: Additional child tax credit

This is the refundable portion of the child tax credit that we explain in "Line 33: Child Tax Credit." To get part of the credit refunded, you have to file **Form 8812, Additional Child Tax Credit.** Flip back to line 33 for a quick refresher. You can find instructions for Form 8812 in Chapter 14.

Line 42: Credit for federal telephone excise tax paid

It may seem extremely picky (tax law usually is), but the IRS has recently been on the losing side in several court cases regarding federal taxes on long distance telephone calls. As a result of these losses, the IRS has decided to stop charging this tax going forward. Good news, but it only gets better. They're also allowing you to claim back amounts you were charged between February 28, 2003 and May 25, 2006.

If you're a careful record keeper and have all your long-distance phone bills back to February, 2003, terrific! Haul those babies out, add up the federal taxes you paid, and place the total on line 42. If you're missing a few of those bills (or more), and can't absolutely reconstruct what you paid, all is not lost. We show you how to calculate the credit on **Form 8913** in Chapter 14. Place your total credit on line 42 of Form 1040A, and be sure to attach **Form 8913** to your return. You want the IRS to see that you didn't pluck this number out of thin air.

Line 43: Total payments

Now you get to add. Find the sum of lines 38, 39, 40a, 41, and 42.

Line 44: We smell refund!

Subtract your total tax (line 37) from your total payments (line 43) — if line 37 is smaller than line 43. Here's your refund! Don't spend it all in one place.

Although refunds are fun, a large refund is a sign that you made the IRS an interest-free loan. More was withheld from your salary than should have been. You can lower the amount of tax withheld by filing Form W-4 with your employer's payroll department. See Chapter 15 for a quick guide through this form.

Lines 45a and 46: What to do with your refund

If you have a refund but think you're going to owe tax in 2007 and can't trust yourself to hang on to the cash, you may want to apply some or all of the refund toward next year's tax (do this on line 46).

Applying the refund toward next year's tax is an excellent option for people who must make quarterly estimated payments, because doing so can significantly reduce the amount of those payments and perhaps even eliminate the first of those payments, which is due on April 16, 2007. This way your money works for you. For example, say you must make an estimated payment of $1,500 for 2007 on April 16, and you've overpaid your 2006 taxes by $1,000 (the amount on line 44 of your 2006 return). If you apply the entire $1,000 overpayment toward the $1,500 estimated tax that is due, you have to pay only $500 instead of paying the full $1,500 and you don't have to wait for your $1,000 refund. After you make this choice, you can't change your mind and ask for it back. You can, however, claim it as an additional payment on your 2007 return.

Lines 45b–d: Direct deposit of your refund

You can speed up the receipt of your refund by almost three weeks and minimize the chances of its loss or theft by requesting that it be deposited directly to your account. *Note:* Consider whether you want to share this type of confidential and personal information — your bank account numbers. See the instructions under "Filling out a 1040EZ," earlier in this chapter. If you want your refund deposited into your bank account, jot down the routing number from one of your checks on line 45b. (That's the nine-digit number shown in Figure 5-2.) On line 45c, check the type of account. Your account number is the number to the right of your routing number as shown in Figure 5-2; enter your account number on line 45d.

If you're interested in splitting your refund between as many as three accounts, now you can. Check out the information in Chapter 8 on what you need to know about **Form 8888, Direct Deposit of Refund**.

Line 47: Amount you owe

Those are three of the most dreaded words in the English language. If the amount on line 37 is greater than that on line 43, subtract line 43 from line 37. Put your Social Security number on the check and write "2006 FORM 1040A" on the line at the bottom left of your check. Make out the check to the United States Treasury.

If you want to charge what you owe on a credit card, read our cautions in "Line 12: Payment due" in the "Filling Out a 1040EZ" section, earlier in this chapter. You can also have the IRS withdraw the balance you owe directly from your account. How's that for a friendlier IRS!

Line 48: Estimated tax penalty

If you owe $1,000 or more in tax, and the sum of the estimated tax payments you made in 2006 plus your withholding doesn't equal either 90 percent of your 2006 tax or 100 percent of your 2004 tax (so-called "Safe Harbor"), you'll be assessed a penalty. You can escape this penalty in a number of ways. **Form 2210, Underpayment of Estimated Tax,** which we discuss in detail in Chapter 15, is used to both compute or to escape the penalty. Chapter 18 has valid excuses that should work.

Final Instructions

If you're filing your return using snail-mail, put your John or Jane Hancock on your form. (That means sign it, okay? Don't get funny and write in *John Hancock;* the IRS doesn't have our sense of humor.) Staple your W-2s and any 1099s where tax was withheld to the front of your return. If you owe money, place your check or money order separately in the mailing envelope; the IRS doesn't want your payment stapled, clipped, taped, or superglued to your return. Mail your return and payment to the IRS Service Center for your area. Check out the IRS Web site (www.irs.gov) for the correct address if you're missing the preaddressed envelope that comes with your Form 1040A instruction booklet.

If you're filing electronically, check out "Finishing up" earlier in this chapter for the instructions for what to do for a 1040EZ. The process to electronically file a 1040A is exactly the same.

Chapter 6

Form 1040: Income Stuff

Surely you remember the old war slogan "Divide and conquer!" (We think Alexander the Great or some other real famous warrior said it.) Well, that's our strategy here. We break down each section and each line of Form 1040 and pound each one into submission.

Note: You're going to be jumping into a deeper section of the pool here. If you're unsure about which Form 1040 to use (EZ, A, or the "long" version), you need to take one step back to Chapter 5. Likewise, if you're unsure of your filing status (single, married filing separately, married filing jointly, head of household), take two steps back to Chapter 4.

Now for Chapter 6, which deals with the guts of the return, the income section (see Figure 6-1). Each heading has the specific line references of Form 1040 listed first. After you go through a segment, plug the correct number onto the same line of your 1040 and move on.

Figure 6-1:
The Income section of Form 1040 lists how much you made in 2006.

Income			
Attach Form(s) W-2 here. Also attach Forms W-2G and 1099-R if tax was withheld.	7 Wages, salaries, tips, etc. Attach Form(s) W-2		7
	8a **Taxable** interest. Attach Schedule B if required		8a
	b **Tax-exempt** interest. **Do not** include on line 8a	8b	
	9a Ordinary dividends. Attach Schedule B if required		9a
	b Qualified dividends (see page 23)	9b	
	10 Taxable refunds, credits, or offsets of state and local income taxes (see page 23)		10
	11 Alimony received		11
	12 Business income or (loss). Attach Schedule C or C-EZ		12
	13 Capital gain or (loss). Attach Schedule D if required. If not required, check here ▶ ☐		13
If you did not get a W-2, see page 22.	14 Other gains or (losses). Attach Form 4797		14
	15a IRA distributions	b Taxable amount (see page 25)	15b
	16a Pensions and annuities	b Taxable amount (see page 25)	16b
Enclose, but do not attach, any payment. Also, please use Form 1040-V.	17 Rental real estate, royalties, partnerships, S corporations, trusts, etc. Attach Schedule E		17
	18 Farm income or (loss). Attach Schedule F		18
	19 Unemployment compensation		19
	20a Social security benefits	b Taxable amount (see page 27)	20b
	21 Other income. List type and amount (see page 29)		21
	22 Add the amounts in the far right column for lines 7 through 21. This is your **total income** ▶		22

Lines 6a–6d: Exemptions

On lines 6a–6d, you need to list everyone for whom you can claim an exemption amount (which reduces your taxes) on this return. Check box 6a for yourself (unless someone else can claim you as his or her dependent). If you're married and filing a joint return, check box 6b, too. List all of your dependents in the 6c table. You need each person's first and last names, their Social Security numbers, and their relationship to you. Check the box next to each name (line 6c (4)) if the dependent qualifies for the child tax credit. Remember, the days of writing "Applied For" in the Social Security boxes are long gone; if you don't list a valid Social Security number here, the IRS will disallow that exemption.

The list to the right of boxes 6a, 6b, and table 6c simply add up all the information you've already indicated.

1. **On the first line, count one for yourself and one for your spouse (maximum of two).**

2. **On the second line, add up the number of dependents you've listed in table 6c who lived with you for a majority of the year.**

3. **On the next line, put the number of dependents you're claiming who didn't live with you due to divorce.**

4. **On the fourth line, put the number of dependents who aren't listed on either of the two lines directly above.**

5. **When you've completed all the lines, add them up, and place the total in the 6d box directly below these numbers.**

   This is the number of exemptions you may claim on this return.

If you're not clear on whether someone is, or isn't, your dependent, or whether they qualify for the child tax credit, check out Chapter 4 for all the dependency rules and regulations.

Lines 7–22: Income

Income is, in brief, money or something else of value that you receive regardless of whether you work for it. Most people know that wages earned from toiling away at jobs are *income*. But income also includes alimony, certain interest, dividends, profits on your investments, and even your lottery winnings or prizes won on *Wheel of Fortune*.

In this chapter, you discover the meaning of all those little slips of paper you receive from your employer, your bank, your investment firms, Social Security, your state government, and anyone else who may have paid you some money during the year. We show you how to use all this information to complete lines 7 through 22, the "Income" section of Form 1040. You can round off to the nearest dollar, so you don't have to fiddle with pennies. It only takes a minute or two; we promise.

Line 7: Wages, salaries, tips

If you work for an employer, you'll receive the famous **Form W-2, Wage and Tax Statement,** which your employer is required to mail to you no later than January 31, 2007. This form helps you find out what you earned during the year and how much your employer withheld from your wages for taxes.

You need to have your Form W-2 in front of you in order to fill in an amount on line 7 (see Figure 6-2). You may notice that you have three or four pages of the same W-2, or that you have multiple copies on the same page. Why? You mail Copy B with your federal return; you file Copy C with your neat and organized tax records; and you affix the state copy (Copy 2) to your state return. If you have a fourth copy, you can either keep it with Copy C, or you can circular file it — the choice is yours. Your employer has already sent Copy A to the folks at the Social Security Administration. If you look at the lower-left corner of your W-2s, you see what to do with each copy.

a Control number		22222	Void ☐	For Official Use Only ▶ OMB No. 1545-0008		

b Employer identification number (EIN)		1 Wages, tips, other compensation	2 Federal income tax withheld

c Employer's name, address, and ZIP code	3 Social security wages	4 Social security tax withheld
	5 Medicare wages and tips	6 Medicare tax withheld
	7 Social security tips	8 Allocated tips

d Employee's social security number	9 Advance EIC payment	10 Dependent care benefits

e Employee's first name and initial	Last name	Suff.	11 Nonqualified plans	12a See instructions for box 12
			13 Statutory employee ☐ Retirement plan ☐ Third-party sick pay ☐	12b
			14 Other	12c
				12d

f Employee's address and ZIP code				

15 State	Employer's state ID number	16 State wages, tips, etc.	17 State income tax	18 Local wages, tips, etc.	19 Local income tax	20 Locality name

Form **W-2** **Wage and Tax Statement** **2006** Department of the Treasury—Internal Revenue Service

Copy A For Social Security Administration — Send this entire page with Form W-3 to the Social Security Administration; photocopies are **not** acceptable.

For Privacy Act and Paperwork Reduction Act Notice, see back of Copy D.

Cat. No. 10134D

Do Not Cut, Fold, or Staple Forms on This Page — Do Not Cut, Fold, or Staple Forms on This Page

Figure 6-2:
Form W-2 shows how much dough you earned and how much various taxes you paid to the government.

If you're self-employed and you don't receive a W-2, you get to skip this line, but you're going to end up doing tons more work completing Schedule C so you can fill in line 12 of the 1040. For farmers, it's Schedule F. Retirees can skip 'em both — one of the many perks of retirement!

If your W-2 is wrong, contact your employer to have it corrected as soon as possible. Otherwise, you'll pay too much or too little tax — and you wouldn't want to do that. If you didn't receive your W-2, call your employer. If that doesn't work, file **Form 4852, Substitute for Form W-2, Wage and Tax Statement,** or **Form 1099-R, Distributions from Pensions, Annuities, Retirement or Profit-Sharing Plans, IRAs, Insurance Contracts, Etc.,** which is a substitute for missing W-2s (and missing 1099-Rs). The magnanimous IRS allows you to estimate your salary and the amount of tax withheld on this form. You then attach Form 4852 to your tax return. You can get that form or any other form by calling the IRS toll-free at 800-829-3676 or downloading it from the IRS Web site at www.irs.gov.

What those W-2 boxes mean

Each of the numbered boxes on your W-2 contains either welcome information (like your gross income, which momentarily makes you feel rich) or the type of information that surely will have you shaking your head in disbelief (such as the total amount of different types of taxes that you paid throughout the year, which effectively makes you feel poor again). If you notice in this discussion that we're skipping over some of those little boxes, rest assured that we explain them when we need to in later chapters.

Box 1: Wages, tips, and other compensation

Your taxable wages, tips, other compensation, and taxable fringe benefits are listed here. This box is a biggie. Everything but the kitchen sink was thrown into box 1. Common examples are your salary, your tips, and the taxable portion of any fringe benefits like the personal-use part of your company car. Other stuff that your employer tossed into box 1 includes back pay, bonuses, commissions, severance or dismissal pay, and vacation pay.

Because box 1 is a catchall, the figure in it may be larger than your actual cash salary. Get it over with — fill in the amount on line 7. If you have one or more W-2s, add 'em up and put in the total.

Box 8: Allocated tips

If you worked in a restaurant and didn't report all your tip income to your employer, box 8 includes the difference between your share of at least 8 percent of the restaurant's income and what you reported. This amount doesn't mean that you're entitled to this money. Your employer figures what 8 percent of the restaurant's income amounts to. This is the minimum amount of tip income the employees have to pay tax on. Your employer then computes your share, which doesn't let you off the hook. The IRS can always audit the restaurant's books and determine, for example, that the tip rate was in fact 15 percent. Ouch! This income isn't reported in box 1. Therefore, you must add it to the amount on Form 1040 (line 7). You must also enter this amount on **Form 4137, Social Security and Medicare Tax on Unreported Tip Income.** You get an earful about this form in Chapter 8.

Box 9: Advance EIC (Earned Income Credit) payment

If you filed a **Form W-5, EIC Advance Payment Certificate,** with your employer in 2006, you may have already received all, or a portion, of the Earned Income Credit (EIC) you're entitled to for 2006. (You can obtain Form W-5 from your employer, by phoning the IRS at 800-829-3676, or by accessing the IRS Web site at www.irs.gov.) If so, you'll find the prepaid amount in box 9 of your Form W-2. When the time comes, you're going to add this amount back to the tax you calculate before subtracting off the full amount of your EIC. This may sound confusing now, but you need to trust us here — it works!

Check out Chapter 8 to find out if your income qualifies you to take the Advanced EIC and the EIC. If you do, we can show you how to fill out Schedule EIC.

Box 10: Dependent-care benefits

If your employer has a daycare plan or provides daycare services, this box includes the reimbursement from your employer for daycare costs or the value of the daycare services that your employer provides. If you have elected to put up to $5,000 into a Section 125 (cafeteria plan) to pay qualified dependent care expenses, the amount you put into that plan will also be included here. Any amount over $5,000 is taxable to you, and has been included in box 1 — don't report it again!

You need to fill out **Form 2441, Child and Dependent Care Expenses** if you're filing a Form 1040, or **Schedule 2, Child and Dependent Care Expenses for Form 1040A Filers** if you're filing a Form 1040A. Other than a slight difference in name, these forms are identical and are used for two reasons:

- ✔ To find out if you qualify for the child and dependent care credit (and how much that will be)
- ✔ To see if any portion of the dependent care benefits shown in box 10 of your Form W-2 is taxable

Take a look at Chapter 14 to discover how to complete these forms. They're not difficult, but you do need to do some information gathering beforehand.

If your box 10 shows less than $5,000, but your Form 2441 (or Schedule 2) indicates that a portion of the amount you had deducted for dependent care is taxable, add that amount to line 7 of your 1040 (or 1040A), and write "DCB" (dependent care benefits) next to it.

Box 12: See instructions for box 12

This cryptic message is meant to direct you to the instructions on the reverse side of your W-2 to find out what the symbols in this box mean. This box includes your 401(k) or 403(b) contributions, the premium on group life insurance of more than $50,000 (that amount also is included in box 1), nontaxable sick pay, employer contributions to your medical savings account, and uncollected Social Security and Medicare taxes on tips that you reported to your employer (and that your employer wasn't able to collect from you — the letter "A" will be next to the amount). Uncollected Social Security tax is added to your final tax bill and is reported on Form 1040 (line 63) along with other taxes that you owe. Next to it, write "UT," which stands for *uncollected tax on tips.* A list of codes, A through BB, on the back of your W-2 explains what each code stands for in box 12. Some of the items entered in boxes 12a through 12d also are entered in box 1 (Wages); others aren't. If an amount in box 12 of your W-2 is already included in box 1, make sure that you don't enter it again on line 7 of your 1040. You don't want to pay more tax than you have to, do you? A silly question, but we thought we'd ask it anyhow.

Box 13: Statutory employee

Full-time life insurance salespeople, agents, commission drivers, traveling salespeople, and certain homeworkers can file as self-employed rather than as employees. This status enables them to deduct their business expenses on **Form 1040, Schedule C (Profit or Loss From Business)** or on **Schedule C-EZ.**

Don't report the amount of your W-2's box 1 on line 7 of your Form 1040 if you want to deduct your business expenses *and* "Statutory Employee" in box 13 is checked. Report your wages and expenses on Schedule C or Schedule C-EZ. By doing it this way, you'll be able to deduct all your travel, entertainment, auto, and other business-related expenses instead of having to claim them as itemized deductions. (See Chapter 11 for loads of Schedule C stuff.) Line 1 of Schedules C and C-EZ has a box to check if you're claiming business expenses as a statutory employee.

Different definitions of what you earned

Many of the boxes on your W-2 include wage information that you don't need to include on your Form 1040. Think of them as FYI boxes. They simply show you the different ways that the IRS computes income for assessing different taxes.

For example, box 3, "Social Security wages," reports the amount of your wages for the tax year that is subject to Social Security taxation (not the benefits that the Social Security Administration is paying you!). Your Social Security wages may differ from your wages as reported in box 1 because some types of income are exempt from income tax but aren't exempt from Social Security tax. For example, if you put $3,000 in a 401(k) retirement plan in 2006, box 3 is going to be $3,000 higher than box 1.

Box 5, "Medicare wages and tips," reports the amount of your wages that is subject to Medicare tax. For most people, their wages that are subject to Medicare equal their total wages that are reported in box 1. Although the amount of your wages that is subject to Social Security tax is 6.2 percent up to $94,200, there is no maximum on wages subject to the 1.45 percent Medicare tax.

Box 7, "Social Security tips," is the amount of tips that you received and reported to your employer. This amount is included in box 1, so don't count it again!

Box 11, "Nonqualified plans," pertains to retirement plans in which you can't defer the tax. Distributions to an employee from a nonqualified or a nongovernmental Section 457 (Deferred Compensation Plan) are reported in box 11 and in box 1. Distributions from governmental Section 457 plans are reported on Form 1099-R. Be thankful that this box applies to only a few people.

Box 12, "See instructions for box 12," is for entering 401(k) contributions (code D), adoption benefits (T), Archer medical savings accounts (R), and excludable moving expenses (P). Taxable fringe benefits, such as your personal use of a company car and reimbursed employee business expenses, are included in box 1 of your W-2 and not here.

The first $5,250 of employer-paid educational expenses is tax-free. Although benefits above that amount are taxable, see Chapter 9, lines 20–26, to determine whether you can claim a deduction for any portion of the taxable amount. The exclusion now applies to graduate-level courses. Aren't you glad you went back to school so that you can understand all this stuff? Up to $205 per month of employer-provided parking and $105 per month for the total of commuter transit passes and commuter van pools are considered tax-free fringe benefits (these are the 2006 amounts). If, however, you opt for the cash, they're taxable.

If the statutory employee box is checked, deducting your business expenses on Schedule C or C-EZ is usually to your advantage. If you take them as a miscellaneous itemized deduction instead, 2 percent of your *adjusted gross income (AGI)* will be subtracted from your total expenses (the infamous 2 percent haircut) and then you may lose even more if your income is too high. Taking these deductions on Schedule C or C-EZ also keeps these expenses out of the clutches of the dreaded *Alternative Minimum Tax (AMT)*, which we explain in Chapter 8. Finally, deducting these expenses on Schedule C lowers your AGI, which means that you pay less tax.

Line 8a: Taxable interest income

Add up all of your interest income from boxes 1 and 3 of all of your **Form 1099-INTs** — if the total is $1,500 or less, enter that amount on this line. If this amount is more than $1,500, you must complete Schedule B (or Schedule 1, if you're filing a Form 1040A). No biggie! Schedule B and Schedule 1 are both easy to complete, and are essentially identical, with the exception of a couple of questions regarding foreign accounts at the bottom of Schedule B. For more information, you have permission to cruise to Chapter 10 to dive further into that schedule. When you get the total, come back and fill it in. With the exception of municipal bonds, all the interest that you earn is taxable. If you need examples, the IRS publications have pages of them. But don't report the interest that you earn on your IRA or retirement account; that interest is taxed only when you withdraw the funds.

If you keep lots of your money in bank accounts, you may be missing out on free opportunities to earn higher interest rates. Chapter 22 discusses money market funds, a higher yielding alternative to bank accounts, and shows you ways to keep more of your investment income.

Line 8b: Tax-exempt interest

Because municipal bond interest isn't taxable, you're not going to receive a 1099. Your year-end statement from your stockbroker includes this information. The IRS wants you to fill in the interest that you received on tax-exempt bonds. Plug it in. Just so you know: Although this interest isn't taxable, the number is used to compute how much of your Social Security benefits may be subject to tax.

Surprisingly, some people who invest money in tax-exempt bonds actually shouldn't. These people often aren't in a high enough income tax bracket to benefit. If your taxable income isn't at least $30,650 and if you're filing as a single (or $61,300 if married filing jointly), you shouldn't be so heavily into tax-exempt bonds. You'd be better off moving at least some of your money into taxable bonds or stocks (where gains can be taxed at rates as low as 5 percent, 10 percent, or 15 percent). See Chapter 22 for more information about investments that are subject to more favorable tax rates.

Line 9a: Ordinary dividends income

In 2003, dividends were much in the news as President George W. Bush pushed through tax changes that reduced the income tax rate on corporate dividends to 15 percent for most people, and a measly 5 percent for lower-bracket (10 or 15 percent) taxpayers. So this change must mean that when you receive your **Form 1099-DIV, Dividends and Distributions,** everything on it will be taxed at no more than 15 percent. Right? Wrong!

Box 1a of your Form 1099-DIV includes the amount of *all* the ordinary dividends (not capital gains), whether qualified for the lower rate or not. If you have more than one 1099-DIV, add together all the amounts in box 1a, and plop the total on line 9a of your 1040 or your 1040A. If you're using Schedule B or 1040A Schedule 1, you'll carry the number from line 6 of those schedules over to line 9a of your 1040 or 1040A. Easy as pie!

Form 1099-DIV includes all kinds of dividends and distributions from all sorts of companies, credit unions, real estate investment entities, and so forth. Some of these may qualify for the special "qualified dividends" tax rates, others don't. If you have an entry in box 1b of your 1099-DIV, make sure you check out Chapter 10 in great detail.

Although you aren't required to file 1040 Schedule B or 1040A Schedule 1 when your dividend income is less than $1,500, if you have more than a couple Form 1099-DIVs arriving in your mailbox, you may want to anyway. One of the most common reasons for the IRS to contact you is because what you report on your return doesn't match the information they've gathered about you from other sources. The more detail you can give on your return, the easier it is to find the discrepancies when they occur. These schedules are probably the easiest IRS forms ever devised, and you'll have absolutely no problems in completing them. Again, check out Chapter 10 to find out how to complete Schedule B.

Line 9b: Qualified dividends

It would be really easy for us to tell you to just add together all the amounts in box 1b of your 1099-DIV and write that number onto line 9b of your Form 1040 or 1040A. Oh, if only life were that simple.

Companies who can attest to whether or not their dividends qualify for the special rates fill out Form 1099-DIVs; what they don't know is whether or not you've held the stock for the required period of time so that your period of stock ownership qualifies. Remember, in order for a dividend to be eligible for these lower rates, not only does the type of dividend payment matter, but also the length of time you've owned the security. Not all dividends reported to you on line 9b qualify; only you can make that determination. Check out the rules in Chapter 10 regarding qualifying dividends.

If you do finally end up with a number in line 9b of your 1040 or your 1040A, *you will overpay your tax* unless you use the tax computation worksheet that we provide at line 44 in Chapter 8 or the qualified dividend and capital gain worksheet in the Form 1040A Instruction Booklet. Paying what you have to is bad enough, but if you ignore our advice and end up paying more, don't expect any thank-yous from the IRS. On the other hand, if you have only $10 of qualified dividends, and you don't have a tax software program that automatically calculates your tax, we understand when you decide that making the computations necessary for your $10 to be taxed at the lower 5 percent or 15 percent rates is hardly worth the hassle.

Because we've been talking about the 1099-DIV extensively here, just a quick heads up — capital gains distributions that have been paid to you from either a mutual fund or from a corporation during 2006 are reported to you here. If you have no other capital gains or losses for 2006, you can list these gains on line 13, which is explained later in this chapter. If you have other capital gains or losses to report, you're going to have to fill our Schedule D first. Sorry!

Line 10: Taxable refunds, credits, or offsets of state and local income taxes

If you itemized your deductions last year and deducted your state or local income tax, *and* if you either received a refund of a portion of that tax or applied a portion of what you paid last year to this year's tax liability, you have to declare that portion as income. When you think about it, adding back this amount that you deducted from your income last year to income this year is only fair. If you didn't itemize your deductions last year and you received a refund, you're off the hook.

State and local tax refunds that you receive are reported on **Form 1099-G,** a form that your state department of revenue sends to you. If you chose to apply part or all of your 2005 state tax overpayment to your 2006 estimated state or local tax payments that you have to make (instead of having it refunded), the overpayment still is considered a refund even though a check wasn't sent to you. Box 2 of Form 1099-G has the amount of your refund.

Check to see what tax year your refund is for before you begin celebrating because you used the standard deduction in 2005. Sometimes (and we can't imagine why this happens), refunds are delayed for months, and years, so the check you may have received recently could be for, say, tax year 2004. If so, you need to check back at those years before you decide to trash the Form 1099-G that's just arrived. The rule regarding whether you need to include these older refund amounts in income this year is based on whether or not you itemized in the year that's being refunded. If you itemized in 2004 and have just received your 2004 refund, you have to declare it as income.

But, like just about every tax rule, there is an exception. For example, your refund isn't taxable if you claimed the standard deduction in a prior year instead of itemizing your deductions.

Even though you may itemize your deductions, only the part of your refund that represents the amount of your itemized deductions in excess of the standard deduction is taxable. That means you have to do some number crunching to make this computation. The following worksheet (see Table 6-1) gives you the answer. Suppose that your 2005 state refund was $800, you filed jointly, and your itemized deductions were $10,500.

Table 6-1	State and Local Income Tax Refund Worksheet		
Example			**Your Computation**
1. Enter the income tax refund from Form(s) 1099-G (or similar statement).		1. $800	1.
2. Enter your total allowable itemized deductions from your 2005 Schedule A (line 28).		2. $10,500	2.
3. Enter on line 3 the amount shown below for the filing status claimed on your 2005 Form 1040: Single — $5,000 Married filing jointly or qualifying widow(er) — $10,000 Married filing separately — $5,000 Head of household — $7,300		3. $10,000	3.
4. If you didn't complete line 39a on your 2005 Form 1040, enter -0-. Otherwise, multiply the number on your 2005 Form 1040, line 39a, by $1,000 ($1,250 if your 2005 filing status was single or head of household) and enter the result.		4. $0	4.
5. Add lines 3 and 4.		5. $10,000	5.
6. Subtract line 5 from line 2. If zero or less, enter -0-.		6. $500	6.
7. Taxable part of your refund. Enter the smaller of line 1 or line 6 here and on Form 1040, line 10.		7. $500	7.

Line 11: Alimony received (by you)

Because the person who pays the alimony can deduct these payments from his or her taxable income (on line 31a), the spouse who receives these payments must include alimony as taxable income. You report alimony received on line 11. You'll know the figure to enter by consulting the divorce decree or separation agreement.

You need to know what alimony is before you can report it as income or deduct it as an expense. The alimony rules aren't simple — why should they be? why simplify divorce? — but we try our best to clear them up. We offer a more detailed explanation of alimony in Chapter 7.

Here's an important tip about alimony and about separate maintenance payments and IRAs. These payments are considered income from employment that entitles you to set up and make deductible contributions to an IRA. Basically, if you receive taxable alimony, you can set up an IRA and deduct what you contribute to it — 100 percent of your alimony and employment income up to $4,000 (or $5,000 if you're age 50 or older), is deductible. However, your deduction may be reduced or eliminated if you're covered by a retirement plan through your work. See Chapter 20 for more on how to set up IRAs. Chapters 7 and 20 give the lowdown on IRAs, which come in deductible and nondeductible varieties, and Roth IRAs, which are always nondeductible.

Line 12: Business income (or loss)

If you're self-employed, you must complete a Schedule C to report your business income and expenses. If you just receive an occasional fee and don't have any business expenses, you can report that fee on line 21 as other income. And remember, if you're a *statutory employee* (a life insurance salesperson, agent, commission driver, or traveling salesperson, for example), report the wages shown in box 1 of your W-2 form on Schedule C along with your expenses. How do you know if you're a statutory employee? Simple, box 13 of your W-2 will be checked. For a quick reminder on this statutory employee title, check out "What those W-2 boxes mean" at the beginning of the chapter.

As a general rule, you're better off reporting your self-employment income on Schedule C, if you're eligible. Although slightly more complicated than entering your income on line 21, you can deduct business-related expenses against your income on Schedule C, and that can lower your income and the tax that you have to pay.

The amount that you enter on line 12 is the result of figuring and jumbling that you do on Schedules C or C-EZ, which is a shorter version. Check out Chapter 11 to dive into that material.

Line 13: Capital gain (or loss)

You don't have to be Bill Gates to have a capital gain or loss. (We bet that Bill has mostly gains. How about you?) You have a capital gain when you sell stocks, bonds, or investment property for a profit. When you sell an asset like your house for a profit, you have a gain that may be taxable (we cover the rules on the exclusion from tax on home sales in Chapter 12), but you have a nondeductible loss if you lose money on the sale of your house. Losses on other investments — such as stocks, bonds, and mutual funds — made outside of retirement accounts are generally deductible. Capital gains and losses get reported on Schedule D with the net result being reported here. If all you have are capital gain distributions from a mutual fund, you can skip Schedule D and enter your capital gain distribution(s) on line 13. Don't forget to check that little box to the left of the amount you entered on line 13, if under this rule you're not required to file Schedule D. See Chapter 12 for a more in-depth explanation of capital gains and losses and of Schedule D.

Line 14: Other gains (or losses)

You guessed it, grab another form — **Form 4797, Sales of Business Property.** Fill out that form and enter the final figure on line 14. Use Form 4797 when you sell property that you've been depreciating (such as a two-family house that you've been renting out). We explain this form in Chapter 12.

Lines 15a and 15b: Total IRA distributions

One of the benefits from all those years of hard work and diligent savings is that someday, hopefully, you'll be able to enjoy and live off the fruits of your labor. When you take distributions from your Individual Retirement Account (IRA), you'll receive a **Form 1099-R, Distributions from Pensions, Annuities, Retirement or Profit-Sharing Plans, IRAs, Insurance Contracts, etc.**

Before we show you how to decipher the information on your Form1099-R, we must share with you some important information if you haven't yet started withdrawals and are getting to the age where you should. (IRAs come in three varieties: deductible, nondeductible, and Roth IRAs. See Chapters 7 and 20 for more on these investment vehicles.)

If you turned 70½ in 2006 and you haven't begun taking distributions from your IRA yet, you must take your first distribution by April 1, 2007. In addition, because you're now required to take annual distributions from your IRA, in 2007 you'll be making two distributions to yourself — one for 2006 (when you turned 70½) and one for 2007.

If you fail to take a required distribution, the IRS assesses a 50 percent penalty on the amount that you should have taken out. For example, a $4,000 required distribution that you didn't take will cost you a cool $2,000 in penalties. Ouch! You can request that the penalty be excused if your failure to make a minimum distribution was caused by a reasonable error or if you're taking steps to remedy the error. Illness, a computational error, or incorrect advice are three examples of a reasonable error. You compute the 50 percent penalty on Form 5329.

Note: The minimum withdrawal rule doesn't apply to Roth IRAs; you can keep money in a Roth IRA for as long as you want.

Don't compound your error. If you discover you should have been taking distributions, start now! The longer you delay, the more penalties will pile up, and the harder it will be for you to make a case to abate penalties that have already been assessed. Only after you've begun taking your distributions should you start trying to talk yourself out of the penalties that the IRS has charged you. You need to attach a statement to your Form 5329 to explain why you didn't make the required distributions, and why you shouldn't be penalized for that. Some good reasons are math errors or illness. Be contrite (I'm sorry, this won't happen again, and I've fixed my mistake), and be convincing. The "dog ate my address book" probably won't work here, but an unanticipated family upheaval probably will.

Computing the amount you must withdraw from retirement accounts

When you reach age 70½, you must start withdrawing at least a minimum amount from your retirement accounts. The minimum amount you must withdraw at 70½ is computed by using the IRS life-expectancy table in this sidebar. An important exception to using this life-expectancy table benefits those of you with spouses who are more than 10 years younger than you. You can use a more advantageous life-expectancy table. Using this other life-expectancy table means that you're not required to take out as much as with the standard life-expectancy table.

Here's an example of how to compute the minimum amount that must be withdrawn: If you turn 70½ in 2007, divide the value of your account on the preceding December 31 — say it was $200,000 — by the number of payout years next to your age in the life-expectancy table. In your case, it's 27.4 years. So in 2007, you must withdraw at least $7,299 ($200,000 ÷ 27.4). In 2008 you'd divide the balance in the account on December 31, 2007, by 26.5.

Minimum Distribution Life Expectancy Table

Age	Payout Years	Age	Payout Years	Age	Payout Years
70	27.4	77	21.2	84	15.5
71	26.5	78	20.3	85	14.8
72	25.6	79	19.5	86	14.1
73	24.7	80	18.7	87	13.4
74	23.8	81	17.9	88	12.7
75	22.9	82	17.1	89	12.0
76	22.0	83	16.3	90	11.4

The IRS Table goes to age 115 and older. Supplement to Publication 590, **Individual Retirement Arrangements** (IRAs) contains the entire table all the way to age 115 (it's Table III), and the life-expectancy table for someone whose spouse is more than 10 years younger (it's Table II). If you're 70, and your spouse is 45, instead of having to use 27.4 years as your life expectancy, Table II in Supplement to Publication 590 enables you to use 39.4 years.

You can find three lifetime-expectancy tables in the Supplement to Publication 590. Table III (illustrated in this sidebar) is the Uniform Lifetime Table that IRA owners use when they're required to start making withdrawals. Table I (referred to as the Single Life Table) is for beneficiaries of an inherited IRA. IRA owners whose spouses are more than 10 years younger can use Table II.

Note: If you have more than one IRA account, you don't have to take a minimum amount out of each account. Tally the total of all your IRAs before computing the minimum amount you must withdraw. You can take that amount from any of your IRAs. With other types of retirement accounts (non-IRAs), you have to withdraw the minimum from each account.

Beginning in 2004, your bank or broker is required to notify the IRS on **Form 5498, IRA Contribution Information** (with a copy to you) that a minimum distribution from your IRA was required. On the 2006 form, box 11 will be checked to indicate that a minimum distribution is required in 2007. They're also obliged to compute the required minimum amount whenever asked to do so.

Even though the IRS instructs you to explain why the penalty should be excused and what steps you have taken to correct the error and to attach that explanation to **Form 5329, Additional Taxes on Qualified Plans (Including IRAs) and Other Tax-Favored Accounts,** the IRS nevertheless requires that you pay the penalty as computed on lines 50–53 of Part VIII, Form 5329. If the IRS believes that you made your case, it will refund the penalty.

Because not parting with your money in the first place is a whole lot nicer, try this suggestion: On lines 50–53 of Form 5329, write "See attached explanation of why the penalty should be excused for reasonable error." Call it our version of "Go now and only pay when you have to." The only downside to taking this step: If the IRS doesn't waive the penalty, you'll have additional interest to pay.

Line 15a is for reporting money that you withdrew from your IRA during the tax year. If you receive a distribution from an IRA, the payer — your bank or broker — sends you Form 1099-R (see Figure 6-3).

☐ VOID	☐ CORRECTED				

PAYER'S name, street address, city, state, and ZIP code	**1** Gross distribution $	OMB No. 1545-0119 **2006** Form **1099-R**	**Distributions From Pensions, Annuities, Retirement or Profit-Sharing Plans, IRAs, Insurance Contracts, etc.**
	2a Taxable amount $		
	2b Taxable amount not determined ☐	Total distribution ☐	**Copy 1 For State, City, or Local Tax Department**
PAYER'S federal identification number / RECIPIENT'S identification number	**3** Capital gain (included in box 2a) $	**4** Federal income tax withheld $	
RECIPIENT'S name	**5** Employee contributions /Designated Roth contributions or insurance premiums $	**6** Net unrealized appreciation in employer's securities $	
Street address (including apt. no.)	**7** Distribution code(s) / IRA/SEP/SIMPLE ☐	**8** Other $ %	
City, state, and ZIP code	**9a** Your percentage of total distribution %	**9b** Total employee contributions $	
/ 1st year of desig. Roth contrib.	**10** State tax withheld $ $	**11** State/Payer's state no.	**12** State distribution $ $
Account number (see instructions)	**13** Local tax withheld $ $	**14** Name of locality	**15** Local distribution $ $

Form **1099-R**   Department of the Treasury — Internal Revenue Service

Figure 6-3: Form 1099-R tells you about distributions made from your retirement accounts.

As a general rule, distributions made from an IRA are fully taxable unless you made nondeductible contributions to the IRA, which we explain in the upcoming instructions for box 2a of the 1099-R. Here's a rundown of the important boxes that you need to read on your 1099-R to report an IRA distribution on Form 1040.

If you turn 70½ in 2006 and wait until 2007 to take a distribution, the distribution you have to take is computed on the balance in your IRA on December 31, 2005, not on December 31, 2006. The second distribution that you must take in 2007 is based on the balance in your account on December 31, 2006.

Box 1: Gross distribution (Form 1099-R)

This box represents the amount of money that you withdrew from your IRA and that was reported to the IRS. Make sure that it's correct by checking to see whether the figure matches the amount withdrawn from your IRA account statement. If you made a nondeductible contribution to an IRA — that's an IRA contribution for which you didn't take a tax deduction and thus filed **Form 8606, Nondeductible IRAs** — write the number from box 1 on line 15a of your Form 1040. The taxable portion of your IRA that you computed on Form 8606 is entered on line 15b. See Chapter 15 for information about how to fill out the form. However, if your IRA distribution is fully taxable (see the next section), don't make an entry on line 15a; write the number on line 15b instead.

Box 2a: Taxable amount

This box contains the taxable amount of your IRA distribution. However, the payer of an IRA distribution doesn't have enough information to compute whether your entire IRA distribution is taxable. Therefore, if you simply enter the amount reported in box 1 on Form 1040 (line 15b) as being fully taxable, you'll overpay your tax if you made nondeductible contributions to your IRA. If you made nondeductible contributions, you must compute the non-taxable portion of your distribution on Form 8606. And you must attach Form 8606 to your return. We show you all you need to know about this form in Chapter 15.

Box 7: Distribution code

A number code is entered in this box if one of the exceptions to the 10 percent penalty for distributions before age 59½ applies:

- ✔ Code 2 — annuity exception
- ✔ Code 3 — disability exception
- ✔ Code 4 — death exception
- ✔ Code 7 — indicated in box 7 if you're at least 59½ years old. That way the IRS knows that the 10 percent penalty for an early distribution doesn't apply. A transfer directly from one IRA account to another doesn't have to be reported to the IRS.

Distributions before 59½

If you withdraw money from your IRA before you turn 59½, not only do you have to include that amount in your income, but you also owe a 10 percent penalty on the taxable amount that you withdrew (your nondeductible contributions aren't subject to the 10 percent penalty). The penalty is computed on **Form 5329, Additional Taxes on Qualified Plans (Including IRAs) and Other Tax-Favored Accounts.** Attach the form to your return and carry over the penalty to Form 1040 (line 60). The penalty doesn't apply to IRA distributions that are paid because of death or disability, paid over your life expectancy, or rolled over to another IRA.

The 10 percent penalty also doesn't apply to withdrawals from an IRA used to pay medical expenses in excess of 7.5 percent of your income. Additionally, anyone receiving unemployment for 12 consecutive weeks can withdraw money to pay health insurance premiums without paying the penalty. Self-employed people out of work for 12 weeks also can make penalty-free withdrawals to pay their health insurance premiums.

The 10 percent penalty doesn't apply to distributions paid over your lifetime or the joint lives of you and your beneficiary. You can switch out of this method after you reach 59½ and after you've used it for five years — for example, you're 56 years old and need some dough. You start taking out annual amounts based on your life expectancy. Read the IRS Supplement to Publication 590 *(Individual Retirement Arrangements)* and then follow the illustration we provide in the sidebar, "Computing the amount you must withdraw from retirement accounts" for the amount you have to withdraw every year. After receiving distributions based on your life expectancy for at least five years, you can switch out of this method. At age 61, you can withdraw the remaining balance or any part of it, if you want. You don't have to make this election for all your IRAs. You can use it with the IRA that has the largest or smallest balance.

Penalty-free (but taxable) withdrawals are allowed for the purchase of a first home and to pay college expenses. This exception to the penalty includes the first home of you and your spouse, child, or grandchild. Penalty-free withdrawals for higher education also apply to you and education expenses of your spouse, child, or grandchild. Withdrawals for graduate school also are penalty-free. No limits are placed on amounts that you withdraw for college expenses. What expenses qualify? Tuition fees, books, and room and board — as long as the student is enrolled at least on a half-time basis.

A first home doesn't mean your first ever — it simply means that you didn't own one within two years of the withdrawal. For example, you sold your home, lived in a rented apartment for three years, and then purchased a new home — this purchase qualifies for the $10,000 penalty-free withdrawal. The homebuyer's exception has a limit of $10,000, but you can stretch the withdrawals over several years. For example, if you withdraw $3,000 in December, you can withdraw $7,000 the following January. You must, however, use the funds within 120 days of withdrawal to buy, build, or rebuild a "first home." Your lifetime limit is $10,000; so after you take out $10,000, that's it.

A married couple can withdraw up to $10,000, penalty-free, from their respective IRAs. For example, David and Betsy have their own IRAs; they can take out $10,000 from each account, but they can't take $20,000 from one account.

The rules for withdrawals from a traditional IRA and a Roth IRA are dramatically varied and different from one another. Chapter 7 has the lowdown on Roth IRAs.

Transfers pursuant to divorce

The transfer of an IRA account as a result of a divorce or maintenance decree isn't taxable to you or your former spouse, nor is it subject to the 10 percent penalty provided your divorce decree requires that you transfer all or part of your IRA to your former spouse, even if one or both of you are younger than 59½.

You can take two approaches to making sure there is no 10 percent penalty assessed when you transfer your IRA to your ex-spouse.

- ✔ Your ex-spouse can open his or her own IRA, and then you make a so-called "trustee-to-trustee transfer" between the accounts.
- ✔ In the case of a total transfer, you may decide just to rename the account you already have, putting your spouse's name and Social Security number on it instead of yours.

Don't allow your current IRA custodian to hand you a check and then attempt to sign it over to your ex-spouse. One hapless taxpayer recently discovered this mistake the hard way. He withdrew the funds from his IRA and endorsed the check over to his ex-spouse. Although the transfer was required by his separation agreement, he ran afoul of the requirement that he didn't transfer his interest in his IRA account. The Tax Court sided with the IRS in determining that his interest in his IRA was extinguished when he withdrew the funds.

Inherited IRAs

When you inherit an IRA, you usually have the option of either withdrawing the money and paying tax on the amount withdrawn or taking the money out in drips and drabs so the IRA can continue sheltering the balance in the account from tax. We say usually, because in some instances the IRA owner predetermines whether at his or her death the account will be paid out all at once or over time. The 10 percent penalty that normally applies to withdrawals made to someone before he or she is 59½ doesn't apply to beneficiaries.

Determining how the money is taken out of the IRA and over what period of time is based on whether the account was left to a spouse (spouses have two additional choices that we explain in the next section) or to someone else.

Surviving spouse

If you're the sole beneficiary of your deceased spouse's IRA, you can choose to roll that IRA over into your own IRA. It can be a new IRA account (which we suggest) or an existing one. A surviving spouse also can redesignate the account as his or her own by converting it to his or her name as the owner. The advantage to rolling over your deceased spouse's IRA into yours or redesignating the account is that if you're younger than 70½, you can delay making withdrawals until you reach that age. The money in the account continues to grow, tax-free. Another plus in electing to treat the account as your own is that you get to name who you want to inherit what's in the account at your death instead of the money going to the beneficiary the original IRA owner selected to succeed you.

If you choose not to treat the IRA as your own, how you take the money depends on whether your spouse was 70½ at the time of death. If your spouse died before the minimum distributions began at age 70½ or April 1 of the following year, you need not start withdrawing the funds until the later of December 31 of the year following your spouse's death or the year in which he or she would have turned 70½. In that year, withdrawals are based on the surviving spouse's life expectancy, which is recalculated every year in accordance with the *Expectancy Table* shown in Table I (single life) in the Supplement to Publication 590 *(Individual Retirement Arrangements)*. If the surviving spouse doesn't start making distributions over his or her life expectancy or waiting until his or her spouse would have turned 70½, then he or she has to withdraw the entire amount in the account by December 31 of the year of the fifth anniversary of his or her spouse's death.

If a surviving spouse dies before the IRA owner would have turned 70½ or before December 31 of the year following the IRA owner's death, the life expectancy of the successor beneficiary is used to determine the minimum distribution that must be made from that point on. In each succeeding year, one is subtracted from that life-expectancy number. Here's how it works. Say the surviving spouse, Florence, age 60, was waiting until her spouse would have turned 70½ before starting to make withdrawals, and she died in 2006. The IRA was left to the couple's daughter, Judy, age 35. Judy decides not to take a distribution until 2007, the year following the year of Florence's death. Based on the Single Life Expectancy (Table I) in Supplement to Publication 590, Judy's life expectancy in 2007 is 48.5 years. The beneficiary's life expectancy begins in the year the distributions start, not the year of death of the IRA owner. In 2007, Judy computes the amount that has to be withdrawn by dividing the balance in the account on December 31, 2006, by 48.5 years. In 2008, her life expectancy is one less, or 47.5 years (48.5 – 1), and so on. If Florence had begun taking distributions because 2006 was the year her spouse would have reached 70½, then Judy would be required to use Florence's life expectancy as determined in 2006, which, based on Table I, is 25.2 years. In subsequent years, Judy would subtract one from that amount to determine how much she needed to withdraw.

When your deceased spouse had already begun taking distributions because he or she had reached that magic age of 70½, the surviving spouse has the following two options:

- ✔ **Elect to treat the IRA as his or her own.** If the surviving spouse elects to treat the IRA as his or her own, the minimum distribution will be based on his or her life expectancy as shown in Table I. When the surviving spouse dies, the succeeding beneficiary uses the surviving spouse's life expectancy in his or her year of death to determine minimum distribution amounts. Subsequent distributions are calculated using that life expectancy minus 1 for each successive year.

- ✔ **Begin distributions by December 31 of the year following the deceased spouse's death.** You have two choices for whose life expectancy can be used in determining the minimum amount that must be withdrawn: yours or your deceased spouse's (for the year he or she died, and then subtracting one in each subsequent year). You get to use the life expectancy that produces the best result. We'd be less than candid if we let you believe that using your deceased spouse's life expectancy is an easy concept to fathom. Unless your deceased spouse was much younger, it's hardly worth the effort. But because you paid good money for this book, we thought we'd better tell you about it.

When a surviving spouse passes away, the succeeding beneficiary uses the surviving spouse's life expectancy in the year of death and then subtracts one in each successive year to determine what must be withdrawn.

If your head's not spinning yet, here's another option: Roll over part of your deceased spouse's IRA and withdraw the rest of it. You have to pay tax on the part that isn't rolled over. But even though you may be younger than 59½, you're not subject to the 10 percent early withdrawal penalty that normally applies when someone withdraws money from an IRA before he or she is 59½, and you likewise won't have to pay a penalty if you choose to receive distributions as a beneficiary of the account.

Because you may be dealing with large sums of money, you may want to seek professional advice or immerse yourself in IRS Publication 590 *(Individual Retirement Arrangements)*. Also, the Roth IRA rules are somewhat different — see Chapter 7 for an explanation of them.

Marital status for calculating the minimum amount that must be withdrawn from an IRA is determined on January 1 of the year for which you're making the withdrawal, so any changes in that status caused by death or divorce are ignored. However, if you divorce during the year and change the beneficiary designation on the IRA, this rule doesn't apply.

Beneficiary other than a surviving spouse

Only surviving spouses can treat inherited IRAs as their own. Other beneficiaries must start receiving distributions from the IRAs. Even if the decedent was under 59½, the 10 percent early withdrawal penalty doesn't apply.

Here is where the rules get hairy. They depend on whether the owner had named a beneficiary. Not only don't large numbers of people have wills, but many folks also simply don't bother to name a beneficiary when setting up an IRA. What happens to the IRA when you don't name a beneficiary? It goes to the persons named in your will. If you don't have a will, it goes to your next of kin. If a person's estate is named as beneficiary, the beneficiaries of the estate don't qualify as IRA beneficiaries, so the IRA is considered to have no beneficiary. If a trust is named as a beneficiary, then under some conditions the beneficiaries of the trust may be considered beneficiaries of the IRA. Check with the attorney who drafted the trust on this one.

If a beneficiary is named, withdrawal amounts are determined by using the beneficiary's life expectancy in the year following the decedent's death and reducing it by 1 in each succeeding year. A minimum distribution, however, must be made in the year of the decedent's death as if he or she were alive.

If no beneficiary was named and the owner of the IRA died before minimum distributions were required (age 70½ or the following April 1), then all the money has to be taken out no later than the end of the fifth year following the owner's death. If the owner died without naming a beneficiary after minimum distributions began, withdrawals may be based on the owner's life expectancy in the year of death. Subtract 1 from that life expectancy in each subsequent year. The payments go to the owner's estate.

Although an estate can be named as a beneficiary, it isn't considered a *designated beneficiary* under the minimum distribution rules, because an estate doesn't have a life expectancy. If the account passes to someone under state law (next-of-kin rule), the IRA also is considered not to have a named beneficiary. However, if the terms of the IRA permit, a beneficiary can be named in a will or by some other election — a letter or note, for example.

Because the age of the eldest beneficiary is used to determine the minimum distribution at death, dividing an IRA into separate accounts makes sense if there are large differences in the ages of your beneficiaries. That way, one account can be for someone age 36 who has a 46.4-year life expectancy and the other for a 15-year-old grandchild who has a 66.8-year life expectancy. Another important change is that you no longer are required to use the life expectancy of the beneficiary you named at your required minimum distribution date. Now beneficiaries can be named after that date.

Make sure that you read the terms of your IRA agreement that you signed when you opened your account so that you understand your withdrawal options.

Withdrawal of nondeductible contributions

If you made nondeductible contributions to your IRA, use **Form 8606** to compute the taxable portion of your withdrawal. You don't have to pay tax on nondeductible contributions that you withdraw — you already have. The total of your IRA distributions is entered on line 7 of Form 8606; enter that same total on line 15a of Form 1040. Carry over the figure from line 15 of Form 8606 to line 15b of the 1040. That's the taxable portion.

Loss on an IRA

You can deduct losses on Roth and nondeductible IRAs. Say that you invest $2,000 in a Roth. The value drops to $1,500. You say, "The heck with it" and withdraw the $1,500. Deduct your $500 loss as a miscellaneous itemized deduction on line 22, Schedule A, Form 1040. To report a loss in a Roth, you have to liquidate all your Roths. This liquidation rule also applies to losses on nondeductible contributions to a traditional IRA.

Lines 16a and 16b: Total pensions and annuities

Here's where you report your retirement benefits from your pension, profit-sharing, 401(k), SEP, or Keogh plans. How these plans are taxed depends on whether you receive them in the form of an annuity (paid over your lifetime) or in a lump sum.

The amounts that you fill in on lines 16a and 16b are reported on a **Form 1099-R** that you receive from your employer or your plan's custodian. If the amount that you receive is fully taxable, complete only line 16b and leave line 16a blank.

Pensions and annuities

If you didn't pay or contribute to your pension or annuity — or if your employer didn't withhold part of the cost from your pay while you worked — then the amount that you receive each year is fully taxable. The amount that you contributed, for which you received a deduction — such as tax-deductible contributions to a 401(k), SEP, IRA, or Keogh — isn't considered part of your cost.

If you paid part of the cost (that is, if you made nondeductible contributions or contributions that were then added to your taxable income on your W-2), you aren't taxed on the part that you contributed, because it represents a tax-free return of your investment. The rest of the amount that you receive is taxable. To compute this amount, you can use either the *Simplified Method* or the *General Rule*.

Simplified Method

You must use the *Simplified Method* for figuring the taxable amount of your pension or annuity if the starting date for your pension or annuity occurred after November 18, 1996, and the payments were from a qualified employee plan, a qualified employee annuity, or a qualified tax shelter annuity. The word *qualified* is tax jargon for a retirement plan approved by the IRS. You can't use this method if you were 75 or older at the starting date and your payments were guaranteed for more than five years at the time the payments began. Who came up with this one? In case you're wondering whether you can use the Simplified Method if your pension began on or before November 18, 1996, the answer is yes, unless, that is, you're required to use the General Rule that we explain in a moment.

Under the Simplified Method, the IRS allows you to declare as nontaxable part of the money that you receive from a certain number of payments made to you or to your beneficiary, based on your age when your pension or annuity started. The nontaxable portion is your after-tax contributions, if any, to the pension. Divide the amount of your contribution to the pension by the number of payments that the IRS allows. Use Table 6-2 to arrive at the nontaxable amount of each payment if your pension is based on one life or if it is based on two life expectancies and the pension starting date was before January 1, 1998. If your pension started before January 1, 1998, and it is based on two lives, use the age of the primary beneficiary, which usually is the employee.

Table 6-2	Simplified Method — One Life	
Combined Age at Annuity Starting Date	*Divide By*	*After 11-18-96*
55 and under	300 payments	360 payments
More than 55 and under 60	260 payments	310 payments
More than 60 and under 65	240 payments	260 payments
More than 65 and under 70	170 payments	210 payments
More than 70	120 payments	160 payments

For reasons that we can't explain, Congress won't make it simple and pick the beginning of a year as the date for making a change. If you started receiving payments after November 18, 1996, you must use the payment schedule in the right-hand column of Table 6-2.

Here's another midstream change. If your retirement began in 1998 or in later years and your pension or annuity is being paid over the life expectancies of two or more retirees — for example, the life expectancies of you and your spouse — you have to use Table 6-3. What's your life expectancy? The IRS determines everything, so send for **IRS Publication 575** (*Pension and Annuity Income*).

Table 6-3	Simplified Method — Two Lives
Combined Age at Annuity Starting Date	*Divide By*
110 and under	410 payments
More than 110 and under 120	360 payments
More than 120 and under 130	310 payments
More than 130 and under 140	260 payments
More than 140	210 payments

Suppose that you retired at age 65 and began receiving $1,000 per month under a *joint and survivor annuity* with your spouse (that is, an annuity that pays a benefit to you or your spouse as long as one of you still is living). Your spouse is 60, and you contributed $31,000 to the pension. Divide the $31,000 by 310 (the amount for your combined age of 125). The resulting $100 is the monthly amount that you receive tax-free. If you live to collect more than the 310 payments, you'll have to pay tax on the full amount of your pension that you receive beyond that point. Your contribution includes amounts withheld from your paycheck and any contributions made by your employer that were reported as additional income.

If you die before you receive 310 payments, your spouse continues to exclude $100 from each payment until the number of payments received, when added to yours, totals 310. If your spouse dies before the 310 payments are made, a miscellaneous itemized deduction on your spouse's final tax return is allowed for the balance of the 310 payments remaining to be paid, multiplied by $100. This deduction isn't subject to the 2 percent adjusted gross income limit. If your spouse dies with 40 payments yet to be made, a $4,000 deduction would be allowed (40 × $100).

If your annuity starting date was after July 1, 1986, but before January 1, 1987, you can take the exclusion as long as you're receiving payments. You don't need to stop at the total number of payments you determined in Table 6-2.

General Rule

You must use the *General Rule* to figure the taxability of your pension or annuity that you receive from a nonqualified (not approved by the IRS) employee plan, or a private or commercial annuity, or from a qualified (IRS-approved) plan if you were 75 or older at the starting date and your payments were guaranteed for more than five years at the time they began. You can use the *General Rule* for a qualified plan that began on or before November 18, 1996 (but after July 1, 1986), if you do qualify or don't choose to use the Simplified Method.

Under the General Rule, a part of each payment is nontaxable because it's considered a return of your cost. The remainder of each payment (including the full amount of any later cost-of-living increases) is taxable. Finding the nontaxable part is extremely complex and requires you to use actuarial tables. For a full explanation and the tables you need, get **IRS Publication 939** *(General Rule for Pensions and Annuities)* or consult a tax advisor.

The nontaxable amount remains the same under the General Rule even if the monthly payment increases. If your annuity starting date was after July 1, 1986, and before 1987, you continue to exclude the same nontaxable amount from each annuity payment for as long as you receive your annuity. If your annuity starting date is after 1986, your total exclusion over the years can't be more than your cost of the contract, reduced by the value of any refund feature. This means that you can't exclude more from tax than you contributed.

If you (or a survivor annuitant) die before the cost is recovered, a miscellaneous itemized deduction is allowed for the *unrecovered cost* on your (or your survivor's) final income tax return. The deduction isn't subject to the 2 percent AGI limit.

Lump-sum distributions

If you were born before 1936, you can elect to have a lump-sum distribution taxed at a special optional method called 10-year averaging. To qualify for this special method, the lump sum must be your entire balance in all your employer's pension plans, and it must be paid within a single tax year. The distribution must be paid because of one of the following reasons:

- You die.
- You leave the firm.
- You're self-employed and become totally and permanently disabled.

Instead of electing the special 10-year averaging, a lump-sum distribution from your employer's pension plan can be rolled over to an IRA or to your new employer's retirement plan. If you don't need the immediate use of the money, a rollover probably is your best bet, because it allows you to continue deferring taxation of the money. (Letting your employer transfer the money on your behalf is also best.) You don't have to roll over the entire amount. The part that you don't roll over is subject to tax and possibly a 10 percent penalty if you aren't 59½. Voluntary after-tax contributions that you made to the plan can now be rolled over, but we advise against doing so, because such contributions are tax-free to you when received and *aren't* subject to the 20 percent withholding tax that lump-sum distributions *are* subject to. See "Tax on early distributions," later in this chapter, for information about how to escape the penalty. A lump-sum distribution is eligible for capital gain or special averaging treatment if the participant was in the plan for at least five years. We discuss these options further in this section.

You can't roll over a hardship distribution from your employer's 401(k) plan to an IRA. It's not allowed. If you try it, you'll be taxed on the distribution from your 401(k) plus will be liable for penalties under the excess contribution rules governing your IRA. You probably weren't looking for this result, were you?

If you have your employer make a direct rollover from the retirement plan to your IRA, tax doesn't have to be withheld. On the other hand, if you receive the lump-sum payment directly, tax must be withheld because the IRS doesn't trust you to complete the rollover in time. *Note:* Remember you have 60 days from the receipt of the money to roll it over into an IRA. This creates a problem, because in order to avoid paying tax on any of the rollover, you're required to put the full amount into the new account, not the full amount less the tax withheld. So, in order to escape without owing a barrel of taxes, you need to cough up the amount of the tax that was withheld when you open the new account with the understanding that the withheld taxes will be refunded to you in the next year. Remember, insisting on a trustee-to-trustee transfer, which doesn't even need to be reported to the IRS is easier, less financially burdensome, and much less stressful.

If you don't roll over your withdrawal within 60 days through no fault of your own, the new law excuses the lateness. Before this change, whenever a financial institution messed up your transfer instructions (depositing the rollover in the wrong account, for example), you were stuck and ended up owing a barrel of taxes due and possibly penalties to boot. Here are some of the other excuses that will fly: being hospitalized, foul-ups by the post office, disasters, or circumstances beyond your control.

A single tax year means exactly that if you want to elect the 10-year averaging method. If, for example, you received $10,000 in 2006 and the balance in 2007, you're out of luck.

If your former employer's retirement plan includes the company's stock (say you work for GE, for example), you may want to transfer the stock to your taxable brokerage account instead of an IRA rollover account. Why? When you take the stock, you pay taxes only on the value at the time you purchased it and not the value when you left the company. For example, you bought shares through your company's retirement account that cost $10,000; the shares are now worth $100,000. You pay tax on $10,000 and not on the current value. And if you're younger than 55, the 10 percent penalty also is computed on the $10,000 value (see the section, "Tax on early distributions," later in this chapter). Only when you sell the shares are you taxed on the appreciation in value, and then you're taxed at capital gain rates that could be as low as 5 percent but no more than the new maximum 15 percent rate.

Capital gains treatment

If you reached the age of 50 before 1986, you can choose to treat a portion of the taxable part of the lump-sum distribution as a capital gain that is taxable at the 15 percent or 20 percent rates. This treatment applies to the portion that you receive for your participation in the plan before 1974. You can select this treatment only once, and you use **Form 4972, Tax on Lump-Sum Distributions,** to make this choice.

The tax on the balance of the lump-sum distribution is computed under the 10-year averaging method described in the next section. For most people, a tidy sum can be saved between the capital gain and averaging methods. Box 3 of Form 1099-R contains the capital gain amount.

Special averaging method

If you reached age 50 before 1986 (you were probably born before 1936, right?), you can elect the 10-year averaging method of the ordinary income portion of your lump-sum distribution. (This procedure also includes the capital gain portion of the distribution if you don't choose capital gain treatment for it.) To qualify, you must elect to use special averaging on all lump-sum distributions received in the tax year.

To use special averaging, you must have been a participant in the plan for at least five full tax years. You can make only one lifetime election to use this method. If you choose the special averaging method, use Form 4972 and figure your tax as if you received the distributions over ten years.

When you treat the distribution as though you received it over ten years, you must use 1986 tax rates. The instructions accompanying Form 4972 contain a 1986 tax-rate schedule. Ten-year averaging can save you a bundle.

You pay the tax on the lump sum in the year that you receive it, even though the tax on the distribution is computed as if you received it over ten years. After you pay the tax, the balance is yours, free and clear.

Form 1099-R

If you receive a total distribution from a retirement plan, you'll receive a **Form 1099-R**. If the distribution qualifies as a lump-sum distribution, box 3 shows the capital gain amount, and box 2a minus box 3 shows the ordinary income amount. Code A is entered in box 7 if the lump sum qualifies for the 10-year special averaging. If you don't receive a Form 1099-R, or if you have questions about it, contact your plan administrator.

Tax on early distributions

Distributions that you receive from your employer's retirement plan before the age of 59½ are subject to a 10 percent penalty and are taxable. But here are some of the exceptions to the 10 percent penalty on employer retirement plans, in the order of how frequently the IRS sees these exceptions:

- ✔ Death.

- ✔ Distributions made after you stopped working (retirement or termination) during or after the calendar year you reach age 55.

- ✔ Distributions made to you (to the extent you have deductible medical expenses in excess of 7.5 percent of your adjusted gross income). You don't have to itemize your deductions for this exception to apply.

- ✔ Distributions made under a Qualified Domestic Relations Order (QDRO), which is a divorce decree or order that spells out in specific detail who is to be awarded the retirement benefit. (See "Transfers pursuant to divorce" on line 15a where we discuss IRA distributions.)

- ✔ Distributions (after separation from service) paid over your lifetime or the joint lives of you and your beneficiary.

- ✔ Distributions to correct excess amounts in the plan.

- ✔ Total and permanent disability.

Pension distributions on Form 1099-R

Pension distributions are reported on Form 1099-R, which is the same one used to report IRA distributions. The difference between how the information on an IRA distribution is reported to you and how the distribution from your pension is reported is as follows:

Box 3: If the distribution is a lump sum, and you were a participant in the plan before 1974, this amount qualifies for capital gain treatment.

Box 5: Your after-tax contributions are entered here.

Box 6: Securities in your employer's company that you received are listed here. The appreciation in value isn't taxed until the securities are sold. Only the actual cost of the shares is taxed when they're received. See the earlier section "Lump-sum distributions."

Box 7: This box informs you if you are receiving a normal retirement payment, a distribution that's subject to the 10 percent penalty because you're under 59½, whether the distribution isn't subject to the penalty or if it's a direct rollover to an IRA, and so on. Here is a list of the codes that you will most likely encounter in box 7:

✔ Code 1 — Early distribution, no known exception

✔ Code 2 — Early distribution, exception to 10 percent penalty applies

✔ Code 3 — Disability

✔ Code 4 — Death

✔ Code 7 — Normal distribution

✔ Code 8 — Excess contributions and earnings, or excess deferrals, taxable in 2006

✔ Code 9 — PS 58 costs (premiums paid for insurance protection taxable in 2006)

✔ Code A — May be eligible for 10-year averaging

✔ Code G — Direct rollover to an IRA or another retirement plan

✔ Code J — Early distribution from Roth IRA and no known exception to the 10 percent penalty applies

✔ Code N — Recharacterized IRA contribution made for 2006 and recharacterized in 2006 (see Chapter 7, line 32)

✔ Code P — Distribution of excess contributions and earnings in the plan

✔ Code Q – Qualified distribution from a Roth IRA

✔ Code R — Recharacterized IRA contribution made in 2005 and recharacterized in 2006 (see Chapter 7, line 32)

✔ Code S — Early distribution from a SIMPLE IRA in first two years, no known exception to 10% penalty

✔ Code T — Roth distribution and an exception to the 10% penalty applies

Box 8: If you have an entry here, seek tax advice.

Box 9a: Your share of a distribution, if there are several beneficiaries.

You report the penalty you have to pay on **Form 5329, Additional Taxes Attributable to Qualified Retirement Plans (Including IRAs) and Other Tax-Favored Accounts,** if none of the exceptions apply. Attach the form to your return and carry over the 10 percent to line 60 on Form 1040.

The penalty-free (but taxable) withdrawals allowed for first-time homebuyers and for paying college tuition don't apply to your employer's pension plan, Keoghs, SEPs, or 401(k)s — only to IRAs.

Minimum distributions

The same rule that applies to IRAs also applies to pension plans for failing to take a minimum distribution by April 1 of the year following the year you turned 70½.

The 70½ rule doesn't apply if you're still employed. You can delay making withdrawals until you retire. This rule doesn't apply to IRAs or to someone who owns 5 percent or more of a business.

Disability income

If you retire on disability, your pension usually is taxable. Sounds unfair, doesn't it? Yep! The way the IRS figures it, pensions are taxable, so how you retire shouldn't make a difference. However, nonpension payments made because of the permanent loss of use of part of the body, or because of permanent disfigurement, are exempt from tax. Sounds like a distinction without a difference.

If you're 65 or older (or if you're younger than 65 and are retired because your disability is total and permanent and you receive disability income), you may be able to claim a credit for the elderly or the disabled. You compute the credit on Schedule R (see Chapter 14).

If you contributed to a plan that paid a disability pension, the part of the pension that you receive that is attributable to your payments isn't subject to tax. You report all your taxable disability on line 7 of your 1040 until you reach the *minimum retirement age* — that is, the age stated in your plan when you're entitled to a regular retirement annuity — and then on line 16a or 16b. You must use the Simplified Method or the General Rule to compute the part of a disability pension that isn't taxable because of your contribution.

Veteran's Administration disability benefits are tax-free. If you're a military retiree and receive disability from other than the VA, don't include in your income the amount of those benefits that are equal to your VA benefits.

Military and government disability pensions that you receive as the result of an injury or sickness that occurred in a combat or extrahazardous area are exempt from tax. So are disability payments made to a government employee as a result of a terrorist attack outside the United States. Since (and because of the events of) September 11, 2001, this provision covers all terrorist attacks, not only those occurring outside the United States and not only for government employees or the military. See Publication 3920 *(Tax Relief for Victims of Terrorist Attacks)*.

Here is a quick reference list on sickness and injury benefits:

- ✔ **Benefits from an accident or health insurance policy:** Not taxable if you paid the insurance premiums.

- ✔ **Compensation for permanent loss, or loss of use of a part or function of your body, or for permanent disfigurement:** Not taxable if paid because of the injury. The payment must be figured without regard to any period of absence from work, because payments for lost wages are taxable.

- ✔ **Compensatory damages:** Not taxable if received for injury or sickness.

- ✔ **Disability benefits:** Not taxable if received for loss of income or earning capacity because of an injury covered by a no-fault automobile policy.

- ✔ **Federal Employees' Compensation Act (FECA):** Not taxable if paid because of personal injury or sickness. However, payments received as continuation of pay for up to 45 days while a claim is being decided and pay received for sick leave while a claim is being processed are taxable.

- ✔ **Life insurance:** Death benefit paid to a beneficiary is exempt from tax.

- ✔ **Reimbursements for medical care:** Not taxable; the reimbursement may reduce your medical expense deduction.

- ✔ **Workers' compensation:** Not taxable if paid under a workers' compensation policy because of a work-related injury or illness.

Effective August 21, 1996, damages received for age, gender, or racial discrimination, and injury to your reputation and emotional distress not related to physical injuries or sickness aren't tax-exempt. Prior to this change, courts had reached differing results on this issue.

Line 17: Rental real estate, royalties, partnerships, S Corporations, trusts

This line is an important one for all you self-starters who are landlords, business owners, authors, taxpayers collecting royalties (like us!), and those people lucky enough to have someone set up a trust fund for them. Jump to Chapter 13 to find out more about this and good old Schedule E — the necessary form to wrestle with for this line.

Line 18: Farm income (or loss)

What comes after E? You got it. If you have farm income or losses, seek ye olde Schedule F (see Chapter 11), fill it out, and fill in the final number on line 18. It's similar to Schedule C.

Line 19: Unemployment compensation

Losing your job was bad enough. And now you receive another nasty surprise — the news that the unemployment compensation that you received is taxable. The government should have sent you a **Form 1099-G** (see Figure 6-4) to summarize these taxable benefits that you received. Unemployment compensation is fully taxable, and you enter it on line 19.

Figure 6-4:
If you repaid some or all of the unemployment compensation benefits you received in 2006, you subtract the amount you repaid from the total amount you received and enter the difference on line 19.

8686	☐ VOID	☐ CORRECTED		
PAYER'S name, street address, city, state, ZIP code, and telephone no.	**1** Unemployment compensation $	OMB No. 1545-0120 20**06** Form **1099-G**	**Certain Government Payments**
	2 State or local income tax refunds, credits, or offsets $		
PAYER'S federal identification number	RECIPIENT'S identification number	**3** Box 2 amount is for tax year	**4** Federal income tax withheld $	**Copy A** **For Internal Revenue Service Center**
RECIPIENT'S name		**5** ATAA payments $	**6** Taxable grants $	**File with Form 1096.** For Privacy Act and Paperwork Reduction Act
Street address (including apt. no.)		**7** Agriculture payments $	**8** Check if box 2 is trade or business income ▶ ☐	Notice, see the **2006 General Instructions for**
City, state, and ZIP code				**Forms 1099, 1098, 5498, and W-2G.**
Account number (see instructions)				

Form **1099-G**   Cat. No. 14438M   Department of the Treasury - Internal Revenue Service

Do Not Cut or Separate Forms on This Page — **Do Not Cut or Separate Forms on This Page**

You can elect to have tax withheld at the rate of 10 percent on your unemployment, so you won't be caught short next April 15. This is one offer most people are likely to refuse.

Why would you have to give back some of your benefits? Because when you're collecting unemployment insurance, you have to be looking for a job. And if you aren't, the folks at the unemployment office may determine that you weren't entitled to all the benefits you received and that you owe some money back. If you gave back the benefits in the same year that you received them, no problem, just subtract what you returned from the total you received and enter that amount on line 19. You also need to enter "REPAID" and the amount that you repaid on the dotted line next to the amount column on line 19.

But if you returned money in 2006 that you paid tax on in 2005, things aren't as easy. Suppose that in 2005 you received and paid tax on $10,000 of unemployment benefits. Then during 2006 you had to repay $2,500, as determined by the unemployment office. The $2,500 you paid back is deductible on Schedule A (see Chapter 9).

If you repaid unemployment compensation (that was less than $3,000) in 2006 that you included in gross income in an earlier year, you may deduct the amount repaid with Form 1040, Schedule A (line 27). If the amount you repaid was more than $3,000, you can take either a deduction for the amount repaid as an itemized deduction or a credit against your tax for the amount of tax you originally paid by including this amount in your income in a prior year.

For example, suppose that in 2006 you repaid $4,000 of unemployment compensation that you received and paid tax on in 2005. Compute your 2005 tax without the $4,000 being included in your income. If your original tax was $10,000 and your tax without the $4,000 of unemployment was $8,416, you can claim the difference ($1,584) as a credit against your 2006 tax. If this credit is more than what you would save by deducting the $4,000 as an itemized deduction in 2005, enter the $1,584 on Form 1040 (line 70), and to the left of the line 70 credit, write "IRC 1341." The credit to which you are entitled is considered an additional tax payment made. The term IRC 1341 comes from Section 1341 of the Internal Revenue Code of 1986. This is known as a *claim of right.*

Lines 20a and 20b: Social Security benefits

Politicians don't want to do away with Social Security; they just want to pay fewer benefits and to tax more of it. As a result, they have made retirement more complicated. Here's how to figure out what to plug in.

Don't forget that if you're married and file a joint return for 2006, you and your spouse must combine your incomes and your benefits when figuring whether any of your combined benefits are taxable. Even if your spouse didn't receive any benefits, you must add your spouse's income to yours when figuring whether any of your benefits are taxable.

Form SSA-1099

Every person who receives Social Security benefits will receive a **Form SSA-1099**, even if the benefit is combined with another person's in a single check. If you receive benefits on more than one Social Security record, you may receive more than one Form SSA-1099. Your gross benefits are shown in box 3 of Form SSA-1099, and your repayments are shown in box 4. The amount in box 5 shows your net benefits for 2006 (box 3 – box 4). This is the amount you use to figure whether any of your benefits are taxable. If you misplaced Form SSA-1099, you can order a duplicate at the Social Security Web site (www.ssa.gov/1099) or by phone.

How much is taxable?

The starting point for determining the taxable portion of your Social Security is your base income, which is your adjusted gross income with a few adjustments. The base income worksheet we give you shows you how to compute this amount. Making the computation is easy, unless you or your spouse were covered by a pension and decided to make a deductible contribution to an IRA because your income was under $70,000 (for joint filers) or $50,000 (for others).

Unless you want to drive yourself crazy, stay away from making deductible contributions to an IRA if you or your spouse were covered by a pension *and* received Social Security. But if you want to do the math in this more-complicated case, we show you how to do the calculations here.

Early retirees, watch your step

People who retire early but continue working part time to supplement their Social Security income may be in for a nasty surprise when they sit down to complete their tax returns.

If you're between the ages of 62 and full retirement age (65 and 6 months if you were born in 1940, 65 and 8 months if you were born in 1941), you lose out on $1 of Social Security benefits for every $2 you earn above $12,480 for 2006. (Remember, this is earned income only; unearned income, such as from investments or a pension, doesn't penalize your benefits.)

This loss of benefits is known as the Social Security giveback, though it seems like a takeback to us. (At full retirement age, you can earn as much as you like without forfeiting any of your benefits.) Every year the full retirement age increases by two months until it reaches age 67.

Not only do you have this giveback to contend with, but more of your Social Security is subject to tax. Married couples with incomes above $44,000, and singles who make more than $34,000, will pay tax on 85 percent of their Social Security income.

Clearly, if you're not careful, working a little extra to add to your income from Social Security income can end up costing you money. Suppose that you earned $2,000 above the year 2006 threshold of $12,480 and, bad luck, it pushed you from the 15 to the 25 percent tax bracket. First, you pay 7.65 percent Social Security and Medicare tax on the extra $2,000 of income, which works out to $153. Next you have to pay income tax on the extra $2,000 you earned, and to make matters worse, that extra income subjected an additional $1,000 of your Social Security to tax. Then you'd have to give back $1,000 of your Social Security benefit. Your cost of making that extra two grand: $1,653!

Our advice to early retirees still younger than the full retirement age: After you reach the 2006 earnings level of $12,480, take a vacation until December 31. One other point: Workers who take early retirement (age 62) and then reach full retirement age in 2006, can earn up to $33,240 in the months before they reach full retirement age without forfeiting benefits. Additionally, you don't lose $1 for every $2 you earn above $33,240. It's $1 for every $3 you earn above $33,240. Think of it as a gift for reaching full retirement age in 2006.

IRS Publication 15 gives you the worksheets you need to figure out what part, if any, of your Social Security benefits you need to include on line 20b of your Form 1040. We provide you an easier set of worksheets right here that give you the same result — just pencil your numbers in over ours.

Base Income Worksheet

For example, you're married filing jointly and have interest and dividend income of $10,000, a $20,000 pension, and you received $16,000 from Social Security.

1. Total income (1040, line 37; 1040A, line 21) before addition of taxable Social Security	$30,000
2. Social Security (box 5, SSA-1099)	$16,000
3. 50 percent of line 2	$8,000
4. Tax-exempt interest income (1040, line 8b; 1040A, line 8b)	$0
5. Foreign earned income and housing exclusion (Form 2555, lines 43 and 48 or Form 2555-EZ, line 18)	$0
6. Qualified U.S. Savings Bond interest (Form 8815, line 14)	$0
7. Adoption benefits (Form 8839, line 30)	$0
8. Certain income of bona fide residents of American Samoa (Form 4563, line 15) or Puerto Rico	$0
9. Student loan interest (Form 1040, line 33 or Form 1040A, line 18)	$0
10. Total of lines 3, 4, 5, 6, 7, 8, and 9	$8,000
11. Base income (add lines 1 and 10)	$38,000

Line 7 really falls under the heading, "Our tax laws are really crazy." How many people drawing Social Security benefits are involved in an adoption?

Now use one of the following worksheets to figure the taxable portion of your Social Security benefits: If line 11 is more than $44,000 (if you're married and filing jointly) or $34,000 (if unmarried), you have to use Worksheet II.

Worksheet 1

1. Base income	$38,000
2. Enter the appropriate amount below.	
Married filing jointly — $32,000	
Married filing separately and living with spouse at any time during year — $0	
All others — $25,000	$32,000
3. Subtract line 2 from line 1.	$6,000
4. 50 percent of line 3	$3,000
5. Social Security (box 5, SSA-1099)	$16,000
6. 50 percent of line 5	$8,000
7. Taxable Social Security — smaller of lines 4 and 6	$3,000

Enter the amount on line 5 ($16,000) on line 20a, Form 1040, and the amount on line 7 ($3,000) on line 20b, Form 1040. For 1040A filers, it's lines 14a ($16,000) and 14b ($3,000).

Worksheet II

Example: Assume the same facts in the example on Worksheet I, except that your AGI is $36,000, your Social Security is $16,000, and your only adjustment to your base income worksheet above is $6,000 in tax-exempt interest.

1. AGI without Social Security	$36,000
2. Tax-exempt interest	$6,000
3. 50 percent of Social Security	$8,000
4. Base income (add lines 1 through 3)	$50,000

Tier-one adjustment

5. Enter the appropriate amount below.	
Married filing jointly — $32,000	
Married filing separately and living with spouse at any time during year — $0	
All others — $25,000	$32,000
6. Subtract line 5 from line 4.	$18,000
7. 50 percent of line 6	$9,000
8. Enter the appropriate amount below.	
Married filing jointly — $6,000	
Married filing separately and living with spouse at any time during year — $0	
All others — $4,500	$6,000
9. The smaller of lines 3, 7, and 8	$6,000

Tier-two adjustment

10. Enter the appropriate amount below.

    Married filing jointly — $44,000

    Married filing separately and living with spouse at any time during year — $0

    All others — $34,000 $44,000

11. Subtract line 10 from line 4. $6,000

12. 85 percent of line 11 $5,100

Taxable portion

13. Add lines 9 ($6,000) and 12 ($5,100). $11,100

14. 85 percent of box 5, SSA-1099 ($16,000) $13,600

15. Taxable Social Security (smaller of lines 13 and 14) $11,100

You would enter the amount in box 5, SSA-1099 ($16,000), on line 20a of Form 1040 and $11,100 from 15 on line 20b, Form 1040. On Form 1040A, it's $16,000 on line 14a and $11,100 on line 14b.

Repayment of benefits

In some cases, your Form SSA-1099 will show that the total benefits you repaid (box 4) are more than the gross benefits you received (box 3). If this situation occurs, your net benefits in box 5 will be a negative figure, and none of your benefits will be taxable. If you receive more than one form, a negative figure in box 5 of one form is used to offset a positive figure in box 5 of another form. If you have any questions about this negative figure, contact your local Social Security Administration office.

Remember, if you and your spouse file a joint return and you both receive an SSA-1099, combine the 1099s to arrive at the total benefits for both of you. That way, even if one of your statements shows a negative amount in box 5, you'll be able to offset that against the other spouse's positive benefits.

Lump-sum Social Security payments

If you receive a lump-sum payment of Social Security benefits in 2006 that includes benefits for prior years, you have two choices. You can consider the entire payment as the amount of Social Security received in 2006 and compute the taxable portion by using Worksheet I or II. Or you can allocate the amount that you received for a prior year as being received in that year.

Doing it the latter way makes sense, if your income was lower in a prior year. If that's the case, maybe none or perhaps less than 50 percent or 85 percent would have been taxable.

If you elect the second way of treating a lump sum that covers more than one year, you don't file an amended return for that year. Here's what you do. You compute the amount of the lump sum that would have been taxable had it been received in the prior year. You then add that amount to your income for the current year.

For example, suppose that you receive a lump-sum payment of $20,000 in 2006 that includes $10,000 of benefits for 2004. If you report the whole amount in 2006, 85 percent, or $17,000, is taxable. If you elect to treat the $10,000 for 2004 as being received for that year, you can save some dough. Why? Because, based on your 2004 income, only 50 percent, or $5,000, of the $10,000 lump-sum income attributed to that year would have to be added to your taxable income. By splitting the payment between the two years (including one where less of your Social Security benefit would have been taxed), you pay tax on only $13,500 ($5,000 for the 2004 benefit, and $8,500 for the 2006 benefit), instead of tax on $17,000 (85 percent of the entire $20,000 benefit). Isn't it better to have to report only $13,500 in 2006 rather than $17,000?

Repayment of benefits received in an earlier year

If the sum of the amount shown in box 5 of each of your SSA-1099s is a negative figure, and all or part of this negative figure is for benefits you included in gross income in an earlier year, you can take an itemized deduction on Schedule A for the amount of the negative figure — or you can claim credit for the tax that was paid on this in a prior year, because you included it in your income. We explain how to make the computation for this *claim of right* in our previous discussion of unemployment insurance on line 19.

If you're married and filing separately, you'll get caught in a special trap. Because the base exemption of $25,000 that single filers enjoy before 50 percent of their Social Security becomes taxable isn't allowed for married couples filing separately, neither are they entitled to the $32,000 single filer base exemption before 85 percent of their benefits becomes taxable. If a married couple lived apart for the entire year and filed separately, then these base exemption amounts apply. However, a recent Tax Court case held that living apart meant separate residences, not separate bedrooms. The long and short of all this is that 85 percent of married individuals' Social Security benefits end up being taxed when they file separately and didn't live apart the entire year.

Line 21: Other income

Line 21 of Form 1040 is a catchall for reporting income that doesn't fit the income categories listed on page one of Form 1040. Hey, even if you *find* some money, the IRS treats it as income! Just report all this miscellaneous income here. Don't forget to write a description of these earnings on the dotted line next to the amount.

Here are some examples of stuff that goes on line 21.

Bartering

Bartering is the trading of your services for goods or other services. You usually must declare the fair market value of goods you receive. If you participate in a barter exchange, you may get a **Form 1099-B** — and the IRS gets a copy, too. For example, suppose that you're a carpenter with a child who needs braces; you agree to make cabinets in a dentist's office in exchange for your child's braces and treatment. Although no cash changed hands, you have to pay tax on what the dentist normally would charge, because that is your income from making the cabinets. The dentist makes out better. Because the cabinets are used in his business, he is entitled to a business deduction equal to the income he has to report. Even poor Jack of Beanstalk fame had taxable income when he traded his cow for those beans.

Not every Form 1099-B is for barter transactions. It's also used to report the sale of stocks and bonds (and other marketable securities) through a broker. Broker, barter – they're both Bs. In some convoluted way, it makes sense. Still, if you have a broker transaction, report it on Schedule D (check out Chapter 12).

Canceled debt

A *canceled debt,* or a debt paid for you by another person, is generally income to you and must be reported. For example, a discount offered by a financial institution for the prepaying of your mortgage is income from the cancellation of the debt. However, you have no income from the cancellation of a debt if the cancellation is a gift. For example, suppose you borrow $10,000 from a relative who tells you that you don't have to repay it. It's a gift! (And be sure to invite *that* relative to Thanksgiving dinner every year.) If you received a sweetheart deal on a loan, make sure that you read the rules on below-market interest rates for loans in Chapter 10.

If your debt is canceled as the result of bankruptcy or because you are insolvent, the cancellation of the debt negates your having to pay tax on the income. And you don't have to report it as income if your student loan is canceled because you agreed to certain conditions to obtain the loan — and then performed the required services.

Under the old law, only student loans from governmental or educational organizations qualified for this exclusion from income rule when professional services were rendered in exchange for the forgiveness of the loan. After August 5, 1997, loans from tax-exempt charities also qualify.

Life insurance

The death benefit paid to the beneficiary of a life insurance contract is exempt from tax. However, this exception doesn't apply to advance payments made to terminally or chronically ill taxpayers.

A limited portion ($250 a day or $91,250 annually) of an advance payment on a life insurance policy won't be subject to tax if paid to a terminally or chronically ill person. Unfortunately, the law gets somewhat ghoulish. A terminally ill person is someone who is certified by a doctor as having a life expectancy of less than 24 months. A person is chronically ill if he or she can't perform at least two normal daily functions, such as eating, bathing, dressing, toileting, and so on. (Only the IRS can make such a distinction.) Amounts above $250 are also excludable if they are used to pay for long-term care. That's an oxymoron if we ever heard one. The tax lingo for these advanced payments is *viatical settlements.* Aren't you glad you took Latin in high school? Report viatical payments and the portions exempt from tax in Section C of **Form 8853, Archer MSAs and Long-Term Care Insurance Contracts.**

To get the name of viatical brokers or companies that advance money before the death of a policyholder, contact either the National Viatical Association at 800-741-9465, or the Viatical Association of America at 800-842-9811.

Other stuff

Here are some more examples of things to include on line 21:

- ✔ **Alaska Permanent Fund distributions (dividends):** See line 13 under 1040A filing section in Chapter 5 for the ins and outs about this kind of income.

- ✔ **Fees that you snare:** Maybe you're a corporate director, or a notary public, and you made some extra cash. Good job!

    If these payments are $600 or more from a single source, you'll receive Form 1099-MISC from the person or company that paid you. If you receive a fee or commission from an activity you're not regularly engaged in for business, you report it instead on line 21. Fees are considered self-employment income, which means that you may owe Social Security tax on them. You compute the Social Security tax you owe on Schedule SE (Self-Employment Tax). The amount of Social Security tax owed is then reported on line 58 of Form 1040, and you get a deduction for half of the tax on line 27.

- ✔ **Free tour:** The free tour you received from a travel agency or the group organizer is taxable at its fair market value. Bon voyage.

- ✔ **Gambling winnings:** Gambling winnings are taxable. But you can also deduct your gambling losses — as long as they don't exceed your winnings — as an itemized deduction on line 27 of Schedule A.

- ✔ **Illegal income:** Al Capone found out about this too late. Remember, he spent time in Alcatraz for tax evasion, not for his health.

- ✔ **Jury duty:** The whopping $7 a day (more or less) that you received for jury duty goes here. If you must repay this amount to your employer because your employer continued to pay your salary while you served on the jury, you can deduct the repayment. The repayment gets deducted on line 34 of Form 1040.

- ✔ **Prizes and awards:** If you get lucky and hit the lottery or win a prize in a contest, the winnings are taxable. Sorry!

  However, some employee achievement awards may be nontaxable. These include non-cash awards, such as a watch, golf clubs, or a TV, given in recognition for length of service or safety achievement. The tax-free limit is $400 if given from a nonqualified employer plan and $1,600 from a qualified plan. Check with your human resources department.

- ✔ **Qualified tuition program payments:** These programs more commonly are known as Section 529 plans in which you prepay a student's tuition or establish an account to pay his or her higher education expenses. To the extent that any earnings are distributed that aren't used to pay higher education expenses, the beneficiary, not the person who established the account, has to pay tax on those earnings. The earnings are reported on Form 1099-Q, box 2. Check out Chapter 24 for details about Section 529 plans as well as other options for saving for educational expenses. Taxable earnings on Coverdell Education Savings Accounts, if you have any, are reported on this line.

- ✔ **Treasure-trove:** Say you buy a used sofa at an auction for $500 and discover a diamond ring under one of the cushions when you get it home. Guess what — you owe the tax on the value of the ring. Unfair! Just think of it as your fellow citizens wanting to share in your good fortune. Forgive us if we confronted you with a moral dilemma on what you have to do.

Frequent-flier miles that you earn on business trips but use for personal travel aren't taxable. One taxpayer stretched this rule too far. He had his travel agent bill the employer for first-class tickets. Next, he purchased coach tickets and used the frequent-flier miles to upgrade to first class. He had the travel agent refund the difference to his personal account. The IRS held that the refunds were taxable.

Deductions

You also use line 21 to claim two types of deductions: a net-operating loss and the foreign earned income and housing exclusion.

Net operating loss (NOL)

This deduction to your income occurs when your business expenses in a prior year exceed your income for that year. Unless you elect otherwise by attaching a statement to your return that says you want to carry the loss forward, you must first carry back the loss to the two prior tax years as a deduction and then forward for the next 20 years — until the total loss is used up. Chapter 18 deals with filing amended returns and how NOLs are carried back and forward. When you carry an NOL forward from a previous year, you enter it as a negative number (for example, <$10,000> on line 21).

Losses incurred before January 1, 1998, can be carried back three years, and then carried forward for 15 years instead of 20. Despite the change, the three-year carryback will still apply to the NOL of small businesses ($5 million or less of income for the past three years) attributable to losses in a presidentially declared disaster area. Farmers are allowed a special break; losses incurred after 1997 can be carried back five years and forward 20 years.

As a result of the events of September 11, 2001, operating losses incurred in 2001 and 2002 can be carried back five years. See Chapter 18.

Foreign earned income and housing exclusion

In 2006, U.S. citizens and permanent residents working abroad are entitled to exclude up to $82,400 of their foreign salary or their self-employed income. (If you've ever considered working abroad, this exclusion may help you make up your mind.) The portion of their foreign housing costs above an annual threshold can also be deducted. The exclusion isn't automatic. You have to file **Form 2555, Foreign Earned Income,** to claim the exclusion and the housing deduction, and attach it to your return. There is also a **Form 2555-EZ.**

To qualify for the exclusion, you must either be a resident of a foreign country or be physically present in a foreign country. Earnings from employment by the U.S. government don't qualify.

To qualify as a resident, you must reside in a foreign country for an uninterrupted period that includes the entire year (January 1 to December 31). So if you start working in London on March 31, 2006, you can't qualify for the exclusion under the entire-year rule, but you can possibly qualify under the *physical presence test.* Brief trips back to the United States don't disqualify you from being a resident of a foreign country.

Under the physical presence test, you must be in a foreign country for 330 days during a 12-month consecutive period. If you weren't physically present or a bona fide resident for the entire year, the $82,400 exclusion has to be reduced based on the number of days you were out of the country.

To determine whether you meet the 330-day test, you may have to apply for an extension of time to file **(Form 2350, Application for Extension to File U.S. Income Tax Return)**. Say you started to work in Paris on July 1, 2006 (great assignment!); you won't know until July 1, 2007, if you meet the 330-day test for the 12-month period of July 1, 2006 to July 1, 2007.

Say that you weren't in a foreign country for 330 days between July 1, 2006, and July 1, 2007. You can still claim a partial exemption for 2006 (half of $82,400) if you meet the bona fide residence test for 2007. If you meet this test, you're considered a bona fide resident since July 1, 2006. While you're waiting to qualify as a bona fide resident for 2007, so that you can claim the foreign earned income exclusion for 2006, you can put off filing your 2006 return until January 30, 2008. Normally, a 2006 return can be extended only until October 15, 2007; Form 2350 will get you the extension to January 30, 2008.

You enter your foreign earnings from Form 2555, line 25 on Form 1040 (line 7). Then you enter the amount of those earnings that you can exclude — plus your foreign housing deduction — as a negative number on line 21 and deduct it from your income.

If your foreign earned income was $82,400 or less and you earned it as an employee (you weren't self-employed), and you're not claiming a foreign housing exclusion or a deduction for moving expenses, the friendly folks at the IRS allow you to use Form 2555-EZ; the difference is 18 lines versus 48.

Line 22: Your total income

Whew! Are you ready to do the math? Don't be stubborn or proud; grab the calculator. Add lines 7 through 21 and put the final figure on line 22. Congratulations! This amount is your total income. Because you don't want to pay tax on this amount, we tell you what deductions and other adjustments to income you're entitled to in the chapters that follow, so you can get away with paying the least amount possible.

Chapter 7

Form 1040, Part II: Adjustments to Income Stuff

. . . .

In This Chapter

▶ Archer MSA deduction

▶ Deduction for certain business expenses of reservists, performing artists, and fee-basis government officials

▶ Health savings account deduction

▶ Moving expenses

▶ The self-employment tax write-off

▶ Keogh and SEP deductions and SIMPLE plans

▶ Self-employed health insurance deduction

▶ Penalty on early withdrawal of savings

▶ Alimony paid (that you deduct!)

▶ IRA deductions

▶ Student loan interest

▶ Return of jury duty pay

▶ Domestic production activities deduction

. . . .

Congratulations! If you're reading this chapter, you've probably made it through the first part of your income tax return. If the amount on line 22 represents all your income, you may now think that all you have to do is figure your tax on that amount. But wait! All you've done so far is figure out your total income. Your taxable income will be much, much less. In this chapter, you can find out about the first set of deductions you can subtract from the total, the so-called *adjustments to income*.

Adjusted Gross Income (AGI)

In this section (see Figure 7-1), you add your adjustments to income on lines 23 through 35 and subtract them from your total income on line 22. The result of this subtraction is called your *adjusted gross income (AGI)*. Your AGI is an important number, because it's used as the benchmark for calculating many allowable deductions — such as medical and miscellaneous itemized deductions — and the taxable amount of your Social Security income. In fact, if your AGI is too high in the eyes of the IRS, we're sorry to say that you may even lose the personal exemptions to which you thought you were entitled — the $3,300 personal exemptions that you can claim for yourself, your spouse, and your dependents.

		Adjusted Gross Income	
Adjusted Gross Income	23	Archer MSA deduction. Attach Form 8853	23
	24	Certain business expenses of reservists, performing artists, and fee-basis government officials. Attach Form 2106 or 2106-EZ	24
	25	Health savings account deduction. Attach Form 8889	25
	26	Moving expenses. Attach Form 3903	26
	27	One-half of self-employment tax. Attach Schedule SE	27
	28	Self-employed SEP, SIMPLE, and qualified plans	28
	29	Self-employed health insurance deduction (see page 30)	29
	30	Penalty on early withdrawal of savings	30
	31a	Alimony paid b Recipient's SSN ▶	31a
	32	IRA deduction (see page 31)	32
	33	Student loan interest deduction (see page 33)	33
	34	Jury duty pay you gave to your employer	34
	35	Domestic production activities deduction. Attach Form 8903	35
	36	Add lines 23 through 31a and 32 through 35	36
	37	Subtract line 36 from line 22. This is your **adjusted gross income** ▶	37

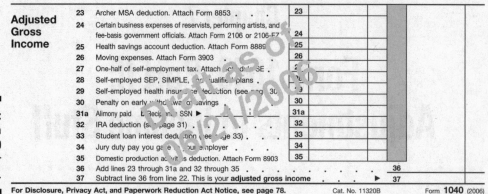

Figure 7-1: This section of Form 1040 may lower your taxes.

For Disclosure, Privacy Act, and Paperwork Reduction Act Notice, see page 78.   Cat. No. 11320B   Form **1040** (2006)

You don't have to itemize your deductions on Schedule A to claim adjustments to income in this section. Everyone gets to make these adjustments.

Here's the line-by-line rundown of the adjustments you may be able to make. The headings refer to line numbers where you plug your data into your 1040.

Line 23: Archer MSA (Medical Savings Account) deduction

This type of account, which is offered by insurance companies and is used to pay your medical bills, is similar to an IRA. For single taxpayers, your MSA must have an annual deductible of at least $1,800 but not more than $2,700. For family coverage the deductible has to be at least $3,650 but not more than $5,450.

You can contribute and deduct up to $4,087.50 if married (75% of the maximum allowable deductible of $5,450) and $1,755 if single (65% of the maximum allowable deduction of $2,700). A nifty feature of MSAs is that, unlike employer-provided flexible spending accounts (FSAs), an MSA isn't subject to the "use it or lose it" rule. Balances in the account can be carried forward from year to year. The earnings on the account accumulate tax-free, and withdrawals to pay medical expenses aren't subject to tax. Like regular IRAs, contributions to an MSA that are made before the April 16, 2007, filing date can be deducted on your 2006 return.

You can be covered under only one high-deductible plan. (Accident, disability, dental care, vision care, long-term care, medical supplemental insurance, and per diem plans that pay a fixed daily rate if you're hospitalized aren't considered additional plans.)

Nonreimbursed medical expenses that can be withdrawn free of tax are the ones that you can deduct as a medical expense on your return if you itemized your deductions. However, the most that can be paid out of the plan for family coverage of out-of-pocket medical expenses (other than for premiums) is limited to $6,650. For single coverage, the out-of-pocket limit is $3,650. Amounts withdrawn that are more than these amounts are taxable. What you can deduct as a medical expense is spelled out in Chapter 9. However, you can't make withdrawals to pay health insurance premiums except for continuation coverage required by federal law, long-term healthcare, or while you're unemployed.

Distributions from an MSA for nonmedical expenses are subject to a 15 percent penalty, plus the tax on the distribution at the rate for your tax bracket. The penalty and income inclusion also apply if you pledge the account for a loan.

After age 65, you can withdraw funds from an MSA for any reason without paying the 15 per-cent penalty (but the funds still are taxable). Although not intended for this purpose, MSAs can potentially be viewed as an additional retirement account.

MSAs were a pilot program, and the provisions, which were originally set to expire on December 31, 2003, have been extended to already existing account holders, although it isn't possible to open a new account at this time. If you owned an MSA on December 31, 2005, you may continue to make contributions to it, or you may choose to roll it over to a Health Savings Account (HSA), which we describe in great detail in "Line 25: Health Savings Account Deduction (Form 8889)."

If you choose to continue funding your MSA, you compute your deduction on **Form 8853, Archer MSAs and Long-Term Care Insurance Contracts.** Every year the deductible and out-of-pocket amounts are indexed and adjusted for inflation. When you've completed Form 8853, take your result and place it gently on line 23.

Line 24: Certain business expenses of reservists, performing artists, and fee-basis government officials

If you believe you fall into the category of an armed forces reservist, a performing artist, or a fee-basis government official, read up! You may be able to deduct certain business expenses from your total income, rather than have them be reduced by a 2-percent-of-income threshold as a "miscellaneous itemized deduction" (see Chapter 9). Before you can decide, though, you need to know if your job and your expenses qualify.

- ✔ **Armed forces reservists** may deduct travel expenses if you're traveling more than 100 miles away from your home in connection with your service.

- ✔ **Performing artists** may deduct all your employee business expenses on line 24, pro-vided that you meet all four requirements:

  - During the tax year, you perform services in the performing arts as an employee of at least two employers.

  - You earn at least $200 each from at least two employers.

  - The business expenses you incur from your performing arts jobs are more than 10 percent than you earn from all your performing arts jobs.

  - Your AGI (see line 37 later in this chapter) isn't more than $16,000 before deduct-ing these business expenses.

  If you're married and either you or your spouse is a performing artist, you need to file a joint return in order to qualify for this deduction unless you lived apart from your spouse for the entire tax year. And, to make matters more interesting, although both you and your spouse must figure the first three requirements separately, the AGI for both of you together can't be more than $16,000. If you can't make any of these require-ments, you have to declare your deductible expenses on Schedule A instead (see Chapter 9).

- ✔ **Government officials** paid on a fee-basis may deduct all your employee business expenses on line 24 if you're employed by your state or local government and are paid in whole or in part on a fee basis ($5,000 to prepare a particular report, for example).

  If you do qualify, you need to fill out Form 2106 or Form 2106-EZ before you fill in an amount on line 24 of your Form 1040.

Line 25: Health Savings Account Deduction (Form 8889)

Health Savings Accounts (HSA) may allow you to pay for unreimbursed medical expenses on a tax-free basis. You may establish an HSA if you're covered by a qualified high-deductible health plan with annual deductibles of at least $1,000 for individuals and $2,000 for families. You may not open or fund one of these accounts if you have other general health insurance (separate dental, accident-only, vision, workers' comp, disability, or long-term care policies don't count against you here). You also can't be claimed as a dependent on someone else's return.

An HSA works similarly to an individual retirement account (IRA). In this case, your HSA is invested and allowed to grow income-tax free until you need to access the money to pay for qualified medical expenses (medical insurance premiums are excluded). Like the Archer Medical Savings Accounts (see "Line 23: Archer MSA (Medical Savings Account) deduction," earlier in this chapter), there's no "use it or lose it" feature here (like there is with Flexible Spending Accounts). Your money continues to grow from year to year until you need to use it. You may contribute a maximum of $2,700 for individuals and $5,450 for families each year. After you enroll in Medicare at age 65, contributions are no longer allowed, although you may continue to take distributions.

If you previously funded an Archer MSA, you're allowed to roll that account into an HSA without paying any tax or penalty. Just like any IRA rollover, though, the safest way to avoid paying any tax or penalty is through a trustee-to-trustee transfer.

If you funded an HSA in 2006 (or from January 1 to April 16, 2007), or rolled your existing Archer MSA over to an HSA, you need to complete **Form 8889, Health Savings Accounts (HSAs).** After you complete that form, take the number from line 11 of the Form 8889 and put it on line 25 of your Form 1040.

These rules for these accounts are fairly intricate, and you really need to consult a pro before setting one up. With health insurance premiums continuing to climb, these accounts, and the high deductible policies that they supplement, are going to become increasingly popular.

Line 26: Moving expenses (Form 3903)

If you incur moving expenses because you have to relocate for job reasons, you can deduct moving expenses for which your employer doesn't reimburse you. Self-employed individuals may also deduct their moving expenses.

In order to claim a moving-expenses deduction, you must meet a couple of pesky requirements. Those requirements are

- The location of your new job must be at least 50 miles farther from your old residence than your last workplace was.

- You must have been employed full-time for at least 39 out of the 52 weeks prior to the move at your old job. If you're self-employed, you must be employed full-time at least 78 weeks out of the 24 months immediately after the move, at least 39 of those weeks happening during the first 12 months.

The place to deduct moving expenses is **Form 3903, Moving Expenses.** You then enter the deductible amount on line 26. See Chapter 15 for more about filling out Form 3903. Don't forget to attach Form 3903 to your return.

Line 27: One-half of self-employment tax

One of the great drawbacks of being self-employed is that you get hit not only with income tax on your earnings but also with Self-Employment Tax. This wonderful invention combines the 7.65 percent ordinary wage earners pay for combined Social Security and Medicare contributions with the employer's matching 7.65 percent. So, because self-employed people are both the employer and the employee, they get stuck with both halves of this tax, or a whopping 15.3 percent of all earnings from self-employment up to $94,200, and 2.9 percent on all earnings above that.

If you're subject to this additional tax (and you know who you are, because you've already filled out **Schedule SE, Self Employment Tax**, which we cover in Chapter 15), line 27 provides some tax relief. You're allowed to deduct one half of your self-employment tax from your total income.

Line 28: Self-employed SEP, SIMPLE, and qualified plans

In case you were looking and you're self-employed, you've just found the place to deduct contributions to your Keogh, SEP, or SIMPLE retirement accounts. These types of accounts allow you to make substantial pretax contributions toward your retirement savings.

A SEP is a combination IRA/profit-sharing plan and is available only for self-employed individuals and their employees (but not corporations). With a SEP (Simplified Employee Pension), you're allowed to stash up to 25 percent of your net income from self-employment, but not to exceed a $44,000 contribution. You can set up your plan and make this contribution for 2006 up to the day that you file your income tax return in 2007, including extensions.

As a self-employed person, you can also set up a Keogh plan. Your contributions to the plan are not only deductible, but also are exempt from tax until you start receiving benefits. But to make a Keogh contribution in 2007 that's deductible on your 2006 return, the plan had to be set up by December 31, 2006. If you already have a Keogh set up by the end of the tax year, see "Keogh contributions," later in this chapter.

Remember, if you have employees and want to contribute to a SEP or Keogh for yourself, you can't ignore your employees. Check out Chapter 20 for the rules on contributions. If you and your spouse are the only ones covered by the plan, you don't have to file an annual information return with the IRS until the plan's assets exceed $100,000. If you're subject to the filing requirements, file **Form 5500EZ.** If you have employees, use **Form 5500.** This form need not be filed for a SEP.

If you forget to set up a Keogh by December 31, 2006, you can't make a deductible contribution to it for 2006. But with a SEP, you can take a deduction for 2006 as long as you set one up and contribute to it by the due date for filing your 2006 return (which can be extended to October 15, 2007). Consider a SEP-IRA for the interim and establish a Keogh by December 31, 2007, so that you can switch over to funding a Keogh for 2007.

Employers with fewer than 100 employees can establish what's known as SIMPLE (Savings Incentive Match Plan for Employees) plans. SIMPLEs come in two forms: a SIMPLE IRA and a SIMPLE 401(k). A *SIMPLE plan* allows an employee to contribute up to $10,000 in pretax dollars with the employer matching a like amount, $12,500 if you turned 50 in 2006. Unlike regular retirement plans, the nondiscrimination coverage rules don't apply, which means you don't have to include your employees in your retirement plan. See Chapter 20 for more about SIMPLE and other small-business retirement plan options.

Regardless of whether you have a SEP, a Keogh profit-sharing, or Keogh pension, you generally can deduct up to 25 percent of your earnings to a maximum deduction of $44,000. You noticed that we said "generally." That's because when it comes to taxes, about every rule has an exception. With a defined-benefit Keogh, you can, depending on your age, put away substantially more than the smaller of 25 percent of your earnings or $44,000. You need to know about a few other wrinkles when deciding which type of plan is best for you, so read on. For example, with a SEP or profit-sharing Keogh, you get to choose the percentage you want to contribute every year. It can be zero or 25 percent or any percentage in between.

Another retirement plan possibility is called the Solo (k), which is a cross between a 401(k) and a profit-sharing Keogh. What's unique about the Solo (k) retirement plan is that business owners without employees — consultants, independent contractors, lawyers and doctors in solo practices, and mom-and-pop shops — can put away significantly more than they can under a conventional Keogh. Here's how it works. Say the earnings of your consulting business are $40,000. Under a regular Keogh, you can contribute and deduct $8,000 (25 percent of $40,000 after deducting the $8,000). With a Solo (k), you get to contribute the $8,000 plus the maximum 401(k) limit of $15,000 for a total contribution of $23,000, as long as the combination of the two contributions doesn't exceed $44,000. There's more! If you're older than 50, you can contribute an additional $5,000 to the 401(k) portion of the plan. This extra amount isn't subject to the overall $44,000 limit. So if your income is $135,000 and you're older than 50, you can contribute $15,000 under the 401(k) arrangement plus $5,000 because you're older than 50, and another $27,000 in normal profit-sharing contributions (25 percent of $135,000 after deducting the $27,000) for a total retirement deduction of $47,000. By comparison, if all you have is a regular Keogh, the most you can contribute is $27,000.

If you're both an employee and a sole proprietor, the most you can contribute to either your employer's 401(k) or the 401(k) feature of your Solo (k) is $15,000. Some taxpayers mistakenly believe they can contribute $15,000 to each 401(k). Don't make that mistake. However, if your employer contributes on your behalf to a profit-sharing plan, you can also contribute to the profit-sharing feature of your plan. However, if you're an owner where you're employed, the profit-sharing plan of your separate business won't be considered a separate plan, meaning that the most you can contribute to both plans is $44,000.

If you find this Solo (k) business intriguing, just click on to www.401khelpcenter.com for a list of companies that sponsor such plans. This Web site also features a calculator that instantly computes the maximum you can contribute. Just enter your age, earnings, and presto! Because the menu options at this site change so often, type in Solo (k) at the search button to go to the "Solo (k) menu."

Computing your SEP and Keogh deductions

We wish we could tell you that all you have to do to figure your Keogh deduction is to multiply your self-employment earnings by 25 percent. Why should the government make it that simple? You must follow two rules to arrive at the amount you are allowed to deduct.

- ✔ **Rule 1.** You have to reduce your earnings by deducting one-half of your self-employment tax and your Keogh contribution to get the amount that you multiply the percentage by, say it's 25 percent.

- ✔ **Rule 2.** The maximum amount of your earnings reduced by this adjustment that you multiply the 25 percent by can't exceed $220,000.

See Table 7-1 to determine your effective contribution rate based on the actual plan percentage that you choose to contribute.

Table 7-1	Keogh and SEP Conversion Table
Actual Plan Rate	*Effective Rate That You Contribute*
1%	.009901
2%	.019608
3%	.029126
4%	.038462
5%	.047619
6%	.056604
7%	.065421
8%	.074074
9%	.082569
10%	.090909
11%	.099099
12%	.107143
13%	.115044
14%	.122807
15%	.130435
16%	.137931
17%	.145299
18%	.152542
19%	.159664
20%	.166667
21%	.173554
22%	.180328
23%	.186992
24%	.193548
25%	.200000

There is a kind of Keogh known as a *defined-benefit retirement plan*. With this type of pension, the annual contribution isn't determined by a percentage of your earnings or by your employees' salaries. You select an annual pension benefit that you want to receive at retirement, say $75,000. Next an insurance actuary determines — based on your age — how much you need to contribute to the pension every year to have a nest egg at retirement that's large enough to pay you $75,000 a year during retirement. If the actuary determines that you need to put away $95,000 a year to accomplish that goal, then you can ignore customary maximum annual deduction limitation of $44,000. Sounds great, but all this red tape is extremely complicated and costly to administer. You can select a retirement benefit as high as $175,000. Because the amount that you can put away every year is based on your age, you can, as a general rule, put away more money under this type of plan at about age 50. That's because at that age, you have fewer years to put money away, so a greater annual contribution to the plan must be made.

If you have a SEP or a profit-sharing plan, you can wait until you file your return in 2007 (including the extension period) to make your contribution to the plan and have it count toward 2006. Extensions of time to file until October 15, 2007, count toward this grace period. On the other hand, if you have a defined-benefit or a regular pension plan (other than a SEP or profit-sharing plan), you must make your contribution by September 15, 2007, regardless of whether you have an extension of time to file until October 15, 2007. Dealing with the IRS rules is a virtual minefield to the unknowing.

Line 29: Self-employed health insurance deduction

If you're self-employed, you may deduct 100 percent of your health insurance premiums from your income, with one caveat: You may not deduct more than your net profit from your business.

A general partner (but not a limited partner), an independent contractor, or a shareholder in an S Corporation may also claim this deduction. The deduction is allowed for premiums paid for you, your spouse, and your dependents. A portion of your long-term care premiums also qualifies for this deduction (see Chapter 9 for the maximum deductible amount).

Line 30: Penalty for early withdrawal of savings

If you withdraw funds from a savings account before maturity or redeem a certificate of deposit before it's due and you're charged a penalty, you can deduct it on your 1040 (line 30). You don't have to itemize to claim this deduction. You can deduct the entire penalty, even when it exceeds the interest income reported on the **Form 1099-INT** that you received. The penalty amount, if any, is shown in box 2 of the 1099, which the bank will send you by January 31, 2007.

Members of the same household

You're members of the same household even if you and your spouse separate yourselves physically in your home (or in your tropical hut, just like Gilligan and the Skipper once did after they had a fight). However, payments made within one month of departure qualify as alimony. For example, suppose that on June 1, while you're still residing in the same residence with your spouse, you make a support payment. If you move out by July 1, this payment is deductible. Any payments made prior to June 1 don't qualify. A technical exception exists, however. If you're not legally separated under a decree of divorce or separate maintenance, a payment made under a written separation agreement, support decree can qualify as alimony even if you are members of the same household. Although this sounds like a distinction without a difference, in plain English this means that temporary payments until the separation or divorce is finalized can be deducted as alimony even if you continue to live in the same residence.

Lines 31a and b: Alimony paid

The alimony you paid is deducted on line 31a; to the left of the amount, you have to enter your former spouse's Social Security number on line 31b. If you don't enter the number, you can expect to hear from the IRS because there is a $50 penalty for making this boo-boo, and your alimony deduction may be disallowed. If you paid alimony to more than one person, enter the total amount of alimony you paid on line 31a, and then list the amount and Social Security number for each recipient on a separate statement, and attach it to your return.

Before you can deduct it as an expense, you need to know what the government defines as alimony. The alimony rules aren't simple, so hang in there.

This is alimony

Payments count as alimony only if *all* the following conditions are met:

- Payments are required by the divorce decree or a separation decree.
- The alimony payer and the alimony recipient don't file a joint return with each other.
- The payment is in cash (including checks or money orders).
- The spouses who are separated or divorced aren't members of the same household (see the sidebar "Members of the same household," later in this chapter).
- The payments aren't required after the death of the spouse who receives the alimony.
- The payment isn't designated as child support.

This isn't alimony

Payments don't count as alimony if *any* of the following conditions are true:

- The payment is a noncash property settlement.
- The payments are a spouse's part of community income.
- The payments are destined to keep up the payer's property.
- The payments aren't required as part of the separation or divorce settlement.

Rules and exceptions to alimony

Looks simple, you say? Sorry. The rules on alimony are one of the most complex areas of the law. The reason for this absurd complexity is that each party to a divorce is trying to achieve opposite goals. The payer usually wants to deduct every payment, and the recipient wants to pay as little tax as possible. To keep everyone honest, regulations breed regulations! The following additional information can help you plug in the right amount on line 11 for alimony received, or line 31a for alimony paid.

- **Cash payments:** A cash payment must be made in cash. (Makes sense, doesn't it?) Therefore, property settlements don't qualify. The transfer of a home or business is considered a property settlement.
- **Payments to a third party:** Payments to a third party qualify as alimony if they are used in place of alimony and are requested in writing by your former spouse. These payments can be for medical expenses, housing costs, taxes, tuition, and so on.
- **Life insurance premiums:** Life insurance premiums on your life insurance qualify as deductible alimony if the payment is required by the divorce or separation agreement and your former spouse owns the policy.

- **Mortgage payments:** Mortgage payments are alimony if you must make mortgage payments (principal and interest) on a home jointly owned with your former spouse — and the terms of the decree or agreement call for such payments. You can deduct half of the total of these payments as alimony. Your spouse reports this same half as income. If you itemize deductions and the home is your qualified residence, you can include the other half of the interest portion in figuring your deductible interest. If the home is your ex's residence, he or she can deduct half of the mortgage interest.

- **Taxes and insurance:** Tax and insurance payments qualify as alimony if you must make them on a home that you hold as tenants in common — which means that your heirs get your share when you die. (The person you own the property with doesn't get your share.) You can deduct half of the tax and insurance payments as alimony, and your spouse reports this amount as income. If you and your ex-spouse itemize deductions, you each may deduct one-half of the real estate taxes. If the property is held as tenants by the entirety or as joint tenants (where the survivor gets it all), none of your payments for taxes and insurance qualify as alimony. If you itemize your deductions, you can deduct all of the real estate taxes.

- **Minimum payment period:** For alimony agreements executed in 1985 and 1986, annual payments in excess of $10,000 had to continue for at least six years. For agreements made after 1986, no minimum payment period exists.

- **Recapture:** To keep people from disguising large divorce settlements as alimony, a recapture provision was enacted for agreements executed after 1986. Recapture means that you have to report as income part of what you deducted during the first two years that you started paying alimony. The recapture rule applies if your average payments decline in the first three years by more than $15,000.

  For example, suppose that in year one and year two, you paid and deducted $25,000 in alimony, but in year three, you paid only $5,000. You triggered the recapture rules, because your payment decreased by more than $15,000. See a tax expert. This area is one you don't want to fool around with. However, recapture doesn't apply if your spouse dies or remarries, or if your alimony payments are geared to a fixed percentage of your income and your income decreases.

- **Payments after death**: Alimony payments must stop at your ex-spouse's death. If you must continue to make payments after your spouse's death — because of the legalese included in the agreement — none of the payments that you made before or after death qualify as alimony that you can deduct.

- **Child support:** A required payment that's specifically designated as child support under your divorce decree isn't deductible as alimony. Even if a payment isn't specially designated as child support, part of it will be considered child support if the payment is to be reduced when your child reaches a specified age, dies, marries, leaves school, or becomes employed.

  For example, suppose that you're required to pay your spouse $2,000 a month. However, when your child reaches age 21, your payment will be reduced to $1,250. Only $1,250 of your $2,000 monthly payment is considered alimony, and the remaining $750 is considered nondeductible child support.

  For pre-1985 divorce decrees, combined spouse and child support payments that are reduced when the child comes of age are treated as alimony. The IRS deemed this deal too good (of course) and thus changed the rules for agreements executed after 1984.

- **Payments to nonresident aliens:** Alimony paid to nonresident aliens is considered U.S. source income. As a result, you have to withhold 30 percent for tax and send it to the IRS, just like your employer does with the tax withheld from your salary. Find out whether the U.S. has a tax treaty with the country of your former spouse — under a number of tax treaties, alimony is exempt from withholding. See IRS Publication 901 (U.S. Tax Treaties) for some really interesting reading!

Normally when a property settlement is reached in a divorce, the transfer isn't taxable to either of the parties. However, there are exceptions (what a surprise!). For example, if you give shares of stock or stock options that you own to your former spouse, the transfer, depending on the type of option, may be a taxable event. However, the spouse who receives the stock or options owes the tax that his or her ex would have owed when the options are exercised or the stock is sold. This rule also applies to other assets. Chapter 12 contains the rules on stock options.

Line 32: You and your spouse's IRA deduction

Saving for your eventual retirement is a good thing, which is why the tax laws are structured to give you all sorts of benefits if you do save for retirement. The IRA is one way that you may sock it away for your golden years.

Originally, IRAs came in plain vanilla. Basically, you were allowed to contribute $2,000 each year into an account and defer paying tax on both your yearly contributions and any money that you earned on your contributions. When you took distributions from your account after retirement, you paid the income tax on the full amount of your distribution at ordinary income rates. What could be easier?

This sort of account still exists, only now it's called a "traditional, fully deductible IRA." Other types of IRAs — essentially variations on a theme, have joined it. Now you may own a traditional deductible IRA, a traditional nondeductible IRA, or even a Roth IRA. Here's how they differ:

- ✔ **Traditional deductible IRA:** You make contributions that you haven't paid tax on yet. When you begin taking money out at retirement, you'll be taxed on the full amount of your distributions.

- ✔ **Traditional nondeductible IRA:** You make contributions into your IRA account with after-tax dollars or money you've already paid tax on. When you begin to take distributions, you're not taxed on the amounts you contributed, but only on the investment earnings — interest, dividends, and capital gains/appreciation — that have accumulated in your account.

- ✔ **Roth IRA:** Just like the traditional nondeductible IRA, you make contributions into your Roth with after-tax dollars. You don't pay any income tax on distributions.

Because line 32 is concerned only with the deduction you can take for a contribution to a traditional IRA, we concentrate on the rules for the deductible IRA here. Even though you don't get a deduction for the nondeductible IRA and Roth IRA, for some people, these accounts can be useful retirement planning tools. You can find out more about all retirement plans in Chapter 20.

You and your spouse (if you're married) are both entitled to contribute and deduct the maximum to your IRAs if you meet the compensation and age requirements that we introduce in this section. This means that, if you're married and able to take advantage of the maximum deduction in 2006, you can exclude up to $8,000 from your total income if you're both under 50, $10,000 if you've both reached that milestone birthday prior to January 1, 2007. These aren't small potatoes!

You have to put real dollars into a real account in order to get the deduction, but you don't have to do it in 2006 in order to get a deduction on your 2006 Form 1040 or Form 1040A. Provided you've put the money into an account by April 16, 2007, you're entitled to take your 2006 IRA deduction.

Types of compensation needed to qualify for an IRA

In order to make contributions to an IRA, you need to have earned income from wages, commissions, tips, self-employment, or the receipt of alimony. If you (or your spouse, if you aren't currently earning from these sources) don't have income from at least one of these, you can't make contributions, so you can't get the deduction.

If you're self-employed, your self-employed earnings for the purpose of determining IRA contribution eligibility are reduced by amounts you contribute to another retirement plan (Keogh or SEP) and by the deduction you're taking for one-half of your self-employment tax. (For more on Keogh or SEPs, see Chapter 20.)

Contribution limits

If you have earned income, congratulations! You've passed the first hurdle. Now you need to figure out how much you can contribute.

For 2006 returns, the maximum you're allowed to contribute to your IRA is $4,000. If you have less than $4,000 of earned income, you may contribute up to 100 percent of your earned income. If you're 50 or older, you can contribute an additional $1,000 (provided you have at least $5,000 of earned income). As long as you turned 50 years old on or before January 1, 2006, you can take advantage of this extra $1,000 amount, which is more commonly referred to as a catch-up contribution. See Chapter 20 for details.

Remember, the earlier in the year that you make your IRA contribution, the sooner it starts growing tax free. For example, if you're turning 50 in December 2006, you don't need to wait until then to make your catch-up contribution. As long as you turn the magic number this year, you can make that contribution at any time during the year.

Age limits

Unlike driving a car, funding an IRA doesn't have a minimum age requirement. Provided you have earned income, you're allowed to make those contributions. However, if you want a traditional IRA, even if it's a nondeductible IRA, you're going to have to stop feeding the kitty in the year in which you turn 70½.

Of course, nowhere is it written that you can't continue to save after you turn 70½ — even in an IRA. At the time you can no longer make traditional IRA contributions, you may be able to contribute to a Roth IRA (see Chapter 20 for more specifics).

Deductible IRA contributions

As a general rule, you can claim a deduction for the contribution that you're allowed to make to your IRA. That rule has only one qualification: If you or your spouse is covered by a retirement plan at work, your ability to claim a deduction may be reduced or eliminated. This restriction doesn't mean you can't make a $4,000 ($5,000 if you're 50 or older) *nondeductible* IRA or Roth IRA contribution.

Table 7-2 shows who may make a deductible contribution to a traditional IRA.

Table 7-2	Who Can Make a Deductible Contribution?	
Filing Status	*Employer's Plan*	*Income Phaseouts/Limits (based on modified AGI)*
Single	No	Fully deductible
or	Yes	Up to $50,000, fully deductible
Head of Household		Between $50,000 and $59,999, partially deductible
		$60,000 and over, no deduction
Married Filing Joint	Neither spouse	Fully deductible
or	One spouse	Up to $150,000, fully deductible for spouse whose employer doesn't have a plan
Qualifying Widow or Widower		Between $150,000 and $159,999, partially deductible for spouse whose employer doesn't have a plan
		$160,000 and over, no deduction
	Both spouses	Up to $75,000 fully deductible
		Between $75,000 and $84,999, partially deductible
		$85,000 and over, no deduction
Married Filing Separately	No	Fully deductible
	Yes	Between $1 and $9,999, partially deductible
		$10,000 and over, no deduction

These limits and phaseouts refer to your "modified adjusted gross income," or "modified AGI" for short. To figure your modified AGI, fill out the worksheet that we include in the sidebar "How to figure partial IRA deductions" later in this chapter.

Are you covered by your employer's plan?

If you're not sure whether or not you (or your spouse) are covered by a pension plan at work, check out box 13 of your W-2. If your employer has some sort of pension plan that you're eligible to participate in, the "Retirement Plan" box will be checked.

You're considered covered, or an active participant, even if you haven't earned the full right (known as *vesting*) to the benefits under your plan. If you switch employers during the year, and one of the employers has a plan and the other doesn't, you're considered covered.

You're also considered covered by a plan when you're both salaried and self-employed, provided that you have your own Keogh, SEP, or SIMPLE plan and you aren't covered by a plan where you're employed. You're also considered covered by a plan if you're self-employed and have a Keogh, SEP, or SIMPLE plan.

If your employer offers you a retirement plan that you can contribute to, such as a 401(k) or 403(b) and you and your employer didn't add any money to your account and no forfeitures were allocated during the tax year, you're not considered covered during the year. Thus, you can make the maximum tax-deductible IRA contribution if your spouse also isn't covered by a pension plan. If he or she is covered by a pension plan, you can still put away, and deduct, the $4,000 maximum, provided your joint income is less than $150,000.

Nondeductible IRA contributions (Form 8606)

Although your deduction for an IRA contribution may be reduced or eliminated because of the AGI modifications, you still can make nondeductible IRA contributions of up to $4,000, or 100 percent of your compensation, whichever is less, plus the $1,000 catch-up amount if you're 50 or older. The difference between your allowable deductible contribution, which is entered on line 32, and your total contributions made, if any, is your nondeductible contribution.

Your total IRA contributions, including deductible, nondeductible, and Roth IRAs, can't exceed $4,000 (or $5,000 if you're 50 or older).

You must report nondeductible contributions to the IRS on Form 8606 even if you don't have to file a tax return for the year. If you're filing a Form 1040, you attach Form 8606 to your 1040. The penalty for not filing your Form 8606 is $50, and if your IRA contributions are more than the permissible amount, you must correct the overpayment; otherwise you may be subject to a 6 percent penalty (see Chapter 8, line 60). The penalty is imposed annually until the excess amount is removed. You can also be penalized an additional $100 if you overstate the computation of your nondeductible contributions on Form 8606.

Say you discovered while preparing your 2006 return that you contributed too much in 2006. Three ways to avoid the penalty are

- **Considering the excess 2006 contribution part of your 2007 IRA contribution.** This way works best. For example, if you contributed $1,000 too much in 2006 and you're entitled to contribute $4,000 for 2007, just change that excess $1,000 contribution for 2006 to a $1,000 contribution to 2007. Now you need to add only an additional $3,000 contribution later in 2007 to reach the maximum $4,000 contribution allowed for 2007. With this simple shift, no penalty will be assessed, and you still manage to contribute the full amounts for both 2006 and 2007.

- **Withdrawing the excess amount by the due date (including extensions) for filing your return.** If you withdraw the excess and the earnings on the excess amount before April 16, 2007, no penalty. However, you'll owe tax on the earnings and, if you're younger than 59½, the earnings are subject to the 10 percent withdrawal penalty discussed in Chapter 6.

- **Withdrawing the excess contribution and paying tax on it when it's too late to use either of the other two methods, even when you didn't claim a deduction for the excess amount.** Ouch!

If after filing your return, you discover that you should have deducted your IRA contribution instead of claiming it as a nondeductible contribution (or vice versa), you can amend your return by filing Form 1040X. You also have to amend Form 8606 and attach it to Form 1040X.

The Roth and other IRAs

Deductible IRAs, nondeductible IRAs, and rollover IRAs for lump sums of your former employer's retirement plan (check out Chapter 6 for more on lump-sum distributions) are only half the story. Be aware of other types of IRAs: MSAs, HSAs, Coverdell Education Savings Accounts (formerly known as Education IRAs), Medicare Plus Choice MSAs, and Roth IRAs. See Chapter 20 for more information about the Roth IRAs and Medicare Plus Choice MSAs. Chapter 24 covers the Coverdell Education Savings Account.

Converting traditional IRAs to Roth IRAs

Although funding your Roth IRA isn't a matter for your Form 1040 or 1040A (which is why we cover it in Chapter 20), you may decide at some point to convert a traditional IRA into a Roth IRA. The conversion of a traditional IRA to a Roth works similarly to any rollover from one pension plan to another, and if you do it properly, you shouldn't have to pay the

10 percent early withdrawal penalty. (We discuss the merits and drawbacks of conversions in Chapter 20). In order to let the IRS know what you've done, you show your conversion on the back of **Form 8606, Nondeductible IRAs.**

If you're considering converting your IRA account, you need to know the following:

✔ In the year of conversion, your income (not including the amount you're converting) must be less than $100,000, including any required distributions from traditional IRA or other retirement accounts.

✔ You may not file as married filing separately.

How to figure partial IRA deductions

You get a partial deduction when your employer has a pension plan that you're eligible to participate in and:

✔ Your modified AGI falls between $50,000 and $60,000 when you're single, or between $75,000 and $85,000 when you're married filing jointly or a qualifying widow or widower.

✔ Your modified AGI falls below $10,000 when you're married filing separately.

If your modified AGI is above the phase-out limits, you aren't entitled to a deduction.

Figure your partial IRA deductions by first determining your modified AGI, which is your AGI from line 37 on Form 1040 (or line 21 on Form 1040A) added to the following deductions:

✔ Your IRA deduction (line 32)

✔ Student loan interest deduction (line 33)

✔ Foreign earned income and housing deductions (this deduction applies only to taxpayers who live and work abroad) per Form 2555 (see Chapter 6)

✔ The exclusion for Series EE U.S. Savings Bond interest (shown on Form 8815) explained in Chapter 10

✔ The exclusion for adoption assistance (Form 8839) — see Chapter 8

If you didn't live with your spouse at any time during the year and you file a separate return, your filing status is considered single for this purpose.

1. Depending on your filing status, enter one of the following:

   $60,000 — single or head of household

   $85,000 — joint or qualifying widow or widower

   $10,000 — married filing separately

   1._____

2. Enter your modified AGI.   2._____

3. Subtract line 2 from line 1.   3._____

4. Your IRA contribution.   4._____

   (See instruction A below.)

5. See instruction B and C below.   5._____

6. Your IRA deduction. Enter   6._____
   the smaller of 4 or 5.

7. Your nondeductible contribution.   7._____
   Subtract 6 from 4.

If line 2 is larger than line 1, you aren't entitled to an IRA deduction — enter zero -0-.

A. Remember, your contribution can't exceed your compensation.

B. If line 3 is $10,000 or more, enter $4,000 (or $5,000 if you're 50 or older in 2006) on line 6 above. No further computations are required.

C. If line 3 is less than $10,000, multiply line 3 by 40 percent (0.40) or 50 percent (0.50) if you were 50 or older by the end of 2006. Round to the nearest $10. If the amount that you arrive at is less than $200, enter $200. Don't ask why. These are the rules. Simply enter the amount you arrive at or the $200 minimum on line 5.

D. Line 6 is your IRA deduction; enter this amount on line 32 (1040) or line 17 (1040A).

E. Your nondeductible IRA contribution is the difference between your maximum IRA contribution, which generally is $4,000, and the portion of the $4,000 you're entitled to deduct (computed on line 6 above). You must also enter this amount on line 1 of **Form 8606, Nondeductible IRAs,** where you keep track of all your nondeductible IRA contributions made through the years. For example, if only $500 of your $4,000 can be deducted, that is the amount you claim on line 32 (1040) or line 17 (1040A). The $3,500 balance is entered on Form 8606.

If a pension doesn't cover you, but does cover your spouse (or vice versa), enter $160,000 on line 1 and complete lines 1 through 7.

If you convert from a traditional IRA to a Roth in 2006 but discover at the end of the year that your income exceeds $100,000, you can have a "do over"! You can "undo" the conversion if you transfer the money back by the due date for filing your return (including extensions) for the tax year in which you made the conversion. The conversion is treated as never having taken place. If your filing date for 2006 is April 16, 2007, you can correct your error regarding your 2006 conversion without any tax consequences if you make a trustee-to-trustee transfer back to a regular IRA by April 16, 2007.

If you convert to a Roth IRA and then the value of the stocks in the converted account head south, you have the option to *recharacterize* (undo a conversion). For example, if you convert an account worth $50,000 in August, and by December, it's worth only $30,000, you probably want to recharacterize the account (and develop a different investing strategy!). Otherwise you have to pay income tax on $50,000 that's now worth only $30,000. You're allowed only one recharacterization a year.

When you recharacterize a Roth back to a traditional IRA, although a conversion is treated as if it never had taken place, because it was *recharacterized,* you must report it on your tax return. Enter the original conversion on line 15a Form 1040 or 11a of Form1040A. Enter zero (-0-) on either line 15b of your 1040 or 11b of your 1040A. These entries show the original conversion and a zero amount as being taxable, because you undid the conversion by means of a recharacterization. Attach a statement to your return showing the amount recharacterized, the original conversion, the earnings or loss while the money was in the Roth, and the amount back in your traditional IRA. If you make a *trustee-to-trustee transfer* when you do a recharacterization, the Roth earnings are considered being earned by the account receiving the recharacterization. A recharacterization can be made on an amended return filed within six months of your original return (including extensions). If you missed the date for recharacterizing a conversion through no fault of your own, the IRS has announced in a number of private-letter rulings that it will excuse missing the deadline.

Your spouse's IRA deduction

Whether or not your spouse is earning wages, tips, commissions, alimony, or income from self-employment, or isn't employed outside the home, he or she is eligible to contribute to an IRA account, and the deductible amount of your spouse's IRA contribution also goes on line 32.

If your spouse isn't employed outside the home, you can set up a spousal IRA account and contribute up to $4,000 for him or her ($5,000 if your spouse is 50 or older) for a total IRA deduction of $8,000. Spouses who are 50 or older also can contribute an extra $1,000.

You can't put the combined total contribution amount into either your account or your spouse's. You each need your own account, and only the maximum contribution per person can be put into either account.

A spouse who isn't working outside the home can set up a fully deductible IRA even if the other spouse is covered by a pension at work, provided the couple's income doesn't exceed $150,000. If their income is between $150,000 and $160,000, a partial deduction is allowed. At $160,000, the deduction is eliminated. See the phase-out worksheet earlier in this chapter to determine whether you qualify for a partial deduction. If this phaseout works against you, don't overlook a nondeductible IRA.

If your spouse is employed

If your spouse is employed during the year — and each of you is younger than 70½ at the end of 2006 — you can each have IRAs and can each contribute up to the $4,000 or $5,000 limits, unless your taxable compensation (or your spouse's) is less than $4,000. Qualifying income ranges are the same as those we explain earlier in this chapter in the section "Compensation needed to qualify for an IRA." For example, Michael and Lisa file a joint return for 2006. Michael earned $28,000, and Lisa earned $1,800. Michael and Lisa can each contribute $4,000 to their respective IRAs for a total of $8,000. Even though Lisa earned less than $4,000, she is deemed to have earned Michael's $28,000 less his $4,000 IRA deduction, or $25,000, as the compensation she needs to qualify for her IRA.

If your spouse isn't employed

If your nonworking spouse decides to set up his or her own IRA, the most the two of you can contribute is 100 percent of your taxable compensation up to $8,000, or $10,000 if both of you are 50 or older. You can divide your IRA contributions between your IRA and your spouse's IRA any way you choose, but you can't contribute more than $4,000 or $5,000 to either IRA (depending on your age). For example, if your salary is $4,500, you can contribute $4,500 — that is, $2,000 for you and $2,500 for your spouse, $1,500 for you and $3,000 for your spouse, or $2,250 for you and $2,250 for your spouse — but no more than $4,500 total. If your salary is more than $8,000, the most you can contribute to your separate accounts is $4,000.

Spouses younger than 70½

You can't make contributions to your own IRA for the year in which you reach age 70½ or in any later year. However, for any year you have compensation, you can continue to make contributions of up to $4,000 or $5,000 (if your spouse is 50 or older) to your spouse's IRA until the year your spouse reaches age 70½.

Line 33: Student loan interest deduction

Although most types of personal interest are no longer deductible, you may deduct up to $2,500 of interest on a loan used to pay higher education and certain vocational school expenses (ask the vocational school whether it qualifies for this deduction if you have to borrow to pay the tab). You can claim this deduction as long as it takes to pay off the loan and as long as you're paying interest on it.

For single filers, the deduction doesn't start to get eliminated until your income hits $50,000 and doesn't completely disappear until $65,000. For joint filers, the phaseout of the deduction starts at the $105,000 income level, with the deduction getting wiped out at $135,000.

The beauty of the student loan interest deduction is that you don't have to itemize your deductions to claim it. You can claim the standard deduction (see Chapter 9) and the student loan deduction. This deduction should be of great benefit to recent graduates.

To take this deduction, you must meet the following requirements:

- ✔ You're not filing as married filing separately and no one else can claim you as a dependent.
- ✔ The loan must be incurred to pay the higher education expenses of you, your spouse, or anyone you claimed as a dependent when you took out the loan.
- ✔ The expenses must be paid within a reasonable amount of time after the loan is taken out. We wish we could tell you what's reasonable, but you know how it is: The IRS knows what's reasonable when it sees it. One way the IRS views as reasonable is when the loan proceeds are used within 60 days before the start or end of an academic semester to pay your allowable higher education expenses.
- ✔ You must be the person primarily responsible for the loan.
- ✔ The student must carry at least half the normal workload of a full-time student or be attributable to a period during which he or she met this requirement.

✔ The loan was taken out to pay higher education expenses for tuition, fees, room and board, books, supplies, and other necessary expenses, such as transportation.

✔ Loans from related family members don't qualify for the deduction.

✔ Revolving lines of credit don't qualify unless you agree that the line will be used only to pay for education expenses.

Students usually take out these loans because they can obtain lower interest rates, but their parents won't be able to claim the deduction, even if they make all the payments. That's because the parents didn't borrow the money. If the student is liable for the loan, the student can't claim the interest deduction when he or she can be claimed as a dependent on someone else's return. But in an interesting twist, if a nondependent student takes the loan, but the parents make the payments, the student may be allowed to take the interest deduction on his or her return.

With these rules, high-income taxpayers may be able to do better with home equity loans (see Chapter 9).

Institutions making education loans are required to issue **Form 1098-E, Student Loan Interest Statement**, listing the interest. Your instruction booklet has a worksheet for 1040 filers to compute the phase-out amount and so do we.

Here's how the phaseout works:

	Single	Married
1. Income.	$53,000	$120,000
2. Threshold amount.	$50,000	$105,000
3. Subtract line 2 from line 1.	$3,000	$15,000
	Single	Married
4. Phase-out range. ($65,000 – $50,000 for singles, $135,000 – $105,000 for joint filers)	$15,000	$30,000
5. Divide line 3 by line 4.	$3,000 ÷ $15,000	$15,000 ÷ $30,000
6. Result.	20%	50%
7. Maximum deduction.	$2,500	$2,500
8. Multiply line 7 by line 6.	$500	$1,250
9. Allowable deduction. (Subtract line 8 from line 7.)	$2,000	$1,250

You figure income for line 1 by adding the following items back to your AGI (line 37, Form 1040 or line 21, Form 1040A):

✔ Student loan interest deduction (line 33)

✔ Foreign earned income and housing deductions (this applies only to taxpayers who live and work abroad) per Form 2555 (see Chapter 6)

✔ Exclusion of income for bona fide residents of American Samoa and the exclusion of income from Puerto Rico

For all those students and former students who have taken advantage of low interest loan consolidations in the past couple of years, remember that you can deduct the interest on your refinanced loan as long as the loan was refinanced with another educational institution or tax-exempt organization.

Line 34: Jury pay returned to your employer

If you have to return jury pay to your employer because your employer continued to pay you while you served on the jury, you can deduct that amount on line 34.

Line 35: Domestic production activities deduction (Form 8903)

One of the lesser-known provisions of the *American Jobs Creation Act of 2004* is the deduction for domestic production activities. This deduction became available in 2005 to taxpayers who produce, and then sell, lease, license, exchange, or otherwise dispose of any product (including manufactured, agricultural, mineral, engineered, cultural, and intellectual) either wholly or significantly within the United States.

The domestic production activities deduction's purpose is to provide an incentive for businesses to keep current jobs, and create new ones, in this country. Accordingly, if you have at least one employee in the United States and you're a builder, a manufacturer, a farmer, a software engineer, an architect or engineer, a film producer or director, a writer, or you own some sort of mining operation that functions primarily inside the United States and sells primarily to consumers in the United States, you'll probably qualify for this deduction if you actually make money at that endeavor. If you don't have employees here, don't even bother trying to calculate this deduction.

For 2006, the deduction is worth the lesser of

- ✔ 3 percent of the smaller "qualified production activities income" or taxable income, or
- ✔ 50 percent of W-2 wages for the employer for the tax year

In order to claim your deduction, you have to complete Form 8903, and then put your result on line 35 of your Form 1040. If you're a member of a partnership or S Corporation, you can find the number you need to use to calculate this deduction on the Schedule K-1 you receive from the partnership or S Corporation tax returns.

If you didn't tackle Form 8903 in 2005, but you think you may qualify for this deduction in 2006, you may want to consult a competent tax advisor this year. Likewise, if your domestic production activities are occurring in a pass-through entity, such as a partnership or an S Corporation, you may want to leave the calculation of this deduction in the hands of a professional. On the other hand, if yours is a fairly straightforward business and you filed Form 8903 last year, you know that calculating this deduction isn't as tough as it looks, after you master the terminology.

Here's how the domestic production activities deduction works. Martin is a builder with one employee. He had gross receipts of $50,000 in 2006, $40,000 of which came from new construction (which is a qualified domestic production activity), and $10,000 from home repairs (which aren't qualified). He paid his employee $10,000 in 2006 (making sure he gave him a Form W-2), and he had other deductions, including the cost of goods sold, of $10,000, leaving a net profit in 2006 of $30,000. Martin's adjusted gross income (line 38 of Form 1040) is $60,000.

The simplest way to calculation Martin's deduction is as follows:

1.	Begin with domestic production gross receipts (DPGR)	$40,000
2.	Subtract pro-rata share of deductions and losses	–4,000
3.	Subtotal (qualified production activities income)	$36,000
4.	AGI without domestic production activities deduction	$60,000
5.	Enter smaller of qualified production activities income or AGI	$36,000
6.	Multiply line 5 by 3 percent	$ 1,080
7.	Enter Form W-2 wages	$10,000
8.	Multiply Form W-2 wages by 50 percent	$ 5,000
9.	Compare lines 6 and 8, and enter the smaller	$ 1,080

Calculating this deduction may seem like a lot of work, but think of this as a practice year. In 2007 through 2009, the percentage of qualified production activities income you can deduct increases to 6 percent, and in 2010, it increases again to 9 percent.

Line 36: Total adjustments

Go ahead, make your day. Add all the figures you have on lines 23 through 35. This total represents your total adjustment — and we hope it's a big number! But alas, it may be zero. Don't despair; there are more deductions to come on the back of Form 1040.

Line 37: Adjusted gross income

The next step is subtracting the amount in line 36 from line 22 (the total income). The result is your *AGI*.

The IRS must think that this is a pretty important number because the good people at the Department of the Treasury have designed an easy-to-find AGI line at the bottom of the 1040 (line 37) where you enter this amount before you turn to the back of the form. Congrats! You're halfway there! This number is used to determine a host of deductions and tax credits. So, as you find out in later chapters, we often refer to this line.

Chapter 8

The Rest of the 1040

*W*hen you turned the page of your Form 1040, you probably had that same sickening feeling that you had as a student when you turned the page on an exam — just to find more junk that you'd never finish before the bell rang! But we think that you can beat the bell this time if you take the 1040 line by line, relax, and let us help you. For some of you, the worst is over; for others, well, you may still have some nasty schedules ahead of you to complete your return, but in this chapter we direct you to the forms you need.

Tax and Credits

You may think that because this section is entitled "Tax and Credits," you're going to calculate how much tax you owe or will be refunded and be on your merry way (see Figure 8-1). Wrong! What you're going to do here is calculate your *taxable income* — that is, the income that you actually owe tax on for the year. Finding out your taxable income isn't the finish line, however, because you may have some *credits* (these are good, because they reduce your tax bill) and some other taxes (these obviously are bad) to report. Then you must settle up with the IRS and determine in *the payments section* whether you paid too much, too little, or just enough tax during the year (yeah, that part will be a little like Goldilocks, the three bears, and the porridge-tasting stuff!).

Line 38: Adjusted gross income

This line is a piece of cake. To complete line 38 at the top of the back page, turn your return back over and copy the entry you made on line 37 — both are your adjusted gross income (AGI)!

Form 1040 (2006)   Page **2**

Tax and Credits			
	38	Amount from line 37 (adjusted gross income)	38
	39a	Check { ☐ **You** were born before January 2, 1942, ☐ Blind. } **Total boxes** if: { ☐ **Spouse** was born before January 2, 1942, ☐ Blind. } checked ▶ 39a ☐	
Standard Deduction for—	b	If your spouse itemizes on a separate return or you were a dual-status alien, see page 35 and check here ▶39b ☐	
	40	**Itemized deductions** (from Schedule A) **or** your **standard deduction** (see left margin) .	40
• People who checked any box on line 39a or 39b **or** who can be claimed as a dependent, see page 36.	41	Subtract line 40 from line 38	41
	42	If line 38 is over $112,875, or you provided housing to a person displaced by Hurricane Katrina, see page 37. Otherwise, multiply $3,300 by the total number of exemptions claimed on line 6d	42
	43	**Taxable income.** Subtract line 42 from line 41. If line 42 is more than line 41, enter -0-	43
	44	**Tax** (see page 37). Check if any tax is from: a ☐ Form(s) 8814 b ☐ Form 4972	44
	45	**Alternative minimum tax** (see page 39). Attach Form 6251	45
• All others:	46	Add lines 44 and 45 . . . . ▶	46
Single or Married filing separately, $5,150	47	Foreign tax credit. Attach Form 1116 if required . . .	47	
	48	Credit for child and dependent care expenses. Attach Form 2441	48	
	49	Credit for the elderly or the disabled. Attach Schedule R .	49	
Married filing jointly or Qualifying widow(er), $10,300	50	Education credits. Attach Form 8863	50	
	51	Retirement savings contributions credit. Attach Form 8880 .	51	
	52	Residential energy credits. Attach Form 5695 . . .	52	
Head of household, $7,550	53	Child tax credit (see page XX). Attach Form 8901 if required	53	
	54	Credits from: a ☐ Form 8396 b ☐ Form 8839 c ☐ Form 8859	54	
	55	Other credits: a ☐ Form 3800 b ☐ Form 8801 c ☐ Form____	55	
	56	Add lines 47 through 55. These are your **total credits**	56
	57	Subtract line 56 from line 46. If line 56 is more than line 46, enter -0- . . . . ▶	57

Figure 8-1: The Tax and Credit section of the Form 1040.

Line 39a

On line 39a, check the box if either you or your spouse was born before January 2, 1942. That makes you 65 or older in 2006 and entitles you to increase the standard deduction to which you're entitled. So you noticed that strange date, but it isn't a misprint. Most logically thinking people believe that if they were born January 1, 1942, their 65th birthdays wouldn't arrive until 2007 and thus wouldn't make them ineligible to increase the standard deduction until 2007. That isn't the IRS's way of thinking. If you were born January 1, 1942, you're considered to be 65 on December 31, 2006 and thereby are entitled to the extra standard deduction amount. Don't ask who came up with this one. We're at a loss to explain it just like you are.

Line 39a also asks you to check a box if you're blind. We realize that most people find this line somewhat puzzling. After all, if someone is blind, how do they know to check the box? We hope the answer is that you bought this book so you could prepare their tax return for them.

If you check one of the boxes on line 39a and you're not itemizing your deductions, see Chapter 9 to compute your increased standard deduction.

Line 39b

If you're married filing separately and your spouse itemizes deductions, then you must also itemize. If one claims the standard deduction, then both must claim it.

If you're legally married but can qualify as head of household, you're treated as if you were unmarried, so you can claim the standard deduction even if your spouse chooses to itemize deductions. See Chapter 9 for the specifics.

Line 40: Itemized deductions (from Schedule A) or your standard deduction

This section refers to what can be a critical choice, so don't make a quick decision between the two choices the IRS offers for deductions. Either choice is good in the sense that the result reduces your taxable income — the income that you owe tax on. HOWEVER, and note, this is a big however: You may be cheating yourself if you automatically jump into the easier of the two choices and take the so-called *standard deduction*.

The standard deduction is tempting to take because, without any complicated figuring, you simply take the deduction that corresponds to your filing status. For example, if you're filing as a single, you can take a standard deduction of $5,150.

If your parent or someone else can claim you as a dependent, the standard deduction to which you're entitled is limited. Check out Chapter 9, which can help you figure your allowable standard deduction.

Itemizing your deductions on Schedule A requires more work than just claiming the standard deduction, but if your total itemized deductions add to more than your standard deduction, don't waste them.

If you're in doubt about whether itemizing saves you money or what expenses you may actually itemize, jump over to Chapter 9 right now. Take a gander at the line items on Schedule A. Even if itemizing can't save you money for this year's return, educating yourself about deductions that are available is a good idea for the future. The major expenses that you may itemize include some home ownership expenses (mortgage interest and property taxes), state income taxes, medical and dental expenses that exceed 7.5 percent of your AGI, gifts to charity, casualty and theft losses that exceed 10 percent of your AGI, job expenses, and other miscellaneous things (that exceed 2 percent of your AGI).

If your AGI (line 38) is more than $150,500 ($75,250 if married filing separately), the itemized deductions that you're entitled to enter here on line 40 have to be reduced. Sorry!

Line 41: Subtract line 40 from line 38

After you've either completed Schedule A for your itemized deductions or elected to take the standard deduction, enter the result on line 40 and then subtract it from line 38 and enter the result on line 41.

Line 42: Exemptions

Multiply the number of exemptions you claimed in the box on line 6d on the front side of your Form 1040 by $3,300. You already filled out line 6d by now (didn't you?), but in case you need to go back to make sure that you grabbed all the exemptions that you are allowed, turn to Chapter 4.

Enter the result of your multiplication on line 42. For example, if you claimed four exemptions on line 6d, enter $13,200 (4 × $3,300) on line 42. Now you understand some of the financial benefits of your children. A bunch of other benefits the kids provide include education credits and deductions and dependent-care and the child tax credits, so read on.

If you housed someone displaced by Hurricane Katrina, you're allowed to claim an additional $500 exemption for each person you housed, up to four people. You can't claim this exemption if your new roommates are related to you, and you had to house them during 2006 for at least 60 days without receiving any compensation from them or from any other source.

Don't forget that if your AGI (line 38) exceeds certain amounts, your deduction for personal exemptions is limited. If your AGI falls into the phase-out ranges in the following bulleted list, flip to Chapter 4 to figure out how much of your $3,300 exemption you lose. And remember, if you're filing a return with more than one exemption on it, a piece of every exemption is lost. The federal government is an equal opportunity taxer! The exemption phase-out amounts are as follows:

- ✔ Married filing separately, beginning at $112,875, completely phased out at $174,125
- ✔ Single, beginning at $150,500, completely phased out at $273,000
- ✔ Heads of household, beginning at $188,150, completely phased out at $310,650
- ✔ Married filing joint, surviving spouse and qualifying widow(er), beginning at $225,750, completely phased out at $348,250

If your income on line 38 (AGI) is less than $112,875, regardless of your filing status, multiply the exemptions you claimed on line 6d by $3,300. None of the thresholds that would send you in search of your calculator apply. Be thankful for small favors.

Line 43: Taxable income

Hey, you get an easy math problem. Subtract line 42 from line 41 and enter the result on line 43. But if line 42 is more than line 41, you get to place -0- (that's a zero) on line 43. If you enter zero on line 43, you could possibly have a *net operating loss* (NOL — see Chapter 18 for more on NOLs). Now you've arrived at another tax landmark — your taxable income, which is your AGI minus your deductions (either standard or itemized) and minus your personal exemptions. Use this amount to begin figuring out what you owe.

Line 44: Tax

The first step to reaching your final tax number is to calculate the total federal tax that's owed on your taxable income (line 43) if you had no other changes.

When your taxable income is less than $100,000, you figure your tax by finding the bracket for your taxable income and filing status in the tax tables located in the back of your 1040 instruction booklet. We explain how to do this in Chapter 5.

If your taxable income on line 43 is more than $100,000, you must use the tax rates for your filing status in the tax-rate schedules, shown in Table 8-1.

Table 8-1	Tax Rate Schedules for 2006	
Filing Status	*Taxable Income*	*Tax Is*
Married Filing Joint, Surviving Spouse and Qualifying Widow(er)	Not more than $15,100	10 percent of taxable income
	Over $15,100 but not more than $61,300	$1,510 plus 15 percent of excess more than $15,100
	Over $61,300 but not more than $123,700	$8,440 plus 25 percent of excess more than $61,300
	Over $123,700 but not more than $188,450	$24,040 plus 28 percent of excess more than $123,700
	Over $188,450 but not more than $336,550	$42,170 plus 33 percent of excess more than $188,450
	More than $336,550	$91,043 plus 35 percent of excess more than $336,550

Filing Status	Taxable Income	Tax Is
Heads of Households	Not more than $10,750	10% of taxable income
	Over $10,750, but not more than $41,050	$1,075 plus 15 percent of excess more than $10,750
	Over $41,050 but not more than $106,000	$5,620 plus 25 percent of excess more than $41,050
	Over $106,000 but not more than $171,650	$21,857.50 plus 28 percent of excess more than $106,000
	Over $171,650 but not more than $336,550	$40,239.50 plus 33 percent of excess more than $171,650
	More than $336,550	$94,656.50 plus 35 percent of excess more than $336,550
Single	Not more than $7,550	10 percent of taxable income
	Over $7,550, but not more than $30,650	$755 plus 15 percent of excess more than $7,550
	Over $30,650 but not more than $74,200	$4,220 plus 25 percent of excess more than $30,650
	Over $74,200 but not more than $154,800	$15,107.50 plus 28 percent of excess more than $74,200
	Over $154,800 but not more than $336,550	$37,675.50 plus 33 percent of excess more than $154,800
	More than $336,550	$97,653 plus 35 percent of excess more than $336,550
Married filing separately	Not more than $7,550	10 percent of taxable income
	Over $7,550, but not more than $30,650	$755 plus 15 percent of excess more than $7,550
	Over $30,650 but not more than $61,850	$4,220 plus 25 percent of excess more than $30,650
	Over $61,850 but not more than $94,225	$12,020 plus 28 percent of excess more than $61,850
	Over $94,225 but not more than $168,275	$21,085 plus 33 percent of excess more than $94,225
	More than $168,275	$45,521.50 plus 35 percent of excess more than $168,275

Here's how using the tax rate schedules works. Suppose that you're single and your taxable income is $118,800. Because your income is between $74,200 and $154,800, here's how to figure your tax:

		Tax
Taxable income	$118,800	
Less: Your starting tax bracket amount $74,200	$74,200	$15,107.50
Balance	$44,600	
Tax bracket percentage for amount more than $74,200	× 28%	$12,488.00
Tax to be entered on line 44		$27,595.50

Capital gains and qualified dividends tax worksheet

If you had capital gains or qualified dividends last year, you know that thinking about making these calculations is worse than actually doing them. If you've never had capital gains or qualified dividends before, don't worry. Just follow the line-by-line instructions. This worksheet actually works!

Qualified dividends and most long-term capital gains are taxed at rates less than your other forms of income. If you have numbers on lines 9b and/or 13 of your Form 1040, or if you have already completed Schedule D (see Chapter 12), then you need to calculate your tax using the Qualified Dividends and Capital Gain worksheet included in your Form 1040 instruction booklet. Otherwise, you're going to pay more tax than you should. The following is an overview of why these items may affect your total tax liability.

Qualified dividends

In 2006, qualified dividends, which we explain in Chapter 10, are taxed at the maximum rate of 15 percent. If your taxable income places you in either the 10 percent or 15 percent bracket, then your qualified dividends will be taxed at a rate of only 5 percent (dropping to 0 percent in 2008). As your children would say, "Sweet!"

Don't get too used to these rates, though; these rates are only here until 2008. In January, 2009, they're scheduled to revert back to the pre-2003 rules, where dividends are taxed as ordinary income.

Capital gains

Like qualified dividends, in 2006, most long-term capital gains are taxed at a maximum 15 percent rate, reduced to 5 percent for taxpayers who are in the 10 percent or 15 percent tax bracket. And, just like qualified dividends, these rates are set to disappear in 2009, reverting back to the pre-2003 rules.

Not every capital gain is eligible for these preferential rates. The maximum rate on the gain on the sale of collectibles is 28 percent. The rate for depreciable real estate is 25 percent on depreciation that's recaptured. If you find this capital gains stuff somewhat confusing, you're not alone. See Chapter 12 for an updated course on the capital gains rules, including what the heck *recapture of capital gain depreciation* is all about and what portion of the gain is taxed at 25 percent and what part is taxed at the lower maximum tax rates. We leave nothing out when it comes to these heady subjects.

We offer a worksheet in Table 8-2 that shows how you calculate your tax if you have qualified dividends or capital gains subject to these lower tax rates.

If you sold your stamp collection or your baseball cards, if you've been enjoying great success on eBay and made profits on your sales, or if you've sold a piece of property that's subject to depreciation recapture (we explain it all in Chapter 12), you can't use the worksheet in Table 8-2. For you, because the IRS knows you're special, you get your very own special worksheet. And it looks grim. The print is tiny, and it has lots of lines. Don't panic. It's essentially the same as the Table 8-2 worksheet with some extra categories thrown in. If you can do the Table 8-2 worksheet, the Schedule D Tax Worksheet will be a piece of cake.

Now that you've determined that you need to use the capital gain worksheet to calculate your tax, Table 8-2 shows you how to do it, using an example of a single taxpayer with $125,000 of taxable income, of which $3,000 comes from qualified dividends and $12,000 comes from long-term capital gains.

	Table 8-2	Qualified Dividends and Capital Gain Tax Worksheet — Line 44		
1.	Enter the amount from Form 1040, line 43.		1.	$125,000
2.	Enter the amount from Form 1040, line 9b.		2.	3,000
3.	Are you filing Schedule D? If so, enter the smaller of line 15 or 16 of Schedule D, but don't enter less than -0-. If not, enter the amount from Form 1040, line 13.		3.	12,000
4.	Add lines 2 and 3.		4.	15,000
5.	If you're claiming investment interest expense on Form 4952, enter the amount from line 4g of that form. Otherwise, enter -0-.		5.	0
6.	Subtract line 5 from line 4. If zero or less, enter -0-.		6.	15,000
7.	Subtract line 6 from line 1. If zero or less, enter -0-.		7.	110,000
8.	Enter the smaller of: The amount on line 1 or $30,650 if single or married filing separately, $61,300 if married filing jointly or qualifying widower, $41,050 if head of household.		8.	30,650
9.	Is the amount on line 7 equal to or more than the amount on line 8? If Yes, skip lines 9 through 11, go to line 12 and check the "No" box. If No, enter the amount from line 7.		9.	N/A
10.	Subtract line 9 from line 8.		10.	N/A
11.	Multiply line 10 by 5 percent.		11.	N/A
12.	Are the amounts on lines 6 and 10 the same? Yes. Skip lines 12 through 15; go to line 16. No. Enter the smaller of line 1 or line 6.		12.	15,000
13.	Enter the amount from line 10 (if line 10 is blank, enter -0-).		13.	0
14.	Subtract line 13 from line 12.		14.	15,000
15.	Multiply line 14 by 15 percent.		15.	2,250
16.	Figure the tax on line 7. Use the tax table or tax computation worksheet, whichever applies.		16.	25,132
17.	Add lines 11, 15, and 16.		17.	27,382
18.	Figure the tax on the amount on line 1. Use the tax table or tax computation worksheet, whichever applies.		18.	29,332
19.	Tax on all taxable income. Enter the smaller of line 17 or line 18. Also include this amount on Form 1040, line 44.		19.	27,382

Wow! That taxpayer just saved a cool $1,950 ($29,332 calculated using tax tables — $27,382 using Qualified Dividends and Capital Gain Tax Worksheet = $1,950 tax savings) by spending a few minutes with this worksheet. If only all your endeavors were this lucrative!

The kiddie tax: Forms 8615 and 8814

Don't jump over to the next line quite yet. If you have children younger than 18 who have investment income, you may need to complete some additional forms (see Chapter 15 for a discussion of Form 8615 and Form 8814). Form 8615 is used if your kid files his or her own return. Use Form 8814 if you qualify to report your kid's investment income on your return. The general rule: If your child is younger than 18, his or her investment income (interest, dividends, and so on) above $1,700 is taxed at your rate, not the child's.

Those tiny boxes on line 43: Forms 8814 and 4972

Form 8814, Parents' Election to Report Child's Interest and Dividends, is the form to use when you elect to report your kids' investment incomes on your own return instead of having the kids file their own returns. See Chapter 15 for a detailed look at your choice.

Form 4972, Tax on Lump-Sum Distributions, however, is more common. If you decide to take all your money out of your employer's retirement plan in a lump sum, use this form to compute your tax under the 10-year averaging method if you're eligible. Using the averaging method can save you a bunch of dough. Refer to Chapter 6 for a complete discussion of this issue. You had to be born before 1936 to qualify.

Line 45: Alternative Minimum Tax (Form 6251)

Just when you thought you were getting this income tax system down (and it was safe to go back into the water), along comes the *Alternative Minimum Tax (AMT),* which is a parallel tax system with its own set of rules and regulations that was designed in 1969 to make higher income taxpayers pay their fair share of the federal government's budget. What qualified as higher income in 1969 doesn't really cut it today; for 2006, taxpayers with income as low as $42,500 could potentially fall into the AMT.

Unfortunately, you can't choose which system you want to be taxed under — you have to complete both calculations. Whichever tax calculation gives you the higher tax, that's the method you have to use. Line 45 is where you put the additional tax you owe if you've been snared by the AMT.

The AMT is a flat tax, assessed at either 26 or 28 percent, depending on your income. It starts with your AGI (line 38 of Form 1040), subtracts your itemized deductions (adjusted to remove items, such as state and local taxes, most miscellaneous itemized deductions, and an additional amount of your itemized medical deductions), and finally a flat exemption amount based on your filing status. The standard deduction doesn't exist in the AMT, and neither do those wonderful personal exemptions that can shave $3,300 per dependent from your taxable income.

The AMT is no longer a tax for just the wealthy; plenty of middle income taxpayers are being hooked by it each year, and it's only expected to get worse. The Taxpayer Advocate, in testimony before Congress in 2006, estimated that 30 percent of taxpayers would be paying the AMT in 2010, or roughly the same number as take a mortgage interest deduction.

Calculate AMT on **Form 6251, Alternative Minimum Tax — Individuals**. Don't assume that you earn too little to have the AMT apply to you — as average incomes rise (even marginally), and income tax rates drop due to tax cuts and inflation, more and more middle income people are finding themselves paying the AMT. If you have any of the following types of income or deductions, you may find yourself subject to it:

- ✔ Job expenses and miscellaneous itemized deductions (line 26 of Schedule A).
- ✔ Medical and dental expenses in excess of 10 percent of your income.
- ✔ Deductions for taxes (line 9 of Schedule A).
- ✔ Home equity mortgage interest not used to buy, build, or improve your home.

- Incentive stock options — the difference between what you paid for the stock and what it was worth when you exercised the option. (See Chapter 12 for the lowdown on handling stock options.)

- Depreciation in excess of the straight-line method.

- Tax-exempt interest from private activity bonds issued after August 7, 1986.

Fortunately, most taxpayers don't need to get that close and personal to Form 6251 with all of 55 lines. The IRS has created a worksheet embedded in the Form 1040 instructions to determine whether or not you need to graduate to Form 6251. And remember, not everyone who has to complete and file Form 6251 has to pay the AMT — the IRS just wants to know that you've been thorough.

Although the preceding listed items are the ones that apply to the majority of affected taxpayers, a slew of other tax preference items aren't allowed under the AMT, such as intangible drilling expenses, circulation expenses, depletion, certain installment sales, passive activities and research, and experimental costs.

Can you avoid the AMT? Defer those deductions and tax incentives that trigger the AMT or accelerate income, so your deductions will be within the AMT limits. Unfortunately, this maneuver requires checking your income and deductible expenses periodically throughout the year. Investing in a tax software program or a tax advisor may help ease the burden.

The AMT in brief

Here is a quick glance at how the AMT works for a couple filing jointly.

	Regular Tax	*AMT*
Income	$150,000	$150,000
Deductions		
Taxes	<20,000>	0
Home Equity Interest (not used to improve your home)	<5,000>	0
Mortgage Interest	<20,000>	<20,000>
Charity	<5,000>	<5,000>
Job Expenses	<15,000>	0
Exemptions (5 ÷ $3,300)	<16,500>	0
AMT Exemption		<62,550>
Taxable Income	$68,500	$62,450
Tax	$10,246	$16,237

The unlucky taxpayer in this example had to cough up $16,237, or a flat 26 percent of his AMT income (or AMTI). That's $5,991 more than what his tax worked out to be under the regular method. You pay the higher of your regular tax or AMT. For simplicity, we didn't take into account all of the various deduction phaseout amounts. If your AMT is higher than your regular tax as computed in this example, the $5,991 difference gets entered here on line 45.

We wish that we could provide you with a general guide on when your AMT will exceed your regular tax, thereby causing you to have to fork over the difference. Unfortunately, we can't. But here is the IRS rule: If your taxable income, combined with your personal exemptions and the items listed earlier in this section, exceeds the following amounts, you could end up paying the AMT:

✔ Married filing jointly and qualifying widow(er) — $62,550
✔ Single or head of household — $42,500
✔ Married filing separately — $31,275

As of 1998, farmers no longer need to include certain installment sales when computing their AMTs.

Line 46: Add lines 44 and 45

Follow the instructions as indicated on the tax form.

Credits: Lines 47 to 55

Now it's time for your *credits* — and each one has a nice form for you to fill out. The credits on lines 47 to 55 may be reduced if your AMT (we discuss it on line 45) exceeds your regular tax. Some credits can't reduce the AMT; others can, such as the Child and Dependent Care (line 48), Elderly and Disabled (line 49), Lifetime Learning and Hope for Education (line 50), Retirement Savings Contributions (line 51), Residential Energy (line 52), Child (line 53), and Adoption credit (line 54). These are the most common credits, and we don't want you to miss them if you're eligible to take them.

Tax credits reduce your tax dollar for dollar. Deductions reduce only your taxable income. A $1,000 tax deduction reduces the tax for someone in the 30 percent tax bracket by only $300. A $1,000 tax credit reduces that tax by $1,000.

Line 47: Foreign tax credit (Form 1116)

If you paid tax to a foreign country on income earned in that country, you're allowed to take a credit for it if you also paid U.S. income tax on that same income. Use **Form 1116, Foreign Tax Credit,** to figure this credit. If you're not itemizing your deductions, you have to claim the foreign tax that you paid as a credit if you want to use it to reduce your tax.

You don't have to be a multinational corporation to pay foreign taxes. With more and more people investing in international mutual funds, the foreign tax credit is being used more than ever before to reduce investors' U.S. tax bills for their share of the foreign taxes paid by the fund.

Unfortunately, the computation of this credit is a killer — and even the IRS agrees. The instructions say that it should take you about 6½ hours to read the instructions, assemble the data, and fill in the form. And that's with all the instructions in English (by and large) and all the parts included! Give it a whirl. If you hate number-crunching, a computer tax software program can help (see Chapter 2). If using a computer isn't your thing, see a tax advisor. Attach Form 1116 to your return and bid it good riddance! You can either claim the foreign tax that you paid as a credit here on line 47 or as an itemized deduction on Schedule A.

As a general rule, taking the credit produces a larger savings. For more on foreign taxes, refer to Chapter 9. You can also use the foreign tax credit for foreign taxes paid on income earned overseas that exceeds the $80,000 exclusion and the housing allowance. (See Chapters 6 and 27 for more about this tax credit.)

You can ignore the fiendish Form 1116 if the foreign tax you paid is $300 or less ($600 for joint filers). Simply enter the foreign tax you paid on line 47 if your foreign tax is less than these amounts. This simplified method of claiming the credit is available if the only type of foreign income you had was from dividends, interest, rent, royalties, annuities, or the sale of an asset.

Line 48: Credit for child and dependent care expenses (Form 2441)

If you hire someone to take care of your children so that you can work for income (doing housework and errands don't cut it), you're entitled to the credit that you figure on **Form 2441**. This credit may save you several hundred dollars. To be eligible, your child must be younger than 13 or a dependent of any age and be physically or mentally handicapped. See Chapter 14 for information on Form 2441.

The maximum credit for one child in 2006 is $1,050 and $2,100 for two children. Employers who provide childcare for their employees are allowed a tax credit for a percentage of their expenses.

The cost of your babysitter, daycare, or after-school care counts toward this credit (but not after-school activities, such as dance, music, and sports); options like summer day camps (overnight camps don't make the grade) do, too. Remember, if you weren't sending your child to that camp in the summer, you'd need to hire a sitter or daycare instead.

Line 49: Credit for the elderly or the disabled (Schedule R)

You use (and attach!) Schedule R for this credit. You're entitled to claim this credit (which can amount to as much as $1,125) if you're married and both you and your spouse are 65 or older — or both of you are disabled and any age. For single taxpayers, the maximum credit is $750. See Chapter 14 for a discussion of Schedule R and the reasons most people are ineligible for this credit. If you qualify, enter this credit on line 49.

Line 50: Education credits (Form 8863)

On this line you claim the *Hope Scholarship Credit* and the *Lifetime Learning Credit*. Remember that credits reduce your tax, dollar for dollar. You claim both credits on **Form 8863, Education Credits (Hope and Lifetime Learning Credits).** Here are snapshots of how these credits work:

✔ **The Hope Scholarship Credit** provides a credit of $1,650 per student per year for the first two years of college. The credit is equal to 100 percent of the first $1,100 of tuition expenses (but not room, board, or books) and 50 percent of the next $1,100 of tuition paid. A student must carry at least one-half the normal course load. The credit can be claimed for you, your spouse, and your dependents. But if you earn too much, you aren't eligible. For married taxpayers (filing jointly only), the credit starts to phase out at $90,000 of income and is gone at $110,000. For single taxpayers, the phaseout starts at $45,000 and is completely wiped out at $55,000. The credit isn't available for anyone convicted of possession or distribution of a controlled substance.

✔ **The Lifetime Learning Credit** is a 20 percent credit on up to $10,000 of tuition expenses (but not room, board, or books). This credit is per family per year, not per student, as is the case with the Hope credit. Unlike the Hope Scholarship, this credit doesn't have a limit on the number of years you may claim it. That's why it's called Lifetime Learning. The same income limits and family-member restrictions that apply to the Hope credit also apply to this credit. Unlike the Hope credit, a student doesn't have to carry at least one-half the normal course load. Any course to acquire or improve job skills qualifies, but not courses involving sports or hobbies.

You can claim the Hope credit for one child and the Lifetime credit for another, but you can't claim both credits for the same student.

Families with more than one child can use both credits in concert, but it requires careful planning. You need to make sure tuition payments are made in the correct tax year for the correct student. Remember, these credits are designed to help you offset the high cost of college and other post-secondary school tuitions.

If you were entitled to claim either credit in 2003, 2004, or 2005 but forgot to, you can correct that error, but time's running out for you to do so. See Chapter 18 on how to amend your 2003 to 2005 returns.

Sometimes students drop classes before the final drop date, and they or their parents receive refunded tuition that affects the amount of either a Hope Credit or Lifetime Learning Credit to which they were entitled. If you fall into this category, read on. If you receive a refund in 2006 or 2007 before you file your 2006 return, subtract your refund from the tuition you paid in 2006 when figuring the credit. If you receive a refund after you file your 2006 return, you have to increase your tax for 2007 by the amount of the credit that the refund gave rise to. For example, in 2006 you paid tuition expenses of $3,000 and claimed a 20 percent Lifetime Learning Credit of $600. In 2007, after you filed your 2006 return, you receive a $1,000 tuition refund. You have to increase your tax on the 2007 return by $200 ($1,000 ÷ 20 percent). You can enter the amount on the dotted line to the left of line 63 and write "Hope or Lifetime Learning Credit" next to it. Make sure that you add this amount to the total you place on line 63.

The IRS can check to see whether you're entitled to either the Hope or Learning Credit because educational institutions now are required to issue **Form 1098-T, Tuition Payments Statement,** which lists the student's name, Social Security number, the amount of tuition paid, whether the student was enrolled for at least half the full-time workload, or whether the courses lead to a graduate-level degree.

The rules regarding which person among family members is eligible to claim the Hope or Lifetime Learning credits have changed dramatically. This change applies to divorced parents where one parent claims the child as a dependent and the other parent foots the tuition bill, or where, because of income phase-out limits, a parent can't claim the credit. A way now exists for the student to claim the credit and shelter any income he or she may have. Say, for example, you're the custodial parent (see Chapter 4) and claim your child as a dependent, but your former spouse pays the tuition. You're considered to have made the payment and may claim an education credit. However, you can twist that stipulation in a number of ways that entitles that person who "is considered to have paid the tuition and related expenses" to claim an education credit. When the student pays the tuition and you claim the student as a dependent, you're still considered to have paid tuition. For example, when someone else, such as a grandparent, pays the tuition, the student is considered to have paid the tuition, which again entitles you to claim an education credit because tuition that's considered paid by the student is considered paid by you.

The Hope and Learning credits provide nifty tax-planning techniques because education credits attach to whoever claims the dependency exemption, the student or the parent. If you can't claim Hope or Learning credits because your income is above the limits ($110,000 when filing jointly or $55,000 for others), maybe you need to consider not claiming the student as a dependent. Because students are considered to have paid their own tuition even though parents may have actually paid it, the students can claim the credit whenever their parents don't claim them as a dependent. Foregoing a $3,300 dependency exemption for someone in the 30 percent bracket costs the parents $990 in tax ($3,300 × 30 percent). On the other hand, the students pick up either the $1,650 Hope or up to $2,000 Lifetime Learning credits.

The scenario in the previous paragraph is based on the student having income that's subject to tax. If the student doesn't have such an income, you may want to try this suggestion: Give the student an investment that has gone up in value followed by a quick sale of that investment. Doing so shifts the income and tax burden from you to the student so the student can apply either of the education credits against the tax, which makes more after-tax money available for the student to pay the tuition. Of course, you need to remember when making any gift that there may be gift tax consequences. By keeping your annual gifts to $12,000 or less per donee ($24,000 or less if you and your spouse are making gifts together), you won't need to file gift tax returns. What a relief!

Don't forget that other tax provisions can help you with the cost of education, including deductible student loan interest (line 33, Chapter 7), and Coverdell Education Savings Accounts (formerly known as Education IRAs), which have become more attractive — see Chapter 24.

Line 51: Retirement savings contributions credit

The retirement savings contribution credit encourages joint filers with adjusted gross incomes of less than $50,000 (heads of household below $37,500 and single filers below $25,000) to save for retirement by enabling them to claim a credit against their tax for a percentage of up to the first $2,000 that they contribute to Roth or traditional IRAs, 401(k)s, or elective deferrals to their employer's retirement plan.

Now for the fine print: If money were taken out of one of these accounts between January 1, 2004, and the due date for filing your 2006 return, including any extension of time to file, you must reduce the maximum $2,000 amount that is subject to the credit by the amount that you withdrew. Whoo! Okay, take a deep breath. For example, say you took $1,500 out of your IRA in 2005. Even though you contributed the $4,000 maximum allowed in 2006 to an IRA, the maximum amount that you can compute the credit on is $500 ($2,000 – $1,500).

In order to claim the credit, you need to fill out yet another form, **Form 8880, Credit for Qualified Retirement Savings Contributions.** Chapter 14 tells you what you need to know to fill out this form correctly and gives you more pointers on the credit for qualified retirement savings contributions.

Line 52: Residential energy credits (Form 5695)

In these days of excessive energy costs, you may already pay serious attention to the gaps in your windows and heat escaping your roof. And the government wants to help. In 2006 and 2007, you can take a credit of up to $500 if you've taken steps to make your home more energy efficient and up to $2,000 if you install a qualified solar water heating or photovotaic system.

Which improvements qualify for this credit? You're allowed to take a credit for 10 percent of the cost of insulation material or other systems designed to reduce heat loss, qualifying exterior windows and skylights (limited to $2,000), and qualifying exterior doors and metal roofs that meet the Energy Star program requirements (your roofer knows if your new roof qualifies). In addition, specific credit amounts range from $50 to $300 for energy efficient heating and cooling systems for your home. In addition, you can take a credit for 30 percent of the cost of a qualified solar energy system, up to a total of $2,000. There's also a 30 percent credit (up to $500 for each ASKW maximum capacity) for the cost of installing a qualified fuel cell or microturbine system: with the government willing to foot so much of the cost, it makes sense (and cents) to explore alternative energy options.

If you've made improvements in 2006 that qualify, calculate your credit on **Form 5695, Residential Energy Credits,** and place the credit on line 52 of Form 1040.

Line 53: Child tax credit

Every dependent child younger than 17 on December 31, 2006 can slice $1,000 off your 2006 income tax bill. That's a dollar-for-dollar credit, so if you have a tax liability of only $2,000 on line 46, and you have two qualifying children, your total tax becomes zero.

The child tax credit comes in two varieties: the nonrefundable *child tax credit* on line 53, and the refundable *additional child tax credit,* which we describe later in this chapter, at line 68. To find out more about these credits, including how to calculate them, check out Chapter 14.

Line 54: Form 8396, Form 8839, and Form 8859

The IRS form designers decided they didn't want to add additional lines to Form 1040. Instead, they've opted to lump some less popular, but very valuable if you qualify, credits here on line 54.

Mortgage interest credit (Form 8396)

You may be eligible for a Mortgage Interest Credit if a state or local government agency issued you a Mortgage Credit Certificate (MCC). These certificates are issued as part of state and local governmental programs that provide taxpayers with financing to help them purchase their principal residence. If you're issued an MCC, it entitles you to a tax credit equal to between 10 percent and 50 percent of the amount of the mortgage interest you paid. If the MCC has a rate that exceeds 20 percent, the maximum credit is limited to $2,000. Amounts of more than $2,000 can be carried over to future years but are subject to the $2,000 annual limit. You must reduce your home mortgage interest deduction on Schedule A by the amount of the credit. A good mortgage broker can assist you in qualifying for a state-sponsored mortgage loan so you can qualify for this credit. If you qualify for this credit, you need to fill out **Form 8396** first before inserting the amount of the credit on line 54 and checking the appropriate box next to the line.

Qualified adoption expenses (Form 8839)

You're entitled to a credit of up to $10,960 in 2006 against your income tax for adoption expenses. Like most other credits, after your income hits certain limits, it begins to be whittled away. Here, the income phaseout range is from $164,410 to $204,410 in 2006. If you adopt a child with special needs, you can claim the credit even if you don't incur adoption expenses in 2006 (see Chapter 24 for how this works). A *child with special needs* means someone with a medical, physical, mental, or emotional handicap; a child whose age makes him or her difficult to adopt; or a member of a minority group. A foreign child can't be considered a child with special needs.

If you suspect that you qualify for this credit, check out Chapter 14, which gives you all the information you need to know to fill out **Form 8839, Qualified Adoption Expenses.**

District of Columbia first-time homebuyer credit (Form 8859)

For a relatively short window of time, first-time homebuyers in Washington, D.C., could qualify for a tax credit of up to $5,000. Unfortunately, this program expired on December 31, 2003. In 2006, the only people able to take this credit will be those who were carrying their credit forward from 2003 or earlier. If this describes you, complete **Form 8859, District of Columbia First-Time Homebuyer Credit,** before you fill in an amount on line 54. If you're using this credit, make sure you check the box for it on line 54, too.

Line 55: Other credits

For the most part, the application of the following credits is extremely limited, and few people are eligible for them. Still, forms and instructions are available either by phoning the IRS (800-829-3676) and asking for the forms and instructions, or on the IRS Web site at www.irs.gov. Here is what boxes a through c on line 55 refer to:

a **Form 3800, General Business Credit:** This form includes a number of credits that qualify as general business credits. If you're claiming more than one of these general business credits, check the Form 3800 box on line 55 of your 1040, and then fill in and attach Form 3800, as well as the forms for the types of credits you are claiming. If you're claiming just one of these general business credits, check the box c Form (specify) on line 55, fill in the form number, and attach that specific form. The following list includes some of the general business credits on Form 3800:

   • **Form 3468, Investment Credit**

   • **Form 5884, Work Opportunity Credit**

   • **Form 5884-A, Credits for Employers Affected by Hurricane Katrina, Rita, or Wilma**

   • **Form 6765, Credit for Increasing Research Activities**

   • **Form 8586, Low-Income Housing Credit**

   • **Form 8820, Orphan Drug Credit**

   • **Form 8826, Disabled Access Credit**

   • **Form 8830, Enhanced Oil Recovery Credit**

   • **Form 8835, Renewable Electricity Production Credit**

   • **Form 8845, Indian Employment Credit**

   • **Form 8846, Credit for Employer Social Security and Medicare Taxes Paid on Certain Employees' Tips**

   • **Form 8847, Credit for Contributions to Certain Community Development Corporations**

   • **Form 8861, Welfare-To-Work Credit**

   • **Form 8864, Biodiesel and Renewable Diesel Fuels Credit**

   • **Form 8874, New Markets Credit (this is a credit for an investment in or a loan to small businesses in low-income communities)**

- **Form 8881, Small Employer Pension Plan Start Up Costs**
- **Form 8882, Employer Provided Child Care Facilities and Services**
- **Form 8910, Alternative Motor Vehicle Credit**

The Small Employer Pension Plan Start Up Costs Credit allows an employer with no more than 100 employees who made more than $5,000 annually, and who didn't have a plan covering the same group of employees in the three immediate past years, to claim a credit of 50 percent of the start-up costs to establish and maintain a company pension. The maximum amount of the credit is $500 and can be claimed for costs incurred for up to three years. The maximum amount of expenses that can be used to compute the credit is $1,000. Start-up expenses above the amount used to compute the credit may be deducted as a business expense.

To claim the start-up credit, the pension plan must cover at least one employee who isn't an owner or who makes at least $5,000, but less than $100,000 (the 2006 amount).

Credits carried over from previous years also are entered on Form 3800.

If you bought a hybrid electric car in 2006, whether for business or personal use (or some combination of both), you calculate and claim your credit for it on Form 8910, Alternative Motor Vehicle Credit, which is one of the forms listed on Form 3800. Check out Chapter 14 for more information on how to claim your credit for your new car.

b **Form 8801, Credit for Prior Year Minimum Tax — Individuals and Fiduciaries.** If you paid the alternative minimum tax in the prior year, you may be entitled to a credit for past payments.

c **Form (specify)_____:** If you're claiming only one of the credits listed in this section, enter the form number and the amount of the credit on this line. If you're claiming more than one of the listed credits, you have to fill out Form 3800 and enter the total of the credits on line a.

Form 8834, Qualified Electric Vehicle Credit — for all you environmentalists. Electric cars come with a maximum $1,000 per-car credit (down from $4,000 in 2005). To claim the credit, enter the form number (8834) on the line by box c and enter the credit to which you're entitled per line 20 of Form 8834 on line 55. Remember, this credit is only for electric vehicles; hybrid vehicle credits are claimed on Form 8910.

Line 56: Total credits

Add lines 47 through 55 and put the sum on line 56. (If you make a mistake, your grade will suffer.)

Line 57: Subtract line 56 from line 46

If line 56 is greater than line 46, just enter "-0-" on line 57.

Other Taxes

What! More taxes? Could be. Read the following sections to see whether any of these taxes apply to you.

Line 58: Self-employment tax (Schedule SE)

If you earn income from being self-employed and from other sources, use Schedule SE to figure another tax that you owe — the Social Security tax and Medicare tax. The first $94,200 of your self-employment earnings is taxed at 12.4 percent (this is the Social Security tax part). There isn't any limit for the Medicare tax; it's 2.9 percent of your total self-employment earnings. For amounts of $94,200 or less, the combined rate is 15.3 percent (adding the two taxes together), and above $94,200, the rate is 2.9 percent. See Chapter 15 for information about filling out Schedule SE.

Line 59: Social Security and Medicare tax on unreported tip income (Form 4137)

If you worked in a restaurant that employed at least ten people and didn't report your share of at least 8 percent of the restaurant's income as tip income, your employer will do it for you. This amount (the difference between what you reported as tip income to your employer and your share of 8 percent of the restaurant's income), which otherwise is known as your allocated tips, is entered on box 8 of your W-2. The amount in box 8 isn't included in box 1 of your W-2 and has to be added to your total wages on Form 1040 (line 7). The Social Security tax that you owe on the amount in box 8 is computed on **Form 4137, Social Security and Medicare Tax on Unreported Tip Income,** and is entered on line 59.

When we say "your share of 8 percent of the restaurant's income," that doesn't mean that you're entitled to this income. It means that the IRS arbitrarily claims that the restaurant generated tip income equal to 8 percent of the restaurant's income. Box 8 of your W-2 is for your share of the total amount of tips. The IRS can always audit the restaurant and determine, for example, that the tip rate was really 14 percent. Ouch!

If your employer wasn't able to collect from you all the Social Security and Medicare tax you owe on your reported tip income, box 12 of your W-2 will show that amount. Code A next to the amount in box 12 is for Social Security tax, and Code B next to the amount in box 12 is for Medicare Tax. Enter the amounts in box 12 on the dotted line to the left of line 63, Form 1040, and to the left of the amount, write "UT," which stands for uncollected tax on tips. Don't forget to enter the amount on the dotted line in the total on line 63.

Line 60: Tax on IRAs, other retirement plans, and other tax-favored accounts (Form 5329)

Try as hard as you may, a day may come when you can't follow the rules exactly on what you should, or shouldn't, be putting in or taking out of your IRA, Roth IRA, Coverdell Education Savings Account, Section 529 (qualified tuition program) Plan, Archer MSAs, or Health Savings Accounts. And that's okay. The IRS understands that the rules for all these are complex and that sometimes people make mistakes. To show how understanding the IRS is, it created **Form 5329, Additional Taxes on Qualified Plans (including IRAs) and Other Tax-Favored Accounts,** that covers these types of accounts and helps you to calculate the penalty you owe for goofing.

Form 5329 is divided into clearly labeled parts. You need to complete only the parts that apply to your situation. If penalties are assessed (and there's a good chance they will be because you're filling out this form in the first place), place the penalty amount on line 60 of your Form 1040.

Line 61: Advance earned income credit payments

If you filed a Form W-5 with your employer in 2006, you've been receiving a portion of your Earned Income Credit (EIC) in each paycheck throughout the year, which is great. This money is in your pocket on a regular basis rather than in one lump sum at the end of the year.

Now that you're filing your tax returns, though, you need to account for the portion of the EIC you've already received. All line 61 does is add the total amount of EIC payments that you've already received back to your total tax. In line 66a, the full amount of the EIC you're entitled to is going to be subtracted. Pretty nifty, eh?

Line 62: Household employment taxes (Schedule H)

Even if you don't expect to hold high political office — or low political office — the provisions of the household employment tax, also known as the *nanny tax,* can save you a tidy sum and simplify the number and type of returns that you have to file. The law covers housekeepers, babysitters, and yard-care workers, as well as nannies.

The nanny tax is figured on **Schedule H,** and the amount you owe is entered on line 61. If you didn't pay cash wages of $1,500 or more in 2006, or $1,000 or more in any calendar quarter, or didn't withhold any federal income tax, you can skip this form. If you paid more than $1,500 in wages in 2006 but less than $1,000 in any calendar quarter, you have to fill out only page 1 and enter the amount from line 8 of Schedule H onto line 62. If you paid more than $1,000 in any quarter, you must fill out page 2 of the form and enter the amount from line 27 of Schedule H onto line 62. See Chapter 15 for more about filling out Schedule H.

Line 63: IRS pop quiz

Find your total tax by adding lines 57 through 62 and placing the amount here.

Payments

This section of the return is where you finally, thankfully, get to tally up how much actual federal tax you paid during the year.

Line 64: Federal income tax withheld

Enter the amounts from box 2 of your W-2s and your W-2Gs, 1099-DIVs, and 1099-INTs, and from box 4 of your Form 1099-Rs, 1099-DIVs, 1099-INTs, and 1099-MISCs on line 64. Make sure that you don't overlook any tax withheld on any other Form 1099.

Line 65: Estimated tax payments

If you made estimated tax payments toward your 2006 tax, fill in the total amount of the payments here. If you applied last year's overpayment to this year's return, don't forget to enter that amount, too! The IRS isn't kind enough to send you a reminder; you have to keep track yourself.

Remember, the IRS doesn't want to wait until April 15, 2008, to collect your 2007 tax. So, if you expect to owe money come next April 15, you must file quarterly estimates if 90 percent of your tax isn't being withheld from your income and you'll owe more than $1,000.

Estimated tax payments are made on **Form 1040-ES, Estimated Tax for Individuals.** The form requires only your name, address, Social Security number, and the amount you're paying. For 2007 estimated payments, make sure that you use the 2006 1040-ES. See Chapter 15 if you need help filling out Form 1040-ES.

Line 66a and 66b: Earned income credit (EIC) and nontaxable combat pay election

The EIC is a special credit for lower-income workers. The credit is refundable — which means that if it exceeds your tax or if you don't owe tax, the IRS will send you a check for the amount of the EIC.

Claiming the EIC doesn't disqualify you from receiving welfare benefits.

Unlike other credits, the EIC is no small piece of change. The credit can be as high as $4,536 for a married couple with two kids. To qualify for the credit, your AGI (line 38 on Form 1040 or line 22 on Form 1040A) or your earned income must be less than the following amounts:

- $32,001 ($34,001 for married filing jointly) if you have one child

- $36,348 ($38,348 for married filing jointly) if you have two or more children

- $12,120 ($14,120 for married filing jointly) if you don't have any children. If you're filing the EIC and you have no qualifying children, you must be at least 25 (but younger than 65), and you may not be claimed as a dependent by anyone else

The rules surrounding the EIC are pretty specific, and the IRS tends to look at these returns carefully. Just because the IRS reads these returns carefully doesn't mean you shouldn't claim this credit if you're entitled to it. It does mean that you need to carefully check out Chapter 14 though. All the rules are laid out for you there in plain English. We even show you how to calculate your EIC.

If you spent a portion of 2006 as a member of the military serving in a designated combat zone, you may elect to include all or a portion of your nontaxable combat pay when calculating the amount of your earned income for the purpose of calculating this credit. If you have very little earned income from other sources in 2006, you may find that using this election helps you get a bigger credit. To make the election, all you need to do is write in the amount of your nontaxable combat pay that you want to include in your EIC calculation on line 66b. Remember that this income is only being counted for the EIC calculation—you still don't have to pay income tax on it.

Line 67: Excess Social Security and RRTA tax withheld

Line 67 applies only if you worked for two employers and your total wages were $94,200 or more. The maximum Social Security tax you're required to pay for 2006 is $5,840.40. So if $6,000 was reported withheld on your W-2s, $159.60 is entered on line 67. Box 4 of your W-2s contains the amount of Social Security tax that was withheld from your salary. If you worked for only one employer and more than $5,840.40 was withheld, skip line 67; you have to get the excess back from your employer.

Line 68: Additional child tax credit (Form 8812)

This credit is the refundable portion of the Child Tax Credit that we explain on line 52 and in Chapter 14. To claim this additional credit, you have to file **Form 8812, Additional Child Tax Credit.**

Line 69: Amount paid with extension request (Form 4868)

If you requested a six-month extension of time by filing **Form 4868, Application for Automatic Extension of Time to File U.S. Individual Income Tax Return,** enter the amount that you paid when you requested the extension. (Unbelievably, despite the millions of taxpayers who file for extensions each year, the IRS still doesn't include this form in the Form 1040 instruction booklet.) See Chapter 4 for more about how to obtain an extension of time to file.

Line 70: Other payments

Here are a couple of the more obscure forms to wonder about:

a **Form 2439, Notice to Shareholders of Undistributable Long-Term Capital Gain:** You'll receive this form if you invested in a mutual fund where the company didn't distribute your share of the long-term capital gains that you were entitled to receive. Enter the amount from line 2 of this form on line 70 and attach a copy of the form to your 1040. See Chapter 12 for information on how to handle the capital gains retained by the fund.

b **Form 4136, Credit for Federal Tax Paid on Fuels:** This form is for claiming a refundable credit for the tax paid on gasoline and gasohol for off-highway use. Bulldozers, forklifts, generators, and compressors used in your business qualify for the credit. Fuel used in motorboats doesn't qualify. Tax paid on undyed kerosene used in home heaters also qualifies for the credit.

c **Form 8885, Health Coverage Tax Credit for Eligible Recipients:** This tax credit allows dislocated workers and uninsured retirees who are receiving pension benefits from the federal government's Pension Benefit Guarantee Corporations (PBGC) to claim a refundable credit equal to 65 percent of their health insurance expenses. This group of people is by no means small. In 2002, the PBGC took over the responsibility for paying the pensions of 95,000 retirees of Bethlehem Steel. Individuals can elect to forego the credit and instead have the government pick up the tab directly for 65 percent of their health insurance premiums.

To be eligible for the credit or the advance payment, you have to be receiving Trade Adjustments Assistance (TAA) allowances under the Trade Act or Alternative Trade Adjustments Assistance (ATAA), or be an uninsured retiree between 55 and 65 who is receiving pension benefits from the PBGC. TAA allowances are paid to workers who lost their jobs because of foreign trade. ATAA benefits are paid to displaced workers under the Trade Acts alternative program. The credit and the advance payment may very well become the prototype for all unemployed workers.

You can obtain TAA or ATAA allowances by submitting a request for determination of eligibility with the U.S. Department of Labor. A special hotline has been set up for the TAA and ATAA programs at 866-628-4282. The Health Coverage Tax Credit (HCTC) Web site is at `www.irs.gov/individuals/article/0,,id=109915,00.html`.

The credit isn't available to individuals who are unemployed and paying health insurance premiums under COBRA unless they meet the eligibility requirements for receiving TAA, ATAA, or PBGC benefits. Coverage under a spouse's health insurance counts toward determining the credit. Individuals covered by Medicare aren't eligible.

Line 71: Credit for federal telephone excise tax paid

A new credit is available for this year only, and available to every taxpayer who has a phone (either landline or cellular) and paid excise taxes on long-distance telephone call. And it's not really a credit, but a refund of taxes you improperly paid during the period from February 28, 2003 through August 1, 2006.

You have two options on claiming this credit. The first, and by far the easiest, is to count up the number of personal exemptions on your return. Claim a $30 credit on line 71 for one exemption, $40 for 2 exemptions, $50 for three exemptions, and $60 if you have four or more exemptions.

If your long-distance bills are large and you have time on your hands to go digging for your old records, you can try the second option, which is to claim the actual amount of federal excise tax you paid on long-distance calls during that period. In order to claim the larger credit, fill out **Form 8913** and attach it to your return.

Line 72: Total payments

You enter the total of the payments (lines 64 through 71) on line 72 and hold your breath (or your nose).

Refund or Amount You Owe

Okay, this is it. Now comes the moment you've worked so hard for. Do you get money back? Do you pay? Read on and find out.

Line 73: The amount that you overpaid

If the amount of your total payments (line 72) is more than your total tax (line 63), subtract line 63 from line 72 (see Figure 8-2). The remainder is the amount you overpaid. Do you like that word "overpaid"?

Other Taxes	58	Self-employment tax. Attach Schedule SE	58	
	59	Social security and Medicare tax on tip income not reported to employer. Attach Form 4137	59	
	60	Additional tax on IRAs, other qualified retirement plans, etc. Attach Form 5329 if required	60	
	61	Advance earned income credit payments from Form(s) W-2, box 9	61	
	62	Household employment taxes. Attach Schedule H	62	
	63	Add lines 57 through 62. This is your **total tax** ▶	63	

Payments	64	Federal income tax withheld from Forms W-2 and 1099	64		
	65	2006 estimated tax payments and amount applied from 2005 return	65		
If you have a qualifying child, attach Schedule EIC.	66a	**Earned income credit (EIC)**	66a		
	b	Nontaxable combat pay election ▶	66b		
	67	Excess social security and tier 1 RRTA tax withheld (see page 59)	67		
	68	Additional child tax credit. Attach Form 8812	68		
	69	Amount paid with request for extension to file (see page 59)	69		
	70	Payments from: a ☐ Form 2439 b ☐ Form 4136 c ☐ Form 8885	70		
	71	Credit for federal telephone excise tax paid. Attach Form 8913 if required	71		
	72	Add lines 64, 65, 66a, and 67 through 71. These are your **total payments** ▶	72		

Refund	73	If line 72 is more than line 63, subtract line 63 from line 72. This is the amount you **overpaid**	73	
Direct deposit? See page 59 and fill in 74b, 74c, and 74d, or Form 8888.	74a	Amount of line 73 you want **refunded to you.** If Form 8888 is attached, check here ▶ ☐	74a	
	▶ b	Routing number	c Type: ☐ Checking ☐ Savings	
	▶ d	Account number		
	75	Amount of line 73 you want **applied to your 2007 estimated tax** ▶	75	

Amount You Owe	76	**Amount you owe.** Subtract line 72 from line 63. For details on how to pay, see page 60 ▶	76	
	77	Estimated tax penalty (see page 60)	77	

Third Party Designee	Do you want to allow another person to discuss this return with the IRS (see page 61)? ☐ **Yes.** Complete the following. ☐ **No**		
	Designee's name ▶	Phone no. ▶ ( )	Personal identification number (PIN) ▶

Sign Here
Joint return? See page 17.
Keep a copy for your records.

Under penalties of perjury, I declare that I have examined this return and accompanying schedules and statements, and to the best of my knowledge and belief, they are true, correct, and complete. Declaration of preparer (other than taxpayer) is based on all information of which preparer has any knowledge.

Your signature	Date	Your occupation	Daytime phone number ( )
▶			
Spouse's signature. If a joint return, **both** must sign.	Date	Spouse's occupation	
▶			

Paid Preparer's Use Only

Preparer's signature ▶		Date	Check if self-employed ☐	Preparer's SSN or PTIN
Firm's name (or yours if self-employed), address, and ZIP code ▶			EIN	
			Phone no. ( )	

Form **1040** (2006)

✱ Printed on recycled paper

Figure 8-2: The rest of the Form 1040. Fill it in and you're done. (Hope you get to fill in the refund line!)

Line 74a: Amount that you want refunded to you

You can speed up your refund by almost three weeks by having your refund wired to your bank account. That way, you can ensure that your refund won't be lost or stolen. To do so, enter your routing number on line 74b. That's the nine-digit number at the bottom left in Figure 8-3. On line 74c, check the type of account: checking or savings. On line 74d, enter your account number. That's the number to right of the routing number in Figure 8-3.

PAUL MAPLE
LILIAN MAPLE
123 Main Street
Anyplace, NY 10000

1234
15-0000/0000

20

PAY TO THE ORDER OF _____ $ ☐

_____ DOLLARS

ANYPLACE BANK
Anyplace, NY 10000

Routing Number (line 73b)
Account Number (line 73d)

For _____

I:250000005I: ⑈200000⑈86⑈ 1234

Figure 8-3: A sample check.

Deciding where to stash your cash when it comes back can be difficult, and too often, this windfall of overpaid taxes just ends up with the money that you use to pay your bills. Now, you no longer have to deposit your entire refund to one account, but can instead choose up to three separate accounts, including your IRA, HSA, Archer MSA, or Coverdell ESA accounts. If you're directing your refund to more than one account, fill out **Form 8888, Direct Deposit of Refund,** with your instructions.

We know that accurate returns are the norm, but on occasion, the amount of your refund may be increased or decreased due to incorrect math, unpaid child or spousal support, federal and/or state taxes, or delinquent student loans. If your refund is decreased, the IRS will subtract any reduction first from the account shown on line 3 of Form 8888, then the one on line 2, and finally from the one listed on line 1. If your refund amount is increased, the additional amount will be tacked onto the last account listed. If you're using your tax refund to fully fund your IRA for 2006, make sure you don't list that account last; if you do, you may run the risk of making an excess contribution. If you're planning on using your refund to fund your 2006 IRA contribution, better make sure that you file your return well in advance of the April 16, 2007 deadline. In order to constitute a valid 2006 IRA contribution, your bank must receive the cash prior to April 16, 2007. Check out Chapter 7 for IRA contribution rules.

Line 75: Amount of line 73 you want applied to your 2007 estimated tax

Here you indicate what amount of your refund you want applied to your 2007 (next year's) estimated tax. After you make this selection and file your return, you can't change your mind and ask for it back. You have to claim it as a credit on your 2007 return.

Line 76: The gosh darn AMOUNT YOU OWE line

If your total tax (line 63) is larger than your total payments (line 72), subtract line 72 from line 63. This is the amount you owe. Sorry. If you want to charge what you owe on a credit card, check out Chapter 5 for the ins and outs of how to do it. The IRS now has a host of alternate payment options. The "new" IRS never stops thinking of ways to separate you from your money. If you want to pay what you owe the old-fashioned way by check, see the section "Finishing Up," which follows.

Line 77: Estimated tax penalty (Form 2210)

If you owe more than $1,000 and haven't paid 90 percent of your tax liability in either quarterly estimates or in withholding, you'll be assessed an underestimating penalty. A number of exceptions either excuse or reduce this penalty. You calculate this penalty on **Form 2210, Underpayment of Estimated Tax.** See Chapter 18 on penalties to see whether one of the exceptions applies to you. Chapter 15 gives you all the facts on the 1040-ES, the estimated tax form, and the penalties that may apply if you don't fill it out. If you got socked for the penalty this year, take time to figure out the rules so it doesn't happen again next year.

Remember, the IRS doesn't want to wait until April 15, 2008, when you file your 2007 tax return, to collect your 2007 tax. You should have paid at least 90 percent of your tax by having tax withheld from your salary, pension, or IRA distributions — or by making estimated quarterly tax payments. If you don't calculate this penalty yourself, the IRS does and will bill you for it. You don't want the IRS to prepare this form, because the IRS will prepare it on the basis of your paying the maximum!

A good tax software program can breeze through this form to see whether you're eligible to have the penalty reduced or eliminated by one of the exceptions. The ability to calculate this form alone is worth the price of the software package.

Finishing Up

If you're filing on paper, sign your return. Attach your W-2s, W-2Gs, 1099s where federal tax was withheld, and all schedules. If you owe money, make sure you write your Social Security number on the front of the check along with the notation "2006 Form 1040." You should also fill out Form 1040-V, Payment Voucher. Mail Form 1040-V and your check (but don't staple them to the return) with your Form 1040 (with all its attachments) to the IRS Service Center for the area in which you live. You can find the addresses in your instruction booklet or on the IRS Web site at www.irs.gov. Check out Chapter 4 for approved ways for filing.

If you're filing electronically, your signature is replaced with a 5-digit (numbers only, and not all zeros) self-selected personal identification number. If you're filing a joint return, both of you need to have PINs. If you have a payment due, you can send it snail-mail with Form 1040-V, arrange an electronic funds transfer (EFT), or pay by credit card. Because you no longer have to physically mail anything to the IRS, make sure that you keep a file with all of your tax information in a safe, and preferably fireproof, place. You'll want to be able to produce these records should the IRS come calling.

Part III
Filling Out Schedules and Other Forms

The 5th Wave   By Rich Tennant

Corporation? Nope.
Limited Partnership?
Not hardly. Ahh —
Soooul Proprietor.

TAX RETURN

In this part . . .

The plain old 1040 isn't just the plain old 1040 — it's really a souped-up version that rides around with a number of schedules and forms, tailored to your specific tax situation. Naturally, these schedules and forms take after the 1040 in their complexity and potential for causing confusion. This part walks you through the schedules and forms that affect most taxpayers, with ways you may be able to take advantage of new tax cuts and tips that help you pay only what you really owe.

Chapter 9

Itemized Deductions: Schedule A

*1*f *Hamlet* were to be written today, we wonder whether Shakespeare would have him lament, "To itemize or to take the standard deduction, that is the question." Forgive the Shakespearean reference, but that is indeed the question that must be answered.

You've reached that point in preparing your return where you must get off the fence and decide to itemize your deductions or not. You've totaled your income and subtracted your allowable adjustments to income. Now to arrive at your taxable income, you have to subtract your standard deduction and exemptions — or take the more difficult road and subtract your itemized deductions.

If you choose to take your standard deduction, you get to subtract that amount of money from your adjusted gross income (AGI), *whether or not you actually paid anything close to that amount for deductible expenses.* But when you're itemizing your deductions, you need to have paid the expenses you're claiming. You aren't allowed to claim expenses paid by someone else, and you can't include amounts that you promised to pay but haven't done so yet.

The Standard Deduction

Every taxpayer, whatever his or her filing status, is entitled to subtract a predetermined amount of money (the *standard deduction*) from his or her AGI and not pay income tax on it. The amount of your standard deduction is based on your filing status, and whether or not someone else may claim you as a dependent on his or her income tax return. For 2006, if you're younger than 65 and aren't blind, the standard deduction amounts are as follows:

✔ Married filing jointly or a qualifying widow(er) — $10,300

✔ Head of household — $7,550

✔ Single — $5,150

✔ Married filing separately — $5,150

If you're married filing separately, you may claim the standard deduction only if your spouse also claims the standard deduction. If your spouse itemizes, you also must itemize. If you decide not to itemize your deductions, enter the standard deduction for your filing status on line 40 of Form 1040, or line 24 of Form 1040A.

Older than 65 or blind

If you're 65 or older, you get to increase your standard deduction by $1,250 if you're single or a head of household, and it's increased by $1,000 if you're married filing jointly or a qualifying widow(er). If you're blind, you're entitled to an extra $1,250 if single and $1,000 if married. For example, if you're single, older than 65 and blind, the standard deduction of $5,150 increases by $2,500 for a total of $7,650.

If you don't want to do the math yourself, Table 9-1 does it for you. Check the appropriate boxes and then find your standard deduction.

Table 9-1	Standard Deduction Chart for People Age 65 or Older or Blind		
Check the appropriate boxes below and total. Then go to the chart.			
You	65 or older ❑	Blind ❑	
Your spouse, if claiming spouse's exemption	65 or older ❑	Blind ❑	
Total number of boxes you checked ___			
If Your Filing Status Is:	*And the Total Number of Boxes You Checked Above Is:*		*Your Standard Deduction Is:*
Single	1		$6,400
	2		$7,650
Married filing joint return	1		$11,300
or qualifying widow(er)	2		$12,300
with dependent child	3		$13,300
	4		$14,300
Married filing separate return	1		$6,150
	2		$7,150
Head of household	1		$8,800
	2		$10,050

If you're claiming an increased standard deduction, you can't use Form 1040EZ; you must use Form 1040A or Form 1040.

Standard deduction for dependents

If you can claim your child or dependent on your own or if someone else can claim that dependent on his or her tax return, the dependent's standard deduction is limited to either $850 or to the individual's 2006 earned income plus $300 for the year (whichever amount is larger — but not more than the regular standard deduction amount of $5,150). So if you're helping your son or daughter prepare his or her return, use the worksheet in Table 9-2 to compute the standard deduction. If your dependent is 65 or older or blind, however, this standard deduction may be higher. Also use Table 9-2 to determine your dependent's standard deduction. Whether you're preparing your own return (as a child being claimed on your parent's return, for example) or you're preparing a return for a dependent that you're claiming, you must complete this worksheet. Otherwise, use the regular standard deduction.

Earned income includes wages, salaries, tips, professional fees, and other compensation that you received for services performed. It also includes anything received as a scholarship that counts as income.

An illustrated example of how to fill out the worksheet in Table 9-2 is provided in Chapter 5 under 1040EZ, line 5.

Table 9-2	Standard Deduction Worksheet for Dependents	
If you are 65 or older or blind, check the boxes below. Then go to the worksheet.		
You	65 or older ❏	Blind ❏
Your spouse, if claiming spouse's exemption	65 or older ❏	Blind ❏
Total number of boxes you checked	_____	
1. Enter your earned income. If none, go on to line 3.	1. _____	
1a. Additional amount allowed in 2006	1a. $300	
1b. Add lines 1 and 1a	1b. _____	
2. Minimum amount	2. $850	
3. Compare the amounts on lines 1b and 2. Enter the larger of the two amounts here.	3. _____	
4. Enter on line 4 the amount shown below for your filing status. Single, enter $5,150. Married filing separate return, enter $5,150. Married filing jointly or qualifying widow(er) with dependent child, enter $10,300. Head of household, enter $7,550.	4. _____	
5. Standard deduction 5a. Compare the amounts on lines 3 and 4. Enter the smaller of the two amounts here. If under 65 and not blind, stop here. This is your standard deduction; otherwise, go on to line 5b.	5a. _____	
5b. If 65 or older or blind, multiply $1,250 by the total number of boxes you checked; if married or qualifying widow(er) with dependent child, use $1,000. Enter the result here.	5b. _____	
5c. Add lines 5a and 5b. This is your standard deduction for 2006.	5c. _____	

Itemized Deductions

Some taxpayers simply compute their tax by using the standard deduction and don't even think about trying to complete Schedule A to compute the amount of their itemized deductions. If you think there is a chance that the total of your deductible expenses exceeds the standard deduction, try completing Schedule A. You may be pleasantly surprised to find that all your deductions do add up to a larger total deduction.

Here's your itemized deduction shopping list:

- Medical and dental expenses that exceed 7.5 percent of your AGI
- Taxes you paid
- Interest you paid
- Gifts to charity
- Casualty and theft losses
- Job-related, investment, and tax-preparation expenses that exceed 2 percent of your AGI
- Other miscellaneous itemized deductions not subject to the 2 percent limit. See the section on line 27 later in this chapter for an in-depth analysis of these types of deductions.

You claim these deductions on Form 1040 with Schedule A. You carry the total on line 28 over to Form 1040 (line 40) where you subtract it from your AGI.

Separate returns and limits on deductions

If you're married and filing separately, you both must itemize your deductions if one of you itemizes deductions, or you both must use the standard deduction. One spouse can't use the standard deduction while the other itemizes.

If you're divorced or legally separated, though, you're now considered single for income tax purposes, and you may make the best choice for yourself without regard to what your former spouse is doing. However, if you opt to itemize, you may claim only those expenses for which you are personally liable. For example, if a residence is in your former spouse's name and you paid the property taxes and the mortgage interest, you can't deduct them. If you were required to pay them under the terms of your divorce or separation agreement, but the property (and therefore the liability) was in your former spouse's name, these expenses wouldn't qualify as itemized deductions, but they may constitute deductible alimony.

Generally, if your home is jointly owned and your divorce or separation agreement requires that you make the mortgage payments, then one half of the payments can be deducted as alimony. Your former spouse reports one half of the payments as taxable alimony and is allowed to deduct one half of the mortgage interest if he or she itemizes his or her deductions. You get to deduct one half of the mortgage interest paid if the home is your residence (which isn't very likely). Payments to a third party (a bank, for example) are treated as received and then paid by your ex. The general rule we just recited for mortgage payments also applies to real estate taxes, provided the title to the home isn't held as *tenants by the entirety* or *in joint tenancy*. We explain the meaning of these legal terms in the alimony section in Chapter 7 and in the sidebar "Separate returns and real estate taxes," later in this chapter. But if you hold title in this manner, here are the rules: None of the payments for real estate taxes are considered alimony payments, and you get to deduct all the real estate taxes.

Deciding who gets to deduct what when a couple divorces is almost as bad as dividing the property. The alimony rules in Chapter 7 explain who gets to claim various deductions. To dig into this further, take a look at IRS Publication 504 *(Divorced or Separated Individuals)*. If you live in a community property state, the rules we just recited are different, so you may want to take a look at IRS Publication 555 *(Federal Tax Information on Community Property)*.

If you and your spouse are separated but don't have a decree of divorce or separate maintenance, you may be able to itemize or use the standard deduction and file as either single or head of household. You can do this if you didn't live with your spouse during the last six months of 2006, and if you maintained a home for more than half of 2006 for you and a child that you are entitled to claim as a dependent, you can use the head of household filing status.

But if you change your mind

Oops! Suppose that you discover you should have itemized after you already filed. Or even worse, suppose that you went to all the trouble to itemize but shouldn't have done so. Just amend your return by filing **Form 1040X, Amended U.S. Individual Income Tax Return.** But if you're married and you filed separately, you can't change your mind unless both you and your spouse make the same change. And if either of you must pay additional tax as a result of the change, you both need to file a consent. Remember that if one of you itemizes, the other no longer qualifies for the standard deduction.

Lines 1–4: Medical and Dental Costs

Your total medical and dental expenses (after what you were reimbursed by your health insurance policy and by pre-tax dollars from your Section 125 medical reimbursement account) must exceed 7.5 percent of your AGI (line 37 of your Form 1040). This detail knocks many people out of contention for this deduction. For example, if your AGI equals $30,000, you need to have at least $2,250 in medical and dental expenses. If you don't, you can cruise past these lines. (Because the threshold is so high, we hope, for your health's sake, that this is one deduction you *can't* take.)

You may deduct medical and dental expenses for you, your spouse, and your dependents. Because medical and dental deductions are claimed in the year in which they're paid, not the year in which the services were originally rendered, you may also be able to deduct the medical expenses of a person for whom you aren't claiming an exemption on your tax return for this year, but who was your dependent when the charges were incurred. If you're not sure whether you're eligible to deduct all the medical expenses you've paid this year, check out **IRS Publication 502, Medical and Dental Expenses,** for more information.

To claim the deduction, you fill in the amounts on lines 1 through 4 on Schedule A (see Figure 9-1). This rule means you can deduct the medical expenses you paid for your child, even though your ex-spouse is claiming him or her. For the purposes of the medical deduction, the child is considered the dependent of both parents (see the sidebar "Special cases — who gets the deduction?" later in this chapter).

Medical and dental expense checklist

Medical and dental expenses consist of more than having a physical and filling the occasional cavity. The list of what qualifies is long and involved, but if you suspect you have something that may qualify, read on.

Adoption and medical expenses

If you adopted a child, you can deduct the medical expenses you paid before the adoption if the child qualified as your dependent when the medical expenses were incurred or paid. If you have an agreement to pay an adoption agency or other persons for medical expenses they paid on behalf of the child, you can deduct the payment as a medical expense. But — bet you knew a *but* was coming — if you pay back medical expenses incurred and paid before the adoption negotiations began, sorry, no deduction.

SCHEDULES A&B	Schedule A—Itemized Deductions	OMB No. 1545-0074

Schedule A&B (Form 1040), Department of the Treasury Internal Revenue Service (99). Schedule A—Itemized Deductions (Schedule B is on back). ► Attach to Form 1040. ► See Instructions for Schedules A&B (Form 1040). OMB No. 1545-0074. 2006. Attachment Sequence No. 07.

Name(s) shown on Form 1040. Your social security number.

Medical and Dental Expenses

Caution. Do not include expenses reimbursed or paid by others.

1 Medical and dental expenses (see page A-2)
2 Enter amount from Form 1040, line 38 | 2 |
3 Multiply line 2 by 7.5% (.075)
4 Subtract line 3 from line 1. If line 3 is more than line 1, enter -0- ... 4

Taxes You Paid

(See page A-2.)

5 State and local income taxes | 5 |
6 Real estate taxes (see page A-5) | 6 |
7 Personal property taxes | 7 |
8 Other taxes. List type and amount ► | 8 |
9 Add lines 5 through 8 ... 9

Interest You Paid

(See page A-5.)

Note. Personal interest is not deductible.

10 Home mortgage interest and points reported to you on Form 1098 | 10 |
11 Home mortgage interest not reported to you on Form 1098. If paid to the person from whom you bought the home, see page A-6 and show that person's name, identifying no., and address ►

| 11 |
12 Points not reported to you on Form 1098. See page A-6 for special rules | 12 |
13 Investment interest. Attach Form 4952 if required. (See page A-6.) | 13 |
14 Add lines 10 through 13 ... 14

Gifts to Charity

If you made a gift and got a benefit for it, see page A-7.

15 Gifts by cash or check. If you made any gift of $250 or more, see page A-7 | 15 |
16 Other than by cash or check. If any gift of $250 or more, see page A-7. You **must** attach Form 8283 if over $500 | 16 |
17 Carryover from prior year | 17 |
18 Add lines 15 through 17 ... 18

Casualty and Theft Losses

19 Casualty or theft loss(es). Attach Form 4684. (See page A-8.) ... 19

Job Expenses and Certain Miscellaneous Deductions

(See page A-8.)

20 Unreimbursed employee expenses—job travel, union dues, job education, etc. Attach Form 2106 or 2106-EZ if required. (See page A-8.) ► | 20 |
21 Tax preparation fees | 21 |
22 Other expenses—investment, safe deposit box, etc. List type and amount ► | 22 |
23 Add lines 20 through 22 | 23 |
24 Enter amount from Form 1040, line 38 | 24 |
25 Multiply line 24 by 2% (.02) | 25 |
26 Subtract line 25 from line 23. If line 25 is more than line 23, enter -0- ... 26

Other Miscellaneous Deductions

27 Other—from list on page A-9. List type and amount ►

27

Total Itemized Deductions

28 Is Form 1040, line 38, over $150,500 (over $75,250 if married filing separately)?
☐ **No.** Your deduction is not limited. Add the amounts in the far right column for lines 4 through 27. Also, enter this amount on Form 1040, line 40. ►
☐ **Yes.** Your deduction may be limited. See page A-9 for the amount to enter.
28

29 If you elect to itemize deductions even though they are less than your standard deduction, check here ► ☐

For Paperwork Reduction Act Notice, see Form 1040 instructions. Cat. No. 11330X Schedule A (Form 1040) 2006

Draft as of 06/08/2006

Figure 9-1:
Use Schedule A to determine the itemized deductions that you can claim.

The following is a list of other items that are deductible, so remember to save all those bills:

✔ Ambulance service.

✔ Breast reconstruction surgery after a mastectomy.

✔ Birth control pills.

- Childbirth classes (but if your husband attends the classes as your coach, his portion of the fee isn't deductible).

- Drugs and medicines prescribed by a doctor.

- Electric wheelchairs (nonelectric ones as well) and electric carts such as The Rascal that you see advertised on TV, including their upkeep and operating cost, are deductible medical expenses. The cost of hand controls or special equipment for a car so a handicapped person can operate it may also be deducted.

- Expenses in obtaining an egg donor.

- Guide dog.

- Hospital bills.

- Laboratory fees and tests.

- Laser eye surgery, including corrective procedures such as LASIK and radial keratotomy. This surgery is deductible because it corrects an eye problem even though a pair of glasses would, arguably, cost considerably less.

- Legal abortion.

- Medical equipment and supplies, crutches, bandages, and diagnosis devices such as blood sugar kits sold over the counter, even though over-the-counter medicines aren't deductible.

- Medical equipment or modifications to your home for needed medical care.

- Medical, hospital, and dental insurance premiums that you pay (but you can't deduct premiums paid by your employer, and you may not deduct premiums that you pay with pretax dollars); don't overlook premiums deducted from your paycheck. This includes a portion of your long-term health-care premiums (flip ahead to insurance premiums for the amounts).

- Medical services (doctors, dentists, opticians, podiatrists, registered nurses, practical nurses, psychiatrists, and so on).

- Oxygen equipment and oxygen.

- Part of life-care fee paid to a retirement home designated for medical care.

- Sexual dysfunction treatment.

- Special school or home for a mentally or physically handicapped person.

- Special items (artificial limbs, contact lenses, and so on).

- Stop-smoking programs. The cost of prescription drugs to alleviate nicotine withdrawal also qualifies as a medical expense, but over-the-counter nicotine gum and patches don't. When will the IRS ever stop making these types of distinctions? A foolish question, we guess, because the IRS is in the business of splitting hairs.

- Transportation for medical care.

- Treatment at a drug or alcohol clinic.

- Wages and Social Security tax paid for worker providing medical care.

- Wages for nursing service.

- Weight-loss programs rooted in a diagnosis of obesity or another disease. However, the restriction against deducting weight reduction costs for purely cosmetic reasons hasn't been lifted. That means you can't deduct the cost of going to Weight Watchers to lose a little weight so you'll look amazing at your 25th class reunion.

Special cases — who gets the deduction?

Sometimes, when two or more people support someone, special rules apply to determine who can claim the medical expenses that were paid.

One tricky case is that of divorced and separated parents. A divorced or separated parent can deduct the medical expenses he or she paid for a child's medical costs — even if the child's other parent is entitled to claim the child as a dependent.

For the purposes of claiming medical expenses, a child is considered the dependent of both parents if all the following conditions are met:

✔ The parents were legally separated or divorced or were married and living apart for the last six months of 2006.

✔ Both parents provided more than half the child's support in 2006.

✔ Either spouse had custody of the child for more than half of 2006.

Just like alcohol or drug treatment addiction programs, where an individual often has to travel away from home to seek treatment, the limited $50 a day deduction for lodging can be claimed for a stay at a weight-reduction clinic. Reduced-calorie diet foods aren't deductible. They are considered a substitute for a person's normal diet.

What about deducting health clubs? Here's the general rule: Health club costs are only considered a deductible medical expense when prescribed by a physician to aid in the treatment of a specific disease or ailment. Remember, though, that obesity is now classified as a disease. Ask your doctor for that all-important prescription and then keep it with all your other income tax documents.

Be aware that many medical and dental expenses can't be deducted. Surprisingly, a number of expenses that you make to improve your health, which should reduce your medical expenses, aren't deductible. You can't deduct these things:

✔ Diaper service

✔ Funeral expenses

✔ Health club or spa dues for activities and services that merely improve your general health

✔ Household help (even if recommended by a doctor)

✔ Life insurance premiums

✔ Maternity clothes

✔ Medical insurance included in a car insurance policy covering all persons injured in or by the car

✔ Nursing care for a healthy baby

✔ Over-the-counter medicines (except insulin); aspirin to relieve pain; toothpaste; toiletries; and cosmetics

✔ Social activities (such as swimming or dancing lessons)

✔ Surgery for purely cosmetic reasons (such as face-lifts, tummy tucks, and so on) — plastic surgery required as the result of an accident is deductible

✔ Teeth whitening — to the IRS, it merely improves a person's attractiveness and doesn't serve to treat an ailment

✔ Trips for general health improvement

Deductible travel costs

The cost of traveling to your doctor or a medical facility for treatment is deductible. If you use your car, you can deduct a flat rate of 18 cents per mile for trips made during 2006. Or you can deduct your actual out-of-pocket expenses for gas, oil, and repairs. You can also deduct parking and tolls. You can't deduct depreciation, insurance, or general repairs.

Deductible travel costs to seek medical treatment aren't limited to just local auto and cab trips — a trip to see a specialist in another city also qualifies for the deduction. Unfortunately, though, transportation costs incurred when you're not going to and from a doctor's office or a hospital are a deduction the IRS likes to challenge (maybe because many taxpayers tried to deduct as a medical expense travel to a warm climate, claiming health reasons!). The cost of transportation to a mild climate to relieve a specific condition is deductible — but the airfare to Arizona, for example, for general health reasons isn't.

Trips to visit an institutionalized child have been allowed when a doctor prescribed the visits.

Travel expenses of a nurse or another person who has to accompany an individual to obtain medical care because he or she can't travel alone are deductible.

In a recent ruling, the IRS said it would allow the deduction for the cost of a medical conference and the travel to get there. This stipulation is a victory for anyone with a chronic illness, or worse, anyone with a child with a chronic illness who knows the frustration of trying to find answers that are often beyond the knowledge of the physician treating the illness. Now if you need to go to a medical conference to find out about the latest treatment options, the cost of the conference and the travel to get there are deductible. Meals and lodging aren't.

Another complicated case is that of a *multiple-support agreement* in which two or more people together provide more than half of a person's total support — but no one on his or her own provides more than half. Such an agreement allows one and only one of the individuals to claim the exemption for the person (even without providing more than half the support). If you are the person entitled to claim the exemption under the agreement, you can deduct the medical expenses you pay. But any other taxpayers who also paid medical expenses can't deduct them.

Special medical expense situations

The deductibility of a medical expense depends on the nature of the services rendered and not on the qualifications, title, or experience of the person providing the service. This means that payments to an unlicensed medical provider are deductible if the provider renders medical care that isn't illegal.

When an expense is generally considered nonmedical, the burden falls on the taxpayer to prove that it meets the definition of a medical expense, which is especially true for expenses incurred for massages, yoga lessons, water filtration systems, and health centers.

Just like every other section of our tax laws, what qualifies as a medical deduction can get hopelessly complex. Here are a few examples:

- You can't deduct marijuana used for medical purposes in violation of federal law, even though you obtained a prescription for it as required under state law.

- You can deduct the cost of a wig purchased on the advice of a doctor to benefit the mental health of a patient who lost all hair as the result of a disease.

✔ You can deduct vitamins only when prescribed by a doctor as part of a treatment for a specific ailment and not merely for nutritional needs.

✔ Special foods that serve as supplements to a regular diet qualify as a medical expense only when prescribed by a doctor to treat a specific ailment. You can't deduct a special diet if it's part of the regular nutritional needs of a person. For instance, diabetics can't deduct the cost of food that doesn't contain sugar. Their sugarless diet merely acts as a substitute for the nutritional needs of a normal diet.

Get the picture? The IRS gives nothing away.

Meals and lodging

Your bill at a hospital or similar institution is fully deductible. That's the *whole* bill, including meals and lodging. You may be able to deduct as a medical expense the cost of lodging not provided in a hospital while you're away from your home if you meet all the following requirements:

✔ The lodging is necessary for your medical care.

✔ A doctor provides the medical care in a medical facility.

✔ The lodging isn't extravagant.

✔ No significant element of personal pleasure, recreation, or vacation is involved in the travel.

The amount that you can deduct as a medical expense for lodging can't exceed $50 a night for you and $50 a night for anyone accompanying you. Only meals that are part of a hospital bill are deductible.

Insurance premiums

Health insurance premiums that you pay that cover hospital, medical, and dental expenses; prescription drugs; and eyeglasses and the replacement of lost or damaged contact lenses are deductible as medical expenses provided that the money you use to pay those premiums is included in your AGI. So is the monthly *Part B and Part D Medicare* premium that gets deducted from your Social Security check. Based on your age, a limited portion of the premium for long-term healthcare also is deductible.

Here are the deductible amounts for long-term healthcare premiums:

Age	Deductible
40 or less	$280
More than 40, but not more than 50	$530
More than 50, but not more than 60	$1,060
More than 60, but not more than 70	$2,830
More than 70	$3,530

Reimbursements and damages

You must reduce your medical expenses by what you were reimbursed under your health insurance policy and from Medicare. Payments that you received for loss of earnings or damages for personal injury or sickness aren't considered reimbursement under a health insurance policy and don't have to be deducted from your medical expenses. If the total reimbursement you received during the year is the same as or more than your total medical expenses for the year, you can't claim a medical deduction.

If you are reimbursed in a later year for medical expenses you deducted in an earlier year, you must report as income the amount you received up to the amount you previously deducted as a medical expense. Your reimbursement isn't taxable if you didn't deduct the expense in the year you paid it because you took the standard deduction or because your medical expenses were less than 7.5 percent of your AGI.

If you receive an amount in settlement of a personal injury suit, the part that is for medical expenses deducted in an earlier year is taxable if your medical deduction in the earlier year reduced your income tax.

In 1997, the IRS ruled that medical expenses or premiums paid by an employer for an employee's domestic partner or the domestic partner's dependent(s) are taxable to the employee and not a tax-free employee fringe benefit. If you live in a state that recognizes domestic partners, civil unions, or same-sex marriages, you may be able to include these premiums on your state income tax return if your state tax calculation allows itemized deductions. Check it out carefully before you file.

Special schooling

You can deduct as a medical expense the cost of sending a mentally or physically handicapped child or dependent to a special school to help him or her overcome a handicap. The school must have a special program geared to the child's specific needs. The total costs, transportation, meals and lodging, and tuition qualify. The types of schools that qualify are ones that do the following things:

- Teach Braille or lip reading
- Help cure dyslexia
- Treat and care for the mentally handicapped
- Treat individuals with similar handicaps

Nursing home

You can include in medical expenses the cost of medical care in a nursing home or home for the aged for yourself, your spouse, or your dependents. This deduction includes the cost of meals and lodging in the home if the main reason for being there is to get medical care. But you can't deduct nonmedical care expenses. For example, if a person enters a nursing home because he or she can't prepare meals or take care of personal needs, then that person can't take a deduction.

You can't deduct the cost of meals and lodging if the reason for being in the home is personal and nonmedical (such as taking up residence in a retirement home). You can, however, include as a deductible medical expense the part of the cost that is for medical or nursing care.

Nursing homes, rest homes, assisted-living facilities, and the like are all accustomed to breaking out their charges into medical and nonmedical amounts. If you're unsure how much of these payments to include on Schedule A, be sure to ask the facility's administrator or billing staff for some guidance.

Improvements to your home

You can deduct as a medical expense the cost of installing equipment and making improvements to your home to help treat a disease or ailment. For example, you can deduct the cost of an air conditioner because you suffer from allergies or asthma. But if the equipment or improvement increases the value of your home, your deduction is limited to the cost of the equipment or improvement minus the increase in the value to your home.

Be prepared to have a battle when making a large improvement to your home for medical reasons. Unless you arrive at the audit in a wheelchair with tears streaming down your cheeks, don't expect an overly sympathetic IRS. On the other hand, deductions for swimming pools have been allowed as a form of therapy in treating a severe ailment or disease. But improvements that merely help improve someone's general health (such as a hot tub or workout room) aren't deductible.

The increase-in-value test for a home doesn't apply to handicapped persons. Modifying stairs and doorways; building ramps, railings, and support bars; and adapting a home to the special needs of the handicapped are allowed. Chairlifts, but not elevators, are also part of the no-increase-in-value category.

Figuring your medical and dental deduction

Your deductible medical and dental expenses equal the total expenses that you've paid minus what you were reimbursed by your insurance policy. The result is then reduced by 7.5 percent of your AGI.

For example, if your medical and dental expenses for the tax year were $4,500 and that your health insurance company reimbursed $500 of that amount, you then have $4,000 of unreimbursed medical expenses. Enter $4,000 on line 1 of Schedule A. On line 2, you enter your AGI from Form 1040 (line 38). On line 3, you enter 7.5 percent of your AGI (if your AGI is $40,000; you would enter $3,000 — that's $40,000 ÷ 0.075). Subtract this amount from the medical expenses reported on line 1 of Schedule A and stick the remainder ($1,000) on line 4.

Lines 5–9: Taxes You Paid

As a general rule, you may deduct only the following tax payments made during the tax year:

- ✔ State and local income taxes
- ✔ Local real estate taxes
- ✔ State and local personal property taxes
- ✔ Other taxes (such as foreign income taxes)

Federal income and Social Security taxes aren't deductible.

Line 5: State and local income taxes

This deduction consists of two elements: the amount of state and local taxes withheld from your salary (boxes 17 and 19 of your W-2) and what you paid in 2006 when you filed your 2005 state tax return. If you made estimated state and local income tax payments in 2006, they're also deductible. You can also deduct taxes relating to a prior year that you paid in 2006.

If you applied your 2005 refund on your state return as a payment toward your estimated 2006 state tax, that's also considered a deductible tax payment. However, if you deducted that amount on your 2005 income tax return, you also have to report the amount as taxable income on Form 1040 (line 10).

Enter the total of your state and local tax payments from boxes 17 and 19 of your W-2(s) on line 5 of Schedule A. Also enter on this line your state and local estimated income tax payments that you made in 2006. And don't forget to add the balance that you paid on your 2005 return. For residents of California, New Jersey, or New York, mandatory payments that you made to your state's disability fund are also deductible. So are disability payments to Rhode Island's temporary fund or Washington State's supplemental workers' compensation fund.

Line 6: Real estate taxes

You can deduct real estate taxes you paid during the year, whether you write a check directly to your city or town or if you place an amount into escrow with the bank that holds your mortgage and the bank pays your taxes.

Calculating the amount of your deduction for real estate taxes is easy! If you pay your tax check(s) directly to your city or town clerk or tax collector, just add up the total you paid in 2006 and insert that number on line 6. If you escrowed your real estate taxes with your mortgage company, your mortgage company will send you an annual mortgage statement in January that tells you how much the company paid to your city or town clerk or tax collector on your behalf. That's the number you put on line 6.

Cooperative apartment

Tenants or stockholders of a cooperative housing corporation may deduct their share of the real estate taxes paid by the corporation. The corporation will furnish you with a statement at the end of the year, indicating the amount of the deduction you're entitled to claim.

Special assessments

Water, sewer, and garbage pickup aren't deductible because they're considered nondeductible personal charges — and so are charges by a homeowners' association. Assessments by the local tax authorities to put in a new street, sewer system, or sidewalks aren't deductible. These types of assessments are added to the tax basis of your home. Either your annual mortgage statement from your bank or the tax collector's bill will indicate whether you're paying a special assessment or a real estate tax.

When you buy or sell real estate

When real estate is bought or sold, the buyer and the seller apportion the real estate taxes between them. This stuff is done at the closing when the buyer and seller are furnished a settlement statement. For example, suppose that you paid $1,000 in real estate taxes for the year on January 1. On June 30, you sell the property. At the time of the sale, your settlement statement should reflect a payment or credit from the buyer for the property taxes you already paid for the remainder of the year. This is how the buyer pays you for the taxes you've effectively paid on his or her behalf for the remainder of the year when the buyer will be in the home. Therefore, you can deduct only the taxes you paid ($1,000) minus what the buyer reimbursed you ($500). That means you deduct only $500 in real estate taxes for the year on line 6 of Schedule A.

You can find this information on your settlement statement and in box 5 of **Form 1099-S, Proceeds from Real Estate Transactions.** The 1099-S is normally issued to you when you sell your home. However, under the new law not all home sales have to be reported on 1099-S. See Chapter 12 for more about this issue.

If the buyer pays back taxes (in other words, taxes that the property seller owed from the time he or she actually owned the home) at the closing or at a later date, they can't be deducted. They are added to the cost of the property. The seller can deduct back taxes paid by the buyer from the sales price when computing the profit that has to be reported on Schedule D (Form 1040). See Chapter 12 for information about handling the sale of your home.

The downside of property tax refunds and rebates

If you receive a refund or rebate in 2006 for real estate taxes you paid in 2006, you must reduce your itemized deductions that you're claiming for real estate taxes by the amount refunded to you. For example, if you paid $2,000 in property taxes during the year and also received a $300 refund because of a reduction in your tax that was retroactively granted, you may claim only $1,700 as the deduction for real estate taxes.

If you received a refund or rebate in 2006 for real estate taxes that you took as an itemized deduction on Schedule A in an earlier year, you must include the refund or rebate as income in the year you receive it. Enter this amount on your 1040 (line 21). In the unlikely event that your refund exceeds what you paid in taxes during the year, you need to include only the portion of the refund up to the amount of the deduction you took in the earlier year. For example, if you claimed a $500 deduction in 2005 and received a $600 rebate in 2006, only $500 of the rebate is taxable. If you didn't itemize your deductions in 2005, you don't have to report the refund as income in 2006.

Line 7: Personal property taxes

Personal property taxes, both state and local, are deductible if the tax charged is based on the value of the personal property. Usually, you pay personal property taxes based on the value of your car and motorboat.

In most states, a registration fee is assessed on cars. These fees aren't deductible unless the fees are based on the car's value. The state agency that invoices you for this fee should state what portion, if any, of the fee, is based on the car's value.

Don't get confused. This section doesn't cover business taxes; they belong on Schedule C. And if you pay sales tax on the purchase of equipment for business use, you can't deduct the sales tax separately; it's added to the cost of the asset, which is depreciated on Schedules C and E.

Separate returns and real estate taxes

When a couple decides to file separate returns, deducting real estate taxes becomes a complicated matter. That's because the deduction is based on how the title to the property is held. If the title is in your spouse's name and you paid the real estate taxes, neither of you can claim a deduction. If your payment is required as a result of your divorce or separation decree, the payment may qualify as an alimony deduction (see Chapter 7).

If property is owned by a husband or wife as *tenants by the entirety* or as *joint tenants* (which means the survivor

inherits the other's share), either spouse can deduct the amount of taxes paid. If the property is held as tenants in common (each owner's share goes to his or her heirs at his or her death), each spouse may deduct his or her share of the taxes paid. However, the rules are somewhat different in community property states; see IRS Publication 555 *(Federal Tax Information on Community Property)*.

Line 8: Other taxes (foreign income taxes)

You can deduct foreign taxes you paid (along with your state or local income taxes) as an itemized deduction on Schedule A, or you can claim a credit for foreign taxes by filing **Form 1116, Foreign Taxes.** *Note:* If your foreign income wasn't subject to U.S. tax (because it was excluded under the $82,400 foreign earned income allowance), you can't claim a deduction or a credit for any foreign taxes paid on the income that you didn't pay U.S. tax on.

As a concession to taxpayers and in recognition of the truly incomprehensible nature of the Form 1116, the IRS allows taxpayers who have $600 or less of foreign tax paid, if married filing joint, or $300 or less for everyone else, to enter the full amount of their foreign tax paid on line 47 of your Form 1040. No Form 1116 is needed here.

In case you're asking yourself what foreign taxes have to do with you, the answer is that if you invested in a mutual fund that invests overseas, the fund may end up paying foreign taxes on some of your dividends. It seems more people are investing in these types of funds than ever before. If your mutual fund paid any foreign taxes, you'll find that information in box 6 of **Form 1099-DIV** that you received.

You can either deduct the foreign tax you paid on this line of Schedule A or claim a credit on Form 1040 (line 47). A deduction reduces your taxable income. A credit reduces the actual tax you owe. So if you're in the 25 percent tax bracket, claiming a deduction for $100 of foreign taxes will reduce your tax bill by $25. On the other hand, if you claim the $100 you paid as a foreign tax credit, you reduce your tax liability by $100, because credits are subtracted directly from the tax you owe.

Lines 10–14: Interest You Paid

The IRS allows you to deduct interest on certain types of loans. According to the IRS, acceptable loans include some (but not all) mortgage loans and investment loans. Interest incurred for consumer debt, such as on credit cards and auto loans — so-called *personal interest,* isn't deductible. Business interest isn't deducted as an itemized deduction; it's deducted from your business income on Schedule C (see Chapter 11).

You can't deduct interest on taxes you owe. It's worth noting, however, that corporations can deduct interest on tax assessments. Doesn't it seem that everyone is allowed a special tax break but you?

Lines 10–11: Home mortgage interest and points reported to you on Form 1098

You can deduct mortgage interest on your main home and a second or vacation home. Why two? We think it's because most representatives in Congress own two homes — one in Washington and one in their district! It doesn't matter whether the loan on which you're paying interest is a mortgage, a second mortgage, a line of credit, or a home equity loan. The interest is deductible as long as your homes serve as collateral for the loan.

Where is the data?

If you paid mortgage interest of $600 or more during the year on any one mortgage, you will receive a **Form 1098, Mortgage Interest Statement,** from your mortgage lender, showing the total interest you paid during the year. Enter the amount from Box 1 of Form 1098 on line 10 of your Schedule A. Enter mortgage interest not reported on a 1098 on line 11. If you purchased a main home during 2006, Form 1098 reports the deductible points you paid. If you paid points that weren't reported on Form 1098, enter the amount on line 12. (If you paid less than $600 in mortgage interest, see your lender.) If the points were reported on Form 1098 (Box 2), add this amount to the interest you are deducting on line 10. The tax treatment of points paid when refinancing a mortgage is discussed on the next page.

You can deduct late payment charges as home mortgage interest. You find these charges on your annual mortgage statement.

If you can pay down your mortgage more quickly than required, don't assume that doing so is not in your best financial interests just because of the deductions allowed for it (see Chapter 23). If you are charged a prepayment penalty, you can deduct that as additional interest.

Limitations on deductions

In most cases, you will be able to deduct all your home mortgage interest. Whether all of it is deductible depends on the date you took out the mortgage, the amount of the mortgage, and how the proceeds from the mortgage loan were used.

Interest on mortgage loans of up to $1 million taken out after October 13, 1987, to buy, build, or improve a first or second home is deductible. Your main home is the home you live in most of the time. It can be a house, a condominium, a cooperative apartment, a mobile home, a boat, or similar property. It must provide basic living accommodations including sleeping space, toilet facilities, and cooking facilities. Your second or vacation home is similar property that you select to be your second home.

In addition, interest on a home equity loan of up to $100,000 taken out after October 13, 1987, is deductible regardless of how the money is used. (Cut these amounts in half if you are married and file a separate return.) The proceeds of a home equity loan don't have to be used to buy, build, or improve your home. They can be used to pay off bills, pay college tuition, or take a vacation.

Interest on a home-improvement loan isn't deductible if it isn't a mortgage loan. The rule is simple: no mortgage, no interest deduction. So if a relative lends you money to buy a home, any interest that you pay isn't deductible unless the relative secures that loan with a mortgage on your house.

Interest on mortgages of any size is tax deductible if you took out your mortgage before October 14, 1987, and you still retain that mortgage. If you've refinanced into a new mortgage since this magical date, you may be out of luck if you refinanced the mortgage for more than you owed prior to refinancing. On the other hand, you're probably saving a bundle because of reductions in your interest rate.

We can think of several reasons why you shouldn't treat the equity in your home like a piggy bank. One reason is that you may find yourself caught in the Alternative Minimum Tax (AMT). Although interest on home mortgages, including home equity debt, is deductible on Schedule A, you may only deduct the amount of interest attributable to the original purchase of your home, as adjusted for additions and improvements to your home, when calculating your AMT. If you've refinanced your mortgage to free up cash to pay for tuitions or cars, or to pay off your credit card debt, you aren't allowed to deduct the interest on that portion of your loan for AMT purposes. Check out Chapter 8 for more information on the AMT.

Interest on refinanced loans

If you refinanced a mortgage on your first or second home for the remaining balance of the old mortgage, you're safe. If the interest on the old mortgage was fully deductible, the interest on the new mortgage is also fully deductible. To the extent of the remaining balance of the old mortgage, the new mortgage is considered a mortgage used to acquire, build, or improve a home.

But, if you refinanced your old mortgage for more than its remaining balance, the deductibility of the mortgage interest on the new loan depends on how you use the excess funds and the amount you refinanced. If the excess is used to improve, build, or buy a first or second home, and the excess plus all other mortgage loans is under $1 million, the interest on the new loan is fully deductible. If any of the excess of a new mortgage loan isn't used to build, buy, or improve your home, the excess is applied to your $100,000 home equity limit. If the excess is under $100,000, you're safe and it's fully deductible. The interest on the part that exceeds $100,000 isn't deductible.

Mixed-use mortgages

You don't need one mortgage to meet the requirement that the mortgage was taken out to buy, build, or improve your home and then one to meet the $100,000 home equity requirement. One mortgage can be considered both, hence the term mixed-use.

Points

The term *points* is used to describe certain upfront charges that a borrower pays to obtain a mortgage. One point equals 1 percent of the loan amount financed. For example, if the loan is for $200,000, two points equal a $4,000 charge. You can deduct the amount you paid in points in 2006 if the loan was used to buy or build your main residence. The points you pay on a second home have to be deducted over the term of the loan.

Points are sometimes referred to as *loan origination fees, processing fees, maximum loan charges,* or *premium charges.* Look for these charges on the settlement statement that the lender (by law) has to provide you.

Points on refinancing

The points paid to refinance a mortgage on a main home aren't usually deductible in full in the year you pay them — even if the new mortgage is secured by your main home. However, if you use part of the refinanced mortgage to improve your main home and you pay the points instead of paying them from the proceeds of the new loan, you can deduct in full (in the year paid) the part of the points related to the improvement. But you must deduct the remainder of the points over the life of the loan. For example, suppose that the remaining balance of your mortgage is $100,000. You take out a new mortgage for $150,000 and use

$25,000 for improvements to your home, $25,000 for personal purposes, and $100,000 to pay off the old loan. The points on the $25,000 used for improvements are deductible in 2006. The points on the $100,000 used to pay off the remaining $100,000 balance of the old mortgage have to be written off over the term of the new loan. The points on the $25,000 used for personal purposes can't be deducted. The $25,000 wasn't used to buy, build, or improve your home. The only way the interest on this $25,000 can be deducted is if it's applied toward your allowance to deduct interest on the first $100,000 on a home equity loan.

Say that you refinanced your home three years ago and you're writing off the points you paid over the 25-year term of the mortgage. If you refinance your mortgage again in 2006, the points remaining to be written off on your old mortgage can be written off in full in 2006. Enter this amount on line 12. The points on your new refinanced loan have to be deducted over the term of the new mortgage.

A penalty for paying off a mortgage early is deductible if the loan qualified for the mortgage interest deduction (the mortgage loan was used to buy, build, or improve your main home).

Seller-paid points

Sometimes, desperate times call for desperate measures. So if the seller pays the points that the buyer normally does, the buyer gets a double windfall. The buyer not only gets the seller to pay the points, but the buyer also gets to deduct them. The buyer also has to subtract the points deducted from the tax basis of the home. Although the seller paid the points, the seller can't deduct them. The points the seller paid are deducted from the selling price.

So if you're a buyer who had the seller pay the points on the purchase of your home but didn't deduct them, you can still do so by filing a **Form 1040X, Amended Return.** But you have to take this step before the three-year statute of limitations expires (see Chapter 18), or you can kiss any refund goodbye. When you file Form 1040X, write "Seller paid points" on the upper-right corner of the form.

Don't overlook your out-of-pocket expenditures

A commonly overlooked deductible charitable expense is your out-of-pocket expenses (money spent) incurred while doing volunteer work for a charity.

For example, you can deduct out-of-pocket expenses (such as gas and oil, but probably not rest-stop candy bars!) that are directly related to the use of your car in charitable work. You can't deduct anything like general repair or maintenance expenses, tires, insurance, depreciation, and so on. If you don't want to track and deduct your actual expenses, you can use a standard rate of 14 cents a mile to figure your contribution (unless you were driving on Hurricane Katrina–related charitable work, in which case your deduction leaps to 32 cents per mile). You can deduct actual expenses for parking fees and tolls. If you must travel away from home to perform a real and substantial service, such as attending a convention for a qualified charitable organization, you can claim a deduction for your unreimbursed travel and transportation expenses, including meals and lodging. If you get a daily allowance (per diem) for travel expenses while providing services for a charitable organization, you must include as income the amount that is more than your travel expenses. Of course, you can deduct your travel expenses that are more than the allowance.

There's one restriction on these deductions: They're allowed only if there is *no significant amount* of personal pleasure derived from your travel. What is the limit the IRS sets on personal pleasure? Well, we can't find an IRS chart, but we can at least assure you that the IRS allows you to enjoy your trip without automatically disqualifying you from this deduction. The IRS doesn't mind if you decide to do some sightseeing, but you can't deduct expenses for your spouse or children who may accompany you. If you go to a church convention as a church member rather than as a representative of the church, you can't deduct your expenses.

You can deduct the cost and upkeep of uniforms that you must wear while doing volunteer work — as long as these uniforms are unsuitable for everyday use. A Boy or Girl Scout uniform, for example, wouldn't be the type of clothing you would wear just anywhere!

Line 12: Points not reported to you on Form 1098

If the points you paid, for some reason, weren't reported on the 1098, based on the rules in the two preceding sections, you'll have to compute this amount on your own. If the points were for the purchase or improvement of your principal residence, you can deduct the points in 2006. If they were for refinancing or for your second home, you have to deduct them over the term of the mortgage. Hunting for this information isn't all that difficult. When the loan was made, you were given a settlement statement by the lender indicating the points you paid.

Line 13: Investment interest

When you borrow against the value of securities held in a brokerage account, the interest paid on what is referred to as a margin loan is deductible. This deduction, however, can't exceed your total investment income. If it does, the excess is carried forward and deducted from next year's investment income — or carried over to future years until it can be deducted. You use **Form 4952, Investment Interest,** to compute the deduction and carry over the result to Schedule A (line 13).

Investment income for the purpose of this deduction includes income from interest, nonqualified dividends (read more in Chapter 10), annuities, and royalties. It doesn't include income from rental real estate or from a *passive activity* (a passive activity — see Chapter 13 — is IRS jargon for a business deal or venture in which you are a silent partner). The following aren't usually considered investment income:

✔ If you borrow money to buy or carry tax-exempt bonds, you can't deduct any interest on the loan as investment-interest expense. If 20 percent of your portfolio consists of tax-exempt bonds, 20 percent of your margin interest on your security account isn't deductible.

✔ Although long-term capital gains and qualified dividends aren't usually considered investment income, you can choose to treat them as investment income in order to deduct the entire amount of the interest you paid on your margin account. There is a trade-off, however. You have to reduce the amount of your capital gains and qualified dividends that are eligible for the maximum long-term capital gain rate (5 or 15 percent, depending on your tax bracket) by the amount of your capital gains and/or qualified dividends you are treating as investment income. For example, suppose you have $2,000 of investment interest paid, $1,000 of investment income, and $10,000 of long-term capital gains and qualified dividends. You may elect to deduct the full $2,000 of investment interest in 2005 if you treat $1,000 of your long-term capital gain and qualified dividends as investment income. Of course, this now means that you receive the preferential tax rate on long-term capital gains and qualified dividends on only $9,000, not $10,000.

✔ Interest expense incurred in a passive activity such as rental real estate, a limited partnership, or an S Corporation isn't considered investment-interest expense unless it is separately stated as "investment interest" on the Schedule K-1 you receive. If your K-1 shows separately stated investment interest, fill out your Form 4952 and claim your deduction on line 13 of Schedule A. Any other type of interest expense shown on your K-1 may be deducted only from your passive-activity income.

Student loan interest isn't investment interest, although we think education is one of the best investments you can make. Even so, you can deduct up to $2,500 of student loan interest, and you don't even have to itemize your deductions. The deduction is claimed as an adjustment to your income along with the other adjustments we discuss in Chapter 7, in the section on line 33.

Here's the fine print on student loan interest: Your income can't exceed $50,000 ($105,000 for joint filers); above these amounts, the deduction gets phased out. So at the $65,000 income level if you're single, and the $135,000 income level if you're married, you can kiss this deduction goodbye.

Lines 15–18: Gifts to Charity

You can deduct your charitable contributions, but the amount of your deduction may be limited, and you must follow a number of strict rules. One good turn doesn't always deserve another!

After you understand the types of things you can and can't deduct, completing this section is a snap. Qualifying contributions that you make by cash and check are totaled and entered on line 15, and those made other than by cash and check (for example, you donate your old *Taxes For Dummies* books to charity when new editions come out) are entered on line 16.

If you make out a check at the end of the year and mail it by December 31, you can deduct your contribution even if the charity doesn't receive the check until January. If you charge a contribution on your credit card, you get to deduct it in the year you charged it — even if you don't pay off the charge until the following year.

If you signed up for a program where a percentage of your credit-card purchases is donated to charity, remember to deduct what the credit-card company paid on your behalf.

Qualifying charities

You can deduct your contributions only if you make them to a qualified organization. To become a *qualified* organization, most organizations (other than churches) must apply to the IRS. To find out whether an organization qualifies, just ask the organization for its tax-exemption certificate.

If for some reason you doubt that an organization qualifies, you can check IRS Publication 78 *(Cumulative List of Organizations)*. Most libraries have Publication 78. You also can call the IRS toll-free tax help telephone number (800-829-3676) to request this publication. If you're Internet-savvy, you can visit the IRS Web site at www.irs.gov and type Publication 78 in the window "Search for Forms and Publication." Click on Publication 78 and then "Search Now," where you can find out whether the charity is a qualified one. Nearly all the tax-exempt charities are listed. If that doesn't work, search www.guidestar.org.

Contributions that you make to the following charitable organizations are generally deductible:

- ✔ Nonprofit schools
- ✔ Organizations such as CARE, the Red Cross, the Salvation Army, Goodwill Industries, the Girl and Boy Scouts, and so on
- ✔ Public park and recreational facilities
- ✔ Religious organizations, including churches, synagogues, mosques, and so on. Keep track of how much money you're putting into the collection plate (and pay by check, if you can). If your church, synagogue, or mosque charges dues, the dues also fall into the charitable donation category.

✔ War veterans' groups

✔ Your federal, state, and local government — if your charitable contribution is only for public purposes

Some people tithe (pay 10 percent of their income) to their church, synagogue, or mosque, and don't think twice about it. Remember, if you're tithing, make sure you include your tithes and take the full amount of your deduction!

If it's your habit to put cash in the collection plate at church or give a cash donation when a charitable solicitor comes to your door, you may want to rethink this strategy if you're planning on claiming these contributions as a charitable donation in 2007. New rules now state that, for tax years beginning after August 17, 2006 (which means the year beginning January 1, 2007 for most individuals), if you can't substantiate your contributions, you can't take them. What constitutes substantiation? Your cancelled check (or a copy of it provided by the bank) works. So does a receipt from the charity or a credit card charge. It doesn't make any difference if you make donations in cash or in kind — you need the substantiation. So now, you may want to cultivate a new habit and put a check in the collection plate instead of cash.

Nonqualifying charities

Generally speaking, contributions or donations made to causes or organizations that just benefit the organization, as opposed to the greater society, aren't deductible. The following are examples of organizations or groups for which you can't deduct contributions:

✔ Dues paid to country clubs, lodges, orders, and so on

✔ Foreign charities (but you can deduct contributions to a U.S. charity that transfers funds to a foreign charity — if the U.S. charity controls the use of the funds). Contributions to charities in Canada, Israel, and Mexico are deductible if the charity meets the same tests that qualify U.S. organizations to receive deductible contributions.

✔ Groups that lobby for law changes (such as changes to the tax code!)

The IRS doesn't want you to deduct contributions to organizations from which you may benefit — so include bingo and raffle tickets in this forbidden group.

✔ Homeowners' associations

✔ Individuals

Big surprise here! So don't try to deduct what you gave to your brother-in-law, because he doesn't count in the eyes of the IRS! The contribution can be to a qualified organization that helps needy and worthy individuals — like your brother-in-law.

✔ Labor unions

But union dues are deductible as an itemized deduction subject to the 2 percent AGI limit on Schedule A.

✔ Lottery ticket costs (gee, we wonder why not?)

✔ Members of the clergy who can spend the money as they want

✔ Political groups or candidates running for public office

✔ Social and sport clubs

✔ Tuition to attend private or parochial schools

This list can go on and on — didn't you suspect that a list of nonqualifying charities would be longer than a list of qualifying ones? — but we think you get the idea. So don't try to deduct the value of your blood donated at a blood bank, and don't even think about trying to deduct your contribution to your college fraternity or sorority!

Contributions of property

Generally, you can deduct the *fair market value (FMV)* of property given to a charity. FMV is the price at which property would change hands between a willing buyer and a willing seller. So if you bought a painting for $2,000 that's worth $10,000 when you donate it to a museum, you can deduct $10,000.

You can use the FMV only if — on the date of the contribution — the property would have produced a long-term capital gain or loss if it had been sold (property held more than one year). If you donate property you held for one year or less or you donate ordinary income property, your deduction is limited to your cost. *Ordinary income property* is inventory from a business, works of art created by the donor, manuscripts prepared by the donor, and capital assets held one year or less. Following are guidelines for deducting contributions of property:

- ✔ **If you contribute property with a fair market value that is less than your cost or depreciated value:** Your deduction is limited to fair market value. You can't claim a deduction for the property's decline in value since you acquired it.

- ✔ **If you have an asset that has declined in value:** Sell that asset to lock in the capital loss deduction (see Chapter 12) and donate the cash for an additional deduction.

  For example, suppose that you paid $12,500 for shares of a mutual fund that invested in Russia that are now worth only $6,000. If you donate the shares, all you can claim is a $6,000 charitable deduction. By selling the shares and donating the cash, not only will you be entitled to a $6,000 charitable deduction, you also will have a $6,500 capital loss that you can deduct.

- ✔ **If you have an asset that has appreciated substantially in value:** Give the asset to the charity rather than sell the asset, get stuck for the tax, and donate the cash you have left. If you donate the asset itself, you get to deduct the full value of the asset, thereby escaping the tax.

One exception to the FMV rule: If you donate a patent or other intellectual property, such as computer software, a copyright, trademark, trade secrets, or general know-how, your deduction is limited to the lesser of fair market value or your basis in the property (what it cost you).

You can't just tell the IRS you've donated property without documenting it, as well. If you've donated property worth $500 or less, just list the value on line 16; for values higher than $500 in the aggregate, you'll also have to complete Form 8283. For values more than $5,000, you may be required to obtain a written appraisal of the property. Depending on the type of property, you may have to attach a copy of that appraisal to your return. If you have donated property with a value in excess of $500, you may want to check out IRS Publication 561 *(Determining the Value of Donated Property)*.

Used clothing and household goods

Clean out those closets for next year so that you can save on your taxes! Hey, even Bill and Hillary Clinton took a deduction for this one! Used clothing and household goods usually have a fair market value that is much less than the original cost. For used clothing, you claim the price that buyers of used items pay in used-clothing stores. See IRS Publication 561 *(Determining the Value of Donated Property — Household Goods section)* for information on the value of items such as furniture and appliances and other items you want to donate.

The records you need: Part I

For contributions of $250 or more, you need a receipt from the charity — otherwise, you could have your deduction tossed out in the event of an audit. The receipt should indicate either the amount of cash you contributed or a description (but not the value) of any property you donated. The receipt must also indicate the value of any gift or services you may have received and you must have the receipt by the time you file your return.

For cash contributions below $250, you can keep a canceled check, a bank record, or a receipt from the charity as proof that you gave the money. But remember, if you donate cash or property valued at $250 or more, you absolutely need a receipt from the charity. If you donate property, you need a receipt from the charity listing the date of your contribution and a detailed description of the property. Every donation is treated as a separate donation for applying the $250 threshold. You don't need a receipt for two $150 checks to the same charity.

If you contribute property worth more than $500, you have to attach **Form 8283, Noncash Charitable Contributions.** On the form, you list the name of the charity, the date of the gift, your cost, the appraised value, and how you arrived at the value. If the value of the property you contributed exceeds $5,000, you need a written appraisal, and the appraiser has to sign off on Part III in Section B of Form 8283. The charity has to complete and sign Part IV of the form. A written appraisal isn't needed for publicly traded stock or nonpublicly traded stock worth $10,000 or less.

Beginning August 17, 2006, you can't donate any old rag and claim a tax deduction. That old rag now needs to be in good or better condition. Who makes that determination? Most likely, you do, but you need to know that the IRS may challenge your assessment of your property. So, if you want to prove that the dress that you've donated was in good and saleable condition, you probably want to have some unassailable proof — a statement from the organization you donated to, or perhaps a photograph. The new regulations also disallow any deduction for items of minimal value (so long, underwear and socks). Of course, there's an exception to this minimal value rule – if a single item has a value of $500 or more and is accompanied by a qualified appraisal, you may still claim the deduction.

What's used clothing or furniture worth? Many charities offer a free printed guide to estimated values. *The Salvation Army Valuation Guide* can be downloaded off the Internet (http://www1.salvationarmy.org/use/www_use.nsf).

Cars, boats, and aircraft

The rules governing how much you may deduct when you contribute a car, boat, or aircraft changed in 2005, and it's not in your favor! Now, when you donate one of these items to a qualified charity, you're limited to deducting the actual gross proceeds from the sale of that used vehicle, rather than a value that you used to assign. How do you know how much to deduct? The charity must provide you with a written acknowledgment of the sales price within 30 days of the sale. What happens if you donate the car at the end of the year, and the charity doesn't have a chance to unload your old clunker before December 31? Just wait to file your tax return until they do. Even if the sale is transacted in the next tax year, your deduction is good for the year in which you transferred the title to the charity.

Of course, this new rule does have a couple of exceptions (when aren't there exceptions?). You need to rely only on the actual sales price of the car, boat, or airplane if the sales price is more than $500, and, if the charity doesn't sell the vehicle, but instead uses it for a charitable purpose, you can go back to the old rules. The old rules, in case you're not current, say that you can assign a reasonable fair market value to that used car by consulting guides such as blue books that contain dealer sale or average prices for recent model years, or any other reasonable method. These guides also give estimates for adjusting values to take into account mileage and physical condition. The prices aren't official, however, and you can't consider a blue book as an appraisal of any specific donated property. But the guides are a good place to start.

If you're thinking of donating your old car, pick up IRS Publication 4303 *(A Donor's Guide to Car Donations)* (available by snail mail or on the Web at www.irs.gov/pub/irs-pdf/p4303.pdf), which can help guide you through this process.

Charitable deduction limits

The U.S. Congress, and by extension, the IRS, thinks that private contributions to charity are good. However, all cash and noncash gifts are subject to some limits. Depending on whether you contributed cash or property, the amount of your deduction may be limited to either 30 percent or 50 percent of your AGI. Contributing cash to churches, associations of churches, synagogues, and all public charities, such as the Red Cross, for example, is deductible up to 50 percent of your AGI. Gifts of ordinary income property qualify for this 50 percent limit.

A 30 percent limit applies to gifts of capital gain property that has appreciated in value if you value your gift for charitable purposes on its *appreciated value* instead of its cost. Otherwise, the 50 percent limit applies. For example, you donate to a museum a painting worth $20,000 that you purchased for $10,000. Your AGI is $50,000. In this case, if you want to use the appreciated value, your deduction will be limited to $15,000, or 30 percent of your AGI of $50,000, and the balance of $5,000 will carry over to 2007. If you elect to use your purchase price, you may claim the entire deduction this year because $10,000 is less than 50 percent of your AGI.

Contributions of capital property may be made only to a church or public charity, and you have to have owned that property for more than a year prior to making the gift. See Chapter 12 for the rules on how the one-year holding period is calculated.

The Pension Protection Act of 2006 contains one very short-lived, but potentially valuable provision for people with large IRAs. For 2006 and 2007, if you're older than age 70½, you may make a direct distribution from your IRA to a charity of your choice of up to $100,000 per year without including that distribution in your income. Of course, because you're not including this income on your Form 1040, you're also not allowed to take a charitable deduction for it on Schedule A.

Contributions that are both qualified and nonqualified

If you receive a benefit from making a valid deductible contribution, you can deduct only the amount of your contribution that is more than the value of the benefit. For example, if you pay to attend a charity function such as a ball or banquet, you can deduct only the amount that is more than the fair market value of your ticket. You can also deduct unreimbursed expenses such as uniforms and actual automobile expenses, or use a standard rate of 14 cents per mile. Just subtract the value of the benefit you received from your total payment. Ask the charity for a receipt that details the actual amount you contributed. Most charities are happy to provide this information. In fact, if the value of your contribution is $75 or more and that is partly for goods and services, the charity must give you a written statement informing you of the amount you can deduct. If you can't easily obtain a receipt, use an estimate based on something the IRS can't disagree with — common sense.

If you're in a generous frame of mind and you meet the age requirements, making donations using this new provision can make a lot of sense. The following are among the reasons why making a direct IRA distribution to a charity may make sense:

- Keeping this distribution out of your adjusted gross income may limit the amount of your Social Security income that is taxed.

- If you itemize your deductions, keeping your AGI lower allows you to deduct more of your medical and miscellaneous itemized deductions, which are reduced by 7.5 percent and 2 percent, respectively, of AGI.

- Paying an IRA distribution directly to charity reduces the chance that your AGI will be so high that your personal exemptions and itemized deductions will start to phase out.

Line 17: (For the world's great humanitarians)

Line 17 is a pretty obscure line. The general rule for cash contributions is that they can't exceed 50 percent of your AGI. For gifts of property like stocks, bonds, and artwork, the amount can't exceed 30 percent of your AGI. So if you contribute more than the IRS permits as a deduction in one year, you can carry over the amount you couldn't deduct and deduct it within the next five years. Enter on line 17 the amount that you couldn't deduct from the last five years and want to deduct this year.

Line 19: Casualty and Theft Losses

We hope that you don't need to use this one. But if you do, and if you've come to view the IRS as heartless, this line may correct that impression. It's not — well, not completely. If you've suffered a casualty or theft loss, you will find that the IRS can be somewhat charitable. Unfortunately, as is the case with any unusual deduction, you've got to jump through quite a few hoops to nail it down.

After you determine whether your loss is deductible, get a copy of IRS **Form 4684, Casualties and Thefts,** on which you list each item that was stolen or destroyed. If your deduction ends up being more than your income — and it does happen — you may have what's known as a *net operating loss*. You can use this type of loss to lower your tax in an earlier or in a later year. This rule is an exception (of course!) to the normal rule that you must be in business to have a net operating loss. See Chapter 18 for more details.

When a casualty loss occurs in a presidentially declared disaster area, a taxpayer has the choice of deducting the loss in the year that it occurred or in the preceding year. By electing to go the prior year route, you can obtain an immediate refund (usually within 45 days) instead of having to wait until the end of the year to receive the full benefit of the loss. Use Form 1040X to claim the loss in the prior year. You have up until the time you file (including extensions) for the year of the loss to make this decision. Remember, the earlier you make it, the quicker you will get your hands on the refund the loss entitled you to. This maneuver also makes sense if you were in a higher bracket in the prior year.

Victims of terrorist attacks or military action

In addition to the casualty-loss deduction, a number of tax relief provisions are available for victims of terrorist or military action and those individuals killed in combat zones. If a member of the U.S. Armed Forces dies while in active service in a combat zone, or from wounds, disease, or other injury received while in a combat zone, his or her income tax liability is forgiven for the tax year of the death, and for any earlier year that ended on or after the first date that person served in a combat zone in active service. So, for example, if a soldier was stationed in a combat zone beginning in 2004, and was wounded in 2005, and eventually died of those wounds in 2006, his or her income tax liability would be forgiven for tax years 2004, 2005, *and* 2006. If taxes were paid in 2004 and 2005, the soldier's family can obtain a refund by filing Form 1040X for those two years.

If an individual (either military or civilian U.S. employee) dies as a result of a terrorist attack or from a military action, regardless of where it happens, his or her income tax is forgiven for the year of death and for any prior year beginning with the year before the year in which the wounds or injury occurred. So, a firefighter who died in 2006 from injuries sustained in the September 11, 2001, terrorist attacks would be eligible to have his or her income tax forgiven for all years beginning with 2000 through 2006. Unfortunately, because the period for filing a claim for refund has already ended for 2000 through 2002, you'll most likely only receive refunds for tax years 2003 through 2005, although the IRS can postpone the filing deadline for those amended returns for up to one year.

Check out IRS Publication 3920 *(Tax Relief for Victims of Terrorist Attacks)* and IRS Publication 3 *(Armed Forces Tax Guide)*. If you feel that dealing with filing refund claims for prior years may just be more than you can handle at the moment, you may want to get a professional to help you. The potential benefits to you and your family at a difficult time are extremely large, but the forms need to be completed and filed in a timely fashion.

The insurance effects

You've got casualty insurance? Great. But there are a couple of things you need to watch out for. First, if you expect to be reimbursed by your insurer but haven't seen any cash by tax-filing time, you need to subtract an estimate of the expected reimbursement from your deductible loss. Second — and this sounds strange — you must reduce the amount of your loss by your insurance coverage even if you don't file a claim. Suppose that your loss is 100 percent covered by insurance, but you decide not to ask for a reimbursement for fear of losing your coverage. You can't claim a deduction for the loss. Only the amount of your loss that's above the insurance coverage would be deductible in that case.

If you're reimbursed by insurance and decide not to repair or replace your property, you could have a taxable gain on your hands. That's because the taxable gain is calculated by subtracting your cost from the insurance proceeds and not the property's fair market value. For example, imagine that your summer cottage, which cost

$150,000 (the cost here refers to the cost of the building and excludes the land costs), burned to the ground. You get $190,000 in insurance money (the house's current FMV), giving you a fully taxable $40,000 gain.

To postpone the gain, you have to replace the property with a similar one, and it must be worth at least as much as the insurance money you received. If the new place is worth less than that, you must report the difference as a capital gain. In addition, you have to replace the property within two years. The two-year period begins on December 31 of the year you realize the gain. If your main home is located in a federally declared disaster area, you have four years, and you can generally get a one-year extension beyond that, if necessary.

For property destroyed in the New York Liberty Zone as the result of the events of September 11, 2001, the replacement period is five years.

Do you have a deductible loss?

Strange as it may seem, the Tax Court has haggled extensively over what is and isn't a casualty. The phrase to remember is *sudden, unexpected, and unusual*. If property you own is damaged, destroyed, or lost as the result of a specific event that is sudden, unexpected, and unusual, you have a deductible casualty. Earthquakes, fires, floods, and storms meet this strict legal test.

But if you dropped a piece of the good china, if Rover chewed a hole in the sofa, if moths ate your entire wardrobe, or if termites gobbled up your brand-new backyard deck, you're doubly out of luck. You've suffered a nondeductible loss. These incidents don't meet the sudden-unexpected-unusual test.

Figuring the loss

Unfortunately, the amount of your deduction isn't going to equal the amount of your loss because the IRS makes you apply a deductible just as your auto insurer does. The IRS makes you reduce each individual loss by $100 and your total losses by 10 percent of your AGI. So if your AGI is $100,000 and you lost $11,000 when the roof caved in, your deduction is only $900. (That's $11,000 minus $100 minus 10 percent of your AGI, or $10,000.)

That stipulation effectively wipes out a deduction for plenty of people. For those whose losses are big enough to warrant a deduction, though, the fun is just beginning. That's because your deduction is limited to either the decrease in the fair market value of your property as a result of the casualty or the original cost of the property — whichever is lower.

Suppose that you bought a painting for $1,000 that was worth $100,000 when damaged by fire. Sorry. Your loss is limited to the $1,000 you paid for it. Now reverse it. You paid $100,000 for the painting, and thanks to the downturn in the market for black-velvet portraits of Elvis, it's worth only $1,000 right before it's destroyed. Your deductible loss is limited to $1,000. And you must apply this rule to each item before combining them to figure your total loss. (One exception is real estate. The entire property, including buildings, trees, and shrubs, is treated as one item.)

The reduction rule ($100 and 10 percent of your income) doesn't apply to property used in a business. It applies only to personal items. Neither is a business casualty limited to the value of the property at the time of the loss. Normally, the loss is what you paid less the depreciation to which you were entitled.

Because your loss is the difference between the fair market value of your property immediately before and after the casualty, an appraisal usually is the best way to calculate your loss. The only problem: The appraiser can't see your property before the casualty, and any photographs or records you may have had probably went up in smoke or floated away. Therefore, it makes sense to videotape both the outside of the property and its contents, including expensive jewelry, and keep the tape in a safe-deposit box, for example. You're not totally out of luck if you don't have before-and-after photos, though. A picture after the casualty and one showing the property after it was repaired comes in very handy when trying to prove the dollar value of your loss. See Chapter 3 for what to do in case all your tax records went up in smoke, for instance.

Casualty losses? You be the judge

Listen to this. A loss as the result of water damage to wallpaper and plaster seems like it ought to be deductible. Not according to the Tax Court, which ruled on such a case in the 1960s. The homeowner failed to prove that the damage came after a sudden, identifiable event. The water had entered the house through the window frames, and the damage could have been caused by progressive deterioration. Now suppose that a car door is accidentally slammed on your hand, breaking the setting of your diamond ring. The jewel falls from the ring and is never found. That lost diamond qualifies as a casualty. On the other hand, if your diamond merely falls out of its setting and is lost, there is no deduction. The number of cases like this is endless. Proving a theft loss can be just as complex. The mere disappearance of cash or property doesn't cut it. You have to prove an actual theft occurred. The best evidence is a police report — and your failure to file one could be interpreted as your not being sure something was stolen.

You need to know that theft losses aren't limited to robbery — they also include theft by swindle, larceny, and false pretense. This very broad definition includes fraudulent sales offers, embezzlement, or losses from identity theft. In one case, a New Yorker was even able to get a theft-loss deduction after handing over a bundle of money to fortune-tellers. The reason? The fortune-tellers were operating illegally.

Normally, you can't deduct the cost of repairing your property because the cost of fixing something isn't really a measure of its deflated fair market value. As with nearly every IRS rule, however, this one has exceptions. You can use the cost of cleaning up or making a repair under the following conditions:

- ✔ The repairs are necessary to bring the property back to its condition before the casualty, and the cost of the repairs isn't excessive.

- ✔ The repairs take care of the damage only.

- ✔ The value of the property after the repairs isn't — because of the repairs — more than the value of the property before the casualty.

Another point is worth knowing: With leased property, such as a car, the amount of your loss is in fact the amount you must spend to repair it.

Although appraisal fees aren't considered part of your loss, they count as miscellaneous itemized deductions. The IRS is required to accept appraisals to get a government-backed loan in a disaster area as proof of the loss.

The IRS can extend the deadline for filing tax returns for up to one year in a presidentially declared disaster area. When the IRS declares a postponement to file and pay, it publicizes the postponement in your area and on its Web site. The postponement also delays the time for making contributions to IRAs. Neither interest nor penalties are charged during the postponement period.

If your casualty or theft loss exceeds your income, you may have a net operating loss (see Chapter 11). This loss enables you to obtain a refund for taxes paid in prior years by carrying it (the loss) back to those years. An amended return has to be filed to accomplish this.

If you have a casualty loss from a disaster that occurred in a presidentially declared disaster area, you can choose to deduct the loss on your return in the year in which the casualty occurred or on an amended return for the preceding year. If you had more earnings in the prior year than in the current one (which is common because of lost earnings due to the disaster), you may gain more benefit from amending the prior return than taking the casualty loss on this year's. If you're not sure whether or not your disaster qualifies, the Federal Emergency Management Agency (FEMA) maintains a list of all the federal disaster zones for the year on its Web site (www.fema.gov/news/disasters.fema).

Lines 20–26: Job Expenses and Most Other Miscellaneous Deductions

Everybody likes to see a deduction that says something about "other." Oh goody, you think, here's my opportunity to get some easy deductions. Unfortunately, if you're like the vast majority of taxpayers, you won't get the maximum mileage out of these deductions. Why? Because the allowable items in this category tend to be small-dollar items. And you have to clear a major hurdle: You get a deduction only for the amount by which your total deductions in this category exceed 2 percent of your AGI. Here's how it works: If your AGI is $50,000 and you have $1,500 of job-related expenses, only $500 is deductible. That's $1,500 minus $1,000 (2 percent of $50,000).

Line 20: Unreimbursed employee expenses

Even if you're not employed by Scrooge International — famous for offering few fringe benefits and not reimbursing job-related expenses — there's a good chance that you're spending at least some out-of-pocket money on your job. Ever take an educational course that helped you get ahead in your career? How about that home fax machine you bought so customers could reach you after hours? If your employer didn't pick up the tab, all is not lost. You can deduct those expenses — or at least a portion of them — from your taxes.

One word of caution: Just about every IRS rule regarding job-related expenses is subject to varying interpretations, which has made the IRS extremely inflexible as to what is and isn't deductible. On the other hand, the Tax Court, which ultimately decides disputes of deductibility, has a tendency to be more liberal than the IRS.

Job search expenses

Job search expenses are deductible even if your job search isn't successful. The critical rule is that the expenses must be incurred in trying to find a new job in the same line of work. So if you're looking to make a career change or seeking your first job, you can forget about this deduction. A taxpayer who retired from the Air Force after doing public relations for the service was denied travel expenses while seeking other employment in public relations. The way the IRS sees the world, any job he sought in the private sector would be considered a new trade or business even if he was performing virtually the same function as he did in the public sector. Go figure.

Here are job search expenses that are considered deductible:

- Cost for placing situation-wanted ads
- Employment-agency and career-counseling fees
- Printing, typing, and mailing of resumes
- Telephone calls
- Travel, meals, and entertaining

Another time, the IRS held that, because a taxpayer had incurred a "substantial break" of more than a year between his previous job and his hunt for a new one, there was a lack of continuity in the person's line of work. No deduction. The IRS is unyielding when it comes to interpreting this rule. Fortunately, the Tax Court sees things differently, tending to consider such gaps as temporary.

If you're away from home overnight looking for work, you can deduct travel and transportation costs, hotels, and meals. The purpose of the trip must be primarily related to searching for a job, though. A job interview while on a golf outing to Palm Springs won't cut it. The IRS looks at the amount of time spent seeking new employment in relationship to the amount of time you are away.

Normally, you deduct job-related expenses on **Form 2106, Employee Business Expenses.** However, unless you're claiming job-related travel, local transportation, meal, or entertainment expenses, save yourself some trouble. You can enter the most basic job-hunting expenses directly on Schedule A (line 20) instead of having to fill out Form 2106. You can use the shorter **Form 2106-EZ, Unreimbursed Employee Business Expenses,** if you weren't reimbursed for any of your expenses and you simply claim the 44.5 cents per mile rate for your job-related auto expenses during 2006.

Job education expenses

If you find that your employer demands greater technical skills, or the fear of being downsized or outsourced has sent you back to the classroom, the cost of those courses is deductible (even if they lead to a degree) under the following conditions:

- You're employed or self-employed.
- The course doesn't qualify you for a new line of work.
- You already have met the minimum educational requirements of your job or profession.
- Your employer or state law requires the course, or the course maintains or improves your job skills.

Up to $5,250 under an employer-paid educational assistance program is a tax-free fringe benefit that you don't want to overlook. This tax-free benefit even applies to graduate level courses.

Like many other tax terms, "maintains or improves job skills" has consistently placed the IRS and taxpayers at odds. The law's intent was to allow a deduction for refresher courses, such as the continuing education classes tax advisors have to take every year.

For example, an IRS agent was denied a deduction for the cost of obtaining an MBA, while an engineer was allowed to deduct the cost of his degree. The rationale: A significant portion of the engineer's duties involved management, interpersonal, and administrative skills. The court felt the engineer's MBA didn't qualify him for a new line of work and was directly related to his job. The IRS agent flunked this test. (There's something strangely satisfying about seeing the IRS turn on its own, isn't there?)

The general rule is that you must be able to prove by clear and convincing evidence how the course is helpful or necessary in maintaining or improving your job skills. So if you can clear that hurdle, here's what's deductible:

- Tuition and books
- Local transportation
- Travel and living expenses while away from home

Travel expenses are allowable if you must go abroad to do research that can only be done there. Travel and living expenses also are deductible when taking a course at a school in a foreign country or away from your home, even if you could have taken the same course locally. Unfortunately, you can't claim a deduction for "educational" trips. For example, say you're a French teacher who decided to spend the summer traveling in the south of France to brush up on your language skills. Nice try, says the IRS, but no deduction.

Instead of claiming a deduction for education expenses, the Hope Scholarship Credit and the Lifetime Learning Credit allow you to take a direct credit against your tax for those expenses. Although the rules you have to meet to qualify for the credits are rather lengthy, we explain them in Chapter 14. Remember, if you're eligible to use either of these credits, they're more valuable to you than taking the deduction here. Don't forget the 2 percent haircut that miscellaneous itemized deductions get!

Miscellaneous job expenses

Just because your job requires you to incur certain expenses doesn't mean they are automatically deductible. Here's a rundown on what generally is deductible:

- Books, subscriptions, and periodicals
- Commuting expenses to a second job (moonlighting, are you?)
- Computers and phones
- Medical exams to establish fitness
- Professional and trade-association dues
- Small tools and equipment
- Uniforms and special clothing
- Union dues
- Unreimbursed travel and entertainment (covered in detail in the next section)

Deductions for computers and cellular phones are hardest to nail down. You must prove you need the equipment to do your job because your employer doesn't provide you with it or because the equipment at work isn't adequate or available. A letter from your employer stating that a computer is a basic requirement for your job isn't good enough. You must also establish that its use is for your employer's convenience and not yours.

For example, suppose that you are an engineer who, rather than staying late at the office, takes work home. You have a computer at home that is similar to the one in the office. Because the use of your computer isn't for the convenience of your employer, you can't claim a deduction. On the other hand, if you need a computer to use while traveling on business, it would be deductible because you now meet the convenience-of-your-employer requirement.

Fax machines, copiers, adding machines, calculators, and typewriters aren't subject to this rigid rule. You must, however, be able to prove that this equipment is job-related and not merely for your own convenience. Although the law requires that you keep a diary or record that clearly shows the computer's or cellular phone's percentage of business use, you don't have to keep a similar record for other office equipment. Be prepared, however, to prove that it is used mainly for business. With a fax machine, for example, it's worth keeping those printouts showing where your calls have been going and where they've been coming from.

We know, this is a crazy thing to ask; after all, are you going to write down every time you use a copier if the copies are for work or personal reasons? But that behavior is exactly what the law requires. Write your representative in Congress and tell him or her what you think. (You'll probably get a reply that says: "Really? When was that law passed?")

Just because your employer requires that you be neatly groomed doesn't mean the cost of doing so is deductible. An airline pilot can't deduct the cost of his haircuts, even though airline regulations require pilots to have haircuts on a regular basis.

Meeting the requirements and keeping the necessary records to deduct job-related expenses can become a part-time job. Unpleasant as it is, though, doing so will almost certainly slash your taxes and save you in the event you're audited.

Job travel (and entertainment!)

Probably no other group of expenses has created more paperwork than travel and entertainment expenses. Taxpayers may spend more time on the paperwork accounting for a business trip than they do planning for it. Unfortunately, this situation can't be changed. But at least we can help you deduct every possible expense in this area. So we begin with the three basic rules regarding travel and entertainment expenses:

- ✔ You have to be away from your business or home to deduct travel expenses. (Makes sense, doesn't it?)
- ✔ You can deduct only 50 percent of your meal and entertainment expenses.
- ✔ You need good records.

Travel expenses that are deductible include taxi, commuter bus, and limousine fare to and from the airport or station — and between your hotel and business meetings or job site. You can also deduct auto expenses, whether you use your own car or lease (see Chapter 11 for more on car and truck expenses), and the cost of hotels, meals, telephone calls, and laundry while you're away. Don't forget tips and baggage handling. Finally, remember the obvious deductions on airplane, train, and bus fare between your *tax home* and business destination.

Your tax home and travel expenses

Yes, we said tax home. This is where the situation gets a little tricky because to be able to deduct travel expenses you must be traveling away from your tax home on business. You are considered to be traveling away from your tax home if the business purpose of your trip requires that you be away longer than an ordinary working day — and you need to sleep or rest so you can be ready for the next day's business. Wouldn't it be nice if the law simply stated that you have to be away overnight?

Your tax home isn't where you or your family reside. Of course not. It's the entire city or general area in which you work or where your business is located. For example, suppose that you work in Manhattan but live in the suburbs. You decide to stay in Manhattan overnight because you have an early breakfast meeting the next morning. You aren't away from your tax home overnight; therefore, you can't deduct the cost of the hotel. The only meal expense you can deduct is the next morning's breakfast — if it qualifies as an entertainment expense.

At this point, you probably want to know how far away from your tax home you have to be. Unfortunately, there isn't a mileage count. When it comes to determining whether you're away from home overnight, the IRS uses that famous U.S. Supreme Court definition: "I can't define it, but I know it when I see it."

Also, your tax home may not be near where you live. For example, if you move from job to job without a fixed base of operation, each place you work becomes your tax home. And travel expenses aren't deductible. And if you accept a temporary assignment that lasts for more than a year, you have moved your tax home to the place of the temporary assignment. Sorry, no deduction. Guess what? It gets worse. Say your assignment is expected to last more than a year but then it doesn't. That sort of assignment isn't considered a temporary assignment (one year or less) that makes your travel and living expenses deductible. It's considered a permanent assignment that doesn't allow you to deduct your travel expenses.

Trips that mix business with pleasure

For travel within the United States, the transportation part of your travel expenses is fully deductible even if part of it is for pleasure. For example, perhaps the airfare and cabs to and from the airport cost $700 for you to attend a business convention in Florida. You spend two days at the end of the convention playing poker with some old friends. Your transportation costs of $700 are fully deductible, but your meals and lodging for the two vacation days aren't.

Transportation costs for travel outside the United States have to be prorated based on the amount of time you spend on business and vacation. Suppose that you spend four out of eight days in London on business. You can deduct only 50 percent of your airfare and four days of lodgings and meals. Any other travel costs (such as taxis and telephone calls while you were conducting business) are deductible.

But this general rule for transportation expenses on travel abroad doesn't apply if you meet any of the following conditions:

- ✔ The trip lasts a week or less.
- ✔ More than 75 percent of your time outside the United States was spent on business. (The days you start and end your trip are considered business days.)
- ✔ You don't have substantial control in arranging the trip.

You are considered not to have substantial control over your trip if you are an employee who was reimbursed or paid a travel expense allowance, aren't related to your employer, and aren't a managing executive. Oh well, *c'est la vie.*

Weekends, holidays, and other necessary standby days are counted as business days if they fall between business days. Great! But if these days follow your business activities and you remain at your business destination for personal reasons, they aren't business days.

For example, suppose that your tax home is in Kansas City. You travel to St. Louis where you have a business appointment on Friday and another business meeting on the following Monday. The days in between are considered tax-deductible business-expense days — you had a business activity on Friday and had another business activity on Monday. This case is true even if you use that time for sightseeing (going up in the Arch!) or other personal activities.

Trips primarily for personal reasons

If your trip was primarily for personal reasons (such as that vacation to Disney World), some of the trip may be deductible — you can deduct any expenses at your destination that are directly related to your business. For example, calls into work are deductible, as well as a 15-minute customer call in Fantasyland. But spending an hour on business does not turn a personal trip into a business trip to be deducted.

Convention expenses

You can deduct your convention-travel expenses if you can prove that your attendance benefits your work. A convention for investment, political, social, or other purposes that are unrelated to your business isn't deductible. Nonbusiness expenses (such as social or sight-seeing costs) are personal expenses and aren't deductible. And you can't deduct the travel expenses for your family!

Your selection as a delegate to a convention doesn't automatically entitle you to a deduction. You must prove that your attendance is connected to your business. For conventions held outside North America, you must establish that the convention could be held only at that site. For example, an international seminar on tofu research held in Japan would qualify if that seminar was unique.

Entertainment: The 50 percent deduction

You can deduct only 50 percent of your entertaining expenses — and that includes meals. People in the transportation industry get a special break, so read on.

You may deduct business-related expenses for entertaining a client, customer, or employee. To be deductible, an entertainment expense has to meet the *directly related or associated test.* That is, the expense must be directly related to or associated with the business you conduct. Under the directly related test, you must show a business motive related to your business other than a general expectation of getting future business (what does the IRS think business entertainment is all about?). Although you don't have to prove that you actually received additional business, such evidence will help nail down the deduction. Don't panic! You can deduct goodwill entertaining and entertaining prospective customers under the associated test. You, or your employee, have to be present, and your entertaining has to be in a business setting. Because the IRS considers distractions at nightclubs, sporting events, and cocktail parties to be substantial, such events don't qualify as business settings. They do under the associated test.

If you have a substantial business discussion before or after entertaining someone, you meet the associated test. For example, suppose that after meeting with a customer, you entertain him and his spouse at a theatre and nightclub. The expense is deductible. Goodwill entertaining and entertaining prospective customers falls under the associated test. But handing a customer two tickets to the Super Bowl and telling him to have a good time doesn't cut it. The reason: There was no business discussion within a reasonable amount of time before or after the game. In such an event the tickets could qualify as a gift. Entertainment includes any activity generally considered to provide amusement or recreation (a broad definition!). Examples include entertaining guests at nightclubs (and social, athletic, and sporting clubs), at theaters, at sporting events, on yachts, and on hunting or fishing vacations. If you buy a scalped ticket to an entertainment event for a client, you usually can't deduct more than the face value of the ticket. Country club dues aren't deductible; only the cost of entertaining at the club is. Meal expenses include the cost of food, beverages, taxes, and tips.

You can't claim the cost of a meal as an entertainment expense if you are also claiming it as a travel expense (this activity is known as *double-deducting*). Expenses also aren't deductible when a group of business acquaintances take turns paying for each other's checks without conducting any business.

With regard to gifts, you can't deduct more than $25 for a business gift to any one person during the year. A husband and wife are considered one person. So if a business customer is getting married, you can't give a $25 gift to each newlywed-to-be and expect to deduct $50.

Standard meal and hotel allowance — or "my city costs more than your city"

Instead of keeping records for your actual meal and incidental expenses (tips and cleaning), you may choose to deduct a flat amount using the *high-low method*. You don't need to keep receipts with this method, but you do have to establish that you were away from home on business. Using the high-low method, you receive a daily meal and incidental expense allowance of $58, and a lodging allowance of $168 if you travel to a high-cost locale (and there aren't many), or a total of $226, and every other area of the country uses $45 per day for food and incidentals and $96 for lodging, or a total of $141 per day for both. (IRS Publication 463 lists high-cost areas.)

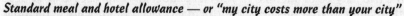

The records you need: Part II

You need a receipt for every travel and entertainment expense that exceeds $75. No receipt, no deduction if you're audited. And a canceled check just won't cut it anymore. The receipt — or a separate diary entry — must also show the business purpose. Although you don't need a receipt if the amount is below $75, you still need an entry in your diary to explain to whom, what, where, when, and why. This $75 rule doesn't apply to your hotel bill. A hotel bill is required, regardless of the amount. For entertainment, you need the name and location of the restaurant or the place where you did the entertaining; the number of people served or in attendance; the date and amount of the bill; and the business purpose, such as "Bill Smith, buyer for Company Z."

A hotel receipt has to show the name and location of the hotel, the dates you stayed there, and the separately stated charges for the room, meals, telephone calls, and so on.

If you want to be more precise in your calculations, you may use the city-by-city per diem rates listed in IRS Publication 1542 instead. For any location not listed in Publication 1542, the rate is $39 for meals and incidentals, $60 for lodging. Employees and self-employed taxpayers can use the standard meal allowance. Whether you use the city-by-city or high-low method, you have to use it consistently throughout the year. For example, you can't use the high-low method for the period before October 1, 2006, and switch to the city-by-city after that date because the rates went up for that city.

Taxpayers in the transportation industry (those involved in moving people and goods) can use a flat rate of $41 a day in the United States and $46 outside the United States for meals and incidental expenses.

People in the transportation industry covered by the U.S. Department of Transportation work rules get to deduct 70 percent of their meal expenses instead of the normal 50 percent limit in 2006. Airline pilots, flight crews, ground crews, interstate bus and truck drivers, railroad engineers, conductors, and train crews are eligible for this break.

Unfortunately, self-employed taxpayers can't use the flat per diem rates listed for hotel-and-meal expenses; only employees can. They can, however, choose to use the part of the rate that applies to meals and incidentals. If you are self-employed, you can compute your travel expense deduction based on $39 a day for meals and incidentals plus your hotel bills. If you're traveling in a high-cost area, it's $58 a day.

The high-low per diem rates change every year on October 1. Why? The federal government is on a fiscal year that starts on October 1, and because the feds set the per diem travel rates, the IRS switched to the federal way of doing things. So, now two rates exist in a given tax year, one for the period January 1, 2006, through September 30, 2006, and another set for the period October 1, 2006, through December 31, 2006. As the result of all this, you have two choices. You can use the per diem rates from January 1 to September 30 for all of 2006, or you can use the rates for travel up to September 30, 2006, and when the new high/low and city-by-city rates come out, you can use those rates from October 1, 2006, through the end of the year.

Don't forget, you don't have to use the high-low per diem rates; you always have the option of using the per diem rates on a city-by-city basis. Check out IRS Publication 1542 for the complete list. The rates are also listed at www.policyworks.gov/perdiem.

If your employer's per diem reimbursement rate is equal to or less than the standard rate, no paperwork is necessary. That's what the standard rate is all about — to keep you from having to attach an accounting of your expenses when you file your return. If your actual expenses or your expenses using the standard meal allowance (your hotel bill plus the standard meal allowance) is more than your per diem allowance, you enter your actual expenses and per diem allowance on **Form 2106, Employee Business Expenses.** Your expenses that are in excess of your per diem allowance per Form 2106 are deducted on Schedule A. If your actual expenses are less than the standard per diem rate, don't look a gift horse in the mouth. You need do nothing. Just say thanks.

If your per diem allowance is more than the standard rate, the excess gets reported in box 1 (Wages) of your W-2. The standard rate, say it was $226 a day, is entered in box 12 of your W-2 with the code L. If your actual expenses are more than the standard rate, you can deduct the excess. Enter your actual expenses on lines 1 through 5 of Form 2106. Enter the amount shown in box 12 of your W-2 on line 7 of Form 2106. The difference between these two amounts gets deducted on Schedule A. If your actual expenses are less than the standard rate in box 12, you aren't entitled to any deduction and you don't have to file Form 2106. What you do get stuck for is the tax on the excess above the standard rate that was included in box 1 (Wages) of your W-2.

You can find all the per diem rates on the IRS homepage at www.irs.gov, or at www.gsa.gov.

The standard meal and hotel allowances don't apply to Alaska, Hawaii, Puerto Rico, or foreign locations, however. A separate schedule can be found at the site for those places and for foreign travel.

You can't use the standard meal and hotel per diem allowances if you're traveling for medical, charitable, or moving-expense purposes. And, if you're employed by your brother, sister, half-brother, half-sister, ancestor, or lineal descendent, you have to collect receipts and substantiate your expenses. Finally, you can't use the standard allowance if your employer is a corporation in which you hold 10 percent or more ownership. So many details!

What IRS form to use

What other form you attach to your Form 1040 depends on whether you are an employee or are self-employed:

- ✔ **If you're self-employed:** You deduct travel on line 24a and the deductible portion of meals and entertainment expenses on line 24b of Schedule C.

- ✔ **If you're employed by someone else:** You must use Form 2106, Employee Business Expenses, or 2106-EZ.

For example, if you are paid a salary with the understanding that you will pay your own expenses, you claim these expenses on Form 2106 and then carry over the amount from line 10 of Form 2106 or line 6 of Form 2106-EZ to Schedule A (line 20) of your Form 1040, where the amount is claimed as an itemized deduction. Form 2106 also allows you to claim travel and entertaining costs that exceed your travel allowance or the amount for which you were reimbursed.

If you received a travel allowance, your employer adds the amount of the allowance to your salary, and it will be included in box 1 of your W-2. So if you received a travel allowance of $10,000 and spent $10,000, the $10,000 isn't completely deductible because it's reduced by 2 percent of your AGI. For example, if your income is $100,000, you can deduct only $8,000 ($10,000 minus 2 percent of $100,000) of your travel expenses. If your income exceeds $139,500, or $69,750 if you are married filing separately, a portion of these deductions is reduced again.

Instead of getting an allowance, have your employer reimburse you for actual expenses that you submit on an expense report. You won't have to file Form 2106, and you won't have to pay tax on the money that you never earned and lose part of your deductions due to silly rules like the 2 percent rule. Neat, huh?

Line 21: Tax preparation fees

You can deduct the fees paid to a tax preparer or advisor! You may also deduct the cost of being represented at a tax audit and the cost of tax-preparation software programs, tax publications, and any fee you paid for the electronic filing of your return. You can also deduct travel expenses when you have to go to a tax audit. This is probably one deduction you wish you weren't entitled to.

Fees paid to prepare tax schedules relating to business income (Schedule C), rentals or royalties (Schedule E), or farm income and expenses (Schedule F) are deductible on each one of those forms. The expenses for preparing the remainder of the return are deductible on Schedule A. That way, more of the fee is deductible, because most of it isn't subject to the 2 percent of AGI rule.

Ready for another tax surprise? *Taxes 2007 For Dummies* is deductible!

Line 22: Other expenses — investment, safe-deposit box, and so on

You may be scratching your head as to how the IRS can throw in a line item here called "other expenses," when we're within the miscellaneous deduction category. The expenses that are most likely to help you on this line to build up to that 2 percent hurdle are fees you incur in managing your investments. Here's a rundown of deductible investment expenses:

- ✔ Accounting fees to keep track of investment income.
- ✔ Financial periodicals.
- ✔ Investment expenses of partnerships, S Corporations, and mutual funds. (You will receive a Schedule K-1 that will tell you where to deduct those expenses.)
- ✔ Investment fees, custodial fees, trust administration fees, and other expenses you paid for managing your investments.
- ✔ Investment fees shown in box 5 of Form 1099-DIV.
- ✔ Safe-deposit box rentals.
- ✔ Trustee's fees for your IRA, if separately billed and paid.

You can't deduct expenses incurred in connection with investing in tax-exempt bonds. If you have expenses related to both taxable and tax-exempt income but can't identify the expenses that relate to each, you must prorate the expenses to determine the amount that you can deduct.

One of the benefits of having so many lawyers in the United States is that when you hire one for a variety of personal purposes, you may qualify to write off the cost. For example, you can deduct a legal fee in connection with collecting taxable alimony and for tax advice related to a divorce if the bill specifies how much is for tax advice and if the bill is determined in a reasonable way.

Part of an estate tax planning fee may be deductible. That's because estate planning involves tax as well as nontax advice. A reasonable division of the bill between the two usually supports a deduction for the portion attributable for tax advice. Legal costs in connection with contesting a will or suing for wrongful death aren't deductible. The same goes for financial planner fees that you pay. The part that applies to tax advice is deductible.

You may deduct legal fees directly related to your job, such as fees incurred in connection with an employment contract or defending yourself from being wrongfully dismissed. You can deduct legal expenses that you incurred if they are business related or in connection with income-producing property.

As a result of the recent unanimous Supreme Court decision in *Commissioner vs. Banaitis,* you must declare the full amount of any taxable settlement you receive as income, and then deduct your attorney's fees (including any contingency fee, where your attorney is paid a percentage of the settlement) as a miscellaneous itemized deduction subject to the 2 percent AGI rule. Unfortunately, doing it this way will probably trigger the Alternative Minimum Tax (See Chapter 8), and the taxpayer will likely end up owing tax on the full amount of the settlement, not just the portion that he or she actually ends up with after paying attorney costs.

If you receive a taxable settlement, for age discrimination or sexual harassment for example, and part of the settlement reimbursed you for medical expenses you incurred to alleviate the symptoms of emotional distress, make sure the settlement agreement accounts for the medical expenses separately. That way you can deduct the medical expenses from the settlement and pay tax on only the net amount.

A legal fee paid to collect a disputed Social Security claim also is deductible to the extent that your benefit is taxable. For example, suppose you paid a $2,000 fee to help collect your Social Security benefits. If 50 percent of your Social Security is taxable, you can deduct $1,000 (50 percent of the fee).

Lines 23–26: Miscellaneous math

Congratulations! You've slogged through one of the parts of the tax return that clearly highlights how politicians and years of little changes add up to complicated tax laws. We know you've spent a lot of time identifying and detailing expenses that fit into these categories. As we warned you in the beginning of this section on job expenses and other miscellaneous deductions, you can deduct these expenses only to the extent that they exceed 2 percent of your AGI. Lines 23 through 26 walk you through this arithmetic.

Line 27: Other Miscellaneous Deductions

More miscellaneous deductions? You bet. These "other miscellaneous deductions" are different from those on lines 20 through 26 in that they aren't subject to the 2 percent AGI limit. Hooray, no convoluted math! These are 100 percent Grade A, no-fat deductions!

- **Estate tax on income you received as an heir:** Enter on line 27 of Schedule A. You can deduct the estate tax attributable to income you received from an estate that you paid tax on. For example, suppose that you received $10,000 from an IRA account when the owner died. You included this amount in your income. The owner's estate paid $2,000 of estate tax on the IRA. You can deduct the $2,000 on line 27. It's called an *IRD deduction.* That's IRS lingo for *income in respect of a decedent,* which means that because the IRA owner never paid income tax on the money in the IRA, guess what? You have to! But you get to deduct a portion of estate tax.

- **Gambling losses to the extent of gambling winnings:** Enter on line 27 of Schedule A.

- **Impairment-related work expenses:** These expenses are allowable business expenses of attendant care services at your place of work and expenses in connection with your place of work that are necessary for you to be able to work. See IRS Publication 907 *(Tax Highlights for Persons with Disabilities)* for more information.

  If you're an employee, enter your impairment-related work expenses on line 10 of Form 2106. This amount is also entered on line 27 of Schedule A. And the amount that is unrelated to your impairment is entered on line 20 of Schedule A.

- **Repayment of income:** If you had to repay more than $3,000 of income that was included in your income in an earlier year, you may be able to deduct the amount you repaid or take a credit against your tax. This is known as a *claim of right.* (See Chapter 6 for help tackling this little gem.) However, if the repayment is less than $3,000, you must deduct it on line 22 of Schedule A.

- **Unrecovered investment in a pension:** If a retiree contributed to the cost of a pension or annuity, a part of each payment received can be excluded from income as a tax-free return of the retiree's investment. If the retiree dies before the entire investment is returned tax free, the unrecovered investment is allowed as a deduction on the retiree's final return. See line 16 in Chapter 6.

- **Work expenses for the disabled:** If you have a physical or mental disability that limits your being employed or that substantially limits one or more of your activities (such as performing manual tasks, walking, speaking, breathing, learning, and working), your impairment-related work expenses are deductible.

Line 28: Total Itemized Deductions

You've (thankfully) reached the end of Schedule A. Warm up that calculator again because you need to do some adding. Sum up the totals that you've written in the far right column on the schedule. Add the amounts on lines 4, 9, 14, 18, 19, 26, and 27. If your AGI on Form 1040, line 38 is $150,500 or less ($75,250 if you're married filing separately), put the total of all those lines on line 28, and then transfer the total to Form 1040, line 40. Before you do, though, just make sure your total on line 28 is greater than your standard deduction amount shown in "The Standard Deduction" section at the beginning of this chapter.

If your AGI is greater than $150,500 ($75,250 if you're married filing separately), wait! You can't just go ahead and enter that total on line 28. Your total itemized deductions are going to be limited.

If your AGI exceeds $150,500 (or $75,250 if you are married filing separately), you have to reduce your total itemized deductions by 3 percent of your income above $150,500. Itemized deductions are never completely phased out, though; the maximum reduction in deductions is 80 percent.

Here's how it works: Your income is $180,500, and you have itemized deductions of $36,000. Because your income exceeds $150,500 by $30,000, your total allowable deductions will be reduced by $900, or $30,000 times 3 percent. By subtracting $900 from your total deductions of $36,000, you arrive at allowable deductions of $35,100. Put this amount on line 28 of Schedule A and line 40 of your Form 1040.

So put this on paper to make the math easier. Use the worksheet in Table 9-3 if your AGI exceeds $150,500 (married filing jointly) or $75,250 (married filing separately) to figure your allowable deductions.

Table 9-3	Itemized Deduction Worksheet		
		Sample	*Your Computation*
1.	AGI line 37 (1040)	$180,500	1. _____
2.	Enter $150,500 ($75,250 if filing separately)	$150,500	2. _____
3.	Subtract line 2 from line 1.	$ 30,000	3. _____
4.	Total itemized deductions (Schedule A)	$ 36,000	4. _____
5.	From Schedule A enter: Medical (line 4) Investment interest (line 13) Casualty loss (line 19) Gambling losses (line 27)	$ 10,000	5. _____
6.	Subtract line 5 entries from line 4.	$ 26,000	6. _____
7.	Multiply line 6 by 80%.	$ 20,800	7. _____
8.	Multiply line 3 by 3%.	$ 900	8. _____
9.	The smaller of lines 7 and 8.	$ 900	9. _____
10.	Your reduced itemized deductions: line 4 less line 9.	$ 35,100*	10. _____

This is the amount you're allowed to deduct. Now you can enter this amount on line 28 of Schedule A and carry it over to line 40 of your Form 1040. Just make sure that the total of your itemized deductions is greater than the standard deduction (see amounts at the beginning of this chapter).

You may be wondering why your medical and dental expenses, investment interest, casualty and theft losses, and gambling losses don't have to reduce these itemized expenses. The IRS doesn't limit or reduce your ability to write off these expenses so that they aren't subject to the 3 percent reduction rule. The IRS *does* want to limit your ability to deduct too much in the way of state and local taxes (including property taxes paid on your home), home mortgage interest, gifts to charity, job expenses, and miscellaneous deductions.

The net effect of the IRS tossing out some of these write-offs is that it raises the effective tax rate that you're paying on your income higher than the IRS tables indicate. This may encourage you, for example, to spend less on a home or to pay off your mortgage faster (see Chapter 23), because you don't merit a full deduction.

Chapter 10

Interest and Dividend Income: Schedule B (1040), Schedule 1 (1040A)

*R*umor has it that John D. Rockefeller once described real wealth as the ability to live off the income from your income. Most people don't achieve that level of wealth, but for some people, their investment income has grown beyond being able to plop a number on the front of their Form 1040 or 1040A and say they're done. If you fall into the category of having more than $1,500 of interest or dividend income, Schedule B of the 1040 (which is located on the backside of Schedule A), or Schedule 1 of the 1040A, is for you. And, if you have a foreign bank account or are involved in a foreign trust, Schedule B has to be filed. Sorry!

So, in the interest of space and time, we tackle both of these forms together because, other than a couple of questions at the bottom of Schedule B concerning foreign bank accounts and foreign trusts, Schedule B and Schedule 1 are identical. Just so you know, with the exception of those foreign bank accounts and trusts, whatever we say about Schedule B (see Figure 10-1) goes for Schedule 1 and vice versa.

Although you may not have sufficient interest and dividend income to file Schedule B, filling it out is still a good idea. It's a good worksheet and a terrific double-check to make sure that all the sources of interest and dividends you showed on last year's returns are accounted for on this year's.

What you need to complete Schedule B are those 1099s (1099-INT and 1099-DIV) that banks, corporations, brokerage firms, and mutual fund companies send by January 31 of the following year. Make sure that you have one of these forms for each and every nonretirement account that you owned during the tax year. If you're missing a form, get on the horn to the responsible financial institution and request it.

If you don't report all your interest or dividend income (or don't furnish the payer with your Social Security number), your future interest and dividend income is subject to backup withholding of 28 percent! To add insult to injury, about a year after filing your taxes, you'll receive a nasty notice called a CP-2000 listing the interest and dividends that you didn't report. You'll end up owing interest and penalties in addition to the tax.

Schedules A&B (Form 1040) 2006

OMB No. 1545-0074   Page **2**

Name(s) shown on Form 1040. Do not enter name and social security number if shown on other side.

Your social security number

Schedule B—Interest and Ordinary Dividends

Attachment
Sequence No. **08**

Part I
Interest

(See page B-1
and the
instructions for
Form 1040,
line 8a.)

Note. If you
received a Form
1099-INT, Form
1099-OID, or
substitute
statement from
a brokerage firm,
list the firm's
name as the
payer and enter
the total interest
shown on that
form.

1 List name of payer. If any interest is from a seller-financed mortgage and the buyer used the property as a personal residence, see page B-1 and list this interest first. Also, show that buyer's social security number and address ▶

Amount

1

2 Add the amounts on line 1 . . . . | 2 |

3 Excludable interest on series EE and I U.S. savings bonds issued after 1989. Attach Form 8815 | 3 |

4 Subtract line 3 from line 2. Enter the result here and on Form 1040, line 8a ▶ | 4 |

Note. If line 4 is over $1,500, you must complete Part III.

Part II
Ordinary
Dividends

(See page B-1
and the
instructions for
Form 1040,
line 9a.)

Note. If you
received a Form
1099-DIV or
substitute
statement from
a brokerage firm,
list the firm's
name as the
payer and enter
the ordinary
dividends shown
on that form.

5 List name of payer ▶

Amount

5

6 Add the amounts on line 5. Enter the total here and on Form 1040, line 9a ▶ | 6 |

Note. If line 6 is over $1,500, you must complete Part III.

Part III
Foreign
Accounts
and Trusts

(See
page B-2.)

You must complete this part if you **(a)** had over $1,500 of taxable interest or ordinary dividends; or **(b)** had a foreign account; or **(c)** received a distribution from, or were a grantor of, or a transferor to, a foreign trust.

| | Yes | No |

7a At any time during 2006, did you have an interest in or a signature or other authority over a financial account in a foreign country, such as a bank account, securities account, or other financial account? See page B-2 for exceptions and filing requirements for Form TD F 90-22.1 . . . . | ☐ | ☐ |

b If "Yes," enter the name of the foreign country ▶

8 During 2006, did you receive a distribution from, or were you the grantor of, or transferor to, a foreign trust? If "Yes," you may have to file Form 3520. See page B-2 . . . . . | ☐ | ☐ |

For Paperwork Reduction Act Notice, see Form 1040 instructions.   Schedule B (Form 1040) 2006

✱ Printed on recycled paper

Figure 10-1:
Had a good
year with
your invest-
ments?
Report your
interest and
dividend
income on
Schedule B.

Although becoming ensnared in backup withholding is unpleasant, don't worry that the amounts withheld by financial institutions from your accounts and sent to the IRS are for naught. They simply represent a forced payment of your expected tax on your interest and dividends. You get "credit" for it on line 64, "Federal income tax withheld," on your Form 1040 (see Chapter 8 for more details). On Form 1040EZ, it's line 7; on Form 1040-A, it's line 38.

Part 1, Lines 1–4: Interest Income

In this first part of the schedule, you need to declare interest income that you earned during the tax year. Although this income can come from a variety of sources, as we tell you about in this chapter, most of it is reported by large, impersonal financial institutions that will send you a computer-generated **Form 1099-INT, Interest Income.**

Before you complete the lines on Schedule B, we want to explain how to read your 1099-INT forms.

Understanding Form 1099-INT

You receive Form 1099-INT from the financial institution, such as a bank, that pays you interest. These forms aren't too difficult to read. The following are brief descriptions of little boxes and other stuff you find on your 1099-INT (see Figure 10-2).

	☐ CORRECTED (if checked)		
PAYER'S name, street address, city, state, ZIP code, and telephone no.	Payer's RTN (optional)	OMB No. 1545-0112	
	1 Interest income $	**2006** Form **1099-INT**	**Interest Income**
	2 Early withdrawal penalty $		
PAYER'S federal identification number / RECIPIENT'S identification number	**3** Interest on U.S. Savings Bonds and Treas. obligations $		**Copy B** **For Recipient**
RECIPIENT'S name	**4** Federal income tax withheld $	**5** Investment expenses $	This is important tax information and is being furnished to the Internal Revenue Service. If you are required to file a return, a negligence penalty or other sanction may be imposed on you if this income is taxable and the IRS determines that it has not been reported.
Street address (including apt. no.)	**6** Foreign tax paid $	**7** Foreign country or U.S. possession	
City, state, and ZIP code	**8** Tax-exempt interest	**9** Specified private activity bond interest	
Account number (see instructions)	$	$	
Form **1099-INT**	(keep for your records)		Department of the Treasury - Internal Revenue Service

Figure 10-2: You receive Form 1099-INT from institutions that pay you taxable interest.

Don't assume that your 1099-INT forms are all correct. Big companies make mistakes, and they often cause taxpayers to pay more tax. Check your 1099-INT forms against the statements that you received throughout the year from the financial firm where you had the account paying the interest. If you receive an incorrect 1099-INT, ask the payer to issue a corrected one on the double! Form 1099-INT lists the telephone number of the person you need to contact in case it has to be revised.

One problem with filing too early is that you may receive a corrected 1099-INT, which means that you'll have to amend your return. And filing one return per year is more than enough for most people!

The amount in box 1 and box 3 of the 1099-INT is the taxable interest that you have to report on line 1 of this schedule. But if you don't have more than $1,500 of total interest income for the tax year, you need not complete this part of Schedule B (you have to complete Part II, "Dividend Income," if you had more than $1,500 in dividend income). If you don't have more than $1,500 in interest, skip Part I and enter the total of your interest income on line 8a of Form 1040. Don't concern yourself with the rest of the boxes on your 1099-INT right now. As we breeze through this chapter, we'll let you know what to do with them.

Completing lines 1–4

Now that you've located and understand Form 1099-INT, you're ready to complete Part I of Schedule B.

Line 1: Taxable interest

Taxable interest includes interest you receive from bank accounts, interest income on loans you made to others, and interest income on loans from most other sources (anything except for municipal bond interest).

Taxable interest doesn't include interest on insurance dividends you leave on deposit with the Department of Veterans Affairs (for people who were in the armed services).

Dividends that are taxed as interest

In the past, savings and loans, credit unions, savings banks, and money market funds often reported the interest you earned as dividends. Now that qualified dividends (we explain this term in "Part II, Lines 5 and 6: Dividend Income") are taxed at a reduced rate, these financial institutions have to clean up their dividend-labeling act. You have to report these so-called dividends as interest even though the interest was reported on **Form 1099-DIV, Dividends and Distributions** by the financial institution instead of Form 1099-INT. Don't you think, sometimes, that everyone out there is trying to confuse you?

Gifts for opening an account

The value of that toaster you received is reported as interest on Form 1099-INT. Enjoy your toast! A gift valued at $10 or less for a deposit of less than $5,000 or $20 for a deposit of $5,000 or more isn't taxable, thanks to a kinder and gentler IRS.

Interest on life insurance dividends

This interest is taxable, but the dividends you receive aren't taxable until the total of all dividends received exceeds the total of all the premiums paid. Keep your annual dividend statements from your company in a file so that you can track that amount versus the premiums you paid.

Interest on EE U.S. Savings Bonds

If you don't have EE bonds, you may happily skip this line. (If you want to know about them, be sure to read Chapter 24.) Otherwise, you need to know that you have a choice regarding how and when to declare the interest you earn on them. You may report all the interest earned over the life of EE bonds when you cash them in. Or, you can choose to report the yearly interest in the year it is earned. Whatever method you choose, you must use the same method for all E, EE, and I bonds that you own.

If your child owns these bonds and has little or no other income, reporting the interest every year may make sense because the first $850 of interest is exempt from tax (see Chapter 24). Attach a statement to your child's return saying that you elect to report the interest annually. If the interest is under $850, you're going to have to file a return even if one isn't required, so that you can make this election for the initial year. After that, as long as the interest is under $850 (an amount that periodically is increased for inflation) and your child doesn't exceed earned income limits, you don't have to file.

Series E bonds stop earning interest after 40 years; Series EE bonds stop earning interest after 30 years. (Series E were issued before 1980, and Series EE were issued after that.) You can avoid paying the tax on the accumulated interest at or before maturity by exchanging these bonds for HH bonds (see the next section, "U.S. H and HH bonds").

When the owner of an E or EE bond dies, the heir pays the tax when the bond is cashed in — unless the interest was reported on the decedent's final return. This choice makes sense if the bond's owner died at the beginning of the year and had little or no income (and was in a lower tax bracket than the heir).

For example, if the owner died on January 10 and filed a return reporting the accumulated EE bond interest of $4,000, no tax would be added because the decedent is entitled to a standard deduction of $5,150 (if single) and a personal exemption of $3,300. On the other hand, if the heir reports the $4,000 of accumulated interest and is in the 25 percent tax bracket, he or she would pay $1,000 in tax.

Say you or the person you inherited a bond from had been reporting the interest on a savings bond annually and you redeem the bond. Guess what? You'll receive a 1099-INT for the entire amount of interest the bond earned through the years. Here's what to do so you don't pay tax on interest you don't have to. Report the entire amount of interest on line 1 of Schedule B and then enter, on the line below, the amount previously reported as a <negative number>. In the space for the name of the payer, write "U.S. Savings Bond Interest Previously Reported." This is how you subtract the interest on which you previously paid tax from the total interest you have to report.

A distribution of savings bonds from a retirement account gets reported as a retirement distribution. The amount you report is the cost of the bond plus the interest up to the time of distribution. When you cash in the bond you will receive a 1099-DIV for all the interest earned through the years. No problem! Just follow the instructions in the preceding paragraph on how to deal with "U.S. Savings Bond Interest Previously Reported."

Here are the rules when you buy a savings bond with someone or in someone else's name. If you buy a bond in the name of another person who is the sole owner, the owner reports the interest. If you buy a bond jointly with your money, you report the interest. If each of you put up the dough, the interest is reported in proportion to what each of you paid. In a community property state, if the bond is community property and you file separately, generally, each spouse reports half the interest.

U.S. H and HH bonds

H and HH bonds are issued only in exchange for E and EE bonds. Interest is paid semiannually, and you receive a Form 1099-INT from the government showing the amount of interest you must report. H bonds have a 30-year maturity, and HH bonds have a 20-year maturity. (In case you really want to know, H bonds were issued before 1980, and HH bonds were issued after that time.)

The amount of interest earned on the E or EE bonds that you exchanged is stated on the H or HH bonds. You report this amount when you cash in the H or HH bonds.

U.S. Treasury bills

U.S. Treasury bills are short-term obligations of the U.S. government, issued at a discount. These bills mature in 1, 2, 3, 6, or 12 months. You report the interest in the year the bill matures, not when you purchase it.

For example, suppose that you purchase a $10,000, 6-month T-bill for $9,700 in December 2005. You report the $300 of interest you earned when the bill matures in 2006. This maneuver is an excellent way to defer income to the next year.

Interest on U.S. Treasury bonds, notes, and bills is exempt from state tax.

I-bonds

I-bonds are similar to EE bonds. The difference is that the interest that is paid at maturity (30 years) or when the bond is cashed in is linked to inflation. I-bonds are issued in denominations as low as $50.

Joint returns, minors, and interest stuff

If your Social Security number is the one that's reported on the 1099-INT, the computers at the IRS check to see whether the interest from the 1099-INT is on your return. On a joint return, either your SSN or your spouse's number can be on the account because you're filing jointly.

But what about an account owned by you and someone other than your spouse (or if you're merely holding the money for someone else)? Suppose that only 50 percent of the $1,200 reported under your SSN is yours. Report the $1,200 on Schedule B, and on the line below, subtract the $600 belonging to the other person. In the space for the name of the payer, write "Nominee Distribution."

Enter the $600 as a negative number <$600>. This is how you subtract the $600 from the total that you must report but that doesn't belong to you. The rules also require that you issue that person Form 1099-INT for their $600. What a pain!

When a minor has an account, make sure that the minor's Social Security number is on the account. If he or she has more than $850 in interest, the minor must file a return. If the minor is under the age of 18, with interest and investment income exceeding $1,700, the excess is taxed at the parent's tax rate (find out more about the Kiddie Tax in Chapter 15).

How do I-bonds stack up against regular inflation-indexed Treasury bonds? A regular inflation-indexed bond carries a fixed rate of interest, with the principal adjusted annually to keep up with inflation. Whereas I-bond holders don't pay tax until the bond is cashed in, holders of regular inflation-indexed bonds have to pay tax every year on the interest payment and the capital gains tax on the inflation-index increase in the value of the bond. Unlike I-bonds, regular inflation-indexed bonds can be purchased only in $1,000 denominations.

Zero-coupon bonds

Zero-coupon bonds don't pay annual interest, but they are issued at a discount very similar to U.S. Savings Bonds. Each year, the bond increases in value equal to the amount of interest it is considered to have earned. In tax lingo, this is referred to as *original issue discount (OID)*. Each year, the issuer or your broker will compute the amount of interest you have to report and send you a Form 1099-OID.

Interest on bonds bought or sold

When you buy a bond between the interest payment dates, you pay the seller the interest that was earned up to the sale date.

For example, suppose that on April 30 you buy a bond that makes semiannual interest payments of $600 on June 30. You must pay the seller $400 for the interest earned up to April 30. You report the $600 in interest that you received for the bond on Schedule B. On the line below, subtract the $400 of interest you paid the seller, and to the left of the $400 amount, write "Accrued Interest Paid." Enter the $400 as a negative amount, <$400>. That's how you subtract the $400 of interest that you paid from the total interest reported.

Unfortunately, paying and receiving bond interest is sometimes not as easy as pie. The following list shows you how to account for a variety of situations where you need to make adjustments to the interest you receive (or pay):

✔ **Sales and purchases between interest dates:** Say you sold a bond for $1,040, $25 of which represents interest on the bond that was earned but not yet paid. Here's how this plays out:

In the year of the sale, $25 is reported as interest income. Next, you reduce the $1,040 you received by the $25. Your selling price for computing your gain or loss is $1,015. If you paid $1,000 for the bond, you have a $15 gain.

When the buyer receives the next interest payment, he is entitled to reduce the payment by the $25 of interest he paid to you. Next, he makes a reduction in his tax basis. He reduces the $1,040 by $25 and uses $1,015 as his tax basis (cost) when he sells the bond to determine whether he has a profit or loss.

✔ **Bond premiums and discounts:** Say you purchase a bond for $1,000 that pays 6 percent ($60) that matures in 10 years at a $100 premium. You can elect to deduct $10 ($100 ÷ 10 years) of the premium each year, so you have to pay tax on only $50. Enter $60 on line 1 of Schedule B. On the next line, enter <$10>, as a negative number. Next to this amount, write "ABP Adjustment," which stands for amortized bond premium. Here's a plain English definition of amortization: It's the $10 deduction you're entitled to. Additionally, every year you have to reduce the $1,100 you paid by the $10 you get to deduct. This is a current deduction that many investors fail to claim. If you don't make this election in the year of purchase, you treat the $100 as part of the cost of the bond in determining your profit or loss on its sale or maturity.

Reversing the earlier example, say you purchased a $1,000, 6 percent bond that matures in 10 years at a $100 discount for $900. When the bond matures, you report the $100 as interest. Suppose you sell the bond for $950 after owning it for only five years; you don't have a capital gain of $50. Instead, you have interest income of $50. Adding a different twist to the example, you sell the bond after 5 years for $960. You report $50 as interest income ($10 × 5 years) and $10 as a capital gain. Instead of doing it this way, you can elect to report a portion of the $100 as interest income ratable over 10 years at a rate of $10 a year. You make this election in the year of purchase by simply reporting the $10 as interest. If you make the election, every year you add the $10 to your tax basis of the bond. You may want to report the income annually because you have a lot of investment interest expense that can't be deducted because you don't have enough investment income to offset the interest expense (see investment interest in Chapter 9, line 13). This rule, which requires that part of the discount be reported as interest instead of capital gain, applies to bonds issued after July 19, 1984, regardless of when you bought them. For tax-exempt bonds, which we will get to in a moment, this rule applies to bonds purchased after April 30, 1993, regardless of when the bond was issued.

Tax refunds

Interest you receive on all tax refunds is taxable interest. You should include only the interest portion of your refund, whether it's federal, state, or local, on Schedule B (1040) or Schedule 1 (1040A). Remember, a refund of federal taxes that you've paid isn't taxable. State and local tax refunds are, and belong on line 10 of Form 1040 (but only if you deducted them on Schedule A in a prior year).

Tax-exempt bonds (municipal bonds)

This year, for the first time, tax-exempt interest (interest on city and state bonds) is reported to you on Form 1099-INT in box 8. You report this income on Form 1040A (line 8b) or on Form 1040 (line 8b). Although this entry on line 8b isn't added to your taxable income, it is used to determine the amount of your Social Security that may be subject to tax.

Most states have a provision that tax-exempt bonds are exempt from state income tax only if the bonds are issued by that state. For example, a New York State resident pays state income tax on a tax-exempt bond issued by Ohio but doesn't pay state income tax on a tax-exempt bond issued by New York.

If you purchase a *municipal* bond at a discount — for example, a $1,000, 10-year, 6 percent bond for $900 — you have $100 of taxable interest at maturity. This isn't a misprint. The $100 is taxable. Say you sell the bond after 5 years for $960. You report $50 as interest and $10 as a capital gain. Here's the math on how this nasty bit of business is computed. Every year during the 10 years until the bond matures, $10 of the discount is considered interest ($100 ÷ 10). This amounts to $50 during the five years you owned the bond. The $50 is reported as interest and is added to the $900 you paid to figure your capital gain. All this probably comes as a surprise to you because you more than likely thought that 100 percent of the income on a municipal bond was tax-exempt. Just like a taxable bond, you can elect to report the discount annually. The interest the bond earns every year is tax-exempt, but not the discount you receive when either the bond matures or is sold.

Line 2: Total interest

Add all the amounts on line 1.

Line 3: U.S. Savings Bonds — education program

One tax shelter that most people are unaware of is that Uncle Sam wants you to put money aside for the education of your children and provides you with a tax exemption to boot. All or part of the interest on certain Series EE or Series I U.S. Savings Bonds used to pay college tuition is exempt from tax under the following conditions:

- ✔ The U.S. Savings Bonds were issued after December 31, 1989.

- ✔ You're 24 years of age or older before the month in which you buy the bonds.

- ✔ The total redemption proceeds — interest and principal — don't exceed the tuition and fees paid for the year. (Room and board aren't considered a part of tuition.) The tuition and fees paid have to be reduced by any nontaxable scholarships.

- ✔ The tuition is for you, your spouse, or your dependents.

- ✔ The exclusion isn't available if you're married filing separately.

- ✔ The bond must be issued in either your name or in your name and your spouse's name as co-owners.

The amount of interest that can be excluded is reduced if your 2006 AGI meets the following requirements:

- ✔ Unmarried taxpayers with an income of $63,100 or less are entitled to a full interest exclusion. Between incomes of $63,100 and $78,100, the exclusion is gradually phased out.

- ✔ Married people filing jointly get a complete interest exclusion if your income is under $94,700 with a phaseout range between $94,700 and $124,700.

- ✔ The preceding income limits are based on your AGI (line 21, Form 1040A or line 37, Form 1040), adding back any student loan interest deduction (line 33, Form 1040 or line 18, Form 1040A), foreign earned income and housing exclusion (Form 2555 or 2555-EZ), and the exclusion from income for employer-provided adoption assistance (line 23, Form 8839).

The amount of interest that you can exclude is computed on **Form 8815, Exclusion of Interest from Series EE and I U.S. Savings Bonds Issued after 1989.** The amount of excludable interest is entered on Schedule B, line 3, and the total interest is listed on line 1. For example, suppose you earned $500 of interest, all of which is excludable interest. You enter the $500 on lines 3 and 1.

You can't redeem a bond and exclude the interest because you're paying higher education expenses and at the same time use those expenses to compute a Hope or Lifetime Learning Credit, nor can you take tax-free distributions from either a Section 529 Plan or a Coverdell Education Savings Account. Choose one; double dipping isn't allowed! Check out Chapter 24 for more on your higher education savings options.

Interest-free loans

Some wise person once said that no good deed ever goes unpunished, and that is never truer than with interest-free loans. If you make an interest-free loan to someone, the IRS assumes the borrower paid you interest anyway. Welcome to the world of *imputed interest,* where the IRS *imputes* (states) what the minimum rate should be and then taxes you on it, whether you've actually charged it or not. In this strange new world, the borrower can deduct the interest he or she is considered to have paid if he or she uses the money to make an investment that produces income, while you are required to report that same amount as income, despite the fact that no money has changed hands. For the applicable minimum rates, go to the IRS Web page (www.irs.gov).

To make this world even more interesting, there are gift tax consequences to this interest-free loan as well. The fact that interest should have been charged but wasn't creates a taxable gift of the interest amount. The person you lent the money to now not only gets the interest-free loan, but also a gift of the amount of interest that he should have paid to you. If it's a small loan, this information may be of little or no consequence to you — you pay the additional income tax and go merrily on your way. If, on the other hand, you've lent someone a large amount, to purchase a house or a business, perhaps, the annual interest you should be charging but you're not could be more than the annual exclusion amount of $12,000. Think before you get involved in interest-free loans — the tax consequences to you could be ferocious!

Rules for interest-free loans also apply to below-market-rate loans.

As with every other IRS rule, there are exceptions to this rule. Here they are:

- Loans under $10,000 aren't subject to the rule.

- For loans between $10,000 and $100,000, interest isn't imputed (that is, assumed to have been made) if the borrower's investment income for the year doesn't exceed $1,000. If the borrower's income exceeds $1,000, the imputed interest is limited to that amount of the person's investment income. Say you lend your son $50,000. If his investment income is under $1,000, no interest is imputed (considered to have been paid). If his investment income is $1,200, that's all the interest you have to report, even if you should have charged him $4,000.

- Certain employee relocation loans to buy a new residence aren't subject to the interest-free loan rule that requires that a minimum rate be charged. See your company's employment benefits office or a tax advisor.

- If the loan exceeds $100,000, you have to deal with the imputed interest rule in its full glory.

Interest-free or below-market-rate-of-interest loans usually occur when a family member taps you for money. In many cases, these types of loans end up not being repaid (see Chapter 12). If scaring someone off with the imputed interest rules doesn't work, try Shakespeare's "neither a borrower nor a lender be."

A lender reporting imputed interest or a borrower claiming an interest deduction must attach a statement to his return indicating how the interest was computed, the loan balance, the name of the borrower or lender, and the borrower's or lender's Social Security number. (If you're the borrower, it's the lender's number, and vice versa.) That should also frighten most would-be borrowers off. As a general rule, when the parties to a below-market-rate-of-interest loan don't make the imputed interest calculations, the IRS ends up drooling over doing it when an audit of either the borrower or the lender uncovers the loan.

Part II, Lines 5–6: Dividend Income

Well, we hope that you made a good bit of extra dough in Part I. Part II provides another opportunity to count your silver coins — er, we mean dividends. You find out about your dividends from another version of a 1099. Anyone who pays you a dividend is required to send you **Form 1099-DIV, Dividends and Distributions** (see Figure 10-3) by January 31, 2007. If your 1099-DIV is incorrect, get the payer to correct it; otherwise, you may pay tax on income you never earned. Getting an incorrect 1099 corrected isn't as much of a headache as it used to be; the telephone number of the person you need to contact is listed on the form.

To report the income from jointly owned stock, follow the rules explained for reporting interest on a joint bank account in the sidebar "Joint returns, minors, and interest stuff," earlier in this chapter.

Watch out for corrected 1099s. If you file really early, you may need to file an amended return. (April 15 comes only once a year; it's best that way.)

Line 5: Name, payer, and amount

Schedule B, Part II, has a column for the payer's name and a column for the amount of the dividend you received. Enter the payer's name in the column that says to list the name of the payer. Enter the amount of the dividend you received in the column that says *amount*. For each 1099-DIV you received, enter the name of the payer and the amount received.

Line 6: Total dividends

This is the easy part. Total all the dividends you listed on line 5 and enter that amount on line 9a of your 1040 or 1040A.

☐ CORRECTED (if checked)

PAYER'S name, street address, city, state, ZIP code, and telephone no.		1a Total ordinary dividends $	OMB No. 1545-0110 **2006** Form **1099-DIV**	**Dividends and Distributions**
		1b Qualified dividends $		
		2a Total capital gain distr. $	2b Unrecap. Sec. 1250 gain $	**Copy B** **For Recipient**
PAYER'S federal identification number	RECIPIENT'S identification number			
RECIPIENT'S name		2c Section 1202 gain $	2d Collectibles (28%) gain $	This is important tax information and is being furnished to the Internal Revenue Service. If you are required to file a return, a negligence penalty or other sanction may be imposed on you if this income is taxable and the IRS determines that it has not been reported.
		3 Nondividend distributions $	4 Federal income tax withheld $	
Street address (including apt. no.)			5 Investment expenses $	
City, state, and ZIP code		6 Foreign tax paid $	7 Foreign country or U.S. possession	
Account number (see instructions)		8 Cash liquidation distributions $	9 Noncash liquidation distributions $	

Figure 10-3: Form 1099-DIV shows you the dividends you reaped in 2006.

Form **1099-DIV** (keep for your records) Department of the Treasury - Internal Revenue Service

Your 1099-DIV: Decoding those boxes

Here's what all those boxes on your 1099-DIV mean:

✔ **Box 1a: Total ordinary dividends.** Enter the total amount of your ordinary dividends on line 5. Make sure you list the payer's name to the left of the amount column.

If the total of your ordinary dividends doesn't exceed $1,500, skip Part II and enter the total on line 9a of Form 1040 or 1040A.

✔ **Box 1b: Qualified dividends.** These dividends are eligible for either the 15 percent or 5 percent rates. Enter this amount on line 9b of Form 1040 or Form 1040A. The portion of your total dividends (line 9a) less your qualified dividends (line 9b) ends up getting taxed at whatever bracket your taxable income (line 43 of Form 1040 or line 27 of Form 1040A) places you in. Now that couldn't be simpler, could it?

✔ **Boxes 2a–2d: Capital gain distributions.** Capital gains, although reported on Form 1099-DIV, aren't entered on Schedule B. Enter them on Schedule D.

- Box 2a has the total capital gain distributions. Enter this amount on Schedule D, line 13 — see Chapter 12. If the only amounts you have to report on Schedule D are capital gain distributions from box 2a because you have no other capital gains or losses and no amounts are entered in boxes 2b through 2d, you don't have to file Schedule D. Enter the amounts from box 2a on Form 1040, line 13a or Form 1040A, line 10.

- Box 2b is for certain real estate capital gain dividends, those tricky unrecaptured Section 1250 gains. This is your opportunity to go directly to the "Unrecaptured Section 1250 Gain Worksheet" located in the Schedule D instructions of your 1040 Instruction Booklet. Follow this worksheet carefully to find out how much, if any, of this number lands on Line 19 of your Schedule D.

- Box 2c indicates the amount of a gain from a small business start-up and specialized small business investment companies; 50 percent of these types of gains can be exempt from tax. The investment has to be in an economically depressed area designated as an Empowerment Zone by the government.

- Box 2d indicates the amount of the total gain in box 2a that gets taxed at 28 percent instead of the lower capital gain rate. This is the rate for the gain on the sale of collectibles (art, antiques, and so on). You get to do another worksheet (come on, they're fun!) found in the Schedule D instructions called "28% Rate Gain Worksheet" before putting any number on Line 18 of your Schedule D.

To make sure you don't overpay the tax on capital gain distributions, flip back to line 44 in Chapter 8, where we show you how to prevent that from happening.

✔ **Box 3: Nondividend distributions.** These used to be called "nontaxable distributions," and that is what they are: nontaxable. These nondividend distributions aren't entered on your return, and you don't currently pay tax on them as dividends. What these distributions do is reduce the basis of your shares when figuring your gain or loss when the shares are sold. For example, suppose that you purchased shares in a company or a mutual fund for $10,000, and you received $500 in nondividend distributions. Your basis for determining gain or loss when you sell the shares is now $9,500.

✔ **Box 4: Federal tax withheld.** Report your federal tax withheld on Form 1040 (line 64). On Form 1040A, it's line 38.

✔ **Box 5: Investment expenses.** This box refers to shares you own in funds not available to the public, so it doesn't apply to most people. We have yet to see a 1099-DIV with an entry in this box! (But it must be there for a reason!) If this box applies to you, it means that you own shares in a nonpublicly traded fund. You can deduct this expense as a miscellaneous itemized deduction on line 22, Schedule A of Form 1040 (see Chapter 9). Publicly traded funds don't pass investment expenses on to shareholders.

✔ **Box 6: Foreign tax paid.** If you own shares in a company or fund that was required to pay tax in a foreign country, your share of the tax is recorded in box 6. You can claim this amount as a credit against your tax or as an itemized deduction. We discuss how to handle this in Chapter 9.

✔ **Box 7: Foreign country or U.S. possession.** This one is easy. It states the country or U.S. possession where the tax was paid. You need this information when you fill out Form 1116, Foreign Tax Credit. See Chapter 14.

✔ **Boxes 8 and 9: Cash and noncash liquidation distributions.** You report these amounts (cash and noncash) on Schedule D (Capital Gains and Losses). If you have entries in these two boxes, see a tax advisor. And check out Chapter 12 to find out more about Schedule D.

Reduced tax rates on dividends

The reduced 15 percent and 5 percent (for those individuals whose taxable incomes, line 43 of Form 1040, or line 27 of Form 1040A, places them in the 10 percent or 15 percent tax bracket) maximum tax rates don't apply to all dividends. Only qualified dividends are entitled to this reduced rate of tax.

Qualified dividends are those dividends paid by

✔ U.S. corporations

✔ A corporation incorporated in a U.S. possession

✔ Foreign corporations traded on a U.S. stock exchange

✔ A foreign corporation whose shares aren't traded on a U.S. market, from a country that has a comprehensive tax treaty with the United States that includes a program providing for the exchange of tax information. Because not many countries have such a comprehensive treaty with the United States, this will probably cause many investors in international funds to rethink whether it makes sense to continue to hold shares that don't entitle them to preferred tax treatment on their dividends.

Not only do you have to know where qualified dividends come from, but you also have to know what dividends aren't considered qualified and eligible for the reduced rates. These are dividends paid by

✔ Banks on certificates of deposits

✔ Bond funds

✔ Credit unions

✔ Farmers' cooperatives

✔ Money market funds

✔ Mutual insurance companies

✔ Real Estate Investment Trusts (REITs)

✔ Savings banks and savings and loans

✔ Tax-exempt corporations

When is a dividend NOT a dividend?

Stock dividends and splits

Stock dividends (not the cash variety) and splits aren't taxable. You now own more shares!

For example, suppose that you own 100 shares. If the stock is split two for one, you now own 200 shares. If you receive a 10 percent stock dividend, you now own 110 shares. Chapter 12 explains how you treat the shares that you received when they are sold.

Life insurance dividends

Life insurance dividends aren't taxable until the total dividends received exceed the total premiums paid.

Savings dividends

So-called dividends from savings and loans, credit unions, savings banks, and bond and money market funds have to be reported as interest.

Three other categories of dividends that aren't considered qualified are:

- Dividends paid on stock purchased with borrowed funds, if the dividend was included in investment income in claiming a deduction for investment interest (line 13, Chapter 9 provides a plain English explanation of what this is all about).

- Payments in lieu of a dividend on a short sale (see Chapter 12).

- Dividends on stock owned less than 60 days in the 121-day period surrounding the ex-dividend date, or the date the stock trades without the announced dividend, which is normally two days before the record day, the day when the company determines who is the record owner of the stock. You need to have owned the stock 60 days out of the 121-day period beginning 61 days before the ex-dividend day.

Qualified dividends that mutual funds receive (from stock holdings) and in turn distribute to you remain qualified and are eligible for the reduced rates. Because qualified dividends received by IRAs, 401(k)s, and retirement accounts are paid in a tax-free environment, you won't pay tax on these dividends as long as the stock is held in one of these accounts. As soon as you begin taking distributions, though, you don't get the reduced rate; all distributions from IRAs (unless you made after tax contributions), 401(k)s, and other retirement accounts are treated as ordinary income, and receive no preferential income tax treatment. Sorry!

Part III, Lines 7–8: Foreign Accounts and Trusts

If you have a foreign bank or security account, you have to check "yes" on line 7a of Schedule B and enter the name of the foreign country. However, if the average balance in the account in 2006 was under $10,000, you can check "no." But if you had more than $10,000 in a foreign bank or security account during the year, then you have to file **Form TD F 90-22.1, Report of Foreign Bank and Financial Accounts,** by June 30, 2007. On this form, you have to list where your account(s) are located, including the name of the bank, security firm, or brokerage firm; its address; and the account number.

Don't treat Form TD F 90-22.1, Report of Foreign Bank and Financial Accounts, lightly. Although the penalties for failure to timely file any IRS form is monetary, the failure to file Form TD F 90-22.1 is a felony, punishable by a five-year prison term. Furthermore, no extensions are allowed. If you need help or aren't sure what to do here, seek advice!

If you're unique enough to have to deal with line 8, it means that you have a foreign trust. You have to check "yes" and complete **Form 3520, Annual Return to Report Transactions With Foreign Trusts and Receipt of Certain Foreign Gifts,** or **Form 926, Return by a U.S. Transferor of Property to a Foreign Corporation** (the trustee completes Form 3520-A). Good luck! (These forms are complicated; consider using a tax advisor.)

If you received a distribution from a foreign partnership or corporation in excess of $12,760 (this amount gets adjusted for inflation every year) that you have treated as a gift, you have to report it to the IRS. If you receive a gift or inheritance from a foreign individual or estate above $100,000, you also have to provide the IRS with the foreigner's name and address. Report this information on Form 3520. You also have to file Form 3520 if you're an owner of a foreign trust or if you received a distribution from one regardless of the amount. The penalty for not filing is 5 percent for each month the return isn't filed, up to a maximum of 25 percent of the amount received. Evidently, a lot of people were claiming that what they earned abroad was a gift or bequest. The amount you report to the IRS as a gift or inheritance isn't taxable. The IRS does, however, want to know about it. A distribution from a foreign trust, partnership, or corporation more than likely is taxable.

The due date for filing Form 3520 is April 16, 2007. File the form separately and don't attach it to your return.

Taxpayers with interest earned in Canadian Registered Retirement Savings Plans are probably unaware that they must file Form 3520. If you haven't been doing this, the good news is that the IRS has pardoned all those who haven't filed the form for all years before 2002. Starting with 2002, you either have to file Form 3520 or attach a statement to your return every year that you're claiming the benefit of Article XVIII (7) of the treaty, including the name of the savings plan's trustee, the account number, and the balance in the account at the beginning of the year. The amount in the plan isn't taxable until distributions are made.

Chapter 11

Business Tax Schedules: C, C-EZ, and F

• •

In This Chapter

▶ Using Schedule C-EZ

▶ Using Schedule C

▶ Reporting income

▶ Tallying and categorizing expenses

▶ Understanding the nuances of Schedule F for farmers

• •

Running your own firm really can be the American dream. In fact, the only thing better than working for yourself is knowing how to keep more of what you earn. It's like giving yourself an immediate raise at tax time.

If you're self-employed, you must report your income on Schedule C (or C-EZ) along with your business expenses. You subtract your expenses from your income to arrive at your profit, on which you have to pay tax. (Farmers use Schedule F instead, but many of the same principles apply.)

Schedule C-EZ

Schedule C-EZ is a three-line form that's relatively EZ to complete. The only catches are that your deductible expenses can't exceed $5,000, you can't have an inventory of items for sale, you must operate only one business as a sole proprietor, and you must use the cash method of accounting (we explain in a moment). You also can't use the C-EZ if you have a net loss from your business, you're claiming expenses for the business use of your home, you had employees, or you're required to file **Form 4562, Depreciation and Amortization** (see our discussion about line 13, later in this chapter, where we explain who has to file this form).

If you do qualify, have a go at it. After you fill in the easy background information in Part I, figure your net profit. So we don't have to constantly repeat ourselves, take a gander two paragraphs down in this chapter at Basic Information (A–E) on how to obtain the information for items B and D. Here's how to fill out this form:

▶ **Line 1:** Fill in the gross income from your business (that's the amount of money you brought in before you started paying for any of your expenses).

▶ **Line 2:** Fill in your business expenses.

▶ **Line 3:** Subtract line 2 from line 1; this amount is your net profit. Remember, if you have a negative number here, you need to use Schedule C to report a loss.

You're done. Carry the profit over to Form 1040 (line 12). Unless you're a statutory employee (see Chapter 6), also carry the profit to line 2 of Schedule SE to calculate your self-employment tax.

Okay, okay, you caught us. If you're deducting automobile expenses on line 2, you have to fill out Part III and answer five (maybe six) more questions so the IRS can be sure that your expenses are legitimate. Four of those questions are Yes/No questions. Don't you wish all IRS forms were like this?

On the other hand, knowing what's taxable and what's deductible can, at times, be confusing. So read on. We take you by the hand to make sure that you don't miss a thing.

Schedule C

This schedule isn't so EZ, but it isn't as bad as it looks (see Figure 11-1) for many small-business owners. In this part, we take you through the line-by-line instructions.

SCHEDULE C (Form 1040) — **Profit or Loss From Business** (Sole Proprietorship) — OMB No. 1545-0074 — **2006**

Department of the Treasury Internal Revenue Service (99)

▶ Partnerships, joint ventures, etc., must file Form 1065 or 1065-B.

▶ Attach to Form 1040, 1040NR, or 1041. ▶ See Instructions for Schedule C (Form 1040).

Attachment Sequence No. 09

Name of proprietor | Social security number (SSN)

A Principal business or profession, including product or service (see page C-2 of the instructions) | B Enter code from pages C-8, 9, & 10 ▶

C Business name. If no separate business name, leave blank. | D Employer ID number (EIN), if any

E Business address (including suite or room no.) ▶
City, town or post office, state, and ZIP code

F Accounting method: (1) ☐ Cash (2) ☐ Accrual (3) ☐ Other (specify) ▶

G Did you "materially participate" in the operation of this business during 2006? If "No," see page C-2 for limit on losses ☐ Yes ☐ No

H If you started or acquired this business during 2006, check here ▶ ☐

Part I Income

1	Gross receipts or sales. **Caution.** If this income was reported to you on Form W-2 and the "Statutory employee" box on that form was checked, see page C-3 and check here ▶ ☐	1	
2	Returns and allowances	2	
3	Subtract line 2 from line 1	3	
4	Cost of goods sold (from line 42 on page 2)	4	
5	**Gross profit.** Subtract line 4 from line 3	5	
6	Other income, including federal and state gasoline or fuel tax credit or refund (see page C-3)	6	
7	**Gross income.** Add lines 5 and 6 ▶	7	

Part II Expenses. Enter expenses for business use of your home **only** on line 30.

8	Advertising	8		18	Office expense	18	
9	Car and truck expenses (see page C-4)	9		19	Pension and profit-sharing plans	19	
				20	Rent or lease (see page C-5):		
10	Commissions and fees	10		a	Vehicles, machinery, and equipment	20a	
11	Contract labor (see page C-4)	11		b	Other business property	20b	
12	Depletion	12		21	Repairs and maintenance	21	
13	Depreciation and section 179 expense deduction (not included in Part III) (see page C-4)	13		22	Supplies (not included in Part III)	22	
				23	Taxes and licenses	23	
				24	Travel, meals, and entertainment:		
				a	Travel	24a	
14	Employee benefit programs (other than on line 19)	14		b	Deductible meals and entertainment (see page C-5)	24b	
15	Insurance (other than health)	15		25	Utilities	25	
16	Interest:			26	Wages (less employment credits)	26	
a	Mortgage (paid to banks, etc.)	16a		27	Other expenses (from line 48 on page 2)	27	
b	Other	16b					
17	Legal and professional services	17					

28	**Total expenses** before expenses for business use of home. Add lines 8 through 27 in columns ▶	28	
29	Tentative profit (loss). Subtract line 28 from line 7	29	
30	Expenses for business use of your home. Attach **Form 8829**	30	
31	**Net profit or (loss).** Subtract line 30 from line 29. • If a profit, enter on **Form 1040, line 12,** and **also** on **Schedule SE, line 2** or **Form 1040NR, line 13** (statutory employees, see page C-6). Estates and trusts, enter on Form 1041, line 3. • If a loss, you **must** go to line 32.	31	
32	If you have a loss, check the box that describes your investment in this activity (see page C-6). • If you checked 32a, enter the loss on **Form 1040, line 12,** and **also** on **Schedule SE, line 2** or **Form 1040NR, line 13** (statutory employees, see page C-6). Estates and trusts, enter on Form 1041, line 3. • If you checked 32b, you **must** attach **Form 6198.** Your loss may be limited.	32a ☐ All investment is at risk. 32b ☐ Some investment is not at risk.	

For Paperwork Reduction Act Notice, see page C-7 of the instructions. Cat. No. 11334P **Schedule C (Form 1040) 2006**

Figure 11-1: Schedule C, Page 1.

Basic Information (A–E)

Lines A through D are pretty easy background stuff. Employer ID Numbers can now be obtained instantly by applying online at www.irs.gov, click on "Businesses," and then click on "More Topics" (both these buttons are on the left of the screen) and you'll be taken to Employer ID Numbers. You can also call 800-829-4933 or go the paper route by sending a completed **Form SS-4, Application For Employer Identification Number,** to the IRS. You can pick up your business code from the list on pages C-7, C-8, and C-9 in your instruction booklet. On line E, simply fill in your business address.

Accounting Method Stuff (F–H)

The two methods to report income are *cash* and *accrual*. With the cash method, you report income when it's actually received, and you deduct expenses when they're actually paid. However, there is (of course) one exception to this rule: If you charge an expense on a credit card, you deduct this expense in the year charged, even if you pay the charge in a later year. (So don't leave home without it!)

Does your business take in $10 million or less? We knew that would get a smile out of you. If so, then you can use the cash method of accounting, but only if a bunch of restrictions don't apply. If you're in a purely service business, then you don't have to worry about these restrictions. You're eligible to use the cash method. You're also eligible to skip the following paragraph.

If your line of business is in the wholesale or retail trade, manufacturing, information services, or mining, then you can't use the cash. However, this rule does have its exceptions: Even if you're in one of these businesses that disqualifies you from using the cash method, you still can use it if providing a service is the main thing you do. For example, you're a publisher (information services) whose main activity is the sale of advertising space. You can use the cash method even though information services isn't one of the businesses normally allowed to use the cash method. The reason? The sale of advertising space is considered a service. When will the IRS ever stop making such distinctions? Similarly, businesses that manufacture or modify a product to a customer's specifications and design can also use the cash method even though manufacturing isn't an eligible business.

 A small business whose average annual income (the current and two previous years) is $1 million or less can use the cash method regardless of its line of business. However, it can deduct the purchase of merchandise for resale only when it's sold and not when it's purchased, so read on.

Even though some people are permitted to use the cash method, if they use materials and supplies that aren't incidental to the services they perform, they face a hitch. Roofing contractors are an example. Even though they use the cash method, they aren't allowed to deduct the cost of the materials they purchase until the later of either when it is used on the customer's job or when they pay for it. Say a contractor paid $5,000 for shingles in December 2006, but didn't install them until January 2007. Sorry, it's a 2007 tax deduction, not a 2006 deduction. (The amount the contractor charges the customer is reported in the year it is received because the contractor is using the cash method.)

Say you must use the accrual method because you operate a clothing store; you report income in the year that sales are made — even when the sales are billed or collected in a later year. You deduct expenses in the year that they're incurred, even if those expenses aren't paid until a later year.

A hybrid method of accounting also exists. Even if you have to use the accrual method to report income and deduct merchandise sold, you nevertheless can use the cash method for the rest of your expenses, rent, telephone, wages, and so on. Doing so can make your bookkeeping less complicated.

If you have the choice, the cash method of accounting gives you more control over when your business sees a profit from year to year. For example, if next year looks like a slower year for you, perhaps because you plan to take a sabbatical, you may elect to push more income into next year. This plan will likely save you tax dollars, because you should be in a lower tax bracket next year. You legally can do this by delaying the sending of invoices until January, for example, that you normally would have mailed in December. Likewise, you can pay more of your expenses in December instead of waiting until January. The general rule is if you're selling merchandise, you have to comply with the accrual method rules. Even though your business involves the sale of merchandise, you still can use the cash method if your average income is $1 million or less. However, you can't deduct your merchandise purchases until you sell those goods. If you're providing a service, you can use the cash method.

This tax cut is the general rule, but it may not apply to everyone. For example, if you operate a business that receives large cash advances from customers before you undertake the work, you're better off using the accrual method. That way you don't have to report the cash advances until you actually do the work.

"Did you 'materially participate' in the operation of the business?" is a trick question designed to limit losses that someone can deduct as a silent partner. If you put up the dough, but someone other than your spouse operated a business that lost money, then *you* can't deduct the loss. The reason? You didn't materially participate in the operation of the business, and (as a result) you're considered to be operating a tax shelter — see the tax shelter rules in Chapter 13. Seven criteria determine *material participation*. Page C-2 of your 1040 instruction booklet has them all. The basic criteria include whether you meet either the 500- and 100-hour rules regarding material participation, whether you were the only one who did the work, or whether you participated on a regular, continuous, and substantial basis. Pass any one of the seven and you're okay.

If you're filing Schedule C to report a working interest in an oil or gas well, you automatically get to check the "Yes" box. Why? Ever heard of the oil and gas lobby?

Part 1, Lines 1–7: Income

Time to tally. This section wants you to find some gross things: gross sales, gross profits, and gross income.

Line 1: Gross receipts or sales

If you operate a service business, enter the income from fees that you actually collected (because you're reporting income under the cash method). If clients have given you Form 1099-MISC to report their payments to you to the IRS, add up the amounts in box 7. Remember, even if you didn't receive a Form 1099-MISC, you're still obligated to report all of the income you received.

If you're filing this form because you're a statutory employee (see Chapter 6, the section about line 7), enter the amount from box 1 of your W-2 and check the "Statutory employee" box on this line. Next, enter your business expenses on lines 8 through 27, and you can ignore our instructions on line 31 about paying Social Security tax, because you already paid it (see lines 4 and 6 of your W-2).

If you're required to use the accrual method, enter the total of all the sales that you billed to your customers on this line.

Line 2: Returns and allowances

If you had to return any fees, enter that amount here. If any customers returned merchandise, that amount also goes on this line, along with any discounts that those customers took.

Line 3: Subtraction quiz

All that you need to do on this line is subtract your returns and allowances (line 2) from your gross receipts and sales (line 1).

Line 4: Cost of goods sold

The IRS must think that you're an accountant; otherwise, the agency would simply tell you to subtract the amount you paid for the merchandise that you sold from your sales to arrive at this figure. Services and other businesses that don't sell products don't have to put an amount on this line.

But because you're not an accountant — thank heavens, you say? — you have to compute the cost of the merchandise that you sold in Part III (on the back of Schedule C). Part III is an eight-line schedule where you enter your beginning inventory, the merchandise that you purchased, the salary that you paid to your production workers (if you manufacture the product that you sell), and the cost of production supplies. You total all these expenses on line 40. From this total, you subtract your ending inventory to arrive at the cost of the goods that you sold. This amount goes back to line 4 (where you are right now!).

Remember, you can't deduct the cost of all the merchandise that you purchased during the year. You can deduct only the cost of merchandise that you sold. That's why you have to subtract your ending inventory, which is the stuff that you didn't sell. You get to deduct what's on hand when it's sold. You enter the amount of the merchandise that you didn't sell (it's called *ending inventory*) on line 41. Your ending inventory gets carried over to your 2007 return. So don't forget to enter the amount from line 41, which becomes your inventory at the beginning of the year, on line 35 of your 2007 Schedule C.

Writing off what a customer doesn't pay

When you use the accrual method to report income, you can write off losses when customers don't pay. However, when you use the cash method, you can't — because you never recorded the income and paid tax on the money that your client owes. The rules regarding when cash-method taxpayers can write off bad debts on loans that they make are similar to the rules regarding when

you can write off a personal loan that goes bad. We explain such things in Chapter 12.

When you're using the accrual method and want to write off what your deadbeat customers owe, you can claim these amounts on Schedule C, line 27.

The following example explains what this inventory business is all about. Say you own a retail furniture store. In 2006, you purchased two identical chairs, one for $1,200 and the other for $1,000. You sold only one chair (we hope business is better next year). Which one did you sell? The inventory method that you select determines that.

Under the *FIFO method* — First In, First Out — the first chair purchased is deemed the first one sold. If that's the $1,200 chair, then enter the cost of the $1,000 chair on line 41, because that's the one considered on hand at the end of the year. Under the *LIFO method* — Last In, First Out — the chair purchased last is deemed to be sold first. Under this method, the $1,000 chair is considered to be sold first, so enter $1,200 on line 41, because that's the cost of the chair that's considered the unsold one. Which method is better? In a period of rising costs, it's the LIFO method. FIFO is better when costs are declining.

Line 33 also requires you to select the method that you used to value your inventory. Three methods are available — cost (box a), lower of cost or market (box b), and other (box c). Skip box c, because it's too complicated. Most people check box a, because it's the easiest. Although using the lower of cost or market method can increase deductions if your inventory declines in value (you get to deduct the amount of the decline), it requires you to revalue your inventory every year.

After you select a valuation method, you can change it only with permission from the IRS.

Line 5: Gross profit

Subtract line 4 from line 3.

Line 6: Other income

Just do what the schedule orders you to do — see page C-3 of the 1040 booklet if you have any questions about other income. Some of the more common — and more obscure — examples of other income include the following:

- Federal and state gasoline or fuel tax credit
- Fee for allowing a company to paint an advertisement on the side of your building
- Interest on accounts receivable
- Scrap sales

Line 7: Gross income

This amount usually is the same as the amount on line 5. But if you had other items of income, such as a refund of a prior year's expense, enter that amount on line 6 and add it to the amount on line 5 to arrive at your gross income.

Part II, Lines 8–27: Expenses

Take a breath and get ready for all those wonderful lines that are split into two columns — so they'd all fit on one page!

Line 8: Advertising

On this line, enter the cost of any advertising that your business does to promote itself — for example, an ad in the Yellow Pages and other forms of advertising, including radio, newspaper, and promotional brochures and mailers. Don't forget the little ads you take out in the affinity magazines for state troopers, police, firefighters, and other service agencies. If they have your name and business information in them, and they're seen by any segment of the public, they're advertising. So is an ad that you take out in your local high school's football program or annual yearbook.

Line 9: Car and truck expenses

If you plan to make an entry on this line, be sure to answer questions 43 through 47b in Part IV on the other side of Schedule C, commonly referred to as Page 2.

When you use your car for business, the expenses of operating your car are deductible. But remember that "using it for business" is the key phrase. You can compute this deduction by using either a flat rate per business mile (see the "Standard mileage rate" sidebar), or you can keep track of actual expenses (gas, oil, repair, insurance, depreciation, and so on). Regardless of which method you use, you're supposed to keep a log or diary so that you can record the business purpose of your trips as well as the mileage ("Dear Diary . . ."). You also have to record the odometer reading at the beginning and end of the year. You need all this information to be able to divide your expenses into personal and business use. But here's a word of caution: Whether you use the flat rate or tabulate your actual expenses, proving that you use your car 100 percent for business is just about impossible. Unfortunately, there's always some personal use!

You don't have to write down the miles that you travel every time you get in and out of your car. Making entries in your diary on a weekly basis meets the IRS requirement that you keep a record of your car's business use near or at the time of its use.

No help from Uncle Sam with commuting expenses

Commuting expenses between your home and office aren't deductible. These expenses are considered personal commuting expenses, no matter how far your home is from your office or place of work. And making telephone calls from your car while commuting or having a business discussion with a business associate who accompanies you doesn't turn your ride into a deductible expense (besides, you should be watching the road). And using your car to display advertising material on your way to the office doesn't count as business use of your auto, either. Finally, the cost of parking at your place of business isn't deductible — but the cost of parking when you visit a customer or client is.

If you use your car to call on clients or customers and don't have a regular office to go to, the mileage between your home and the first customer that you call on — and the mileage between the location of the last customer that you call on and your home — is considered commuting. If your office is in your home, you can deduct all your auto expenses for calling on clients or customers. Use line 44 to split out your commuting miles from your business miles.

Second job

If you moonlight after work, you can deduct the cost of getting from one job to the other. But transportation expenses going from your home to a part-time job on a day off from your main job aren't deductible. A meeting of an Armed Forces Reserve unit is considered travel to a second job, however. If the meeting is held on the same day as your regular job, it's deductible.

Temporary job site

If you have a regular place of business and commute to a temporary work location, you can deduct the cost of the daily round trip between your home and the temporary job site.

If you don't have a regular place of work (but ordinarily work at different locations in the general area where you live), you can't deduct the daily round trip between your home and your temporary job site. But if you travel to a job site outside your general area, your daily transportation is deductible. Sounds like a distinction without a difference, right? But if this exception applies to you, don't look a gift horse in the mouth.

You can deduct the business portion of the following: depreciation, leasing and rental fees, garage rent, licenses, repairs, gas, oil, tires, insurance, parking, and tolls.

If you're self-employed, you can deduct the business portion of interest on a car loan; if you're an employee, you can't. Fines for traffic violations aren't deductible, either — so slow down!

Sales tax can't be deducted separately — it's added to the car's tax basis for the purposes of determining the amount of depreciation that you're entitled to claim. If you're an employee, you can deduct personal property tax on your car if you itemize your deductions on Schedule A. (See Chapter 9 for more info.) If you're self-employed, you deduct the business portion of your personal property tax on line 23 and the personal part on Schedule A.

Standard mileage rate

Instead of figuring your actual expenses with those maddening depreciation computations, you can use a flat rate of 44.5 cents for every business mile you drive in 2006, whether you're self-employed or you work for someone else.

If you drove your car 15,000 miles in 2006 for business, you'd be entitled to a $6,675 deduction (15,000 × 44.5 cents). If you aren't self-employed, you can claim this deduction on page 2 of **Form 2106, Employee Business Expenses.**

Although Form 2106 is intended for employees who are deducting auto expenses, self-employed Schedule C filers will find Part II of the form helpful in computing their deductible automobile expenses.

When you're calculating your business mileage deduction on Form 2106, if you were reimbursed for any of your car expenses that weren't included in box 1 of your W-2 as taxable wages, a code L appears next to the amount of the reimbursement in box 12 of your W-2. You must deduct this amount from your total auto expenses (whether you use actual numbers or base it on the flat-rate mileage calculation) and enter it on line 7 of Form 2106.

If you choose the flat-rate method, you can't claim any of your actual expenses, such as depreciation, gas, oil, insurance, and so on. If you want to use this method, you must choose it the first year that you start using your car for business. If you don't use the standard mileage rate in the first year, you can't use the standard mileage rate in a subsequent year. But if you use the standard mileage the first year, you can switch to deducting your actual expenses, but you probably won't want to after you take a look at the rules in the IRS Publication 463 *(Travel, Entertainment, Gift, and Car Expenses).*

If you trade in your car, you can use the flat rate for both cars because you owned them at different times.

You can use the standard mileage rate whether you own or lease a vehicle.

If you sell your car, you have to reduce its tax basis by the amount of depreciation built into the flat rate so that you can determine whether you made a taxable profit or loss. A table (of course) in IRS Publication 463 shows you how to make this computation.

Standard mileage rate or actual expenses?

You can deduct either the business portion of your actual expenses or use the standard mileage rate for your business miles (see the "Standard mileage rate" sidebar). The standard mileage method relieves you of the task of keeping track of your expenses. It only requires that you track your miles. Deducting your actual expense requires both. Whichever method you use, Part II of Form 2106 (although intended for employees) contains an excellent worksheet to help you compute your deduction.

Depreciation

Car depreciation rules are always tricky, and tax year 2006 is no exception. Still, if you feel you're going to have a better result using your actual car expenses instead of the standard per mile flat rate (44.5 for 2006), you're going to have to figure them out. Look at the "Depreciation" section, later in this chapter to find out which method of depreciation you're supposed to use for your car for 2006. Strangely enough, even though it relates directly to your car and is one of the valid car and truck expenses, all of your auto depreciation gets lumped together on line 13 of Schedule C.

Leased autos

If you lease a car rather than buy it, you're probably asking yourself why we waited so long to discuss how leased autos are deducted. There are two reasons:

✔ First, a special rule applies, which we explain later in this chapter at "Lines 20a or b: Rent or lease" (this is your lucky day!).

✔ Secondly, lease payments for cars aren't deducted on line 9, they're deducted on line 20a. All your other car-related expenses, such as gasoline, oil changes, and insurance, are still deducted here on line 9.

Line 10: Commissions and fees

The fees that you paid to sell your merchandise or to bring in new clients (as in referral fees) go on this line.

However, if you pay someone who isn't your employee more than $600 in a year, you have to file **Form 1099-MISC** with the IRS and send the person that you paid a copy of the form by January 31. IRS Publication 334 *(Tax Guide for Small Business)* explains how to comply with this requirement.

Line 11: Contract labor

This line is meant to clearly identify businesses using independent contractors. The IRS is zeroing in on businesses that pay workers as independent contractors instead of as employees where the employer is obligated to withhold and pay Social Security and Medicare Taxes on their salaries. If someone works on your premises and under your control, he or she is probably your employee, and the rules about withholding taxes and Social Security apply. However, if treating these types of workers as independent contractors is standard in your industry (that is, at least 25 percent of your industry treats them this way) and you issue these workers a Form 1099 at the end of the year, you may have an escape hatch. IRS Publication 1779 *(Independent Contractor or Employee)* and IRS Publication 15-A *(Employer's Supplemental Tax Guide)* address the independent contractor issue in greater detail.

Line 12: Depletion

This line applies if your business deals with properties such as mines, oil and gas wells, timber, and exhaustible natural deposits. You can compute depletion two ways, and, of course, you want to use the one that produces the larger deduction. To be on the safe side, take a look at IRS Publication 535 *(Business Expenses)*.

Line 13: Depreciation

Depreciation is the annual deduction that enables you to recover the cost of an investment (that has a useful life of more than one year) in business equipment or in income-producing real estate. Or, as an accountant friend of one of us explained (in a ten words or less challenge), depreciation is "recovering an asset's value ratably over its useful economic life." The word "depreciation" is itself enough to send most readers to the next chapter, we know, but just think of depreciation as a way of reducing your tax! Now, are you more excited about depreciation possibilities? Unless you elect the special provision that allows you to deduct the first $108,000 of equipment or furniture used in your business (we explain this provision later in the chapter in "The Section 179 buying bonanza: The $108,000 depreciation deduction"), you have to write off your purchase of these assets over their respective useful lives — as established by the IRS (see Table 11-1). You can't depreciate land and works of art. (So you can't depreciate your van Goghs!) See Chapter 21 for a discussion of the pros and cons of depreciating versus taking an outright deduction.

Table 11-1	Useful Life
Type of Property	*Useful Life (Years)*
Computers and similar equipment	5
Office machinery (typewriters, calculators, copiers)	5
Autos and light trucks	5
Office furniture (desks, files)	7
Appliances (stoves, refrigerators used in residential buildings)	5
Shrubbery	15
Residential buildings	27.5
Nonresidential buildings after 5/12/93	39
Nonresidential buildings before 5/12/93	31.5
Goodwill, customer lists, franchise costs, and covenants not to compete	15

If you're an employee claiming auto expenses, you claim the depreciation for the auto on Form 2106, Employee Business Expenses; Form 4562 isn't required. For rental income reported on Schedule E, use Form 4562 for property that you started renting in 2006. For property that you started renting before 2006, you don't need to file Form 4562.

We'd be lying if we said that calculating depreciation is quick and easy. It's not. But calculating it isn't impossible. Still, you may have questions along the way or want to check with someone else after you've finished to make sure you've done it right. Consider asking a tax professional to double-check your depreciation calculations after you're done to make sure they're correct.

To file (or not to file) Form 4562

You compute your depreciation deduction for business property that you started using in 2006 on **Form 4562, Depreciation and Amortization.** Carry the amount of depreciation that you calculate on this form over to line 13 of Schedule C.

The depreciation you normally can deduct every year is determined by an item's useful life. Based on that, you then take a percentage of the item's cost as a deduction. Before we get into explaining how that works, you need to know about a depreciation deduction that you can take right off the bat, the $108,000 deduction.

The $108,000 deduction (Section 179 depreciation)

You can deduct up to $108,000 of the cost of new or used business equipment that you purchased and started to use in 2006, provided that all of the property you placed into service in your business in 2006 didn't exceed $430,000. If you fall into this category, you don't have to fuss with the standard depreciation tables to claim this depreciation deduction. We show you the ins and outs of this in just a moment. Whether you purchased new or used equipment doesn't matter. It only has to be used more than 50 percent of the time in your business. If the equipment, machinery, or office furniture that you purchased for your business didn't exceed $108,000, simply deduct what you spent on Form 4562 and on line 13 of Schedule C.

If you are only depreciating property you started using prior to 2006, Form 4562 isn't required. On line 13 of Schedule C, just enter the amount to which you're entitled based on the useful life of the asset from the applicable schedule that we provide in this chapter. For example, if you want to depreciate an asset that has a five-year useful life, use Table 11-2. If you're depreciating cars, computers, or cellular phones, or other so-called listed property, however, you must use Form 4562, because you can depreciate only the business portion of those kinds of items.

IRS depreciation percentages

To calculate the amount of depreciation that you're entitled to claim, glance at the IRS depreciation tables (Tables 11-2 through 11-6). For business property other than real estate, you'll notice that each table has two categories: *half-year convention* and *mid-quarter convention*. Usually, you use the half-year convention, because the mid-quarter convention comes into play when the business assets you acquired and started using in the last three months of the year exceed 40 percent of all business assets that you placed in service during the year. Got that? Read on and follow the examples for both types of depreciation conventions.

Table 11-2	MACRS (Modified Accelerated Cost Recovery System): 5-Year Property				
Year	**Half-Year Convention**	**Mid-Quarter Convention**			
		First Quarter	**Second Quarter**	**Third Quarter**	**Fourth Quarter**
1	20.00%	35.00%	25.00%	15.00%	5.00%
2	32.00	26.00	30.00	34.00	38.00
3	19.20	15.60	18.00	20.40	22.80
4	11.52	11.01	11.37	12.24	13.68
5	11.52	11.01	11.37	11.30	10.94
6	5.76	1.38	4.26	7.06	9.58

Table 11-3   MACRS: 7-Year Property

Year	Half-Year Convention	Mid-Quarter Convention			
		First Quarter	Second Quarter	Third Quarter	Fourth Quarter
1	14.29%	25.00%	17.85%	10.71%	3.57%
2	24.49	21.43	23.47	25.51	27.55
3	17.49	15.31	16.76	18.22	19.68
4	12.49	10.93	11.97	13.02	14.06
5	8.93	8.75	8.87	9.30	10.04
6	8.92	8.74	8.87	8.85	8.73

Table 11-4   MACRS: 15-Year Property

Year	Half-Year Convention	Mid-Quarter Convention			
		First Quarter	Second Quarter	Third Quarter	Fourth Quarter
1	5.00%	8.75%	6.25%	3.75%	1.25%
2	9.50	9.13	9.38	9.63	9.88
3	8.55	8.21	8.44	8.66	8.89
4	7.70	7.39	7.59	7.80	8.00
5	6.93	6.65	6.83	7.02	7.20
6	6.23	5.99	6.15	6.31	6.48

Table 11-5   Residential Rental Property (27½-Year)

Use the row of the month of the taxable year that the property was placed in service.

Month	Year 1	Year 2	Year 3	Year 4	Year 5	Year 6
Jan	3.485%	3.636%	3.636%	3.636%	3.636%	3.636%
Feb	3.182	3.636	3.636	3.636	3.636	3.636
Mar	2.879	3.636	3.636	3.636	3.636	3.636
Apr	2.576	3.636	3.636	3.636	3.636	3.636
May	2.273	3.636	3.636	3.636	3.636	3.636
Jun	1.970	3.636	3.636	3.636	3.636	3.636
Jul	1.667	3.636	3.636	3.636	3.636	3.636
Aug	1.364	3.636	3.636	3.636	3.636	3.636
Sept	1.061	3.636	3.636	3.636	3.636	3.636
Oct	0.758	3.636	3.636	3.636	3.636	3.636
Nov	0.455	3.636	3.636	3.636	3.636	3.636
Dec	0.152	3.636	3.636	3.636	3.636	3.636

Residential real estate is depreciated over 27½ years. Nonresidential real estate, a factory or office building for example, placed in use after May 12, 1993, is depreciated over 39 years. If it was *placed in service* (that's the IRS term for when you started using it) after 1986 and before May 13, 1993, it's depreciated over 31½ years. You can get the depreciation rates for these two periods from IRS Publication 946 *(How To Depreciate Property)*. For prior periods, you have to use the rates in IRS Publication 534 *(Depreciating Property Placed in Service before 1987)*.

Table 11-6	Commercial Property (31½ Years and 39 Years)			
Use the row of the month of the taxable year that the property was placed in service.				
Month	**(31½ Years)**		**(39 Years)**	
	Year 1	**Later Years**	**Year 1**	**Later Years**
Jan	3.042%	3.175%	2.461%	2.564%
Feb	2.778	3.175	2.247	2.564
Mar	2.513	3.175	2.033	2.564
Apr	2.249	3.175	1.819	2.564
May	2.273	3.175	1.605	2.564
Jun	1.720	3.175	1.391	2.564
Jul	1.455	3.175	1.177	2.564
Aug	1.190	3.175	0.963	2.564
Sept	0.926	3.175	0.749	2.564
Oct	0.661	3.175	0.535	2.564
Nov	0.397	3.175	0.321	2.564
Dec	0.132	3.175	0.107	2.564

For example, say you purchased the building where you operate your business in March 2006 for $225,000. Because it is nonresidential property purchased after May 12, 1993, you have to depreciate it over 39 years. You make a reasonable determination that the land is worth $25,000, so you have a depreciable basis of $200,000. Next you look up the rate in the 39-year column for March (2.033 percent). Your depreciation for 2006 is $4,066 ($200,000 × 2.033 percent). In later years, it is $5,128 ($200,000 × 2.564 percent).

Real estate isn't eligible for the special $108,000 depreciation deduction.

Additions or improvements to property

An addition or improvement that you make to your property is treated as a separate item for the purposes of depreciation — regardless of how you depreciate the original asset. For example, you own a house that you've rented since 1984 and have been depreciating over 19 years (you were allowed to use that short of a useful life back then). And in 2006, you added a new roof. The roof has to be depreciated over 27½ years and at the rate in the IRS depreciation tables for residential real estate. The depreciation tables reproduced in this chapter go up to only six years. For tables that go beyond six years, send for IRS Publication 946 *(How to Depreciate Property)*.

Suppose that you're depreciating a computer that you purchased for $5,000 in 2006. First, you must look up its useful life (Table 11-1). According to the IRS, computers have a useful life of five years, so use the depreciation percentages for five-year property. Okay, easy enough so far.

Under the half-year convention for five-year property (Table 11-2), you find 20 percent as the amount. For 2006, you're entitled to a $1,000 depreciation deduction ($5,000 × 20 percent). In 2007, you'd multiply the $5,000 cost by 32 percent, for a deduction of $1,600. And then you use 19.20 percent, 11.52 percent, 11.52 percent, and 5.76 percent in each of the succeeding years. Of course, you only have to make these calculations if you choose not to use (or you've already maxed out) the special $108,000 depreciation you're allowed. Fun calculations, right? Based on the convention rules, the write-off period for stuff is one year longer than its useful life. That's because in the first year you're entitled to only a half-year's worth of depreciation. The half-year convention rule means that all assets are considered to have been purchased on July 1 — which entitles you to only half the normal amount of depreciation in the first year.

Half-year convention versus mid-quarter convention depreciation

As if trying to figure out what type of property you have isn't confusing enough, you also need to figure out the rules regarding how much depreciation you can take in the first year. Basically, the IRS makes an assumption that you'll purchase equal amounts of business property all through the year, putting some into service each month. Rather than have you track each and every purchase on your tax return, the IRS allows you to average it all together by using the half-year convention. The half-year convention considers that all property you purchased in 2006, regardless of the date it is actually purchased and put into service, was put into service on July 1.

For new tenants or lessors leasing office space in 2006, depreciation rules on improvements to property, whether indoor or outdoor, reverted on January 1, 2006, to a standard 39 years (as opposed to a 15-year recovery for some improvements that was in effect for 2005). Keep in mind, that when the lease ends, you may deduct any part of the cost of the improvements that you haven't depreciated if you're a tenant. If you're the lessor, you must continue depreciating improvements you made unless you remove them. If the tenant makes improvements, you won't recognize income unless the improvements are really intended as rent.

Not everyone purchases equal amounts of property throughout the year, though. Many people load their purchases into the last quarter of the year, when they have an idea of how much money they'll have to pay tax on if they don't sink some if it back into their business pronto. If you've purchased more than 40 percent of your total depreciable property in 2006 in the last quarter of 2006 (October through December), you must use the mid-quarter convention for each asset. These two designations mean that you have to keep track of when you purchased property and when you put it into service in order to be able to depreciate it properly.

For example, say you bought a calculator for $500 on February 1, 2006, and a copier for $1,000 on October 1, 2006, and chose not to claim the special depreciation deduction. Under the half-year convention, you're entitled to a depreciation deduction of $300 ($1,500 × 20 percent). But because more than 40 percent of all your business property was bought and placed into service the last three months of the year, you have to switch to the mid-quarter convention for each asset. So here's how you have to separately compute the depreciation for these two pieces of equipment.

Under the mid-quarter convention for five-year property (see Table 11-2), for an asset purchased in the first quarter, the depreciation rate is 35 percent. Therefore, you're entitled to a $175 depreciation deduction ($500 × 35 percent) for the calculator. For the copier, you have to use the 5 percent rate for property bought during the fourth quarter ($1,000 × 5 percent), which entitles you to a $50 deduction.

The long and the short? By using the mid-quarter convention, you can claim only half the depreciation that you normally would. At this point, you're probably scratching the back of your head and wondering who thinks of these things. We must confess that we don't know either. Just play along.

You can save yourself the headache that this mid-quarter convention causes and get a larger deduction to boot by claiming *up to $108,000 of Section 179 depreciation,* which we point out in the next section.

The Section 179 buying bonanza: The $108,000 depreciation deduction

Instead of computing depreciation by using the standard depreciation tables, you can elect to deduct up to $108,000 of the cost of new and used business equipment that you purchased and started using in your business in 2006. Actually, this amount isn't a one-time deduction; you can take the deduction every year. One taxpayer that we know of liked this deduction so much that he deducted the same amount every year. Remember, however, that you must have actually spent up to $108,000 in 2006 to get the write-off. This bonanza is known in IRS terms as Section 179 depreciation.

Be aware that the *Community Renewal Tax Relief Act of 2000* allows businesses in economically depressed areas called Empowerment Zones to expense the first $143,000 of business property. IRS Publication 954 *(Tax Incentives for Empowerment Zones and Other Distressed Communities)* has the lowdown on this extra depreciation deduction and on a number of tax credits that are available in these zones. Publication 954 lists the areas designated as Empowerment Zones and Communities. To see if your exact business location falls within one of these general areas, call the Department of Housing and Urban Development (HUD) at 800-998-9999 or check out their Web site at www.ezec.gov.

If you buy a few items, you can pick and choose which ones you want to write off completely and which ones you don't. If you want the largest possible deduction for all your listed property, allocate your $108,000 Section 179 depreciation first against property with the longest life, and work your way toward property with the shortest life. On the other hand, some property with a short-listed life has an even shorter actual life, such as computers. You may want to allocate Section 179 depreciation first to property that you know you won't own for the full depreciation term. Only after you've written off the cost for those items, you can then use the remainder to write off your longest-life property.

If you're married filing separately, you can deduct only $54,000, unless you and your spouse agree upon how much of the $108,000 buying bonanza each of you is entitled to deduct.

If you buy equipment costing more than $430,000, the $108,000 that you're entitled to deduct is reduced dollar for dollar by the amount over $430,000. So if the total cost is $538,000 or more, you can kiss any part of your $108,000 write-off goodbye. Here's how this works: Say you purchased equipment costing $434,000. You have to reduce the maximum $108,000 you can write off by $4,000.

The beauty of the $108,000 limit (besides the immediate deduction) is that it keeps you from having to wade through the depreciation tables to compute your depreciation. The second rule regarding the $108,000 expensing is that this deduction can't produce a loss from all your business activities. Suppose that your consulting income — after all other expenses — is $10,000, and you bought $24,000 worth of equipment. You can expense only $10,000. The $14,000 balance carries over to the next year. If you have enough consulting income after your other expenses, you can deduct it then. If you don't, keep carrying it over until you do.

But there is a pleasant surprise. You can count all your earned income to determine whether you pass the *no-loss test.* So in the preceding example, if you or your spouse had at least $14,000 in wages (in addition to your $10,000 consulting income), you can deduct the whole $24,000 of the equipment you purchased.

Listed property: Cars used 50 percent or more in your business

Listed property is an IRS term for autos, telephones, computers, boats, and airplanes — items that the IRS suspects you may use more for pleasure than for business. With listed property, you not only need to tell the IRS what you purchased and put into service in 2006, but also what percentage of the time you used that property for your trade or business. Although you still calculate depreciation using the Tables 11-2 through 11-6, now you also need to multiply your potential total depreciation result by your amount of business use to get your actual depreciation amount.

The largest single item piece of listed property for most people is their car. The IRS considers cars to have a useful life of five years, which is the starting point to determine the amount of depreciation on the auto that you can deduct.

If the business use of your car is more than 50 percent of its total use, you compute your depreciation (under *MACRS — Modified Accelerated Cost Recovery System*) according to what is known as the *half-year convention*. The half-year convention means that assets, in the year of purchase, regardless of the month they were acquired, are considered to have been purchased on July 1, and you're, therefore, entitled to a half-year's depreciation. In subsequent years, you're entitled to a full-year's depreciation for that year provided that you continue to own the property for the full year.

If you put that new car into service between October and December 2006, and if its value (added to whatever else you bought in that period) is greater than 40 percent of the value of the total property you put into service in 2006, you need to switch to the mid-quarter convention that we describe in the "Half-year convention versus mid-quarter convention depreciation" section earlier in this chapter.

Of course, before you begin to calculate the depreciation on that car that you put into service in 2006, you need to know that the IRS has some interesting ideas of what constitutes a car suitable for your business. Unless that new car cost you less than $14,800 (or $16,300 for a truck or van with a gross unloaded weight of less than 6,000 pounds), your new vehicle is subject to the luxury car rules, which will limit your deduction. Check out Table 11-7 to find the depreciation limits for your new chariot.

Table 11-7	Depreciation Deductions for New and Used Cars Subject to the Luxury Car Limits	
	Limits for a Car	*Limits for a Truck or Van*
2006	$2,960	$3,260
2007	$4,700	$5,200
2008	$2,850	$3,150
Later years	$1,775	$1,875

Cars are listed property with a five-year life, so these amounts represent the maximum amount of depreciation you may take. If your business usage is less than 100 percent, you get depreciation only for the business use of your car. If you did not elect Section 179 depreciation, just multiply the depreciation deduction by the percentage of business use.

If your vehicle cost more than $14,800 ($16,300 for a truck or van) and is subject to the luxury car limits, you can't claim any additional Section 179 depreciation because your regular depreciation deduction is already greater than the first-year depreciation limit.

If you managed to snag a car for less than the luxury car limit, you can claim an additional Section 179 expense deduction, but the sum of your Section 179 allowance and regular depreciation deduction using Table 11-2 can't exceed the first-year limit ($2,960 for a car and $3,260 for a truck or van). If on the other hand you splurged, and bought something really high-end for more than the allowed $14,800, skip the calculation, and use the maximum depreciation numbers shown in Table 11-7. Remember, if you used that car at all for personal reasons, you need to reduce that maximum depreciation amount by the percentage of personal use.

For example, if you buy a car for $20,000, using the mid-year convention, you'd ordinarily be entitled to 20 percent of the purchase price ($4,000). Unfortunately, this is more than the total allowed, so you need to reduce the available depreciation to $2,960. Then, if you use that car only 60 percent of the time for your business, the deduction you're allowed to claim is 60 percent of the total possible, or $1,776. Next year, when you begin your depreciation calculations for this car, just multiply the $20,000 cost by 38 percent — the second-year depreciation percentage from Table 11-2 — which is $7,800. Compare this number to the second-year depreciation limit of $4,700. Because the limit is lower, you can only claim $4,700 multiplied by your percentage of business use for this year.

Listed property: SUVs, vans, and heavier trucks

If the new car you bought to use for your business is really one of the larger SUVs, a van, or a heavier truck, you may not be subject to the luxury car rules. What does this exemption from the luxury car rules mean to you? The limits on depreciation in Table 11-7 don't apply to you. You're allowed to follow the regular depreciation rules, and you may even deduct up to $25,000 using the Section 179 depreciation described earlier in this chapter, in the section "The Section 179 buying bonanza: The $108,000 depreciation deduction" earlier in this chapter.

Which SUVs and trucks qualify? An SUV or truck must rate as weighing at least 6,000 pounds unloaded in order to meet this requirement. You can check these figures out with your local car dealer when you're researching your next SUV or truck purchase.

A heavy SUV must be built on a truck chassis to avoid the luxury car rules and get the benefit of the $25,000 expense deduction. Most heavy SUVs are built on truck chassis but a few are built on a car chassis. Again, ask you dealer about this before making your purchase. Furthermore, you can't claim a $25,000 Section 179 expense deduction on a heavy truck that has a cargo bed that is less than 6 feet long. The short-bed rule affects some big trucks with an extended cab. A heavy truck with a short bed is still exempt from the luxury car limits though. You just can't get that extra $25,000 deduction.

One exception to the 6,000-pound weight rule does exist (one always does!). If you've purchased a truck or van in 2006 that weighs less than 6,000 pounds, you may still be able to follow the regular depreciation rules if the truck or van is somehow modified so that it could be used only for your trade or business. The IRS is looking for modifications such as:

- Adding ladder racks and a tool chest on a truck or van
- Having only a shelf-type seat in the front (with no seating in the back)
- Including shelving in a van
- Providing space for carrying merchandise and equipment

If you use your SUV, van, or truck some of the time for personal use, you can't claim Section 179 expense deduction or depreciation deduction for the cost that is attributable to personal use. Here's how it works. Say you buy a big SUV for $70,000, and you use it 60 percent of the time for business. Of your $70,000 purchase price, only $42,000 ($70,000 × 60 percent)

is available for expensing and depreciating. You can expense $25,000, which leaves you with $17,000 ($42,000 – $25,000) to depreciate. You're allowed to take 20 percent of that (using the half-year convention), resulting in an additional $3,400 depreciation. Your total deduction is $28,400 ($25,000 + 3,400).

Listed property: Cars used 50 percent or less for business

If the business use of your car is 50 percent or less, you must depreciate it using the *straight-line method* under the *alternative depreciation system (ADS)* (see Table 11-8). Straight-line depreciation is relatively easy, right? Wrong . . . in this case. Remember, this calculation is for a car with a business use of less than 50 percent, so the IRS makes you reduce the amount of depreciation that you're allowed under the straight-line method by the percentage of personal use.

Table 11-8	Straight-Line Method under ADS for Auto Depreciation	
Year	5-Year Property	Maximum Yearly Limit*
1	10%	$2,960
2	20%	$4,700
3	20%	$2,850
Each succeeding year	20%	$1,775

Remember that this amount is the maximum deduction if your car was used 100 percent for business.

So if you used your car for business 40 percent of the time, the maximum depreciation allowed by law in the first year is $1,184 ($2,960 × 40 percent).

In coming years, you calculate your depreciation deduction the same way. In years 2 through 5, you use a depreciation rate of 20 percent according to Table 11-8, and then 10 percent for year 6. Any depreciation that you can't claim in years 1 through 6 (because of the yearly maximum limits) is deducted in subsequent years at $1,775 a year, less your personal use, until your car is fully depreciated.

You can't claim any Section 179 deduction on a car, truck, or SUV (or any other type of "listed" property) that is used 50 percent or more for personal purposes. If you claim the deduction in the year you buy the vehicle and in a later year your personal use increases to at least 50 percent, part of it can be added back to your income along with some of the depreciation you claimed.

All this auto depreciation stuff is almost enough to make you start using your feet to call on clients. But then, there's no depreciation allowance for shoes.

A tax software program can save you from all this mind-numbing number crunching. (See Chapter 2 for more information about selecting a tax software program.)

If you started depreciating your car prior to 2006, Table 11-9 shows you the maximum yearly depreciation limits for 2006.

Table 11-9	2006 Annual Depreciation Ceiling for Cars Put into Service Prior to 2006								
Year	1997	1998	1999	2000	2001	2002	2003	2004	2005
2006	$1,775	$1,775	$1,775	$1,775	$1,775	$1,775	$1,675	$2,960	$4,800

Electric and hybrid vehicles

Hybrid (combination gasoline/electric) cars follow the same depreciation rules as standard, gasoline-powered ones. Electric vehicles get more of a depreciation break. The maximum annual depreciation limit for an electric vehicle purchased in 2006 is $8,980. For that same car, next year, you'll be able to deduct a maximum of $14,400, while your year three maximum depreciation drops to $8,650, and year four and beyond, $5,225, until you've completely recovered the cost of that car.

Although a vehicle has to be 100 percent electric powered to qualify for the increased depreciation limits, both electric and hybrid vehicles qualify for the Alternative Motor Vehicle Credit (see Chapter 14). The government is encouraging you to save fuel and the environment; this credit can be as high as $4,000 for an electric car, and $3,400 for a hybrid, depending on fuel efficiency. You do need to split the credit between **Form 3800, General Business Credits,** and **Form 8910, Alternative Motor Vehicle Credit,** based on your business usage.

Remember, when figuring your annual depreciation deduction, you first need to subtract the total amount of your credit from the cost of the car.

Line 14: Employee benefit programs

Enter here the premiums that you paid for your employees' accident, health, and group term life insurance coverage — but don't count the cost of your own insurance benefits here. See Chapter 7 to find out how you may be able to deduct 100 percent of your personal health insurance premiums.

Line 15: Insurance (other than health)

Enter on this line the premiums that you paid for business insurance, such as fire, theft, robbery, and general liability coverage on your business property.

Line 16a: Mortgage interest

If you own the building in which you operate your business, deduct any mortgage interest you paid on line 16a. If you're claiming a deduction for the business use of your home, the mortgage interest you paid is deducted on line 10 of **Form 8829, Expenses for Business Use of Your Home.** The amount of the deduction is stated on **Form 1098, Mortgage Interest Statement,** that you should receive in January 2007 from your bank.

Line 16b: Other interest

You can deduct interest on business loans here. If you took out a mortgage on your house and used the proceeds of the loan to finance your business, deduct the interest here — and not on Schedule A. If you borrowed money for your business from other sources, such as a bank or even your credit card, deduct the interest on those loans here as well.

You can't deduct the interest you paid on the taxes you owed on your personal tax returns. You can, however, deduct late interest paid on employment taxes (Social Security, Medicare and withholding taxes) that as an employer you paid. See Chapter 9 for more information on the interest that you paid.

Line 17: Legal and professional services

On this line, enter any fees that you paid for tax advice, for preparing tax forms related to your business, and for legal fees regarding business matters. Professional services include fees for accounting and engineering work that you pay for. Garden variety consulting work gets entered on line 10, contract labor.

If you pay someone more than $600 (your accountant, for example), you have to provide him or her with Form 1099-MISC by January 31 — just like we told you to do with commissions and contract labor that you deducted on lines 10 and 11.

The IRS must love lawyers. You must report all payments that you made to your lawyer — even for the reimbursement of expenses that you were billed. Additionally, the present exemption saying that payments made to corporations don't have to be reported to the IRS on Form 1099 no longer applies to lawyers. Know any good lawyer jokes?

Line 18: Office expense

Enter your costs for stationery, paper supplies, postage, printer toner, and other consumable items that you use in the operation of your office or business.

Line 19: Pension and profit-sharing plans

Enter your contribution to your employees' Keogh, SIMPLE, or SEP account(s). As for your own Keogh or SEP, enter that amount on Form 1040 (line 28). See Chapter 7.

Employers with fewer than 100 employees may establish what's known as SIMPLE retirement plans. These plans have none of the mind-numbing rules to follow or forms to file that regular retirement plans have. A SIMPLE plan can also cover the owner(s) of a farm (see Chapter 20 for more about SIMPLE plans and other small business retirement plans).

Lines 20a and b: Rent or lease

If you rented or leased an auto, machinery, or equipment, enter the business portion of the rental payments on line 20a. But if you leased a car for more than 30 days, you may have to reduce your deduction by an amount called the *inclusion amount* if your leased car's value exceeded the following amounts (see Table 11-10) when you started leasing it.

Whether you're entering your car lease payments here or on Form 2106, Employee Business Expenses, you aren't allowed to deduct the full amount of the lease payments on a new Bentley! In fact, you're not allowed to lease much of anything and claim the full amount of the lease payments. Just like there are luxury car rules for calculating depreciation, there are essentially luxury car rules for leased cars, as well (only the IRS refers to *inclusion amounts* for leased cars, or the amount by which your lease payments must be reduced, as opposed to luxury car rules). The inclusion amounts and luxury car rules do the same thing — they both effectively limit your deduction.

You can find charts with the lease inclusion amounts for cars, SUVs, vans, light trucks, and electric cars in IRS Publication 463 *(Travel, Entertainment, Gift, and Car Expenses)*. These numbers are adjusted annually for inflation, so you do need to check every year. Fortunately, IRS Publication 463 is easy and cheap to obtain (it's free), either by calling 800-829-3676, or on the Internet at www.irs.gov.

Even though you reduce your rental payments by the lease-inclusion amount, leasing may still provide you with a larger deduction than purchasing. But remember, lease payments that are payments toward the purchase price of a car aren't deductible. The IRS considers such leases a purchase contract, because you end up owning the jalopy at the end of the lease. If you have such a lease agreement, you must depreciate the car based on its value, and doing so sends you right back to the annual limit that you can claim for auto depreciation.

Table 11-10	Inclusion Amounts
Year Lease Began	*Amount*
2006	$15,200
2005	$15,200
2004	$17,500
2003	$18,000
2002	$15,500
2001	$15,500
2000	$15,500
1999	$15,500
1998	$15,800

On line 20b, enter your office rent, for example.

Line 21: Repairs and maintenance

Enter the cost of routine repairs — such as the cost to repair your computer — on this line. But adding a new hard disk isn't a repair; that cost must be depreciated over five years unless it qualifies for the special election to write off the first $108,000 of business assets.

A repair (as opposed to an improvement) keeps your equipment or property in good operating condition. A repair that also prolongs the life of your equipment has to be depreciated, so make the most of the $108,000 deduction instead of depreciating the cost over its useful life.

If you're confused about what qualifies as a repair and what qualifies as an improvement, you're not alone. Through the years, the Tax Court has been clogged with cases dealing with repairs as current write-offs versus improvements that have to be depreciated. We suggest that you contact a tax advisor to evaluate your specific situation. The $108,000 immediate write-off should solve this problem.

Line 22: Supplies

If your company manufactures a product, you report factory supplies here. In other words, you deduct the cost of supplies that contribute to the operation of the equipment that you use in your office or business. For example, if you operate a retail store, you enter the cost of mannequins, trim, packaging, and other such items on this line.

Line 23: Taxes and licenses

On this line you deduct your business taxes, such as Social Security and unemployment insurance taxes for your employees. You also enter the costs of permits and business licenses. You don't deduct the Social Security tax that you pay because you're self-employed; you can deduct half of this tax on line 27 of your 1040 (see Chapter 7 for more on how this deduction works).

Lines 24a–b: Travel, meals, and entertainment

To find out what you can deduct for travel, meals, and entertainment, see the explanation in Chapter 9. No point repeating all that stuff here!

You can deduct 100 percent of the money you spent on airfare and hotels on line 24a. But be careful — money you spend on room service is limited to 50 percent, unless you work in the transportation industry. Because you can deduct only 50 percent of your meals and entertainment expenses, only enter the 50 percent you're allowed to deduct on line 24b.

If you're in the transportation industry and are subject to the Department of Transportation restrictions on the number of hours you can work, you're allowed to deduct 70 percent of your meals and entertainment, so enter 70 percent of your total meals and entertainment on line 24b.

If you don't have all your receipts but you still want to take this deduction, check out Chapter 9 for the per diem rules and regulations.

Line 25: Utilities

Can you imagine what this line is for? If you're thinking of electric and telephone bills, for example, you hit the nail on the head. However, if you're claiming a home office deduction (discussed in further detail later in this chapter), your utility costs belong on **Form 8829, Expenses for Business Use of Your Home,** and not here.

Line 26: Wages

Enter here the wages that you paid your employees. However, make sure you deduct payments to independent contractors on line 11. Deduction of independent contractor expenses is a hot issue with the IRS. So flip back to line 11.

Line 27: Other expenses

On the reverse side of Schedule C is Part V, a schedule where you list your expenses whose descriptions defy the neat categories of lines 8–26. Here you can enter dues, subscriptions to related business periodicals, messenger services, overnight express fees, and so on. If you have more than nine items in the other expense category just add another Part V page, but enter the grand total on line 48 of only one of the forms.

Line 28: Total expenses

Addition time — add lines 8–27. This amount is what it costs to operate your business.

Line 29: Tentative profit (loss)

Subtract line 28 from line 7. If line 28 is more than line 7, you have a loss, and you enter it as a negative number. For example, if you lost $10,000, enter it as <$10,000> (a negative number).

Line 30: Form 8829

Yes, you can deduct home office expenses. If you work out of your home, the rules for claiming a deduction for a home office are now more lenient. That's the good news. The bad news? You must use **Form 8829, Expenses for Business Use of Your Home,** to claim the deduction for the portion that you use for business. You can find detailed instructions for filling it out and other rules you must follow to nail down this deduction in Chapter 15. You can't take a loss because of the home office deduction. You can, however, carry over an excess deduction amount to another year's tax return.

Because only a portion of your total mortgage interest and real estate taxes are deducted as part of your home office expenses, don't forget to deduct the balance of your total mortgage interest that you entered on line 10(b) of Form 8829, and the balance of your total real estate taxes from line 11(b) of this form. Your mortgage interest balance goes on line 10 of Schedule A; the real estate taxes balance goes on line 6 of Schedule A. These two amounts represent your mortgage interest and taxes related to the portion of the house you live in.

Line 31: Net profit (or loss)

After you arrive at your net profit or loss, copy it onto Form 1040 (line 12) and then on Schedule SE (line 2) so that you can compute the amount of Social Security tax that you have to pay. See Chapter 15 to find out how to complete Schedule SE.

Lines 32a and b: At-risk rules

Suppose that you borrow money to go into business. The at-risk rules limit the amount of business losses that you can deduct on borrowed money that you're personally not liable to repay. For example, you need $20,000 to go into business. You invest $10,000, and your rich uncle gives you $10,000. You lose the entire $20,000. You can deduct only the $10,000 that you personally invested in your business. See Chapter 13 for more details on the at-risk rules. Basically, if you're personally responsible for all the liabilities of your business, check box 32a. If you are, you can deduct all your losses. If you're not at risk for all the investment that was made in your business, check 32b. Guess what? You have to fill out **Form 6198, At Risk Limitations.** This form determines how much of your loss you're allowed to deduct.

If you aren't personally responsible, see a tax professional, because the rules in this area are anything but clear or simple.

Start-up expenses

Start-up expenses are the expenses incurred in getting into business before the business actually begins operating. The types of expenses usually incurred during this period are market studies, consulting and professional services, and travel in securing prospective suppliers, customers, and feasibility studies. Whether you can deduct these expenses depends on whether you actually start the business.

If you go into business, you can elect to deduct these expenses over 60 months. You make the election in the year that you start the business by attaching a statement to your return describing the expenditures, the dates incurred, the month the business opened, and the number of months you are electing to deduct the expenditures. You can elect more than 60 months but not less. The deduction is computed on **Form 4562, Part VI, Depreciation and Amortization.**

If you don't go into business, you can deduct some of your start-up expenses in the year that your attempt to go into business failed. Now you're probably asking, which ones? The answer isn't all that clear. You can deduct your business start-up expenses but not investigatory expenses. What's the difference, you ask? Here's what the IRS says the difference is. *Investigatory expenses* are costs incurred in reviewing a prospective business prior to reaching a final decision to acquire or enter the business. *Start-up expenses* are costs incurred after you decide to go into business but prior to the time the business actually begins to operate. If you guessed that a lot of taxpayers end up in Tax Court as the result of how they decided to separate the two, you're right. Start-up expenses are deducted on Schedule C.

Operating Loss

Suppose that you start a business and it produces an operating loss. In other words, your costs — not just equipment, but rent, salaries, and other expenses — exceed your income. You may write off that loss against any other income that you and your spouse made that year.

If the loss is greater than your combined income in the current year, you have what is known in IRS jargon as a *net operating loss (NOL)* that you can carry back over each of the past two years and obtain a refund on the tax that you paid at that time. Whenever the loss still isn't used up by carrying it back, you can carry it forward to offset your income during the next 20 years. The carryback is mandatory unless you elect to carry it only forward. Making the election is simple. Just attach a statement to your return, indicating: "I choose to carry my loss forward." After you've made this election, you can't change your mind. See Chapter 18 for information about amending a prior year's return and carrying back losses.

Losses incurred before January 1, 1998, can be carried back three years and forwarded for only 15 years. The three-year carryback still applies to the NOLs incurred by small businesses in presidentially declared disaster areas. A small business is one that earned $5 million or less of income in each of the three preceding years. Farmers get to carry back losses five years.

NOLs incurred in 2001 and 2002 had to be carried back five years. This treatment of your NOL was mandatory unless you informed the IRS in a written statement attached to your return that you wanted to either carry back the NOL two years, three years if you qualified, or if you wanted to carry it forward instead. This action had to be taken when you filed your return, which could have been extended to October 15 if you had a valid extension of time to file until then. If you didn't attach such a statement to your return stating what you wanted to do, the NOL had to be carried back five years.

Keep in mind, however, that you can't operate a part-time business, for example, that continually loses money. This situation is known as a hobby loss. If you don't show a profit in at least three of every five consecutive years, you may have a fight — with the IRS — on your hands. You must show a profit in at least three of every five consecutive years, or the IRS can declare your business a hobby and disallow your losses. The IRS doesn't consider your enterprise a business when you have continuing losses. No business, no business deductions. Some taxpayers have challenged this rule in Tax Court and won. They were able to prove that they ran their enterprises like a business and anticipated making a profit but didn't. The three-out-of-five-year rule was established to keep the IRS off your back. If you meet this requirement, the IRS can't claim that the losses in the two other years can't be deducted because the business is a hobby. Not making a profit in three out of five years doesn't automatically make the venture a hobby, but it's a strong indication that it may be.

Schedule F: Profit or Loss from Farming

Schedule F, Profit or Loss from Farming, is the form that you use to report the income and expenses from selling crops or livestock. All types of farms and farming income are included here, including farms that produce livestock, dairy, poultry, fish, aquaculture products, bee products, fruit, or a truck farm (because produce isn't the only thing farmers raise and harvest). Even though Schedule F is titled "Profit or Loss from Farming," you use this form to tell the IRS what you took in from operating a plantation, ranch, nursery, orchard, or oyster bed. Schedule F isn't as bad as it looks. In fact, it's set up in exactly the same way as Schedule C, Profit or Loss from Business. Although a business is a business (and farming is certainly a business), the IRS clearly thought that there were enough tax items that were peculiar to farming that it deserved its own schedule.

In this section, we take you through the highlights of Schedule F (check out Figure 11-2).

Once upon a time, all taxpayers could reduce their taxes by averaging their incomes over a number of years whenever their incomes suddenly shot up. However, all that ended in 1986. In 1998, farmers, but not other taxpayers, got a break. If farmers' incomes suddenly shoot up, they can once again reduce their taxes by averaging their incomes over the past three years.

When you get to line 44 of your Form 1040 — the line where you compute your tax — use **Schedule J, Form 1040, Income Averaging for Farmers and Fishermen.** Make sure that you attach this schedule to your return.

Before you even attempt to prepare your Schedule F, obtain a copy of IRS Publication 225 *(Farmer's Tax Guide),* either by calling 800-829-3676, or from the Internet at www.irs.gov.

SCHEDULE F (Form 1040) Department of the Treasury Internal Revenue Service (99)	**Profit or Loss From Farming** ► Attach to Form 1040, Form 1040NR, Form 1041, Form 1065, or Form 1065-B. ► See Instructions for Schedule F (Form 1040).	OMB No. 1545-0074 **2006** Attachment Sequence No. **14**

Name of proprietor · Social security number (SSN)

A Principal product. Describe in one or two words your principal crop or activity for the current tax year.   **B** Enter code from Part IV ►

C Accounting method: (1) ☐ Cash   (2) ☐ Accrual   **D** Employer ID number (EIN), if any

E Did you "materially participate" in the operation of this business during 2006? If "No," see page F-2 for limit on passive losses.   ☐ Yes   ☐ No

Part I **Farm Income—Cash Method.** Complete Parts I and II (Accrual method. Complete Parts II and III, and Part I, line 11.)
Do not include sales of livestock held for draft, breeding, sport, or dairy purposes. Report these sales on Form 4797.

1	Sales of livestock and other items you bought for resale	1		
2	Cost or other basis of livestock and other items reported on line 1	2		
3	Subtract line 2 from line 1		3	
4	Sales of livestock, produce, grains, and other products you raised		4	
5a	Cooperative distributions (Form(s) 1099-PATR)	5a		
		5b Taxable amount	5b	
6a	Agricultural program payments (see page F-2)	6a		
		6b Taxable amount	6b	
7	Commodity Credit Corporation (CCC) loans (see page F-3):			
a	CCC loans reported under election		7a	
b	CCC loans forfeited	7b		
		7c Taxable amount	7c	
8	Crop insurance proceeds and federal crop disaster payments (see page F-3):			
a	Amount received in 2006	8a		
		8b Taxable amount	8b	
c	If election to defer to 2007 is attached, check here ► ☐ 8d Amount deferred from 2005		8d	
9	Custom hire (machine work) income		9	
10	Other income, including federal and state gasoline or fuel tax credit or refund (see page F-3)		10	
11	**Gross income.** Add amounts in the right column for lines 3 through 10. If you use the accrual method, enter the amount from Part III, line 51 ►		11	

Part II **Farm Expenses—Cash and Accrual Method.**
Do not include personal or living expenses such as taxes, insurance, or repairs on your home.

12	Car and truck expenses (see page F-4). Also attach **Form 4562**	12		25	Pension and profit-sharing plans	25	
13	Chemicals	13		26	Rent or lease (see page F-5):		
14	Conservation expenses (see page F-4)	14		a	Vehicles, machinery, and equipment	26a	
15	Custom hire (machine work)	15		b	Other (land, animals, etc.)	26b	
16	Depreciation and section 179 expense deduction not claimed elsewhere (see page F-4)	16		27	Repairs and maintenance	27	
				28	Seeds and plants	28	
				29	Storage and warehousing	29	
17	Employee benefit programs other than on line 25	17		30	Supplies	30	
18	Feed	18		31	Taxes	31	
19	Fertilizers and lime	19		32	Utilities	32	
20	Freight and trucking	20		33	Veterinary, breeding, and medicine	33	
21	Gasoline, fuel, and oil	21		34	Other expenses (specify):		
22	Insurance (other than health)	22		a	- - - - - - - - - - - - - -	34a	
23	Interest:			b	- - - - - - - - - - - - - -	34b	
				c	- - - - - - - - - - - - - -	34c	
a	Mortgage (paid to banks, etc.)	23a		d	- - - - - - - - - - - - - -	34d	
b	Other	23b		e	- - - - - - - - - - - - - -	34e	
24	Labor hired (less employment credits)	24		f		34f	

| 35 | **Total expenses.** Add lines 12 through 34f. If line 34f is negative, see instructions ► | 35 | |
| 36 | **Net farm profit or (loss).** Subtract line 35 from line 11.
• If a profit, enter on **Form 1040, line 18,** and also on **Schedule SE, line 1.**
If you file **Form 1040NR,** enter the profit on **Form 1040NR, line 19.**
• If a loss, you **must** go to line 37. Estates, trusts, and partnerships, see page F-6. | 36 | |

Figure 11-2:
Schedule F,
Profit or
Loss from
Farming.

| 37 | If you have a loss, you **must** check the box that describes your investment in this activity (see page F-6).
• If you checked 37a, enter the loss on **Form 1040, line 18,** and **also** on **Schedule SE, line 1.**
If you file **Form 1040NR,** enter the loss on **Form 1040NR, line 19.**
• If you checked 37b, you **must** attach **Form 6198.** Your loss may be limited. | 37a ☐ All investment is at risk.
37b ☐ Some investment is not at risk. |

For Paperwork Reduction Act Notice, see page F-6 of the instructions.   Cat. No. 11346H   Schedule F (Form 1040) 2006

Figuring out Schedule F

Even though Schedule F is very similar to Schedule C, it does include some crucial differences between farms and other kinds of business. Here are some of the more important differences:

Line C: Accounting method

Most farmers use the cash method because it's the easier of the two methods. You total what you received and subtract what you paid. You don't need to figure out what you owe and who owes you. You don't need to determine your inventory at the end of the year (for crops or animals that you didn't sell). A slight exception to this rule also exists, however. If you bought livestock or other items for resale, you must keep a separate record of the items that you didn't sell. These purchases can't be deducted until they're sold. And thanks to depreciation rules, farm structures and equipment can't be deducted in the year you paid for them. They have to be depreciated over their useful lives.

Under the *accrual method,* you report income in the year sales are made — even if the sales are billed or collected in a later year. You deduct expenses in the year in which the expenses are incurred, even if you don't pay these expenses until later.

Under both cash and accrual methods, you report all income and expenses for the calendar year ending December 31. You choose one of the two accounting methods in the year that you file your first Schedule F. After you select a method, you can't change an accounting method without IRS permission.

The cash method of accounting gives you more control over when your farm sees a profit from year to year. For example, if next year looks like a slower year for you, you may elect to claim more of your income next year. Doing so will likely save you tax dollars, because you're more likely to be in a lower tax bracket that year (if it is, in fact, a less profitable year for you). You can legally shift your income by deferring sales or by delaying sending out bills until January (bills that you otherwise would have mailed in December, for example). Likewise, to lower your taxable income this year, you can pay more of your expenses in December instead of waiting until January.

Another reason for selecting the cash method of accounting is that you don't have to fill out lines 38 through 51 in Part III of Schedule F. That part is for accrual method folks. Isn't that reason enough?

If you're operating a farm and aiming to produce a tax deduction (commonly referred to as a *tax shelter*) rather than a profit, you're required to use the accrual method.

Part 1: Farm Income — Cash Method

If you're able to use the cash method of accounting, you need to fill out Part I in order to arrive at your gross income. Unlike Schedule C, which is fairly unspecific about what to include and where to include it, Schedule F lists out each category of income. All you need do is pop in the numbers and add them up on line 11.

Cash basis means that you actually received payment in order for it to count as income in the current year. The fact that you sent an invoice for an item in 2006 doesn't mean you need to include it in your 2006 income; if your customer doesn't pay you until 2007, that income becomes next year's problem.

Part 11: Farm Expenses — Cash and Accrual Method

Part II covers what you paid during 2006 for goods and services related to your farm, and every farmer filing a Schedule F has to fill out this part, whether you're a cash basis or accrual basis taxpayer.

Once again, most of the expenses are similar or even identical to those expenses you'll find on Schedule C; however, several do require additional explanation:

Line 13: Chemicals

On line 13, enter the total amount you paid for pesticides and herbicides.

Line 14: Conservation expenses

Want to see a farmer get really mad just before April 15? Just tell him that the $10,000 he spent to clear a pasture or cut diversion channels can't be deducted until he sells the land. Thankfully, though, these types of expenses are deductible, if they're consistent with a government conservation program. But limits do exist. Conservation expenses can't exceed 25 percent of your total farming income. The 75 percent you can't deduct is carried over to 2007 and subject to that year's 25 percent limit. You can deduct the following conservation expenses:

- Conditioning
- Constructing diversion channels, drainage ditches, irrigation ditches, earthen dams, outlets, or ponds
- Contour furrowing
- Eradicating brush
- Grading
- Leveling
- Planting windbreaks
- Restoring soil fertility
- Terracing

Line 15: Custom hire (machine work) expenses

If you paid someone to spray your crop, plow a field, or harvest a crop, enter the amount you paid here. Tax auditors are trained to investigate this deduction to find out whether you're deducting land-clearing expenses or paying someone to build structures that have to be depreciated.

Remember two things: Land-clearing can be deducted only as a conservation expense and is subject to the limit explained on line 14. And if you pay a custom hire more than $600, you have to file Form 1099-MISC with the IRS by February 28, 2007, and furnish a copy to the person you paid by January 31, 2007.

Line 16: Depreciation and Section 179 expense deduction

Farmers are entitled to deduct the cost of their equipment over its useful economic life. And for most items, such as cars, farmers do it the same way as everyone else (see the explanation for Schedule C, line 13 earlier in this chapter). However, all farm property may not be depreciated in the same way as other business property. Although other businesses must depreciate using the General Depreciation System (GDS) (described on line 13, Schedule C earlier in this chapter), farms may elect to use the Alternate Depreciation System (ADS).

What's the difference? Depreciation using GDS involves using uniform capitalization rules, whereas ADS depreciation doesn't. When the property involved is a computer or some other form of machinery that is productive from the time you put it into service, using uniform capitalization rules makes sense. When you're talking about fruit trees that take years and years before becoming truly productive, uniform capitalization isn't such a positive concept. Check out IRS Publication 225 (*Farmer's Tax Guide*) to find out more about your depreciation options.

Choosing what method you need to use to depreciate your farm property is never easy, and after you make an election to use ADS depreciation, changing it is hard. Talking with a tax professional makes a great deal of sense. Make sure that you choose one who deals extensively with farmers. As the number of farmers continues to decrease, finding a professional with ample experience in this area is becoming increasingly difficult.

Line 24: Labor hired (less employment credits)

On line 24, enter the amount you paid in cash wages — that is, the total amount you pay your employees *before* you withhold income tax and Social Security and Medicare taxes. The cost of any meals and lodging that you provide isn't considered wages, which means that employees don't have to pay tax on it. However, you're allowed to deduct those costs as a valid "other expense." On line 34, you can deduct the cost of food you buy for your employees.

Any cash allowance that you give employees to buy meals is considered part of their wages. Normally, you can deduct only 50 percent of the cost of meals. (See "Lines 24a–b: Travel, meals, and entertainment" earlier in this chapter for more information.)

If more than half of all the employees to whom you provide meals are furnished the meals for what the law calls "the convenience of the employer," then all the meals you furnish your employees are fully deductible (but the value of the meals isn't included in your employees' income). No 50 percent "haircut" for farmers who meet this "convenience" test. Convenience of the employer means just that — they provide the food and the place for the employees to eat at a time of their choosing in order for the employees to be able to work.

If you pay your employees *in-kind,* you can deduct (as a labor expense) the value of the goods they received. For example, suppose that you give an employee a horse worth $1,500 as payment for painting your barn. You can then deduct the $1,500 as a labor expense. However, remember that you must also report (as income) the $1,500 as if you sold the horse to your employee because bartering is a taxable event (and you need to fill out a Form 1099-B to report the barter's value).

The wages you paid and the income tax and Social Security and Medicare taxes that you're required to withhold are reported to the government on **Form 943, Employer's Annual Federal Tax Return for Agricultural Employees.** You must file this form by January 31, 2007. If you withheld less than $2,500 for the year, you can pay what you owe when you file Form 943. But as soon as you withhold $2,500 or more, you have to turn over to the government what you withheld for the month by the 15th of the following month. If you withheld $50,000 or more during 2005, you must remit your withholding taxes electronically (directly from your bank by wire transfer on a semiweekly basis). You'd think that if you're required to wire your withholding taxes in 2007, you'd have to do so because you withheld more than $50,000 in 2006 and not 2005. Guess what? You'd be wrong. If you operate more than a mom-and-pop family farm (that includes everyone who withholds $2,500 or more during the year), get your hands on IRS Publication 51 (Circular A, *Agricultural Employer's Tax Guide*). This publication explains more than you want to know about this subject in all its glorious detail.

The wages you pay to a child under the age of 18 aren't subject to Social Security and Medicare taxes. So, as long as the child's wages total less than $5,150 (the standard deduction for tax year 2006), the child doesn't have to pay any tax at all (as long as that $5,150 is the child's *only* source of income). And even better, you get to deduct the $5,150 as a labor expense. The only requirement is that the amount you pay for the child's services must be reasonable. For example, you can't claim that you paid your 3-year-old $5,150 to clean out the barn. And because the standard deduction is tied to the rate of inflation, every year it goes up.

Lines 37a and 37b: At risk

If you have a loss and are personally liable to pay back every dime that you borrowed to go into business, check line 37a. If not, check line 37b and check out line 27 of Schedule C earlier in this chapter to find out more. The rules are complex regarding the deduction of losses when you have no economic risk.

Identifying tax issues specific to farmers

Unfortunately, you still have to cope with a few additional issues that we explain in the following sections.

Estimated taxes

The IRS doesn't want to wait until April 15 to collect what you owe. If two-thirds of your income was from farming in 2005 or 2006, you have to make an estimated income tax payment by January 15, 2007, for what you owe for 2006, or file your return (including your full tax payment) by March 1, 2007. If you don't make an estimated payment, you'll be charged a penalty equal to current market interest rates. The penalty is computed on **Form 2210-F, Underpayment of Estimated Tax by Farmers and Fishermen.**

The amount of your required estimated tax payment is 66⅔ percent of your 2006 actual tax or 100 percent of your 2005 tax, whichever is the smaller amount. For example, suppose that your 2006 tax is $10,000 and your 2005 tax was $1,000. Because your 2005 tax of $1,000 is smaller than $6,667 (⅔ of your 2006 tax of $10,000), you need to pay only $1,000 on January 15, 2007. The $9,000 balance can be paid when you file on April 16.

If you file your return by March 1, 2007, and pay what you owe, you can skip having to make the January 15 payment.

Even though you file your return by March 1, 2007, you have until April 16, 2007, to make and deduct your IRA contribution (see Line 32, Chapter 7). If two-thirds of your income in 2005 or 2006 wasn't from farming, then the regular estimated tax rules apply. See Chapter 15.

If you're hearing about all this information for the first time — sorry. Mark your January 2008 calendar so you don't face it again when you file your 2007 return.

Operating at a loss

When operating any business, you must show a profit in at least three of every five consecutive years, or the IRS will term your business a hobby and disallow your losses, a situation known as *hobby losses*. If you're breeding, training, showing, or racing horses, however, you must make a profit in *two out of seven years* to keep the tax collector away. The IRS doesn't consider your enterprise a business if you have continuing losses — no business, no business deductions.

The three-out-of-five rule was established to keep the IRS off your back. If you meet this requirement, the IRS can't claim that the losses in the two other years can't be deducted because the business is a hobby. Not making a profit in three out of five years or two out of seven years doesn't automatically make the venture a hobby, but it is a strong indication that it may be.

However, if your farm does incur a net loss in 2006, you can write off that loss against any other income you and your spouse made that year. And there's more — if the loss is greater than your combined income in the current year, you can carry the loss back over each of the past five years and obtain a refund on the tax you paid at that time. If carrying it back still doesn't use up the loss, you can carry it *forward* to offset your income in the *next 20* years. You can also choose not to carry the loss back and use it only in future years instead. See Chapter 18 for more information on amending a prior year's return and carrying losses back as well as forward.

Your Social Security tax

This tax is commonly referred to as the self-employment tax. Check out Chapter 15 to find out how to compute this amount and take a deduction for half of what you pay in Social Security tax.

Farmers have an optional method for computing this tax. The computation is made in Part II of Schedule SE. Here's how it works. If your gross income (from line 11 on Schedule F) is $2,400 or less, or your net income (line 36) was less than $1,733, you can report two-thirds of your gross income as *your net farm income from self-employment.* Remember, you use this amount to compute your Social Security tax (not for figuring the amount on which you pay income tax). For example, suppose that your gross income was $1,800 and your net income (profit) was $500 — you can elect to report $1,200 (⅔ of $1,800) as your self-employment income, for the purpose of computing your Social Security tax. (However, you pay income tax on only the $500 of net income that you earned.) Why do all this?

- ✔ You receive credit for Social Security coverage.
- ✔ Your dependent childcare deduction and earned income credit increase with this method.

According to the IRS, dividends from a farm cooperative are income that are subject to self-employment tax and not investment income, which isn't subject to this tax. If you receive part of a crop from a tenant farmer, it's considered rental income, which isn't subject to self-employment income if you didn't materially participate in overseeing your tenant's activities.

Investment credits

The law allows an *investment credit,* which is similar to a direct payment of tax, for what you spent on reforestation or to rehabilitate historic structures and buildings placed in service before 1936. For reforestation, the law allows a credit for up to $10,000 of these expenditures. If you rehabilitate a historic structure, you can take an investment credit equal to 20 percent of your expenses. The *energy credit* equals 10 percent of what you spend installing solar or geothermal energy-producing equipment. These credits are computed on **Form 3468, Investment Credit.** Also check out the tax incentives for empowerment zones and other distressed communities in IRS Publication 954 *(Tax Incentives for Distressed Communities),* and **Form 8850, Work Opportunity and Welfare-to-Welfare Credits.**

Fuel credits

You can claim a credit for the off-highway use of fuels on your farm. The credit is computed on **Form 4136, Credit for Federal Tax Paid on Fuels.** *Note:* The definition of *off-highway* use doesn't apply to pleasure boats.

You can also buy dyed diesel fuel tax-free for use on a farm. Ask the vendor for an exemption certificate. Fill it out, hand it back, and watch the price drop.

You can now claim a credit or refund for the excise tax on undyed kerosene or diesel fuel for home use.

Electric and clean fuel–burning vehicles

Don't overlook the Alternative Motor Vehicle Credit (refer to Chapter 14) if you purchased a new electric or hybrid vehicle in 2006.

Sale of a farm or equipment

The sale of a farm or farm equipment gets tricky — you must consider many different factors, such as recapture of depreciation, credits, and basis (cost) adjustments to the property being sold. These types of sales are reported on **Form 4797, Sales of Business Property.** For more information on capital gains, see Chapter 12.

Cash-method farmers who use the installment method for reporting the sale of farm property don't have to take installment sales into account when determining whether they're subject to the Alternative Minimum Tax. See information in Chapter 8 if you're subject to this fiendish tax because you're claiming too many deductions.

Chapter 12

Capital Gains and Losses: Schedule D

. . . .

In This Chapter

▶ Tax basis background stuff

▶ Your introduction to Schedule D

▶ Short-term and long-term capital gains and losses

▶ How to handle Form 4797 (if you need to)

▶ How to deal with the sale of your home, worthless securities, stock options, and bad debts

. . . .

*I*f you sell a security, such as a stock, bond, or mutual fund (or any other investment held outside of a tax-sheltered retirement account), and you sell it for more than you paid for it, you owe capital gains tax on the profit. Conversely, when you sell an investment at a loss, the loss is tax deductible. Although it may seem unfair, a loss on the sale of your home, auto, jewelry, art, and furniture isn't deductible. That's a cruel reality regarding the sale of personal items.

Schedule D is the place where you plug in your profit or loss on the following examples:

- ✔ Your coin or stamp collection
- ✔ Your home (if you can't exclude all the gain)
- ✔ Household furnishings
- ✔ Jewelry and art
- ✔ Stocks and bonds

In this chapter, you discover the wonderful world of capital gains. You see what sorts of property qualify for preferential tax treatment when you sell them and what kinds don't. You figure out the rules surrounding the sale of your home (one of the last, truly great tax breaks out there), and find out the difference between short-term and a short sale. Most of all, though, this chapter tells you what you need to know, and where to find all the information you need to successfully complete your Schedule D.

Collectibles and Real Estate

The maximum rate on the sale of *collectibles* (art, antiques, stamp collections, memorabilia, and so on) is 28 percent.

> ## Property defined
>
> Definitions are the spice of life for IRS agents. Here's an important one.
>
> When most people refer to property, they mean real estate. But when the IRS talks about property, it can be anything that you own, such as stocks, bonds, cars, boats, or computers. So when you see the term property on a form, the government is talking about more than the old homestead. For example, a landlord's payment to a tenant to give up a rent-controlled apartment is considered the sale of property subject to lower capital gain tax rates.

One additional capital gains rate of 25 percent kicks in when you sell depreciable real estate. In that case, part of the profit — equal to the depreciation that you deducted through the years — is taxed at 25 percent, and the balance of the profit is taxed at the lower capital gains rate. Taxing all the depreciation at 25 percent relates only to real estate that you started to depreciate after 1986. If you started to depreciate it prior to 1987, part of the depreciation gets taxed at 25 percent and part at regular tax rates. Our advice: If you sell real estate that you started depreciating before 1987, see a tax pro.

What Part of Schedule D?

After you determine that you have a capital sale you need to report, you need to figure out where to report it. The face of Schedule D gives you two options: Part I, Short-term capital gains and losses (for property held one year or less), and Part II, Long-term capital gains and losses (for everything that you've owned for longer than one year). The length of time you owned the property determines whether you complete Part I or Part II. If you have a capital gain that is subject to the 25 percent or 28 percent rates, you must also use the worksheet in your instruction booklet. Finally, Part III summarizes all that you've done on Parts I and II and the worksheets for 28 percent and 25 percent gains that you find in your instruction booklet.

You list all your individual capital gains and losses on line 1 or 8. Line 1 is for short-term gains and losses, and line 8 is for long-term gains and losses.

Accuracy counts when preparing your Schedule D. Be precise when figuring your holding period because there's a big difference between long-term and short-term capital gains tax rates. And make sure, because the IRS checks its records, that the total of line 3 and line 10 of Schedule D match the total from all your **Forms 1099-B, Proceeds from Broker and Barter Exchange Transactions.**

Schedule D: Columns

After you determine whether the security that you sold goes in the short-term (Part I) or long-term (Part II) section, you're ready to work your way across the page. Take a look at Figure 12-1, Schedule D, to familiarize yourself with the layout of this form before you begin.

Details for figuring short term or long term

In most cases, whether you've held a security or other asset for more than 12 months is obvious. Here are some details that may help in less-clear cases. For securities traded on an established securities market, you begin counting the days in your holding period the day after the trading date on which you bought the securities, and stop on the trading date on which you sold them. For holding-period purposes, ignore the *settlement date* — this is the date when you actually pay the broker for a purchase or get paid from the broker for a sale.

For property that you received as a gift, you're considered to have purchased the property on the same day that the donor did — and not on the date of the gift — if you use the donor's tax basis as your basis. However, the holding period starts on the date of the gift if you sell it at a loss, and you're required to use the fair market value (FMV) of the property when it was given to you. Property inherited via someone's estate is treated as a sale of a long-term capital asset, even if you sold the shares or property the day after you received them. The more-than-12-months-rule is ignored.

When you purchase assets such as stocks or bonds by exercising an option, the holding period starts the day after the option is exercised — and not on the day that you received or purchased the option.

Here's how it works: Suppose that you sold 100 shares of Wonder Widget stock for $4,000 on April 17, 2006. Because you paid $6,000 for the shares on April 16, 2005, you have a capital loss of $2,000. To figure out whether the loss is long term or short term, start counting on April 17. The 17th of each month starts the beginning of a new month. Because you sold the shares on April 17, 2006 — one day more than 12 months — the loss is long term, so you'll place this transaction in Part II of Schedule D. (Had you sold them on April 16 — exactly 12 months after buying them — the loss would have been short term.) Here's how to show the IRS exactly what happened.

Column (a) Description of the property

100 shares of Wonder Widget

Column (b) Date acquired

4-16-05

Column (c) Date sold

4-17-06

Column (d) Sales price

$4,000

Column (e) Cost or other basis

$6,000

Column (f) Gain or <loss>

<$2,000>

If you need more spaces because lines 1 and 8 accommodate only five stock transactions each, use Schedule D-1 to list the rest of your stock trades.

SCHEDULE D
(Form 1040)

Department of the Treasury
Internal Revenue Service　(99)

Capital Gains and Losses

► Attach to Form 1040 or Form 1040NR.　► See Instructions for Schedule D (Form 1040).

► Use Schedule D-1 to list additional transactions for lines 1 and 8.

OMB No. 1545-0074

2006

Attachment
Sequence No. 12

Name(s) shown on Form 1040

Your social security number

Part I Short-Term Capital Gains and Losses—Assets Held One Year or Less

(a) Description of property (Example: 100 sh. XYZ Co.)	(b) Date acquired (Mo., day, yr.)	(c) Date sold (Mo., day, yr.)	(d) Sales price (see page D-6 of the instructions)	(e) Cost or other basis (see page D-7 of the instructions)	(f) Gain or (loss) Subtract (e) from (d)
1					

2　Enter your short-term totals, if any, from Schedule D-1, line 2 . . . . | **2** | | |

3　**Total short-term sales price amounts.** Add lines 1 and 2 in column (d) . . . . | **3** | | |

4　Short-term gain from Form 6252 and short-term gain or (loss) from Forms 4684, 6781, and 8824 | **4** |

5　Net short-term gain or (loss) from partnerships, S corporations, estates, and trusts from Schedule(s) K-1 | **5** |

6　Short-term capital loss carryover. Enter the amount, if any, from line 10 of your **Capital Loss Carryover Worksheet** on page D-7 of the instructions . . . . | **6** (.) |

7　**Net short-term capital gain or (loss).** Combine lines 1 through 6 in column (f) . . . . | **7** |

Part II Long-Term Capital Gains and Losses—Assets Held More Than One Year

(a) Description of property (Example: 100 sh. XYZ Co.)	(b) Date acquired (Mo., day, yr.)	(c) Date sold (Mo., day, yr.)	(d) Sales price (see page D-6 of the instructions)	(e) Cost or other basis (see page D-7 of the instructions)	(f) Gain or (loss) Subtract (e) from (d)
8					

9　Enter your long-term totals, if any, from Schedule D-1, line 9 . . . . | **9** | | |

10　**Total long-term sales price amounts.** Add lines 8 and 9 in column (d) . . . . | **10** | | |

11　Gain from Form 4797, Part I; long-term gain from Forms 2439 and 6252; and long-term gain or (loss) from Forms 4684, 6781, and 8824 . . . . | **11** |

12　Net long-term gain or (loss) from partnerships, S corporations, estates, and trusts from Schedule(s) K-1 . . . . | **12** |

13　Capital gain distributions. See page D-1 of the instructions . . . . . . | **13** |

14　Long-term capital loss carryover. Enter the amount, if any, from line 15 of your **Capital Loss Carryover Worksheet** on page D-7 of the instructions . . . . | **14** (.) |

15　**Net long-term capital gain or (loss).** Combine lines 8 through 14 in column (f). Then go to Part III on the back . . . . . | **15** |

Figure 12-1:
Schedule D,
Page 1.

For Paperwork Reduction Act Notice, see Form 1040 instructions.　　Cat. No. 11338H　　**Schedule D (Form 1040) 2006**

Calculating Your Adjusted Basis

Most of the columns on Schedule D are fairly self-explanatory. The description of the property, the date sold, and the sales price can be lifted directly from **Form 1099-B, Proceeds from Broker and Barter Exchange Transactions** (in the case of marketable securities) or from your HUD settlement sheet if you've sold your house and have to report a taxable gain.

Column (e), your cost or other *basis* in the property, is where you tell the IRS how much money you have invested in this particular piece of property, either personally or because you received it as a gift, an inheritance, or as part of a divorce settlement. Here are some items to consider when calculating your adjusted tax basis.

What's the starting point?

Figure out when this particular property came into your possession and by what method. Remember, you didn't need to necessarily buy it — you may have inherited it, earned it, received it as a gift from Great-Aunt Sadie, or obtained it from your ex-spouse as part of the property settlement. With whatever method, it came in with a cost already attached to it.

Dealing with purchased property

If you purchased a security from a broker, you should have received a sales confirmation. The confirmation lists the number of shares, the stock's name, the price per share, the gross price for your total purchase, any commissions and fees that were charged when you bought, and the date you placed the trade. Keep that confirmation in a permanent file so you can access that information whenever you need it. For your home, you'll have received a HUD settlement sheet. And if you buy collectibles (artwork, baseball cards, and the like), keep your sales receipts.

Looking at inherited property and property received by gift, for services or in advance

Obtain from the estate's executor the property value on the date of the decedent's death, or if the executor elects, the alternate valuation date six months after date. Your acquisition date in the stock is the decedent's date of death. The following types of property have different requirements.

- **Gifted property:** To figure the basis of property that you received as a gift, you must know the donor's basis at the time the gift was made, its fair market value (FMV) at the time the gift was made, and any gift tax that the donor paid.

  - If the FMV at the time of the gift was more than the donor's basis, then your basis for figuring a gain or loss is the donor's basis.

  - If the FMV at the time of the gift was less than the donor's basis, your basis for figuring a gain is the donor's basis, and your basis for figuring a loss is the FMV at the time of the gift.

- **Property received for services:** The amount that you're required to include in your income becomes your basis. Suppose that for putting a deal together you receive 100 shares of stock valued at $10,000. Because you had to pay tax on the value of the shares, your tax basis for the 100 shares is $10,000.

- **Property received in a divorce:** You use your spouse's basis. Generally, neither spouse is required to pay tax on property transferred as part of a divorce settlement.

Making adjustments to your basis

For many people, tracking their basis in property is like shooting at a moving target — the darned thing just won't stay put. Still, keeping track of your basis in property isn't impossible if you know what you're supposed to look at. The following list includes some of the more common basis adjustments:

- **Dividend reinvestment plans:** Some people opt to increase their investment in a particular security or mutual fund by reinvesting their ordinary dividends, their capital gain distributions, or both. This is nothing more than using the cash dividends you would have received to purchase additional shares. Doing so adds not only shares to your holding, but also to the basis. For example, at the beginning of 2005, you owned 1,000 shares of XYZ Corp, with a basis of $20,000. XYZ Corp paid a $1 per share dividend during 2005, providing you a total dividend of $1,000, which you declared and paid tax on as dividend income in 2005. You reinvested the $1,000, buying shares at $20/share. At the end of 2005, you now had 1,050 shares of XYZ Corp, with a total basis of $21,000.

Be careful when tracking the basis with dividend reinvestment plans; your holding period on each batch of new shares purchased is the dividend payment date, not the date of your original investment. If you sell those 1,050 shares at the beginning of 2006, the original 1,000 will have a long-term holding period (they were purchased prior to 2005), while the 50 shares purchased during 2005 through the dividend reinvestment program are a short-term asset.

✔ **Improvements and/or casualty losses to your home or rental property:** Increase your home's basis by the cost of any improvements you make plus the costs connected with purchasing the property — such as the fee that you paid the title company and your attorney. An added room, remodeled kitchen, or fancy landscaping all add to your basis. On the other hand, maintenance and repairs don't, so there's no basis adjustment for painting the house or repairing the plumbing. If you have a casualty loss, the basis in your home is reduced by the amount of basis you assign to that part of the property. For example, if you purchase property including a house and a barn for $100,000, of which $10,000 belongs to the barn, if the barn blows down in a hurricane, you need to reduce your basis by that $10,000. If you own rental real estate, or if you have a home office, depreciation and any casualty losses that you may have deducted (see Chapter 13 for more details) reduce your basis.

✔ **Original Issue Discount, market discount, and bond premium adjustments:** When you buy a bond and pay a different amount for it than its face value, you've paid either a premium (more) or received a discount (less). The IRS requires that you make adjustments over the bond's life to make your tax basis in that bond equal the bond's face value on the date the bond matures. Sounds simple, doesn't it? In fact, every year that you own the bond, you're going to declare interest on your tax return that you haven't actually received (in the case of a discounted bond), or subtract interest that you have received (in the case of a premium bond), and add or subtract those amounts to your basis on a year-by-year basis. Chapter 10 explains how this works in more detail. Just remember, every year you make an adjustment on Schedule B, you need to carry that adjustment to your basis records to keep them up-to-date.

✔ **Sale of partial holding:** You may decide to sell only part of what you own of stock ABC (many people do sell partial holdings). If you do, you need to either identify the shares that you're selling before the sale if you own multiple lots of that security that were purchased on multiple days, or accept the IRS default determination that the first shares you buy are the first shares you sell (FIFO — first in, first out method). Check out Chapter 22 to find out more about the tax benefits of selecting specific shares to sell rather than using FIFO. Chapter 22 also explains about the average cost method that's particularly useful when dealing with your mutual fund shares.

✔ **Stock dividends, splits, and returns of capital:** If you receive additional stock as part of a nontaxable stock dividend or stock split, you must reduce the per-share basis (but not the total basis) of your original stock. You make this computation by dividing the cost of the stock by the total number of shares that you now have. You must, however, reduce your basis when you receive nontaxable cash distributions (that number in box 3 of Form 1099-DIV that no one seems to know what to do with), because this transaction is considered a return on your investment.

✔ **Undistributed capital gains:** If your mutual fund had capital gains that it didn't distribute to its shareholders, you can increase your basis by that amount, which will reduce the amount of capital gains tax you'll owe when you eventually sell. We often see undistributed capital gains with technology and biotech funds. You'll be sent **Form 2439, Notice to Shareholders of Undistributed Long-Term Capital Gains.** You report your share of the undistributed gains and get a credit for the tax paid by the fund (entered on line 70 [and check box a], Form 1040). Your tax basis in the fund is increased by the difference between the capital gain that was retained by the fund and the actual tax paid by the fund on your behalf.

Tracking basis is a long and often tedious process, but it's worth it in the end. Keep a permanent file folder handy, ready to receive all those important receipts, confirmations, and other information so that you can find them when you need them. If you use computer software to track your finances, make sure you enter all your transactions so that your records are accurate.

Now that you know how and where to find the information that you need to tackle your 2006 Schedule D, you can confidently begin.

Part 1, Lines 1–7a and b: Short-Term Capital Gains and Losses — Assets Held One Year or Less

Line 1 should be a breeze if you fine-tuned your form skills in the preceding Wonder Widget example. Now you use your own short-term financial gains and losses as examples and complete the columns for line 1. If you have more than five items, you can list more on Schedule D-1.

Line 2: Enter your short-term totals, if any, from Schedule D-1, Line 2

Why is Schedule D-1 needed? Because line 1 has space for only five trades. If you had more, enter them on Schedule D-1, add them all up, and enter the total sales price from Schedule D-1 in column (d) of this line. Enter the profit or the <loss> that you computed on Schedule D-1 in column (f) on this line as well.

Line 3: Total short-term sales price amounts

Follow the instructions. Add column (d) of lines 1 and 2. Why? The IRS wants to compare the stock trades that you're reporting with the trades that your broker said you made and reported to the IRS on Form 1099-B.

Line 4: Short-term gain from Form 6252, and short-term gain or <loss> from Forms 4684, 6781, and 8824

All these form numbers! Because these forms rarely apply to most people, you may as well use them to play the lottery. Seriously, most people are going to deal with only **Form 4684, Casualties and Theft,** at some specific point in their lives. We cover this form in Chapter 9.

For those of you who are curious, **Form 6252** is for installment sales, **Form 8824** is for like-kind exchanges, and **Form 6781** is for commodity straddles. You can find more on **Form 6252** later in this chapter; if the other two forms apply to you, we suggest that you consult a tax advisor. Enter the short-term gains or losses from these forms on line 4 of Schedule D.

Line 5: Net short-term gain or <loss> from partnerships, S Corporations, estates, and trusts from Schedule (s) K-1

Short-term gains or losses from a partnership, an S Corporation, an estate, or a trust are reported on a schedule called a K-1. On line 5, enter the short-term gain or loss as indicated on the K-1 (short-term gains and losses only; long-term gains and losses go to line 12).

Line 6: Short-term capital loss carry-over

If you had more short-term losses than you were able to use last year, you may carry over the amount you weren't able to use to this year's return. You need your 2005 Schedule D in order to complete the Capital Loss Carryover Worksheet contained in the Schedule D instructions. After you calculate your 2005 short-term loss carry-over on the worksheet, insert your result on line 6, Schedule D.

You never need to go back any farther than last year's return to find your capital loss carry-over. Even if that carry-over loss was due to a sale that happened many years ago, you've been carrying the loss forward from year to year on your Schedule D.

Line 7: Net short-term gain or <loss>

On line 7, combine lines 1 through 5 in column (f) and enter the total. If it's a loss, make sure you enter it as a negative number.

Part II, Lines 8–15: Long-Term Capital Gains and Losses — Assets Held More than One Year

You want long-term capital gains because the government taxes them at lower rates.

Line 8: Columns (a), (b), (c), (d), (e), and (f)

As you did in Part I, fill in the columns for your long-term gains and losses. Schedule D-1 is available to list all your trades in case you had more than can fit on line 8 of this form.

When estates or heirs sell property that they inherited, they automatically get the long-term rate. If you're selling inherited property, put the date of death in as the acquisition date. If you're handwriting the form, also place the word "inherited" either in the space for the acquisition date or next to it. If you're using any computer software, check for a place in the interview form where you can code the acquisition as a sale of inherited property — the software will do the rest.

Line 9: Enter your long-term totals, if any, from Schedule D-1, Line 9

Just like you did on line 2 for short-term gains or losses, enter the totals of your long-term gains or losses from Schedule D-1 here. The total sales price goes in column (d). Enter your gain or <loss> in column (f).

Line 10: Total long-term sales price amounts

Add column (d) of lines 8 and 9. The IRS compares this figure to determine whether you reported all the sales that your broker reported to the IRS. If this number doesn't agree with what your broker reported on Form 1099-B, you can expect to hear from the IRS in about 12 months that you didn't report all your sales and that you owe additional tax and interest.

Line 11: Gain from Form 4797, Part 1; long-term gain from Forms 2439 and 6252; and long-term gain or <loss> from Forms 4684, 6781, and 8824

Here are some more lottery numbers. Everything that we said in our discussion of line 4 applies here — plus **Form 2439, Notice to Shareholder of Undistributed Long-Term Capital Gains,** and **Form 4797, Sales of Business Property.**

Form 2439, Notice to Shareholders of Undistributed Long-Term Capital Gains

Mutual fund companies are required to distribute the income they earn to their shareholders each calendar year by January 31 of the following year. When they do, the mutual fund company shareholders (that's you and me) pay the tax on the income, and the company doesn't. Sometimes, though, long-term capital gains aren't paid to the shareholders, and the company then must pay the tax. When this happens, the company will issue **Form 2439** to the shareholders, alerting them to the fact that there was additional long-term capital gain income that has already been taxed. When this happens, plug in the amount you see on line 1a of Form 2439 here, on line 11 of Schedule D. To be sure you don't pay taxes twice on this money (remember, the mutual fund company already has), fill in the amount of taxes paid shown on line 2 of Form 2439 on line 70 of Form 1040 and check the box labeled "Form 2439."

Form 4797, Sales of Business Property

The odds of having to complete any of those other nasty forms thankfully are small. But just in case you sell a business property, such as a building or an office copier, and have to deal with Form 4797, here are some tips to help you get through that form.

First of all, you need to know that the reason for a separate form is that the tax treatment of this type of sale is extremely complex. So what's new? The government believes that the new maximum rates are too good of a deal — many taxpayers were claiming a depreciation deduction on business assets they owned, including real estate, and then having any gain when they sold the property taxed at the lower capital gains rate. Form 4797 changes all that, forcing you to recapture all the depreciation you've claimed, pay tax at your ordinary income tax rates for that amount (with the exception of real estate depreciation recapture, which rate is capped at 25 percent for post-1986 depreciation), and then, if there's any additional gain, you get to apply capital gains rates to those.

For the purposes of depreciation, business property is divided into two types:

- ✔ Auto, business equipment, and machinery
- ✔ Real estate

Here's how this depreciation recapture rule for real estate works. Say you sold a building for $400,000 that you originally paid $200,000 for. Through the years, you claimed depreciation of $100,000, which reduces your tax basis for figuring your profit to $100,000. You have a $300,000 profit — $400,000 minus your cost ($200,000) reduced by your depreciation ($100,000). Of the $300,000 profit, the $100,000, representing deductions that you took for depreciation, is taxed at 25 percent, and the $200,000 balance is taxed at 5 or 15 percent, depending on what your tax bracket is without taking this gain into consideration.

If you think *depreciation recapture* sounds complicated, you need to remember that this rule is for real estate that you started to depreciate after 1986. For depreciation claimed before 1987, part is taxed at the regular rate and part at 25 percent. Which part? See a tax professional.

For all other property, the recapture rules work like this: Suppose that you purchased machinery for $10,000 and that you used it in your business for three years before selling it for $12,000. In the three years that you owned it, you took depreciation deductions totaling $7,120. This step reduces your tax basis to $2,880 ($10,000 cost – $7,120 depreciation). Ordinarily, if you sold property with a basis of $2,880 for $12,000, you'd have a capital gain of $9,120. But because a portion of those proceeds represents depreciation you have to recapture, you have a capital gain of only $2,000; the remaining amount of gain of $7,120 equals the amount of depreciation you need to recapture and pay ordinary income tax rates on. When you sell property for more than your adjusted basis, but less than its original cost, all the gain represents recaptured depreciation, and will be taxed at your ordinary income rates.

The depreciation recapture rules don't apply to business property sold at a loss. The loss is deductible from your income without limitation. The part of the profit that's recaptured and taxed at your regular tax rate is carried over from Form 4797 to Form 1040 (line 14). The long-term capital gain portion is carried over from Form 4797 to Schedule D (line 11). Use the long-term capital gain worksheet in Chapter 8 to make sure that you don't overpay.

This stuff may be more than you care to know about the sale of business property. But before you even contemplate the sale of business property, seek advice. If the amount involved is large, make sure that you get the best advice possible. See Chapter 2 for information about how to pick a good tax specialist.

Form 6252, Installment Sale Income

Here's the story on **Form 6252, Installment Sale Income.** Suppose that you sold a parcel of land for $60,000 in 2006. You paid $15,000 for it and will receive $10,000 in 2006 — and $10,000 a year for the next five years. You don't report the $45,000 profit that you made in 2006. You report a percentage of the profit as each installment is received.

You report the $10,000 that you receive every year on Form 6252, but you pay tax on only $7,500 of it, or 75 percent of what you received. (Your $45,000 profit is 75 percent of your $60,000 selling price.) The $2,500 that you don't pay tax on is the recovery of your cost. The $7,500 profit that you owe tax on is transferred to Schedule D.

You may elect out of the installment method and report the entire gain in the year of sale. You may want to go this way if you have a great deal of itemized deductions that would be wasted because they're more than your income (or if you're in an Alternative Minimum Tax [AMT] situation). See Chapter 8 for more about this tax.

If you have more deductions than income, you'll waste those excess deductions unless you can come up with more income in a hurry. Here's where opting out (for tax purposes) of an installment sale agreement makes sense. Looking at the previous example, if you have $10,000 in salary income and personal exemptions and itemized deductions come to $55,000, you could report another $45,000 of income before you have to pay a dime in tax. So reporting all the income from an installment sale in the year of the sale makes sense in this example.

If you're running a business, you can't use the installment method for sales of merchandise to customers. And, you need to charge interest on the unpaid installments. If you charge an unrealistically low rate of interest on the sale, the IRS will impute a rate of interest equal to the *Applicable Federal Rate (AFR)* that it publishes monthly on its Web site. Say you make a sale of $100,000 that's due in one year and you don't charge the buyer interest when the AFR should have been 5 percent. The IRS will recast the sale as follows: $5,000 will be considered interest, and $95,000 will be considered the amount of the sale that qualifies as a capital gain.

Line 12: Net long-term gain or <loss> from partnerships, S Corporations, estates, and trusts from Schedule(s) K-1

Line 12 is similar to line 5. You report any long-term gains and losses, as indicated on Schedule K-1, from partnerships, S Corporations, estates, and trusts on line 12. We discuss these entities in Chapter 13.

Line 13: Capital gain distributions

Mutual fund distributions are reported on Form 1099-DIV, boxes 2a–2d. Capital gain distributions received from a partnership, an S Corporation, an estate, or trust are reported on a schedule called a K-1. You enter these distributions on line 13.

If your Form 1099-DIV shows numbers in boxes 2b–2d, these numbers are included in the total in box 2a, but they're not eligible for the 15 percent maximum capital gains tax. Copy the number in box 2a onto line 13 of Schedule D to help you reach your total capital gain result. The Schedule D instructions and worksheets can guide you in calculating the tax on each portion of gain, whether it's 5 or 15 percent maximum gain property, 25 percent gain property, or 28 percent gain property. Enjoy!

If all you have are capital gain distributions from mutual funds and no other capital gains or losses, you can skip Schedule D. If you qualify under this rule, tally all your capital gain distributions and enter the total on line 13 of Form 1040, which is titled "Capital gain or (loss)," or line 10 of Form 1040A, which is titled "Capital gain distributions." If you're filing Form 1040, make sure you check the box to the left of line 13, indicating that Schedule D isn't required. See Chapter 8 to find out how to capture the information in box 2 from Form 1099-DIV, and to make certain you don't overpay your capital gains tax.

Line 14: Long-term capital loss carry-over

Enter your long-term capital losses that you couldn't deduct in previous years because you didn't have any capital gains in those years on this line. "Line 6: Short-term capital loss carry-over" explains how to handle carry-overs.

Line 15: Combine lines 8–14 in column (f)

Just follow the instructions. Add lines 8–14 in column (f). It couldn't be easier, and besides, you're almost finished. Remember, if you have a loss, enter it as a negative number.

Part III, Lines 16-22: Summary of Parts I and II

Hey, this part should be easy, right?

Line 16: Combine lines 7 and 15

If this line is a loss, skip lines 17 through 20 and move ahead to line 21. If it's a gain, enter this number on your Form 1040, line 13.

Line 17: Comparing lines 15 and 16

If lines 15 (gross long-term capital gain) and 16 (combined long-term and short-term capital gain) are both gains, check the "Yes" box and go to line 18. If line 16 is a gain, but line 15 shows a loss, check the "No" box and go straight to line 22.

Line 18: 28 percent gains

If you were fortunate enough to sell your Honus Wagner baseball card (one recently sold at auction for a cool $1.25 million) and can now retire in comfort, you first need to pay capital gains tax on your collectible baseball card. This line is where you segregate the gains from the sales of collectibles from the rest of your capital gains. To figure out what number to put here, first fill out the **28% Rate Gain Worksheet** you can find with your Schedule D instructions.

Line 19: 25 percent gains

If you're the recipient of a capital gain from the sale of depreciated real estate and need to recapture some or all of that depreciation, here's where you tell the IRS just how much that was. First, though, you're going to have to complete the **Unrecaptured Section 1250 Gain Worksheet** in your Schedule D instructions.

Line 20

If you don't have any numbers on lines 18 or 19, move to the head of the class. Complete your Form 1040 through line 43, and then calculate your tax using the **Qualified Dividends and Capital Gain Tax Worksheet** that's included in your instruction booklet. We also give you instructions on how to do this in Chapter 8. Put the answer to your tax calculation on line 44 of Form 1040.

If you have a number on either or both of lines 18 or 19, you get to complete the **Schedule D Tax Worksheet** located in your Schedule D instructions. It looks long, but it's really not so bad. All you're doing is calculating the tax on each category of income you have, and then adding them together. Be methodical; you'll do fine!

If you have numbers on lines 18 or 19, don't complete lines 21 or 22 of Part III. You're finished with Schedule D.

Line 21: Capital losses

If you've had an unfortunate year with your investments, you determine how much of that misfortune you can use to wipe out ordinary, taxable income this year on this line. For any filing status except married filing separately, if your loss on line 16 is less than $3,000, enter the amount of your loss here and on line 13 of your Form 1040. If it's greater than $3,000, enter $3,000 on line 21 and also on line 13 of your Form 1040. Remember, if you're married but filing separately from your spouse, you can claim losses up to only $1,500 — your spouse gets the same.

Line 22: Qualified dividends

Qualified dividends, which we discuss in Chapter 10, are taxed at a maximum rate of 15 percent. If you have qualified dividends on line 9b of your 1040, check the "Yes" box and fill out the **Qualified Dividends and Capital Gain Tax Worksheet** that's located in your Form 1040 instruction booklet and also in Chapter 8. If you don't have any qualified dividends, go back and complete the rest of your Form 1040.

Using Schedule D When You Sell Your Home

Selling your home may be one of the biggest financial decisions you make in your life. It may also provide you with one of the largest tax breaks that's available to the average Joe and Jane. Believe it or not, a married couple can exclude up to $500,000 of the profit they make on the sale of their home. A single person is entitled to a $250,000 exclusion from the capital gains tax.

Of course, nothing's that simple. You need to qualify. Here's how:

- If you're married, you or your spouse must have owned the residence for at least two of the past five years, and both of you must have used it as your primary residence for two out of the past five years; a vacation home can't meet this test.

- If you're single, you must have owned and used the residence as your primary residence for two of the past five years.

How does the two-out-of-the-past-five-years rule works? The look-back starts on the date of the sale. For example, suppose that you sold your home on July 1, 2006. Between July 1, 2001, and July 1, 2006, you must have owned and used your home as your principal residence for any two years during this period. The periods don't have to be consecutive as long as they add up to two years.

Tips for the newly widowed, married, or divorced

The ownership and use as a primary residence includes the period that a deceased spouse used and owned the residence.

The exclusion is available on an individual basis, which means that the $250,000 exclusion is available for the qualifying principal residence of each spouse for those who file jointly but live apart — not an uncommon arrangement these days. If you happen to marry someone who used the exclusion within the two-year period before your marriage, you're entitled to your $250,000 exclusion and vice versa.

If a residence is transferred in a divorce, the time period that the ex-spouse owned the residence is taken into account to determine whether the ownership-and-use tests have been met.

If you're a surviving spouse and owned your home jointly, your basis for the half-interest owned by your spouse is one-half of the fair market value (FMV) on your spouse's date of death. (Don't let the term basis throw you. For a quick, one-sentence explanation, check out the sidebar "Property defined," earlier in this chapter.) The basis in your half-interest is one-half the tax basis of the house as computed in the next paragraph (usually the cost plus improvements).

For instance, if your home cost $200,000 and was worth $400,000 when your spouse died, your new basis is $300,000 (½ of the $200,000 cost plus ½ of the $400,000 FMV).

In community property states, when a spouse dies, the FMV at the date of death becomes the tax basis of the entire house. So in the previous example, the surviving spouse's tax basis is $400,000 (the FMV) and not $300,000.

Say you shuttle between two residences, one in New Jersey and one in Florida, the one that you use most of the time will ordinarily be considered your primary residence. Where it's a close call, the IRS looks at these factors to determine which residence is the primary one:

- The taxpayer's place of employment
- Where the taxpayer's family lives most of the time
- The address listed on tax returns, driver's license, auto registration, and a voter registration card
- The mailing address for bills and correspondence
- The location of the taxpayer's religious institutions and recreational clubs he or she is a member of
- Location of the taxpayer's bank

The $500,000/$250,000 exclusion replaces the old once-in-a-lifetime $125,000 exclusion that was available only to taxpayers older than 55. Age no longer matters. In addition to raising the exclusion limits, the new provision is more generous in another way: You may use it repeatedly, but not more often than every two years.

The two-year rule is waived for both singles and couples when they have to sell their homes within two years because a new job requires them to move (the new place of employment must be 50 miles farther from the old home than the old home was from the old workplace — see the moving expense deduction in Chapter 9 for more about the 50-mile rule), they move for health reasons (it must be a specific illness and not just for general health), or they move for other unforeseen circumstances (more details in this section). The sale for health reasons must involve the health of:

- The taxpayer, his or her spouse, or the co-owner
- A member of the taxpayer's household

✔ Members of the taxpayer's family — children, their descendents, brothers and sisters and their descendents and their children, parents, aunts, uncles, stepchildren, step-brothers, stepsisters, stepparents, and in-laws, as well as descendents of the taxpayer's grandparents. I bet you thought this list would never end!

Here is the official IRS list of "unforeseen circumstances":

✔ Becoming eligible for unemployment insurance

✔ A change in employment that leaves you unable to pay your mortgage or basic living expenses

✔ Damage to the residence resulting from a natural or man-made disaster or an act of war or terrorism

✔ Death

✔ Divorce or legal separation

✔ Multiple births resulting from the same pregnancy

For example, say you buy a house on August 1, 2005, for $350,000, and you sell it for $550,000 on August 1, 2006 (if we're going to make up a story, why not make it a good one?), because you're moving from New York to Los Angeles to start a new job. You're single. Because you owned the house for only 12 months of the required 24-month period, you're entitled to one-half of the $250,000 exclusion, or $125,000. That means that only $75,000 of your $200,000 profit is subject to tax.

The $500,000/$250,000 exclusion may have given you the idea that, because of the increased exclusion amount, you no longer have to keep records of your purchases or improvements. Although this premise may be true for many people, it doesn't necessarily apply to everyone. Suppose that you're single and buy a house for $300,000. Because you don't know what you'll sell the house for in 20 years, you'd better hang on to the receipts for any improvements that you paid for. Suppose that you sell your house for $600,000 — a $300,000 profit — but you're entitled to only a $250,000 exclusion. Good records can help you reduce the profit even further.

The sale of vacant land adjacent to a principal residence qualifies for the $250,000/$500,000 exclusion if it's used as part of the principal residence. This qualification applies even if the land is sold separately, as long as the land sale occurs within the two-year period before or after the sale of the dwelling place. Say the land was sold in 2005, and the dwelling was sold in 2006. Because the adjacent land had to be reported on your 2005 return, you have to file an amended return for 2005 if the sale of the land and the dwelling are less than the exclusion. You're entitled to obtain a refund for the tax you paid on the land in 2005.

In order to not unduly burden members of the military, who often buy a house at one base, only to be transferred to another before they qualify for the full exclusion amount, the Congress, through the *Military Families Relief Act,* has authorized the IRS to issue rules allowing you to suspend the five-year holding period under these circumstances. This act provides that, if you buy a house in 1998 for $150,000, live there for three years, and then are transferred to other active military postings for the next five years, when you sell that house in 2006 for $400,000, you're still qualified to take the full $250,000 exclusion, even though you weren't actually living there for two out of the last five years.

How do you know if you can suspend your holding period? If you're on qualified official extended duty at a posting at least 50 miles from your main home, or you're ordered to live in government quarters, you can. In addition, if you're ordered to active duty for a period of more than 90 days, or indefinitely, you also qualify.

Even better, the IRS has made this holding period suspension retroactive to the sale of your principal residence after May 6, 1997. If you sold a home after that date, but paid capital gains tax on all or a portion of your gain because you were disqualified from taking the full exclusion under the old rules, you can amend your tax return and claim a refund using Form 1040X. Complete the form per its instructions, and write across the top "Military Family Tax Relief Act." Remember, though, you can only claim a credit or refund within three years from the date you filed your original return, or two years from the date you paid the tax.

A couple of caveats are attached to this offer. First, you can't suspend your holding period for longer than ten years, and second, you can suspend the holding period on only one property at a time.

Computing your profit

Computing the profit on the sale of your home is simple.

From the sales price, subtract the following expenses in connection with the sale:

- ✔ Advertising costs
- ✔ Attorney fees
- ✔ Real estate broker's commission
- ✔ Title closing costs

From the sales price after the expenses of the sale, subtract the following (in this order):

- ✔ Original cost of your castle
- ✔ Improvements
- ✔ Closing costs and attorney fees at the time of purchase

What constitutes an improvement? An improvement is anything that adds to your house's value or prolongs its life. Drapery rods, Venetian blinds, termite proofing, and shrubbery all fit the bill. If you own a condo or co-op, your cost basis also includes special assessments to improve the building, such as renovating the lobby or installing a new heating system. Co-op owners get an additional boost, because the part of their maintenance charges that goes to paying off the co-op's mortgage also is added to their cost.

From your profit, subtract the exclusion that you're entitled to. If you're single, it's $250,000; for couples, it's $500,000. If this exclusion exceeds your profit, you can stop right there because there's nothing more to do. You need not report the sale on your return; the entire profit is tax-free. If your profit exceeds the exclusion, you owe tax and have to report the sale on Schedule D. For example, your profit is $410,000, and you're entitled to only exclude $250,000. You have to report the sale and pay tax on $160,000.

On the other hand, if your profit is $410,000 and you're entitled to exclude $500,000, you need not report the sale on your return.

If you have a loss, it isn't deductible. Profits above the exclusion amounts are. We're sure that you've heard this before: "Heads, they win; tails, you lose."

You can find an excellent worksheet in the IRS Publication 523 *(Selling Your Home)* that can guide you through your profit computation. This publication also has a nifty list of examples of the types of improvements that increase the tax basis of a home. So don't overlook it.

Reporting a profit that exceeds the exclusion

You report the sale of your residence on Schedule D only if the profit exceeds the exclusion you're entitled to.

Normally, the purchaser (typically via the title company) reports the sale on **Form 1099-S, Proceeds from Real Estate Transactions.** If you're single and the sale is for $250,000 — or $500,000 or less for couples — and you meet the other requirements such as the two-year principal residence test, you can sign a certificate at the time of the sale so that a Form 1099-S doesn't have to be sent to the IRS.

Here's how you compute the profit on the sale of your home and report the profit on Schedule D if you are required to:

1. **Figure your tax basis by adding your original cost, closing costs, and cost of improvements.**

2. **Compute your net selling price.**

   That's your selling price less your selling and closing expenses.

3. **Subtract your tax basis from your net selling price.**

   For example, you sold your home for $610,000. Your closing costs were $10,000, and the original cost of your home plus improvements and closing costs was $400,000.

Congratulations, you made a $200,000 profit ($610,000 – $10,000 – $400,000). If you're single or married, you don't have to report the profit on Schedule D, because your exclusion ($250,000 for singles or $500,000 if married) exceeds your profit.

If your profit exceeds your exclusion, you have to report the profit on Schedule D. Here's how you do it. Report the entire gain on line 8, filling out columns (a) through (f). Because you qualify for the exclusion, enter it on the line directly below the line where you reported the gain. Write Section 121 exclusion in column (a) and the amount of the exclusion in column (f) as a loss (in parentheses). For example, $250,000 is written as <$250,000> in column (f). If you're married, enter <$500,000>.

If you used part of your home as an office or rented out your home, the exclusion doesn't apply to any depreciation that you claimed after May 6, 1997. For example, if you claimed $10,000 in depreciation after May 6, 1997, and you're entitled to a $500,000 exclusion and the gain on the sale of your home is $400,000, you can exclude only $390,000 of that gain. You owe tax on the $10,000 of depreciation claimed after May 6, 1997.

Following the home office and rental rules

Under the old rule, the IRS considered a taxpayer's home sale (where the home was partially used for business) the sale of two pieces of property — the portion used as the residence that qualified for the $250,000 or $500,000 exclusion, and the portion used for business that didn't. For example, if someone used 20 percent of his or her home for business and then sold the home at a $150,000 profit, $30,000 would be considered the sale of business property that has to be reported on Form 4797, Sales of Business Property, and would be taxed. The remaining $120,000 is considered the gain on the sale of a principal residence that is exempt from tax because it's less than the exclusion. At the end of 2002, the IRS had a change of heart!

Under the new rule, only the depreciation claimed after May 6, 1997, is taxable. The rest of the profit on the sale is eligible for the $250,000/$500,000 exclusion. You report the depreciation on **Form 4797, Sales of Business Property,** and carry it over to line 11 of Schedule D. This profit is subject to the 25 percent maximum capital gains tax.

If under the old rule you paid tax on the part of the profit from the sale of your in-home office, file an amended return and get your money back (see Chapter 18 to find out how to file an amended return).

If the portion of your home that's used for business is separate from the dwelling unit, the new rule doesn't apply, and you're considered to have sold two parcels: the business portion, which is taxable, and the residence, which is eligible for the exclusion. The clearest example: You have a townhouse with a finished basement that you convert into a separate unit and close off by removing the interior stairway that leads to the rest of the house.

Use Schedule D for Other Issues Involving Stocks (Worthless and Otherwise)

You can use Schedule D to handle such issues as worthless securities, wash sales, stock options, stock for services, and appreciated employer securities.

Worthless securities

Suppose that you felt certain that Company X was going to make a comeback, so you invested $15,000. But you were wrong. Not only has Company X failed to make this comeback, but also its shares are no longer even being quoted in the morning paper.

Great! So at least $15,000 is a write-off, right? No. The problem with this scenario is that you must be able to prove — with an identifiable event — that your investment is in fact *completely worthless.* Being partially worthless doesn't cut it. In one case, bondholders in a company canceled 30 percent of the face value of their bonds to keep the company afloat. But they couldn't deduct the portion of the debt they canceled because their investment hadn't become completely worthless. Likewise, the fact that the shares of a company are no longer being quoted doesn't make them worthless.

We wish that we could tell you that convincing the IRS that you're entitled to write off your $15,000 investment is as easy as losing it. It's not — and this is an area of the law that's more confusing than most. You may think that bankruptcy, going out of business, liquidation, the appointment of a receiver, or insolvency indicates that your investment no longer had any value. But these events only prove that the company is in financial trouble, not that its shareholders won't receive anything in liquidation. In order to claim a deduction for worthless securities, your investment must be completely worthless.

When is an investment worthless? As a general rule, you can say that an investment is worthless when a company is so hopelessly insolvent that it ceases doing business or it goes into receivership, leaving nothing for its stockholders. If you're not sure, one source worth checking is CCH Inc. (which also does the technical editing of this book). This outfit.

publishes an annual list of worthless securities as part of its "Capital Changes Reports." Most major brokerage firms and public libraries subscribe to this service, or you can reach the company directly at 800-TELL-CCH (800-835-5224).

If proving when unmarketable shares in a company actually became worthless is so difficult, why not lock in a loss by finding some accomplice — the broker who sold them to you, for example — to take the shares off your hands for a penny apiece? Nice try, but no go. A number of taxpayers have attempted to "structure sales" in this fashion, but both the IRS and the Tax Court have denied the losses because these sales weren't considered legitimate. Instead, the taxpayers were told to hang on to their investments and deduct them only when they became certifiably worthless. In other words, they were back to square one.

Securities that became worthless in a given tax year are considered to have become worthless on the last day of that year and reported in the short-term section of Schedule D. Enter your cost and zero (-0-) for the sales price because the investment is worthless. So, as you can see, Schedule D has a few other handy uses as well.

Wash sales

Suppose that you own a stock that has declined in value. You think that it will recover, but you want to deduct the money that you lost. If you sell the stock and buy back the shares within 30 days of the sale, you can't deduct the loss. This type of trade is called a wash sale. The loss can't be deducted in the year of the trade. The loss is deducted when you sell the new shares.

Here is an example of how the wash sale rule works. You paid $15,000 for a stock that has declined in value to $6,000. You sell it incurring a $9,000 loss. Then the stock starts to rebound, and you get that sense that it's going to stage a comeback. Two weeks later you buy the stock back for $7,000. You can't deduct your $9,000 loss, because you sold and repurchased shares of the same company within a 30-day period. Your $9,000 loss is added to the $7,000 you paid for the new shares. The cost you use to determine any gain or loss when the new shares are sold is now $16,000.

Small business stock

You can deduct up to $50,000 ($100,000 if filing jointly) of a loss from the sale, or from worthlessness of *small business stock* (more commonly called "Code Section 1244 stock"). A corporation qualifies as a "1244 corp." if at the time its stock is issued, the amount of money it receives doesn't exceed $1 million. That means if you're married and sustained a $150,000 "1244 loss," you can deduct $100,000 from your income. The $100,000 loss is computed on Form 4797, line 10. The $100,000 is then carried over to line 14 of Form 1040 as a negative number in parentheses. The $50,000 balance is considered a capital loss and is entered on Schedule D. How do you know whether the company you invested in is a "1244 corp."? Find out before you put up your dough. But, if you're reading about small business stock for the first time, track down the company's accountant or attorney. You must be the original owner of the shares. Additional contributions of capital don't qualify as "Section 1244 stock."

Stock options

Stock options, those opportunities to buy shares in a company in the future at a price that is set at the time the option is created, usually come in two varieties: *statutory options,* which have to meet certain IRS rules to qualify for special tax advantages, and *nonstatutory stock options,* which are also subject to special rules even though the tax savings aren't as great. Statutory stock options include incentive stock options and options under an employee stock purchase plan.

Incentive stock options (ISOs)

You aren't subject to tax when an *incentive stock option* is granted. You realize income or loss only when you sell the stock that you acquired by exercising the ISO.

You must exercise the option within 10 years from the date that it was granted. The option price has to be at least equal to the value of the stock on the day that the option was granted. For example, you can't receive an option to buy shares for $10 a share when the shares are selling for $18 a share. In any one year, you can't receive an option to buy shares that are worth more than $100,000 on the date that the option was granted. If you go over $100,000, the excess isn't considered an ISO, so read on until you get to the section "Nonstatutory stock options."

When you sell stock that you acquired by exercising an ISO, you have a long-term capital gain if you held the shares for more than one year from the date when you exercised the option and more than two years after the ISO was granted. For example, say you exercise an option for $15,000. You later sell the shares for $25,000. You have a long-term capital gain of $10,000 if you meet the one- and two-year rules. If you don't meet these rules, the $10,000 gain is divided into two parts. The difference between the exercise price and the value on the day that you exercised the option is taxed as ordinary income. The difference between the value on the day that you exercised the option and the value on the day that you sold the stock is treated as a capital gain (either short- or long-term). In the previous example, if the shares were worth $20,000 on the day that you exercised the option, then $5,000 of the gain would be taxed as ordinary income, and $5,000 (the difference between the sales price, $25,000, and the $20,000 value on the day the option was exercised) is taxed as a long-term capital gain.

Although the spread between the option price and the value on the day that you exercised the option isn't subject to tax for regular tax purposes, it is subject to the fiendish Alternative Minimum Tax (AMT). So take a peek at the section about the AMT in Chapter 8, or better yet, speak to a good tax pro.

The holding period for determining long- or short-term capital gains on shares acquired by exercising a stock option starts on the day after you exercise the option. We explain the holding period rules earlier in this chapter, in the sidebar "Details for figuring short term or long term."

If an ISO is transferred, say in a divorce, it loses its special tax treatment. An ISO transferred at death doesn't.

Employee stock purchase plans

Employee stock purchase plans allow you to buy your company's stock at a discount. The discount isn't taxed until you sell the shares. If you hold the shares for more than two years after the option was granted and more than one year after you acquired the shares, the discount is taxed as ordinary income, and the difference between the value on the day that you acquired the shares is a capital gain (either short- or long-term). For example, you sold shares for $25,000 that you had purchased under an employee plan for $16,000. On the day that the options were granted, the shares were worth $18,000. Of the $9,000 gain, $2,000 ($18,000 − $16,000) is taxed at ordinary rates, and $7,000 ($25,000 − $18,000) is taxed as a capital gain, either short- or long-term.

If you sold the shares before the end of the two-year period, substitute the value of the shares on the day that you purchased them in place of the value when the option was granted to determine the ordinary income portion of the $9,000 gain. Suppose that the value of the shares on the day that you purchased them was $20,000. Of the gain, $4,000 ($20,000 – $16,000) is taxed as ordinary income, and the $5,000 balance ($25,000 – $20,000) is taxed as a capital gain. Is there a way around these maddening rules? Hold the shares for more than two years.

Nonstatutory stock options

Because nonqualified stock options don't have to meet any IRS rules, there are no restrictions on the amount of these types of options that may be granted. If a nonstatutory stock option doesn't have an ascertainable value when it's issued (which is usually the case for options that aren't traded on a stock exchange), no income is realized when you receive the option. When you exercise the option, you're taxed on the spread. For example, you exercise a $4,000 option to purchase stock trading at $10,000; you realize ordinary income of $6,000. Your tax basis for figuring a gain or loss when you sell the shares is $10,000. If the option has an ascertainable value, the value of the option is taxed as additional salary. For example, you receive an option to buy 100 shares that you can sell for $1,000 on the day that you receive the option. The bad news: You owe tax on the $1,000. The good news: When you exercise the shares, the $1,000 is added to the cost of the shares when determining whether you have a profit or loss when you sell the shares.

Unlike an ISO, a nonstatutory stock option can be transferred tax-free in a divorce.

Options that have expired

Say you paid $1,500 in December 2005 to purchase an option to buy 1,000 shares of a stock for $60 a share that was good for 60 days, and you let the option expire in 2006 because you lost your bet when the stock never increased in value. You have a $1,500 short-term loss that you can deduct in 2006.

The reason we're warning you about this situation is because options that have expired aren't reported on the year-end tax statement that your broker is required by law to send. Only sales are reported, and consequently, many people tend to overlook this deduction. Don't be one of them.

Short sales

Not many people get involved with short sales, but we thought you should know about them. When an investor believes a stock is going to tank and wants to take advantage of that fact, he or she "shorts" the stock by selling it. How can you sell, you say, something that you don't own? You borrow the shares you sell from your broker. If you're right and the stock goes down, you can buy the stock down the road for much less than you sold it for and replace the shares you borrowed from the broker. Doesn't everybody wish they had done this before the market took a nosedive?

With a short sale, your gain or loss is reported when you buy the shares you have to return to the broker. Only, the normal rule (that you always use the trade date and not the settlement date) doesn't apply to short sales. If you made a profit, it's the trade date. If you have a loss, it's the settlement date. This rule is important at the end of the year. For example, you make a short sale and then buy the shares you're going to return to the broker on December 31, but that purchase doesn't settle until January 4. If you made a profit, you report it in 2006. A loss, on the other hand, gets reported in 2007.

If, at the end of the year, you have an open short position (you hadn't returned the shares to the broker), your year-end tax statement (remember the IRS gets a copy of it) will probably report the short sale as a regular one. Report the sale on your return so that you and the IRS are in sync. By using the sales price as your cost, you obtain the net effect of showing a zero gain or loss on your Schedule D. That way you won't be reporting any actual income, and the IRS won't start up with you by claiming you failed to report all your sales. Report the sale when you buy the shares that you owe the broker.

Short sales are considered short-term because with a short sale your holding period starts with the day you purchase the shares that you return to the broker, which usually is one day.

If your short position was open for more than 45 days, and your broker charged you for any dividends that you owed to the owner of the shares you borrowed, that charge gets deducted on line 13 of Schedule A as investment interest. See why good records are so important?

Stock for services

Stock for services is taxed as additional salary or fee income if you're an independent contractor. However, special rules apply as to when you have to report the income. If the stock is subject to restrictions, you report as income the value of the stock when the restrictions are lifted. For example, a restriction may be that you have to work for the company for three years; otherwise, you forfeit the shares.

Even if the shares are subject to restrictions, you can elect to report the value of the shares as income in the year you receive them. This is known as a Section 83(b) election. Why would you want to do this? Say you receive shares in a start-up venture that have little value at the time you receive them. If you wait to report the value of the shares as income five years from now, when the restrictions are lifted and the shares are worth a great deal, you could be taxed at rates which currently are as high as 35 percent, or 39.6 percent when rates are scheduled to revert back to that rate in 2010, on the value at that time. On the other hand, if the shares currently are worth only a few thousand dollars, reporting the income now and paying a small amount of tax makes sense, because when you sell the shares after they've increased dramatically in value, the profit will be subject to the maximum 15 percent (or perhaps the lower 5 percent) capital gain rate. Remember, such a tactic is a gamble. If the company goes bust, you'll have paid tax on shares that ended up being worthless, but you will have a worthless stock deduction for the amount of income you paid tax on when you made the Section 83(b) election.

Appreciated employer securities

Many taxpayers overlook a special rule that applies when shares of the company where they work are distributed to them as part of a lump-sum distribution from a retirement plan. The value of the shares isn't subject to tax at the time you receive them. Only the cost of the shares when they were purchased is. For example, shares of your employer's stock that you bought through your employer's retirement plan for $50,000 now are worth $200,000. Only the $50,000 is subject to tax when you receive the shares. If you sell the shares the following year for $225,000, you have to report a $175,000 capital gain that year.

If you don't hold the shares for more than one year, part of the gain is taxed as a short-term sale. In the previous example, if you didn't hold the shares for more than a year after they were distributed, $25,000 of the gain is short-term, and $150,000 is long-term. The difference between the cost and the value on the day that they were distributed is treated as long-term ($200,000 – $50,000), and the difference between the sales price and the value on the date of distribution is short-term ($225,000 – $200,000).

Using Schedule D for Nonbusiness Bad Debts

Suppose that you lent your best friend $2,500 on New Year's Eve, and you haven't seen him since New Year's Day. All is not lost. You can deduct the $2,500. This news comes as a surprise to many people, because you can usually deduct losses only on investment and business transactions. But you must be able to prove that a valid debt existed, that the debt is worthless, and that you previously paid tax on the money that you lent.

- ✔ **What is worthless?** As with securities, there must be some identifiable event — such as bankruptcy, legal action, or the disappearance of the debtor — to prove that you can't collect what you're owed. You don't necessarily have to sue the debtor or even threaten to take legal action. This is one of the few instances where the IRS is on your side, not your lawyer's!

- ✔ **The right to sue:** To prove that you have a valid debt, you should be able to show that you have a right to sue. This situation creates a special problem with loans to family members. The IRS tends to view such loans as gifts. So if you had your brother sign a promissory note and put up collateral when you lent him money, you could prevail if the IRS ever questioned whether it was a valid debt. Yet, as you probably know, most dealings between family members are done a little more casually than that. See Chapter 10 for more on this painful subject.

- ✔ **Is the debt deductible?** Finally, to establish that a debt is deductible, you must have paid tax on what you lent. Suppose that you worked in a local bookstore in anticipation of being paid later. The bookstore went out of business, and you weren't paid. Sorry. Because you never received the bookstore income and didn't report it on your tax return, you're not entitled to a deduction if it's not paid.

You deduct nonbusiness bad debts on good old Schedule D as a short-term loss, regardless of how long the money was owed. If you don't have capital gains to offset the deduction, you can deduct up to $3,000 of the loss and carry over the balance to next year, just like with other investment losses. Additionally, you must attach a statement to your return explaining the nature of the debt, name of the debtor and any business or family relationship, date the debt became due, efforts made to collect the debt, and reason for determining that the debt is entirely worthless (only business debts can generate a deduction if they're partially worthless).

Don't confuse nonbusiness bad debts with business-related bad debts that can be deducted on your business tax returns. Refer to Chapter 11 for more on business-related bad debts.

Day traders

There are tax advantages to being considered a trader rather than a mere investor. Vast sums of money, however, have been lost day trading, and the tax impact has been significant (see Chapter 22 for more on investing and taxes). Most people are investors because they purchase securities they hold for a long time in anticipation the investment will appreciate in value and produce income (dividends). An investor reports gains and losses on Schedule D. If losses exceed gains, an investor is limited to an annual deductible of $3,000 with a lifetime to carry over the remaining loss to future years to offset gains. Investment expenses are deducted as miscellaneous itemized deductions. A home office deduction isn't allowed no matter how much time investors spend analyzing their investments because they're not carrying on a trade or business.

A *day trader,* on the other hand, typically tries to capture short-term swings in the market. A trader reports his expenses on Schedule C and trading gains and losses on Schedule D. Traders can claim a home-office deduction because they're carrying on a trade or business. A trader can deduct all margin interest on Schedule C. Investors deduct theirs on Schedule A, provided it doesn't exceed their investment income. Gains aren't subject to Self-Employment

Tax, nor can a deduction for a contribution to an IRA or retirement plan based on the gain be claimed, because the gain isn't considered earned income. Traders are subject to the same $3,000 annual limit on trading losses that exceed gains. The wash sale rule also applies. To be a trader, your trading has to be, in IRS jargon, "sufficiently frequent and substantial." Like so many IRS definitions it falls under the heading of, "I can't define it, but I know it when I see it." The IRS tends to take the position that you can't be a trader if you have another regular job. They like to reserve trader status for people who trade on a full-time basis to the exclusion of other activities. This is plainly wrong. You can be a part-time trader. The New York Stock Exchange defines a trader as someone who buys and sells a stock in the same trading session at least four times a week.

Mark-to-market traders

A *mark-to-market trader* elects to treat any stocks he or she holds at the end of the trading day on December 31 as being sold on that day. Any of these deemed gains or losses are reported on the mark-to-market trader's return. For true day traders, this requirement shouldn't be of any consequence, because they typically don't own securities at the end of any day. A position trader, on the other hand, who has an open position December 31, and who makes a mark-to-market election, loses the ability to use the year-end tax strategy of selling the losers and holding the winners. On the following January 1, a mark-to-market trader must adjust the tax bases of the securities deemed to have been sold. Gains that were reported because of the election are added to the basis of the securities held on December 31 and losses are subtracted from its basis.

A mark-to-market trader reports expenses on Schedule C and trading activity as ordinary gains and losses on Form 4797. The wash-sale rule doesn't apply to this type of trading. If net losses occur, all these losses can be used to offset other income; the $3,000 limit doesn't apply. If the losses produce a net operating loss (exceeding your other income), they can be carried back to a prior year to obtain a refund and then forwarded to future years. Trading gains aren't subject to Self-Employment Tax, and no IRA or retirement deduction can be claimed.

A true mark-to-market trader isn't the same as a day trader. All gains and losses received by a day trader are treated as short-term capital gains (so that you may deduct only a maximum of $3,000 of net loss against ordinary income), whereas the mark-to-market trader treats gain income as ordinary income.

That the gains are treated as ordinary income doesn't mean that mark-to-market traders can't have long-term capital gains taxed at the favorable lower rates. By holding investment securities in a separate account, a mark-to-market trader can still generate long-term capital gains.

It's too late to make the mark-to-market election for 2006. You have to make the election a year in advance. To be effective for 2007, it has to be made on your tax return (2006) or on an extension of time to file (Form 4868) that is filed by April 16, 2007. After you make the election, it applies to all future years unless you obtain IRS permission to change. Make the election by attaching the following signed statement to your return or extension request:

> I hereby elect to use the mark-to-market method of accounting under Section 475(f) of the Internal Revenue Code for my trade and business of trading securities. The first year for which this election is effective is the taxable year beginning January 1, 2007.

> _____ (Signed)

> (Your name and date)

Chapter 13

Supplemental Income and Loss: Schedule E

. . . .

In This Chapter

▶ Defining supplemental income

▶ Completing Schedule E

▶ Discussing tax shelter

. . . .

Don't let the words *supplemental income* throw you. That's just IRS-speak for the income you receive from rental property or royalties, or through partnerships, S Corporations (corporations that don't pay tax; the owners report the corporations' income or loss on their personal tax returns), trusts, and estates. To report your rental or royalty income, you use Schedule E, which is laid out in the form of a profit or loss statement (income and expenses). From your income, you subtract your expenses. The remainder is your *net income,* the income that you have to pay taxes on. If you have a loss, the rules get a little sticky as to whether you can deduct it. (Isn't that a surprise?)

Remember that if you're a self-employed taxpayer receiving royalties, such as a musician, you use Schedule C. The information in this chapter applies to people who receive royalties and aren't self-employed. For example, George Gershwin received royalties from *Porgy and Bess* and reported them on Schedule C. But he has passed away, and now his heirs receive royalties that must be reported on Schedule E.

First-time authors get a break. They aren't subject to self-employment tax (Social Security tax on royalties), because being an author, at this point, isn't considered their regular line of work. Thanks to a Tax Court case, first-time authors don't become subject to self-employment tax until their particular book is revised or they start on a second one.

Part 1: Income or Loss from Rental Real Estate and Royalties

If you receive rent or royalties, you should receive Form 1099-MISC. Box 1 is for rent, and box 2 is for royalties. (Even if you rent your summer home to the Queen of England, you report your rent and royalties separately.)

Just because you didn't receive a Form 1099-MISC from the tenants renting your summer house or the family who rents the other side of your two-family house doesn't mean you're off the hook and don't need to report that income. You're required to report all income, whether or not it is reported to the IRS on a Form 1099, on your income tax return.

Line 1: Kind and location of each real estate property

On line A, enter the location. For example: Two-family home, Albany, New York. The line provides enough room for listing three properties. If you have more than three properties, enter the additional properties on another Schedule E, but use the total column on only one Schedule E to enter the total of all the properties.

Line 2: Vacation home questions

Here, you're asked whether you used any of the properties listed on line 1a, 1b, or 1c, and for how long. For example, you may have rented out your beach home for July and August, but you used it in June and September. See the "Vacation homes" sidebar later in this chapter for information about vacation home expenses you can and can't deduct.

Lines 3–4: Income

Copy the amounts from box 1, rent, and box 2, royalties, of your 1099-MISC onto lines 3 and 4 of Schedule E.

You may wonder whether some unusual cases of rent are counted as income. Rent paid in advance, for example, is counted as rent. If you sign a lease in December 2005 and collect January's rent of $1,000, this amount should have been included in 2005's rent income on this schedule, even though it applies to 2006's rent due. Security deposits that you must return aren't rental income. And if your tenant pays you to cancel the lease, the amount you receive is rent — it isn't considered a tax-free payment for damages. Although expenses paid by the tenant and applied against the rent are considered rental income, you're entitled to deduct those expenses. Finally, if you're a Good Samaritan and charge a relative or friend less than the fair rental value, your deductions for depreciation and maintenance expenses can't exceed the rent you collect.

Lines 5–18: Expenses

On these lines, you tabulate the amounts that you're allowed to deduct. Good bookkeepers to the head of the line. If you have good records, you can save a tidy sum. The expense lines apply to both royalties and rents.

If you rent out half of a two-family house and you occupy the other half, for example, you can deduct only 50 percent of your expenses, unless the expenses relate specifically to the rental unit. If it's a three-family unit and you occupy one of the units, you can deduct only 66 percent of the expenses. So, if you make repairs in your tenant's kitchen, you get to deduct the full amount, but you'll be able to deduct only a portion of roof repairs. Get the picture? But remember that the portion of your mortgage interest and property taxes that relates to the part you occupy gets deducted on Schedule A (see Chapter 9).

Line 5: Advertising

You're allowed to deduct the cost of newspaper ads, for example, if you had to run ads to find renters for your property. The same goes if you had building signs made.

Line 6: Auto and travel

Travel to inspect your rental property is deductible. But if you live in Buffalo and go to Florida in January to inspect a vacation home that you rent out part of the time, be prepared for a battle with the IRS. Refer to the guidelines for deducting travel in Chapter 9 and your auto expenses in Chapter 11.

Line 7: Cleaning and maintenance

You can deduct your costs for cleaning and maintenance, such as your monthly fee for the window washer and your payment to the guy who tunes up your furnace before the cold weather sets in.

Line 8: Commissions

You can deduct commissions paid to a real estate broker to find a tenant. The norm is 5 percent to 10 percent.

Line 9: Insurance

We hope that you carry insurance to protect against your building burning down, lawsuits, and other perils such as floods and earthquakes. You can deduct the cost of these policies. One tricky area to be aware of is if you pay for an insurance premium that covers more than one year. In that case, you deduct only the portion of the premium that applies to each year's Schedule E. For example, suppose that in 2006 you pay a $900 premium that covers a three-year period. You deduct $300 in 2006, another $300 in 2007, and the final $300 in 2008.

Line 10: Legal and other professional fees

Legal fees incurred in the purchase of the property must be added to the cost of the building and deducted as part of your depreciation deduction (coming later). Legal fees for preparing a lease are deductible. And the part of your tax-preparation fee used to prepare this Schedule E is deductible. See line 17, Chapter 11, about having to issue Form 1099.

Line 11: Management fees

You can deduct the costs of managing the property — collecting the rent, seeing to all repairs, paying a management company (if you have one), and so on.

Line 12: Mortgage interest paid to banks (Form 1098)

This amount comes right off **Form 1098, Mortgage Interest Statement,** which you get from the bank that holds the mortgage. The bank sends you this statement by January 31. A copy goes to the IRS so it can check whether you're deducting the correct amount.

Line 13: Other interest

If the person from whom you purchased the property provided the financing and holds a mortgage on the property, the interest is entered here because this is where the interest that wasn't paid to financial institutions goes. All the fees you paid when you took out the mortgage are deducted over the duration of the loan. You also put the interest on a second mortgage here, as well as the interest on short-term installment loans for the purchase of appliances and other assets.

Unlike with a personal residence, points and fees to obtain a mortgage on rental property aren't deductible in the year that you pay them. You must write off these amounts over the term of the loan and deduct them on this line. If you didn't receive a Form 1098, enter the interest you paid on this line.

Interest paid on an income tax bill can't be deducted. You can deduct interest on employment taxes that you were late in paying.

Line 14: Repairs

Repairs are deductible in full in the year in which you pay for them. Improvements are deducted over 27½ years for residential property and over either 31½ or 39 years, depending on when it was acquired, for commercial or nonresidential property (refer to Chapter 11 to obtain the rate of depreciation that you can claim every year). A *repair* — such as fixing a leaky roof — keeps your property in good operating condition. It doesn't materially add to the value of the property or prolong its life. An *improvement*, such as adding an entire new roof, on the other hand, adds to the property's value or prolongs its life and thus is written off over its useful life.

Line 15: Supplies

You can deduct such things as cleaning supplies, light bulbs, and small items that you buy at a hardware store.

Line 16: Taxes

This line includes real estate taxes on the property. Additionally, if you employ a superintendent or a janitor, this line is where you enter the Social Security and unemployment taxes that you must pay. The bank holding the mortgage sends you an annual mortgage statement that gives you the tax information. The Social Security and unemployment taxes will be listed on your quarterly payroll tax return.

Line 17: Utilities

Why don't you just go ahead and enter your electric, gas, fuel, water, sewer, and phone costs for your property here? We would.

Line 18: Other

This is one of those catchall lines for things whose descriptions don't fit on the preceding lines, such as gardening and permits.

Lines 19–26

Add lines 5 through 18 and enter the total on line 19. Then you get to do more figuring. Read on.

Line 20: Depreciation expense or depletion (Form 4562)

The tax law allows you to claim a yearly tax deduction for depreciation. You can't depreciate land. So, for example, you can depreciate only 85 percent of your cost (because, as a rule, at least 15 percent of a building's purchase price must be allocated to land). You can make this allocation based on the assessed value for the land and the building or on a real estate appraisal. You compute your depreciation deduction on **Form 4562, Depreciation and Amortization,** and you attach this form to your 1040 only if you first started to claim a deduction for a particular item in 2006. If you started claiming depreciation on an asset in an earlier year, the form isn't required. Compute the depreciation and enter the amount here. An annual depreciation rate schedule for residential real estate is available in Chapter 11. IRS Publication 946 (How to Depreciate Property) has the complete depreciation schedule for commercial real estate. Also in Chapter 11 check out an abridged schedule for commercial property, which must be depreciated over either 31½ or 39 years. We provide a detailed example of exactly how depreciation is computed.

Even though an apartment building must be depreciated over 27½ years, furniture and appliances used in the building must be depreciated over only 7 years. Don't forget though, that even though you can't use Section 179 depreciation for the building, you may use it for furnishings. Check out Chapter 11 to see how Section 179 depreciation works, and whether it makes sense for you to use it here.

Line 21: Total expenses

Add lines 19 and 20 and place the total on this line.

Line 22: Income or loss from rental real estate or royalty properties

The first part is just basic arithmetic. Subtract line 21 from your income from line 3 or 4. If your number is positive, you have, as the title of Schedule E announces, supplemental income; if your total is negative, you have a loss. On line 22, you'll notice a reference to Form 6198. This notice refers to the wonderful at-risk rules. Don't concern yourself with these rules unless you were lucky enough to get a mortgage for which you aren't personally liable for the payments. We get to the at-risk rules on line 27.

Line 23: Deductible rental real estate loss (Form 8582)

If your real estate property showed a loss for the year (on line 22), you may not actually be able to claim that entire loss on your tax return. If you didn't show a loss, skip ahead to the next line.

Line 23 is where you enter how much of the loss on line 22 can be deducted. Rental real estate is considered a passive activity, and you normally have to complete **Form 8582, Passive Activity Loss Limitations,** to determine the portion, if any, that you're allowed to deduct. However, if you meet all the following conditions, you're spared from Form 8582 (keep your fingers crossed):

- ✔ Rental real estate is the only passive activity you're involved in. (Remember that passive activity is a business or investment where you act as a silent partner — you aren't actively involved.)

- ✔ You actively participated in making management decisions or arranged for others to provide services, such as repairs.

- ✔ Your rental real estate loss didn't exceed $25,000 — or $12,500 if you're married and filing separately.

- ✔ You didn't have rental or passive activity losses that you couldn't deduct in a prior year.

- ✔ If you're married and filing separately, you must have lived apart from your spouse for the entire year.

- ✔ Your modified adjusted gross income (see the following worksheet) is less than $100,000 (or $50,000 if you're married and filing separately).

- ✔ You don't hold any interest in rental real estate as either a limited partner or as a beneficiary of an estate or trust.

If you meet all seven of these criteria, congratulations, you can skip the dreaded Form 8582 and write your deductible real estate loss right here on line 23.

If you have to fill out Form 8582 to compute your rental losses on Schedule E (line 22) because your modified adjusted gross income (AGI) is more than the limit (or you were involved in other passive activities), you have to be familiar with tax-shelter and other rules that allow you to deduct up to $25,000 of losses from rental real estate that you actively manage. If Form 8582 applies to you, oh taxpayer, you need a tax advisor! *Note:* You don't necessarily need professional tax help every year, but you do need to consult with an advisor in the year that you purchase the property to make sure you understand all the tax rules that you must obey. As long as nothing monumental changes in the future, you'll do perfectly fine on your own with just *Taxes 2007 For Dummies.* If we went into the tax-shelter rules in complete detail, we'd need a second volume to this book.

Worksheet to determine whether you need to file Form 8582

This little worksheet helps you compute your modified AGI so that you can determine whether it exceeds the limits that we just mentioned. If it does, off you go to Form 8582. Remember, enter every number here as a positive, even if it's a loss.

1. AGI from Form 1040 (line 37) — $_____

2. Taxable portion of Social Security (line 20b of Form 1040) — $_____

3. Subtract line 2 from line 1 — $_____

4. Your IRA deductions (line 32 of Form 1040) — $_____

5. Student loan interest (line 33) — $_____

6. One-half of self-employment tax (line 27 of Form 1040) — $_____

7. Passive activity losses (line 4 of Form 8582) — $_____

8. Interest from Series EE and I Savings Bonds used to pay education expenses (Form 8815) — $_____

9. Exclusion for adoption assistance payments, Form 8839, line 30 — $_____

10. Add lines 4–9 — $_____

11. Add line 10 to line 3; which equals your modified AGI — $_____

If line 11 is less than $100,000, or less than $50,000 if you're married and filing separately, you don't have to file Form 8582 (as long as you meet the other six criteria we mentioned earlier).

If you have only rental or royalty income or losses, you don't need to turn the page of your Schedule E. You're done! After you follow all those little instructions about what lines to add, take the amount from line 26 over to your 1040 (line 17). But, if you must continue, bear up. You're halfway there.

The $25,000 special allowance

Here's why that $100,000 modified AGI figure is so important. You can deduct up to $25,000 of the losses you incurred in rental real estate if you actively participate in the management of the property and own at least 10 percent — which means that you have to make management decisions regarding the approval of new tenants and rental terms, approving expenditures, and other similar decisions. So if you turn an apartment or home that you own over to a real estate agent to rent and manage, the $25,000 loss-deduction rule doesn't apply. You may be able to pull off this deduction, however, if you reserve the right to approve all expenditures and improvements that have to be made.

Now for the ever-present exception to the general rule: If your income exceeds $100,000, the $25,000 limit is reduced by 50 cents for every dollar of income you earn that's more than $100,000. When your income reaches $150,000, the $25,000 allowance is completely phased out. The loss that's phased out (the portion that you can't deduct in any year) doesn't just disappear. You carry it over and enter it on line 1c of **Form 8582, Passive Activity Loss Limitations** (this is IRS-speak for a tax shelter) to determine the amount of the carryover that's deductible in a future year. When you eventually sell the property, all your suspended losses for that property can be deducted in the year of the sale. We explain all this in greater detail in the section "The tax shelter rules" later in this chapter.

The $25,000 figure is reduced to $12,500 if you're married, filing separately, and living apart from your spouse for the entire year; the phaseout begins at $50,000 of your AGI (not $100,000) and is completely phased out at $75,000. If you lived with your spouse at any time during the year and you're filing separate returns, you can't use the $12,500 exception (half of $25,000). Please don't ask us about the reason for this one; it's way too complicated. On Form 8582, you compute the portion of the $25,000 allowance to which you're entitled.

IRS math quiz

Complete Part I of Schedule E by adding the positive amounts on line 22 and entering them on line 24. Line 24 is where you gather your profits. So, if you have a profit in column A of line 22 and a loss in column B, you enter the profit on line 24 and the loss on line 25. For reasons we can't explain, the IRS form makes you snake your way through line 22 and separate the profits from losses. After you complete this process, add any royalty losses from line 22 to your real estate losses from line 23 and enter the total on line 25. Finally, add the amounts on lines 24 and 25 and enter that total on line 26. Carry this total over to line 17 of Form 1040.

Think twice before converting your personal residence you lived in to a rental property, because you may be forfeiting the $250,000 ($500,000 for couples) exclusion on your potential profit if you do. Because a residence must be your principal residence for two of the five years looking back from the date of the sale (see Chapter 12 for the rules on sales of a residence), after you've rented your former home for more than three years, you can kiss the exclusion goodbye.

The tax shelter rules

If you rent out your vacation home or part of a two-family house, you're operating a tax shelter — and you always thought that tax shelters were something that only movie stars and high-income athletes were involved with!

In 1986, Congress decided to kill tax shelters and passed an anti-tax-shelter law. As a result, you can deduct a loss from a *passive activity* (that's what a tax shelter is now called in IRS jargon) only if you have income from another passive activity. If you don't, the loss is *disallowed*. Disallowed losses are suspended and carried over to future years. If you have passive income (that's income from a shelter) next year, you can deduct the loss. If you don't have passive income next year, you keep carrying over the loss until you do, or until you sell the property or your interest in the tax shelter.

For example, suppose that you have a rental loss of $5,000 in 2006 and no other passive income. You can't deduct any of the $5,000 loss in 2006 (but see "The $25,000 special allowance" earlier in this chapter). The loss is carried over to 2007. If in 2007 the property generates a $4,000 profit, you can deduct $4,000 of the suspended loss and carry over the $1,000 balance to 2008. If you sell the property in 2008, the $1,000 can be deducted — even if you don't have any rental income in 2008.

If you have two or more passive activities, you combine them to determine whether a loss in one can be used to offset a profit in another. For example, suppose that you own one building that you rent out at a $6,000 loss and another building that produces a $5,000 profit. You can use $5,000 of the $6,000 loss to offset the $5,000 profit from the second building, and the $1,000 balance is carried over to the next year.

If you have a passive activity loss, you compute the amount of the loss that can be deducted or that has to be carried over to future years on **Form 8582, Passive Activity Loss Limitations.** On this form, you combine your passive activity losses and income. If income exceeds losses, you have a deduction. If it doesn't, you have a suspended loss. But remember: If you sell the property, the loss, together with any suspended losses, is deductible.

Vacation homes

Determining the expenses you can deduct on a vacation home is no fun in the sun because you have to allocate the operating expenses based on how many days you rent your home and on how many days you use it. What's deductible and what's not are based on the following three mind-numbing rules:

✔ **Rule 1:** If you rent your home for fewer than 15 days, you don't have to report the rent you collected, and none of the operating expenses are deductible. Your mortgage interest and real estate taxes still are deducted as itemized deductions.

✔ **Rule 2:** If you rent your home for 15 or more days and your personal use of your home is more than the greater of 14 days or 10 percent of the total days it's rented, then the property isn't considered rental property, and the expenses allocated to the rental period can't exceed the rental income. Expenses that are allocated to the rental period but can't be deducted are carried forward to future years. These expenses can be deducted to the extent of your future rental income or until you sell the property. If you have a profit on the rental of a vacation home, this rule doesn't apply. Tax shelter rules apply only to losses.

In figuring the rental days, count only the days the home actually was rented. The days that you held the property out for rent, but it wasn't rented, don't count as rental days. After making this computation, you allocate your rental expenses based on the total number of days rented divided by the total number of rented days plus the days you used it. For example, suppose that your beach cottage was rented for 36 days and you used it for 36 days. In such a case, 50 percent of the operating expenses for the year would be allocated to the rental period, 36 days rented ÷ 72 days (36 rented and 36 personal days). Don't count any days that you worked full time to repair the property as personal days.

The Tax Court is on your side when it comes to deducting mortgage interest and taxes, which don't have to be allocated under the preceding formula. You can allocate this stuff on a daily basis. So, in the example, only 10 percent (36 rental days ÷ 365) of your taxes and mortgage interest would have to be allocated to the rental period, leaving the other 90 percent to be deducted on Schedule A as an itemized deduction. This court decision means that a larger amount of your other rental expenses can be deducted from your rental income, and (better yet) you get to deduct 90 percent of your mortgage interest and taxes as an itemized deduction rather than just 50 percent.

✔ **Rule 3:** If the personal use of your residence doesn't exceed the greater of 14 days or 10 percent of the total days it's rented, then your vacation home is treated as rental property. If the total amount of your rental expenses exceeds your rental income, your loss is deductible if you have other passive income (or if the $25,000 special allowance permits). You still have to allocate the expenses of running the property between personal and rental days.

Have a nice vacation.

When isn't a loss a loss? When you have a sweetheart deal. In a recent Tax Court case, a taxpayer was denied a rental loss deduction because she gave her brother a big break on the rent. The court considered the days she rented to her brother as personal use. She therefore ran afoul of the 14 days or 10 percent of the days rented rule (see the "Vacation homes" sidebar in this chapter). And it doesn't end there: Any loss on a subsequent sale of the house isn't deductible. The low rent she charged shows she lacked a profit motive. No profit motive, no deductible loss.

Part 11: Income or Loss from Partnerships and S Corporations

The average taxpayer finds page 2 of Schedule E the most daunting. You report income and losses from partnerships, S Corporations, estates, and trusts on that page. Instead of the nice, long, symmetrical columns of page 1, Schedule E's flip side looks as if it was designed to confuse rather than clarify.

Partnerships and S Corporations are called pass-through entities. As that term implies, all the income and deductions of whatever type of a partnership or an S Corporation pass through to each partner or shareholder based on ownership percentage, with the income and deductions maintaining their character (interest remains interest, charitable deductions remain charitable deductions, and so on). Every year, each partner or shareholder receives a form called a Schedule K-1 that reflects the income, loss, or deduction that belongs on the return. Schedule K-1 is actually filed as part of the partnership (Schedule 1065-K-1) or S Corporation's income tax returns (Schedule 1120S K-1), as well as a copy being sent to you.

Line 27: The at-risk and other tax shelter rules

You can hardly consider line 27 a simple yes or no question. Here you are asked whether you're reporting losses that weren't allowed in prior years because of at-risk or basis limitations, passive losses not reported on Form 8582, Passive Activity Loss Limitation (the name alone is enough to frighten most people), or unreimbursed partnership expenses.

The purpose of the at-risk rules is to prevent investors from deducting losses in excess of what they actually stand to lose. This rule prevents you from investing $10,000 and deducting $30,000 when the partnership loses an additional $20,000 on money it borrowed that you weren't personally responsible for. The K-1 that you receive indicates what your risks are (see item F). At-risk rules are extremely complex and are an area where we recommend that you consult a tax advisor for help. Typically, the at-risk rule comes into play when you invest $30,000: $10,000 in cash and you sign a *promissory note* for $20,000 bearing the language "without recourse against the maker (you)." Because you can't be forced to pay the $20,000, you're not at risk and, therefore, you can deduct losses only up to your $10,000 cash investment.

The basis limitation rule prevents you from limiting the amount you can lose when you make an investment and deduct more than that amount. Say you invest $25,000 . . . that's all you can deduct regardless what your share of the entity's loss amounts to.

The question about passive losses not reported on Form 8582 was new in 2003. Its purpose is to flush out taxpayers who are deducting losses they claim aren't passive when they actually are. For a quick refresher, passive losses are those losses in which you didn't materially participate.

What this question is all about is that sometimes, when a tax shelter entity runs out of dough, partners are called upon to pay some of the expenses personally to keep the business afloat. When partners try to deduct these expenses, the IRS invariably claims they can't. The question on line 27 is an attempt to bring these expenses out in the open instead of burying them along with other deductions. However, a court case states that when an investor and a partner are essentially in the same type of business, any unreimbursed expenses that the investor pays on behalf of the partnership are deductible.

Lines 28–32: Name . . . and so on!

Now you have to deal not only with line numbers but also with letters! Here's what you enter in the following columns of line 28:

(a) Enter the name of the partnership or S Corporation.

(b) Enter P for partnership or S for S Corporation.

(c) Put a check here if it's a foreign partnership.

(d) Scribble in the tax identification number for the partnership or S Corporation. (Hey, this line is pretty easy so far!)

(e) This column is the easiest of all. Place a check mark here if you're not at risk for any of the liabilities of the entity.

Passive income and loss

If the *passive income amounts* (that's rent or ordinary income from a partnership or an S Corporation, but not dividends, interest, or capital gains, which don't get entered here) on the Schedule K-1 are negative, and if you have enough positive passive income from all your partnerships and S Corporations to offset them, you enter the negative number in column (f). Because figuring these amounts out on the fly is tough, you need to go to Form 8582 first to compute what amount of loss is allowable before you fill out this part of Schedule E.

In column (g), enter the income from the passive activity in this lovely column. Refer to "The tax shelter rules," earlier in this chapter, for the definition of passive income and losses.

Nonpassive income and loss

Column (h) deals with nonpassive income and losses. If you're a working partner in a partnership or a working shareholder in an S Corporation, line 1 of the K-1 shows the share of the loss you're entitled to deduct. Enter that amount here.

For column (i), the wonderful K-1 also shows the amount of the partnership's or S Corporation's special depreciation that you get to deduct — line 9 of the K-1 for partnerships and line 8 for S Corporations. Enter it here.

In column (j), enter the amount of income from Schedule K-1 in this column — it's the amount on line 1.

Lines 29 through 32 are strictly addition. What a relief!

Where do you put all the other stuff, like interest, dividends, capital gains, charitable contributions, investment interest expense, and whatever else the partnership or the S Corporation decides to report to you? Look next to each line on your Schedule K-1, and it will clearly show you where to insert the information on each line into your tax return so that interest and dividends are put on Schedule B, charitable contributions on Schedule A, and so forth. Your Schedule K-1 should also arrive with pages of instructions. If what you're looking at on the front of the schedule isn't as clear as you want, look for the answers to your questions buried in the instruction's fine print.

Part III: Income or Loss from Estates and Trusts

In this part, you enter income or loss from an estate or trust of which you're a beneficiary. You should receive a Schedule K-1 from either the estate or the trust, and the K-1 also indicates income such as dividends, interest, and capital gains. Interest and dividends go on Schedule B (see Chapter 10), and capital gains go on Schedule D (see Chapter 12). The ordinary income or loss reported on the K-1 is what goes on in this section of Schedule E. Maybe that's why the IRS gives only two lines to work with in this part of the form — and that's down from *three* lines a couple of years back!

Lines 33–37: Name . . . and so on!

In column (a), carefully enter the name of the estate or trust.

In column (b), enter the identification number for the trust or estate.

Passive income and loss

In column (c), you put the passive loss allowed from Form 8582.

In column (d), you enter passive income from the K-1s and Form 8582.

When calculating the amounts that are passive, remember that only ordinary income and rental income qualify here — all other forms of income shown on this Schedule K-1 are reported elsewhere on your return. Check the K-1 instructions carefully to see where to put all those other numbers.

Nonpassive income and loss

Columns (e) and (f) are mostly for show, because most heirs or beneficiaries don't participate in the management of the estate or trust, and so it is rare for an heir or beneficiary to have nonpassive income or loss.

Lines 34 through 37 are the simple part of this section. All it requires is simple addition.

Part IV: Lines 38–39: Income or Loss from Real Estate Mortgage Investment Conduits (REMIC)

If you've invested in a Real Estate Mortgage Investment Conduit (REMIC), which is a company that holds a pool of mortgages, you'll most likely receive interest on **Form 1099-INT, Interest Income,** or **Form 1099-OID, Original Issue Discount.** But if you received **Form 1066, Schedule Q,** from the REMIC, enter the amounts, names, and so on from that form on line 38. Add columns (d) and (e) and enter the total on line 39.

Part V: Summary

Unless you're a farmer and file Form 4835 (line 40) or a real estate professional (line 43), everything on Schedule E is pulled together on line 41. Do the math and transfer the amount to Form 1040 (line 17) and take a break. You deserve it.

If you rent out your farm, you report your rental income and expenses on **Form 4835, Farm Rental Income and Expenses.** Donald Trump — or rather, his accountant — is an example of one who has to fill out line 43, Reconciliation for Real Estate Professionals.

Chapter 14

Giving Credits Where Credits Are Due

- -

In This Chapter

▶ Finding your way around the credit for Child- and Dependent-Care Expenses (Form 2441 or Schedule 2)

▶ Understanding credit for the elderly and disabled (Schedule R or Schedule 3)

▶ Educating yourself about Education Credits (Form 8863)

▶ Figuring out the Child Tax Credit and the Additional Child Tax Credit

▶ Crediting certain contributions to Retirement Savings (Form 8880)

▶ Profiting from the Residential Energy Credit and the Alternative Motor Vehicle Credit

▶ Adopting the Adoption Credit

▶ Calculating the Earned Income Credit

▶ Taking the Credit for Federal Telephone Excise Taxes Paid

- -

To paraphrase Rudyard Kipling, a deduction is only a deduction, but a good tax credit can mean real cash in your pocket. Tax credits are a dollar-for-dollar reduction of tax, unlike deductions, which reduce only taxable income. The results to your personal bottom line as you wend your way toward the end of your Form 1040 or 1040A may be spectacular.

Just like deductions, credits are designed to promote certain social policies, like having children, adopting children, looking after those children, and educating them beyond high school. They may help you save for your retirement, save energy, or pay you back for taxes you've already paid, such as foreign taxes on income.

In order to qualify for these tax savings, you need to fill out yet another form (or forms, if you qualify for more than one of these credits). This chapter shows you how to maneuver your way through the most popular of these additional forms to give you the best (legal) result possible.

Credits: Refundable versus nonrefundable

Just when you thought you had the difference down between a deduction and a credit, along comes another distinction: Some credits are refundable, while others aren't. What's the difference?

A refundable credit is one that you'll receive credit for and cash back in a refund, *even if you don't have enough tax showing on lines 46 or 63 of your 1040 (or line 28 of your 1040A) to offset it.* If you're eligible for refundable

credits, you may receive a larger tax refund than what you paid in withholdings during the year.

A nonrefundable credit, on the other hand, can offset only taxes shown on line 46 of your 1040 or 28 of your 1040A. If you don't have enough tax on those lines to use all, or even a part, of the credits to which you'd otherwise be entitled, tough! You're out of luck this year — better luck next!

Child- and Dependent-Care Expenses: Form 2441 (1040) and Schedule 2 (1040A)

If you hire someone to take care of your children so you can work, you're entitled to the credit that you figure on **Form 2441 (1040)** or **Schedule 2 (1040A).** Because both of these forms are nearly identical, what we say in this section for one goes for the other unless we specify otherwise.

For the purpose of taking this credit, you're not just limited to what you paid your babysitter. Nursery school, summer and vacation day camps, after-school programs, and daycare expenses also qualify for this credit. In order to be eligible to claim this credit, your child must be under the age of 13 or a dependent of any age who is physically or mentally handicapped. You're also entitled to the credit if your spouse is handicapped or is a full-time student and you incur expenses getting care for your kids so that you can work. Here are the ins and outs of the Child- and Dependent-Care Credit:

✔ You can claim childcare expenses while you're working or looking for work, as long as you have some earned income. However, if you don't find a job and don't have any earned income, you can't claim the credit.

What constitutes *earned income?* Wages, tips, strike benefits, disability pay reported as wages, voluntary salary deferrals such as for a 401(k) plan, meals and lodging furnished for the convenience of the employer (regardless of whether these fringe benefits are subject to tax), and earnings from being self-employed after deducting expenses — add all these up and that's what's called earned income. Want a shorter definition? What were you paid for working? But, because this is a tax book, we have to give you every last item.

✔ If you're married, you both must have a job or at least be looking for work. Looking for work assumes that you're planning on finding work; if you look for work all year, but never find a job and have no earned income, you can't take the credit.

Your spouse is considered to be working and having earned income if he/she is a full-time student or unable to care for himself or herself.

✔ For your expenses to be considered work-related, they must help to enable you to work or look for work.

✔ Sleep-away camp doesn't qualify as a childcare expense.

✔ Payments to relatives count even if they live in your home, provided they're not your dependent. If the relative providing the care is your child, the child must be 19 by the end of the year and not your dependent for the payment to count as childcare expenses.

✔ Although nursery school counts as a childcare expense, after the child enters the first grade, any tuition you pay must be allocated between the schooling expenses (if your child attends a private school) and the expenses incurred for childcare.

✔ Expenses incurred while you're out sick don't qualify. They weren't incurred for the purpose of enabling you to work. You incurred the expenses because you were sick and couldn't take care of your kids.

✔ Medical expenses incurred on behalf of a spouse or dependent who is unable to care for himself or herself count as work-related expenses. But you can't claim these expenses as both medical and work-related. You must claim one or the other. Claim medical expenses on Schedule A, Form 1040. (See Chapter 9.)

If you're unsure whether you're eligible to take this credit, refer to Chapter 4 to read all about the new, uniform tests to determine your qualified child.

Parts 1 and 11

To claim the Child and Dependent Care Credit, you can be single, a head of household, qualifying widow(er) with dependent child(ren), or married filing jointly. Here's how to fill out Form 2441 or Schedule 2:

✔ **Line 1** requires that you report the name, address, Social Security number, or Employer Identification Number (EIN) of the person or organization providing the care, and the amount that you paid to the provider. If you're paying your nanny or babysitter under the table (illegally), you can't claim this credit. However, if your annual payment to any one individual is less than $1,500, you're not liable for the payment of Social Security taxes for your childcare provider. See Chapter 15 for the nanny tax rules.

   If you didn't receive dependent-care benefits from your employer, you need to complete only Part II in addition to line 1. If you did receive these benefits, you have to complete Part III on the back of the form. Employer-provided dependent-care benefits are noted in box 10 of your W-2.

✔ **On line 2,** enter the qualifying person's name (that's IRS jargon for your child), the child's Social Security number, and what it costs to care for the child so that you can work. However, you can't enter more than $3,000 for one child or $6,000 for two or more children. Just because you're limited to a maximum of $6,000 of qualifying expenses doesn't mean those expenses need to be split evenly between your children. You can, for example, have one child with $4,000 of qualifying expenses, and another with only $2,000. The total for all your children, however, can't exceed $6,000.

✔ **On line 3,** enter the amounts from line 2, keeping in mind the $3,000 limit for one child and $6,000 limit for two or more kids. If you completed Part III, enter the amount from line 28.

✔ **On line 4,** enter your earned income.

✔ **On line 5,** if you're married and filing jointly, enter your spouse's earned income. If your spouse doesn't have any income, you can't claim this credit; however, a spouse who is either a full-time student or unable to care for himself is considered to have earned income even if he or she didn't receive any wages. In this exception, your spouse is deemed to have income of $200 per month if you have one qualifying child or dependent, and $400 per month if you have two or more qualifying children or dependents.

   A second rule linked to this deemed-income business: Your credit is based on the lower of your spouse's income or your allowable childcare expenses. If this rule sounds more complex than most rules, here's how it works. Say your spouse was a full-time student for six months, and you have $3,000 in childcare expenses for caring for your 2-year-old daughter. Your spouse is deemed to have earned $1,200, six months times $200. Because this amount is lower than your actual expenses, it's the amount the credit is based on.

   If you're not married and filing jointly, put the amount that you had on line 4 on line 5 as well.

✔ **On line 6,** enter the smaller of lines 3, 4, or 5.

✔ **On line 7,** enter your adjusted gross income (AGI) from line 38 of your 1040 or line 22 of your 1040A.

   Based on your AGI, use the chart below line 8 to find out what percentage of line 6 you can claim as a credit. For example, if your amount on line 7 was more than $43,000, you're entitled to a credit equal to 20 percent of the amount you entered on line 6. Enter that percentage on line 8 and do the math to get the figure on line 9. For example, if line 6 is $6,000 (you have two kids), your credit is $1,200 ($6,000 × 20 percent).

✔ **On line 10,** enter the amount from Form 1040, line 46 minus the amount from Form 1040, line 47 (your foreign tax credit, if you have any), or the amount from Form 1040A, line 28.

✔ **On line 11,** you're going to enter the smaller of the numbers on line 9 and line 10. This is the amount of your credit.

Many states also allow a credit for child- and dependent-care expenses. For example, New York bases its tax credit on the amount of the federal credit. Check with your state's tax office to find out what credit, if any, you can take.

Looking ahead, find out whether your employer offers you the ability to have money deducted from your paycheck — before taxes — into a dependent-care spending account. You may be able to use this account in the future and save even more tax dollars instead of taking this credit (you can't do both).

Part III

If your employer has a daycare plan or provides daycare services under a qualified plan, the reimbursement paid to you or your care provider may not be completely tax-free. To determine whether any portion is taxable, you need to complete Part III of Form 2441. The amount your employer paid for daycare costs or the value of the daycare services that your employer provides is indicated in Box 10 of Form W-2. The amount that is excludable from tax is limited to the smallest of

✔ The amount in Box 10 Form 1040

✔ The total of your child- and dependent-care expenses

✔ Your earned income

✔ Your spouse's earned income

✔ $5,000 ($2,500 if married, filing separately)

The portion of tax-free childcare benefits that you received reduces the amount of child- and dependent-care expenses eligible for the child-care credit.

Credit for the Elderly or the Disabled: Schedule R (1040) and Schedule 3 (1040A)

You're entitled to claim this credit (which may amount to as much as $1,125) if you're married and both you and your spouse are 65 or older — or both of you are disabled and any age. For single taxpayers, the maximum credit is $750.

At face value, giving a tax credit to the elderly and/or disabled sounds like a great idea. But wait, some requirements may make most people ineligible for this credit: You have to reduce the amount of the income that's eligible for the credit by the nontaxable portion of your Social Security and other pension and disability benefits. Also, if your income is more than $7,500 if you're single (or $10,000 if you're married), the amount of your income that's eligible for this credit is reduced further.

If ever there was an argument for automatically building cost-of-living increases into the tax code, this is it. The Credit for the Elderly or the Disabled hasn't moved with the times, and in almost every instance filling out these forms is an exercise in futility.

If you think you may be eligible for this credit, have the IRS figure it for you. Fill out page 1 of the form, which asks questions about your age, filing status, and whether you're disabled. Attach the form to your return, and on Form 1040, line 49 or Form 1040A, line 30, write "CFE" (an acronym for "credit for the elderly") on the dotted line. Remember: Always check the computation for a form that you asked the IRS to calculate to make sure that the IRS's computation is right. The IRS isn't infallible.

Don't be disappointed if you don't qualify for this credit. Almost no one does!

Education Credits (Form 8863)

Whether you're filing a Form 1040 or a Form 1040A, if you think you're eligible for either the Hope Scholarship Credit or the Lifetime Learning Credit, you've come to the right place to find the answer. If you're not sure whether you, your spouse, or your dependent child qualifies, or which credit you qualify for, look at Chapter 8 for a host of useful information about these credits.

Although you can't claim both credits for the same student, if you're the fortunate payer of more than one student's tuition bills, you may claim the Lifetime Learning Credits for multiple students so long as the total qualifying tuition and fees don't exceed $10,000, and the Hope Credit for different student(s) in the same year. What a bargain!

Here's how the **Form 8863, Education Credits (Hope and Lifetime Learning Credits)** works:

- ✔ **Line 1** is the meat of the information for the Hope Credit. In (a), fill in the name(s) of your qualifying students, in (b), their Social Security numbers, (c), the amount of qualified expenses you paid up to $2,200 per student, and (d), the lesser of $1,100 or the qualified expenses you paid. Double these amounts if the institution your student attends is located in the Gulf Opportunity Zone created in response to Hurricanes Katrina and Rita (the school will let you know). In (e), write the answer you get when you add (e) to (d). And in (f), write one-half of the amount in column (e). Sounds simple, right?

- ✔ **On line 2,** add the amounts in (f) from line 1. If you have no students eligible for the Lifetime Learning Credit, you may now skip to line 7.

- ✔ **On line 3,** provide the information on your qualifying student for whom you're claiming the Lifetime Learning Credit. In Column (a), write the student's name, in (b), his or her Social Security number, and (c), the amount of the qualifying expenses you paid. If you're unsure of what qualifies, remember, only tuition and fees apply — no room and board, books, or other sundries.

- ✔ **On line 4,** add up all the amounts you listed in line 3(c). Easy!

- ✔ **On line 5a,** enter the smaller of line 4 or $10,000. Remember, that's the maximum amount you can calculate this credit on. On line 5b, put the smaller of your actual expenses or $10,000 if your student attended an eligible institution in the Gulf Opportunity Zone. Subtract line 5b from line 5a, and put the result on line 5c.

- ✔ **On line 6a,** multiply the amount on line 5b by 40 percent (.40). On line 6b, multiply line 5c by 20 percent (.20). Add lines 6a and 6b together, and place the total on line 6c. This is your tentative Lifetime Learning Credit.

- ✔ **On line 7,** add the amounts you have on lines 2 and 6c.

The rest of the Form 8863 determines whether or not your credit is going to be limited, or even completely disallowed, because you earn too much money. Remember, the phaseouts for education limits begin at $90,000 of AGI (1040 line 38 or 1040A, line 22) for married filing joint returns, and $45,000 for single, head of household, or qualifying widow(er), and the credits completely disappear if your AGI hits $110,000 for married filing joint returns and $55,000 for single, head of household, or qualifying widow(er). If your AGI is above these limits, sorry, but you're out of luck this year. Congress thinks you earn enough to send your students through school without any help from the taxpayers.

Child Tax Credit

If you have qualifying children, the ability to wipe $1,000 off your income tax bill per adorable urchin seems like manna from heaven. Still, not everyone gets to take the credit — people who earn too much and people who earn too little may be out of luck.

Like so much else that's good in the Internal Revenue Code, the Child Tax Credit has phase-outs. After your income exceeds $110,000 if filing jointly, $75,000 filing as single or head of household, or $55,00 if married filing separately, the amount of your credit is reduced by $50 for every $1,000, or part thereof, that your income exceeds the above thresholds. This phaseout is on a per-child basis. For example, for joint filers with one child, the credit is completely phased out when their income reaches $130,000. If they have two children, a complete phaseout of the credit doesn't occur until their income reaches $150,000.

A quick formula — for every $20,000 of income above the phase-out levels, you lose the $1,000 credit for one kid. At $40,000 you lose the credit for two kids.

To claim the credit, your child must be eligible under the new standardized rules listed in Chapter 4. In addition, he or she must also be a U.S. citizen or resident who was younger than 17 on December 31, 2006. In certain circumstances (children of divorced parents are one case that comes to mind), it's possible to claim this deduction for a child who isn't your dependent. To do so, though, you have to complete **Form 8901, Information on Qualifying Children Who Are Not dependents (Child Tax Credit Only).** Not to worry — Form 8901 is as easy as pie to complete. It's just looking for your child's name, Social Security number, and relationship to you. What could be simpler?

This child tax credit comes in two varieties: *The Child Tax Credit* that most people find easy to compute and the *Additional Child Tax Credit* that comes into play when the regular Child Tax Credit exceeds your tax. When your potential credit is greater than your tax, part of the credit may be refundable. People with three or more kids get to compute the refundable credit two ways and then choose the one that produces the largest refund. People with fewer kids get only one shot, which by the way, is the simpler method to compute. To determine the additional credit, you have to fill out **Form 8812, Additional Child Tax Credit.**

Here is how the refund works. Say, for example, that your tax is $1,800 and you're entitled to a $2,000 credit (2 kids × $1,000). By filling out Form 8812, you may discover that you're entitled to a refund of the $200 difference.

To compute the amount of your Child Tax Credit, use the worksheet in your 1040 instruction booklet.

If you have more than two children or the amount of the credit you've calculated on the worksheet exceeds the amount of your tax on either line 28 of Form 1040A or line 44 of Form 1040, you may be entitled to take the Additional Child Tax Credit (Form 8812). So don't overlook this opportunity. You can claim the Additional Child Tax Credit on line 42 of Form 1040A or line 68 of Form 1040.

If you've received nontaxable combat pay in 2006, you may find that you don't have a large enough tax liability to take full advantage of the child tax credit. Not to worry — you're allowed to include that nontaxable combat pay in your calculations for this credit if it gives you a larger credit than you'd receive without including that pay. Remember, doing so doesn't mean you're signing on to pay tax on these nontaxable amounts; you're only using the additional income to give yourself a larger credit. But, if you do choose to calculate your credit using your nontaxable combat pay, you have to use all of your nontaxable combat pay, not only a portion.

Retirement Savings Contributions Credit (Form 8880)

If your AGI (line 38 of Form 1040 or 22 of Form 1040A) is $50,000 or less if married filing jointly, $37,500 or less if head of household, or $25,000 or less if single, and if you were able to make a contribution into a retirement plan, this credit was designed expressly for you. For people who qualify, this credit can be a whopping tax credit of up to $1,000 per person ($2,000 per married couple). In order to get the credit, you have to complete **Form 8880, Credit for Qualified Retirement Savings Contributions.**

Form 8880 is one of the better-designed IRS forms, and the directions are actually in understandable English. There's just one place that the IRS may have made clearer, so here's our best shot to make the instructions plainer:

Line 2 refers to *elective deferrals to a 401(k) or other qualified employer plan, voluntary employee contributions, and 501(c)(18)(D) plan contributions for 2006.* The amounts that the IRS is looking for here are your contributions into your company's retirement plans or your contributions into your traditional or Roth IRA accounts. Only include on this line amounts that you put into your retirement accounts and not amounts your employer contributed.

This credit is designed for full-time working people, not students working a part-time job, so three additional rules apply:

✔ You have to be born before January 1, 1989.

✔ You may not be someone else's dependent.

✔ You may not be a student enrolled on a full-time basis during any five months of 2006, which means graduates of the class of June 2007 aren't eligible to claim this credit, unless they went to school only part-time.

Residential Energy Credits (Form 5695)

In these days of higher fuel costs, Congress has tried to lessen the blow by providing a variety of credits for improving your home's energy efficiency. If your 2005 fuel bills pushed you to make changes to your home in 2006, you may qualify for some, or all, of these credits. These credits, which you calculate on **Form 5695,** cover a large array of improvements, including:

✔ 10 percent of the cost of adding insulation or other heat-saving systems

✔ 10 percent of the cost (limited to $2,000) of qualified exterior windows, including skylights

✔ 10 percent of the cost of qualified exterior doors

✔ 10 percent of the cost of a treated metal roof that meets Energy Star program requirements

✔ Up to $300 for residential energy property costs, including the purchase and installation of qualified electric heat pump water heaters, electric heat pumps, geothermal heat pumps, central air conditioners, and natural gas, propane, or oil water heaters

✔ Up to $150 for qualified natural gas, propane, or oil furnaces or hot water boilers

✔ Up to $50 for certain advanced main air circulating fans used in natural gas, propane, or oil furnaces

You aren't limited by the number of improvements you can make; however, your aggregate credits for these types of improvements can't exceed $500.

In addition to the above improvements, there are additional credits available, including:

✔ 30 percent of the cost of purchasing and installing solar panels to produce electricity, not to exceed a $2,000 credit

✔ 30 percent of the cost of purchasing and installing qualified solar water heating in your home, not to exceed a $2,000 credit

✔ 30 percent of the cost of purchasing and installing qualified fuel cell property, not to exceed a $1,000 credit per kilowatt capacity produced.

To qualify for these nonrefundable credits, your house must be located in the United States, and the improvements must be new, must meet certain energy efficiency standards, and they must reasonably be expected to stay in use for at least five years. If you've gone to town and turned your home into the ultimate in energy efficiency, you may find that you have more credits showing on line 29 of Form 5695 than you can use this year. You can carry excess credits forward to 2007.

Adoption Credit (Form 8839)

If you adopted a child in 2006, if you began or completed adoption proceedings in 2006, or if you tried unsuccessfully to adopt a child in 2006, read on. Expenses that you incurred during the adoption process may be eligible for a tax credit. In order to be able to claim that credit on your Form 1040 or your Form 1040A, you need to complete and attach **Form 8839, Qualified Adoption Expenses**.

Understanding the adoption credit and exclusion rules

The Adoption Credit has specific rules that include the following:

✔ If your AGI is $164,410 or less, you're entitled to the full credit. Between $164,410 and $204,410, the credit is phased out. At $204,411, it's gone. If you claimed a foreign income exclusion or housing deduction (Form 2555 or Form 2555-EZ) because you're working abroad, because you're claiming an income exclusion from Puerto Rico, or because you're a resident of American Samoa (Form 4563), you have to adjust your income for the purpose of calculating your credit by adding these amounts to your AGI shown on line 38, Form 1040 when figuring whether your income is more than the income threshold.

- ✔ The adopted child must be younger than 18 or physically or mentally incapable of self-care.

- ✔ Adopting your spouse's child doesn't qualify, nor does a surrogate parenting arrangement.

- ✔ Adoption expenses can't be paid with funds received from any federal, state, or local adoption program.

- ✔ The credit can't exceed your tax minus any credits claimed on lines 47 through 51, and 53 on Form 1040 plus the nonbusiness energy credit from line 12 of Form 5695 and the mortgage interest credit from line 11 of Form 8396.

- ✔ Any unused credit can be carried forward for five years until you use it up.

- ✔ Married couples must file a joint return. However, if you're legally separated for the last six months of the year, you're eligible to file a separate return and claim the credit.

The types of expenses that qualify for the credits include adoption fees, court costs, attorney fees, traveling expenses (including meals and lodging) and other expenses directly related to adopting an eligible child.

In addition to the Adoption Credit, you may also exclude up to $10,960 from your income for adoption expenses paid by your employer under an adoption-assistance program. For example, you incur $21,920 in adoption expenses. You pay $10,960, and your employer pays $10,960 as part of an adoption-assistance program. You're entitled to a $10,960 credit for the expenses you paid, and you're not taxed on the $10,960 paid by your employer.

As a practical matter, owners or principal shareholders of a business aren't eligible to participate in an employer adoption–assistance program.

For a U.S. adoption, if you pay adoption expenses in any year prior to the year the adoption becomes final, the credit is taken in the year following the year the expenses are paid. If you pay adoption expenses in the year the adoption becomes final, you claim the credit in that year. If you pay adoption expenses in a year after the adoption becomes final, you claim the credit for those expenses in the year of payment.

For example, you incur $10,000 of adoption expenses in 2006 but pay $8,000 in 2006 and $2,000 in 2007 when the adoption is finalized. You have to wait until 2007 to claim the credit for the $8,000 of expenses, which is added to the $2,000 you paid in 2007. Had the adoption become final in 2006, you could claim the credit based on the $8,000 you paid in 2006. In this scenario, in 2007 you would base the credit on the $2,000 paid that year.

With a foreign adoption, you can't claim the credit or the exclusion until the adoption becomes final. Adoption expenses paid in an earlier year are considered paid in the year the adoption becomes final.

Regardless of the year paid, your adoption expenses or adoption exclusion can't exceed $10,960 for any child.

Figuring out Form 8839

You compute both the credit and the exclusion on **Form 8839, Qualified Adoption Expenses.** Enter the amount of the credit (line 18) on line 54 (Form 1040). Carry forward any unused credit that you had in 2005 to your 2006 Form 8839 on line 13. The phase-out income limits don't apply to carryovers. The phaseout is applied only once in the year that generated the credit.

The amount of taxable employer–provided adoption expenses is computed in Part III of Form 8839. The taxable portion, if any, on line 31, gets reported on line 7 of Form 1040. Next to line 7, write "AB" for adoption benefit. How could you have a taxable benefit? Say your employer paid $7,000 in benefits, but you were entitled to exclude only $4,000 because your income exceeded $164,410. In that case, $3,000 of the benefit would be taxable.

You can claim the adoption credit for expenses on an unsuccessful adoption. On line 1 of Form 8839 where the child's name goes, enter "See page 2." At the bottom of page 2 of Form 8839, indicate the name and address of the agency or attorney that assisted in the attempted adoption. Then complete the form as if the adoption had taken place. We know that this probably is painful, and we wish we knew what to say to ease that pain.

Alternative Motor Vehicle Credit (Form 8910)

If you purchased a new hybrid gas/electric car or light truck, whether for business or personal use, or a combination of the two in 2006, you may know that you're entitled to a pretty hefty credit (ranging from $250 to $3,400, depending on fuel economy) as a governmental thank-you for helping the environment. Use Form 8910 to figure this credit.

If you purchased your new vehicle for business or a combination of business and personal use, you calculate the percentage of the business credit in Part II of Form 8910, and then place the result on line 1v of Form 3800. Place the personal use percentage of the credit (calculated in Part III of Form 8910) on line 55 of Form 1040.

This credit is not only limited by date (it ceases to exist in all cases on vehicles purchased after December 31, 2010), but also by the success of the individual manufacturers. The credit begins to phase out in the second calendar quarter after the company sells its 60,000th hybrid. The good news: If you bought your hybrid prior to October 1, 2006, you'll get the full amount of the credit. The bad news: Toyota sold its 60,000th hybrid to its dealers in the quarter ending June 30, 2006. Accordingly, beginning October 1, 2006, the credit for qualifying Toyota and Lexus hybrids was cut in half. On April 1, 2007, the credit will be reduced to 25 percent of the original amount, and it will disappear entirely on October 1, 2007. So far, Toyota (including Lexus) is the only company to have the credit limited for its hybrids. If you're anticipating purchasing a hybrid, refer to the IRS Newsroom at www.irs.gov/newsroom for the most recent updates on which models and years qualify, the amount of credit per model, and whether or not the credit has begun to phase out for that particular company's cars and light trucks.

Earned Income Credit (EIC)

The largest (in most cases) of the refundable credits, the Earned Income Credit (EIC) has come to represent the link between making it and not making it financially in many households that live from paycheck to paycheck. Because receiving this credit may be so important to the health and well-being of your finances, take a moment to understand who it's designed to help, how it works, and how to prepare the tax forms correctly.

As its name suggests, the EIC is restricted to taxpayers with earned income. What the name doesn't tell you is that it's restricted to low-income taxpayers who earn the vast majority of their income from wages, tips, commissions, salaries, union strike benefits, or net earnings from self-employment (for the purpose of this credit, net earnings from self-employment less one-half of your self-employment tax).

Even though you must have earned income in order to qualify for the credit, you must also meet the AGI guidelines. Table 14-1 shows you where the phaseouts begin and end, depending on your family's size.

Table 14-1	Earned Income Credit Phaseouts					
	With No Qualifying Children		With One Qualifying Child		With Two or More Qualifying Children	
Filing Status	Beginning Phaseout Amount	Completely Phased Out	Beginning Phaseout Amount	Completely Phased Out	Beginning Phaseout Amount	Completely Phased Out
Single or Head of Household	$6,740	$12,120	$14,810	$32,001	$14,810	$36,348
Married Filing Jointly and Qualified Widow(er)	$8,740	$14,120	$16,810	$34,001	$16,810	$38,348

Earned income doesn't include the following:

- ✔ Alimony or child support
- ✔ Interest and dividends
- ✔ Pensions or annuities
- ✔ Social Security benefits
- ✔ Taxable scholarships or fellowships that weren't reported on your W-2
- ✔ Unemployment insurance
- ✔ Veterans' benefits
- ✔ Welfare benefits

Rules that everyone must follow include the following:

- ✔ You need a valid Social Security number.
- ✔ Your filing status can't be married filing separately.
- ✔ You must be a U.S. citizen or resident alien for the entire year.
- ✔ You can't file Form 2555 or 2555-EZ (see Chapter 6).
- ✔ Your investment income must be $2,800 or less.
- ✔ You must have earned income.

In an effort to ease the burden on military families, you may elect to include the full amount of nontaxable combat pay you received in 2006 in calculating your earned income for the purpose of the EIC. It's important to calculate the credit both with and without your non-taxable combat pay in order to figure out which benefits you the most.

Figuring the EIC

If you meet all the requirements, figuring the EIC is easy. No math is required. The credit to which you're entitled usually is based on the lower of your earned income and adjusted gross income (AGI). If your earned income and AGI are the same, look up that amount for the corresponding income bracket in the Earned Income Credit Table and read across to the appropriate column: No qualifying child, one child, or two children under your filing status, single or head of household, or married filing jointly. For example, your EIC is $2,747 if your earned income and AGI is $12,240 and you're filing as head of household with one qualifying child. If your earned income and AGI aren't the same, your EIC is based on the lower of these two figures. However, if your AGI is less than $6,740 ($8,740 for married filing jointly), and you don't have any children, or if your AGI is less than $14,810

($16,810 for married filing jointly), and you have one or more children, then you base your EIC on your earned income. Attach the EIC Schedule to your return and enter the credit on Form 1040, line 66(a) or Form 1040A, line 41.

If you're currently eligible for the EIC, and you want to receive a portion of that credit for 2007 during the year, file a **Form W-5, EIC Advance Payment Certificate,** with your employer. Go back to Chapter 4 to see how this works.

If you don't want to risk putting the wrong number down on your Form 1040 or 1040A, you can take the easy way out and let the IRS figure your EIC. Complete and attach Form 1040 EIC to your return and write EIC to the right of Form 1040, line 66(a) or 1040A, line 41. Make sure that you complete all the other lines on your return.

If you're thinking of electing to include your nontaxable combat pay, here's how this election works: Mark is married with one child. He was deployed in a combat zone for eleven months of 2006. He and his wife earned only $4,000 of taxable earned income for the year, while he earned $16,000 of nontaxable combat pay. If Mark and his wife calculate the EIC on the basis of $4,000 of earned income, their credit is only $1,369. If they elect to add Mark's $16,000 of combat pay (for a total of $20,000) for the purpose of calculating the credit, their credit is now $2,233. Remember, Mark's not electing to pay tax on his combat pay, but only to use it to give him, and his family, a bigger credit. All Mark and his wife need to do to make this election is to fill in the amount of nontaxable combat pay on line 66b of Form 1040 or 41b of Form 1040A.

Singles and couples with no children are entitled to take this credit if they meet the income requirements (plus you must have maintained a home in the United States for more than six months, file a joint return if married, not be a dependent of another, and be at least 25 but younger than 65). However, the EIC is really focused on single and two-parent families, and these people derive the greatest benefit. Not every family is equal in the eyes of the IRS, though. In order for your family to qualify as such, the child (or children) you're claiming as a qualifying child must pass *all* the uniform tests in Chapter 4. In addition, your qualifying child (or children) can't be another person's qualifying child. Similarly, you can't be the qualifying child of another person when you have a child who qualifies.

What do you do when your qualifying child could also be someone else's qualifying child? How do you choose who gets the qualifying kid and the larger EIC? You don't have to play "rock, paper, scissors." Instead, tiebreaking rules govern. If one of the taxpayers is the qualifying child's parent, the parent gets to claim the qualifying child. If neither taxpayer is the parent, the person with the highest AGI claims the child. Finally, if both parents seek to claim the credit, but don't file jointly, the parent with whom the child resided longest during the year claims the child. If a tie still results, the qualifying child designation goes to the parent with the highest AGI.

To compute the credits, go to the EIC Table in your tax-instruction booklet. Based on your income and the number of qualifying children, read across for your earned income line to the amount of credit that you can claim.

If you don't list your dependent's Social Security number on the EIC form, you get *no credit*. If investment income exceeds $2,800, you get *no credit*. Investment income includes capital gains, interest, dividends, and tax-exempt interest. Add them up (capital losses and rental losses aren't included) to see if you exceed the limit. Also, if you're married filing separately, you aren't entitled to the credit.

Anyone who fraudulently claims the EIC is ineligible to claim it for ten years. For those individuals who are reckless or intentionally disregard the rules, the penalty is two years. If you feel the IRS seems to be more interested in finding EIC infractions than any other kind of tax dodge, you may be right. The IRS is very concerned about rooting out fraudulent EIC claims and is examining returns with the EIC extremely closely. You may not be able to avoid the scrutiny if you file for the EIC, so make certain that your claim is a valid one.

Credit for Federal Telephone Excise Tax Paid (Form 8913)

We know that you probably have better things to do with your time than to dig through almost three and a half years of paid bills, but if you were curious and had a rainy afternoon to play detective, you could calculate the amount you actually paid in federal long-distance excise taxes on bills dated between February 28, 2003 and August 1, 2006. If you choose to take this route, Form 8913 is where you need to show your work. Just make sure that you attach this form to your Form 1040, 1040A, or 1040EZ.

If, on the other hand, after seeing how little you paid for this tax on one month's bill, you can think of better ways to spend your time, you can still claim this credit. Just count up the number of personal exemptions on your return. Without digging out a single old phone bill, you get to claim $30 for one exemption, $40 for two, $50 for three, and $60 for four or more. Just place the appropriate credit on line 71 of Form 1040, line 42 of Form 1040A, or line 9 of Form 1040EZ. How much easier does it get?

Chapter 15

Other Schedules and Forms to File

In This Chapter
▶ Form 1040-ES (the estimated tax)
▶ Form 3903 (moving away)
▶ Forms 8606, 8615, 8814, and 8829 (IRAs, kiddie taxes, and home office expenses)
▶ Form W-4 (tax withholding)
▶ Schedules H and SE (for household employees and the self-employed)

Most taxpayers want to think that they need to fill out only the front and back of their 1040 or 1040A, and then they're done. Oh, if only life were so simple. The fact is that your life isn't (that's why you're not filing Form 1040EZ), and you probably need to file a variety of other tax schedules and forms to accompany your 1040 or 1040A. These additional forms are tailored to specific tax situations, and trust us, there's something for everyone. This chapter discusses the more common forms and schedules.

Estimated Tax for Individuals (Form 1040-ES)

The U.S. tax system actually has a simple rule that most people never think about: It's a pay-as-you-owe system, not a pay-at-the-end-of-the-year one. That's why *withholdings* (having your taxes deducted from your paycheck and sent directly to the government) are great — what you don't see, you don't miss, and your tax payments are made for you. If you're self-employed or have taxable income, such as retirement benefits, that isn't subject to withholding, you need to be making quarterly estimated tax payments on Form 1040-ES.

When you don't pay your taxes on your income as you earn it, you may get hit with penalties and interest when you do pay them, on or before April 15 of the following year.

You can avoid paying a penalty on tax underpayments if you follow these guidelines: You must pay in at least 90 percent of your current year's tax, either in withholdings or in estimated tax payments, as you earn your income, or you can use the Safe Harbor method.

Calculating your Safe Harbor estimated tax payments

If your income isn't constant or regular, you may choose to follow the so-called Safe Harbor rule, and pay 100 percent of last year's tax on an equal and regular basis during this current tax year. This method is simpler than it sounds. If, for example, you have a $3,000 tax liability showing on your 2006 Form 1040, line 63, you may choose to either withhold $3,000 from your 2007 income or make four quarterly payments of $750 in 2007. Provided that you do one or the other, you won't owe any penalty for a 2007 tax underpayment, even if your 2007 tax liability is $15,000. Remember, though, you still do have to pay the balance of tax due by April 15, 2008, in order to avoid late payment penalties and interest.

Because the Safe Harbor rule is so easy, we never use anything else to calculate estimated taxes. The 90 percent rule is tricky to calculate, your amounts need to be adjusted every time during the year that your income rises or falls, and using it leads to a mountain of increased paperwork. Still, because it is one of the rules, we explain how to calculate your estimated taxes using the 90 percent rule in this section.

If your 2006 income is more than $150,000, you have to make estimated tax payments equal to 110 percent of your 2006 tax to escape a 2007 underestimating penalty if your 2007 tax turns out to be substantially more than your 2006 tax. For example, if your 2006 tax is $100,000 (and your income is much higher), you need to make estimated tax payments of $110,000 ($100,000 × 110 percent) in order to qualify for Safe Harbor in 2007. Then, even if your tax in 2007 is $150,000, you won't have to pay any penalty or interest on the $40,000 balance due, even though your estimated tax payments were less than 90 percent of your tax. This rule doesn't apply to farmers or fishermen.

Completing and filing your Form 1040-ES

You need to accompany your estimated tax payments with **Form 1040-ES (payment voucher), Estimated Tax for Individuals.** This small form requires only your name, address, Social Security number, and the amount that you're paying. For 2007 estimated payments, make sure that you use the 2007 1040-ES. Write your checks to the "United States Treasury," making sure your name, Social Security number, and the words "2007 Form 1040-ES" are written on the face of the check, and then mail to the address listed in the Form 1040-ES booklet.

Quarterly estimated tax payments are due for the 2007 tax year on April 16, June 15, September 17, 2007, and January 15, 2008. If you file your completed 2006 tax return and pay any taxes due by January 31, 2008, you can choose not to pay your fourth quarter estimate (due January 15, 2008) without incurring any penalty.

If you're not sure how much you need to pay in estimates, Form 1040-ES (2007) also contains instructions and a worksheet to help you calculate your 2007 estimated tax payments. If you're using the Safe Harbor method to calculate your estimated tax requirements and you have nothing withheld from any source, you can skip the worksheet, take the number from line 63 of your 2006 Form 1040, divide it by 4, and drop that number into each of the vouchers. You're done! Now you just need to remember to pay your quarterly bills.

If, on the other hand, some, but not all, of your income has taxes withheld on it, or you want to only pay 90 percent of your 2007 tax liability upfront (maybe because your income in 2007 is going to be considerably less than it was in 2006), you're going to have to complete the worksheet that comes in the Form 1040-ES packet to calculate your estimated payment amounts.

The 2007 Estimated Tax Worksheet contained in the Form 1040-ES packet is a preview of your 2007 tax return, or what you think that tax return will show. On it you include your adjusted gross income (AGI), your deductions, whether you itemize or take the standard deduction, any credits you may be entitled to, and any additional taxes you may be subject to. The worksheet can help you calculate the minimum amount you must pay during 2007 in order to avoid paying penalties and interest at the end of the year.

You're only estimating here. If your circumstances change and your income rises or falls, you can adjust any payments you haven't yet made. After you make a payment, though, you're stuck with it, and will need to wait until you file your income tax return for 2007 before you can claim a refund.

Don't include your first estimated tax payment for 2007 with your 2006 Form 1040 or Form 1040A. Instead, mail it separately to the address shown in the instructions for Form 1040-ES. The IRS routes different types of payments to different post office boxes to help eliminate confusion on their end, and a payment sent to the wrong address may be credited against the wrong year.

Moving Expenses (Form 3903)

If you incur moving expenses because you have to relocate for your job, you can deduct moving expenses for which your employer didn't reimburse you. Self-employed individuals may also deduct their moving expenses. And, unlike other deductible expenses, this deduction isn't subject to varying interpretations. It's subject to two mathematical tests. The first one: The distance between your new job location and your former home must be at least 50 miles more than the distance between your former home and your former job location. Allow us to run these specs by you one more time:

A. Miles from your old home to new workplace

B. Miles from your old home to old workplace

C. Subtract line B from line A.

If line C is at least 50 miles, you're entitled to a moving-expense deduction. For someone just entering the workforce, the new job must be at least 50 miles from his or her old residence.

The second test requires that you remain employed on a full-time basis at your new job location for at least 39 weeks during the 12-month period immediately following your arrival. You don't have to work for the same employer. In other words, you can't claim a deduction unless you pass the distance test and satisfy the employment-duration requirement.

The rule is even tougher on self-employed people. To get the deduction, you must work full time in the general area of your new workplace for 78 weeks (that's a year and a half) during the 24 months after your arrival. To save you this bit of math, a part-time job doesn't satisfy the 39- or 78-week test.

If you work outside the United States, you're eligible for a special exemption: You can deduct expenses for a move to a new home in the United States when you permanently retire. The move doesn't have to be related to a new job. This exemption also applies to a survivor of someone who worked outside the United States.

Members of the Armed Forces aren't subject to either the distance or length-of-employment requirements at the new location, provided that the move is the result of a permanent change of station.

You can deduct moving expenses in either the year in which they're incurred or the year in which they're paid, which will most likely be the same year, because moving companies typically demand their money before they'll begin to unload the truck, and the move-it-yourself truck rental companies aren't going to let their trucks out of sight until they know they have your credit card information.

Meals, temporary living expenses, and expenses incurred in the sale or lease of a residence aren't deductible. You may deduct only the cost of moving and storage of your household goods and personal effects from your former residence to your new one, plus travel and lodging costs for you and members of your household while traveling to your new residence. The cost of storing and insuring your household goods and personal effects can be deducted for any 30 consecutive days after the day your possessions were removed from your former home and before they are delivered to your new home. You can deduct lodging on the day of your arrival and lodging within the area of your former home within one day after you couldn't live in your former home because your furniture had been removed. Deductible moving expenses include connecting and disconnecting utilities, shipping an auto, and transporting household pets — so don't forget Fido. Meals are never deductible, even while traveling from one area to another. These are the federal rules. Some states allow a deduction for moving expenses — your state rules may or may not be similar to the federal rules.

The place to deduct moving expenses is **Form 3903, Moving Expenses.** If you haven't met the 39- or 78-week test by the time that you file your return, don't worry. You're still allowed to claim the deduction if you expect to meet the test. However, if it turns out that you fail the 39- or 78-week test, you must report the deduction as income on next year's tax return. No fun at all.

You've lucked out with Form 3903; it's only five lines to get through! Here's what you do:

- ✔ **Line 1:** Enter the cost of transporting and storing your household and personal goods plus the other deductible moving expenses we discuss earlier in this section.

- ✔ **Line 2:** Enter the travel and lodging expenses you're allowed for you and members of your household that you incurred in traveling from your old home to your new home, plus the one-day lodging expenses on the day of arrival and departure. Remember, you can claim only the costs for a single trip from your old residence to your new one. If you use your car, you can claim 18 cents a mile plus tolls and parking for 2006.

- ✔ **Line 3:** Add lines 1 and 2 (your total moving expenses). All these expenses must be incurred within one year from the time you start to work at the new location. Expenses incurred beyond a year are deductible for reasons such as allowing a child to finish school.

- ✔ **Line 4:** Enter the amount that your employer reimbursed you for your moving expenses. Here is where things can become confusing and you can end up not deducting all that you're entitled to deduct or paying tax on part of the moving expenses that you were reimbursed. When your employer reimburses you for moving expenses of the type that you could deduct if you had paid them directly, the reimbursement will be noted in box 12 of your Form W-2 with a code P next to it. If you didn't incur deductible moving expenses in excess of what you were reimbursed, you have nothing to deduct and need not file Form 3903.

    If, on the other hand, your employer gave you a specific amount, say $15,000, to cover your moving expenses, that amount will be reported in box 1 of your W-2 as taxable wages. Nothing will be entered in box 12 of your W-2. If that is the case, you couldn't be making a bigger mistake by believing that because you were reimbursed you have nothing to deduct. Because the $15,000 shows up as taxable wages, you're entitled to claim your deductible moving expenses. If you don't find out from your employer how the $15,000 was reported to the IRS, it's going to cost you dearly, because you'll pay more tax than you have to by not deducting the moving expenses to which you're entitled. Enter your deductible moving expenses on lines 1 and 2, and don't enter what you were reimbursed, because it's already been included in your taxable wages.

    If your employer reimbursed you for moving expenses of the type that you could have deducted if you had paid them directly and for moving expenses that you can't deduct, the reimbursement for the deductible expenses will be noted in box 12 of your Form W-2 with a code P. The nondeductible moving expenses included in the reimbursement are included in box 1 of your W-2 as taxable wages. Temporary living expenses paid by your employer are the type that can't be deducted if you had paid them. Sorry, you owe tax on this amount. If this situation occurred, enter all your deductible moving expenses on lines 1 and 2 of Form 3903 and what your employer reimbursed you as indicated in box 12 of your W-2 on line 4.

    If your employer didn't reimburse you, box 12 will have nothing in it, and nothing will be added to your taxable wages. Enter your deductible moving expenses on lines 1 and 2 and put a zero (-0-) on line 4 of Form 3903.

✔ **Line 5:** Subtract line 4 from line 3. The result is the amount of your deductible 2006 moving expenses. Now enter this amount on your Form 1040 (line 26).

If line 3 is less than line 4, subtract line 3 from line 4 and include the amount on line 7, Form 1040, labeled "wages, etc." The reason? If you receive a reimbursement from your employer that's larger than your deductible moving expenses, you have to pay tax on the difference and can't enter any amount on line 5 of Form 3903.

Nondeductible IRAs (Form 8606)

If you made contributions to a traditional nondeductible IRA or a Roth IRA in 2006; took distributions from a traditional, SEP, or SIMPLE IRA; converted from a traditional, SEP, or SIMPLE IRA to a Roth IRA, either in whole or in part; or took a distribution from your Roth IRA, you need to complete **Form 8806, Nondeductible IRAs,** and attach it to your return. This form is divided into three parts, and on this form is where you figure out what part, if any, of your distribution is taxable:

✔ Part I: Nondeductible Contributions to Traditional IRAs and Distributions from Traditional, SEP, and SIMPLE IRAs

✔ Part II: 2006 Conversions from Traditional, SEP, or SIMPLE IRAs to Roth IRAs

✔ Part III: Distributions from Roth IRAs

Part 1: Traditional IRAs

This section is important if you made or are making nondeductible contributions or if you're taking money out of a traditional IRA to which you've made nondeductible contributions. This form tells you how much money you have to pay tax on every time you withdraw money from your nondeductible IRA account.

✔ **Line 1:** Enter your 2006 nondeductible IRA contribution, including the dough that you put in between January 1, 2007, and April 16, 2007. Enter your $4,000 (or $5,000 if you're older than 50) contribution on this line if you meet either of the following criteria:

  • You're contributing the $4,000 (or $5,000) maximum, you're covered by a pension plan where you work, and you earned more than $85,000, if married, or $60,000, if single.

  • You can't make any part of a Roth IRA contribution because your income exceeds $160,000 for couples or $110,000 if single.

If only a portion of your contribution qualifies for an IRA deduction or a Roth IRA and you elect to have the remaining balance treated as a nondeductible contribution, enter that amount here. For example, if you want to contribute $4,000, but because of the income phaseouts discussed in Chapter 6, you can deduct only $2,000 on line 32 of your Form 1040 or line 17 of your Form 1040A, enter the remaining $2,000 on line 1 of Form 8606.

If you're able to deduct a portion of your contribution, refer to Chapter 7 for a worksheet that helps you calculate your deduction amount. Whatever amount is left is what you'll use on Form 8606.

✔ **Line 2:** Now you need to look back at your Form 8606 from last year's return (or whenever you last made a nondeductible IRA contribution), and pick up the number from line 14. Remember, keeping track of how much money you've put into your nondeductible IRA is one good reason why you always keep copies of your prior years' income tax returns.

✔ **Line 3:** This part of the form is really easy. Add lines 1 and 2, and enter the total here.

If you didn't withdraw any money from this IRA, enter the amount from line 3 on line 14. Sign and date the form, and attach it to your return. Nothing else is required.

If you withdrew any money from your nondeductible IRA, you have to tackle lines 4 through 13. They may look complicated, but they really aren't — just a lot of adding and subtracting, so get your calculator ready.

✔ **Line 4:** If you withdrew money from your nondeductible IRA and you made your nondeductible contribution for 2006 between January 1, 2007, and April 16, 2007, you have to enter that amount again on this line. Why? To determine how much of your withdrawal is taxable, you must compare the total of all of the nondeductible contributions that you made through December 31, 2006, with the value of your IRA on that date. You know the rules. Apples to apples!

✔ **Line 5:** Subtract line 4 from line 3. This amount is the total of all your nondeductible contributions through December 31, 2006.

✔ **Line 6:** Enter the value of all your IRAs on December 31, 2006.

✔ **Line 7:** Enter what you withdrew in 2006. Don't include any amounts you rolled over to a Roth IRA.

✔ **Line 8:** Enter the net amount you converted, if any, from a regular IRA. The IRS allows you to make this conversion if you pay the tax on the entire conversion in the year that you make it in exchange for not paying taxes on distributions when you take them. *Note:* This is the net amount; don't include any amounts that you converted and then recharacterized (check out Chapter 7 or the "Recharacterizations" sidebar in this chapter to refresh your memory on this provision).

✔ **Line 9:** Add lines 6, 7, and 8. This amount is what your IRAs would've been worth on December 31, 2006, if you hadn't withdrawn any money.

✔ **Line 10:** Get out your calculator. Divide the amount on line 5 by the amount on line 9 and enter it as a decimal on line 10. For example, if the total basis (your nondeductible contributions) of your IRAs is $10,000 (line 5) and the total value of your IRAs is $100,000 distribution (line 9), divide $10,000 by $100,000 to get 0.1 (or 10 percent). Enter that number on line 10.

✔ **Line 11:** On this line you begin to calculate the amount of tax you owe on your Roth conversion. Multiply the amount on line 8 by the decimal on line 10 to arrive at the portion of your conversion that won't be taxed because it represents your previously taxed contributions.

✔ **Line 12:** Multiply line 7 (the amount that you withdrew in 2006) by line 10 to arrive at the amount of your distribution from a traditional, SEP, or SIMPLE IRA that isn't taxable (because you already paid the tax on your contribution amounts).

✔ **Line 13:** Add lines 11 and 12. Line 13 is the nontaxable portion of what you withdrew.

✔ **Line 14:** Subtract line 13 from line 3. The IRS refers to this amount as your *tax basis,* or the amount of money that is still sitting in your IRA after you've taken your distribution or made your conversion on which you've already paid tax. Remember, if you've paid income tax on it once, you don't have to pay tax on it again.

✔ **Line 15:** Subtract line 12 from line 7 and enter the difference here. This amount represents that taxable portion of your withdrawal. Enter this amount on line 15b, Form 1040, or on line 11b, Form 1040A.

Sign and date the form if you aren't attaching it to your return, and hang on to it for dear life. If you ever need to prove to the IRS the amount of your nondeductible contributions, your Form 8606 from all the years in which you made contributions should be invaluable evidence.

Recharacterizations

Recharacterization is a fancy word for changing your mind and undoing the IRA–to–Roth IRA conversion. You need to consider recharacterization if the value of your Roth dropped after you made the conversion. You have to do a recharacterization if you misfigured your 2006 income and it ended up being more than $100,000, which is the permissible limit. (Chapter 7 explains how recharacterizations are treated on your return.)

You must file Form 8606 to report nondeductible contributions even if you don't have to file a tax return for the year. If you file a Form 1040, you must attach Form 8606 to your 1040. There is a $50 penalty for not filing your 8606! Also, if your IRA contributions are more than permissible amounts, you may be subject to a 6 percent penalty, and you must withdraw the overpayment.

Part II: Conversions from traditional IRAs to Roth IRAs

If you converted from a traditional, SEP, or SIMPLE IRA to a Roth IRA in 2006, you need to complete this section.

- ✔ **Line 16:** Enter the amount you converted from your traditional (simple) IRA to your Roth IRA. If you already completed Part I of this form, just pick up the amount on line 8.

- ✔ **Line 17:** Enter the amount from line 11 if you converted a nondeductible IRA.

- ✔ **Line 18:** Subtract line 17 from 16 and carry it over to line 15b of your 1040 or line 11b of 1040A. This is the taxable amount of your Roth conversion.

Part III: Distributions from Roth IRAs

In this part, you compute the taxable portion, if any, on nonqualified distributions from your Roth IRA. For a quick review on how a Roth is taxed, check out Chapter 7. Remember, you have to keep money in a Roth for at least five years in order to have the entire withdrawal escape tax.

- ✔ **Line 19:** Enter the amount you withdrew from your Roth IRA.

- ✔ **Line 20:** Every rule has an exception, and this exception is the one for nonqualified Roth distributions. If you took a distribution so you could pay qualified first-time home-buyer expenses, such as your down payment, construction costs, mortgage points, or other closing costs, you don't have to pay the penalty on the nonqualified distribution. And, if you think that first-time homebuyer expenses are a thing of the past for you, think again: The IRS defines a first-time homebuyer as anyone who hasn't held an ownership interest in a principal residence for at least two years prior to signing the contract on this home.

- ✔ **Line 21:** Subtract line 20 from line 21. This amount represents the total of your nonqualified distribution.

- ✔ **Line 22:** Enter the basis (what you contributed to your Roth) of what you withdrew. It sounds tough, but it's not. Here's how to compute Roth basis: Enter the total amount of all your Roth contributions on this line less any amounts you've withdrawn previously. For example, if you've contributed a total of $10,000 to your Roth since you started it in 2001, and in 2005, you withdrew $1,500, your basis in 2006 is $8,500 ($10,000 − $1,500).

✔ **Line 23:** Subtract line 22 from 21. Enter zero (-0-) if line 22 is more than line 21.

✔ **Line 24:** If you've made Roth conversions, enter your basis here. Calculate this number the same as you did for your Roth contribution basis in line 20.

✔ **Line 25:** Subtract line 24 from line 23. If line 24 is more than line 23, enter zero (-0-). If not, carry this amount over to line 15b of your 1040 or line 11b of 1040A. This is the amount on which you have to pay tax. If you're under age 59½, this amount may also be subject to a 10 percent penalty.

Forms 8615 and 8814, the Kiddie Tax

Beginning in 2006, if you have children under age 18 (yup, they raised the age from 14) who have investment income, you may need to complete Form 8615 or Form 8814. After a child reaches age 18, the kiddie tax doesn't apply — the child pays whatever his or her tax rate is.

Form 8615 is the form that you use when your child files his or her own return; use **Form 8814** when you elect to report your kid's investment income on your return. (See the sidebar "Why your 3-year-old may be in the 35 percent tax bracket" for more on making this election.)

Here's how the kiddie tax works. If a child has $2,700 in interest income, for example, the first $850 is exempt from tax. The next $850 is taxed at the child's tax rate (10 percent), which comes to $85. The remaining $1,000 is taxed at the parent's rate. So if the parent is in the 33 percent tax bracket, the kiddie tax amounts to $330 ($1,000 × 33 percent), plus the child's portion of $85, for a total bill of $415.

Children whose investment income is more than $850 must file a return, but if their income is less than $1,700, they can file their return by using the less complicated Form 1040A. If they don't have any taxable investment income (you invested the money that their grandparents gave them in tax-exempt bonds), they don't have to file a return until their earned income, such as income from a part-time job, exceeds $5,150. Unless your child was 18 by the end of 2006, here's how to compute the kiddie tax.

1. **Enter your Social Security number and taxable income on Form 8615.**

2. **Add the amount of your child's investment income that's in excess of $1,700 to your taxable income.**

3. **Recompute your tax.**

   The difference between the tax on your return and the recomputed figure is the kiddie tax.

   A good tax software program can save you all this math (see Chapter 2).

But if you don't have a tax software program and your child's investment income in excess of $1,700 is $1,000, add the $1,000 to your taxable income. Now compute your tax on this amount. For example, if the tax on this amount is $9,305 and the tax on your return is $9,000, the $305 difference is the kiddie tax. Enter that amount plus $85 (the tax on the $850 that isn't exempt from tax, per the tax tables) on your child's return on Form 1040 (line 44).

If your kid gets stuck for the kiddie tax, you have to use Form 1040 when filing his or her return. The computation of the kiddie tax on Form 8615 doesn't affect the tax that you have to pay. Your taxable income is used only to determine the tax rate to apply to your kid's income above $1,700. It only feels like you're being taxed twice.

Why your 3-year-old may be in the 35 percent tax bracket

Once upon a time, if you were in the 70 percent tax bracket (rates were that high before 1981), it made sense to make a gift of investment property to your children, because the income the property produced would be taxed at the child's tax rate — which could have been as low as 11 percent. But that was back in the good old days (that is, if you think anything is nostalgic about 70 percent tax rates).

This tax savings scheme ended in 1986. Nowadays, if a child is under the age of 18, all investment income higher than $1,700 is taxed at the parents' tax rate — which can be as high as 35 percent. The reason for the change is to remove the incentive for higher-income earners to transfer lots of money to their kids just to save tax dollars by benefiting from lower tax brackets.

But there's more. (There always is.) If you and your spouse file separate returns, you enter the larger of either your or your spouse's taxable income on Form 8615. If you're separated or divorced, the parent who has custody of the child for the greater part of the year uses his or her taxable income when completing Form 8615. But if you and your spouse live apart and qualify to file as unmarried (single or head of household), the custodial parent's taxable income is used on Form 8615.

And it gets worse (as it always seems to)! If you have two or more kids, you enter the total of all their investment income on Form 8615. The kiddie tax is computed and allocated among them. For example, suppose that your daughter's investment income in excess of $1,700 is $3,000, and your son's is $2,000; you enter $5,000 on each child's Form 8615. Then each child's share of the total kiddie tax is allocated. Your daughter's share is three-fifths of the tax, and your son's share is two-fifths.

By now you're looking for a way to avoid having to file a separate tax return because your child has $1 more than $850. Is there a way, you ask? Yes. If your child has investment income of only $8,500 or less and it's all from interest and dividends, you can report the income on your return by filing Form 8814. That's $8,500 for each child. But we don't recommend this course of action because the kiddie tax is higher on your return than it would be on the child's return, and your tax could also be higher. To find out more about the smartest ways to invest in your child's name, read Chapter 24. The $8,500 threshold is indexed for inflation.

Form 8829, Expenses for Business Use of Your Home

Your home office no longer has to be the place where you meet customers or the principal place where you conduct business. You're entitled to claim a home office deduction if you have a dedicated space in your house that you use for your business, even if it's used only to conduct administrative or management activities of your business, provided you have no other office or other place of business where you can perform the same tasks. So a person who brings work home is out of luck. So is the person who spreads out over the dining room table. So long as you eat there, that table isn't dedicated solely to the pursuit of your business. A carpenter who sets up his computer and desk in a corner of that dining room so that he can price jobs and bill his clients has a valid deduction, because that corner of his dining room is set aside solely for the administrative and management activities of his business.

The rule allowing taxpayers to claim a deduction for the portion of their home they use to perform administrative and management activities was designed to help doctors who perform their primary duties in hospitals, salespeople who spend most of their time calling on customers at their customers' offices, and house painters and other tradespeople who spend their time at job sites but use an office in their home to do all their paperwork. Use **Form 8829, Expenses for Business Use of Your Home,** to claim the deduction.

If you use part of your residence for business, you can deduct the mortgage interest, real estate taxes, depreciation, insurance, utilities, and repairs related to that part of your house. Renters get to deduct their business portion of the rental expenses.

If you use a portion of your home to store inventory or samples, you're also entitled to deduct your home office expenses. Say that you sell cosmetics and use part of your study to store samples. You can deduct expenses related to the portion of your study used to store the cosmetics, even if you use the study for other purposes.

A home office deduction can't produce a loss. For example, suppose that your business income is $6,000. You have $5,000 in business expenses and home office expenses of $1,500 (of which $1,000 is for the portion of your mortgage interest and real estate tax allocated for the use of the office). First, you deduct the interest and taxes of $1,000, which leaves a balance of $5,000 for possible deductions. Then you deduct $5,000 of business expenses, which brings your business income to zero. You can't deduct the remaining $500 of your home office expenses, but you can carry it over to the next year. If you don't have sufficient income to deduct the $500 next year, you can carry it over again.

If you're a renter, filling out Form 8829 correctly means that you first determine your total rent — including insurance, cleaning, and utilities. Then you deduct the portion used for business. If you rent four rooms and one room is used for business, you're entitled to deduct 25 percent of the total. (If the rooms are the same size, you can use this method. If not, you have to figure out the percentage on a square-footage basis.)

For homeowners, you compute the total cost of maintaining your home, depreciation, mortgage interest, taxes, insurance, repairs, and so on. Don't forget to deduct the cost of your cleaning service if your office is cleaned in addition to the rest of the house. Then deduct the percentage used for business.

Measuring your home office

Complete lines 1 through 7 on Form 8829 to find out how much of your home you used exclusively for your business.

- ✔ **Line 1:** Enter the area, in square feet, of the part of your home that you used for business: for example, 300 square feet.

- ✔ **Line 2:** Enter the total area, in square feet, of your home: for example, 1,500 square feet.

- ✔ **Line 3:** To determine the percentage of your home that you used for business, divide line 1 by line 2 and enter the result as a percentage here. In the earlier example, you would enter 20 percent (300 ÷ 1,500). Keep this percentage handy; it's the percentage of the expenses for the whole house — such as interest, real estate taxes, depreciation, utility costs, and repairs — that you use on Form 8829 to determine your deduction.

- ✔ **Line 7:** Unless you use your home as a daycare facility, you can skip lines 4 through 6 (which calculate the percentage of your home that you use for your daycare) and enter your deduction percentage from line 3 onto line 7. If you use your home to provide daycare services, multiply the result from line 6 by the number on line 3, and enter the result here.

Figuring your allowable home office deduction

Lines 8 through 34 on Form 8829 involve megacomputations, much more than our space allows. In this section, we take you through the basics that apply to most people. Take a peek at IRS Publication 587 *(Business Use of Your Home)* for additional information.

- ✔ **Line 8:** Enter the amount from line 29 of your Schedule C (this amount is what you earned after expenses). Your home office deduction can't exceed this amount.

- ✔ **Lines 9 through 20, column (a):** Expenses that apply exclusively to your office go in this column. Repairs and maintenance, such as painting your office, are two such items.

- ✔ **Lines 9 through 20, column (b):** Enter your expenses that apply to the entire house on these lines. The IRS refers to them as indirect expenses.

  If you rent, instead of owning your home, the rent that you paid goes on line 20, column (b).

- ✔ **Lines 21 through 34:** It's number-crunching time — enough to make us wonder who came up with this form!

- ✔ **Line 34:** This is your allowable deduction. Carry it over to line 30 on Schedule C.

If you had more home office expenses than you could use last year, don't forget to add the amount you had left over from your tax year 2005 Form 8829, line 41 onto line 23 of your tax year 2006 Form 8829. The same goes for excess depreciation and casualty losses from line 42 of your tax year 2005 Form 8829. Enter that amount on line 29.

Determining your home office's depreciation allowance

You also have to apply your home office deduction percentage (from line 7 of Form 8829) to your home's depreciation allowance. This section includes a line-by-line breakdown of the appropriate part on Form 8829.

Line 35: Your home's value

Here's where you compute your depreciation deduction. You get to write off the percentage of your home that you claim as a home office (in our earlier example, 20 percent) over either 31½ or 39 years, depending on when you set up your office. Residential property usually is written off over 27½ years, but because the office is used for business, it's considered business property and has a longer life.

On line 35, enter the smaller of what you paid for your home (including the original and closing costs, as well as any improvements you've made to the property) or its fair market value at the time you first started to use it for business. You don't have to make this comparison every year — only when you started claiming a home office deduction.

Line 36: Land not included

Because you can't depreciate land, you have to subtract the value of the land that your home sits on from the cost of your home so that you calculate the house's net cost. A value of 15 percent for the land is a safe subtraction unless you know for certain what you paid for your building lot.

Line 37: Basis of building

Subtract line 36 from line 35. This amount is your home's basis after subtracting the value of the land that you can't depreciate.

Line 38: Business portion of your home

Multiply line 37 by your home office deduction percentage from line 7. In our continuing example, that's the 20 percent of the house used for business that you can write off.

Line 39: Depreciation percentage

If you set up your office before May 12, 1993, it's a 31½-year write-off. Use the depreciation table in IRS Publication 587 *(Business Use of Your Home)*.

If you set up your office after May 12, 1993, the write-off is over 39 years. Use Table 15-1 to determine your depreciation percentage.

Table 15-1			39-Year Depreciation Schedule for Business Use of Home (%)									
Use the column for the month of the year you set up your office.												
Year	Jan	Feb	Mar	Apr	May	Jun	Jul	Aug	Sep	Oct	Nov	Dec
1	2.461	2.247	2.033	1.819	1.605	1.391	1.177	0.963	0.749	0.535	0.321	0.107
2–39	2.564	2.564	2.564	2.564	2.564	2.564	2.564	2.564	2.564	2.564	2.564	2.564

For example, if you set up your office in June 2003, enter 1.391 percent on line 39 of Form 8829. Every year thereafter you use 2.564 percent.

Line 40: Depreciation allowable

Multiply line 38 by line 39. This number is your depreciation deduction, based on the business use of your home. Enter this amount on lines 40 and 28 of this form.

Deducting what's left

Remember that you can't take a loss because of the home office deduction. You can, however, carry over an excess deduction amount to another year's tax return.

On lines 41 and 42, compute the amount of your home office deduction that you couldn't deduct. You get to deduct it in future years, provided that you have enough income.

On Schedule A, don't forget to deduct the balance (in our example, 80 percent) of your total mortgage interest that you entered on line 10(b) of Form 8829, and the balance of your total real estate taxes from line 11(b) of this form. Your mortgage interest balance goes on line 10 of Schedule A; the real estate taxes balance goes on line 6 of Schedule A.

Form W-4, Employee Withholding

If you owe a bundle to the IRS for 2006, chances are you aren't withholding enough tax from your salary. Unless you don't mind paying a lot on April 16 (remember that April 15 is a Sunday, so you get an extra day), you need to adjust your withholding in order to avoid interest and penalties if you can't pay what you owe when it's due.

Too many exemptions

If you claimed more than ten withholding exemptions on your **Form W-4, Withholding Allowance Certificate,** or if you earned more than $200 per week and claimed an exemption from all withholding, your employer must submit the W-4 to the IRS.

If the IRS determines that you overstated the number of exemptions to which you're entitled, it will either notify your employer that your withholding certificate is inaccurate or ask you for written verification of why you believe you're entitled to the extra exemptions that you claim. If the IRS asks you for this information, it sends you the **Form 6355, Worksheet to Determine Withholding Allowances.** The three-page Form 6355 is more detailed than the W-4 that you completed.

If, after reviewing Form 6355, the IRS determines that you aren't entitled to the number of exemptions that you claimed, it notifies your employer to disregard your W-4 and to withhold tax based on the number of exemptions it says you're entitled to. This edict remains in effect until the IRS approves a new W-4. To get approval to change the number of your exemptions, you must file a new W-4 with your employer, who again submits the W-4 to the IRS. You also must attach a written statement explaining why you're requesting a change.

If you don't have reasonable basis for the number of exemptions that you claim, you'll be assessed a $500 penalty. A simple error or an honest mistake won't result in penalty. Phew!

Relying on the worksheet on Form W-4 to accurately calculate the correct number of exemptions you should be claiming would be easy, but it's not that simple, especially if you're married and both you and your spouse are working. If you fall into this category and your combined taxable income is greater than $123,700, you'll have to deal with the marriage penalty (which we talk about in Chapter 4). Check out the IRS Web site (www.irs.gov), which has a nifty W-4 calculator that you can use at any time during the year to make sure you're having enough tax withheld from your paychecks. The calculator is easy to use, and gives a reasonably accurate picture of how much you'll owe (or have refunded) next April 15.

To access this calculator, type "W-4 Calculator" in the box labeled "Search IRS Site for" and hit "Go." It's that easy!

Household Employment Taxes: Schedule H (the Nanny Tax)

If you have household workers (including housekeepers, babysitters, yard-care workers, and nannies) who earned more than $1,500 from you in 2006, you may be required to pay employment taxes for them (that's the employer's half of the Social Security and Medicare taxes, plus federal unemployment [FUTA] taxes). Please see Chapter 21 for help in making the determination. If your workers meet the employee test, fortunately, you don't need to figure out the ordinary employment tax forms, which need to be filed either monthly or quarterly; instead, if you qualify, you may use Schedule H to calculate what you owe.

Prior to the nanny tax, which is retroactive to January 1, 1994, household employers had to file quarterly reports and pay Social Security taxes if they paid household help more than $50 in a quarter. Now you don't have to withhold and pay Social Security taxes unless you pay a domestic worker more than $1,500 during the year. If you're just figuring out the change in the law and didn't pay more than $1,400 in 2003, 2004 or 2005, but filed quarterly returns, you can get your money back by filing **Form 843, Claim for Refund and Request for Abatement.** After April 15, 2007, you can no longer get back any 2003 tax you incorrectly overpaid. See Chapter 18 to find out more about the statute of limitations on refunds.

Here are two important provisions of the nanny tax that you should be aware of:

✔ You're not required to pay Social Security tax for domestic employees under the age of 18 (for any portion of the year), regardless of how much you pay them. The exemption doesn't apply if the principal occupation of the employee is household employment. So you're off the hook for payroll taxes for your 12-year-old mother's helper, or the 16-year-old down the street who babysits occasionally.

✔ You don't have to file quarterly payroll tax forms. Any Social Security, Medicare, or federal unemployment (FUTA) taxes, and income taxes that you choose to withhold can be paid when you file your return in April.

If your withholding or estimated tax payments aren't enough to cover the Social Security, Medicare, and FUTA (we explain these taxes later in this section) taxes that you owe, a penalty will be assessed. So make sure that you pay in enough.

Although the nanny tax simplifies your IRS filings, you still have to keep filing quarterly state unemployment tax returns, unless your state elects to conform to the IRS method of filing annually.

Schedule H looks more formidable than it really is. Here's the lowdown on what it's really about:

✔ If you paid your household help less than $1,500 in 2006 and didn't withhold any income tax, you don't have to file this form.

✔ If you paid any one household employee less than $1,500 during 2006, but you withheld federal income tax, you need to fill out only Part I beginning with line 5.

For example, suppose that you pay someone $60 a week. That's $780 a quarter and $3,120 for the year. You have to answer only questions A, B, and C on the form and fill out the eight lines in Part I. It's strictly simple math stuff. You have to multiply the $3,120 in cash wages that you paid by the 12.4 percent Social Security rate and the 2.9 percent Medicare tax rate. Add both of these taxes together on line 8 of the form and carry this amount over to line 62 of Form 1040. Sign and date the form at the bottom of page 2 if you aren't attaching it to your return.

Don't forget that you also have to furnish your employee with a W-2 stating the amount that you paid, as well as the amount of Social Security, Medicare, and income tax that you withheld. Withholding income tax is optional on your part. One further chore: You have to file a copy of the W-2 and Form W-3 (if more than one W-2 is being filed) with the Social Security Administration in Wilkes-Barre, Pennsylvania, by February 28, 2007. Your employees must get their W-2s by January 31, 2007.

✔ If you had one or more household employees in 2006, and paid wages totaling $1,000 or more in any calendar quarter in either 2005 or 2006, you have to fill out Parts II and III of Schedule H. Not only do you owe Social Security and Medicare taxes, you also have to pay federal unemployment tax, commonly known as FUTA. Of course, if you had no employees in 2006, but did in 2005, you're not required to fill out Schedule H at all.

Check with your state tax department to find out whether you have to register and pay state unemployment tax on a quarterly basis. Also check with your insurance broker to see whether your homeowner's insurance covers domestic employees or whether you need a separate workers' compensation policy. Don't play fast and loose in this area. If your nanny gets hurt or injured, you may have to pay a bundle if you don't have insurance coverage.

The immigration law requires that you verify that every new employee is eligible to work in the United States. You do this by completing **Form I-9, Employment Eligibility Verification.** You can get this form from the Immigration Service (800-521-1504). The form doesn't get filed. Hang onto it in case someone from the Immigration Service knocks on your door.

Schedule SE: Self-Employment Tax Form

If you earn part or all of your income from being self-employed, use Schedule SE to figure another tax that you owe — the Social Security tax and Medicare tax. The first $94,200 of your self-employment earnings is taxed at 12.4 percent (this is the Social Security tax part). The Medicare tax doesn't have any limit; it's 2.9 percent of your total self-employment earnings. For amounts of $94,200 or less, the combined rate is 15.3 percent (adding the two taxes together), and for amounts above $94,200, the rate is 2.9 percent. If your self-employment earnings are under $400, you aren't subject to this tax.

Your self-employment earnings may be your earnings reported on the following:

- ✔ Schedule C (line 31)

- ✔ Schedule C-EZ (line 3)

- ✔ Schedule K-1 (line 15a), Form 1065 — if you're a partner in a firm

- ✔ Schedule F (line 36)

- ✔ Form 1040 (line 21) — your self-employment income that you reported as miscellaneous income

You can use Section A of Schedule SE, called the *short worksheet,* if your only income subject to Social Security and Medicare tax is self-employment income. If you're self-employed and also are employed by someone else, you have to use the long form; otherwise, you may end up paying more Social Security than you're required to because Social Security tax has already been withheld from your salary. To prevent this disaster, enter the total of the amounts from boxes 3 and 7 of your W-2 on line 8a of page 2 of Schedule SE. (And if you file **Form 4137** on unreported tips, enter the amount from line 9 of that form on line 8b of Schedule SE.)

Remember, half of your self-employment tax is deductible. Complete Schedule SE and note the following: The amount on line 5 of Schedule SE is the amount of tax that you have to pay; you carry it over to Form 1040 (line 58) and add it to your income tax that's due. Enter half of what you have to pay — the amount on line 6 of Schedule SE — on Form 1040 (line 27).

Wouldn't it be nice if this form simply said, "If you are self-employed, use this form to compute how much Social Security and Medicare tax you have to pay"? Paying this tax ensures that you'll be entitled to Social Security when you're old and gray.

You have three choices when filling out this form:

- ✔ **Section A — Short Schedule SE:** This section is the shortest and easiest one to complete — 6 lines. But if you were employed on a salaried basis and had Social Security tax withheld from your wages, you will pay more self-employment tax than required if you use the short schedule. Moonlighters beware.

- ✔ **Section B — Long Schedule SE:** Use this part of the form if you received wages and are self-employed. Suppose that you have wages of $40,000 and have $55,000 in earnings from your business. If you use the Short Schedule SE, you'll end up paying Social Security tax on $95,000 when the maximum amount of combined earnings that you're required to pay on is only $94,200. You pay Medicare tax, however, on the entire $95,000.

    This section isn't all that formidable. Make use of it so you don't end up paying more Social Security tax than you have to.

- ✔ **Part II — Optional method:** If your earnings are less than $1,600, you can elect to pay Social Security tax on at least $1,600, so you'll build up Social Security credit for when you become 65.

If you need to complete Section B or Part II of Schedule SE, check out **IRS Publication 533, Self-Employment Tax,** for all the help you could possibly need. If your needs are simpler, here's the lowdown on Section A — Short Schedule SE:

- ✔ **Line 1:** If you're not a farmer, you can skip this line. If farming is your game, enter the amount from line 36 of Schedule F or box 14, Code A, Form 1065, Schedule K-1 for farm partnerships.

- ✔ **Line 2:** Enter the total of the amounts from line 31, Schedule C (line 3, Schedule C-EZ) and box 14, Code A, Schedule K-1 (for partnerships). This is how each partner pays his or her Social Security and Medicare tax. You may also have to pay Social Security and Medicare tax on the miscellaneous income reported on line 21. What kind of income do you have to pay on? The answer: directors' fees, finders' fees, and commissions.

  The following aren't subject to self-employment tax: jury duty, notary public fees, forgiveness of a debt even if you owe tax on it, rental income, executor's fees (only if you're an ordinary person, and not an attorney, an accountant, or a banker, who might ordinarily act in this capacity), prizes and awards, lottery winnings, and gambling winnings — unless gambling is your occupation.

- ✔ **Line 3:** A breeze. Add lines 1 and 2.

- ✔ **Line 4:** Multiply line 3 by 92.35 percent (0.9235). Why? If you were employed, your employer would get to deduct its share of the Social Security tax that it would have to pay, and so do you.

- ✔ **Line 5:** If line 4 is $94,200 or less, multiply line 4 by 15.3 percent (0.153) and enter that amount on line 58 of Form 1040. For example, if line 4 is $10,000, multiply it by 15.3 percent, and you get $1,530.

  If line 4 is more than $94,200, multiply that amount by 2.9 percent (0.029) and add that amount to $11,680.80. (This is the maximum Social Security tax that you're required to pay.) For example, if line 4 is $95,000, multiply that amount by 0.029 (2.9 percent is your Medicare tax), which comes to $2,755. Now add your Medicare tax ($2,755) to your Social Security Tax ($11,680.80) for a grand total of $14,435.80. Enter $14,436 on line 58 of Form 1040. Remember, you get to use cents on Schedule SE, but the IRS wants you to use the whole dollar method on Form 1040.

- ✔ **Line 6:** Multiply line 5 by 50 percent. You can deduct this amount on line 27 of your 1040.

Part IV
Audits and Errors: Dealing with the IRS

The 5th Wave — By Rich Tennant

"Our goal is to maximize your upside and minimize your downside while we protect our own backside."

In this part . . .

Good news and bad news arrives via the U.S. Postal
Service. One letter that you hope doesn't find its way
to you is an official, thin envelope from the IRS announcing
that you've won its special drawing. Perhaps you were
hoping that the return that you hadn't filed wouldn't be
missed. Maybe you're a law-abiding citizen and can't
understand why the tax folks are hassling you again.
You could choose to ignore the IRS's queries, but we
don't recommend making the IRS angry.

In this part, you find out how to deal with just about
everything the IRS can throw at you during the year. If
you didn't file in time or couldn't pay all your taxes, we
provide a shoulder to cry on as well as sound counsel
for how to make things better.

Chapter 16

The Dreaded Envelope: IRS Notices, Assessments, and Audits

· ·

In This Chapter

▶ Deciphering assessment and nonassessment notices

▶ Understanding the different types of audits

▶ Preparing for an audit

▶ Querying repetitive audits

▶ Making the statute of limitations work for you

▶ Keeping the IRS out of your accounts and property

· ·

Most people don't know that they have a one-in-three chance of receiving a notice from the IRS stating that they failed to report all their income, filed late, didn't pay what they owed, or made an error in preparing their return. Perhaps you have committed one or even a combination of these infractions!

Of course, even worse than a simple notice is the letter that informs you that you've been selected for either a full or partial audit. And, because returns that are audited are often selected at random, you may not have done anything wrong, but you're still placed in the position of proving the information contained on your return is, in fact, correct and accurate.

Face it, getting any mail (other than your refund check) from the IRS strikes fear in the hearts and souls of even the most confident and honest taxpayers. In this chapter, we show you what to do and how to respond when the IRS comes to you looking for more info.

Finding Strength in Numbers

If you think that you received an IRS notice simply because you're unlucky, you may be mistaken. Winning the IRS notice lottery is easy, and you're hardly in exclusive company! Each year, the IRS issues millions of the following:

✔ Penalty notices

✔ Notices informing taxpayers that they didn't report all their income

✔ Notices to taxpayers stating that they failed to file a tax return

✔ Notices citing math or clerical errors

✔ Notices to taxpayers that they failed to pay what they owed

And every year, millions of beleaguered taxpayers write back saying that the notices they received are either incorrect or unclear.

When you're dealing with the IRS, remember the three "P"s — promptness, persistence, and patience! Don't let yourself become discouraged when matters move more slowly than you'd like. Don't forget that although you may feel like the IRS is a huge, impersonal bureaucracy; it's actually filled with individuals who may be able to help you, if you let them. "I shall overcome" should be your motto.

One of the biggest headaches in dealing with the IRS is that the agency can be big and impersonal. That's why this part of this book provides you with suggested strategies and sample response letters developed from the decades of experience that have helped our clients deal with those daunting IRS notices. These strategies and letters work. When an IRS form can work better and faster than a letter, we include that form and suggest using it.

Understanding the IRS Notice Process

If you've never had a pen pal, you have one now. And you don't even have to write back — the letters just keep coming. However, disregard this pen pal at your peril; the IRS doesn't just get mad when you hide from it, it has the power to take your money.

Receiving your typical notice

There are seemingly zillions of points the IRS may decide to check on your return, and there seems to be just as many ways they can usher you into the twilight realm of notices, adjustments, and increasing assessments. Really, though, all of this paper follows a timeline, no matter what the name or number of the first letter you receive from the IRS.

Typically, when the IRS decides to check with you about your tax return, it sends you a first notice of adjustment, such as the **CP-2000, Notice of Proposed Adjustment for Underpayment/Overpayment,** the **CP-13, We Changed Your Account,** or a 30-day letter (notifying you of an audit's results). If you fail to respond to this first notice, if the IRS isn't satisfied with your reply, or if you fail to exercise your appeal rights, a Statutory Notice of Deficiency is issued. Remember that adjustments merely correcting a math or processing error — or assessing a penalty — don't require the issuance of a Statutory Notice unless the error results in you owing more tax. We get into what you should do when you receive a Statutory Notice in "Receiving a Statutory Notice of Deficiency," later in this chapter.

If you don't respond, the IRS then may make an assessment. That amount, plus penalties, is entered into the service center's computer under your Social Security number. The service center then sends up to four notices (you can stop the notices at any time by paying the assessment). The first three come at approximately five-week intervals, covering a 15-week period. All three notices ask for payment within ten days. The fourth notice announces that things are about to hit the fan.

The first notice either informs you that there is a balance due (you filed but didn't pay what you owed), that there was a math error, or that an adjustment was made to your account (for example, you didn't make all the tax payments you claimed). It explains the reason(s) for the change plus any penalties that are being assessed. Unfortunately, interest is always charged when a balance is owed.

After you receive that first notice, you know that if you ignore it, the second will soon be winging its way to you. The second form is Form CP-503. It's marked, **"IMPORTANT immediate action is required."** It lists how much the IRS now thinks you owe and how much time you have to pay it.

And, if that doesn't get your attention, the third notice, **Form CP-504,** bears the legend, **"Urgent! We intend to levy certain assets. Please respond NOW."** Now you'll find additional penalties and interest tacked on to your last balance, plus it gives you another deadline to pay the full amount owing or enter into a payment agreement.

The fourth notice is sent by certified mail 30 days after the third notice (the law requires that it be sent this way before the IRS can start seizing someone's property or wages). This notice bears the legend **Final Notice of Intent to Levy and Notice of Your Right to a Hearing.** This notice informs you that if payment isn't received within 30 days or you don't request a collection hearing within that period, the IRS has the right to seize your property and garnish your wages. (Remember, the IRS defines property as more than just your residence; it has its eye on your car, boat, personal property, other real estate, bank accounts, and investments, too.) Ouch! You can expect to receive this type of notice (letter) about 20 weeks after the first notice.

Don't think you can fob off the folks at the IRS. The IRS can and will use any and all means within its extensive arsenal to collect the tax it feels is due. If you ignore the IRS, don't expect the IRS just to go away. Instead, respond promptly and courteously. They aren't robots or monsters on the other end of the telephone, but just IRS employees trying to do their job.

Now for some good news: You can now appeal a notice of intent to levy or a notice that a lien has been filed. When you do, the IRS must stop all collection activity while your appeal is pending. Thanks to the 1998 law that overhauled the IRS, a separate notice is now sent informing you of your appeal rights. For more information, see "Appealing a lien or levy," later in this chapter.

If you receive a Final Notice and can't pay what you owe, see Chapter 18 to review your options. If you haven't paid the balance or contacted the IRS to arrange payment within ten days after receiving a Final Notice, the contact section of the Automated Collection System (ACS) takes over, unless the IRS has what's known as *levy source information* — that is, the IRS knows where it can get your cash; it knows where to find your property or income. In that case, a Notice of Levy will be issued against your salary and bank accounts, for example. The contact section handles cases where the payment of tax can't be satisfied by levy. The ACS contacts you by telephone, and if it can't get you to pay, the ACS turns the case over to a revenue officer.

Deciphering a notice

Don't panic! If you're like most taxpayers, you'll look at the notice, see a dollar figure, and decide it's too painful to look at again. Do yourself a favor, take a peek at it again; the dollar figure might be a refund — but it isn't likely.

One critical bit of advice: The computers at the service centers won't tolerate being ignored. Maybe they hooked you by error, but there's no satisfying them until they reel you in, or until you convince the IRS that their computer made an error. To do so, you must respond quickly to a notice. Otherwise, you severely prejudice your appeal rights and end up with no recourse but to pay the tax and forget the whole thing — or to pay the tax and then try to get your money back. The latter isn't as impossible as it sounds. We tell you how to get back what is rightfully yours in Chapter 17.

Every notice contains the following:

- Date of the notice
- Taxpayer Identification number — your Social Security or Employer Identification number for businesses (make sure that it's yours)

- ✔ The form number you filed — 1040, 1040A, or 1040EZ
- ✔ Tax period — the year
- ✔ A control number (evidently your name, address, and Social Security number aren't enough)
- ✔ Penalties charged
- ✔ Interest charged
- ✔ Amount owed
- ✔ Tax payments you made

Both you and the IRS are able to track any missing tax payment by a long series of numbers printed on the back of your check. The first 14 numbers make up the IRS's control or tracking number; the next nine are your Social Security number, followed by a four-letter abbreviation of your name. The next four numbers are the year the payment was applied (0512 means the year ending December 2005), and the last six digits record the date on which the payment was received.

More and more banks have stopped returning cancelled checks with their monthly statements; however, you can still retrieve a copy of both the front and back of your cancelled tax check from your bank when you need it, although you may have to pay a fee to do so. Don't let the fee deter you — pay up and get the information you need.

Unfortunately, not every notice provides all the information necessary to precisely determine what went wrong — IRS notices are famous for their lack of clarity. Our favorite is a client's notice that indicated that either an error was made, an outstanding balance existed, not all the payments listed on the return were made, or a penalty was being assessed. The notice went on to promise that the IRS would send a separate notice (which, by the way, never came) stating which explanation applied.

All is not lost if you receive an IRS notice and after careful inspection, you still don't understand it. Call the IRS at the telephone number indicated on the notice or at 800-829-1040 and request a Record of your Tax Account Information, which takes about seven to ten days to arrive. This printout lists every transaction posted to your account. With this additional information, you should be able to understand why you were sent the notice.

If the transcript of your tax account fails to clarify why you received the notice in the first place, write to the IRS and ask it to provide a better or more exact explanation. See Chapter 17 to find out more about getting a better explanation.

Assessing Assessment Notices

Assessment notices usually inform you of one of the following situations:

- ✔ You weren't given credit for all the tax payments that you claim you made.
- ✔ You made a math error or used the wrong tax table or form.
- ✔ You filed a return but neglected to pay what you owed.
- ✔ You agreed to the results of a tax examination.
- ✔ You owe a penalty.

General assessment notices — the CP series forms and other notices

The IRS uses one of the CP series forms to inform you that your refund is being reduced or eliminated. This may be the case if your refund is being applied to other taxes you owe, which will be announced on Form CP-49. Or it may be the result of one of the reasons from the list in the preceding section. The IRS also intercepts refunds to pay nontax governmental debts, such as defaults on student loans and nonpayment of child support. We discuss the IRS refund interception program in greater detail in Chapter 17.

In addition to the CP series notices, you may receive other correspondence from the IRS. If you've failed to pay your income taxes in the past, or you haven't given your correct Social Security number to your bank, brokerage, or any other institution, partnership, trust or estate, or any other entity that is paying you income, the IRS may require these payers withhold income tax from any payments they make to you. Likewise, if you're thinking to avoid withholdings on your wages by some judicious fudging on your Form W-4, think again. Your employer is required to submit extreme withholding exemptions to the IRS, and it may ask you for clarification.

The IRS also sends a general assessment notice to assess a penalty for filing or paying late, failing to make timely estimated tax payments, failing to report all your income, or overstating credits or deductions on your return. Watch out!

Income verification notice — Form CP-2501

The IRS will send you a Form CP-2501 when information on your income tax returns doesn't match information it's received about you from a third party on either a Form W-2 (wages and tips), a Form 1098 (mortgage interest), or a Form 1099 of any variety (which covers most other types of income). Don't believe that just because the notice is coming from the IRS that it's necessarily correct. As an example, here's what happened to one of the authors of this book: A 1099 for $820 was wrongly entered into the IRS's computer as $82,000. Based on that entry, the IRS issued a bill for additional tax, interest, and penalties totaling $50,000. One of our form letters in Chapter 17 corrected the error in a matter of weeks. No one is immune from such errors. Getting a notice from the IRS that you owe $50,000 doesn't exactly make your day, even if you happen to be a tax expert.

Income verification notices ask you to explain differences between the income and deductions you claimed on your return and the income and deductions reported to the IRS by banks, your employer, and brokerage firms. The IRS assumes that the information it collects from these third parties is correct and that you have made a mistake on your return.

Ignore an income verification request, and you'll receive a subsequent notice adjusting your account and billing you for penalties, interest, and additional tax. Often, the IRS doesn't bother sending an income verification notice; it simply assumes that the information about you in its computer is correct and sends **Form CP-2000, Notice of Proposed Adjustment for Underpayment/Overpayment,** which we discuss in "Receiving your typical notice," earlier in this chapter.

One of the quickest ways we know to become separated from your money is to ignore one of these nice little notices. If the notice you receive is wrong or unclear, you need to notify the IRS. To find out how to do this, see Chapter 17.

In 2002, the IRS sent out 1.5 million CP-2000 notices that picked up a cool $2.5 billion from taxpayers who didn't report all their income. If you fail to report all your income, you can expect to receive a CP-2501 or CP-2000 within 12 to 15 months after filing your return.

Request for your tax return — Forms CP-515 and CP-518

Form CP-515, Request for your tax return, and **CP-518, You didn't respond regarding your tax return,** are reserved as the nonfilers' first notice and then final notice of overdue returns. These notices go to approximately 2 million people each year, asking why they didn't file a tax return.

The fact that the IRS expects you to file a return doesn't mean that you are actually required to. See Chapter 4 to verify if your income falls below certain limits, which means you don't need to file a return. Still, if the IRS comes calling, looking for that return, you need to be able to answer.

Here are some of the reasons the IRS may be looking for a return from you when you don't feel you need to file one:

- ✔ The income that the IRS says you didn't report is exempt from tax.

- ✔ The income that the IRS says you failed to report isn't yours. For example, you opened a bank account for your child or for a relative, and you inadvertently gave the bank your own Social Security number.

- ✔ The IRS counted the income twice. Perhaps you reported interest income on a schedule other than the proper one. Or your broker reported your total dividends to the IRS as having been paid by the broker, while you reported those dividends on your return according to the names of the corporations that paid them.

- ✔ You reported income in the wrong year. Maybe someone paid you at the end of the year, but you didn't receive this income until the beginning of the next year — and you reported it in that year.

- ✔ You made a payment to the IRS for which you weren't given credit.

If you think that the IRS's conclusions about your return are wrong, turn to Chapter 17 to find out how to respond to the various types of IRS notices.

Hardship, IRS style

If backup withholding creates a hardship — that is, you need the dough to live on — you can request that it be stopped. IRS regulations state that undue hardship exists in several forms. For example, you're under hardship if backup withholding — when combined with other withholding and estimated tax payments — produces a substantial overpayment of tax. Or perhaps your ability to pay medical expenses might be affected. Maybe you rely upon interest and dividend income to meet basic living expenses, or you live on a modest fixed income. You're also a hardship case if you've filed a bankruptcy petition or if you're an innocent spouse who had no knowledge of your mate's failure to report all income.

See Chapter 18 for more information on the latter topic. Every October 15, the IRS makes a determination on whether backup withholding should be stopped, such as where there is no underreporting of interest and dividends or the underreporting has been corrected. If the IRS decides in your favor, backup withholding stops on January 1 of the following year. The two exceptions to the January 1 rule: If the IRS determines that there was no underreporting or that you would suffer undue hardship, it notifies you and informs the payer either not to start backup withholding or to stop backup withholding within 45 days of its determination.

We are proposing changes to your tax return — CP-2000

This form cuts right to the chase. It assumes the information that the government received regarding your income and that doesn't appear on your return is correct. No questions are asked about whether this information is correct or not. The IRS assumes it's correct, and you're billed for additional tax and interest.

Backup withholding notice

As a trade-off for repeal of the short-lived mandatory withholding on interest and dividends, Congress enacted a system of backup withholding if you fail to furnish a payer of taxable income with your Social Security number. The IRS also notifies the payer that backup withholding should be started if you failed to report interest and dividend income on your tax return.

If the IRS determines that backup withholding is required, the payer is informed to withhold tax at the rate of 28 percent. What type of income most often gets hit for this type of withholding? Interest and dividends, payments of more than $600 per year to independent contractors, sales of stocks and bonds, and annual royalties in excess of $10 are usually targeted.

Backup withholding usually applies only to interest and dividend income. Other payments, however, are subject to withholding if you fail to provide the payer with your Social Security number. The IRS doesn't notify you that you're subject to backup withholding — it instead notifies the payer, who is required by law to notify you.

By notifying your local *Taxpayer Advocate* — the IRS problem-solving official (see Chapter 17) — you can stop backup withholding under certain circumstances:

✔ You didn't underreport your income.

✔ You did underreport — but you paid the tax, interest, and penalties on the unreported income.

✔ The backup withholding will cause you undue hardship, and the underreporting probably won't happen again.

If you get hit with backup withholding, file all your returns for delinquent years, start reporting all your income, or pay what you owe. If you do this, the IRS will automatically stop backup withholding on January 1 if everything is in order by the preceding October 15.

Federal tax lien notice — Form 668 (F)

A statutory lien automatically goes into effect when you neglect or refuse to pay the tax the IRS demands. This type of lien attaches to all property that you own. A statutory lien is sometimes referred to as a secret lien because its validity doesn't depend on its being filed as a matter of public record. Statutory simply means that, under the law, the IRS has the right to do it. They don't have to prove that you failed to pay what you owe before they file a lien. Guilty unless proven innocent?! Yup!

Because a statutory lien places the rights of only the IRS ahead of yours, the IRS will usually file a Notice of Lien so that it places itself first in line before your other creditors. (No cutting in line, please!) A federal tax lien covers all of a taxpayer's property, including real estate, cars, bank accounts, and personal property. These liens are filed in accordance with state law, usually with the county clerk, town hall, or court where the taxpayer lives.

You should be aware that credit agencies routinely pick up liens that have been filed against you. After a credit agency has this information, your credit is marked as lousy. Even if paid, a lien stays on your credit history for seven years. But wait, it gets even better. If you're unable to pay the taxes you owe, the unpaid lien remains on your credit report for up to 15 years!

Although the law requires that the IRS release a lien within 30 days after it has been paid, the IRS doesn't always comply. Upon paying the tax, you can obtain a release of the lien by either contacting the revenue officer who filed the lien or by following the procedure in **Publication 1450, A Certificate of Release of Federal Tax Lien.**

Collection Due Process Hearing

When the IRS files a Notice of Tax Lien or issues a Levy Notice, the law requires it to inform you of your right to a hearing before the IRS's Appeals Office, where you can protest the filing of the lien, the amount of tax the lien or levy is for, request an installment agreement, make an offer in compromise, or request innocent spouse relief. This is called a Collection Due Process Hearing. You'll receive **Form 12153, Request for Collection Due Process Hearing,** along with the lien or levy notice. You have 30 days from the date you receive the notice to make the request. The Taxpayer Bill of Rights (discussed in Chapter 17) tells you what to do when the IRS fails to release a lien. The IRS is liable for damages if it fails to release an erroneous lien or a lien that has been paid.

What you can't do at these hearings is reargue the same issue that you addressed at previous hearing. The law considers such actions a stalling tactic and allows no second chances when you're caught stalling. You can challenge the underlying amount of tax due only if you never received a Statutory Notice of Deficiency (explained in "Receiving a Statutory Notice of Deficiency" later in this chapter) or if you had no prior opportunity to dispute the tax liability.

If your appeal is rejected, you can appeal to the U.S. Tax Court. If, for some reason, the Tax Court lacks jurisdiction, you can appeal to a federal district court.

Property levy notice — Form 668-A (c)

A Notice of Levy is used to seize your property, and that includes your bank and brokerage accounts. You can kiss your money good-bye 30 days after this levy is served. A Notice of Levy usually isn't issued until after the IRS has exhausted all other possible collection procedures, however. The IRS makes an effort to contact you to try to arrange a payment schedule, and it usually sends at least four prior notices. Remember, you filed a tax return indicating where you work, where you bank, and where you have other assets!

Whenever the IRS issues a Levy Notice, you have the right to request a Collection Due Process Hearing. So flip back to that heading. You can't miss it; it's only a few paragraphs back.

You may be interested in knowing that some assets are exempt from levy:

- A taxpayer's principal residence — if the amount of the levy doesn't exceed $5,000. When a levy exceeds this limit, the IRS can't grab a residence unless it has the written consent of a U.S. district court judge. Property used in a taxpayer's business can't be seized unless approved by a district director or an assistant district director (the head IRS official for your district), or if the collection of tax is in jeopardy.

- 85 percent of unemployment benefits.

- Tools and books of a taxpayer's trade, business, or profession up to a value of $3,710. (This amount is for 2006. It's adjusted every year for inflation.)

✔ Schoolbooks. (The IRS doesn't want you to stop studying!)

✔ Court-ordered child-support payments.

✔ Wearing apparel.

✔ $7,430 worth of furniture and personal effects, livestock, and poultry. (This amount is for 2006. It's adjusted every year for inflation.)

✔ Undelivered mail.

✔ 85 percent of worker's compensation and non-means–tested welfare payments.

✔ Military service disability payments.

✔ Certain AFDC (Aid to Families with Dependent Children), Social Security, state and local welfare payments, and Job Training Partnership Act payments.

✔ Certain annuity and pension payments.

✔ A minimum weekly exemption for wages, salaries, and other income (see "Wage levy notice — Form 668-W(c)" later in this chapter).

Wage levy notice — Form 668-W(c)

Form 668-W(c), Notice of Levy on Wages, Salary, and Other Income, is given to your employer (instead of you) and is used to take a portion of your wages to pay your outstanding tax liability. Whereas a Notice of Levy (see the preceding section) attaches only to property held by a third party (such as a bank) at the time the levy is issued, a wage levy is a continuing one — it applies to all wages, salaries, and commissions owed and to future wages, salaries, and commissions.

Continuous levies that apply to what you'll receive in the future not only cover your salary, but they also cover 15 percent of any unemployment, worker's compensation benefits, and non-means–tested welfare payments you are scheduled to receive. The meek won't inherit the world; the IRS will.

But part of every taxpayer's wages is exempt from levy. This exemption is equal to a taxpayer's standard deduction plus the number of personal exemptions he or she is entitled to, divided by a 52-week year. Therefore, in 2006, a married taxpayer entitled to four exemptions (husband, wife, and two children) would be entitled to a weekly exemption of $451.92, computed as follows:

Standard deduction	$10,300
Personal exemptions (4 × $3,300)	$13,200
Total	$23,500
	$23,500 ÷ 52 = $451.92 per week

In 2007, these numbers will be adjusted for inflation, and will probably rise to about $465 for the same family. Don't spend it all in one place. *IRS Publication 1494 (Table for Figuring Amount Exempt From Levy on Wages, Salary, and Other Income)* has the exemption amounts.

A taxpayer claims the amount of the exemption from levy to which he or she is entitled on **Form 668-W(c), Part 6, Statement of Exemptions.** If you don't fill out Part 6 and return it to your employer so it can be sent to the IRS, your employer is required to compute your exemption as married filing separately with one exemption, which works out to only $162.50 a week. (Yikes — better fill out Part 6!) The amount of wages that can be exempted can be increased for the amount of court-ordered child support payments.

If your employer fails to furnish you with **Form 668-W(c), Part 6, Statement of Exemptions,** send a letter to the IRS revenue officer in charge of your case, giving that person all the relevant information. Make sure to include your name, address, Social Security number, your marital status, and all the exemptions to which you're entitled. Don't forget to include the names and Social Security numbers of your spouse and your child, and the amount of any court-ordered child-support payments you're required to make.

If, by levying your wages, the IRS pushes you below the poverty level, or you wind up not being able to meet your basic living expenses, see Chapter 18 to free yourself from this forced slavery.

Handling Nonassessment Notices

The IRS usually issues a nonassessment notice to inform you of one of the following situations:

- ✓ You forgot to sign a return.
- ✓ You failed to attach a W-2.
- ✓ You omitted a form or schedule.
- ✓ You didn't indicate filing status.

If you receive a nonassessment notice, simply write across it in bold lettering: "INFORMATION REQUESTED IS ATTACHED." Then attach the requested information to the notice and return it to the IRS in the envelope provided. After you provide the IRS with the requested information, the matter usually is closed — unless the information you submit conflicts with information previously reported on your return. If this situation occurs, the IRS will send a notice that assesses additional tax, interest, and possibly a penalty, or that instructs you to contact a particular person at the IRS.

A notice correcting a refund due to you (usually made on Form CP-49) shouldn't be viewed as a nonassessment notice. Just because a notice doesn't demand that you write a check, don't think that the IRS isn't billing you for something. Quite often, the IRS reduces a refund when it assesses additional tax or penalties.

Paying interest on additional tax

The IRS must send a notice of additional tax due within 18 months of the date when you file your return. If it doesn't send a notice before the 18 months are up, it can't charge interest after this 18-month period. Nor can the IRS resume charging interest until 21 days after it gets around to sending a notice.

This provision doesn't cover all notices, so here's what you should know about this 18-month rule:

- ✓ Your return had to be filed on time — otherwise, you're not entitled to this suspension of interest.
- ✓ The failure to file or to pay penalties isn't covered by this rule.
- ✓ Additional tax due as the result of an audit isn't covered.

So what is covered? Suppose that you forgot to report $1,000 of income on your 2006 return that you filed October 15, 2007 (assuming that you obtained a six-month extension), and the IRS didn't send a notice until November 1, 2009. You owe interest from April 16, 2007 (filing an extension doesn't stop the running of interest from the original due date) through April 15, 2009 (18 months from October 15, 2007). However, interest is suspended from April 15, 2009, through November 21, 2009 (21 days from the November 1, 2009, notice date).

Receiving a delinquent tax return notice

You should treat a delinquent tax return notice as seriously as it sounds. If your tax return is delinquent, you may be contacted by mail, by telephone, or in person. Remember that the IRS has the right to issue a summons commanding you to appear with your tax records and explain why you didn't file a tax return. Any taxpayer who receives a delinquent return notice should consider seeking the services of a qualified tax advisor (see Chapter 2).

Failure to file a required tax return or returns is a criminal violation of the Internal Revenue Code and can result in time in the big house. Usually, the IRS isn't terribly interested in prosecuting the small potatoes who don't owe a huge amount of tax, and save their prosecutorial dollars for the big spuds who owe the farm. These cases make big headlines, serving as morality tales for everyone else who wonders what would happen if, just once, they "forgot" to file. Extra! Extra! Read all about it!

If you file late returns — even in response to an IRS inquiry — and don't owe a substantial amount of tax (what's considered substantial is known only to the IRS), the IRS probably will accept the return and assess a penalty for late payment and possibly fraud instead of trying to send you to prison (although they do have that option).

If you don't reply to a delinquent return notice, the IRS can take one of the following steps:

✔ Refer the case to its Criminal Investigation Unit.

✔ Issue a summons to appear.

✔ Refer you to the Audit Division.

✔ Prepare a "substitute" return.

If the IRS decides to prepare a *substitute return* for you, it will use the information that it has on you in its master file, using the married-filing-separately or filing as single tax table, the standard deduction, and one exemption. Having the IRS prepare your return is the quickest way we know to become separated from your money. Although no fee is involved, you're likely to pay unnecessary tax. Remember, the IRS isn't interested in saving you money.

Why not beat the IRS to the punch? The IRS has an official policy of usually not prosecuting anyone who files a return prior to being contacted and makes arrangements to pay what is owed. Penalties and interest, however, will be assessed. This procedure is called a *voluntary disclosure*. The IRS wants customers back in the fold so badly that it lists voluntary disclosures in a prominent location on its Web site.

What You Must Know about Audits

On a list of real-life nightmares, most people would rank tax audits right up there with having a tooth pulled without Novocain. The primary trauma of an audit is that it makes many people feel like they're on trial and are being accused of a crime. Don't panic.

You may be audited for many reasons, and not necessarily because the IRS thinks you're a crook. You may receive that audit notice because some of the information on your return doesn't match up with information from third parties, because an IRS data entry operator added (or subtracted) a zero off a number on your return, or because your return deviates from average returns in your neighborhood or your income range. Finally, some returns are plucked at random, and searching for a reason will just make you crazy! About 15 percent of audited returns are left unchanged by the audit — that is, the taxpayers don't end up owing more money. In fact, if you're the lucky sort, you may be one of the rare individuals who actually gets a refund because the audit finds a mistake in your favor! Unfortunately, it's more likely that you'll be one of the roughly 85 percent of audit survivors who end up owing more tax money, plus interest. How much hinges on how your audit goes.

Most people would agree that not knowing what to expect in a situation is what's most terrifying about it. This is even truer when dealing with the IRS. Here's what you need to know about audits:

- ✔ **You needn't attend your audit.** An EA, CPA, or attorney can go in your place.

- ✔ **If at any time during the audit you feel hopelessly confused or realize that you're in over your head, you can ask that the audit or interview be suspended until you can speak to a tax pro.** When you make this request, the IRS must stop asking questions and adjourn the meeting so you can seek help and advice.

- ✔ **The burden of proof is on you.** You're considered to be guilty until proven innocent. Unfortunately, that's how our tax system operates. However, if you and the IRS end up in court, the burden of proof switches to the IRS, provided you meet the IRS's substantiation and recordkeeping requirements and present credible evidence. What all this means is that you can't just sit in court and say, "Prove it" to the IRS.

- ✔ **Unless a routine examination reveals the likelihood of unreported income, the IRS can't conduct a financial status audit by demanding that you fill out Form 4822, Statement of Annual Estimated Personal and Family Expenses, so the IRS can determine how you lived on the income reported on your return.**

- ✔ **Although it's true that fewer people are being audited than in the past, that's only part of the story.** The IRS's computers constantly compare the information received from employers, banks, and brokers with the information reported on people's returns. Because of these constant comparisons, millions of taxpayers each year are sent bills totaling billions of dollars.

- ✔ **Through a major shift of its audit priorities, the IRS is now targeting high-income earners, self-employed taxpayers, small businesses, and workers who receive tip income because it believes that these groups possess the greatest ability to not report all their income.** Low-income taxpayers haven't escaped the wrath of the IRS, though. The IRS continues to crack down on perceived Earned Income Tax Credit (EIC) abuse, so returns with Schedule EIC often receive extra scrutiny.

Surviving the Four Types of Audits

Thankfully, only four types of audits exist: office audits, field audits, correspondence audits, and random statistical audits, more commonly referred to as the audits from hell. With all four types of audits, maintaining good records is the key to survival. (Chapter 3 tells you what to do if you're audited and can't produce the needed evidence. If you haven't already taken out the trash and lost all your evidence, you can also refer to Chapter 3 for help filing and organizing the documents you may need.)

Office audits

An office audit takes place at an IRS office. The IRS informs a taxpayer that it is scheduling an office audit by sending **Notice 904.** The front of this notice lists the date, time, and place of the audit, and the back lists the items that the IRS wants to examine.

The audit date isn't chiseled in granite. If you can't gather the information necessary to substantiate the items the IRS is questioning, you can request a postponement. As a general rule, the IRS grants only two postponements unless you can demonstrate a compelling reason for an additional delay, such as an illness or the unavailability of certain tax records.

If you need more time but can't get an additional postponement, go to the audit with the records you have, put on your most confident face, and calmly inform the tax examiner that you need more time to secure the documents you need so that you can substantiate the remaining items the IRS is questioning. The tax examiner then prepares a list of the additional items the IRS needs to complete the audit, together with a mailing envelope so you can mail copies of the requested documents to the IRS.

Never, ever, mail originals. If the additional documents don't lend themselves to easy explanation through correspondence, then schedule a second appointment to complete the audit.

Most office audits are concerned with employee business expenses, itemized deductions such as medical expenses, charitable contributions, tax and interest expense deductions, miscellaneous itemized deductions, deductions for personal exemptions, and moving-expense deductions. Lately, the IRS has expanded office audits to include small-business returns, income from rental property, and income from tips and capital gains.

If the IRS is trying to verify your income, it may want to know about your lifestyle. How will the IRS find out about your lifestyle? You'll tell them, that's how. Auditors are trained to control the interview. They feign ignorance, use appropriate small talk, use "silence" and "humor" appropriately, and avoid overtly taking notes so as not to distract the taxpayer, and they pay attention to the taxpayer's nonverbal language. The IRS even has a form to flush out lifestyle information, **Form 4822, Statement of Annual Estimated Personal and Family Expenses,** which — thank heaven — the IRS can now only spring on you when a routine examination has established the likelihood of unreported income. The form asks all about your expenses, from groceries to insurance — anything you and your family would spend money for as consumers. We don't know what it is about this form, but when the IRS shoves it under someone's nose, many taxpayers can't resist the urge to respond, "I'll show them what it costs to live in this country." What most people are unaware of is that you're under no obligation to fill out this form. The law only requires you to fill out and file a tax return. Statistical research has revealed that the IRS can collect more tax by examining sources of income than by examining deductions. If you operate a small business or have rental income, be prepared to explain where every deposit into your bank account came from.

Field audits

Field audits are conducted at a taxpayer's place of business. These audits focus on business returns and complex individual returns. If you file Form 1040, Schedule C, you're a likely candidate for a field audit.

Again, be prepared to verify the source of every deposit into your bank account. Field agents are required to survey both your preceding and subsequent years' tax returns to determine whether similar items were treated in a consistent manner. If an audit results in a significant increase in tax, you are now suspect, and the tax examiner will audit your subsequent years' tax returns (which normally are only surveyed).

An office audit specifies what items will be examined from the very beginning of the process. Not so with a field audit — tax examiners have a great deal of discretion as to what items they review and to what depth they review the items. Count on having to verify your total income, travel and entertainment expenses, gifts, automobile expenses, commissions, payments to independent contractors, and any expenses that appear large in relation to the size of your business.

Deciding where your audit happens

Both field and office audits are conducted in the district where a return was filed. This practice may create a burden if you live in one district and are employed or have your business located in another. For example, if you work or your business is located in Manhattan and you live in Connecticut, you normally would be contacted by the examination branch in Connecticut. If your tax records are in Manhattan or you spend most of your time there, you can request that the examination be transferred to the Manhattan District.

Besides gaining the convenience of having the audit conducted where your records, your advisor, or your business is located, you also get a little more time to pull together your tax data.

To transfer an audit from one district to another, call the IRS auditor and tell him or her why you want to transfer the audit to a different district. The transfer usually takes two to three months. The IRS also requires that you request the transfer in writing.

The following note will suffice when requesting that a tax examination be transferred from one IRS district to another:

[your address]

[date]

District Director

[address of district that issued exam notice]

Re: [your name and your Social Security number]

[exam year]

Dear District Director:

Because my tax records are located in [for example, Manhattan] and I spend most of my time there, I respectfully request that the audit you have scheduled be transferred to the [for example, Manhattan] District.

You may contact me during business hours at [telephone number]. Thank you in advance for your prompt attention to this request.

Very truly yours,

[your name]

Enclosed: Copy of exam notice

A tax examiner may examine each and every deduction or merely select a month or two of expenses and examine them on a sample basis. If they don't turn up any discrepancies, the examiner will accept the rest of the expenses for that category as correct.

Correspondence audits

Correspondence audits are exactly what the name suggests. The IRS conducts correspondence audits completely by mail and limits them to a few key areas of individual returns, such as itemized deductions, casualty or theft losses, employee business expenses, IRA and Keogh plan payments, dependency exemptions, childcare and earned income credits, deductions for forfeited interest on early withdrawals from savings accounts, and exclusion from income of disability payments. Income items may also be examined by a correspondence audit.

If you're ever the proud subject of a correspondence audit, the IRS gives you a return envelope in which to submit your documents, canceled checks, bills, and statements to substantiate the items the IRS questions. Again, never send original documents — only copies. Retaining the originals is crucial in case you have to stare down further inquiries, or if the IRS does the unthinkable and loses your documentation.

When it comes to substantiating any deduction, the burden of proof is on you. If what you must substantiate is complex or requires a detailed explanation, you can ask for an interview in which you can explain in person.

Random statistical audits

Although it is extremely unlikely, your return may be selected for an audit under the National Research Program. The IRS conducts these audits to gather statistical information that can be used to determine pockets of tax cheating. The IRS, however, never uses that word. It refers to failing to report income or inflating deductions as "noncompliance."

Under its research program, the IRS annually selects certain types of taxpayers' returns (waiters, taxi drivers, freelance writers, and so on) so it can measure the degree of tax compliance for particular industries, trades, or professions. On the basis of these audits, the IRS National Office determines which areas require stricter or greater enforcement efforts. Although being on the receiving end of one of these audit notices is never fun, in this environment of large federal budget deficits, the IRS is unlikely to suspend this current project.

Under the National Research Program, the IRS may audit your return in the following ways: computer checking, correspondence, and face-to-face. Everything is subject to verification, but in most cases, only certain lines will be checked. Be prepared, though, to provide your children's birth certificates to prove you're entitled to claim your kids as dependents. If something smells fishy or doesn't look right, you can count on being questioned in detail about the matter. The IRS looks under every rock, including matching up cash settlements you may have received in a personal injury lawsuit, for example.

Questioning Repetitive Audits

It is IRS policy not to examine an individual's tax return if the taxpayer has been examined for the same issue(s) in either of the two preceding years and the audit resulted in no (or only a small) tax change.

If you receive a notice of an audit questioning the same item(s) questioned in a previous audit, call the agent and inform him or her that the IRS audited the same issue(s) in one of the two prior years with little or no change in tax. (And do note that the IRS has never bothered to define *little*. Changes of less than a few hundred dollars in tax, however, should meet this criterion.) The tax examiner will ask you to furnish proof. Mail the examiner a copy of the IRS notice that your prior return was accepted without change, or mail the notice that adjusted your return.

If you can't document that the IRS is questioning items that it *already* questioned — with no change in tax — in one of the two preceding years, the lack of documentation doesn't mean that you can't get the current examination canceled. Just inform the examining agent by telephone about the prior year's tax examination. The tax examiner will postpone the audit and request a Record of your Tax Account Information from the two preceding years. If your tax account supports your contention, the IRS will cancel the audit.

Getting Ready for an Audit

Preparing for an audit is sort of like preparing for a test in school: The IRS informs you of which sections of your tax return the agency wants to examine so that you know what to "study." The first decision you face when you get an audit notice is whether to handle it yourself or to turn to a tax advisor to represent you. Hiring representation costs money but saves you time, stress, and possibly money.

Who can represent you in an audit?

The IRS permits three types of individuals to fully represent taxpayers before the IRS: enrolled agents, certified public accountants, and attorneys. All three are bound by IRS rules of practice. (Tax preparers can represent you at an audit but not in any appeals beyond that.)

Enrolled agents (EAs) become enrolled to practice before the IRS by passing a two-day written examination administered by the IRS in which their knowledge of the tax code is tested. Alternatively, they must have at least five years of experience as an IRS tax auditor. Attorneys and certified public accountants are the other two groups permitted to

represent taxpayers before the IRS. Many states have continuing education requirements for CPAs and attorneys. The IRS requires that EAs also meet continuing education requirements.

Probably the best way to find a qualified tax professional is to ask a relative or friend for a recommendation of someone whose level of service and performance they are more than satisfied with. To figure out which of these tax practitioners may be best suited to help you in an audit, be sure to read Chapter 2.

If you normally prepare your own return and are comfortable with your understanding of the areas being audited, represent yourself. If the IRS is merely asking you to substantiate deductions, you'll probably do all right on your own. However, make sure you read "What You Should Know about Audits," earlier in this chapter.

What constitutes substantiation may at times involve a somewhat complicated interpretation of the law and its accompanying regulations. If the amount of tax money in question is small compared to the fee you'd pay a tax advisor to represent you, self-representation is probably the answer. However, if you're likely to turn into a babbling, intimidated fool and are unsure of how to present your situation, hire a tax advisor to represent you.

Changing your mind regarding representation part way through the audit is okay. At any time during the examination — such as when you feel a dizzy sensation, and before you throw up in the examiner's lap — the Taxpayer Bill of Rights allows you to request that the audit be suspended until you have time to consult with either an enrolled agent, a certified public accountant, or an attorney. After you make this request, the IRS agent must stop asking questions or requesting documents until you are properly represented.

But if you do decide to handle the audit yourself, get your act together sooner rather than later. Don't wait until the night before to start gathering receipts and other documentation. You may discover, for example, that you can't find certain documents.

You need to document and be ready to speak with the auditor about the areas the audit notice said were being investigated. Organize the various documents and receipts in folders. You want to make it as easy as possible for the auditor to review your materials. Don't show up, dump shopping bags full of receipts and paperwork on the auditor's desk, and say, "Here it is — *you* figure it out."

Don't bring documentation for parts of your return that aren't being audited, either. Besides creating more work for yourself, you're required to discuss only those areas mentioned in the audit letter.

Whatever you do, don't ignore your *audit request letter.* The Internal Revenue Service is the ultimate bill-collection agency. And if you end up owing more money (the unhappy result of most audits), the sooner you pay, the less interest and penalties you'll owe.

Winning Your Audit

Two people with identical situations can walk into an audit and come out with very different results. The loser can end up owing much more in taxes and having the audit expanded to include other parts of the return. The winner can end up owing less tax money.

Here's how to be a winner:

- ✔ **Treat the auditor as a human being.** Although this seems like obvious advice, your anger and resentment at being audited won't win you any points with your examiner. The examiner is just doing his or her job and knows you are busy and have other things to do. Ranting and raving in front of the auditor is likely to make him or her search extra hard for places where your return may be dicey. Treating the examiner with respect and courtesy will make the audit a much easier experience for everyone concerned.

- ✔ **Stick to the knitting.** You're there to discuss only the sections of your tax return in question. Don't volunteer other information unless you want the examiner to look at those areas as well.

- ✔ **Discuss and don't argue.** State your case. If the auditor wants to disallow a deduction or otherwise increase the tax you owe and you don't agree, state only once why you don't agree. If the auditor won't budge, don't get into a knockdown, drag-out confrontation. He or she may not want to lose face and will only feel inclined to find additional tax money — that's the auditor's job. Remember that you can plead your case with several layers of people above your auditor. If that course fails and you still feel wronged, you can take your case to Tax Court.

- ✔ **Don't be intimidated.** Just because IRS auditors have the authority of the government behind them, that doesn't make them right or all-knowing. The audit is only round one. If you disagree with the results, you have the right to appeal.

- ✔ **Appeal the results of an audit, if necessary.** If you're dissatisfied with the results of an audit, refer to "Appealing the results of an audit" later in this chapter to figure out how to make an appeal.

- ✔ **Go to Tax Court.** If you receive a Statutory Notice of Deficiency (this notice comes after you have exhausted all your appeals within the IRS or if you don't respond to a notice that the IRS wants to audit your return), you have 90 days to appeal your case to the U.S. Tax Court. If you don't appeal, the IRS can enforce collection on the 91st day. Refer to "Receiving a Statutory Notice of Deficiency" at the end of this chapter for more information.

Understanding the Statute of Limitations on Audits

The IRS must make any assessment of tax, penalties, or interest within three years from the due date for filing a tax return. If the IRS grants you an extension of the filing deadline, the statute of limitations is extended to include the extension period. If the due date falls on a legal holiday or a Saturday or Sunday, the due date is postponed to the next business day.

Here's how the statute of limitations works: The IRS must make an assessment regarding a 2006 tax return by April 16, 2010, three years from the April 16, 2007, due date. After the 2010 deadline, the IRS can make no demand for additional tax. If a return is filed after the due date, the three-year period starts on the date the return is filed. However, if you file your return on or before April 16, 2007, the three-year statute of limitations still expires on April 16, 2010.

Your state tax return and the IRS

The IRS and 48 states have an agreement calling for the exchange of information about taxpayers. Only Nevada and Texas haven't signed on. Under these agreements, individual states and the IRS notify each other about tax-payers who failed to file returns and when either a state or the IRS has adjusted a taxpayer's taxable income.

The tax laws of most states provide that if the IRS has adjusted your tax return, you must file an amended state income tax return with that state within 30 to 90 days of the IRS's adjustment. The amended state return must reflect the adjustments made by the IRS, and you must pay any additional tax plus interest. If an amended return isn't filed, your state's tax collector, upon receiving notice of the adjustments from the IRS, will send a demand for additional tax and interest, and possibly a penalty for not notifying the state within the required time frame.

If more than 25 percent of the income that you're required to report is omitted from your return, the statute of limitations extends to six years. No statute of limitations runs on a false or fraudulent return. Thus, if a false or fraudulent return was filed, there's no time limit on when the government can assess additional tax. The same goes for not filing a return; there's no time limit.

Extending the statute of limitations

If the statute of limitations is about to expire and you haven't resolved your problems with the IRS, you'll be asked to agree to extend the statute of limitations. If you don't agree, the IRS will immediately assess your tax based on the information it has.

The only way to stop the IRS from forcing you to pay the tax is to file a petition with the Tax Court within a 90-day period. Although IRS Publication 1035 *(Extending the Tax Assessment Period)* explains this process, our advice is to see a professional if you ever get into water this hot.

The statute of limitations on tax collection is . . .

Ten years — period. After ten years, the IRS can't collect a dime. The ten-year assessment period starts on the day the IRS receives your return or on April 15, whichever is later. For purposes of the statute of limitations, returns filed early are considered filed on April 15. However, if the government increases your tax or makes an adjustment, the ten years on the additional tax owed starts to run from the date of the additional assessment. The reason the IRS still can go after financier Marc Rich (the second most famous tax evader after Al Capone) after all these years for the hundreds of millions he owes is because the 10-year statute of limitations is suspended when a taxpayer (if you can call him that) is continuously out of the country for more than six months.

If the ten-year period is about to expire, the IRS usually attempts to extend the period by getting you to sign **Form 900, Tax Collection Waiver.** More often than not, the IRS will threaten to seize everything under the sun that you own unless you agree to sign. Here's when you absolutely need professional help — and not just any tax advisor, but someone who is an expert and specializes in these types of cases. Ask people that you trust for suggestions of people to contact.

Since January 1, 2000, the IRS is allowed an extension of the 10-year statute of limitations on collection only where it has issued a levy, entered into an installment, or instituted court action. Such suits, however, are rare.

If you have an installment agreement in force, the ten-year period isn't automatically extended until you pay off what you owe. The terms of the agreement at the time you and the IRS entered into it govern how long the government has to collect what you owe. If the agreement is silent as to the collection statute, it's 10 years. So be careful what you sign when you request an installment agreement.

Appealing the results of an audit

The IRS issues **Form 4549-A, Income Tax Examination Changes,** and **Form 1902-B, Report of Individual Tax Examination Changes,** after an audit has been completed. Form 4549-A spells out any adjustments to income and expenses that have been made and any penalties and interest that are due.

These notices often are referred to as *30-day letters*. Within 30 days after receipt of an audit notice, you must agree to the adjustment, submit additional information explaining why an adjustment shouldn't be made, or request a hearing before the Appeals Division.

If you disagree with the proposed adjustment, and the amount of tax is more than $25,000, a written protest must be filed. IRS Publication 5 *(Your Appeal Rights and How To Prepare a Protest If You Don't Agree)* is extremely helpful in preparing a protest. Consider retaining a tax advisor when protesting large sums. This written protest is akin to a legal brief lawyers submit in outlining a case.

Appeals, you guessed it, are made to the Appeals Office, whose purpose is to settle disputes. The IRS agent who examined your return has no authority to take into account the time and expense to the IRS and the possibility that the IRS may lose in court. An appeals officer can. Approximately 90 percent of all cases referred to the Appeals Office are settled.

If the amount involved isn't more than $25,000, a formal written protest isn't required. A simple statement explaining the changes you don't agree with and why you feel your deduction should be allowed is all that is necessary.

The IRS also issues a 30-day letter if you fail to show up for an audit. In such an instance, the examining agent will review your return and make adjustments to both income and deductions that he or she deems warranted.

If you receive a 30-day letter because you failed to show — even if you missed the audit because you never received the original notice scheduling it — contact the agent at the number given on the letter and schedule an audit appointment. If you make a new appointment within 30 days, the examining agent or appointment clerk will place a hold on your adjusted return (that is, it won't be processed), pending the outcome of the rescheduled audit.

After completing the audit, the IRS issues a new notice of income tax changes that supersedes the preceding one. If you agree to the audit changes and sign off on them, you can pay what you owe at that time, or you can wait to be billed.

Receiving a Statutory Notice of Deficiency

Although a notice (such as one proposing income tax changes) informs a taxpayer that additional tax is due, the IRS can't legally enforce the collection of additional tax until a Statutory Notice of Deficiency — often referred to as a *90-day letter* — is sent to a taxpayer by certified mail at the taxpayer's last known address.

A Statutory Notice of Deficiency isn't required if additional tax is due because of a math error. Statutory Notices are generally required only if additional tax is due as the result of the IRS adjusting a taxpayer's income, deductions, or credits from what was originally reported on the tax return the taxpayer filed. Unless a petition is filed with the U.S. Tax Court in Washington within 90 days of receipt of a Statutory Notice, the IRS can initiate collection action at the end of the 90-day period. If you file a petition with the Tax Court, all collection action is delayed until 60 days after the court renders its decision. If you live outside the United States, the 90-day period for filing a petition is extended to 150 days. The address of the Tax Court is included on the notice, but we give it to you here anyway, just in case:

400 Second Street, N.W.

Washington, DC 20217

The notice will indicate when the 90-day period expires. If your petition gets lost in the mail or arrives late, you're out of luck. However, a certified mail, FedEx, DHL, Airborne, or UPS receipt showing that the petition was sent to the Tax Court within the 90-day period will save the day.

Chapter 17

Fixing Mistakes the IRS Makes

In This Chapter
▶ Demystifying IRS mistakes
▶ Responding to notices
▶ Mastering the generic response form
▶ Dealing with a non-responsive IRS
▶ Finding a lost refund

*W*e know you may probably be surprised to hear, but on rare occasion, the IRS goofs. And when the IRS does goof, you may feel as though the sky has fallen in. You may not be able to control the IRS, but you can control how you respond when the IRS makes a mistake. You can choose to scream, shout, run around in circles, clutch at your heart, or tear your hair out by the roots when that notice appears in your mailbox. Or, you can sit back calmly, take a careful look at what's in that letter, and then determine if it's reasonable or in error.

Face it, most tax problems arrive uninvited, unannounced, and unexpected. Unfortunately, most people don't have a clue how to legally, swiftly, and inexpensively get Uncle Sam off their backs. Stay tuned as we explain how to fix a variety of problems caused by the IRS — without breaking a sweat or having a heart attack. (Did you know taxes continue even after you're dead?)

Although the IRS is reluctant to admit it, it does make mistakes. In fairness to the IRS, collecting taxes from more than 130 million individuals (not to mention all the returns from corporations, partnerships, trusts, estates, and other assorted entities) under an extraordinarily complex tax system is, to say the least, difficult. The number of errors can appear to be limitless, but most errors occur for simple reasons.

Pointing the Finger: Common IRS Flubs

We wish that we could explain why the IRS can't get it right the first time. We can't. But we can give you an idea of the number of mistakes made, the types of mistakes, and the action that you can take. We also can — and do! — offer tips to keep you away from the IRS paper trail.

The IRS processes more than a billion transactions a year. So, math wizard, what does an error rate of, say, 1 percent translate into? Ten million errors! That's a whole bunch of errors. The following is a long list of the types of flubs the IRS can make:

- **Misapplied payments:** The IRS may not have posted tax payments that you made to your tax account (under your Social Security number). Payments are sometimes posted to the wrong year or type of tax. Perhaps the IRS didn't properly post over-payments from a preceding or subsequent year.

- **Misunderstood date:** The IRS may claim that you didn't file or pay tax on time. Computers at a service center may not acknowledge that the due date for filing or paying fell on a legal holiday or on a Saturday or Sunday and may therefore blame you for filing late, when in fact you filed on the first business day following a legal holiday or a Saturday or Sunday. Or perhaps you had a valid extension of time to file, but the IRS said that you filed your tax return late.

- **Wrong Social Security/ID number:** A data processing clerk may incorrectly input your Social Security number, or you may have been assigned two numbers. Because all data on a joint return is recorded under the Social Security number of the spouse whose name is listed first, any payments or credits that the other spouse made may not be posted under the first spouse's number. This situation frequently occurs when taxpayers file jointly for the first time or when a taxpayer files separately after having filed jointly in a prior year.

- **Wrong income:** Income earned by another person may be inadvertently reported under your Social Security number. This often happens when a taxpayer opens a bank account for a child or another relative.

- **Exempt income:** Money you earned on your IRA, Keogh, pension account, or from municipal bond investments was reported to the IRS as being taxable.

- **Double-counted income:** Income earned from a taxpayer's business or profession may be recorded as income from wages — or vice versa — and the IRS moved the income to the line or schedule on the taxpayer's return where it correctly belongs. That's okay, but sometimes the IRS moves the income without removing it from the line or schedule where it first was incorrectly entered!

- **Lost return:** The IRS or the U.S. Postal Service may have lost your return and payment, leaving you in the unenviable position of having to prove the timely filing of the return. Hope you made a copy and sent the original by an approved method, either Certified Mail from the post office, or an approved private delivery service (Airborne, DHL, FedEx, and UPS)!

- **Partially corrected error:** The IRS may have corrected only one of the errors that was previously made. For example, an IRS error may be corrected, but the penalties and interest that were incorrectly charged were not removed.

- **Data processing error:** A computer bug — or another unexplained phenomenon — may have caused a notice to be issued stating that a math error on your return was made where no error exists. Or someone may have failed to input all the data from the schedules attached to your return into the IRS computer.

Data processing errors are common with Form 2210, Underpayment of Estimated Tax by Individuals, Estates, and Trusts, where a taxpayer claims an exemption from the penalty for underestimating the amount of his or her required estimated tax payments. This type of error usually causes the IRS either to assess a penalty when it shouldn't or to issue a refund for the underestimating penalty that the taxpayer has paid.

✔ **Incorrect 1099:** The IRS may receive an incorrect Form 1099 from a bank or brokerage firm — either the amount of income reported on the form is wrong or the income isn't yours. Even if the payer corrects it (and files the correction with the IRS), the correction may never make it into the IRS computer. Don't you just hate it when that happens?

Fixing IRS Mistakes: Just the Facts, Ma'am

There is elegance in simplicity when corresponding with the IRS. Keep to the point. No letter should be longer than one page. A half page gets even quicker results. Remember, the tax examiner reviewing your inquiry could have little experience in the area you're writing about. Such people are, however, extremely conscientious in performing their duties. You stand a better chance of achieving the results you want by making their jobs as easy as possible. Don't succumb to the temptation to go into a narrative on how unfair our tax system is or how you are paying more than your fair share. Save that stuff for your representative in Congress.

Your letter to the IRS should contain the following items — and nothing more:

✔ Vital facts: name, mailing address, Social Security number on the tax return, and the year of the disputed tax return.

✔ The control number from the notice, type of tax, and a copy of the notice you received — refer to Chapter 16 to find out how to get your hands on this information.

✔ The type of mistake the IRS made.

✔ The action you want the IRS to take.

✔ Copies of the documents necessary to prove your case — canceled checks, corrected Form 1099s, mailing receipts — but never send the originals.

Address your letter to the Adjustments/Correspondence (A/C) Branch at the service center that issued the notice. You should note the type of request you are making at the extreme top of the letter — REQUEST TO ADJUST FORM [form number]. Use the bar-coded envelope that was sent with the notice to mail your letter.

Include a simple thank you and the telephone number where you can be reached in case the clerk at the IRS Service Center has any questions. Telephone contact between you and an IRS employee can take weeks off the Adjustments/Correspondence process. See Figure 17-1 for an example of a generic Dear John, er, we mean Dear IRS, letter. This example addresses an adjustment to be made to Form CP-2000.

Upon receipt of your letter, the A/C Branch is supposed to stop the computer from sending further notices until the matter is resolved, although you'll likely receive the next notice that was already in the pipeline. If your problem can't be resolved in seven days, you will be sent a letter indicating when it can be resolved. If you receive a second notice, don't be alarmed. This delay isn't unusual. The IRS doesn't move all that fast.

If 30 days go by and you haven't heard from the IRS or you receive a third notice, see the section "Getting Attention When the IRS Ignores You," later in this chapter.

Request to Adjust Form CP-2000

[your address]
[date]

Adjustments/Correspondence Branch
Internal Revenue Service Center
[address]

Re: [your name, Social Security
number]
[tax year, DLN]

Dear IRS:

I have received your notice dated [date], in which you claim that I failed to report [$] of interest on my tax return.

Please be advised that your notice, a copy of which is enclosed, is incorrect. The interest that you claimed I earned was in fact earned on my daughter's bank account. Her Social Security number is [number], which should have been given to the bank, instead of mine, when the account was opened.

Please adjust your notice to reflect that no additional tax is due. Thank you for your prompt attention to this request. I can be reached at [phone number] should you require any additional information.

Very truly yours,
[your name]

Figure 17-1:
Here's how to compose a Dear IRS letter that gets right to the point.

Sending a Simple Response to a Balance Due Notice

If you receive a balance due notice for a tax that already has been paid, simply mark the front of the notice:

"This balance has been paid. Enclosed is a copy, front and back, of my canceled check that you failed to give me credit for having paid. Please remove all penalties and interest charges that were assessed."

You can obtain the information that the IRS requires to properly credit your payment from the back of your canceled check. On the back of the check, you'll notice the date, the location of the IRS service center, where it was endorsed, and the serial number stamped on it. See Chapter 16 to find out what these numbers relate to.

If any of this information isn't legible or you can't readily cull it from the back of the check, simply photocopy the check (front and back) and send the photocopy — along with the notice — in the envelope provided. Write across the notice:

"This has been paid — copy of check enclosed."

Sending Generic Responses to Generic Notices

If you're like us, you probably dislike form letters with a passion. At times, however, you have no choice but to fight fire with fire. To simplify things, we have included an all-purpose generic response letter (see Figure 17-2).

Generic Response Letter
Request to adjust Form [number]
[your address]
[date]

Adjustments/Correspondence Branch
Internal Revenue Service Center
[address]

Re: [your name, Social Security
number]
[tax year, DLN, Form number]

Dear IRS:

I am in receipt of your notice dated [date] (copy enclosed). Please be advised that your notice is incorrect.

[Insert generic paragraph(s) we have provided pertaining to one of the issues to be corrected.]

I would appreciate your adjusting the notice that you sent me now that you have the information contained in this letter that was previously unknown to you.

I would also appreciate your abating any penalties and interest that were incorrectly assessed.

I thank you in advance for your prompt attention to this request. I can be reached at [number] should you have any questions.

Very truly yours,
[your name]

Enclosed: Notice [number]

Figure 17-2:
You can get down and dirty with the IRS folks by using this battle-proven generic letter. Just insert the correct generic paragraph from the section where indicated.

You can use this letter simply by inserting any one of the following responses to frequent IRS errors. To keep it simple, we list the IRS error you want to address as the heading, and the response you can use appears right below it in a different typeface between quotation marks. We also include some explanatory text without quotes.

Misapplied payments

"Enclosed is a copy of my canceled check, front and back, showing that the tax was paid."

Misunderstood due date

Here are several solutions to common problems with due dates.

Due date for filing or paying fell on Saturday, Sunday, or legal holiday

"Please be advised that your notice incorrectly penalizes me for filing/paying late. The due date for filing/paying fell on a [Saturday], and I made payment/filed on the next business day. Enclosed is a copy of my check dated [date], which is dated the date of the extended due date, as allowed by law. The serial number on the back of the check clearly indicates that the IRS negotiated my check on [date].

"Please correct your records to reflect that my return/payment was timely and remove all penalties and interest that were charged."

If the return in question is for a year prior to 2004 and you don't have a mailing receipt, you may have to request a copy of the envelope in which you mailed your return from the service center before requesting an adjustment. Your mailing envelope becomes a permanent part of your return.

Beginning with the 2004 tax year, if the IRS says it hasn't received your return, you're required to show that you did, indeed, file it on time. If you mailed it, make sure to keep track of your Certified Mail or other receipt that clearly shows the date you sent it. You can't say that you put it in the mail by the due date, but that the letter carrier failed to pick it up. This argument no longer works. If you can't prove otherwise, you're on the hook for late filing penalties and interest if the IRS says you filed late. Check out Chapter 4 for the best way to file paper returns.

Valid extension of time to file

"Your notice incorrectly assesses a penalty for late filing. Enclosed is a copy of my extension that granted me an extension of time to file until [date]. I filed my return prior to the expiration of the extension on [date].

"Please correct your records by removing the penalties and interest that were incorrectly assessed."

Enclose a copy of any canceled check that may have accompanied the extension and refer to the check in the letter. If you have it, also enclose a copy of your Certified Mail or private delivery service receipt, clearly showing the postmark or other date it was mailed.

Late filing

If you mailed your return on time with a balance due that you didn't pay — and the IRS sent a notice demanding the balance plus an erroneous late-filing penalty — be prepared for lengthy correspondence with the IRS. If you don't have a postal mailing receipt for years prior to 2004, you'll have to write to the service center and request a copy of the mailing envelope in which your tax return was mailed so that you can check the postmark. For tax years beginning 2004 and going forward, if you don't have proof of timely mailing, you're out of luck.

"Your notice incorrectly assessed a late-filing penalty in the amount of [amount]. Please be advised that my return was timely filed on [date].

"I am enclosing a copy of my Certified Mail Receipt that clearly shows this return was timely filed."

Or, for tax years prior to 2004 that you didn't use Certified Mail,

"By checking the postmark on the envelope in which my return was mailed, you will see that I didn't file late and therefore no penalty should be assessed. I would appreciate your sending me a copy of my mailing envelope when responding to this inquiry."

If the IRS can't locate your envelope (which sometimes happens) or the envelope bears a crazy, illegible postmark date, you have a problem. If this is the only time you were notified that you filed your return late, you'll have to request that the penalty be abated because of reasonable cause — and because of your record of always filing on time. (We hope that you've always filed on time.) For more about reasonable cause, see Chapter 18.

If you file on time and enter into an agreement to pay in installments, the late payment penalty gets reduced from 0.5 percent a month to 0.25 percent a month while you're making payments. See Chapter 18 if you can't pay on time. The total late payment penalty that can be charged can't exceed 25 percent of the tax owed.

Wrong income

"The income on which you claim I owe additional tax per your notice isn't my income. The bank/broker/insurance company [or whatever] incorrectly reported the income that was earned on this account as belonging to me. This account, in fact, belongs to my [mother, for example], who reported it on her tax return for the year in question. Her Social Security number is [123-45-6789].

"Enclosed, please find a copy of my [mother's] tax return and a statement from her stating that the balance in the account you are questioning belongs to her. I have instructed the bank to correct its records. Please correct yours so that my tax account reflects that no tax is owed."

Exempt income

We're constantly amazed when we review returns that clients prepared themselves. One thing that crops up all the time is how often they pay tax on income when they don't have to. Here are two prominent examples and the appropriate response when the IRS sends a bill for tax due on tax-exempt income.

Keogh — IRA

"The income on which you claim I owe additional tax is income earned from my [Keogh or IRA] account and is exempt from tax. Enclosed is a copy of my year-end statement of that account. Please note that the number of this account is the same as the number that appears on your notice. Please correct your records so my tax account shows that no additional tax is owed your agency."

Municipal bonds

"The income on which you claim I owed additional tax is tax-exempt municipal bond interest. Enclosed is a corrected statement from my broker/bank that clearly identifies that the amount of income reported on your notice is tax-exempt municipal bond interest. Please correct your records so my tax account shows that no tax is owed your agency."

Double-counted income

"The interest income you claim I failed to report on my tax return for the year in question was, in fact, reported on Schedule C of my return (copy enclosed). By adjusting Schedule B (Interest and Dividend Income) of my tax return without adjusting my Schedule C, you are requiring me to pay tax on the same item of income twice by double-counting it. Please correct your records so my tax account reflects that no tax is owed your agency."

Lost return

This is a tough one. But one secret the IRS closely guards is that it frequently loses or misplaces tax returns. The IRS even has a form letter when this happens. The letter requests that you send a duplicate. Unfortunately, when you do, you're likely to receive a follow-up notice saying that the IRS received the duplicate, but that it was filed late! When you file a duplicate return, always mark the top in bold lettering: "Duplicate — Original Filed (insert date)."

Refund return

"Enclosed is a copy of my return that your notice claimed was not filed. Please be advised that this return, which indicated a refund due, was filed on [date]."

If you have a postal mailing receipt, enclose a copy of it.

For tax years prior to 2004, if someone other than you mailed your return, or if another person saw you mail your return, get a statement to that effect and enclose it. (Of course, if the person you asked to mail your return forgot, you can always try to get him or her to pay your late-filing penalty.)

Balance due return

"Enclosed is a copy of the return that your notice (copy enclosed) dated [date] claimed was not filed. Please be advised that my return was mailed on [date]. However, as of this date, my check number [number] dated [date] that accompanied my tax return hasn't been returned to me by my bank.

"I call your attention to *Estate of Wood,* 92TC No.46 and *Sorrentino,* 171 FSupp2d 1150, cases in which the courts held that a timely mailed return is presumed to have been received by the IRS.

"I would appreciate your correcting your records to reflect that this return was timely filed. If you would be kind enough to send me a bill for the balance I owe without reference to any penalties, I will remit full payment on receipt of your bill."

If, in fact, you included a check for the balance due with your return that has now been lost, verify that your bank hasn't already cashed it before you issue another. A cashed check supports your assertion that you timely filed the original return, and you don't want to pay the taxes twice. If your bank has cashed the check, then get a front-and-back copy and send it with your duplicate return. If your check hasn't cleared, stop payment on it, and send a new one with the duplicate return. Sending a copy of the stop-payment order is a good idea; remember that you're trying to establish that the original return was timely filed. The more proof you can provide, the likelier the IRS will see things your way.

Enclose any proof of mailing that you have. Remember, saying that you placed it in the mailbox before the filing deadline now only works for years prior to 2004; after that, you need your Certified Mail or other approved private delivery receipt as proof.

Lost check

"Please be advised that my check, number [number], dated [date], was attached to my return that I filed on [date]. Because my bank still hasn't returned my check, I am placing a stop payment on it and have issued a new check for the same amount as the original check. I am enclosing a copy of my bank's stop-payment order. Kindly abate the interest that you charged on your notice. It would be unfair to charge me interest because your agency can't locate my check."

Tax assessed after statute of limitations

By filing a **Form 911, Taxpayer Application for Assistance Order,** or TAO, you put the IRS on notice that it could be liable for damages and costs up to $1 million resulting from its reckless and intentional behavior in dunning you. If the IRS's actions merely are negligent, you can collect damages and costs up to $100,000. TAOs are covered under the Taxpayer Bill of Rights, which we discuss in Chapter 18. This form is filed with the office of the IRS's Taxpayer Advocate in your area. You can get a copy of Form 911 by calling 800-829-3676. The downside of filing this form is that the statute of limitations is extended while this application is pending (see Chapter 16).

To cover all bases, write to the Adjustments/Correspondence Branch at the service center that issued the assessment.

> "Please be advised that your assessment for additional tax, penalties, and interest was issued in violation of the statute of limitations. The time for making an additional assessment for the year in question expired on [date].

> "Please remove this assessment from my tax account, along with any interest or penalties that were charged. The assessment you made is in direct violation of the law. An assessment must be made within three years after the return is filed. This assessment doesn't comply with that requirement."

Refer to Chapter 16 for more on the statute of limitations.

Partially corrected error

> "Please make the following adjustment [insert] as requested in my original letter of [date] (copy enclosed) that your current notice [date] failed to adjust."

At this point, you may want to refer the matter to the local Taxpayer Advocate Office. (See "Getting Attention When the IRS Ignores You," later in this chapter.)

Erroneous refund

Remember what your mother told you about keeping money that doesn't belong to you? She was right, of course — maybe because she had to deal with the IRS. As a practical matter, if you want to save yourself a great deal of time corresponding with the IRS, deposit the check, but don't spend the money (sorry). You ultimately will receive a bill for it. You may be asking, "Why not just return the check?" The problem with doing that is if the IRS doesn't get its paperwork right, you won't have the money, but you will have a bill from the IRS demanding repayment.

You returned a refund check

> "Enclosed is a refund check that was incorrectly issued to me."

Return the check to the service center where you filed your return, not to the Treasury Department office that issued the check. Send this letter by certified mail.

You didn't return a refund check sent to you by mistake

> "Your notice demanding interest on a refund sent to me in error is assessed in violation of the law. I discovered the error only when I received your notice demanding repayment. I call your attention to the fact that Section 6404(e)(2) of the Internal Revenue

Code states that no interest may be charged if a taxpayer who receives an erroneous refund of $50,000 or less repays it when the IRS demands payment. Enclosed please find my check in the amount of the tax that was incorrectly refunded. Please correct your notice by removing the interest that you shouldn't have charged me."

If this approach doesn't work, contact the IRS Taxpayer Advocate in your area.

Data processing error

A data-processing problem is probably the most difficult to cope with.

"Your notice incorrectly states that [choose appropriate problem(s)]:

(a) A mathematical error was made.

(b) I used the wrong tax table in computing my tax.

(c) I incorrectly claimed a credit.

"Please be advised that I rechecked my return and do not believe that any error was made. Enclosed is a copy of my return. Please review it and advise me exactly where you believe an error was made.

"I thank you in advance for your prompt attention to this request."

Incorrect 1099

Use (a) or (b) when appropriate.

(a) "Your notice incorrectly claims that I failed to report all the income I received from [name]."

(b) "Please be advised that the 1099 information that you received from [name] is incorrect."

"I have enclosed a copy of a corrected 1099 that [name] has reissued to me."

"I would appreciate your adjusting my tax account to reflect the information contained in the corrected 1099. When this is done, you will readily see that no additional tax is due."

Always try to get the 1099 corrected and send along a copy of the new one. Forms 1099 have to, by law, list the names, addresses, and telephone numbers of whom you can contact when the 1099 is wrong.

Wrong year

"The miscellaneous income your notice claims I failed to report for the year in question was not received until the following year and was reported on that year's return (copy enclosed). Additionally, I am enclosing a copy of my bank statement for the month in which this income was received. You will notice that this bank statement bears the following year's date."

Never received prior notices

"You don't have my correct address, which is probably why I never received your prior notices. Please send me copies of these notices so I can determine whether the most current notice that I enclose is correct. If it is, I will pay the amount I owe upon receipt of the prior notices I never received. If it is not correct, I will contact you. I thank you in advance for your prompt attention to this request."

To speed up the process, call the IRS at the number indicated on the notice and request a copy of the Record of your Tax Account Information. To obtain a copy of your tax account, flip back to Chapter 3. This document reflects all postings made by the IRS for tax, interest, penalties, and payments. Also, send the **IRS Form 8822, Change of Address.**

Getting Attention When the IRS Ignores You

At times, it seems that a black hole ravages every IRS service center, devouring loads of taxpayer correspondence. Naturally, the IRS won't respond right away in these cases. If you don't get a response, the IRS has a special office that handles these problems: the office of your local Taxpayer Advocate.

Getting to know your local Taxpayer Advocate

The local Taxpayer Advocate Office is the complaint department of the IRS. Every one of the 33 IRS districts, as well as each of the 10 service centers, has an advocate. An advocate's function is to resolve taxpayer problems that can't be resolved through normal channels.

The National Taxpayer Advocate, who is appointed by the Secretary of the Treasury, oversees all functions of the local Taxpayer Advocates and their employees. The national and local taxpayer advocates operate independently from the IRS and report directly to Congress. The purpose behind this independence is to provide taxpayers with a "customer-friendly" problem-solving office. Being independent of all other IRS offices enables the office of the local advocate to cut through red tape.

Local Taxpayer Advocates don't interpret tax law, give tax advice, or provide assistance in preparing tax returns. They resolve procedural, refund, notice, billing, and other problems that couldn't be fixed after one or more attempts by a taxpayer. A local advocate can abate penalties, trace missing tax payments, and credit them to a taxpayer's account. An advocate also can approve replacement refund checks for originals that were either lost or stolen, release a lien, and — of greatest importance — stop IRS collection action.

Meeting the criteria for a Taxpayer Advocate case

Under its Problem Resolution Program, caseworkers (called Associate and Senior Associate Advocates) working under the local Taxpayer Advocate are the folks that do the actual problem solving. They accept cases for a variety of reasons. The following types of cases are ones that you can cry on their shoulders about:

✔ You call or write the IRS about a problem. After 30 days, you contact the IRS again, but the IRS still ignores you.

✔ You file your return expecting a nice refund, but after 60 days, you're still waiting. You contact the IRS, but nothing happens.

✔ You receive a letter from the IRS promising to respond to your particular inquiry by a certain date, but the IRS forgets about you.

✔ You're suffering a hardship or are about to suffer one, such as the loss of your credit or livelihood.

If the Advocate takes your case

Taxpayer Advocate caseworkers are committed to resolving your problem in seven working days. If they can't, you'll be informed — usually by telephone — when you can expect the problem to be resolved. Most cases are closed in 30 days or less. If an advocate asks for certain information and it isn't sent, the case won't be held open indefinitely; after two weeks, it will be closed, in which case you must make a new Taxpayer Advocate contact. A caseworker closes a case by writing to the taxpayer and explaining what corrective action has been taken, if any. (If no corrective action can be taken, the advocate's letter offers an explanation.)

Although an Associate Advocate can be helpful, keep in mind that they don't work for a charitable organization. They're experts at cutting through red tape. If the advocate won't take your case, he or she will refer it to the IRS office that should have handled it from the start.

Contacting the local Taxpayer Advocate

Except in emergency cases, such as when a levy has been filed and the taxpayer owes no money, taxpayers should write to the advocate in the district where they reside. Your letter should contain the following:

- ✔ A complete description of the problem
- ✔ Copies of the fronts and backs of canceled checks (if applicable)
- ✔ A signed copy of your tax return (if applicable)
- ✔ Copies of all notices received from the IRS
- ✔ Copies of previous letters written to the IRS regarding the problem
- ✔ The number of phone calls you made to the IRS, whom you spoke with, the dates, and what was discussed
- ✔ Any other documents or information that might help the advocate expedite the resolution of this problem
- ✔ A telephone number where you can be reached during the day

In emergency situations, contact the Taxpayer Advocate by phone. The advocate can immediately take a variety of actions. For example, the advocate can issue a **Taxpayer Assistance Order (TAO),** if a notice of levy has been incorrectly issued. A TAO stops the original IRS action that the IRS never should have undertaken.

The Taxpayer Advocate toll-free phone number (877-777-4778) can direct you to the office of your local advocate, or you can find that information at www.irs.gov by plugging "Taxpayer Advocate" into the keyword search.

Finding Your Refund When It Doesn't Find You

If you didn't receive your refund, you may be one of about 90,000 taxpayers whose refund checks are returned to the IRS by the U.S. Postal Service. According to the IRS, these checks are undeliverable because of incorrect addresses or because the taxpayer moved and failed to leave a forwarding address. So if you move, make sure that you notify the IRS by filing **Form 8822, Change of Address.** That way, you'll be sure to get your refund.

The actual figures on how many taxpayers never receive their refund checks are substantially higher when you take into account the refund checks that are either lost or stolen. There are also a number of other reasons why a taxpayer may not have received a refund. For example, the refund could have been used to offset another year's tax bill or to pay what was owed on a delinquent student loan or past-due child support.

How to locate your refund

Yes, the IRS does have a lost-and-found department. You can find out the status of your refund by using the "Where's My Refund" system, either through the IRS automated TeleTax System (dial 800-829-4477 on a touch-tone phone and answer the automated questions), or through the IRS Web site (www.irs.gov; click on "Where's My Refund").

Whether you use the TeleTax System or the IRS Web site to access this information, you'll have to give them some info: your Social Security Number, your filing status, and the exact amount of your refund.

You shouldn't start asking about your refund until at least four weeks after you filed your return. It takes about that much time for the IRS to process a tax return and input the information into its computers. Only after the IRS inputs the information on your return into its computer can you find out about the status of your refund.

If a mistake was made, the refund may have to be processed manually, which may take an additional four to six weeks. Whatever the reason for the delay, the "Where's My Refund" system informs you of the date your refund check was mailed or when it will be mailed.

If more than ten days to two weeks have elapsed since the date that a refund check was scheduled to be mailed, and you still haven't received it, the check probably was lost or stolen. In situations like this, you can do one of three things:

- ✔ Fill out **Form 3911, Taxpayer Statement Regarding Refund,** and send it to the service center where you filed. This one-page form asks whether you ever received the check, or whether you received it and lost it. Allow four to six weeks for processing.

- ✔ Contact the office of your local Taxpayer Advocate. See "Getting Attention When the IRS Ignores You," earlier in this chapter, for more information.

- ✔ Contact the IRS refund section at 800-829-1040. You'll have the opportunity to speak to an IRS employee instead of a machine.

Uncashed refund checks

You have to cash a refund check within 12 months. When your refund check isn't cashed within the required 12-month period, that doesn't mean you're not entitled to your refund. You are. A new refund check must be issued and the uncashed one returned to the IRS. This procedure can be accomplished by filing **Form 3911, Taxpayer Statement Regarding Refund,** with the service center where you filed your return. Across the top of the form, write:

"The enclosed refund check cannot be cashed; 12 months have passed since it was issued. Please issue a replacement check."

You aren't entitled to additional interest on a replacement check because you failed to deposit or cash your refund. But you are entitled to interest if the IRS is late in issuing your refund. See the very next section.

Interest on refunds

If the IRS doesn't issue your refund within 45 days of filing your return, it must pay you interest. So if you file by April 15 and you don't receive your refund by May 30, interest is due.

Refunds and estimated tax payments

If you requested that your refund be applied to next year's tax, you can't change your mind and subsequently request a refund. You can get your overpayment back only by taking credit for it on next year's tax return. No interest is paid on an overpayment of tax credited to next year's tax bill.

Joint refunds

When married couples divorce or separate, or when a dispute exists as to how much of the refund each is entitled to, Revenue Ruling 80-7 provides a formula for determining each spouse's share of the refund. Again, this is one of those times when consulting a tax advisor is a must. If the parties can't decide how to divide the refund, either spouse may request that the IRS issue a separate refund check by filing **Form 1040X, Amended U.S. Individual Income Tax Return,** and making the computation required by Revenue Ruling 80-7. The IRS will accept a joint 1040X with only one signature from a divorced or separated taxpayer requesting a separate refund check. The worksheet on the back of **Form 8379, Injured Spouse Allocation,** can guide you through the computation. Attach this form to your amended return. The refund belongs to the spouse whose income, deductions, and tax payments produced the refund. Filing jointly doesn't change who is entitled to the refund. Filing jointly only determines the amount of tax a couple has to pay.

Revenue Ruling 80-7 must be modified for taxpayers residing in community property states (Arizona, California, Idaho, Louisiana, New Mexico, Nevada, Texas, Washington, and Wisconsin).

Joint estimated payments

Where joint estimated payments have been made and a husband and wife file separate returns, the estimated payments may be divided in any manner the couple sees fit. However, if a couple can't agree on how estimated payments are to be divided, the payments will be divided in the same manner as joint refunds, as required by Revenue Ruling 80-7.

Deceased taxpayer

If a refund is due a deceased taxpayer, **Form 1310, Statement of Person Claiming Refund Due a Deceased Taxpayer,** must be attached to the return unless you're the surviving spouse filing a joint return. If the form isn't attached, the IRS will send back the return along with Form 1310. The refund is processed only after the IRS receives the completed Form 1310.

Statute of limitations

To get a refund, you must file a return within three years of its due date, including extensions of time to file (or within two years of the date tax was paid, if that's later). After that time, you can kiss your refund goodbye. A return that's filed before the due date is considered to have been filed on the due date. For example, if the due date for filing a return is April 16, 2007, an amended return must be filed by April 16, 2010. After that date, no refund will be allowed.

If the April 16, 2007, filing date is extended to October 15, 2007, an amended return must be filed by October 15, 2010. Your acceptance of a refund doesn't bar a future claim for a refund if you subsequently discover that you made a mistake in computing the amended return and now realize that you're entitled to an even greater refund than you computed on your amended return.

The statute of limitations is suspended when you become *financially disabled,* meaning that a disability has rendered you unable to manage your financial affairs. This change in the tax code was brought about by the case of a senile taxpayer who erroneously overpaid the IRS $7,000, and a timely (within three years) refund claim wasn't filed. Assuming that adequate proof of a medical disability can be provided, this taxpayer, under the new law, can still get his $7,000 back. How disabled does someone have to be? The disability or impairment must be expected to result in death or expected to last continuously for at least a 12-month period.

This rule doesn't apply when a taxpayer's spouse, or another person such as a guardian, a conservator, or someone acting with a power of attorney, is authorized to act for the taxpayer on tax matters. In these cases, the normal three-year statute of limitations applies.

Protective claims

Sometimes you must file a tax return and pay tax even though you know the information on the return is incomplete, and that you probably shouldn't owe any tax at all. And sometimes the resolution of these issues may take years, such as in a complex litigation. In those circumstances, you may file a so-called *protective claim* with your income tax return that will suspend the statute of limitations regarding refunds while the litigation is pending. If you feel that you fall into this category, use your big, black marker and write the words "Protective claim under Reg. Sec. 301.6402-2(a)" across the top of your original return, and make sure you file on time (as properly extended). Check with your attorney, accountant, or enrolled agent to make sure you qualify for this break, and to be certain you've complied with every hiccup in the regulation.

If your protective claim request is successful, you'll be able to file an amended return for the year in question and receive your refund (plus interest) even after the normal statute of limitations on refunds has expired.

Refund offset program

Yes, Virginia, if you or your spouse owes back taxes, a non-tax federal debt (student loans, anyone), or delinquent child support, the refund you thought you were getting may be history. The IRS will use the refund money first to offset back taxes. With what's left, the Treasury will try to recover delinquent student loan amounts and/or child support payments. What if only one of you owes this money, though? If the past due amounts clearly belong to only one of you, you may recover the portion of the refund that belongs to you. In this case, the nonobligated spouse must file **Form 8379, Injured Spouse Allocation,** to claim his or her share of the refund. Revenue Ruling 80-7 explains how to divide the refund. Every year, the IRS intercepts several million refunds as part of this program. Yes, Big Brother is watching and has long tentacles.

Just remember: To err is human, to forgive divine. And we never accused the IRS of not being human.

Chapter 18

Fixing Your Own Mistakes

●●

In This Chapter

▶ Fixing bad returns

▶ Making a deal with the IRS

▶ Abating penalties and interest

▶ Understanding the Taxpayer Bill of Rights

●●

*E*veryone makes mistakes. To make them is human; typically, to admit that they're your fault isn't. Still, in most cases, when you've made a mistake on your tax return, the sooner you fix it, the happier and less poor you'll be. In some cases, you need to complete more paperwork; in others, you have to personally persuade an IRS employee. Regardless, here's our advice for how to do it now, do it right, and be done with it!

Amending a Return

Through the years, when taxpayers discovered that they failed to claim a deduction or credit in a prior year, they often asked whether they could claim that deduction on *this year's* return. They couldn't, and you can't, either.

If you discover that you forgot to claim a deduction and the statute of limitations hasn't expired, you have to file an amended return. Similarly, if you discover that a deduction was improperly claimed, you must file an amended return and pay any additional tax plus interest.

Not surprisingly, more amended returns are filed when the flow of funds is going in a taxpayer's direction rather than in the government's. Although this discovery isn't a startling one, it has more to do with letting sleeping dogs lie than with people's honesty. It will take a sociologist to properly address this issue, and we aren't quite qualified to pull it off.

If you forgot to claim a deduction in a prior year, you must file an amended return within three years from the date of filing your original return, or within two years from the time the tax was paid, whichever is later. **Form 1040X, Amended U.S. Individual Income Tax Return,** is used to correct a prior year's tax return.

Suppose you filed your 2005 return on April 17, 2006. If you want to amend this return, you must do so by April 17, 2009. However, if you filed your return on or before April 17, 2006, the three-year statute of limitations still expires on April 17, 2009. If you had an extension of time to file until October 16, 2006, the three-year period starts to run from that date. Remember, the statute of limitations on tax year 2006 returns will run until April 16, 2010, because April 15, 2007, is a Sunday.

This three-year rule is suspended for anyone suffering from a serious disability that renders him or her unable to manage his or her financial affairs. We're not talking about an ingrown toenail type of disability, but truly incapacitating illness or disability that is expected to result in death or reasonably last for at least a year. This provision enables such taxpayers to recover tax that was erroneously overpaid in instances where the three-year statute of limitations would normally bar a refund. However, when a taxpayer's spouse or another person such as a guardian is authorized to act on the disabled taxpayer's behalf, this new rule doesn't apply. The IRS believes that the person looking after the disabled person's financial affairs should be bound by the same three-year rule that everyone else has to follow.

In most cases, filing an amended return doesn't affect the penalty for underestimating your tax. For example, suppose that you were assessed a $1,000 penalty for underpayment of your estimated tax. Your amended return is for half the tax on your original return. The $1,000 underestimating penalty can't be reduced. This is one mistake that can't be amended.

Amended returns also are useful for changing how you reported an item on your original return. You can change your mind in the following situations:

- ✔ You filed separately but now want to file jointly. It is important to note that you can't do this in reverse — you can't switch to filing separately if you originally filed jointly.

- ✔ You want to change from itemizing your deductions to claiming the standard deduction, or vice versa.

- ✔ You reported something incorrectly. This situation may occur if you claimed a deduction or an exemption of income to which you weren't entitled. An example could be when a noncustodial parent incorrectly claimed an exemption for a child or claimed head of household filing status.

Some decisions to treat an item in a certain manner are irrevocable, such as using the straight-line depreciation method and taking a net operating loss forward instead of backward.

More expenses than income (net operating losses)

An amended return is permitted whenever you incur a *net operating loss (NOL)*. You have an NOL if the amount of money you lost (in a business or profession) exceeds all your other income. You can carry back an NOL to offset your taxable income in the two previous years, and doing so entitles you to a refund for both years. If the NOL isn't completely used up by carrying it back, it can be carried forward for 20 years until it's used up.

Any part of an NOL that the owner of a small business (provided that the person's income for each of the preceding years was under $5 million) resulting from a casualty, or theft loss, and NOLs attributable to losses in a presidentially declared disaster area can be carried back for three years.

NOLs incurred in 2001 and 2002 were allowed to be carried back five years. This mish-mash of rules also provided for a selection process. In these two years you could have chosen whether you wanted to take the loss back five, three, or two years, or not at all. If you didn't select a specific carryback period, then you were bound by the five-year rule for 2001 and 2002 NOLs. The tax code has returned to the two-year carryback rule, unless the three-year casualty or disaster area loss rules apply.

Telling the IRS what you want to do (we know what you want to tell the IRS) couldn't be easier. Simply attach a statement to your return that indicates whether you want the two- or three-year carryback rule to apply. So for a 2006 loss governed by the two-year carryback rule, the loss is applied first against your 2004 income. If the loss exceeds that year's income, the balance is carried over to 2005 and then on to future years. Under three-year rule, your 2003 income would be where your 2006 loss carryback would start.

When filing your return for the NOL year, you can elect to carry the NOL forward instead of having to amend your returns for the preceding years. This choice may make sense when your income or tax rates are rising. The reverse would be true when tax rates are declining the way they currently are. The election to only carry a loss forward to future years would also make sense if you were in a lower tax bracket in prior years. Remember, make sure that you really want to carry the NOL forward, because you can't change this election by filing an amended return. However, if you filed your return and didn't make this election, but now you want to, you have six months from April 16, 2007, to file an amended return and make the election. See Publication 536, Net Operating Losses (NOLs).

In order to carry back your NOL, use **Form 1045, Application for Tentative Refund,** if you're able to file it within one year of the year you had the NOL; otherwise use **Form 1040X, Amended U.S. Individual Income Tax Return.**

If you and your spouse weren't married to each other in all the years involved in figuring the carryback and carryover, then only the spouse who incurred the loss can carry it back or forward.

The tax benefit rule

Whenever you deduct an expense in one year and part or all of that expense is reimbursed in a subsequent year, you usually have to report the reimbursement as income. For example, suppose that you deducted $10,000 in medical expenses in 2005, and were reimbursed $3,000 by your insurance company in 2006. You have to report the $3,000 as income in 2006.

However, if the original deduction didn't result in a tax savings, you don't have to report the reimbursement. For example, you may receive a state tax refund for a year in which you claimed the standard deduction instead of itemizing your deductions — you don't have to report the refund.

When You Can't Pay Your Taxes

"If you can't pay," goes the old saw, "you can owe." That's certainly the way the IRS looks at things. Every year, the IRS receives millions of returns from taxpayers who can't pay what they owe before the April 15 deadline, and that amounts to tens of billions of dollars of taxes due *each* year.

If you find yourself among the millions of Americans who can't pay all or any part of what they owe, you have four options:

✔ You can pay it off in installments, which millions of taxpayers currently are doing.

✔ You can put it off until you have more money.

✔ You can try to convince the IRS to take less than it wants. The IRS doesn't accept every offer that is made, but it is fairly pragmatic, and in recent years, has reached agreement in almost 25 percent of cases. From where the IRS sits, receiving some of what it is owed is better than receiving nothing. This acceptance rate is actually much higher when you consider that a third of the offers can't be processed because they don't contain all the information necessary to make them processible. The average settlement is around 13 percent of what is owed.

✔ You can file for bankruptcy in the absolute worst-case scenario.

Whatever you do, don't confuse filing with paying. More people get into hot water because they mistakenly believe that they need to put off filing until they can pay. If you're one of the approximately 2 million non-filers that the IRS currently is looking for, file your return as soon as possible — even if you can pay only part of what you owe. Owing the IRS money is expensive, but owing money and tax returns is far worse! Although the interest rates the IRS charges are lower than what you'll get on your credit card (IRS rates in 2006 have ranged between 7 and 8 percent and are refigured every three months), interest compounds daily on the balance you owe, in addition to a late-payment penalty of half a percentage point per month. That kind of interest adds up quickly! If you haven't filed your tax return, though, the IRS tacks on additional non-filing penalties of 5 percent per month, up to a maximum of 25 percent.

At first, the IRS comes after you through the mail. If you owe money, either from the findings of an audit or because you simply couldn't pay it all on April 15, you'll get four notices from the IRS at five-week intervals. If you don't pay everything you owe on April 15, the fourth and last letter arrives by certified mail around Labor Day. That's when things start to get ugly.

In our experience, many taxpayers freeze when they receive one of these notices and then place the unopened envelope in a pile to be dealt with when the cows come home or hell freezes over. Bad idea! Whether or not you've actually opened the envelope, you're still responsible to respond to the requests inside, even if to tell the IRS that you can't pay right now. If you fail to respond, your account is considered delinquent and is forwarded to the IRS Automated Collection System (ACS), which means you'll start getting telephone calls demanding payment — at home and, if the IRS can't reach you at home, at work, at your club, anywhere the IRS has a number for you. Although the IRS is trying to be a friendlier place, the collections are collections, and they want their money! If the ACS isn't successful in getting you to pay up, your account may be transferred to an IRS revenue officer who will contact you in person.

Because the IRS usually has what it refers to as *levy source information* about you in its files, it has the option to place a levy on your assets or salary, or to simply seize your property. IRS collection agents are especially fond of cars — used or new, they don't discriminate. Keep in mind that from the return you filed the IRS already knows where your income comes from and how much you make and has the right to get additional information about you from credit and governmental agencies, such as the Department of Motor Vehicles, passport agencies, and the U.S. Postal Service. It can make you pay in more ways than one. And every time you make a payment, the IRS makes a permanent record of your bank account.

To avoid that hassle, if there's any way that you can get the money together, send a partial payment when filing your return, a partial payment with the first, second, and third notices, and the balance (including interest and penalties) with the fourth notice.

When the IRS sends a bill for less than $100,000, you have 21 interest-free days to pay it. When the amount you owe is more than $100,000, you have ten *business days* before you're charged interest.

The IRS must notify you of your right to protest a levy of your salary or property. You have 30 days from the date the IRS sends you a Levy Notice by Certified Mail to request what is known as a Collection Due Process Hearing. We explain how to request this type of hearing and what it's all about in Chapter 16.

Requesting an installment agreement

In some cases, people need more time to pay what they owe. If you need more time, you can request to pay in installments by attaching **Form 9465, Installment Agreement Request,** to your return or to any of the notices you receive. Then send it to the IRS Service Center where you file or to the center that issued the notice. You also can request an installment agreement by telephoning the IRS Taxpayer Services office at 800-829-1040.

If you owe less than $10,000 and can pay off what you owe in 36 months, the IRS is required by law to grant your request to pay in installments. However, some strings are attached. During the past five years, you had to have filed and paid your tax on time. Even if this rule knocks you out of contention, the IRS has a new policy that automatically grants installment agreements when the amount owed is less than $25,000 and can be paid off in 60 months. When you request an installment agreement, the IRS mails you an acceptance letter that tells you where to send the money. You won't have to provide a financial statement, and the IRS won't file federal tax lien, which is no small matter, because a tax lien can affect your credit rating for seven years, even if you pay off your tax liability in a shorter period of time. There's a $43 charge for an installment agreement and a $24 charge for either changing an existing agreement or reinstating an agreement that's defaulted on. The installment agreement requires that you don't fall behind in filing or paying.

Be careful not to fall behind on your payments, or you may have to apply for an installment plan all over again. The IRS allows you to make payments using a variety of methods. Checks, money orders, electronic fund transfers, and credit cards (but no postage stamps, please) are all acceptable forms of payment. You can use cash, but only if you pay in person at an IRS office (for safety and security reasons, we don't recommend this latter method!). If you want to be sure you don't fall behind on your payments, you can either pay by Direct Deposit (use Form 9465) or by Payroll Deduction (use Form 2159, available by calling the number on your notice or by visiting your local IRS office). If you can't make a payment, contact the IRS. You stand a good chance of being able to skip a payment if you have a plausible reason. Although the IRS isn't all that charitable, it reserves its wrath for taxpayers who ignore the agency.

Installments get trickier when you owe more than $25,000 or want to stretch your payments out for more than 60 months. You can either use Form 9465 or go straight to the IRS, either by mail or by phone. (A representative, such as an enrolled agent, a CPA, or an attorney, can make this request on your behalf.) When you owe this higher amount, you'll need to file a financial statement listing your assets, liabilities, and monthly income and expenses, which is submitted on **IRS Form 433-A, Collection Information Statement for Individuals.** Use Form 433-A if you're self-employed. For a business, use **Form 433-B.**

After reviewing the form, the IRS will recommend one of the following courses of action or a combination of them. The IRS may tell you to

- ✔ Make immediate payment by liquidating some of your assets.
- ✔ Obtain a cash advance from a credit line.
- ✔ Borrow against the equity in any assets you may have, such as your residence.
- ✔ Make an installment agreement.

There is a fifth option: If there's just no way you can pay, the IRS will stop bothering you for the money. Yes, if you get the fifth option, the IRS will prepare **Form 53, Report of Taxes Currently Not Collectible,** and you'll be off the hook — for a while. However, the IRS will contact you every 9 to 12 months for a new financial statement to find out whether your financial condition has changed. Remember, the IRS has ten years to collect what you owe before the statute of limitations on collections expires. Also keep in mind that just because the IRS isn't currently collecting from you, interest and penalties continue adding to your unpaid tax.

You can appeal any rejection of a request for an installment agreement to the IRS Appeals Office (see Chapter 16). Although the IRS doesn't have a specific form for this, you can try using **Form 12153, Request for a Collection Due Process Hearing.**

If you filed your return on time and enter into an installment agreement, the late-payment penalty gets reduced from 0.5 percent a month to 0.25 percent a month while you're making your payments. The total late-payment penalty that can be charged can't exceed 25 percent of the tax owed. On $10,000 of tax owed, this reduction amounts to a $25-per-month savings.

Making an offer

What if you think there's no way you'll ever be able to pay it all off? The IRS, believe it or not, often takes partial payment. First, you need to fill out **Form 656, Offer in Compromise.** This nine-line form requires you to complete only three lines in addition to your name, address, and Social Security number. You merely check one of the three boxes in Item 6, which include "Doubt as to Liability" — "I do not believe I owe this amount" — to which you need to attach an explanation; "Doubt as to Collectibility" — "I have insufficient assets and income to pay the full amount" — to which you need to attach a complete financial statement (Form 433-A, or Form 33-B); or "Effective Tax Administration" — "I owe this amount and have sufficient assets to pay the full amount, but due to my exceptional circumstances, requiring full payment would cause an economic hardship or would be unfair and inequitable" — to which the financial statement must be attached. Unlike the application for an installment plan, this financial statement *will be audited,* not merely reviewed.

The 1998 law that restructured the IRS created two additional reasons for submitting an Offer in Compromise. They are known as the *equity offer* and the *hardship offer.* The equity option may be used when the collection of the full liability creates "such an inequity as to be detrimental to voluntary tax compliance." Don't laugh! We're quoting directly from the law. The hardship offer may be submitted when full collection would otherwise create an unreasonable hardship. What qualifies under this provision are situations where seizing or selling your assets or having to make payments would leave you without enough to pay reasonable, basic living expenses.

An Offer in Compromise is a matter of public record and, if accepted, may come with strings attached. You may have to agree that for a period of years, perhaps as many as five, you'll pay more than you offered in the event your financial condition improves. An aging Joe Louis had to accept such terms, just in case he ever started earning millions again by going back into the boxing ring.

Underestimating estimated taxes

If you have income that isn't subject to withholding, the IRS doesn't want to wait until April 15 to be paid; it wants you to pay what you owe in quarterly estimates. The penalty kicks in when you owe $1,000 or more when you file your return and you haven't made tax payments equal to 90 percent of your tax during the year or 100 percent of your prior year's tax liability.

The penalty for underestimating your tax may be abated because of a casualty, disaster, or another unusual circumstance. It also can be abated by filing **Form 2210, Underpayment of Estimated Tax,** if you meet one of the following conditions:

✔ You paid estimated 2006 taxes equal to 100 percent of your 2005 tax. If your 2005 income exceeded $150,000, however, you need to pay 110 percent of your 2005 tax to be certain you'll escape the penalty for 2006.

✔ You met the 90 percent tax payment of your 2006 tax liability requirement.

✔ You filed a return for the preceding year that showed no tax liability.

✔ You retired at age 62 or older, or became disabled, and your underpayment was due to reasonable cause.

If you operate a seasonal business or didn't earn your income evenly throughout the year, you may be able to reduce or eliminate the penalty by using the annualized income installment method. Not many taxpayers use it because of its complexity, but if you think it will save you money, IRS Publication 505 *(Tax Withholding and Estimated Tax)* explains how it works. For example, say you earned nothing for 11 months and then had income in the 12th month. You're required to make only one estimated payment instead of four.

To get the penalty waived, attach an explanation to Form 2210 along with any documentation that will prove you shouldn't be charged a penalty. See Chapter 8 for details about this fiendish penalty.

Who are candidates for Offers in Compromise? All types of taxpayers: senior citizens with few or no assets or in poor health, spendthrifts who earned large sums of money and squandered it, athletes and actors whose earning potential has diminished, casualties of downsizing, and people whose relatives are reluctant to leave them money because of their tax problems.

You can appeal an offer that is rejected. While an offer is pending, the IRS is prohibited from levying your salary or property. Use Form 12153 to request an appeal.

In 2006, the IRS instituted significant changes in the Offers in Compromise program. For offers submitted after July 15, 2006, the IRS now requires, in addition to a $150 application processing fee, a 20 percent payment with a lump-sum offer or the first installment on your proposed period payment offer. The $150 application fee and additional down-payment is waived if the offer is based solely on doubt as to liability or if the income of the person making the offer is below the poverty level.

Don't be fooled by what you may have heard. The IRS is anything but a pushover when it comes to agreeing to accept less.

Declaring bankruptcy

After many years of talking about it, in 2005, Congress finally acted to make it more difficult to discharge your debts in bankruptcy. The result is the *Bankruptcy Abuse Prevention and Consumer Protection Act of 2005,* which now applies a means test to determine whether or not you can completely wipe out your debts, or whether you'll have to enter into a five-year payment plan. What does this act mean to you? If things are really dire, you may still decide that declaring personal bankruptcy is the only way out; however, now you'll receive six months of credit counseling before you can apply. And, after you do file for bankruptcy, if you earn more than the median income for a family of your size in your locale, you may be required to repay a portion of your debts, including your unpaid taxes, over a five-year period. Although the provisions of this new law are definitely tougher than those provisions of the prior law, filing a bankruptcy petition still stops the IRS from garnishing your salary or seizing your property.

Of course, if your income falls below the median for a family of your size in your area, you can still file for a complete discharge of your debts, including unpaid income tax liabilities that are more than three years old. If you fall into this category, you're still required to have six months of credit counseling prior to visiting the bankruptcy court.

You can recover up to $1 million in damages if the IRS willfully violates the bankruptcy law's prohibition against seizing your salary or property.

Even if your tax liability isn't completely wiped out in bankruptcy court, as often happens, the IRS won't have as much power over you anymore. For example, you don't have to get IRS approval on an installment plan. If the bankruptcy court allows your repayment plan because the bankruptcy judge finds it fair and equitable, the IRS has to accept it.

Filing bankruptcy, in addition to being emotionally charged, has its pros and cons. Bankruptcy is a technical and difficult area of the law and one that you may not wish to negotiate by yourself. If you find that you're contemplating filing for bankruptcy, you may want to use the services of a competent bankruptcy attorney. Your choice of an attorney is key; you can find a list of local bankruptcy attorneys through Martindale-Hubbell, an attorney database available at your local law firm, public library, or online at www.martindale.com. *Bankruptcy: Is It the Right Solution to Your Debt Problems?* by Robin Leonard (Nolo Press) can help you figure out the right questions to ask in order to choose the best attorney.

Filing for bankruptcy is a drastic step. Before heading down that road, be sure to analyze your overall financial situation, level of debt relative to your income, and your current spending. Eric's *Personal Finance For Dummies* (Wiley) can assist you with that analysis.

Planning ahead to avoid these problems

Making adequate provisions in the first place is your best defense against not being able to pay your tax bill on April 15. Routinely review your withholding allowances (Form W-4) to make sure that the proper amount of tax is being withheld from your salary. (See Chapter 15 if you need help determining how much to withhold.) If you're self-employed or have income that isn't subject to withholding, you need to make quarterly estimated payments using **Form 1040-ES.**

Abating a Penalty

Although the Internal Revenue Code contains about 150 penalties, some are more common than others. The most common penalties include

- ✔ Accuracy errors (the IRS defines accuracy errors as either negligence or disregard of the rules)
- ✔ Failure to file
- ✔ Failure to pay
- ✔ False Withholding Exemption Certificate (Form W-4)
- ✔ Underestimating tax

Many taxpayers who receive a penalty notice believe that a penalty wouldn't have been charged unless it was correct, and they simply pay it. After all, penalties are asserted on official-looking documents. Never assume that any notice is correct. Thoroughly reading the notice is the primary requirement for making sure that you don't pay what you don't owe.

The IRS assesses tens of millions of penalties each year totaling tens of billions of dollars. And almost 50 percent of the penalties are abated or forgiven because taxpayers questioned them and had either reasonable cause or because the penalty in question was improperly assessed. Taxpayers can look to several sources — the *Internal Revenue Manual,* court cases, IRS Rulings and Announcements, and regulations to the Internal Revenue Code — to determine whether they meet the definition of reasonable cause.

Unlike some taxes, penalties never are deductible. Because some penalties are additions to the tax you must pay, interest is computed on the total amount due — tax plus penalties.

The Internal Revenue Manual (IRM)

The Internal Revenue Manual is the IRS bible. It contains the rules that IRS employees must follow when applying the law (not that it helps you any when they don't). According to the manual, the following situations constitute reasonable cause for abating a penalty:

- ✔ Your return was mailed on time but was not received until after the filing date, regardless of whether the envelope bears sufficient postage.
- ✔ Your return was filed on time but was received by the wrong IRS office.

✔ You relied upon erroneous information provided to you by an IRS officer or employee.

✔ Your return was filed late because of the death or serious illness of the taxpayer or a close family member.

✔ You were unavoidably away on the filing date.

✔ Your place of business, residence, or business records was destroyed because of fire or other casualty. Victims of natural disasters, take note!

✔ You applied to the IRS district director for proper tax forms prior to the filing deadline, but these forms weren't furnished in sufficient time.

✔ You presented proof of having visited an IRS office before an IRS expiration date for filing returns to secure information on how to properly complete your return, but you weren't able to meet with an IRS representative.

✔ You were unable, for reasons beyond your control, to obtain the records necessary to determine the amount of tax due, or, for reasons beyond your control, you weren't able to pay. For example, you couldn't get your money out of a bankrupt Savings & Loan to pay your taxes, or your account was attached by a lien or court order. Perhaps you earned money in a foreign country that you couldn't convert into dollars, or a person who was needed to cosign a check was ill or away.

✔ Your tax advisor incorrectly advised you that you didn't need to file a return, even though you provided him or her with all the necessary and relevant documents, or the advisor prepared the return incorrectly.

Your ignorance of the law may be considered reasonable cause for a late return if other factors, such as a situation in which you are filing a return for the first time, support this contention. However, you must demonstrate that you exercised ordinary care and prudence.

Court cases that define reasonable cause

You're not the first person to think you have a reasonable excuse why you shouldn't be charged a penalty. Many others have gone before you and fought until they got the result they were looking for. Here are some court cases that favored taxpayers. These legal precedents create guidelines that the IRS should follow. Be cautious, though, when using legal precedents to buttress your arguments to the IRS; your facts will almost never be identical to the facts in the case, and the IRS may just be itching to point out the differences to you.

Ignorance

The taxpayer's limited education and business experience, together with his reliance on the advice of an attorney, caused his failure to file to be due to reasonable cause. *C.R. Dexter, 306 F. Supp 415.*

Litigation

The taxpayer's late filing was due to reasonable cause when litigation was necessary to determine the taxability of income received. *F.P. Walker* (CA-9), 326 F. 2nd 261 (Nonacq).

Timely mailed and presumed received

Beginning in 2004, the IRS began to require that taxpayers, if asked, prove that they had filed their returns on time. Now, in order to be able to provide the necessary proof, you should be sure to file your paper returns by the due date using Certified Mail or another approved method of filing. If the return in question was for a year prior to 2004, you can still use the argument that it was timely filed if the postmark on the envelope shows it was mailed by the due date. *Sorrentino,* 171 FSupp2d 1150.

Reasonable cause — an important definition

With the exception of fraud penalties, just about every penalty can be abated for what is known as reasonable cause. The IRS defines reasonable cause as follows: "If the taxpayer exercised ordinary business care and prudence and was nevertheless unable to file or pay within the prescribed time, then the delay is due to reasonable cause."

Return executed but misplaced

Tax returns were signed and given to an employee whose duty was to mail the returns. Instead, the employee by error then placed the returns in a file together with copies of the returns of many other corporations. When the IRS sent a notice a year later, the error was discovered and the returns were filed at that time. *Bouvelt Realty,* 46 BTA 45.

Return misplaced by the IRS

The Commissioner failed to refute the taxpayer's evidence that the tax returns were timely filed but misplaced by the IRS. *J.J. Carlin,* 43 TCM (CCH) 22.

Mailing of return on time

The IRS asserted that a return due on the 15th hadn't been received for filing until the 17th. The corporate officer who had mailed the return had died, and because of the Commissioner's failure to produce the envelope in which the return was mailed, it was held that no penalty should attach. *Capento Securities Corp.,* 47 BTA 691 (Nonacq) Aff'd CA-1.

Honest belief

The taxpayer's honest but mistaken belief that an extension of time to file allowed him to delay the filing of his tax return until he had sufficient funds to pay his tax constituted reasonable cause for the late filing of his tax return. *M.S. Alba,* DC, East.Dist.MO.No.80-764.

In another case, a taxpayer — while separated from her husband — attached her W-2 to a joint return that she gave back to her husband to file. The honest belief that the return was filed didn't constitute willful neglect. *E. Barker,* 22 TCM 634.

Illness

The taxpayer's illness and hospitalization constituted reasonable cause for failure to file a tax return. *C. Freeman,* 40 TCM 1219, Dec. 37,236 (M).

Reliance on accountant

Where a corporate taxpayer selects a competent tax expert, supplies the expert with all necessary information, and asks the expert to prepare proper tax returns, the taxpayer has done all that ordinary business care and prudence can reasonably demand. *Haywood Lumber & Mining Co. v Comm.,* (CA-2) 178 F.2nd 769.REV'D CA-2.

Excuses that won't fly

The dog-ate-my-taxwork excuse won't work, nor will these.

Delegation of authority

In a landmark case, the Supreme Court held that the reliance on an attorney as to the filing date of a return didn't constitute reasonable cause. *R.W. Boyle,* SCT. 105 S. Ct. 687. The Supreme Court held in this case that a qualified tax advisor's incorrect advice as to whether a tax return should be filed constitutes reasonable cause, but that the tax advisor's mistaken advice as to the correct date a return must be filed does not.

But subsequent to *U.S. v Boyle,* a disabled taxpayer's reliance on an attorney to timely file a return was considered reasonable cause. *C. Brown v U.S.,* 57 AFTR 2d (M.D. Tenn. 1985).

Incarceration

The Tax Court rejected a taxpayer's claim that incarceration constituted reasonable cause. *R. Llorente,* 74 TC 260.

IRS rulings and announcements

Some taxpayers are amazed when they discover that the IRS rather than Congress creates most of the tax rules that they must follow. That's because most tax laws include the following language: "in accordance with rules and regulations to be promulgated by the Secretary of the Treasury" — meaning that the Treasury Department makes and enforces the rules. Therefore, you must pay special attention to IRS rulings and announcements — there's a whole lot of promulgating going on.

Partnership returns — Rev. Proc. 84-35

If a partnership is composed of ten or fewer partners and each of the partners reports his or her share of the partnership's income and deductions, the partnership won't be charged a penalty for either not filing or filing late.

Erroneous advice given by IRS employees over the telephone

According to IRS Information Release IR-88-75, incorrect advice given over the telephone by an IRS employee may constitute reasonable cause. The only problem with this provision is how you prove that you called the IRS and received erroneous advice. The IRS will consider that a taxpayer received incorrect advice over the telephone, if a taxpayer provides the following information:

- Whether the taxpayer tried to find the answer to the question in IRS forms, instructions, or publications.
- The questions asked and the specific facts given to the IRS employee.
- The answer the taxpayer received.
- The IRS employee's name and ID number. Yes, every employee has one.
- The date and time of the call.

If you're reading this provision for the first time, it's probably too late. But the next time you call the IRS for advice, make sure that you jot all this information down.

Erroneous written advice by IRS

Both the tax and the penalty attributable to the incorrect written advice can be abated. You can do this by filing **Form 843, Claim for Refund and Request for Abatement,** and checking box 4a.

IRS criteria for determining reasonable cause

This IRS ruling spells out the criteria for reasonable cause. Here they are:

- Do the taxpayer's reasons address the penalty that was assessed?

- Does the length of time between the event that caused the late filing and the actual filing negate the fact that the taxpayer attempted to correct the situation in a timely fashion?

- Does the continued operation of a business after the event that caused the taxpayer's noncompliance negate the taxpayer's excuse?

- Should the event that caused the taxpayer's noncompliance or increased liability have been reasonably anticipated?

- Was the penalty the result of carelessness, or does the taxpayer appear to have made an honest mistake?

- Has the taxpayer provided sufficient detail (dates, relationships) to determine whether he or she exercised ordinary business care and prudence? Is a nonliable individual being blamed for the taxpayer's noncompliance? What is the nature of the relationship between the taxpayer and this individual? Is the individual an employee of the taxpayer or an independent third party, such as an accountant or a lawyer?

- Has the taxpayer documented all pertinent facts?

- Does the taxpayer have a history of being assessed the same penalty?

- Does the amount of the penalty justify closer scrutiny of the case?

- Could the taxpayer have requested an extension or filed an amended return?

Critical to getting the IRS to accept your reasons for late filing or paying is the time frame between the event that was clearly beyond your control and the date of your ultimate compliance with your obligation to file or pay. What the IRS considers to be an acceptable amount of time between these two events is based on the facts and circumstances in each case. Figure 18-1 shows a reasonable cause sample letter.

Penalty appeals

If the Adjustments/Correspondence Branch (see Chapter 17) rejects your request to have a penalty abated, you may appeal. Every service center has a penalty appeals unit. The A/C Branch notice informing taxpayers that their request was rejected will also inform them of their appeal rights and how to exercise them.

Payment of the penalty isn't a prerequisite to requesting an appeal. No official IRS form exists for requesting this type of appeal. Although some appeals within the IRS need not be in writing, this one must. Your original letter requesting an abatement can be used with one simple modification: Your opening sentence should state that you are requesting an appeal from a tax examiner's determination (which you are enclosing) that you failed to establish reasonable cause.

Some IRS offices require that the tax and interest be paid before they will consider a penalty abatement. No specific law requires this; the IRS is famous for making up its own rules.

Sample Reasonable Cause Letter

Request to abate penalty
[your name and address]
[today's date]

Adjustments/Correspondence Branch
Internal Revenue Service Center
[address]

Re: [your name]
[Social Security number]
[tax year]

Dear IRS:

I am in receipt of your notice of [date] in which you asserted a late filing and payment penalty in the amount of [penalty $] plus interest on this amount of [interest $].

Please be advised that my late filing and payment were due to reasonable cause and, according to tax law, should be abated.

On [date], I was ill with [illness]. I was hospitalized and didn't recover sufficiently until [date]. When I was well enough to assemble the data necessary to file a return and pay what was owed, I immediately did so. Enclosed is a letter from my physician confirming the nature of my illness and the length of my recovery, as well as the hospital bill.

Regulation 301.6651-1(c) provides that:

> "If a taxpayer exercised ordinary business care and prudence and was nevertheless either unable to file the return or pay within the prescribed time, the delay is due to reasonable cause."

Thank you in advance for your prompt attention to this request. If you require further clarification of any point, I can be reached at [number].

Very truly yours,

[your name]

Enclosed: Form CP-22A (Statement of Change to Your Account)
                   Letter from physician and hospital

Figure 18-1:
A sample
reasonable
cause letter.

You may want to include any additional reasons that constitute reasonable cause, or any proof, such as

- ✔ Your passport showing that you were out of the country
- ✔ Medical records stating that you were ill
- ✔ A statement from a third party who saw you mail the return on time
- ✔ A police or insurance report showing that the loss of your records was caused by a theft or other casualty

These documents, whenever available, need to be sent with the original abatement request. Hold nothing back!

At times, for inexplicable reasons, tax examiners take the position that a taxpayer should have quickly estimated his or her income and filed a return based on this estimate. In such instances, you should point out that the event that took place was the reasonable cause that prevented you from preparing an estimate.

The IRS has a policy that no collection action will be taken while a penalty appeal is pending — unless, that is, the case already was assigned to a collection officer who determined that the appeal was requested solely to postpone or delay payment. Whenever you're being bugged for the penalty, contact the office of your local Taxpayer Advocate to get the IRS Collection Division off your back. A Taxpayer Advocate has authority to do this. (See Chapter 17 for a Tax Advocate's duties.)

Be patient when requesting an abatement of a large penalty or when appealing a penalty abatement decision. The process isn't speedy.

Abating Interest

Whereas the IRS has the power to abate a penalty for reasonable cause, it doesn't have — as a general rule — the authority to abate interest. But like every IRS rule, there are some limited exceptions when interest can be abated.

When interest is incorrectly charged

If interest was assessed after the expiration of the statute of limitations or was assessed illegally, then it's probably correct to assume that the underlying tax also was incorrectly assessed. If this is the case, the interest, as well as the tax, can be abated.

Interest and tax that were incorrectly or illegally assessed may be abated in one of two ways. You can use **Form 911, Application for Taxpayer Assistance Order,** or you can write to the Adjustments/Correspondence Branch at the service center (or district office) that issued the notice. Figure 18-2 shows a sample letter with two possible reasons.

You can collect damages when the IRS willfully or negligently collects tax that isn't owed.

Erroneous refunds

The IRS is required to abate interest on a demand for repayment of a refund that was issued in error. For this rule to apply, the refund must be less than $50,000, and the taxpayer must in no way be responsible for causing the refund. On an erroneous refund, the IRS can charge interest only from the point in time when it demanded repayment and not for the period prior to the taxpayer being asked to repay it.

For example, suppose that you should have received a $100 refund, but instead, you received a $1,000 refund. No interest can be charged on the $900 for the period of time you held the money. If interest is assessed on the $900, filing **Form 843, Claim for Refund and Request for Abatement,** will get back the interest that you paid.

Sample Letter
[your name and address]
[today's date]

Internal Revenue Service Center
[address]

Re: [your name]
[Social Security number]
[tax year]

Dear IRS:

I respectfully request that you abate the tax assessment in the amount of [amount] that your agency made by error pursuant to the enclosed notice.

Reason (1): Section 6404(e) specifically allows for the abatement of tax that was assessed as the result of an IRS mathematical or clerical error.

Reason (2): Your assessment was made after the three-year statute of limitations had expired. Such assessments are prohibited by law.

I may be reached by telephone during the day at [number] should you require any further information.

Very truly yours,

[your name]

Enclosed: Copy of notice

Figure 18-2:
A sample
letter to
abate
interest.

IRS delays

The Tax Reform Act of 1986 gives the IRS the authority to abate interest on any tax deficiency when an IRS official fails to perform a *ministerial act* and instead moves at a snail's pace in handling routine matters. (In this case, a ministerial act has nothing to do with performing the prescribed rituals of your favorite religious institution; the IRS official must appropriately and in a timely manner perform the prescribed rituals of your "favorite" government agency.) The IRS has the right to abate interest, but it isn't compelled to do so. When the failure to perform a ministerial act has occurred, interest is required to be abated from the time when the IRS first contacted you, not from the due date of your tax return, which normally is the case.

Here's how the IRS decided whether interest could be abated in the following cases:

✔ You moved from one state to another. Your return was selected for audit. You request the audit to be transferred to your new location, and the transfer is approved. But the IRS delays in transferring your case. Interest can be abated.

✔ An audit reveals that additional tax is due. You and the IRS have agreed on the amount of additional tax due, but the IRS delays in sending you a bill. Interest can be abated.

✔ You deducted a loss from a tax shelter that is being audited. The audit of the shelter takes a long time to complete. Interest can be abated.

✔ The agent auditing your return is assigned to a training course, and, during the training course, your audit is neither worked on nor reassigned to a different agent. Interest can be abated.

Form 843, Claim for Refund and Request for Abatement, is used to abate interest in situations where the IRS has caused a delay. Check box 4a (Interest Caused by IRS Errors and Delays).

Although delays by the IRS caused by loss of records, transfer of personnel, extended illness, leave, or training now are causes for abating interest, be forewarned that getting interest abated on an IRS delay nevertheless is a tough nut to crack. The IRS has the authority but, again, isn't compelled to abate interest when managerial acts cause delay.

When the IRS doesn't send a bill

When you sign off on the results of a tax examination or notice of proposed adjustments to your return, the IRS must send you a bill for payment within 30 days. If it doesn't, the agency can't charge interest until a bill is sent. Use Form 843 to abate any interest charges after the 30-day period.

When the IRS sends a bill

If the amount that you owe is less than $100,000, you have 21 interest-free days to pay it. If the amount you owe is more than $100,000, you have 10 business days before you're charged interest.

The 18-month rule

The IRS must send a notice of additional tax due within 18 months of filing your return. If it doesn't, it has to stop charging interest after 18 months and until 21 days after it sends a notice. Look in Chapter 16 to see how this rule works.

Not all IRS notices are covered by this provision. For example, audit notices aren't. See Chapter 16 for the ins and outs of how this provision works.

Protecting Yourself with Innocent Spouse Relief

Innocent spouse relief, like the Tooth Fairy and the Loch Ness Monster, used to belong to the category of whimsy, possible in some far-fetched way, but never actually experienced. Fortunately for many members of either troubled marriages or marriages where spouses keep their financial dealings separate and private, innocent spouse relief (including separation of liability and equitable relief) is now a useful area of tax law instead of a fantasy that exists on the books but not in reality. The IRS explains it in great detail in Publication 971, Innocent Spouse Relief (and Separation of Liability and Equitable Relief), which is available by mail or through the IRS Web site, www.irs.gov.

Essentially, an innocent spouse is one who signs a joint tax return on which there is an understatement of tax while not knowing whether the information contained on the return is correct. Signing a joint return ordinarily makes you jointly or severally liable for all the tax due on that return, even if it is your spouse's income. (See Chapter 4 for the specific details about filing a joint return.) That means that if your spouse is a deadbeat and doesn't pay any tax owed, you may end up paying more than your fair share of the tax, or maybe all of it. However, a so-called innocent spouse may be able to convince the IRS that he or she knew nothing about the underreported income or overreported deductions and/or credits that created this additional tax.

If you live in a one of the community property states (Arizona, California, Idaho, Louisiana, Nevada, New Mexico, Texas, Washington, or Wisconsin), even if you filed married filing separately, you may be liable for a portion of your spouse's understatement of tax; however, innocent spouse rules will work for you, too. You just need to apply them a little differently by separating out what is your liability from what belongs to your spouse (or ex-spouse). Publication 971 can help you with all the flowcharts and worksheets you could possibly desire.

If you receive a bill from the IRS for additional tax and you had no knowledge of the extra income excluded and/or the extra deductions and credits claimed, you may be entitled to relief. In the innocent spouse rules, three forms of relief are available:

✔ Innocent spouse relief

✔ Relief by separation of liability

✔ Equitable relief

Getting innocent spouse relief: Determining if you're eligible under the new rules

If you've just received a notice or bill from the IRS referring to income or deductions you know nothing about, you may qualify as an innocent spouse. In order for the IRS to consider your request (which you're going to file on **Form 8857,** aptly named **Request for Innocent Spouse Relief**), you need to meet *all* of the following conditions:

✔ You filed a joint return that has an understatement of tax due to erroneous items of your spouse or former spouse.

✔ At the time that you signed the joint return, you didn't know and had no reason to know that the tax shown on the return was understated.

✔ Taking into consideration the facts and circumstances, holding you responsible for the underpayment of tax is unfair.

For example, your spouse plays the horses on the side, and one day, wins $10,000 at the racetrack. Your spouse never tells you about the money and spends it without your knowledge. When the time comes to complete your joint tax return, he or she figures that what you don't know won't hurt you and leaves the $10,000 off the return. The IRS, on the other hand, knows about the money because the racetrack has reported the information, and comes looking for the income tax due on the $10,000. In this case, you're clearly an innocent spouse, and provided you file your Form 8857, you won't be liable for the additional tax on the $10,000. You're still on the line for any other tax shown on the return that you know about.

You really have to be clueless in order to obtain any type of innocent spouse relief. Being told that money that you're receiving isn't taxable still constitutes knowledge, because you know about the money. And, if you and your spouse are transferring assets back and forth between yourselves or a third party in the hopes of hiding taxable income from the IRS, that's fraud, and that's not allowed.

If, on the other hand, the IRS is hounding you for back taxes and you really think innocent spouse relief might apply, give it a try. You can't be penalized for applying, and who knows, you may just be successful!

Receiving relief by separation of liability

The IRS may separate any additional tax liability into his and hers (so-called "separation of liability") if you are no longer married to, are widowed, or are legally separated from the spouse with whom you filed a joint return, or you weren't a member of the same household as an estranged spouse during any point of the 12-month period preceding the filing of Form 8857.

The IRS is fussy when determining whether or not you're living in the same household as your estranged spouse. In order for you to qualify on that point, you really must be living apart, in separate houses or apartments, and not just as a trial or convenience. For example, couples who live in different cities because of job reasons but who are together for all other purposes don't qualify. Neither will your living in an RV parked in your spouse's driveway.

Once again, just as in traditional innocent spouse relief, you must have no knowledge of the erroneous items. If you even had an inkling that your spouse was cheating on your joint taxes, you both are liable for the additional tax even if you received no benefit.

Under what circumstances can the IRS say you aren't responsible for all or part of any unpaid tax? Your spouse runs off in the middle of the night with all your dough and jewelry. Suppose that the IRS then discovers an additional $20,000 of income, $5,000 of which the IRS proves you had knowledge of. You and your spouse are responsible for the tax on the $5,000 that you knew about. Your spouse is solely responsible for the tax on the remaining $15,000.

Obtaining equitable relief

If you aren't eligible for either innocent spouse relief or separation of liability relief, you may still qualify for relief under the IRS's guidelines for equitable relief. Equitable relief is different from either traditional innocent spouse relief or separation of liability because the IRS will, given the right set of circumstances, give you partial or full relief not only for a tax understatement, but also for a tax underpayment (where you signed a return, but the taxes showing weren't paid).

In addition, the requirements for equitable relief are specific, and you must meet them all. They are

- You and your spouse or ex didn't transfer assets between yourselves as part of a fraudulent scheme.

- Your spouse or ex-spouse didn't transfer property to you with the intention of avoiding tax.

- You didn't file or fail to file your return with the intention of committing fraud.

- You didn't pay the tax.

- You're able to establish that, given all the facts, holding you liable for either the understatement or underpayment of the tax would be unfair.

- The relief which you seek must be attributable to your present or ex-spouse unless you live in a community property state, the item is in your name but you're able to prove it's not really yours, you didn't know that money you intended for tax payments were misappropriated by your spouse (or ex), or you're able to establish that you were a victim of abuse before signing the return and that you signed the return under duress.

Additional innocent spouse rules

You must elect innocent spouse relief within two years from the day the IRS begins to enforce collection, either by a garnishment or notice of intent to levy, or a lawsuit by the IRS against you. For example, if the IRS sends you a notice of intent to levy, you have two years from that date to file Form 8857. If all you receive is a notice demanding payment, no time limits are placed on when you can no longer request innocent spouse relief.

Relief is available under this provision for all taxes, no matter how old. You can apply for relief even if you were denied innocent spouse relief under the old law.

No collection activity may be undertaken while your application for relief is pending. And if relief is denied, you can appeal to the U.S. Tax Court. You have 90 days after the notice of denial to make your appeal.

Now for the bad news: The IRS must notify your ex and give him or her the opportunity to object to what you're doing.

When a married couple separates, the IRS should be informed of each spouse's new address so that all notices received by one spouse are received by the other. You can take care of this by filing **Form 8822, Change of Address.**

The Taxpayer Bill of Rights enacted in 1996 enables you to ask what the IRS is doing to get your ex-spouse to pay and how much he or she has paid. Because of possible hostility toward an ex-spouse, the IRS won't reveal the ex-spouse's home or business address.

The Taxpayer Bill of Rights

This great republic was founded on the principle that taxation without representation is tyranny. But if you've ever had a run-in with the IRS, you know that taxation *with* representation isn't so hot, either. To feed its insatiable appetite for spending, Congress has given the IRS almost unlimited authority to collect taxes — an authority that, sadly, can be abused in all sorts of horrible ways.

In response to congressional hearings and a flurry of taxpayer horror stories in 1998, Congress enacted the so-called *Taxpayer Bill of Rights.*

Now, whenever you get a notice of any kind from the IRS, you get a two-page summary of the taxpayer bill, entitled "Your Rights as a Taxpayer." This remarkably readable document explains how to appeal an IRS decision, suggests where you can get free information, and assures you that you're entitled to "courtesy and consideration" from IRS employees. Reading it, you almost get the impression that the IRS is a friendly place that wants only what's best for you. Use your common sense here – remember, at the end of the day, the IRS is trying to get money that you're trying to hang onto. You and the IRS are still adversaries; the Taxpayer Bill of Rights just makes you more civilized adversaries!

The Taxpayer Bill of Rights has been through a few incarnations. The original Taxpayer Bill of Rights contained two significant points:

- At any time during an audit or interview, you may ask to speak with an enrolled agent, attorney, or CPA. Whenever that happens the IRS must stop what it's doing and let you do so.

- The IRS may not take money or property from you on the same day that you comply with a summons. In other words, the IRS can't demand that you appear and then seize your car when you get to its office — something that used to happen a lot.

Increased taxpayer rights in a nutshell

In 1998, the IRS received quite a bit of negative press after congressional hearings revealed the abuse taxpayers were routinely being subjected to. It made great headlines, "IRS horror stories." After hearing from individual taxpayers who thought they'd been put through the wringer by the tough guys down at IRS Central, Congress decided to come to the rescue and give taxpayers more protection and rights. We have to chuckle a bit at all this — after all, Congress was the organization that created all these ambiguous and cumbersome tax laws in the first place.

Here are the major provisions that supposedly benefit taxpayers. We say supposedly because the actual benefit often is far, far less than meets the eye:

✔ **Burden of proof falls (more) on the IRS.** Unlike the criminal justice system, which operates under the premise that when charged with a crime, you're presumed innocent until proven guilty, the U.S. tax system has operated under the reverse, perverse presumption that you're guilty until proven innocent. However, to benefit from being presumed innocent until the IRS proves otherwise, your tax disagreement must actually land in court, and you must meet other requirements, including having good records and having been cooperative and compliant to that point.

✔ **Taxpayers have new protections regarding collections.** In recent years, the IRS got itself into trouble with the way it handled certain tax collections. In some cases, taxpayers experienced unjustified and confrontational seizure of property and other assets, even for small amounts of tax owed. Now, for example, the IRS needs a court order to sell someone's home and a higher level of approval within the IRS to seize someone's business.

✔ **Innocent spouse rules are enhanced.** As we discuss in this chapter, married couples heading toward divorce don't always cooperate about money and taxes. The tax bill passed in 1998 beefs up a spouse's ability to file separately while still married to avoid being held responsible for the other spouse's tax negligence. Although this option may sound attractive, we fear that it will increase total costs for both spouses, especially if you factor in the costs of a divorce lawyer wrangling over tax liabilities.

✔ **Advice given by tax advisors to taxpayers is confidential.** With legal matters, what a client tells his or her attorney is largely confidential. With tax issues, that same standard of confidentiality hasn't been applied to what a taxpayer tells his or her preparer or advisor. Taxpayers can now consult with tax advisors in the same confidential and privileged manner as they do with lawyers. Remember, however, that information disclosed in preparation of a tax return isn't covered by this rule!

Despite those important rights, the original Taxpayer Bill of Rights left much to be desired. In too many cases, it allowed the IRS itself to interpret your rights. It's like having the same person as prosecutor, judge, jury, and executioner.

The Taxpayer Bill of Rights — Parts 2 and 3

Our complaint with the original Taxpayer Bill of Rights was that it didn't have teeth. Now it does. But not a full set. And, unlike in the Rocky movies, the Taxpayer Bill of Rights Part 2 that became law on July 30, 1996, and Part 3, which came about when the IRS was overhauled in 1998, don't see to it that the underdog always wins. Here's what the improved Taxpayer Bill of Rights does for you:

✔ Abates the penalty for failing to deposit payroll taxes for first-time filers of employment tax returns.

✔ Enables you to file a joint return after a separate return has been filed without having to pay the full joint tax.

✔ Allows the return of levied property, including your salary, if you have an installment agreement to pay what you owe and it would be a hardship (you can't pay your bills) not to return it. Under the old rules, once the IRS "glommed" your dough, it couldn't return it.

✔ Requires that 1099s have the name, address, and telephone number of whom to contact in case the reported amount is incorrect and needs investigating.

✔ Shifts the burden to the IRS to prove that its position was substantially justified when you prevail in a suit with the IRS. If the IRS position wasn't substantially justified, you can collect for legal fees and court costs from the IRS. Under the old rule, you had to prove that the IRS's position wasn't substantially justified.

✔ Requires that the IRS, upon a taxpayer's request, make every reasonable effort to contact private creditors when a Notice of a Tax Lien has been withdrawn.

The bill also includes the following helpful provisions:

✔ If a few people, namely the owners or officers of a business, are personally responsible for payment of taxes that were withheld from their employees' salaries and one of these individuals pays more than his or her share, that person can sue to recover that amount from the others. The IRS now is obliged to tell what each person paid and what the IRS is doing to collect what is owed from the others. Because the IRS usually goes after the owner where it will have least difficulty in collecting the entire amount that business owes, that poor soul now has the right to know what his partners have paid so he can make them pay their share of what he was forced to pay.

✔ The IRS must notify taxpayers if it receives a payment that can't be applied against what is owed, instead of merely depositing the check and holding it in limbo.

✔ If you owe the IRS, the IRS must send you at least an annual bill so you know where you stand. The statement must include a detailed computation of the interest charged.

✔ For taxes that you and an ex-spouse jointly owe, you can ask the IRS what it is doing to get your ex-spouse to pay the tax, and you have the right to be told how much has been paid. Because of possible hostility toward an ex-spouse, the IRS, however, won't reveal the ex-spouse's home or business addresses.

✔ The innocent spouse rules have been made more lenient in a number of ways. Relief can also be obtained on an apportioned basis.

✔ If the IRS doesn't send a notice adjusting a taxpayer's return within 18 months, it must stop charging interest after 18 months and until 21 days after a notice is sent. See Chapter 16, because not all IRS notices are covered under this rule.

✔ You can collect up to $1 million in damages if the IRS acts with reckless or intentional disregard of the rules in collecting tax. If the IRS is merely negligent, the limit is $100,000. The IRS has the authority — but, again, isn't compelled — to abate interest because of delays on its part. Delays caused by loss of records, transfer of personnel, extended illness, leave, or training programs now are causes for abating interest.

✔ If someone issues you a fraudulent 1099, you can sue for damages of up to $5,000.

✔ Proof under the timely-mailing-is-filing rule requires that a document or return had to be sent by either certified or registered mail. Using FedEx, DHL, Airborne, or UPS now is equivalent to sending a return or document by certified or registered mail.

A mailing receipt that you receive from the post office other than for certified or registered mail isn't considered valid proof of meeting the timely-mailing-is-timely-filing rule.

✔ Financial status audits to scrutinize a taxpayer's lifestyle are allowed only when a routine examination has established a likelihood of unreported income. See Chapter 16.

✔ Taxpayers have a 30-day period to appeal a lien or levy. See Chapter 16.

✔ The rejection of an Offer in Compromise or a request for an installment agreement can be appealed.

✔ While an Offer in Compromise or a request for an installment agreement is pending or on appeal, the IRS can't levy against a taxpayer.

✔ Your residence can't be seized unless authorized in writing by a U.S. district court judge. Business assets can't be seized unless authorized by a district or assistant district director.

✔ The law shifts the burden of proof from the taxpayer to the IRS in court proceedings.

Part V
Year-Round Tax Planning

The 5th Wave   By Rich Tennant

"Annuities? Equity income? Tax-free municipals? I say we stick the money in the ground like always, and then feed this guy to the sharks."

In this part . . .

Taxes aren't a financial island unto themselves. Just about every major financial decision you make involves a tax angle and has tax consequences. With just a little bit of knowledge and advance planning, you can make your money work much harder for you. In fact, the worse you are at managing your finances, the more money you can put back into your pocket, if you figure out how to make tax-wise financial decisions. This part helps you make the most of your money year-round. Just don't forget that it's here!

Chapter 19

Tax-Wise Personal Finance Decisions

In This Chapter

▶ Viewing your finances holistically

▶ Learning from common mistakes

▶ Overcoming tax-planning hurdles

Managing your personal finances involves much more than simply investing money. It includes making all the pieces of your financial life fit together. And, just like designing a vacation itinerary, managing your personal finances means developing a strategy to make the best use of your limited dollars and being prepared to deal with some adversity and changes to the landscape.

Taxes are a large and vital piece of your financial puzzle. The following list shows some of the ways that tax issues are involved in making sound financial decisions throughout the year:

✔ **Spending:** The more you spend, the more taxes you'll pay for taxed purchases and for being less able to take advantage of the many benefits in the tax code that require you to have money to invest in the first place. For example, contrary to the hucksters on late-night infomercials, you need money to purchase real estate, which offers many tax benefits (see Chapter 23). And because taxes are probably your largest or second biggest expenditure, a budget that overlooks tax-reduction strategies is likely doomed to fail. Unless you have wealthy, benevolent relatives, you may be stuck with a lifetime of working if you can't save money.

✔ **Retirement accounts:** Taking advantage of retirement accounts can mean tens, perhaps even hundreds of thousands more dollars in your pocket come retirement time. Who says there are no free lunches? Check out Chapter 20.

✔ **Investing:** Many tax angles factor into wise investing. Merely choosing investments that generate healthy rates of return isn't enough. What matters is not what you make but what you keep — after paying taxes. Understand and capitalize on the many tax breaks available to investors in stocks, bonds, mutual funds, real estate, and your own business. See Chapter 21 for the details.

✔ **Protecting your assets:** Some of your insurance decisions also affect the taxes you pay. You'd think that after a lifetime of tax payments, your heirs would be left alone when you pass on to the great beyond — wishful thinking. Estate planning can significantly reduce the taxes to be siphoned off from your estate. Peruse Chapter 25 to find out more about estate planning.

Taxes infiltrate many areas of your personal finances. Some people make important financial decisions without considering taxes (and other important variables). Conversely, in an obsession to minimize or avoid taxes, other people make decisions that are counterproductive to achieving their long-term personal and financial goals. Although this chapter shows you that taxes are an important component to factor into your major financial decisions, *taxes should not drive or dictate the decisions you make.*

Taxing Mistakes

Even if some parts of the tax system are hopelessly and unreasonably complicated, there's no reason why you can't learn from the mistakes of others to save yourself some money. With this goal in mind, this section details common tax blunders that people make when it comes to managing their money.

Seeking advice after a major decision

Too many people seek out information and hire help after making a decision, even though seeking preventive help ahead of time generally is wiser and less costly. Before making any major financial decisions, educate yourself. The book you're holding in your hands can help answer many of your questions.

If you're going to hire a tax advisor to give advice, do so *before* making your decision(s). Read Chapters 2 and 29 for tips about finding a good tax advisor. The wrong move when selling a piece of real estate or taking money from a retirement account can cost you thousands of dollars in taxes!

Failing to withhold enough taxes

If you're self-employed or earn significant taxable income from investments outside retirement accounts, you need to be making estimated quarterly tax payments. Likewise, if, during the year, you sell an investment asset at a profit, you may need to make a (higher) quarterly tax payment.

Not having a human resources department to withhold taxes from their pay as they earn it, some self-employed people dig themselves into a perpetual tax hole by failing to submit estimated quarterly tax payments. They get behind in their tax payments during their first year of self-employment and thereafter are always playing catch-up. Don't be a "should've" victim. People often don't discover that they "should've" paid more taxes during the year until after they complete their returns in the spring — or get penalty notices from the IRS and their states. Then they have to come up with sizable sums all at once.

To make quarterly tax payments, complete **IRS Form 1040-ES, Estimated Tax for Individuals.** This form and accompanying instructions explain how to calculate quarterly tax payments — the IRS even sends you payment coupons and envelopes in which to mail your checks. We walk you through the essentials of completing this form in Chapter 15.

Although we — and the IRS — want you to keep your taxes current during the year, we don't want you to overpay. Some people have too much tax withheld during the year, and this overpayment can go on year after year. Although it may feel good to get a sizable refund check every spring, why should you loan your money to the government interest-free? When you work for an employer, you can complete a new W-4 to adjust your withholding. Turn the completed W-4 in to your employer. When you're self-employed, complete Form 1040-ES, Estimated Tax for Individuals. (See Chapter 15 for instructions on completing your W-4.)

If you know that you'd otherwise spend the extra tax money that you're currently sending to the IRS, then this forced-savings strategy may have some value. But you can find other, better ways to make yourself save. You can set up all sorts of investments, such as mutual funds (see Chapter 22), to be funded by automatic contributions from your paychecks (or from a bank or investment account). Of course, if you happen to prefer to loan the IRS money — interest-free — go right ahead!

Overlooking legal deductions

Some taxpayers miss out on perfectly legal tax deductions because they just don't know about them. Ignorance is not bliss when it comes to your income taxes . . . it's costly. If you aren't going to take the time to discover the legal deductions available to you (you bought this book, so why not read the relevant parts of it?), then spring for the cost of a competent tax advisor at least once.

Fearing an audit, some taxpayers (and even some tax preparers) avoid taking deductions that they have every right to take. Unless you have something to hide, such behavior is costly and silly. Remember that a certain number of returns are randomly audited every year, so even when you don't take every deduction to which you're legally entitled, you may nevertheless get audited! And how bad is an audit, really? If you read Chapter 16, you can find out how to deal with your audit like a pro. An hour or so with the IRS is not as bad as you might think. It may be worth the risk of claiming all the tax breaks to which you're entitled, especially when you consider the amounts you can save through the years.

Passing up retirement accounts

All the tax deductions and tax deferrals that come with accounts such as 401(k)s, Keoghs, and IRAs were put in the tax code to encourage you to save for retirement. So why not take advantage of the benefits?

You probably have your reasons or excuses, but most excuses for missing out on this strategy just don't make good financial sense. Most people underfund retirement accounts because they spend too much and because retirement seems so far away. Many people also mistakenly believe that retirement account money is totally inaccessible until they're old enough to qualify for senior discounts. See Chapter 20 to find out all about retirement accounts and why you should fund them.

Ignoring tax considerations when investing

Suppose that you want to unload some stock so that you can buy a new car. You sell an investment at a significant profit and feel good about your financial genius. But, come tax time, you may feel differently.

Don't forget to consider the taxes due on profits from the sale of investments (except those in retirement accounts) when making decisions about what you sell and when you sell it. Your tax situation also needs to factor in what you invest outside retirement accounts. When you're in a relatively high tax bracket, you probably don't want investments that pay much in taxable distributions such as taxable interest, which only add to your tax burden. See Chapter 22 for details on the tax considerations of investing and which investments are tax-friendly for your situation.

Not buying a home

In the long run, owning a home should cost you less than renting. And because mortgage interest and property taxes are deductible, the government, in effect, subsidizes the cost of home ownership.

Even if the government didn't help you with tax benefits when buying and owning a home, you'd still be better off owning over your adult life. If you instead rented, all your housing expenses are exposed to inflation, unless you have a great rent-controlled deal. So owning your own abode makes good financial and tax sense. And don't let the lack of money for a down payment stand in your way — methods exist for buying real estate with little upfront money. See Chapter 23 to find out about real estate and taxes.

Ignoring the financial aid tax system

The college financial aid system in this country assumes that the money you save outside tax-sheltered retirement accounts is available to pay educational expenses. As a result, families who save money *outside* instead of *inside* retirement accounts may qualify for far less financial aid than they otherwise would. So in addition to normal income taxes, an extra financial aid "tax" is effectively exacted. Be sure to read Chapter 24, which covers the best ways to save and invest for educational costs.

Neglecting the timing of events you can control

The amount of tax you pay on certain transactions can vary, depending on the timing of events. If you're nearing retirement, for example, you may soon be in a lower tax bracket. To the extent possible, you need to delay and avoid claiming investment income until your overall income level drops, and you need to take as many deductions or losses as you can now while your income still is high. Following are two tax-reducing strategies — income shifting and bunching or shifting deductions — that you may be able to put to good use when you can control the timing of either your income or deductions.

Shifting income

Suppose that your employer tells you in late December that you're eligible for a bonus. You find out that you have the option of receiving your bonus in either December or January (ask your payroll and benefits department if this is an option). Looking ahead, if you're pretty certain that you're going to be in a higher tax bracket next year, request to receive your bonus in December. (See Chapter 1 to find out about your tax bracket.)

Or suppose that you run your own business and operate on a cash accounting basis and think that you'll be in a lower tax bracket next year. Perhaps business has slowed of late or you plan to take time off to be with a newborn or take an extended trip. You can send out some invoices later in the year so that your customers won't pay you until January, which falls in the next tax year.

Bunching or shifting deductions

When the total of your itemized deductions on Schedule A (see Chapter 9) is lower than the standard deduction, you need to take the standard deduction. This itemized deduction total is worth checking each year, because you may have more deductions in some years than others, and you may occasionally be able to itemize.

When you can control the timing of payment of particular expenses that are eligible for itemizing, you can *shift* or *bunch* more of them into select years when you're more likely to have enough deductions to take advantage of itemizing. Suppose that because you don't have many itemized deductions this year, you use the standard deduction. Late in the year, however, you feel certain that you'll itemize next year, because you plan to buy a home and will therefore be able to claim significant mortgage interest and property tax deductions. It makes sense, then, to shift and bunch as many deductible expenses as possible into next year. For example, if you're getting ready to make a tax-deductible donation of old clothes and household goods to charity, wait until January to do so.

In any tax year that you're sure you won't have enough deductions to be able to itemize, shift as many itemizable expenses as you can into the next tax year. If you don't know what types of expenses you can itemize, be sure to peruse Chapter 9.

Be careful when using your credit card to pay expenses. These expenses must be recognized for tax purposes in the year in which the charge was made on the card and not when you actually pay the credit card bill.

Not using tax advisors effectively

If your financial situation is complicated, going it alone and relying only on the IRS booklets to figure your taxes usually is a mistake. Many people find the IRS instructions tedious and not geared toward highlighting opportunities for tax reductions. Instead, you can start by reading the relevant sections of this book. You can figure out taxes for yourself, or you can hire a tax advisor to figure them out for you. Doing nothing isn't an advisable option!

When you're overwhelmed with the complexity of particular financial decisions, get advice from tax and financial advisors who sell their time and nothing else. Protect yourself by checking references, clarifying what advice, analysis, and recommendations the advisor will provide for the fee charged. If your tax situation is complicated, you'll probably more than recoup a preparer's fee, as long as you take the time to hire a good one (see Chapter 2 for tips on hiring help).

Remember that using a tax advisor is most beneficial when you face new tax questions or problems. If your tax situation remains complicated, or if you know that you'd do a worse job on your own, by all means keep using a tax preparer. But don't pay a big fee year after year to a tax advisor who simply plugs your numbers into the tax forms. If your situation is unchanging or isn't that complicated, consider hiring and paying someone to figure out your taxes one time. After that, go ahead and try completing your own tax return.

Comprehending the Causes of Bad Tax Decisions

When bad things happen, it's usually for a variety of reasons. And so it is with making financial blunders that cause you to pay more tax dollars. The following sections describe some common culprits that may be keeping you from making tax-wise financial maneuvers and what you can do about them.

"Financial planners" and brokers' advice

Wanting to hire a financial advisor to help you make better financial decisions is a logical inclination, especially if you're a time-starved person. But when you pick a poor planner or someone who isn't a financial planner but rather a salesperson in disguise, watch out!

Unfortunately, many people calling themselves financial planners, financial consultants, or financial advisors actually work on commission, which creates enormous conflicts of interest with providing unbiased and objective financial advice. Brokers and commission-based financial planners (who are also therefore brokers) structure their advice around selling you investment and other financial products that provide them with commissions. As a result, they tend to take a narrow view of your finances and frequently ignore the tax and other consequences of financial moves. Or they may pitch the supposed tax benefits of an investment they're eager to sell you as a reason for you to buy it. It may provide a tax benefit for someone, but not necessarily for you in your specific situation.

The few planners who work on a *fee basis* primarily provide money-management services and charge 1 percent to 2 percent per year of the money they manage. Fee-based planners have their own conflicts of interest, because all things being equal, they want you to hire them to manage *your money.* Therefore, they can't objectively help you decide whether you should pay off your mortgage and other debts, invest in real estate or a small business, or invest more in your employer's retirement plan. In short, they have a bias against financial strategies that take your investment money out of their hands.

Be especially leery of planners, brokers, and money-managing planners who lobby you to sell investments that you've held for a while and that show a profit. If you sell these investments, you may have a hefty tax burden. (See Chapter 22 for more insight on how to make these important investing decisions.)

Advertising

Another reason you may make tax missteps in managing your personal finances is advertising. Although reputable financial firms with terrific products advertise, the firms that spend the most on advertising often are the ones with inferior offerings. Being bombarded with ads whenever you listened to the radio, watched television, or read magazines and newspapers was bad enough, but now e-mail boxes are stuffed full of spam, and fax machines are blitzed with promos too.

Responding to ads usually is a bad financial move, regardless of whether the product being pitched is good, bad, or so-so, because the company placing the ad typically is trying to motivate you to buy a specific product. The company doesn't care about your financial alternatives, whether its product fits with your tax situation, and so on. Many ads try to catch your attention with the supposed tax savings that their products generate.

Advice from publications

You read an article that recommends some investments. Tired of not taking charge and making financial decisions, you get on the phone, call an investment company, and — before you know it — you've invested. You feel a sense of relief and accomplishment — you've done something.

Come tax time, you get all these confusing statements detailing dividends and capital gains that you must report on your tax return. Now you see that these investment strategies generate all sorts of taxable distributions that add to your tax burden. And you may be saddled with additional tax forms to complete by April 15. You wish you had known.

Articles in magazines, newspapers, newsletters, and on Web sites can help you stay informed, but they also can cause you to make ill-advised financial moves that overlook tax consequences. Article writers have limited space and often don't consider the big picture or ways their advice can be misunderstood or misused. Even worse is that too many writers don't know the tax consequences of what they're writing about.

Overspending

Far too many tax guides go on and on and on, talking about this tax break and that tax break. The problem is that to take advantage of many of the best tax breaks, you need to have money to invest. When you spend all that you earn, as most Americans do, you miss out on many terrific tax benefits that we tell you about in this book. And the more you spend, the more taxes you pay, both on your income and on the purchases you make (through sales taxes).

Just like losing weight, spending less *sounds* good, but most people have a hard time budgeting their finances and spending less than they earn. Perhaps you already know where the fat is in your spending. If you don't, figuring out where all your monthly income is going is a real eye-opener. The task takes some detective work — looking through your credit card statements and your checkbook register to track your purchases and categorize your spending.

Financial illiteracy

Lack of education is at the root of most personal financial blunders. You may not understand the tax system and how to manage your finances, because you were never taught how to manage them in high school or college.

Financial illiteracy is a widespread problem not just among the poor and undereducated. Most people don't plan ahead and educate themselves with their financial goals in mind. People react — or, worse, do nothing at all. You may dream, for example, about retiring and never having to work again. Or perhaps you hope that someday you can own a house or even a vacation home in the country or by the shore.

You need to understand how to plan your finances so you can accomplish your financial goals. You also need to understand how the tax system works and how to navigate within it to work toward your objectives.

If you need more help with important personal financial issues, pick up a copy of the latest edition of Eric's *Personal Finance For Dummies* (Wiley).

Chapter 20

Reducing Taxes with Retirement Accounts

· ·

In This Chapter

▶ Understanding the advantages and potential pitfalls of retirement accounts

▶ Comparing the different types and rules of retirement accounts

▶ Prioritizing account options, and understanding transfers and withdrawals

· ·

*S*aving and investing through retirement accounts is one of the simplest yet most powerful methods to reduce your tax burden. Understanding the myriad account options and rules isn't simple, but we do our best at explaining them in this chapter.

Unfortunately, most people can't take advantage of these plans because they spend too much of what they make. So not only do they have less savings, but they also pay higher income taxes — a double whammy. And don't forget, the more you spend, the more sales tax you pay on purchases. To be able to best take advantage of the tax savings that come with retirement savings plans, you should spend less than you earn. Only then can you afford to contribute to these plans.

Identifying Retirement Account Benefits

Retirement may seem like the distant future to young people. It's often not until middle age that warning bells start stimulating thoughts about what money they'll live on in their golden years. The single biggest mistake people at all income levels make with retirement accounts is not taking advantage of them. When you're in your 20s and 30s (and for some individuals in their 40s and 50s), spending and living for today and postponing saving for the future seems a whole lot more fun than saving for retirement. But assuming that you don't want to work your entire life, the sooner you start saving, the less painful it is each year, because your contributions have more years to grow and because you have more years to cultivate the savings habit.

Each decade that you delay contributing approximately doubles the percentage of your earnings that you need to save to meet your goals. For example, if saving 5 percent per year in your early 20s gets you to your retirement goal, waiting until your 30s may mean socking away 10 percent; waiting until your 40s, 20 percent . . . it gets ugly beyond that!

So the longer you wait, the more you'll have to save and, therefore, the less that will be left over to spend. As a result, you may not meet your goal, and your golden years may be more restrictive than you hoped.

We use this simple lesson to emphasize the importance of considering *now* the benefits you achieve by saving and investing in some type of retirement account.

Contributions are (generally) tax-deductible

Spend money today and you get some instant gratification. Put some of that same money into a retirement account, and you might yawn with excitement and then get a headache figuring where to invest it!

Retirement accounts really should be called *tax-reduction accounts*. If they were, people might be more eager to contribute to them. For many people, avoiding higher taxes is the motivating force that gets them to open the account and start the contributions.

If you're a moderate-income earner, you probably pay about 30 to 35 percent in federal and state income taxes on your last dollars of income (see Chapter 1 to identify your tax bracket). Thus, with most of the retirement accounts described in this chapter, for every $1,000 you contribute to them, you save yourself about $300 to $350 in taxes in the year that you make the contribution. Contribute five times as much, or $5,000, and whack $1,500 to $1,750 off your tax bill! Thanks to tax bills passed in the early 2000s, the contribution limits on retirement accounts have greatly increased in recent years and will continue to rise in the years ahead (the details are later in this chapter).

Check with your employer's benefits department because some organizations match a portion of employee contributions. Be sure to partake of this free matching money by contributing to your retirement accounts.

Special tax credit for lower-income earners

In addition to the upfront tax break you get from contributing to many retirement accounts, lower-income earners may receive tax credits worth up to 50 percent on the first $2,000 of retirement account contributions. Like employer-matching contributions, this tax credit amounts to free money (in this case from the government), so you should take advantage!

As you can see in Table 20-1, this relatively new retirement account contribution tax credit phases out quickly for higher-income earners, and no such credit is available to single taxpayers with adjusted gross incomes (AGIs) of more than $25,000 and to married couples filing jointly with AGIs of more than $50,000. (*Note:* This credit isn't available to taxpayers who are claimed as dependents on someone else's tax return or who are under the age of 18 or full-time students.)

Table 20-1	Tax Credit for the First $2,000 in Retirement Plan Contributions	
Single Taxpayers Adjusted Gross Income	**Married Couples Filing Jointly Adjusted Gross Income**	**Tax Credit for Retirement Account Contributions**
$0 to $15,000	$0 to $30,000	50%
$15,001 to $16,250	$30,001 to $32,500	20%
$16,251 to $25,000	$32,501 to $50,000	10%

Tax-deferred compounding of investment earnings

After money is placed in a retirement account, any interest, dividends, and appreciation add to the amount of the account without being taxed. You get to defer taxes on all the accumulating gains and profits until you withdraw the money, presumably in retirement. Thus more money is working for you over a longer period of time.

Retirement account penalties for early withdrawals

One objection that some people have to contributing to retirement accounts is the early withdrawal penalties. Specifically, if you withdraw funds from retirement accounts before age 59½, you not only have to pay income taxes on withdrawals, but you also may pay early withdrawal penalties — typically 10 percent in federal and state charges. (There's a 25 percent penalty for withdrawing from a SIMPLE plan within the first two years, which decreases to 10 percent thereafter.)

The penalties are in place for good reason — to discourage people from raiding retirement accounts. Remember, retirement accounts exist for just that reason — saving toward retirement. If you could easily tap these accounts without penalties, the money would be less likely to be there when you need it during your golden years.

If you have an emergency, such as catastrophic medical expenses or a disability, you may be able to take early withdrawals from retirement accounts without penalty. You may withdraw funds from particular retirement accounts free of penalties (and, in some cases, even free of current income taxes) for educational expenses or a home purchase. We spell out the specifics of this loophole in the "Penalty-free IRA withdrawals" section later in this chapter.

What if you just run out of money because you lose your job? Although you can't bypass the penalties because of such circumstances, if you're earning so little income that you need to tap your retirement account, you'll surely be in a low tax bracket. So even though you pay some penalties to withdraw retirement account money, the lower income taxes that you pay upon withdrawal — as compared to the taxes that you would have incurred when you earned the money originally — should make up for most or all of the penalty.

Know also that if you get in a financial pinch while you're still employed, some company retirement plans allow you to borrow against a portion of your cash balance. Just be sure that you can repay such a loan — otherwise, your "loan" becomes a withdrawal and triggers income taxes and penalties.

Another strategy to meet a short-term financial emergency is to withdraw money from your IRA and return it within 60 days to avoid paying penalties. We don't generally recommend this maneuver because of the taxes and potential penalties invoked if you don't make the 60-day deadline.

In the event that your only "borrowing" option right now is a credit card with a high interest rate, you should save three to six months' worth of living expenses in an accessible account before funding a retirement account to tide you over in case you lose your income. Money market mutual funds are an ideal vehicle to use for this purpose.

You may be interested in knowing that if good fortune comes your way and you accumulate enough funds to retire "early," you have a simple way around the pre-age-59½ early withdrawal penalties. Suppose that at age 50 you retire and want to start living off some of the pile of money you've stashed in retirement accounts. No problem. The IRS graciously allows you to start withdrawing money from your retirement accounts free of those nasty early withdrawal penalties. To qualify for this favorable treatment, you must commit to withdrawals for at least five continuous years, and the amount of the withdrawals must be at least the minimum required based on your life expectancy.

Your retirement tax rate need not be less than your tax rate during your working years for you to come out ahead by contributing to retirement accounts. In fact, because you defer paying tax and have more money compounding over more years, you can end up with more money in retirement by saving inside a retirement account, even if your retirement tax rate is higher than it is now.

The tax rate on *long-term capital gains* — investments held more than one year — and stock dividends (see Chapter 22) is significantly lower than the rate on ordinary income. Even though recently passed rules lowered the tax rate on some investment returns produced outside retirement accounts, most people will still come out ahead investing through retirement accounts.

And remember this: You may get an added bonus from deferring taxes on your retirement account assets if you're in a lower tax bracket when you withdraw the money. You may well be in a lower tax bracket in retirement because most people have less income when they're not working.

I need how much for retirement?

On average, most people need about 70 percent to 80 percent of their pre-retirement income to maintain their standard of living throughout their retirement. For example, if your household earns $40,000 per year before retirement, you'll likely need $28,000 to $32,000 (70 percent to 80 percent of $40,000) per year during retirement to live the way that you're accustomed to living.

Remember that 70 percent to 80 percent is just an average. You may need more or less. If you currently save little or none of your annual income, expect to have a large mortgage payment or growing rent in retirement, or anticipate wanting to travel or do other expensive things in retirement, you may need 90 percent or perhaps even 100 percent of your current income to maintain your standard of living in retirement.

On the other hand, if you now save a high percentage of your earnings, are a high-income earner, expect to own your home free of debt by retirement, and anticipate leading a modest lifestyle in retirement, you may be able to make do with, say, 60 percent of your current income.

If you've never thought about what your retirement goals are, looked into what you can expect from Social Security (stop laughing), or calculated how much you should be saving for retirement, now's the time to do it. The latest edition of *Personal Finance For Dummies,* written by Eric Tyson (Wiley), goes through all the necessary details and even tells you how to come up with more to invest and do it wisely.

Note: When you're near retirement and already have money in a tax-sheltered type of retirement account (for example, at your employer), by all means continue to keep it in a tax-favored account if you leave. You can accomplish this goal by rolling the money over into an IRA account. If your employer offers good investment options in a retirement plan and allows you to leave your money in the plan after your departure, consider that option, too.

Don't go overboard

Over the years, we've seen some clients "over" contribute to retirement accounts. We don't literally mean that these well-intentioned souls broke the contribution limit rules. We're talking about unusual situations where people have contributed more to their retirement accounts than what makes good financial and tax sense.

For example, it may not make sense for a taxpayer who is temporarily in a very low tax bracket (or owing no tax at all) to contribute to retirement accounts. Ditto the person who has a large estate already and has piles inside retirement accounts that could get walloped by estate and income taxes upon their passing. Few people, of course, have this perhaps enviable "problem."

When in doubt and if you have reason to believe you should scale back on retirement account contributions, consult with a competent financial/tax advisor who works for an hourly fee and doesn't sell products or manage money. Please see the latest edition of Eric's *Personal Finance For Dummies* (Wiley) for more details.

Naming the Types of Retirement Accounts

When you earn employment income (or receive alimony), you have the option of putting money away in a retirement account that compounds without taxation until you withdraw the money. In most cases, your contributions are tax-deductible. The following sections discuss the major types of "IRS-approved" retirement accounts and explain how to determine whether you're eligible for them and some other nitpicky but important rules.

Employer-sponsored plans

You should be thankful that your employer values your future enough to offer these benefits and grateful that your employer has gone to the trouble of doing all the legwork of setting up the plan, and in most cases, selecting investment options. If you were self-employed, you'd have to hassle with establishing your own plan and choosing a short list of investment options. All you have to do with an employer plan is save enough to invest and allocate your contributions among the (generally few) investments offered.

401(k) plans

For-profit companies generally offer 401(k) plans. The silly name comes from the section of the tax code that establishes and regulates these plans. A 401(k) generally allows you to save up to $15,000 per year for tax year 2006. Your employer's plan may have lower contribution limits, though, if employees don't save enough in the company's 401(k) plan. Your contributions to a 401(k) generally are excluded from your reported income and thus are free from federal and, in some cases, state income taxes, but not from Social Security and Medicare taxes (and from some other state employment taxes).

Older workers — those at least age 50 — are able to put away even more — up to $5,000 more per year than their younger counterparts. For 2007 and after, the contribution limit on 401(k) plans and the additional amounts allowed for older workers will rise, in $500 increments, with inflation.

Some employers don't allow you to start contributing to their 401(k) plan until you've worked for them for a full year. Others allow you to start contributing right away. Some employers also match a portion of your contributions. They may, for example, match half of your first 6 percent of contributions (so in addition to saving a lot of taxes, you get a free bonus from the company). Check with your company's benefits department for your plan's details.

Smaller companies (those with fewer than 100 employees) can consider offering 401(k) plans, too. In the past, it was prohibitively expensive for smaller companies to administer 401(k)s. If your company is interested in this option, contact a mutual fund or discount brokerage organization, such as T. Rowe Price, Vanguard, or Fidelity (see Chapter 22). In some cases, your employer may need to work with a separate plan administrator in addition to one of these investment firms.

403(b) plans

Many nonprofit organizations offer 403(b) plans to their employees. As with a 401(k), your contributions to these plans generally are federal and state tax-deductible. 403(b) plans often are referred to as tax-sheltered annuities, the name for insurance-company investments that satisfy the requirements for 403(b) plans. For the benefit of 403(b) retirement-plan participants, no-load (commission-free) mutual funds also can be used in 403(b) plans.

Nonprofit employees generally are allowed to contribute up to 20 percent or $15,000 of their salaries, whichever is less. Employees who have 15 or more years of service may be allowed to contribute beyond the $15,000 limit. Ask your company's benefits department or the investment provider for the 403(b) plan (or your tax advisor) about eligibility requirements and details about your personal contribution limit.

As with 401(k) plans, the contribution limit for workers age 50 and older is $20,000. After 2006, the contribution limit on 403(b) plans and the additional amounts allowed for older workers will rise, in $500 increments, with inflation.

After-tax 401(k) and 403(b) contributions

Some employer-based retirement plans allow for after-tax contributions. Historically, it made sense to consider such options after exhausting contributions that provide a tax break. The merit of an after-tax contribution is that it can compound without taxation until withdrawal, at which point you would owe taxes on the investment earnings withdrawn.

Tax legislation passed earlier in this decade introduced another way to make after-tax retirement plan contributions. Specifically, effective tax year 2006, employers can allow employees to make after-tax Roth contributions to both 401(k) and 403(b) plans.

Like Roth IRA contributions, Roth 401(k) and Roth 403(b) contributions not only grow tax-deferred but also allow

for tax-free withdrawal of investment earnings. This extra tax break (the Roth tax-free withdrawal of investment earnings) is the new part of being able to make after-tax contributions to 401(k) and 403(b) plans.

Generally speaking, you still will likely be better off making pretax retirement plan contributions before considering after-tax (Roth) contributions. Most people are best served taking the sure tax break than waiting many years for an unspecified tax break. Please see our discussion in the section "To Roth or not to Roth?" later in this chapter for further information.

If you work for a nonprofit or public-sector organization that doesn't offer this benefit, make a fuss and insist on it. Nonprofit organizations have no excuse not to offer 403(b) plans to their employees. Unlike 401(k) plans, 403(b) plans have virtually no out-of-pocket setup expenses or ongoing accounting fees. The only requirement is that the organization must deduct the appropriate contribution from employees' paychecks and send the money to the investment company handling the 403(b) plan. If your employer doesn't know where to look for good 403(b) investment options, send them to Vanguard (800-662-2003), Fidelity (800-343-0860), or T. Rowe Price (800-492-7670), all of which offer solid mutual funds and 403(b) plans.

SIMPLE plans

Employers in small businesses have yet another retirement plan option, known as the SIMPLE-IRA. SIMPLE stands for Savings Incentive Match Plans for Employees. Relative to 401(k) plans, SIMPLE plans make it somewhat easier for employers to reduce their costs, thanks to easier reporting requirements and fewer administrative hassles. (However, employers may escape the nondiscrimination testing requirements — one of the more tedious aspects of maintaining a 401(k) plan — by adhering to the matching and contribution rules of a SIMPLE plan, as described later in this section.)

The contribution limits for SIMPLE plans is $10,000 for tax year 2006 for younger workers ($12,500 for those age 50 and older). The contribution limits will increase in increments of $500 with inflation after 2006.

Employers must make small contributions on behalf of employees. Employers can either match, dollar for dollar, the employee's first 3 percent that's contributed or contribute 2 percent of pay for everyone whose wages exceed $5,000. Interestingly, if the employer chooses the first option, the employer has an incentive not to educate employees about the value of contributing to the plan because the more employees contribute, the more it costs the employer. And, unlike a 401(k) plan, greater employee contributions don't enable higher-paid employees to contribute more.

Self-employed plans

When you work for yourself, you obviously don't have an employer to establish a retirement plan. You need to take the initiative. Although setting up a plan means work for you, you can select and design a plan that meets your needs. You can actually do a better job than many companies do; often, the people establishing a retirement plan don't do enough homework, or they let some salesperson sweet-talk them into high-expense (for the employees, that is) investments. Your trouble will be rewarded — self-employment retirement plans generally enable you to sock away more money on a tax-deductible basis than most employers' plans do.

If you have employees, you're required to make contributions comparable to the company owners' (as a percentage of salary) on their behalf under these plans. Some part-time employees (those working fewer than 500 to 1,000 hours per year) and newer employees (less than a few years of service) may be excluded. Not all small-business owners know about this requirement — or they choose to ignore it, and they set up plans for themselves but fail to cover their employees. The danger is that the IRS and state tax authorities may, in the event of an audit, hit you with big penalties and disqualify your prior contributions if you have neglected to make contributions for eligible employees. Because self-employed people and small businesses get their taxes audited at a relatively high rate, messing up in this area is dangerous. The IRS has a program to audit small pension plans.

Don't avoid setting up a retirement savings plan for your business just because you have employees and you don't want to make contributions on their behalf. In the long run, you can build the contributions you make for your employees into their total compensation package — which includes salary and other benefits like health insurance. Making retirement contributions need not increase your personnel costs.

To help small-business owners defray some of the costs of establishing and maintaining a retirement savings plan, Congress established a new tax credit. Eligible small employers can claim 50 percent of the costs to set up and administer a retirement plan (to a maximum of $500 per year) for up to three years. The employer's plan must cover no more than 100 employees and at least one employee who isn't deemed highly compensated by the IRS's definition. Highly compensated individuals for 2006 include those who make more than $100,000 per year.

To get the most from your contributions as an employer, consider the following:

✔ Educate your employees about the value of retirement savings plans. You want them to understand how to save for the future, but more important, you want them to value and appreciate your investment.

✔ Select a Keogh plan that requires employees to stay a certain number of years to vest in their contributions and allows for "Social Security integration" (see the discussion in the upcoming section on Keogh plans).

✔ If you have more than 20 or so employees, consider offering a 401(k) or SIMPLE plan, which allows employees to contribute money from their paychecks.

SEP-IRAs

Simplified Employee Pension Individual Retirement Account (SEP-IRA) plans require little paperwork to set up. Each year, you decide the amount you want to contribute to your SEP-IRA; no minimums exist. Your contributions to a SEP-IRA are deducted from your taxable income, saving you big-time on federal and usually state taxes. As with other retirement plans, your money compounds without taxation until withdrawal.

SEP-IRAs allow you to sock away about 20 percent of your self-employment income (business revenue minus expenses), up to a maximum of $44,000 for tax year 2006.

Keoghs

Keogh plans require a bit more paperwork to set up and administer than SEP-IRAs. The historic appeal of certain types of Keoghs was that they allowed you to put away a greater amount of your self-employment income (revenue less your expenses).

Keogh plans now have the same contribution limit ($44,000 and 20 percent of net self-employment income) that SEP-IRA plans do. The future contribution limit of Keogh plans will increase in $1,000 increments with increases in the cost of living, just as with SEP-IRA plans.

So, with Keogh and SEP-IRA plans having the same contribution limits, you may wonder why you should consider a Keogh plan if such plans generally require more paperwork and hassle. Well, an appeal of Keogh plans is that they allow business owners to maximize their contributions relative to employees in two ways that they can't with SEP-IRAs:

✔ Keogh plans allow vesting schedules, which require employees to remain with the company for a specified number of years before they earn the right to their full retirement account balances. *Vesting* refers to the portion of the retirement account money that the employee owns. After a certain number of years, an employee becomes fully vested and, therefore, owns 100 percent of the funds in his retirement account. If an employee leaves prior to being fully vested, he loses the unvested balance, which reverts to the remaining plan participants.

✔ Keogh plans allow for Social Security integration. Integration effectively allows the high-income earners in the company (usually the owners) to receive larger percentage contributions for their accounts than the less highly compensated employees. The logic behind this is that Social Security taxes top out after you earn more than $94,200 (for tax year 2006). Social Security integration enables self-employed business owners and key employees earning in excess of this amount to make up for this ceiling.

Just to make life complicated, Keoghs come in several flavors, which we've ordered from simplest to more complex:

✔ **Profit-sharing plans:** These plans have the same contribution limits as SEP-IRAs. So why would you want the headaches of a more complicated plan when you can't contribute more to it? Profit-sharing plans appeal to owners of small companies who want to use vesting schedules and Social Security integration, which can't be done with SEP-IRA plans.

✔ **Money-purchase pension plans:** Historically, you could contribute more to these plans than you could to a profit-sharing plan or a SEP-IRA. Now all these plans have the same maximum tax-deductible contribution limit — the lesser of 20 percent of your self-employment income or $44,000 per year.

✔ **Defined-benefit plans:** These plans are for people who are able and willing to put away more than the Keogh and SEP-IRA contribution limit of $44,000 per year. Of course only a small percentage of people can afford to do so. Consistently high-income earners older than age 45 to 50 who want to save more than $44,000 per year in a retirement account should consider these plans. If you're interested in defined-benefit plans, you need to hire an actuary to calculate how much you can contribute to such a plan.

Individual Retirement Accounts (IRAs)

A final retirement account option is an Individual Retirement Account (IRA). Because your IRA contributions may not be tax-deductible, contributing to an IRA generally makes sense only after you've exhausted contributing to other retirement accounts, such as the employer- and self-employed–based plans discussed earlier, which allow for tax-deductible contributions. The following sections discuss your IRA options.

"Regular" IRAs

Anyone with employment (or alimony) income can contribute to a *regular* or *traditional* IRA — in other words, the original type of IRA that existed before Congress monkeyed with the laws and created more IRA flavors. You may contribute up to $4,000 each year.

If you don't earn $4,000 a year, you can contribute as much as you want (and can afford) up to the amount of your employment or alimony income. If you're a nonworking spouse, you're also eligible to put $4,000 per year into a so-called spousal IRA.

By tax year 2008, the annual contribution limit for IRAs (both regular and the newer Roth IRAs, see "Nondeductible IRA contributions") will rise to $5,000. People age 50 and older will be able to contribute even more — an extra $1,000 per year starting in 2006 (see Table 20-2).

Table 20-2	IRA (Regular and Roth) Contribution Limits	
Year	*Contribution Limit for Those Under 50*	*Contribution Limit for Those 50 and Older*
2006–2007	$4,000	$5,000
2008	$5,000	$6,000

Your contributions to a regular IRA may or may not be tax-deductible. For tax year 2006, if you're single and your adjusted gross income (AGI) is $50,000 or less for the year, you can deduct your IRA contribution in full. If you're married and file your taxes jointly, you're entitled to a full IRA deduction if your AGI is $75,000 per year or less. *Note:* These AGI limits will increase in future tax years (more details in a moment).

If you make more than these amounts, you can take a full IRA deduction if and only if you (or your spouse) aren't an *active participant* in any retirement plan. The only way to know for certain whether you're an active participant is to look at your W-2 form, that smallish (4-inch x 8½-inch) document your employer sends you early in the year to file with your tax returns. An X mark in a little box in section 13 on the W-2 form indicates that you're an active participant in an employer retirement plan.

Married couples with AGIs of $150,000 or less are no longer disqualified from taking a tax deduction for an IRA contribution because one person is an active participant in an employer's retirement plan. At an AGI of between $150,000 and $160,000, a partial deduction is allowed. At an AGI of $160,000 or more, no IRA deduction is allowed for spouses of active retirement account participants.

For tax year 2006, if you're a single-income earner with an AGI above $50,000 but below $60,000, or married filing jointly with an AGI above $75,000 but below $85,000, you're eligible for a partial IRA deduction, even if you're an active participant. The size of the IRA deduction that you may claim depends on where you fall in the income range. For example, a single-income earner at $55,000 is entitled to half ($1,000) of the full IRA deduction because his or her income falls halfway between $50,000 and $60,000. (See Chapter 7 to find out how to calculate your exact deductible IRA contribution.)

Table 20-3 shows how a gradual rise in the AGI ceiling for fully deductible IRA contributions breaks down for future tax years. (Remember that these figures represent the beginning of a $10,000 phaseout range. In 2007, for example, IRA deductibility phases out between $50,000 and $80,000 for single taxpayers.)

Table 20-3	The Adjusted Gross Income Ceiling for Fully Tax-Deductible IRA Contributions	
Tax Year	*Single*	*Married Filing Jointly*
2006	$50,000	$75,000
2007 and beyond	$50,000	$80,000

Why so many different types of retirement accounts?

The different types of retirement plans — 401(k)s, 403(b)s, SEP-IRAs, Keoghs, regular IRAs, Roth IRAs, and SIMPLE — and the unique tax laws governing each are enough to drive taxpayers and some tax preparers wacky. The complexity of the different rules is another reason that some folks don't bother with these accounts.

As with the other complicated parts of our tax laws, retirement account regulations have accumulated over the years. Just like the stuff that you toss into your spare closet, attic, basement, or garage, the regulations just keep piling up. No one really wants to deal with the mess.

Our neighbors to the north in Canada have a retirement account system that we could learn from. In Canada, they have but one account — it's called the Registered Retirement Savings Plan (RRSP). Everyone with employment income can establish this account and contribute up to 18 percent, or up to a maximum annual total contribution of $18,000 — simple, equitable, and easy to understand. Why don't we do it? Go talk to the boneheads in Congress who brought us this supposedly "simple, equitable, and easy" tax system you're reading about!

Nondeductible IRA contributions

You can contribute to an IRA even if you can't deduct a portion or all of an IRA contribution because you're already covered by another retirement plan and your adjusted gross income is greater than the income limits in Table 20-3.

An IRA contribution that isn't tax-deductible is called, not surprisingly, a nondeductible IRA contribution. (We've never accused the IRS of being creative.) To make a nondeductible contribution, you have to have employment income during the year equal to at least the amount of your IRA contribution.

The benefit of this type of contribution is that the money can still compound and grow without taxation. For a person who plans to leave contributions in the IRA for a long time (a decade or more), this tax-deferred compounding may make nondeductible contributions worthwhile. However, before you consider making a nondeductible IRA contribution, be sure to read about the newer Roth IRAs that may offer better benefits for your situation.

If you end up making a nondeductible IRA contribution, you may wonder how the IRS will know not to tax you again on those portions of IRA withdrawals (because you've already paid income tax on the nondeductible contribution) in retirement. Surprise, surprise, you must fill out another form, **Form 8606**, which you file each year with your tax return to track these nondeductible contributions. We show you how to complete this form in Chapter 15. If you haven't filed your year 2006 tax form yet, you may still make your IRA contribution.

Roth IRAs

For years, some taxpayers and tax advisors (and book authors and financial counselors) have complained about the rules and regulations on regular IRAs. The income limits that allowed for taking an IRA deduction were set too low. And many people who couldn't take a tax deduction on a contribution were unmotivated to make a nondeductible contribution, because earnings on the contribution still would be taxed upon withdrawal. (Granted, the tax-deferred compounding of earnings is worth something — especially to younger people — but that's a more complicated benefit to understand and value.)

So, rather than addressing these concerns by changing regular IRAs, Congress decided to make things even more complicated by introducing another whole IRA known as the Roth IRA, named after the Senate Finance Committee chairman who championed these new accounts. (Perhaps if congressional representatives couldn't name accounts after themselves, removing some of the incentive to continue creating new retirement accounts, we might someday have real tax reform!)

Should you convert your regular IRA to a Roth IRA?

If the Roth IRA's tax-free withdrawals of accumulated earnings appeal to you, you may be interested in knowing that the tax laws allow taxpayers to transfer money from a regular IRA to a Roth IRA without having to pay any early withdrawal penalties. The catch (you knew there'd be one) is that you must pay income tax on the amount transferred, and such a transfer is available only to taxpayers with AGIs of less than $100,000 (this income limitation disappears after 2009).

Whether you'll come out ahead in the long run by doing this conversion depends largely on your time horizon and retirement tax bracket. The younger you are, the higher the tax bracket you think that you'll be in when you retire, and the smaller the account you are thinking of converting, the

more such a conversion makes sense. On the other hand, if you drop into a lower tax bracket in retirement, as many retirees do, you're probably better off keeping the money in a standard IRA account. For assistance with crunching numbers to see whether a conversion makes financial sense, visit the investment firm T. Rowe Price's Web site at `www.troweprice.com` and check out the analytic tools in the "IRA Calculator" section.

Of course, if you can't afford to pay the current income tax you'll owe on the conversion, then don't do it. And again, remember that a future Congress could reverse some of the benefits of the Roth IRA. Thus we generally don't advise many people to convert a regular IRA into a Roth IRA.

Understanding the Roth IRA

The Roth IRA allows for up to a $4,000 annual contribution for couples with AGIs under $150,000 and for single taxpayers with AGIs under $95,000. (Those individuals age 50 and older may contribute $5,000.) The $4,000 limit is reduced for married taxpayers with AGIs above $150,000 ($95,000 if single) and is eliminated for couples with AGIs above $160,000 ($110,000 for singles). As with regular IRAs, the contribution limit for Roth IRAs will rise to $5,000 by 2008 and to $6,000 for those age 50 and older (refer to Table 20-2).

Although this newer IRA doesn't offer a tax deduction on funds contributed to it, it nevertheless offers benefits not provided by regular IRAs and some other retirement accounts. The distinguishing feature of the Roth IRA is that the earnings on your contributions aren't taxed upon withdrawal as long as you're at least age 59½ and have held the account for at least five years.

An exception to the age-59½ rule is made for first-time homebuyers, who can withdraw up to $10,000 from a Roth IRA to apply to the purchase of a principal residence. Remember, however, that your Roth IRA must be in existence for five years before you're allowed an income tax–free withdrawal for a home purchase.

Another attractive feature of the Roth IRA: For those not needing to draw on all their retirement accounts in the earlier years of retirement, the Roth IRA, unlike a standard IRA, doesn't require distributions after the account holder passes age 70½.

To Roth or not to Roth?

Before you go running out to contribute to a Roth IRA, keep in mind that the lack of taxation on withdrawn earnings is in no way guaranteed for the future. Congress can giveth tax benefits, and Congress can taketh them away. If the government is running large deficits in future years, turning around and taxing Roth IRA withdrawals, especially for the more affluent, would increase tax revenue. (On the other hand, retired voters vote, and members of the Congress that tap the short-term benefit of taxing too many of these accounts may face a voter backlash.)

Consider contributing to a Roth IRA if you've exhausted your ability to contribute to tax-deductible retirement accounts and you aren't allowed a tax deduction for a regular IRA contribution because your AGI exceeds the regular IRA deductibility thresholds. If you find yourself in the fortunate situation that your high income disallows you from funding a Roth IRA, then that would be a good reason to contribute to a nondeductible regular IRA (after having maxed out your contributions to other tax-deductible retirement accounts). Sorry, but you can't contribute $4,000 in the same tax year to both a regular IRA and a Roth IRA; the sum of your standard and Roth IRA contributions may not exceed $4,000 in a given year. (If you're so enamored of the Roth IRA's benefits and think you'd rather put your money into a Roth IRA than make a tax-deductible retirement account contribution, check out T. Rowe Price's Web site retirement tools described in the "IRA Calculator" section at www.troweprice.com.)

Penalty-free IRA withdrawals

Except for a few situations having mostly to do with emergencies, such as a major illness and unemployment, tapping into an IRA account before age 59½ (called an *early withdrawal*) triggers a hefty 10 percent federal income tax penalty (in addition to whatever penalties your state charges). Now, however, you're allowed to make a penalty-free early withdrawal from your IRA for two specific expenses. First-time homebuyers — defined as not having owned a home in the past two years — may withdraw up to $10,000. Amounts also may be withdrawn for *qualified higher education costs* (college expenses for a family member such as a child, spouse, the IRA holder, or grandchildren).

Early withdrawals from regular IRA accounts still are subject to regular income tax in the year of withdrawal. Withdrawals from a Roth IRA (discussed in the next section) can be both penalty-free and federal income tax-free as long as the Roth IRA account is at least five years old.

Newer Roth IRA accounts also are exempt from the normal retirement account requirement to begin taking minimum distributions at age 70½ if you aren't working.

Annuities

Annuities, like IRAs, allow your capital to grow and compound without taxation. You defer taxes until withdrawal. Annuities carry the same penalties for withdrawal prior to age 59½ as IRAs do. However, unlike all other retirement accounts except a Roth IRA, you aren't forced to begin withdrawals at age 70½; you may leave the money in an annuity to compound tax deferred for as many years as you desire.

And, unlike an IRA that has an annual contribution limit, you can deposit as much as you want in any year into an annuity — even $1 million if you have it! As with a so-called nondeductible IRA, you get no upfront tax deduction for your contributions. Thus, consider an annuity only after fully exhausting your other retirement account options.

What exactly is an annuity? Well, *annuities* are peculiar investment products — contracts, actually — that insurance companies back. If you, the annuity holder (investor), die during the so-called accumulation phase (that is, prior to receiving payments from the annuity), your designated beneficiary is guaranteed to receive the amount of your original investment.

Because annuities carry higher fees (which reduce your investment returns) because of the insurance that comes with them, you should first make the maximum contribution that you can to an IRA, even if it isn't tax-deductible. Also, consider annuities only if you plan to leave the money in the annuity for 15 years or more. The reasons are twofold. First, it typically takes that long for the tax-deferred compounding of your annuity investment to make up for the annuity's relatively higher expenses. Second, upon withdrawal, the earnings on an annuity are taxed at ordinary income tax rates, which are higher than the more favorable long-term capital gains and stock dividend tax rates. If you don't expect to keep your money invested for 15 to 20-plus years to make up for the annuities' higher ongoing fees and taxes on the back end, you should simply invest your money in tax-friendly investments in non-retirement accounts (see Chapter 22).

Taxing Retirement Account Decisions

In addition to knowing about the different types of retirement accounts available and the importance of using them, we know from our work with counseling clients that you're going to have other problems and questions. This section presents the sticky issues that you may be struggling with, along with our recommendations.

Prioritizing retirement contributions

When you have access to more than one type of retirement account, prioritize which accounts to use by what they give you in return. Your first contributions should be to employer-based plans that match your contributions. After that, contribute to any other employer or self-employed plans that allow tax-deductible contributions. When you've contributed the maximum possible to tax-deductible plans or don't have access to such plans, contribute to an IRA (read the sections earlier in this chapter about choosing between a regular IRA and a Roth IRA).

If you've maxed out on contributions to an IRA or don't have this choice because you lack employment income, consider an annuity or tax-friendly investments (see Chapter 22).

We hate to bring it up, but some spouses worry about whether the bulk of their retirement account contributions will end up in the other spouse's account. You may be concerned about this situation because of the realities of a potential divorce. In a divorce, money in retirement accounts (regardless of how much is in which person's name) can be divided up like the other assets. But rather than worrying about the possibility of divorce, how about investing in the effort to make your relationship stronger to avoid this problem? If you dislike paying taxes, you're going to hate a divorce wherein you could face a 50 percent "tax rate" — that's the amount of your combined assets your spouse could walk away with!

Transferring existing retirement accounts

With employer-maintained retirement plans, such as 401(k)s, you usually have limited investment options. Unless you are the employer or can convince the employer to change, you're stuck with what is offered. If your employer offers four mutual funds from the Lotsa Fees and Lousy Performance Fund Company, for example, you can't transfer this money to another investment company.

After you leave your employer, however, you generally have the option of leaving your money in the employer's plan or transferring it to an IRA at an investment company of your choice. The process of moving this money from an employer plan to investments of your choice is called a *rollover*. And you thought you weren't going to be reading anything fun today!

When you roll money over from an employer-based retirement plan, don't take personal possession of the money. If your employer gives the money to you, the employer must withhold 20 percent of it for taxes. This situation creates a tax nightmare for you because you must then jump through more hoops when you file your return. You also should know that you need to come up with the extra 20 percent when you do the rollover, because you won't get the 20 percent back that your employer withheld in taxes until you file your tax return. If you can't come up with the 20 percent, you have to pay income tax and maybe even excise taxes on this money as a distribution. Yuck!

After you leave the company, you can move your money held in SEP-IRAs, Keoghs, IRAs, and many 403(b) plans (also known as *tax-sheltered annuities*) to nearly any major investment firm you please. Moving the money is pretty simple. If you can dial a toll-free number, fill out a couple of short forms, and send them back in a postage-paid envelope, then you can transfer an account. The investment firm to which you're transferring your account does the rest. Here's the lowdown on how to transfer retirement accounts without upsetting Uncle Sam or any other tax collector:

1. **Decide to which investment firm you want to move the account.**

   When investing in stocks and bonds, mutual funds are a great way to go. They offer diversification and professional management, and they're low-cost. (For more information on mutual funds, see *Mutual Funds For Dummies,* by Eric Tyson [Wiley].)

2. **Call the toll-free number of the firm you're transferring the money to and ask for an account application and asset transfer form for the type of account you're transferring — for example, SEP-IRA, Keogh, IRA, or 403(b).**

   The reason for allowing the new investment company to do the transfer for you is that the tax authorities impose huge penalties if you do a transfer incorrectly. Allowing the company to which you're transferring the money do the transfer for you is far easier and safer. If the company screws up (good investment firms don't), the company is liable.

3. **Complete and mail back the account application and asset transfer forms to your new investment company.**

   Completing this paperwork for your new investment firm opens your new account and authorizes the transfer. If you have questions or problems, the firm(s) to which you're transferring your account has armies of capable employees waiting to help you. Remember, these firms know that you're transferring your money to them, so they normally roll out the red carpet.

   Transferring your existing assets typically takes a month to complete. If the transfer isn't completed within a month, get in touch with your new investment firm to determine the problem.

   If your old company isn't cooperating, a call to a manager there may help to get the ball rolling. The unfortunate reality is that too many investment firms will cheerfully set up a new account to accept your money on a moment's notice, but they will drag their feet, sometimes for months, when it comes time to relinquish your money. If you need to light a fire under their behinds, tell a manager at the old firm that you're sending letters to the National Association of Securities Dealers (NASD) and the Securities and Exchange Commission (SEC) if they don't complete your transfer within the next week.

Taking money out of retirement accounts

Someday, hopefully not until you retire, you'll need or want to start withdrawing and enjoying the money that you socked away in your retirement accounts. Some people, particularly those who are thrifty and good at saving money (also known, by some, as cheapskates and tightwads), have a hard time doing this.

You saved and invested money in your retirement accounts to use at a future date. Perhaps you're in a pinch for cash and the retirement account looks as tempting as a catered buffet meal after a day of fasting. Whatever the reason, here's what you need to consider *before* taking the money out of your retirement accounts.

Lower taxes for working seniors

Increasing numbers of seniors may find that they need to work more years to make financial ends meet. Now, rather than being able to draw full Social Security retirement benefits at age 65, people have to wait longer to get their full Social Security benefits — the current full retirement age is age 65 years and eight months in 2006. The age at which you can draw full Social Security benefits will gradually rise in the years ahead until it reaches age 67 for those born after 1959.

Under prior tax law, some Social Security recipients ages 65 to 69 who were working faced stiff taxes. Specifically, working seniors had to give back $1 of Social Security benefits for every $3 they earned above $17,000 in a tax year. Thus, in addition to owing federal and state income on their earnings, seniors earning in excess of $17,000 annually paid an effective tax rate of 33 percent in lost Social Security benefits!

Now, seniors reaching full retirement age for Social Security purposes and drawing Social Security benefits can earn as much as they like without being penalized (those under age 65 who are receiving Social Security benefits can earn up to $12,480 in 2006; the earnings limit is $33,240 for those individuals reaching full retirement age in 2006). Thus working seniors need not end up having to pay back up to half or more of their earnings in excess of $17,000 per tax year. For seniors needing to continue working for financial reasons, this tax law change is a huge relief. This change also should reduce the number of seniors driven from the workforce because, after paying taxes on their employment earnings, working for pay isn't worth their time.

When should you start withdrawing from retirement accounts?

Some people start withdrawing funds from retirement accounts when they retire. This option may or may not be the best financial decision for you. Generally speaking, you're better off postponing drawing on retirement accounts until you need the money. The longer the money resides inside the retirement account, the longer it can compound and grow, tax-deferred. But don't wait if postponing means that you must scrimp and cut corners — especially if you have the money to use and enjoy.

Suppose that you retire at age 60 and, in addition to money inside your retirement accounts, you have a bunch available outside. If you can, you're better off living off the money outside retirement accounts *before* you start tapping the retirement account money.

If you aren't wealthy and have saved most of the money earmarked for your retirement inside retirement accounts, odds are you'll need and want to start drawing on your retirement account soon after you retire. By all means, do so. But have you figured out how long your nest egg will last and how much you can afford to withdraw? Most folks haven't. Take the time to figure how much of your money you can afford to draw on per year, even if you think that you have enough.

Few people are wealthy enough to consider simply living off the interest and never touching the principal, although more than a few people live like paupers so that they can do just that. Many good savers have a hard time spending and enjoying their money in retirement. If you know how much you can safely use, you may be able to loosen the purse strings.

One danger of leaving your money to compound inside your retirement accounts for a long time after you're retired is that the IRS will require you to start making withdrawals by April 1 of the year *following* the year you reach age 70½. It's possible that because of your delay in taking the money out — and the fact that it will have more time to compound and grow — you may need to withdraw a hefty chunk per year. This procedure could push you into higher tax brackets in those years that you're forced to make larger withdrawals.

This forced distribution no longer applies to people who are working for a company, and also doesn't apply to money held in the newer Roth IRAs (see "Roth IRAs" earlier in this chapter). Self-employed individuals still have to take the distribution.

If you want to plan how to withdraw money from your retirement accounts so that you meet your needs and minimize your taxes, consider hiring a tax advisor to help. If you have a great deal of money in retirement accounts and have the luxury of not needing the money until you're well into retirement, tax planning will likely be worth your time and money.

If you've reached the magic age of 70½ and are required to take an IRA distribution but you don't need that additional income and you really don't want to pay any additional tax, you can now direct your minimum distribution amount (or more, if you're feeling generous) be paid directly to a qualified charity of your choice. The distribution qualifies as your annual required distribution, but the payment to charity excludes it from your adjusted gross income or your taxable income.

Naming beneficiaries

With any type of retirement account, you're supposed to name beneficiaries who will receive the assets in the account when you die. You usually name *primary beneficiaries* — your first choices for receiving the money — and *secondary beneficiaries,* who receive the money in the event that the primary beneficiaries also are deceased when you pass away.

The designations aren't cast in stone; you can change them whenever and as often as you desire by sending written notice to the investment company or employer holding your retirement account. Note that many plans require spousal consent to the naming of a beneficiary other than the spouse.

Do the best you can in naming beneficiaries, and be thankful that you don't have to designate someone to raise your children in your absence! You should know that you can designate charities as beneficiaries. If you want to reduce the amount of money that's required to be distributed from your retirement accounts annually, name beneficiaries who are all at least ten years younger than yourself.

The IRS allows you to calculate the required minimum distribution based on the joint life expectancy of you and your oldest named beneficiary. However, you can't use a difference of greater than ten years for a nonspouse. If a nonspouse is named as the beneficiary and is more than ten years younger, for tax purposes of calculating required withdrawals, they are considered to be just ten years younger than you. (Maybe that's why some rich, older men like marrying younger women!)

Perplexing pension decisions

As discussed earlier in the chapter, if you've worked for a larger company for a number of years, you may have earned what is known as a *pension benefit.* This term simply means that upon attaining a particular age, usually 55 to 65, you can start to receive a monthly check from the employer(s) you worked for. With many pension plans today, you earn (vest) a benefit after you have completed five years of full-time work.

Make sure to keep track of the employer(s) where you have earned pension benefits as you move to new jobs and locations. Mail address changes to your previous employers' benefits departments. If they lose track of you and you forget that you've earned a benefit, you could be out a great deal of money.

What age to start?

With some plans, you may be able to start drawing your pension as early as 50 years of age — as long as you've worked enough years somewhere. The majority of plans, however, won't give you payments until age 55 or 60. Some plans even make you wait until age 65.

If you don't have a choice as to what age you want to start drawing benefits, that situation surely simplifies things for you. Before you become perplexed and overwhelmed if you do have options, remember one simple thing: Smart actuaries have created the choices available to you. Actuaries are the kinds of people who score 800s (a perfect score, in case you forgot) on their math SATs. These folks work, eat, breathe, and sleep numbers.

The choices you confront show you that the younger you elect to start drawing benefits, the less you are paid. Conversely, the longer you can wait to access your pension, the more you should receive per month. That said, here are some pointers:

- ✔ Some pensions stop offering higher benefits after you reach a certain age — make sure that you don't delay starting your benefits until after you've reached this plateau. Otherwise, make your decision as to what age to start drawing benefits based on when you need the money and/or can afford to retire. Run the numbers or hire a competent tax or financial advisor.

- ✔ If you're still working and earning a healthy income, think twice before starting pension benefits — these benefits are likely to be taxed at a much higher rate. You're probably going to be in a lower income tax bracket after you stop working.

- ✔ If you know that you're in poor health and won't live long, consider drawing your pension sooner.

Attempting to calculate which age option will lead to your getting more money isn't worth your time. So many assumptions, such as the rate of inflation and the number of years you'll live, are beyond your ability to predict accurately. The actuaries have done their homework on these issues, and that's why the numbers vary the way they do.

Which payment option for you married folks?

Besides deciding at what age you'll elect to start receiving benefits, you may have other choices if you're married, such as how much money you'll receive when you begin your pension benefit versus how much your spouse will receive if you pass away.

Before we dig into these choices, remember that actuaries are smart — don't make your selection based on age differences between you and your spouse. For example, if you're married to someone much younger, you may be tempted to choose the pension option that maximizes the amount your spouse receives upon your death because you're likely to predecease your spouse. However, each person's pension options already reflect the age differences between spouses, so don't waste your time with this line of thinking. Remember those smart actuaries.

Although the actuaries know your age and your spouse's age, they don't know or care about your ability and desire to accept financial risk. Pension options differ from one another in how much money you can receive now versus how much your spouse is guaranteed to receive in the event that you die first. As with many things in life, there are tradeoffs. If you want to ensure that your spouse continues to receive a relatively high pension in the event of your passing, you must be willing to accept a smaller pension payment when you start drawing the pension.

Understanding the mandatory retirement account distribution rules

If you're self-employed or retired from a company, on April 1 of the year following the year you turn 70½, you have to make some important decisions about how the money will come out of your regular IRA. (This policy isn't applicable to Roth IRAs.) The first choice: whether you receive yearly distributions based on your life expectancy or based on the joint life expectancies of you and your beneficiary. If your aim is to take out as little as possible, you'll want to use a joint life expectancy. That choice will stretch out the distributions over a longer period.

Next, you have to decide how you want your life expectancy to be calculated.

Sometimes, tax law changes actually make things simpler. You'll be happy to know that recently approved IRS regulations make required minimum distribution calculations much easier.

Under the prior laws, retirees had several confusing methods for calculating their mandated retirement account withdrawal amounts. With the new regulations, in most cases, seniors can simply take their retirement account balances and divide that by a number from an IRS life expectancy table.

Another benefit of these new rules is that the new table generally produces lower required distributions and, therefore, a greater ability to preserve the account tax-free than was possible under the old regulations.

See Chapter 6 for more details.

The actuaries also don't know about your current health. All things being equal, if you're in poor health because of a chronic medical problem when you choose your pension option, lean toward those that provide your spouse with more.

The following are some of the typical options, which are ranked in order of providing the most to the fewest dollars at the beginning of retirement. The first choices, which provide more cash in hand sooner, are the riskiest from the standpoint of surviving spouses. The latter choices, which offer less cash in hand today, are the least risky for surviving spouses:

- ✔ **Single Life Option:** This option pays benefits only as long as the pensioner (the person who earned the pension benefit) is alive. The survivor receives nothing. The single life option offers the highest monthly benefits but is also the riskiest option. For example, the pensioner receives $1,500 per month for as long as he or she is alive. The spouse receives nothing after the pensioner's death. Consider this option only if you have sufficient assets for your spouse to live on in the event of your dying early in retirement.

- ✔ **Ten Years' Certain Option:** This option pays benefits for at least ten years, even if the pensioner passes away within the first ten years of drawing the pension. The pensioner continues receiving benefits for as long as he or she lives, even if he or she lives more than ten years. For example, a pensioner receives $1,400 per month for at least ten years until his or her death. The spouse then receives nothing.

- ✔ **50 Percent Joint and Survivor Option:** With this option, the survivor receives 50 percent of the pensioner's benefit after his or her death. For example, a pensioner receives $1,350 per month. Upon the pensioner's death, his or her spouse receives a reduced benefit of $675 per month.

- ✔ **Two-thirds Joint and Survivor Option:** With this option, the survivor receives 66 percent of the pensioner's benefit after his or her death. For example, a pensioner receives $1,310 per month. Upon the pensioner's death, his or her spouse receives a reduced benefit of $865 per month.

✔ **75 Percent Joint and Survivor Option:** With this option, the survivor receives 75 percent of the pensioner's benefit after his or her death. For example, a pensioner receives $1,275 per month. Upon the pensioner's death, the spouse receives a reduced benefit of $956 per month.

✔ **100 Percent Joint and Survivor Option:** With this option, the survivor receives 100 percent of the pensioner's benefit after his or her death. For example, a pensioner receives $1,200 per month. Upon the pensioner's death, the spouse continues to receive $1,200 per month.

Choosing the best pension option for you and your spouse isn't unlike selecting investments. What's best for your situation depends on your overall financial circumstances and desire, comfort, and ability to accept risk. The Single Life Option is the riskiest and should be used only by couples who don't really need the pension — it's frosting on the financial cake — and are willing to gamble to maximize benefits today. If the surviving spouse is very much dependent on the pension, select one of the survivor options that leaves a high benefit amount after the pensioner's death.

Beware of insurance salespeople and "financial planners" (who also sell life insurance and are therefore brokers and not advisors) who advocate that you purchase life insurance and take the Single Life Option. They argue that this option enables you to maximize your pension income and protect the surviving spouse with a life insurance death benefit if the pensioner dies. Sounds good, but the life insurance expense outweighs the potential benefits. Choose one of the survivor pension options that effectively provides life insurance protection for your survivor. This method is a far more cost-effective way to "buy" life insurance.

Chapter 21

Small Businesses and Tax Planning

*W*hether *you* are your entire company or you have many employees for whom you're responsible, running a business can be one of the most frustrating, exhilarating, rewarding — and financially punishing — endeavors of your adult life. Many Americans fantasize about being their own boss. Tales of entrepreneurs becoming multimillionaires and multibillionaires focus our attention on the financial rewards without teaching us about the business and personal costs associated with being in charge.

The biggest challenges business owners face are the personal and emotional ones. It's sad to say, but these challenges rarely get discussed among all the glory tales of rags to riches. Major health problems, divorces, the loss of friends, and even suicides have been attributed to the passions of business owners consumed with winning or overwhelmed by their failures. Although careers and business success are important, if you really think about it, at best these things need be no higher than fourth on your overall priority list. Your health, family, and best friends can't be replaced — but a job or business can.

Business owners know the good and the bad. Consider the countless activities that your company has to do well to survive and succeed in the rough-and-tumble business world. You need to develop products and services that the marketplace will purchase. You have to price your wares properly and promote them. And your business will always face competitors who continually change the landscape.

With money flowing into and out of your coffers, you need to document your income and expenses. Otherwise, preparing your business's tax returns will be a frustrating endeavor. Being audited under these circumstances can produce a never-ending nightmare. And, unlike working for a corporation, owning a small business makes you responsible for ensuring that the right amount of tax is withheld and paid on both the state and federal levels.

This chapter can help you to make tax-wise decisions that will boost your business profits and yet comply with myriad tax regulations that annoy many entrepreneurs like you.

Organizing Your Business Accounting

If you're thinking about starting a business or you're already in the thick of one, you need to keep a proper accounting of your income and expenses. If you don't, you'll have a lot more stress and headaches when it comes time to file the necessary tax forms for your business.

Real versus bogus businesses and hobby loss rules

This chapter is about how small-business owners can make tax-wise decisions while running their businesses. It's not about how to start up a sideline business for the primary purpose of generating tax deductions.

Unfortunately, some self-anointed financial gurus claim that you can slash or even completely eliminate your tax bill by setting up a sideline business. They say that you can sell your services while doing something you enjoy. The problem, they argue, is that — as a regular wage earner who receives a paycheck from an employer — you can't write off many of your other (that is, personal) expenses. These hucksters usually promise to show you the secrets of tax reduction if you shell out far too many bucks for their audiotapes and notebooks of inside information.

"Start a small business for fun, profit, and huge tax deductions," one financial book trumpets, adding that, "The tax benefits alone are worth starting a small business." A seminar company that offers a course on "How to Write a Book on Anything in 2 Weeks . . . or Less!" (we must be doing something wrong) also offers a tax course entitled "How to Have Zero Taxes Deducted from Your Paycheck." This tax seminar tells you how to solve your tax problems: "If you have a sideline business, or would like to start one, you're eligible to have little or no taxes taken from your pay." Gee, sounds good. Where do we sign up?

Suppose that you're interested in photography. You like to take pictures when you go on vacation. These supposed tax experts tell you to set up a photography business and start deducting all your photography-related expenses: airfare, film, utility bills, rent for your "home darkroom," and restaurant meals with potential clients (that is, your friends). Before you know it, you've wiped out most of your taxes.

Sounds too good to be true, right? It is. Your business spending must be for the legitimate purpose of generating an income. According to the IRS, a sideline activity that generates a loss year in and year out isn't a business but a hobby.

Specifically, an activity is considered a hobby if it shows a loss for at least three of the past five tax years. (Horse racing, breeding, and so on are considered hobbies if they show losses in at least five or more of the past seven tax years.) Certainly, some businesses lose money. But a real business can't afford to do so year after year and still remain in business. Who likes losing money unless the losses are really just a tax deduction front for a hobby?

When the hobby loss rules indicate that you're engaging in a hobby, the IRS will disallow your claiming of the losses. To challenge this ruling, you must convince the IRS that you are seriously attempting to make a profit and run a legitimate business. The IRS will want to see that you're actively marketing your services, building your skills, and accounting for income and expenses. The IRS also will want to see that you aren't having too much fun! When you're deriving too much pleasure from an activity, in the eyes of the IRS, the activity must not be a real business.

What's the bottom line? You need to operate a legitimate business for the purpose of generating income and profits — not tax deductions. If you're thinking that it's worth the risk of taking tax losses for your hobby, year after year, because you won't get caught unless you're audited, better think again. The IRS audits an extraordinarily large number of small businesses that show regular losses.

Besides helping you over the annual tax-filing hurdle, you want accurate records so that you can track your business's financial health and performance during the year. How are your profits running compared with last year? Can you afford to hire new employees? Analyzing your monthly or quarterly business financial statements can help you answer these important business questions.

 Here's a final reason to keep good records: The IRS may audit you, and if that happens, you'll be asked that dreaded question: "Can you prove it?" Small-business owners who file Schedule C, Profit or Loss From Business, with their tax returns are audited at a much higher rate than other taxpayers. Although that dubious honor may seem like an unfair burden to business owners, the IRS targets small businesses because more than a few small-business owners break the tax rules and many areas exist where small-business owners can mess up.

The following sections cover the key tax-organizing things that small-business owners need to keep in mind.

Leave an "audit" trail

When it comes time for filing your annual return, you need the documentation that enables you to figure your business income and expenses. At a minimum, set up some file folders in which you can collect receipts and other documentation — perhaps one folder for tabulating your income and another for compiling your expenses. Computer software (see Chapter 2) also may help you with this chore, but you still must go through the hassle of learning a new program and then continually entering the data.

It doesn't matter whether you use file folders, software, or a good old-fashioned shoebox to collate this important financial information. What does matter is that you keep records of expenses and income.

You'll probably lose or misplace some of those little pieces of paper that you need to document your expenses. Thus one big advantage of charging expenses on a credit card or of writing a check is that these transactions leave a paper trail, which makes it easier to total your expenses come tax time and deal with being audited when you need to prove your expenses.

Just remember to be careful when you use a credit card, because you may buy more things than you can really afford. Then you're stuck with a lot of debt to pay off. On the other hand (as many small-business owners know), finding lenders when you need money is difficult. Borrowing on a low-interest-rate credit card can be an easy way for you to borrow money without shamelessly begging a banker for a loan.

Likewise, leave a trail with your revenue. Depositing all your receipts in one account helps you when tax time comes or if you're ever audited.

Separate business from personal finances

One of the IRS's biggest concerns is that as a small-business owner, you'll try to minimize your business profits (and therefore taxes) by hiding business income and inflating your business expenses. Uncle Sam thus looks suspiciously at business owners who use personal checking and credit card accounts for business transactions. You may be tempted to use your personal account this way (because opening separate accounts is a hassle — not because you're dishonest).

Take the time to open separate accounts. Doing so not only makes the feds happy, it also makes your accounting easier.

Please don't make the mistake of thinking that paying for an expense through your business account proves to the IRS that it was a legitimate business expense. If they find that the expense was truly for personal purposes, the IRS then will dig deep into your business's financial records to see what other shenanigans are going on.

Keep current on income and payroll taxes

When you're self-employed, you're responsible for the accurate and timely filing of all your income taxes. Without an employer and a payroll department to handle the paperwork for withholding taxes on a regular schedule, you need to make estimated tax payments on a quarterly basis.

When you have employees, you also need to withhold taxes on their incomes from each paycheck they receive. And you must make timely payments to the IRS and the appropriate state authorities. In addition to federal and state income taxes, you must withhold and send in Social Security and any other state or locally mandated payroll taxes and annually issue W-2s for each employee and 1099-MISCs for each independent contractor paid $600 or more. Got a headache yet?

For paying taxes on your own self-employment income, you can obtain **Form 1040ES, Estimated Tax for Individuals.** This form comes complete with an estimated tax worksheet and the four payment coupons to send in with your quarterly tax payments. It's amazing how user-friendly government people can be when they want your money! The form itself has some quirks and challenges, but you'll be happy to know that we explain how to complete Form 1040ES in Chapter 15.

To discover all the amazing rules and regulations of withholding and submitting taxes from employees' paychecks, ask the IRS for **Form 941.** Once a year, you also need to complete **Form 940** for unemployment insurance payments to the feds. And, unless you're lucky enough to live in a state with no income taxes, don't forget to get your state's estimated income tax package.

If your business has a part-time or seasonal employee and the additional burden of filing **Form 941** quarterly, the IRS has just made the paperwork a tad easier. Beginning for 2006, you may be able to file **Form 944, Employer's Annual Federal Tax Return,** if your tax withholding on behalf of employees doesn't exceed $1,000 for the year (which translates to about $4,000 in wages). If you qualify, you need to file only once each year. If you think you may qualify, call the IRS at 800-829-0115 or visit its Web site at www.irs.gov. If you do qualify, the IRS will send you something in writing.

Falling behind in paying taxes ruins some small businesses. When you hire employees, for example, you're particularly vulnerable to tax landmines. If you aren't going to keep current on taxes for yourself and your employees, hire a payroll company or tax advisor who can help you to jump through the necessary tax hoops. (Refer to Chapter 2 for advice on selecting a tax advisor.) Payroll companies and tax advisors are there for a reason, so use them selectively. They take care of all the tax filings for you, and if they mess up, they pay the penalties. Check with a tax advisor you trust for the names of reputable payroll companies in your area.

Minimizing Your Small-Business Taxes

Every small business has to spend money to make money. Most businesses need things like phone service, paper, computers and printers, software, a bottle of extra-strength aspirin, and a whole bunch of other things you probably never thought you'd be purchasing.

But don't spend money on business stuff just for the sake of generating tax deductions. In some cases, business owners we know buy all sorts of new equipment and other gadgets at year's end for their business so that they can reduce their taxes. Although we endorse reinvesting profits in your business and making your company more efficient and successful, keep in mind that spending too much can lead to lower profits. Remember that nothing is wrong with paying taxes. In fact, it's a sign of profits — business success!

What follows is an overview of what you can do and what not to do to be a tax-wise spender for your business.

Depreciation versus deduction

When you buy equipment such as computers, office furniture, bookshelves, and so on, each of these items is supposed to be depreciated over a number of years. Depreciation simply means that each year, you get to claim as a tax deduction a portion of the original cost of purchasing an item until you depreciate the entire cost of the purchase. Depreciation mirrors the declining value of equipment as it ages.

For example, suppose that you spend $3,000 on computer equipment. According to the IRS, computer equipment is to be depreciated over five years. Thus each year you can take a $600 deduction for depreciation of this computer if you elect straight-line depreciation (which we define in Chapter 11).

By expensing or deducting (by using what's called a Section 179 deduction) rather than depreciating, you can take as an immediate deduction the entire $3,000 you spent on computer equipment (unless it contributes to your business showing a loss or a larger loss). As a small-business owner, you can take up to a $108,000 deduction for tax year 2006 for purchases of equipment for use in your business.

Wanting to expense the full amount of equipment immediately is tempting, but that isn't always the best thing to do. In the early years of your business, for example, your profits may be low. Therefore, because you won't be in a high tax bracket, the value of your deductions is limited. Looking ahead — when you have reason to be optimistic about your future profits — you may actually save tax dollars by choosing to depreciate your purchases. Why? By delaying some of your tax write-offs until future years (when you expect to be in a higher tax bracket because of greater profits), you save more in taxes.

Shifting income and expenses

Many small-business owners elect to keep their business accounting on what's called cash basis. This choice doesn't imply that all business customers literally pay in cash for goods and services or that the business owners pay for all expenses with cash. *Cash basis* accounting simply means that, for tax purposes, you recognize and report income in the year it was received and expenses in the year they were paid.

By operating on a cash basis, you can exert more control over the amount of profit (income minus expenses) that your business reports for tax purposes from year to year. If your income fluctuates from year to year, you can lower your tax burden by doing a little legal shifting of income and expenses.

Suppose that you recently started a business. Assume that you have little, but growing, revenue and somewhat high start-up expenses. Looking ahead to the next tax year, you can already tell that you'll be making more money and will likely be in a much higher tax bracket (see Chapter 1 for the personal income tax brackets and later in this chapter for corporate tax brackets). Thus you can likely reduce your tax bill by paying more of your expenses in the next year. Of course, you don't want to upset any of your business's suppliers. However, some of your bills can be paid after the start of the next tax year

(January 1) rather than in late December of the preceding year (presuming that your business's tax year is on a normal calendar year basis). *Note:* Credit card expenses are recognized as of the date you make the charges, not when you pay the bill.

Likewise, you can exert some control over when your customers pay you. If you expect to make less money next year, simply don't invoice customers in December of this year. Wait until January so that you receive more of your income next year. Be careful with this revenue-shifting game. You don't want to run short of cash and miss a payroll! Similarly, if a customer mails you a check in December, IRS laws don't allow you to hold the check until January and count the revenue then. After you receive the payment, it's supposed to be recognized for tax purposes as revenue.

One final point about who can and who can't do this revenue and expense two-step. Sole proprietorships, partnerships, S Corporations, and personal service corporations (which we discuss later in the chapter) generally can shift revenue and expenses. On the other hand, C Corporations and partnerships that have C Corporations as partners may not use the cash accounting method if they have annual receipts of more than $5 million per year.

Cars

If you use your car for business, you can claim a deduction. The mistake that some business owners (and many other people) make is to buy an expensive car. This purchase causes two problems. First, the car may be a waste of money that could be better spent elsewhere in the business. Second, the IRS limits how large an annual auto expense you can claim for depreciation (see Chapter 11 for details about business deductions for cars).

The IRS gives you a choice of how to account for business automobile expenses. You can either expense a standard mileage charge (44.5 cents per mile for tax year 2006) or keep track of the actual operating expenses (such as gas, insurance, repairs, and so on), plus take depreciation costs.

With expensive cars, the mileage expense method will probably shortchange your deduction amounts for auto usage. Now you have another reason not to spend so much on a car! When you buy a reasonably priced car, you won't need to go through the headache of tracking your actual auto expenses (in addition to not wasting money), because the mileage expense method probably will lead to a larger deduction. Tracking mileage and using the mileage expense method is so much easier.

Auto dealers often push automobile leasing. For the auto dealers and salespeople in the showrooms, leases have the marketing appeal of offering buyers a monthly payment that's often lower than an auto loan payment — without the perceived noose around your neck of a large car loan. Don't be fooled. If you do your homework and hunt for a good deal on a car, buying with cash is the best way to go. Borrowing with an auto loan or leasing are much more expensive (leasing generally being the highest cost) choices and tempts car buyers to spend more than they can afford.

Travel, meal, and entertainment expenses

The IRS clamps down on writing off travel, meal, and entertainment expenses because some business owners and employees abuse this deduction, trying to write off nonbusiness expenses. Some books, seminars, and unscrupulous tax preparers have effectively encouraged this abuse. So, be honest — not only because it's the right thing to do, but also because the IRS looks long and hard at expenses claimed in these areas. Travel must be for a legitimate business purpose. If you take a week off to go to Bermuda, spend one day at a business convention, and then spend the rest of the time sightseeing, you may have a great time — but only a portion of your trip expenses may be deductible.

One exception exists: If you extend a business trip to stay over on a Saturday to qualify for a lower airfare — and you save money in total travel costs by extending your stay — you can claim the other extra costs incurred to stay over through Sunday. If your spouse or friend tags along, his or her costs most definitely are not deductible.

Only 50 percent of your business expenses for meals and entertainment are deductible. In addition, the IRS doesn't allow any deductions for club dues (such as health, business, airport, or social clubs), entertainment facilities (such as executive boxes at sports stadiums), apartments, and so on. Please see Chapter 11 for details.

Home alone or outside office space?

When you have a truly small business, you may have a choice between setting up an office in your home or getting outside office space. You may be surprised to hear us say that the financial and tax sides of the home office decision actually aren't important — certainly not nearly as important as some business owners make them out to be. Why? First, the cost of office space you rent or purchase outside your home is an expense that you can deduct on your business tax return. If you own your home, you already get to claim the mortgage interest and property taxes as deductions on your personal tax return. So don't set up a home office thinking that you'll get all sorts of extra tax breaks. You'll qualify for some minor ones (such as deductions for utilities, repairs, and insurance) for the portion of your home devoted to business. Please see Chapter 15 for details.

The one extra home-based office deduction that you can take if you're a homeowner is depreciation. (See Chapter 23 to find out more about the other tips to avoid paying taxes on the profits from the sale of your home.)

Try as best you can to make your decision about your office space based on the needs of your business and your customers, along with your personal preferences. If you're a writer and you don't need fancy office space to meet with or impress anyone, working at home may be just fine. If you operate a retail or service business that requires lots of customers to come to you, getting outside office space is probably the best choice for all involved — and may be legally required. Check with governing authorities in your town, city, and county to find out what regulations exist for home-based businesses in your area.

Independent contractors versus employees

If you want to give yourself a real bad headache, read the tax laws applying to the classification of people that a business hires as either employees or independent contractors. When a business hires an employee, the business is required to withhold federal and state taxes and then send those taxes to the appropriate taxing authorities. The government likes the employee arrangement better because independent contractors (as a group) tend to pay less in taxes by underreporting their incomes. Contractors are also entitled to take more business deductions than are allowed for regular employees.

When a business hires independent contractors to perform work, the contractors are responsible for paying all their own taxes. However, business owners now are required to file **Form 1099** with the IRS and some state tax agencies. On Form 1099, you report the amount of money paid to contractors who receive $600 or more from the business. This form enables the IRS to keep better tabs on contractors who may not be reporting all their incomes.

Unless a company offers benefits to an employee (insurance, retirement savings plans, and so on), a hired hand should prefer to be an independent contractor. Contractors have more leeway to deduct business expenses, including the deduction for a home office. Contractors can also tax-shelter a healthy percentage of their employment income in a self-employed retirement savings plan, such as a SEP-IRA or Keogh (see Chapter 20 for details on retirement accounts). However, one additional expense for contractors is their obligation to pay the full share of Social Security taxes (although they can then take half of these Social Security taxes as a tax deduction on their returns). An employer, by contrast, would pay half the Social Security and Medicare taxes on the employee's behalf.

So how do you, as the business owner, decide whether a worker is to be classified as a contractor or as an employee? Some cases are hard to determine, but the IRS has a set of guidelines to make most cases pretty clear-cut.

✔ The classic example of an independent contractor is a professional service provider, such as legal, tax, and financial advisors. These people are considered contractors because they generally train themselves and, when hired, figure out how they can accomplish the job without much direction or instruction from the employer. Contractors usually perform work for a number of other companies and people, and they typically hire any others they need to work with them.

✔ On the other hand, employees usually work for one employer and have set hours of work. For example, a full-time secretary hired by a business would be considered an employee because he or she takes instructions from the employer regarding when, where, and how to do the assigned work. Another indication of employee status is whether the secretary's presence at the work site is important for completing the assigned work.

What do you do if your situation falls between these two types, and you're perplexed about whether the person you're hiring is a contractor or an employee? Ask a tax advisor or contact the IRS for the handy-dandy **Form SS-8, Determination of Worker Status for Purposes of Federal Employment Taxes and Income Tax Withholding.** Complete the form, mail it in, and let the IRS make the call for you. That way, the IRS can't blame you — although you may rightfully feel that you're letting the fox guard the henhouse!

Insurance and other benefits

A variety of insurance and related benefits are tax-deductible to corporations for all employees. These benefits include the following:

✔ Health insurance

✔ Disability insurance

✔ Term life insurance (up to $50,000 in benefits per employee)

✔ Dependent-care plans (up to $5,000 per employee may be put away on a tax-deductible basis for childcare and/or care for elderly parents)

✔ Flexible spending or cafeteria plans, which allow employees to pick and choose the benefits on which to spend their benefit dollars

For businesses that are *not* incorporated, the business owner(s) can't deduct the cost of the preceding insurance plans for themselves — but they can deduct these costs for employees.

All in the family

When you hire family members to perform real work for fair wages, you may be able to reduce your tax bill. If your children under the age of 18 are paid for work performed, they're probably in a much lower tax bracket than you are. And, if they're working for you, the parent, they need not pay any Social Security tax like you do. You can even get your kids started on investing by taking some of their earnings and helping them to choose some investments or contribute some of their earnings to an Individual Retirement Account.

Thus, as a family, you may pay less in total income taxes. But you can't simply pay a family member for the sole purpose of reducing your family's taxes. The family member you're paying must be doing legitimate work for your business, and you must be paying a reasonable wage for the type of work being done.

If you earn more than the $94,200 cap (in 2006) for full Social Security taxes, hiring a family member who isn't your minor child may lead to more Social Security taxes being paid by your family. Why? When you earn more than $94,200, you don't pay Social Security taxes on the amount above $94,200. If you instead pay a family member for working in the business and that person is earning less than the $94,200 threshold, then, as a family, you'll end up paying more in total Social Security taxes. Although it's true that earning more helps you qualify for more Social Security benefits come retirement, given the future of the Social Security system, your family member will be lucky to get back all of what he or she is paying into the system.

Self-employed people can deduct 100 percent of their health insurance costs for themselves and their covered family members.

Retirement plans

Retirement plans are a terrific way for business owners and their employees to tax-shelter a healthy portion of their earnings. If you don't have employees, regularly contributing to one of these plans is usually a no-brainer. When you have employees, the decision is a bit more complicated but often a great idea. Self-employed people may contribute to Keoghs, Simplified Employee Pension Individual Retirement Accounts (SEP-IRAs), or SIMPLE plans. Small businesses with a number of employees also should consider 401(k) plans.

Recent tax law changes increase the amount of money that both small employers and employees can sock away in retirement plans. A new tax credit also helps small employers recoup some of the costs of establishing and maintaining a retirement plan. We discuss all these plans and the impact of the new tax rules in detail in Chapter 20.

To Incorporate or Not to Incorporate

Starting a business is hard enough. Between mustering up the courage and swinging it financially, many business owners meet their match trying to decide what should be a reasonably straightforward issue: whether to incorporate. Just about every book that addresses the subject (and just about every lawyer or accountant who advises business owners) steers clear of giving definitive answers.

In some instances, the decision to incorporate is complicated, but in most cases, it need not be a difficult choice. Taxes may be important to the decision but aren't the only consideration (Eric Tyson and Jim Schell's *Small Business For Dummies,* published by Wiley, offers additional information). This section presents an overview of the critical issues to consider.

Liability protection

The chief reason to consider incorporating your small business is for purposes of liability protection. Attorneys speak of the protection of the *corporate veil.* Don't confuse this veil with insurance (or with the veil a bride normally wears on her wedding day). You don't get any insurance when you incorporate — or when you get married! You may need or want to buy liability insurance instead of (or in addition to) incorporating. Liability protection doesn't insulate your company from being sued, either.

When you incorporate, the protection of the corporate veil provides you with the separation or division of your business assets and liabilities from your personal finances. Why would you want to do that? Suppose that your business is doing well and you take out a bank loan to expand. The next year, however, the government enacts a regulatory change that makes your services or product obsolete. Before you know it, your business is losing money and you're forced to close up shop. If you can't repay the bank loan because of your business failure, the bank shouldn't be able to go after your personal assets if you're incorporated, right?

Unfortunately, many small-business owners who need money find that bankers ask for personal guarantees, which negate part of the liability protection that comes with incorporation. Additionally, if you play financial games with your company (such as shifting money out of the company in preparation for defaulting on a loan), a bank may legally be able to go after your personal assets. So, you must adhere to a host of ground rules and protocols to prove to the IRS that you're running a bona fide company. For example, you need to keep corporate records and hold an annual meeting — even if it's just with yourself!

A business can be sued if it mistreats an employee or if its product or service causes harm to a customer. But the owner's personal assets should be protected when the business is incorporated and meets the other tests for being a legitimate business.

Before you call a lawyer or your state government offices to figure out how to incorporate, you need to know that incorporating takes time and costs money. So if incorporating doesn't offer enough benefits to outweigh the hassles and costs, don't do it. Likewise, if the only benefits of incorporating can be better accomplished through some other means (such as purchasing insurance), save your money and time and don't incorporate.

Corporate taxes

Corporations are taxed as entities separate from their individual owners. This situation can be both good and bad. Suppose that your business is doing well and making lots of money. If your business isn't incorporated, all the profits from your business are taxed on your personal tax return in the year that those profits are earned.

If you intend to use these profits to reinvest in your business and expand, incorporating can potentially save you some tax dollars. When your business is incorporated (as a regular or so-called C Corporation), the first $75,000 of profits in the business should be taxed at a lower rate in the corporation than on your personal tax return (see Table 21-1). One exception to this rule is personal service corporations, such as accounting, legal, consulting, and medical firms, which pay a flat tax rate of 35 percent on their taxable incomes.

Table 21-1	2006 Corporate Tax Rates for Regular (C) Corporations
Taxable Income	*Tax Rate*
$0–$50,000	15%
$50,001–$75,000	25%
$75,001–$100,000	34%
$100,001–$335,000	39%
$335,001–$10,000,000	34%
$10,000,001–$15,000,000	35%
$15,000,001–$18,333,333	38%
More than $18,333,333	35%

Another possible tax advantage for a corporation is that corporations can pay — on a tax-deductible basis — for employee benefits such as health insurance, disability, and up to $50,000 of term life insurance. The owner usually is treated as an employee for benefits purposes. (Refer to the "Insurance and other benefits" section earlier in this chapter for details.) Sole proprietorships and other unincorporated businesses usually can take only tax deductions for these benefit expenses for employees. Benefit expenses for owners who work in the business aren't deductible, except for pension contributions and health insurance, which you can deduct on the front of **Form 1040.**

Liability insurance — a good alternative (if you can get it)

Before you incorporate, ask yourself (and others in your line of business or advisors who work with businesses like yours) what actions can cause you to be sued. Then see whether you can purchase insurance to protect against these potential liabilities. Insurance is superior to incorporation because it pays claims.

Suppose that you perform professional services but make a major mistake that costs someone a lot of money — or worse. Even if you're incorporated, if someone successfully sues you, your company may have to cough up the dough. This situation not only costs a great deal of money but also can sink your business. Only insurance can cover such financially destructive claims.

You can also be sued if someone slips and breaks a bone or two. To cover these types of claims, you can purchase a property or premises liability policy from an insurer.

Accountants, doctors, and a number of other professionals can buy liability insurance. A good place to start searching for liability insurance is through the associations that exist for your profession. Even if you aren't a current member, check out the associations anyway — you may be able to access any insurance they provide without membership, or you can join the association long enough to get signed up. Incorporating, however, doesn't necessarily preclude insuring yourself. Both incorporating and covering yourself with liability insurance may make sense in your case.

Resist the temptation to incorporate just so you can have your money left in the corporation, which may be taxed at a lower rate than you would pay on your personal income (see Chapter 1 for the personal income tax rates). Don't be motivated by this seemingly short-term gain. If you want to pay yourself the profits in the future, you can end up paying more taxes. Why? Because you pay taxes first at the corporate tax rate in the year your company earns the money, and then you pay taxes again on these same profits (this time on your personal income tax return) when you pay yourself from the corporate till in the form of a dividend.

Another reason not to incorporate (especially in the early days of a business) is that you can't immediately claim the losses for an incorporated business on your personal tax return. You have to wait until you can offset your losses against profits. Because most businesses produce little revenue in their early years and have all sorts of start-up expenditures, losses are common.

S Corporations

Subchapter *S Corporations,* so named for that part of the tax code that establishes them, offer some business owners the best of both worlds. You get the liability protection that comes with being incorporated, and the business profit or loss passes through to the owner's personal tax returns. So if the business shows a loss in some years, the owner may claim those losses in the current year of the loss on the tax returns. If you plan to take all the profits out of the company, an S Corporation may make sense for you.

The IRS allows most — but not all — small businesses to be S Corporations. To be an S Corporation in the eyes of the almighty IRS, a company must meet *all* the following requirements:

- ✔ Be a U.S. company
- ✔ Have just one class of stock
- ✔ Have no more than 75 shareholders (who are all U.S. residents or citizens and aren't partnerships, other corporations, or, with certain exceptions, trusts)

Limited liability companies (LLCs)

Just in the past generation, a new type of corporation has appeared. Limited liability companies (LLCs) offer business owners benefits similar to those of S Corporations but are even better in some cases. Like an S Corporation, an LLC offers liability protection for the owners. LLCs also pass the business's profits through to the owners' personal income tax returns.

Limited liability companies have fewer restrictions regarding shareholders. For example, LLCs have no limits on the number of shareholders. The shareholders in an LLC can be foreigners, and corporations and partnerships also can be shareholders.

Compared with S Corporations, the only additional restriction LLCs carry is that sole proprietors and professionals can't always form LLCs (although some states allow this). All states now permit the formation of LLCs, but most state laws require you to have at least two partners and not be a professional firm. (The IRS has stated that one-owner LLCs will be treated as sole proprietorships and must file Schedule C for tax purposes unless the owner elects to file as a corporation on Form 8832.)

Other incorporation issues

Because corporations are legal entities distinct from their owners, corporations offer other features and benefits that a proprietorship or partnership doesn't. For example, corporations have shareholders who own a piece or percentage of the company. These shares can be sold or transferred to other owners, subject to any restrictions in the shareholders' agreement.

Corporations also offer *continuity of life,* which simply means that corporations can continue to exist despite the death of an owner — or the owner's transfer of his or her share (stock) in the company.

Don't incorporate for ego purposes. If you want to incorporate to impress friends, family, or business contacts, you need to know that few people would be impressed or even know that you're incorporated. Besides, if you operate as a sole proprietor, you can choose to operate under a different business name ("doing business as" or *d.b.a.*) without the cost — or the headache — of incorporating.

If you've weighed the pros and cons of incorporating and you're still on the fence, our advice is to keep it simple. Don't incorporate. Remember that after you incorporate, it takes time and money to unincorporate. Start off as a sole proprietorship and then take it from there. Wait until the benefits of incorporating for your particular case outweigh the costs and drawbacks of incorporating.

Where to get advice

If you're totally confused about whether to incorporate because your business is undergoing major financial changes, getting competent professional help is worth the money. The hard part is knowing where to turn, because it's a challenge to find one advisor who can put all the pieces of the puzzle together. And be aware that you may get wrong or biased advice.

Attorneys who specialize in advising small businesses can help explain the legal issues. Tax advisors who do a lot of work with business owners can help explain the tax considerations. If you find that you need two or more advisors to help make the decision, it may help to get them together in one room with you for a meeting — which may save you time and money.

Investing in Someone Else's Business

Putting money into your own business (or someone else's) can be a high-risk but potentially high-return investment. The best options are those you understand well. If you hear about a promising business opportunity from someone you know and trust, do your research and make your best judgment. The business may well be a terrific investment. But keep in mind that people are always willing to take more risk with other people's money than with their own — and that many well-intentioned people fail at their businesses.

Before investing in a project, ask to see a copy of the business plan. Talk to others (who aren't involved with the investment!) about the idea and learn from their comments and concerns. But don't forget that many a wise person has rained on the parade of what turned out to be a terrific business idea.

Avoid limited partnerships and other small-company investments pitched by brokers, financial planners, and the like. They want you to buy limited partnerships because they earn hefty commissions from the sales. If you want a convenient way to invest in businesses and earn tax breaks, buy some stock mutual funds inside a retirement account.

Buying or Selling a Business

When you're buying or selling an existing business, consider getting the help and advice of competent tax and legal advisors. As a buyer, good advisors can help you inspect the company you're buying and look for red flags in the financial statements. Advisors can also help structure the purchase to protect the business you're buying — and to gain maximum tax benefits. When you're a seller, your advisors can help you prepare your business for maximum sale value and minimize taxes from the sale price.

If your business is worth a lot, make sure to read Chapter 25 on estate planning, because hefty taxes may be owed upon your death if you don't structure things properly. Your heirs may be forced to sell your business to pay estate taxes!

For more information about successfully starting, buying, selling, and running a small business, check out the latest edition of *Small Business For Dummies,* by Eric Tyson and Jim Schell (Wiley).

Chapter 22

Your Investments and Taxes

. . . .

In This Chapter

▶ Understanding tax-friendly investment strategies

▶ Comprehending the tax ramifications of reinvesting and dollar-cost averaging

▶ Knowing which tax-favored investments are best

▶ Deciding what investments to sell when and how

▶ Understanding special tax issues with mutual funds and stock options

. . . .

*W*hen you have money to invest or you're considering selling investments that you hold outside a retirement account, taxes should be an important factor in your decisions. But tax considerations alone should not dictate how and where you invest your money and when you sell. You also need to weigh issues such as your desire (and the necessity) to take risks, your personal likes and dislikes, and the number of years you plan to hold on to the investment.

Note: This chapter focuses on tax issues relating to investments in mutual funds, stocks, bonds, and other securities. Other chapters in this part of the book cover tax matters for investing in real estate or small businesses, investing for your children's future, and protecting your assets from estate taxes.

Tax-Reducing Investment Techniques

For investments that you hold inside *tax-sheltered* retirement accounts such as IRAs and 401(k) plans (see Chapter 20), you don't need to worry about taxes. This money isn't generally taxed until you actually withdraw funds from the retirement account. Thus you should never invest money that's inside retirement accounts in other tax-favored investments, such as tax-free money market funds and tax-free bonds (discussed later in this chapter).

You're far more likely to make tax mistakes investing *outside* of retirement accounts. Consider the many types of distributions produced by nonretirement account investments that are subject to taxation:

✔ **Interest:** Bank accounts, for example, pay you interest that is fully taxable, generally at both the federal and state levels. Bonds (IOUs) issued by corporations also pay interest that is fully taxable. Bonds issued by the federal government, which are known as Treasury bonds, pay interest that is federally taxable.

✔ **Dividends:** Many companies distribute some of their profits to shareholders of stock (shares of company ownership) as dividends.

Much lower tax rates apply to stock dividends — just 5 percent for those in the federal 10 and 15 percent tax brackets, and only 15 percent for those in all higher tax brackets.

✓ **Capital gains:** The profit from the sale of an investment at a price higher than the purchase price is known as a capital gain. Capital gains generally are federally and state taxable. Lower tax rates apply to capital gains for investments held for the long term (see the next section).

The following sections detail specific strategies for minimizing your taxes and maximizing your *after-tax returns* — that is, the return you actually get to keep after payment of required taxes.

Buy and hold for "long-term" capital gains

A *long-term* capital gain, which is the *profit* (sales proceeds minus purchase price) on an investment (such as a stock, bond, or mutual fund) that you own for more than 12 months, is taxed on a different tax-rate schedule. *Short-term* capital gains (securities held for one year or less) are taxed at your ordinary income tax rate.

The maximum federal tax rate on long-term capital gains is currently just 15 percent for holding periods of more than 12 months. For investors in the two lowest federal income tax brackets — 10 percent and 15 percent — the long-term capital gains tax is 5 percent for assets held more than 12 months.

When investing outside retirement accounts, investors who frequently trade their investments (or who invest in mutual funds that do the same) should seriously reconsider these strategies and holdings. With longer-term capital gains being taxed at lower tax rates, trading that produces short-term gains (from investments held 12 months or less), which are taxed at ordinary income tax rates, penalizes higher bracket investors the most. The sane strategy of buying and holding not only minimizes your taxes but also reduces trading costs and the likelihood of being whipsawed by fluctuating investment values.

Why, you may wonder, is there a set of capital gains' tax rates that are different from (lower than) the regular income tax rates presented in Chapter 1? In addition to the possibility that our government wants to make our tax lives more difficult, some logic lies behind the lower long-term capital gains tax rates. Some argue that this lower tax encourages investment for long-term growth. However, others complain that it's a tax break that primarily benefits the affluent.

When you buy and hold stocks and stock mutual funds outside retirement accounts, you can now take advantage of two major tax breaks. As we discuss in this section, appreciation on investments held more than 12 months and then sold is taxed at the low capital gains tax rate. Stock dividends (not on real estate investment trusts) are also taxed at these same low tax rates — just 5 percent for those in the federal 10 and 15 percent tax brackets and 15 percent for everyone else.

Pay off high-interest debt

Many folks have credit card or other consumer debt, such as auto loans costing 8 percent, 9 percent, 10 percent, or more per year in interest. Paying off this debt with your savings is like putting your money in an investment with a guaranteed tax-free return that's equal to the interest rate you were paying on the debt. For example, if you have credit-card debt outstanding at a 15 percent interest rate, paying off that loan is the same as putting your money to work in an investment with a guaranteed 15 percent annual return. Because the interest on consumer debt isn't tax-deductible, you actually need to earn more than 15 percent on your other investments to net 15 percent after paying taxes.

Still not convinced that paying off consumer debt is a great "investment"? Consider this: Banks and other lenders charge higher rates of interest for consumer debt than for debt on investments (such as real estate and businesses). Debt for investments is generally available at lower rates of interest and is tax-deductible. Consumer debt is hazardous to your long-term financial health (because you're borrowing against your future earnings), and it's more expensive.

In addition to ridding yourself of consumer debt, paying off your mortgage quicker may make sense, too. This financial move *isn't always* the best one because the interest rate on mortgage debt is lower than that on consumer debt and is usually tax-deductible (see Chapter 23).

Fund your retirement accounts

Take advantage of opportunities to direct your employment earnings into retirement accounts. If you work for a company that offers a retirement savings plan such as a 401(k), try to fund it at the highest level that you can manage. When you earn self-employment income, look into SEP-IRAs and Keoghs. See Chapter 20 for all the details on retirement accounts.

You get three possible tax bonuses by investing more of your money in retirement accounts.

- ✔ Your contributions to the retirement accounts come out of your pay before taxes are figured, which reduces your current tax burden.
- ✔ Some employers provide matching contributions, which is free money to you.
- ✔ The earnings on the investments inside the retirement accounts compound without taxation until withdrawal. Funding retirement accounts makes particular sense if you can allow the money to compound over many years (at least 10 years, preferably 15 to 20 years or more).

If you need to save money *outside* retirement accounts for short-term purposes such as buying a car or a home, by all means, don't do all your saving inside sometimes-difficult and costly-to-access retirement accounts. But if you accumulate money outside retirement accounts with no particular purpose in mind (other than that you like seeing the burgeoning balances), why not get some tax breaks by contributing to retirement accounts? Because your investments can produce taxable distributions, investing money outside retirement accounts requires greater thought and consideration, which is another reason to shelter more of your money in retirement accounts.

Use tax-free money market and bond funds

A common mistake many people make is not choosing a tax-appropriate investment given their tax bracket. Here are some guidelines for choosing the best type of investment based on your federal tax bracket:

- ✔ **33 percent or higher federal tax bracket:** If you're in one of these high brackets, you definitely need to avoid investments that produce taxable income. For tax year 2006, the 33 percent federal bracket started at $154,800 for singles and $188,450 for married couples filing jointly.
- ✔ **25 or 28 percent federal tax bracket:** If you invest outside retirement accounts, in most cases, you should be as well or slightly better off in investments that don't produce taxable income. This may not be the case, however, if you're in tax-free money market and bond funds whose yields are depressed because of a combination of low interest rates and too high operating expenses.

✔ **10 or 15 percent federal tax bracket:** Investments that produce taxable income are generally just fine. You'll likely end up with less if you purchase investments that produce tax-free income, because these investments yield less than comparable taxable ones even after factoring in the taxes you pay on those taxable investments.

When you're investing your money, it isn't the return that your investment earns that matters; what matters is the return you actually get to keep after paying taxes. The following sections describe some of the best investment choices you can make to reduce your overall tax burden and maximize your after-tax return.

If you're in a high enough tax bracket (federal 33 percent or higher), you may come out ahead with tax-free investments. Tax-free investments yield less than comparable investments that produce taxable earnings. But the earnings from tax-free investments can end up being greater than what you're left with from taxable investments after paying required federal and state taxes. See the sidebar "Determining whether tax-free funds will pay more," later in this chapter, to find out how to compare the yields.

Should you change investment strategies with new tax laws?

Given the tax law changes that reduced the tax rate on most stock dividends (a lot) and capital gains (a little bit more), should you alter your investment strategy?

All things being equal, assets that have appreciation potential (like stocks) and which pay corporate dividends (stocks again) have been given a boost. "Anything which increases the after-tax return of stocks is good for the stock market," says Catharine Gordon, principal with the Vanguard Group.

Your goals and willingness to take on risk should still drive your overall asset allocation. So, don't skew your asset allocation to dividend-paying stocks instead of income-producing bonds. The fundamental characteristics of stocks compared with bonds haven't been altered by these recent tax law changes. In the short term, bonds tend to be less volatile than stocks, but in the long run, stocks generally produce higher returns.

You won't benefit from these lower long-term capital gains tax rates and stock dividends tax rates (now just 15 percent and only 5 percent for those in the 10 and 15 percent federal income tax brackets) for investments held inside retirement accounts. When investment earnings are withdrawn from all retirement accounts except Roth IRAs, those returns are taxed as ordinary income. (With a Roth IRA, qualified withdrawals are free of taxation.)

Despite the fact that some of the many tax benefits of retirement accounts have been negated by this new tax bill, an analysis by the investment firm T. Rowe Price shows that investors should still generally take advantage of funding retirement plans that provide for immediate tax reductions. "When taking into account the advantage of investing on a pre-tax basis in the tax-deferred account versus an after-tax basis in the taxable account, the tax-deferred account proves more advantageous, though its relative advantage compared with the taxable account is not as great as it would be under current law," says the T. Rowe Price report.

With regards to funding an annuity or other retirement account which are done on an after-tax basis, T. Rowe Price's analysis found that after factoring in taxes, it takes about 25 years for the nondeductible retirement account to be worth as much on an after-tax basis as an equally funded taxable account.

Christine Fahlund, senior financial planner with T. Rowe Price, adds, "Don't change asset allocation because of these new laws, but you may want to change the location of where you hold some assets. For example, put taxable bond funds inside retirement accounts," because bond interest payments don't receive favorable tax treatment in a nonretirement account. "It may be better to hold dividend-paying stocks outside retirement accounts," says Fahlund, to take advantage of the low tax rate on stock dividends.

Tax rates and laws can and will change again. Don't develop long-term investing strategies based upon short-term tax law changes. Also, be sure to consider your individual situation and goals.

Tax-free *money market funds,* offered by mutual fund companies, can be a better alternative to bank savings accounts that pay interest (which is subject to taxation). The best money market funds pay higher yields and give you check-writing privileges. If you're in a high tax bracket, you can select a *tax-free* money market fund, which pays dividends that are free from federal and/or state tax. You can't get this feature with bank savings accounts.

Unlike bank savings accounts, the FDIC (Federal Deposit Insurance Corporation) doesn't insure money market mutual funds. For all intents and purposes, though, money market funds and bank accounts have equivalent safety. Don't allow the lack of FDIC insurance to concern you, because fund companies haven't failed. And in those rare instances when a money fund's investments have lost value, the parent company has infused capital to ensure no loss of principal on the investor's part.

Just as you can invest in a tax-free money market fund, so too can you invest in tax-free bonds via a tax-free bond mutual fund. These funds are suitable for higher tax bracket investors who want an investment that pays a better return than a money market fund without the risk of the stock market. Bond funds are intended as longer-term investments (although they offer daily liquidity, they do fluctuate in value).

Some companies offering competitive yields on tax-free money market funds and bond funds are Vanguard (800-662-7447; www.vanguard.com), USAA (800-382-8722; www.usaa.com), and Fidelity (800-343-3548; www.fidelity.com). Fidelity's Spartan series funds generally require higher minimums to open ($10,000 or more versus the other firms' $3,000).

Invest in tax-friendly stock mutual funds

All too often, when selecting investments, people mistakenly focus on past rates of return. We all know that the past is no guarantee for the future. But an even worse mistake is choosing an investment with a reportedly high rate of return without considering tax consequences. Numerous mutual funds effectively reduce their shareholders' returns because of their tendency to produce more taxable distributions (dividends and capital gains).

Historically, however, many mutual fund investors and publications haven't compared the tax-friendliness of similar mutual funds. Just as you need to avoid investing in funds with high sales commissions, high annual operating expenses, and poor relative performance, you also should avoid tax-unfriendly funds when investing outside of retirement accounts.

When comparing two similar funds, most people prefer a fund that averages returns of 14 percent per year instead of a fund earning 12 percent. But what if the 14 percent-per-year fund causes you to pay a lot more in taxes? What if, after factoring in taxes, the 14 percent-per-year fund nets just 9 percent, while the 12 percent-per-year fund nets an effective 10 percent return? In that case, you'd be unwise to choose a fund solely on the basis of the higher reported rate of return.

Capital gains + dividend distributions = more taxes!

All stock mutual fund managers buy and sell stocks during the course of a year. Whenever a mutual fund manager sells securities, any gain from those securities must be distributed, by year's end, to the fund shareholders. Securities sold at a loss can offset those liquidated at a profit. When a fund manager has a tendency to cash in more winners than losers, significant capital gains distributions can result.

Choosing mutual funds that minimize capital gains distributions, especially short-term capital gains distributions that are taxed at the higher ordinary income tax rates rather than the favored long-term capital gains rates we discuss earlier in this chapter, can help investors defer and minimize taxes on their profits. By allowing their capital to continue compounding, as it would in an IRA or other retirement account, fund shareholders receive a higher total return. (You can find the historic capital gains distribution information on a fund by examining its prospectus.)

Long-term investors benefit the most from choosing mutual funds that minimize capital gains distributions. The more years that appreciation can compound in a mutual fund without being taxed, the greater the value to the fund investor. When you invest in stock funds inside retirement accounts, you need not worry about capital gains distributions.

In addition to capital gains distributions, mutual funds produce dividends that are subject to normal income tax rates (except in the case of qualified stock dividends, which are taxed at the same low rates applied to long-term capital gains). Again, all things being equal, non-retirement account investors in high tax brackets should avoid funds that tend to pay a lot of dividends (from bonds and money market funds). Hold such funds inside of tax-sheltered retirement accounts.

Timing of fund purchases affects tax bill

Investors who purchase mutual funds outside tax-sheltered retirement accounts also need to consider the time of year they purchase shares in funds, so they can minimize the tax bite. Specifically, investors should try to purchase funds *after* rather than just before the fund makes the following types of distributions:

- **Capital gains distributions:** December is the most common month in which mutual funds make capital gains distributions. If making purchases late in the year, investors may want to find out whether and when the fund may make a significant capital gains distribution. Often, the unaware investor buys a mutual fund just prior to a distribution, only to see the value of the fund decline. But the investor must still pay income tax on the distribution. The December payout is generally larger when a fund has had a particularly good performance year and when the fund manager has done a lot of trading that year.

- **Dividend distributions:** Some stock funds that pay reasonably high dividends (perhaps because they also hold bonds) tend to pay out dividends quarterly — typically on a March, June, September, and December cycle. Try to avoid buying shares of these funds just before they pay. Make purchases early in each calendar quarter (early in the months of January, April, July, and October). Remember that the share price of the fund is reduced by the amount of the dividend, and the dividend is taxable.

Determining whether tax-free funds will pay more

If you're in the federal 33 percent tax bracket or higher, you will usually come out ahead in tax-free investments. Making the comparison properly means factoring in federal and state taxes. For example, suppose that you call a fund company and the representative tells you that the company's taxable money market fund currently yields 5.1 percent. The yield or dividend on this fund is fully taxable.

Further suppose that you're a resident of California — home to beautiful beaches and rumbling earthquakes — and that the same fund company's California money market fund currently yields 3.4 percent. The California tax-free money market fund pays dividends that are free from federal and California state tax. Thus you get to keep all 3.4 percent that you earn. The income you earn on the taxable fund, on the other hand, is taxed.

So here's how you compare the two:

Yield on tax-free fund ÷ yield on taxable fund

.034 (3.4%) ÷ .051 (5.1%) = 0.67

In other words, the tax-free funds pay a yield of 67 percent of the yield of the taxable fund. Thus, if you must pay more than 33 percent (1.0 − 0.67) in federal and California state tax, you net more in the tax-free fund (see Chapter 1 for details on how to determine your federal and state tax rate).

If you do this analysis comparing some funds today, be aware that yields do change. The difference in yields between tax-free and taxable funds widens and narrows a bit over time.

Don't get *too* concerned about when funds make distributions, because you can miss out on bigger profits by being so focused on avoiding a little bit of tax. If you want to be sure of the dates when a particular fund makes distributions, call the specific fund you have in mind.

Understanding the tax virtues of index funds

Mutual fund managers of actively managed portfolios, in their attempts to increase their shareholders' returns, buy and sell individual securities more frequently. However, this trading increases the chances of a fund needing to make significant capital gains distributions. Index funds, by contrast, are mutual funds that invest in a relatively fixed portfolio of securities. They don't attempt to beat the market averages or indexes. Rather, they invest in the securities to mirror or match the performance of an underlying index.

Although index funds can't beat the market, they have the following advantages over actively managed funds:

✔ Because index funds trade much less often than actively managed funds, index fund investors benefit from lower brokerage fees.

✔ Because significant ongoing research need not be conducted to identify companies in which to invest, index funds can be run with far lower operating expenses. All factors being equal, lower brokerage and operating costs translate into higher shareholder returns.

✔ Because index funds trade less often, they tend to produce lower capital gains distributions. For mutual funds held outside of tax-sheltered retirement accounts, this reduced trading effectively increases an investor's total rate of return. Thus index mutual funds are tax-friendlier.

The Vanguard Group (800-662-7447; www.vanguard.com), headquartered in Valley Forge, Pennsylvania, is the largest mutual fund provider of index funds. Vanguard also offers some of the best *exchange traded funds,* which are index funds that trade during the trading day on the major stock exchanges. Exchange traded funds may offer an even lower-cost way for some investors to buy and hold a broad market index for the longer-term.

Tax-Favored Investments to Avoid

Investment and insurance brokers and "financial planners" (who sell products, work on commission, and are therefore salespeople) love to pitch investment products that supposedly save you on your taxes. Salespeople generally don't examine your entire financial situation. Therefore, the salesperson may sell you an inappropriate or lousy investment that pays (the salesperson!) hefty commissions. The following sections discuss the main investments these commission-driven folks try to sell you — along with the reasons why you shouldn't buy them.

Limited partnerships

Avoid limited partnerships (LPs) sold through brokers and financial planners. They are fundamentally inferior investment vehicles. That's not to say that no one has ever made money on one, but they are burdened with high sales commissions and ongoing management fees that deplete your investment. You can do better elsewhere.

Limited partnerships invest in real estate and a variety of businesses, such as cable television and cellular phone companies. They pitch that you can get in on the ground floor of a new investment opportunity and make big money. They also usually tell you that while your investment is growing at 20 percent or more per year, you get handsome dividends of 8 percent or so each year. Sound too good to be true? It is.

Many of the yields on LPs have turned out to be bogus. In some cases, partnerships have propped up their yields by paying back investors' original investment (principal) — without clearly telling them, of course. The other LP hook is the supposed tax benefit. The few loopholes that did exist in the tax code for LPs have largely been closed. (Amazingly, some investment salespeople hoodwink investors into putting their retirement account money — which is already tax-sheltered — into LPs!) The other problems with LPs overwhelm any small tax advantage, anyway.

The investment salesperson who sells you this type of investment stands to earn a commission of up to 10 percent or more — so only 90 cents, or less, of your dollar actually gets invested. Each year, LPs typically siphon off another few percentage points for management fees and other expenses. Most partnerships have little or no incentive to control costs. In fact, the pressure is to charge *more* in fees to enrich the managing partners.

Unlike with a mutual fund (which you can sell if it isn't performing), with LPs you can't vote with your dollars. If the partnership is poorly run and expensive, you're stuck. LPs are *illiquid*. You can't get your money out until the partnership is liquidated, typically seven to ten years after you buy in.

The only thing limited about a limited partnership is its ability to make you money. If you want to buy investments that earn profits and have growth potential, stick with stocks (preferably using mutual funds), real estate, or your own business. For income as opposed to longer-term growth potential, invest in bonds.

Cash-value life insurance

Life insurance that combines life insurance protection with an account that has a cash value is usually known as *universal, whole,* or *variable life.* Life insurance should *not* be used as an investment, especially if you haven't reached the maximum allowable limit for contributing money to retirement accounts. Agents love to sell cash-value life insurance for the high commissions.

The cash value portion of such policies grows without taxation until withdrawn. However, if you want tax-deferred retirement savings, you should *first* take advantage of retirement savings plans, such as 401(k)s, 403(b)s, SEP-IRAs, and Keoghs, which give you an immediate tax deduction for your current contributions. These accounts also allow your investments to grow and compound without taxation until withdrawal.

Money paid into a cash-value life insurance policy gives you no upfront tax breaks. When you've exhausted contributing to tax-deductible retirement accounts, you may find that a nondeductible IRA and then, possibly, variable annuities can provide tax-deferred compounding of your investment dollars. Some company retirement plans also allow you to make nondeductible contributions, the benefit of which is that your investment earnings compound without taxation over the years. A recent tax law change increased the contribution limits for Roth IRA accounts and introduces after-tax Roth contributions for some employer plans. Roth retirement accounts allow for tax-free compounding and tax-free withdrawal of investment earnings, something that cash value life policies don't do. See Chapter 20 for the details on retirement accounts.

The only real financial advantage cash-value life insurance offers is that, with proper planning, the proceeds paid to your beneficiaries can be free of estate taxes. You need to have a fairly substantial estate at the time of your death to benefit from this feature. And numerous other, more cost-effective methods exist to minimize your estate taxes (see Chapter 25 for more details on estate planning).

Reinvesting and dollar-cost averaging tax issues

When you make small purchases in a particular non-retirement account investment over time, you increase your accounting complexity and tax-filing headaches. For example, if you buy shares in a mutual fund, you'll be asked if you want the dividends and capital gains paid out to you as cash or reinvested into buying more shares in the fund. Increasing numbers of individual companies allow you to reinvest dividends on individual stock holdings. These plans are known as dividend reinvestment plans, or DRIPs. Some discount brokers also offer this service for free for individual stocks.

If you're retired or need to live off your investment income, receiving cash payments probably works best. If you don't need the money, reinvesting dividends allows your money to continue compounding and growing in the investment. Although reinvesting complicates your tax situation, because you're buying shares at different times at different prices, the benefits should outweigh the hassles. (But please take note: You still must pay current taxes on reinvested distributions in nonretirement accounts.)

Another investing approach is dollar-cost averaging, which can also cause tax headaches when you sell investments held outside of retirement accounts. Dollar-cost averaging simply means that you're investing your money in equal chunks on a regular basis, such as once a month. For example, if you have $60,000 to invest, you can choose to invest $2,000 per month until it's all invested, which takes a few years. The money that awaits future investment isn't lying fallow. You keep it in a money-market-type account, where it earns a bit of interest while it waits its turn.

The attraction of dollar-cost averaging is that it enables you to ease a large chunk of money into riskier investments instead of jumping in all at once. The possible benefit is that if the price of the investment drops after some of your initial purchases, you can buy more later at a lower price. If you had put all your money at once into an investment and then the value dropped like a stone, you'd kick yourself for not waiting.

The flip side of dollar-cost averaging is that if your investment of choice appreciates in value, you may wish that you had invested your money faster. Another possible drawback of dollar-cost averaging is that you might get cold feet as you continue to invest money in an investment that's dropping in value. People who are attracted to dollar-cost averaging out of fear of buying before a price drop can become scared to continue boarding what may look like a "sinking ship."

Dollar-cost averaging is most valuable when the money you want to invest represents a large portion of your total assets, and you can stick to a schedule. It's best to make your contributions automatic so that you're less likely to be frightened off should prices begin falling after you start investing. If you aren't investing a lot of money, or the amount is a small portion of your total holdings, don't bother with dollar-cost averaging.

When you buy an investment via dollar-cost averaging or dividend reinvestment at many different times and prices, accounting is muddied as you sell portions of the investment. Which shares are you selling: the ones you bought at a higher price or the ones you bought at a lower price?

For record-keeping purposes, save your statements detailing all the purchases in your accounts. Most mutual fund companies, for example, provide year-end summary statements that show all transactions throughout the year. Be sure to keep these statements. For purchases made in recent years, and in the future, fund companies should also be able to tell you what your average cost per share is when you need to sell your shares.

Load mutual funds and the like

Load simply means sales commission — up to 8.5 percent of your investment dollars are siphoned off to pay some broker a commission. Although mutual funds are good investment vehicles, you don't need to pay a sales commission or load — loads are additional and unnecessary costs that are deducted from your investment money. Load funds don't perform any better than no-load (commission-free) funds. Why should they? Commissions are paid to the salesperson, not to the fund manager.

Another problem with buying load funds is that you miss out on the opportunity to objectively assess whether you should buy a mutual fund at all. For example, maybe you should pay off debt or invest somewhere else. But salespeople almost never advise you to pay off your credit cards or mortgage, or to invest through your company's retirement plan instead of investing through them.

Salespeople who sell mutual funds usually push other stuff as well. Limited partnerships, life insurance, annuities, futures, and options hold the allure of big commissions. Salespeople often don't take the time to educate investors, tend to exaggerate the potential benefits, and obscure the risks and drawbacks of what they sell.

✔ In addition to load mutual funds, you may be pitched to buy a unit investment trust or *closed-end fund.* For the most part, these funds are similar to other mutual funds, and they also pay brokers' commissions.

✔ Beware of brokers and financial planners selling bogus no-load funds, which are actually load funds that simply hide the sales commission.

You may be told something along the line that — as long as you stay in a fund for five to seven years — you won't have to pay the back-end sales charge that would apply upon sale of the investment. This claim may be true, but it's also true that these funds pay investment salespeople hefty commissions. The brokers are able to receive this commission because the fund company charges you high ongoing operating expenses (usually 1 percent more per year than the best funds). So one way or another, these salespeople get their commissions from your investment dollars.

Invest in no-loads and avoid load funds and investment salespeople. The only way to be sure that a fund is truly no-load is to look at the fund's prospectus. Only in the prospectus, in black and white and without marketing hype, must the truth be told about sales charges and other fund fees. Never buy an investment without looking at its prospectus.

Annuities

Annuities are a peculiar type of insurance and investment product — sort of a savings-type account with slightly higher yields that are backed by insurance companies.

Insurance agents and financial planners working on commission happily sell annuities to many people with money to invest. The problem is, annuities are suitable investments for relatively few people. If annuities do make sense for you, you can buy no-load (commission-free) annuities by bypassing salespeople and dealing directly with mutual fund companies.

The major selling hook of annuities is the supposed tax savings. "Why pay taxes each year on your investment earnings?" the agent or financial planner will ask. As in other types of retirement accounts, money that's placed in an annuity compounds without taxation until withdrawal. However, unlike most other types of retirement accounts (discussed in Chapter 20) — 401(k)s, SEP-IRAs, and Keoghs — your contributions to an annuity give no upfront tax deductions. And, unlike Roth retirement accounts, you get no tax break upon withdrawal of your investment earnings from an annuity. The only annuity income tax benefit, as with cash-value life insurance, is that the earnings compound without taxation until withdrawal. Thus it makes sense to consider contributing to an annuity only after you fully fund your tax-deductible and Roth retirement accounts.

Because annuities carry higher annual expenses due to the insurance that comes with them, they generally make sense only if you have many years to allow the money to compound. So annuities are *not* appropriate if you're already in or near retirement. Also, the lower tax rate on long-term capital gains and stock dividends (which we discuss earlier in this chapter) makes investing money in annuities relatively less attractive than simply investing in tax-friendly nonretirement account holdings. All earnings on an annuity are taxed upon withdrawal at ordinary income tax rates, whereas with a nonretirement account investment, much of your profits could be deferred into lower taxed long-term capital gains and lower taxed stock dividends.

Selling Decisions

After you've owned a stock, bond, or mutual fund for a while, you may want to contemplate selling some or all of it. Taxes should factor into the decision when you consider selling investments that you hold outside tax-sheltered retirement accounts. For investments held inside retirement accounts, taxes aren't an issue because the accounts are sheltered from taxation (unless you're withdrawing funds from the accounts — see Chapter 20 for the details). In most cases, you need not waste your money or precious free time consulting a tax advisor. In the sections that follow, we outline issues for you to consider in your selling decisions.

Selling selected shares

Before we get into the specific types of investment decisions you're likely to confront, we must deal with a rather unpleasant but important issue: accounting methods for security sales. Although this stuff gets a little complicated, with some minimal advance planning, you can acquire sound methods to reduce your tax burden. If you sell all the shares of a security that you own, you can ignore this issue. Only if you sell a portion of your shares of a security should you consider *specifying* which shares you're selling.

Suppose that you own 200 shares of stock in Intergalactic Computer Software, and you plan to sell 100 shares. You bought 100 of these shares ten years ago at $50 per share, and then another 100 shares two years ago for $100 per share. Today, the stock is worth $150 per share. What a savvy investor you are!

So, which 100 shares should you sell? The IRS gives you a choice, from a tax-accounting standpoint. You can identify the *specific* shares that you sell. In the case of Intergalactic, you would opt to sell the last or most recent 100 shares you bought, which would minimize your tax bill — because these shares were purchased at a higher price. At the time you want to sell the shares through your brokerage account, identify the shares you want to sell by noting the original date of purchase and/or the cost of those shares. So in the case of your Intergalactic stock holdings, simply tell your broker that you want to sell the 100 shares that you bought two years ago (give the date) at $100 per share. (The broker should include this information on the confirmation slip you receive for the sale.) Please note that if these shares had been bought within the past year and you had a gain, you may not want to sell those shares, because the profit *wouldn't* be taxed at the lower long-term capital gains tax rate discussed earlier in this chapter.

The other method of determining *which* shares you're selling is the method the IRS forces you to use if you don't specify before the sale which shares are to be sold — the *first-in-first-out (FIFO) method*. FIFO isn't a dog with a funny name; it's an accounting term that means that the first shares you sell are the first shares that you bought. Not surprisingly, because most stocks appreciate over time, the FIFO method leads to paying more tax sooner. In the case of Intergalactic, FIFO means that the first 100 shares sold are the first 100 shares that you bought (the ones you bought ten years ago at the bargain-basement price of $50 per share).

Although you'll save taxes today if you specify that you're selling the shares you bought most recently, don't forget (and the IRS won't let you) that when you finally sell the other shares, you'll then owe taxes on the *larger* profit you realize from those shares. The longer you hold these shares, the greater the likelihood that their value will rise, realizing a larger profit for you (although you end up paying more taxes). Of course, the risk always exists that the IRS will raise tax rates in the future or that your particular tax rate will rise. If you sell some of your investments, keep your life simple by considering selling all your shares of a specific security. That way, you don't have to hassle with all this accounting nonsense for tax purposes.

To be able to choose, or specify, which shares you're selling, you must select them before you sell. If you don't, the IRS says that you must use the FIFO method. You may wonder how the IRS knows whether you specified which shares before you sold them. The IRS doesn't know. But if you're audited, the IRS will ask for proof.

Selling securities with (large) capital gains

Capital gains tax applies when you sell a security at a higher price than you paid for it. As we explain earlier in this chapter, the long-term capital gains rate is lower than the tax rate you pay on ordinary income (such as from employment earnings or interest on bank savings accounts). Odds are, the longer you hold securities such as stocks, the greater the capital gains you'll accrue, because stocks tend to appreciate over time.

Suppose that your parents bought you 1,000 shares of XYZ company stock ten years ago, when it was selling for $10 a share. Today, it's selling for $20 per share; but you also vaguely recall that the stock split two-for-one a few years ago, so now you own 2,000 shares. Thus, if you sell XYZ stock for $40,000 today, you'd have a capital gain of $30,000 on which to pay taxes. So why would anyone want to sell?

The answer depends on your situation. For example, if you need the money for some other purpose — buying a home, taking a yearlong trip around the world — and the stock is your only source of funds, go for it. If you can't do what you want to do without selling, don't let the taxes stand in the way. Even if you pay state and federal taxes totaling some 25 percent of the profit, you'll have lots left over. Before you sell, however, do some rough figuring to make sure that you have enough to accomplish what you want.

What if you hold a number of stocks? To diversify and meet your other financial goals, all you need to do is prioritize. Give preference to selling your largest holdings (total market value) that have the smallest capital gains. If some of your securities have profits and some have losses, sell some of each to offset the profits with the losses. (Gains and losses on securities held one year or less are taxed at your ordinary income tax rates — see Chapter 12 for more details.)

Don't expect to obtain objective, disinterested, tax-wise advice regarding what to do with your current investments from a stockbroker or from most financial planners. If they earn commissions on the products they sell, their bias will be to tell you to sell. Even though some financial planners don't get commissions, they can charge fees on what they manage. When you seek objective help with these "sell versus hold" decisions, turn to a competent tax or financial advisor who works on an hourly basis.

Selling securities at a loss

Perhaps you own some losers in your portfolio. If you want to raise cash for some particular reason, you may consider selling some securities at a loss. Don't hold on to an investment just because its value now is less than what you paid for it. Waiting until its value rises to what you originally paid is a natural, but silly, human desire. Selling a loser now frees up your money for better investments. Losses can also be used to offset gains (investments sold at a profit) — just remember that long-term losses will offset long-term gains first. Only after you've completely exhausted your long-term gains can you use them against short-term gains, which are taxed at a higher rate.

Both short-term and long-term losses can be deducted against ordinary income, subject to limitations. If you want to sell securities at a loss, be advised that you can't claim more than $3,000 in short-term or long-term losses on your federal tax return in a given tax year. If you sell securities with losses totaling more than $3,000 in a year, the losses must be carried over to future tax years. This situation not only creates more tax paperwork, but also delays realizing the value of deducting a tax loss. So try not to have net losses (losses plus gains) exceeding $3,000 in a year.

Some tax advisors advocate doing *year-end tax-loss selling.* The logic goes that if you hold a security at a loss, you should sell it, take the tax write-off, and then buy it (or something similar) back. Sounds good in theory, but when you eventually sell the shares that you bought again at the lower price, you'll owe tax on the increased price anyway. (When you sell other stocks during the year at a profit, tax-loss selling to offset these taxable gains makes more sense.) But many people who sell an investment that has declined in value don't want to buy the same investment again. This reluctance can cause other investment blunders. For example, suppose you had the misfortune to buy some stocks back in 2000. In the next couple of years, your stocks plummeted about 30 percent or more, it wasn't because of your poor stock-picking ability. You simply got caught in the U.S. stock market downdraft. You'll make a bad situation worse by panicking and selling at reduced price levels just to take a tax loss. If anything, under such circumstances consider doing the opposite — take advantage of the sale and buy more!

If you do decide to sell for tax-loss purposes, be careful of the so-called wash sale rules. The IRS doesn't allow deduction of a loss for a security that you sell if you buy that same security back within 30 days. As long as you wait 31 or more days, you will have no problem. When you're selling a mutual fund, you can easily sidestep this rule simply by purchasing a fund similar to the one you're selling.

When you own a security that has ceased trading and appears worthless (or even if you've made a loan that hasn't been repaid — even if to a friend), you can probably deduct this loss. See Chapter 12 for more information on what situations are deductible and how to claim these losses on your annual tax return.

Mutual funds and the average cost method

In the United States, you never have a shortage of choices — so why shouldn't it be the same with accounting methods? When you sell shares in a mutual fund, the IRS allows you an additional method — the *average cost method* — for determining your profit or loss for tax purposes. (This information doesn't apply to money market funds, which don't fluctuate in value.)

If you bought fund shares in chunks over time and/or reinvested the fund distributions (such as from dividends) into more shares of the fund, tracking and figuring what shares you're selling can be a real headache. So the IRS allows you to take an average cost for all the shares you bought over time.

Be aware that after you elect the average cost method, you can't change to another method for accounting for the sale of the remaining shares. If you plan to sell only some of your fund shares, and it would be advantageous for you to specify that you're selling the newer shares first, choose that method (as we describe in the "Selling selected shares" section earlier in this chapter).

Stock options and taxes

Some companies grant particular employees *stock options*. If you're the proud holder of this type of option, congratulations! You're either an important employee or work for a company that believes in sharing the success of its growth with its employees.

If you have statutory stock options, sometimes known as *incentive stock options,* you face a number of important decisions that can have significant tax consequences. Basically, stock options grant you the right to buy shares of stock from your employer at a predetermined price. For example, suppose that you take a job with a large discount retailer and the company tells you that, after December 31, 2006, you may "exercise the right" to purchase 1,000 shares of its stock at $50 per share.

In the years ahead, you and other store employees help the company to continue growing and expanding. Suppose the company's stock price eventually rises to $75 per share in the next year. Thus, because your options enable you to buy company stock for $50 per share, and it's now at $75 per share, you have a profit on paper of $25,000 (1,000 shares × $25 profit per share)!

To realize this profit, you must first exercise your option (your company benefits department can tell you how). After you are the proud owner of the shares, you can sell them if you want to. However — and this is a big *however* — if you sell the shares within a year of having exercised the options, or within two years after the grant of the option (whichever is later), you will owe ordinary income tax on the profit. If you hold the shares for the required period of time, then you will pay the lowest possible long-term capital gains tax. (You may also be subject to the Alternative Minimum Tax, or AMT — see Chapter 8 to find out more about this tax.)

When you're a high-income earner, holding on to your exercised stock options for more than 12 months so that you qualify for the favorable capital gains tax treatment is normally to your advantage. The risk in waiting to sell is that your profits shrink as the stock price drops.

Nonstatutory stock options are a bit different type of option. Unlike incentive stock options, nonstatutory stock options aren't given special tax treatment. With nonstatutory stock options, you must pay tax on the options either when you receive them (if you can determine their fair market value) or when you exercise them. You must also pay income tax on the difference between the fair market value of the stock at the time you exercise the option minus the value of the option on which you pay tax. After you exercise the option, the decision on when to sell (and the tax consequences) is the same as for incentive stock options. If you don't know which type of option your employer offers, ask the benefits department.

If you aren't a high-income earner and waiting to sell offers no tax advantage, selling your shares as the shares become exercisable is usually prudent. When the stock market plunged in the early 2000s, a number of employees, especially in high-tech companies, got clobbered with taxes on nonstatutory stock options on stock that they held onto that then plummeted in value. So the employees ended up being out a lot of dough in taxes and in some cases holding worthless or near worthless stock. We should also note that having too much of your wealth tied up in the stock of your employer is dangerous. Remember that your job is already on the line if the company's success wanes.

Selling securities whose costs are unknown

When you sell a security or a mutual fund that you've owned for a long time (or that your parents gave you), you may not know the security's original cost (also known as its cost basis). If you could only find the original account statement that shows the original purchase price and amount . . .

If you can't find that original statement, start by calling the firm through which you purchased the investment. Whether it's a brokerage firm or mutual fund company, it should be able to send you copies of old account statements. You may have to pay a small fee for this service. Also, increasing numbers of investment firms (particularly mutual fund companies) automatically calculate and report cost basis information on investments that you sell through them. The cost basis they calculate is generally the average cost for the shares that you purchased. See Chapter 3 for more ideas on what to do when original records aren't available.

Chapter 23

Real Estate and Taxes

In This Chapter

▶ Home ownership tax breaks

▶ Home-buying and mortgage decisions and taxes

▶ Strategies for keeping the IRS at bay when selling your house

▶ Tax considerations when investing in real estate

Tax benefits are a significant reason why many people, especially people in the real estate business — such as real estate agents, bankers, mortgage brokers, and others in the lending business — advocate property ownership.

Buying a home or investing in real estate *can* provide financial and psychological rewards. And tax breaks can help reduce the cost of owning real estate. On the other hand, purchasing and maintaining property can be time-consuming, emotionally draining, and financially painful.

Surveying Real Estate Tax Breaks

Just as contributing money to retirement accounts (see Chapter 20) yields tax breaks, so does buying a home and investing in other real estate. The U.S. tax system favors property ownership because of the widely held belief that owners take better care of their property when they have a financial stake in its future value. Arguing with this logic is difficult if you have visited almost any government-subsidized tenement.

All the powerful real estate lobbies also contribute to the addition and retention of real estate tax benefits in our tax code. Builders, contractors, real estate agents, the banking industry, and many other real estate–related sectors have an enormous financial stake in the American hunger to own and improve properties.

You should understand the tax aspects of owning a home and investing in other real estate so that you can make the most of these tax-reduction opportunities. Making wise real estate decisions also requires that you know how to fit real estate into your overall financial picture. After all, you have limited income and other options on which to spend your money.

Don't make the mistake of depending on those individuals involved in the typical real estate deal to help you see the bigger picture. Remember that these folks make their livings off your decision to buy real estate, and the more you spend, the more they make.

We know that you can't wait to uncover the real estate tax breaks available for the taking. But before we get to them, we kindly ask that you never forget two important caveats to gaining these property tax advantages:

- ✔ You have to spend money on real estate — acquiring property, paying the mortgage and property taxes over the years, and improving the property while you own it — to even be eligible for the tax breaks. As we discuss in this chapter, if you're a high-income earner or make the wrong financial moves, you may not be able to claim some of the real estate tax benefits available.

- ✔ Always remember that the price of real estate in the United States reflects the fact that buyers and sellers know about the tax deductions. This is a major reason why so many people are willing to pay sums with many zeroes for a piece of the American Dream. Other countries that don't offer tax breaks for home ownership, such as Canada, have comparatively lower prices because buyers can't afford to pay higher prices when they can't bank on a tax deduction to help subsidize the cost.

The following sections offer an overview of the tax goodies available to U.S. homeowners. The benefits are similar to, but different from, the tax benefits for rental or income property owners, which we discuss later in this chapter.

Mortgage interest and property tax write-offs

When you buy a home, you can claim two big ongoing expenses of home ownership as tax deductions on Schedule A of Form 1040. These expenses are your property taxes and the interest on your mortgage.

You're allowed to claim mortgage-interest deductions on a primary residence (where you actually live) and on a second home for mortgage debt totaling $1 million. You're also allowed to deduct the interest on a home equity loan of up to $100,000 (see Chapter 9).

Property taxes also are fully deductible on Schedule A, whether you purchase a $50,000 shack in an unpopulated rural area or a multimillion-dollar mansion overlooking the ocean.

Dealing with "excess" housing profits

Although the house-sale capital gains tax laws benefit many people, the rules do have a negative twist. If you live in an area with relatively inexpensive real estate, you may find this difficult to believe: Some longer-term homeowners, especially in the higher-cost sections of the country, may have profits in excess of the law's limits ($250,000 for singles and $500,000 for married couples filing jointly).

For those in that admittedly enviable position, the tax laws offer no escape hatch. At the time of sale, single homeowners with accumulated profits (which also include those profits rolled over, under the old tax laws, from previous sales) greater than $250,000 and couples with profits greater than $500,000 must pay capital gains tax on the excess.

When they start to bump up against the maximum amounts that can be shielded from capital gains taxation, long-term homeowners and those buying expensive homes may want to consider selling and moving, even if it's within the same neighborhood.

Those whose homes have appreciated well in excess of the limits may want to consider, if possible, holding their homes until their deaths, at which point, under current tax laws, the IRS wipes the capital gains slate clean (see Chapter 25). Please also be aware that increasing numbers of taxpayers are finding themselves subject to the dreaded Alternative Minimum Tax (AMT) for many reasons including the realization of larger capital gains.

Also keep in mind that although relatively few homeowners today have housing profits in excess of these seemingly high limits, the bounds are fixed and aren't scheduled to increase with inflation. Thus, in the years ahead, increasing numbers of homeowners will be affected by the limits. That's why you should heed our advice to keep receipts for your home improvements, which allow you to increase your home's cost basis for tax purposes and thus reduce your potentially taxable capital gain. See the section, "Tracking your home expenditures," later in this chapter.

Home ownership capital gains exclusion

Normally, when you make an investment in a stock or business, for example, and you later sell it for a profit (also known as a *capital gain*), you owe tax on the profit. Some real estate, however, receives special treatment in this regard.

The tax laws pertaining to the sale of a primary residence now allow for a significant amount of profit to be excluded from taxation: up to $250,000 for single taxpayers and up to $500,000 for married couples filing jointly. Moreover, to take advantage of this tax break — unlike under the old house-sale rules — house sellers need not be over a particular age or buy a replacement residence of equal or greater value to the one just sold.

So, if you're longing to move to a less-costly housing market, you're largely free of tax constraints to do so. This tax break also benefits empty nesters and others nearing or in retirement who want to buy a less-costly home and free up some of their home equity to use toward retirement.

House losses aren't deductible

Some homeowners have learned firsthand that real estate prices go down as well as up. If it's time for you to sell your house and move on, you may be disappointed to discover that you can't deduct the loss if your house sells for less than what you paid for it. If you lose money investing in the stock market, on the other hand, those losses are usually deductible (see Chapter 22). Although you may think it's unfair that home ownership losses aren't tax-deductible, don't forget that you're already getting many tax perks from your home — the mortgage interest and property tax deductions.

Converting rental property to save on taxes

If you want to sell appreciated rental property, the new house-sale rules may benefit you as well. How? By moving into a rental property that you own and making it your primary residence for at least two years, you can shield the profits from the sale of the property from taxation. (Obviously, this strategy is feasible only for certain types of properties that you would be willing or able to live in. Also, it doesn't apply to depreciation taken after May 7, 1997 — see Chapter 12.)

When you move from your house, rent it out for a period of time, and then sell it, the IRS may consider that you have converted your home from a primary residence to a rental property. Thus you may lose the privilege of excluding tax on the profit from the sale. The only exception: You actively tried to sell the house after you moved and only rented it temporarily to help defray the costs of keeping it until you sold it.

Home office deductions

When you run your business out of your home, you may be able to take additional tax deductions beyond the mortgage interest and property taxes that you already claim as a homeowner. Check out Chapter 21 for a more in-depth discussion of this issue.

Purchasing Your Humble Home

Financially speaking, you really shouldn't buy your own place unless you anticipate being there for at least three years, and preferably five years or more. Many expenses accompany buying and selling a property, such as the cost of getting a mortgage (points, application and credit report fees, and appraisal fees), inspection expenses, moving costs, real estate agents' commissions, and title insurance. And remember, most of these expenses are *not* tax-deductible (at best, they can only be added to your home's tax basis as we explain in the section, "Tracking your home expenditures" later in this chapter). To cover these transaction costs plus the additional costs of ownership, a property needs to appreciate a fair amount before you can be as well off financially as if you had continued renting. A property needs to appreciate about 15 percent just to offset these expenses, even factoring in the tax benefits that homeowners enjoy.

If you need or want to move in a couple of years, counting on that kind of appreciation is risky. If you're lucky (that is, if you happen to buy before a sharp upturn in housing prices), you may get it. Otherwise, you'll probably lose money on the deal.

Some people are willing to buy a home even when they don't expect to live in it for long because they plan on turning it into a rental when it's time to move on. Holding rental property can be a good long-term investment, but don't underestimate the responsibilities that come with rental property. (Rent the movie *Pacific Heights* and talk to friends and colleagues who've been landlords!)

Exploring the tax savings in home ownership

To quickly estimate your monthly tax savings from home ownership, try this simple shortcut: Multiply your marginal federal tax rate (refer to Chapter 1) by the total monthly amount of your property taxes and mortgage. (Technically, not all your mortgage payment is tax-deductible; only the portion of the mortgage payment that goes to interest is tax-deductible. However, in the early years of your mortgage, the portion that goes toward interest is nearly all of the payment. On the other hand, your property taxes will probably rise over time, and you can also earn state tax benefits from your deductible mortgage interest and property taxes.)

Keep track of your tax bracket

When you first consider purchasing a home or purchasing a more expensive home, it usually pays to plan ahead and push as many so-called itemizable deductions as you can into the tax year in which you expect to buy your home.

For example, suppose that this year you're using the standard deduction because you don't have many itemized deductions. You decide late in the year that you expect to buy a home next year and therefore will have mortgage interest and property taxes to write off and you'll probably be able to itemize the next year. It makes sense, then, to collect as many deductible expenses as possible and shift them into next year. For example, if the solicitations surrounding the December holidays prompt you to contribute money to charities, you can wait until January to donate. Take a look at the deductible items on Schedule A (see Chapter 9) to determine what else you may want to postpone paying.

Also, be aware that your income tax bracket may change from year to year. Thus, when possible, you can choose to pay more or less of some itemizable expenses in one year versus another. Suppose that you receive your annual property tax bill in the fall of the year, and it's payable in two installments. You must pay one installment before the end of the year, whereas you have until the next spring to pay the other installment. If for some reason you expect to be in a lower tax bracket next year — perhaps you're going to take a sabbatical and will earn less income — you may choose to pay the entire property tax bill before the current year ends. In this case, the property tax deduction has greater value to you in the current year because you're in a higher tax bracket.

Be sure to read Chapter 1, which explains how to figure your current and future expected tax bracket for planning purposes to minimize your taxes.

To figure out more precisely how home ownership may affect your tax situation, try plugging some reasonable numbers into your tax return to guesstimate how your taxes may change. You can also speak with a tax advisor.

When you buy a home, make sure to refigure how much you're paying in income taxes, because your mortgage interest and property tax deductions should help lower your income tax bills (federal and state). Many homebuyers skip this step and end up getting a big tax refund the next year. Although getting money back from the IRS and state may feel good, it means that, at a minimum, you made an interest-free loan to the government. In the worst case, the reduced cash flow during the year may cause you to accumulate debt or miss out on contributing to tax-deductible retirement accounts. If you work for an employer, ask your payroll/benefits department for Form W-4 (see Chapter 15 for information about how to fill out this form). If you're self-employed, you can complete a worksheet that comes with Form 1040-ES (see Chapter 15).

Deciding how much to spend on a home

When you fall in love with a home and buy it without looking at your monthly expenditures and long-term goals, you may end up with a home that dictates much of your future spending. Real estate agents and mortgage lenders are more than happy to tell you the maximum that you're qualified to borrow. They want your business, and the more money you spend, the more they make. But that doesn't mean that you should borrow the maximum.

Typical is the advice of this real estate broker who also happens to write about real estate:

> "The first step is to find out what price you can afford to buy. The easiest way to do this is to make an appointment with a loan agent or a mortgage broker."

Easy, yes. But doing so probably won't get you the right answer. Like real estate agents, mortgage brokers tell you the maximum loan you can qualify for. This amount isn't necessarily what you can "afford." Remember, mortgage and loan agents get a commission based on the size of your loan. Taking into consideration your other financial goals and needs, such as saving for retirement, isn't part of their job description (nor generally their expertise).

In addition to analyzing your retirement planning, questions you should ask yourself before buying a home may include how much you spend (and want to continue spending) on fun stuff, such as travel and entertainment. If you want to continue your current lifestyle (and the expenditures inherent in it), be honest with yourself about how much you can really afford to spend as a homeowner.

Often, first-time homebuyers are apt to run into financial trouble because they don't know their spending needs and priorities and don't know how to budget for them. Buying a home can be a wise decision, but it also can be a huge burden. Some people don't decrease their spending as much as they should, based on the large amount of debt they incur in buying a home. In fact, some homeowners spend even more on all sorts of gadgets and furnishings for their homes. Many people prop up their spending habits with credit. For this reason, a surprisingly large percentage of people — some studies say about half — who borrow additional money against their home equity use the funds to pay other debts.

Don't let your home control your financial future. *Before* you buy property or agree to a particular mortgage, take stock of your overall financial health, especially in terms of retirement planning if you hope to retire by your mid-60s.

Tread carefully if you purchase a vacation home

Part of the allure of a second or vacation home is the supposed tax and financial benefits. Even when you qualify for some or all of them, tax benefits only partially reduce the cost of owning a property. We've seen more than a few cases in which the second home is such a cash drain that it prevents its owners from contributing to and taking advantage of other attractive investments, including tax-deductible retirement savings plans.

If you can realistically afford the additional costs of a second home, we aren't going to tell you how to spend your extra cash. But please don't make the all-too-common mistake of viewing a second home as an investment. The way most people use them, they aren't.

Investment real estate is property that you rent out. Most homeowners with second homes rent out their other property 10 percent or less of the time. As a result, second homes usually are cash drains, not moneymakers.

If you don't rent out a second home property most of the time, ask yourself whether you can afford such a luxury. Can you accomplish your other financial goals — saving for retirement, paying for your primary residence, and so on — with this added expense? Keeping a second home is more of a consumption decision than an investment, if you don't rent it out. Most people can't afford such an extravagance.

Also, be aware that if your vacation home appreciates in value, the IRS doesn't allow you to sell this type of home without taxation of your capital gains the way it does with primary residences (see the discussion earlier in this chapter).

Tracking your home expenditures

Although it may be a bit of a hassle, documenting and tracking money spent improving your property is in your best interest. For tax purposes, you can add the cost of these improvements to your original purchase price for the home. So, when you sell the property someday, you get to reduce your profit, for tax purposes, accordingly. Keep in mind that under the current tax laws, most people won't owe capital gains tax from the sale of a house. Single people can make a $250,000 profit, and married couples filing jointly can realize $500,000 in profit without paying tax on the proceeds of the sale. However, you still need to track your home improvement expenditures because it's impossible to know while you're living in your home if your future sale, which could be many years off, could trigger capital gains tax. Who knows how much real estate will appreciate in the interim or what changes could happen to the tax laws?

As we discuss later in this chapter, when you sell your house, you may need to report to the IRS, on **Schedule D, Capital Gains and Losses,** the selling price of the house, the original cost of the house, and how much you spent improving it. Therefore, we strongly advise setting up a simple file folder, perhaps labeled "Home Improvements," into which you deposit receipts for your expenditures.

The challenging part for most people is simply keeping the receipts organized in one place. Another task is correctly distinguishing between spending on *improvements*, which the IRS allows you to add to your cost of the home, and spending for *maintenance and repairs*, which you can't add to the original purchase price of the home.

Improvements include expenses such as installing an alarm system, adding or remodeling a room, planting new trees and shrubs in your yard, and purchasing new appliances. These improvements increase the value of your home and lengthen its life. Maintenance and repairs include expenses such as hiring a plumber to fix a leaky pipe, repainting, repairing a door so that it closes properly, and replacing missing roof shingles.

You're okay if you rent

Don't believe that you aren't a success if you aren't a homeowner. And, as we discuss earlier in this chapter, don't feel pressured to buy a home just because of the tax breaks or because that's what nearly everyone else you know seems to be doing. Remember that the value of those tax breaks is reflected in higher U.S. home prices versus lower home prices in other countries where real estate owners don't receive such tax deductions.

Some financially successful long-term renters include people who pay low rent — because they've made sacrifices to live in a smaller rental, for example, or live in a rent-controlled building. One advantage of low rental costs is that you may be able to save more money. If you can consistently save 10 percent or more of your

earnings, you will probably meet your future financial goals, house or no house.

Another advantage of being a long-term renter is that you won't have a great deal of money tied up in your home. Many homeowners enter their retirement years with a substantial portion of their wealth in their homes. As a renter, you can have all your money in financial assets that you can probably tap into far more easily.

Some renters are tempted to invest in a property elsewhere and rent it to others or use it when they want. This decision is neither straightforward nor simple. Make sure that you read the sections later in this chapter that discuss investment property and second homes.

It's interesting to note that if you hire a contractor to do home improvements, the IRS allows you to effectively add the cost of the contractor's time (the labor charges) into the overall improvements that reduce your home's profit for tax purposes. On the other hand, if you elect to do the work yourself, you gain no tax benefit for your sweat. You can't add a cost for the value of your time — the IRS assumes that your time isn't worth anything. You work for free! Now you have another reason for hiring someone to do the work for you.

Also, don't forget to toss into your receipt folder the *settlement statement,* which you should have received in the blizzard of paperwork you signed and received when you bought your home. Don't lose this valuable piece of paper, which itemizes many of the expenses associated with the purchase of your home. You can add many of these expenses to the original cost of the home and reduce your taxable profit when it comes time to sell. You also want to keep proof of other expenditures that the settlement statement may not document, such as inspection fees that you paid when buying your home.

Reporting revenue if you sometimes rent

The IRS allows you to rent your home or a room in your home for up to 14 days each year without having to declare the rental income and pay income taxes on it. Renting your home or a portion thereof for more than 14 days requires that you report the income when you file your annual tax return. You can declare real estate rental income by filing Schedule E. (Refer to Chapter 13 for more information.)

Making Tax-Wise Mortgage Decisions

The largest expense of property ownership is almost always the monthly mortgage payment. In the earlier years of a mortgage, the bulk of the mortgage payment covers interest that generally is tax-deductible. In this section, we discuss how to factor taxes and your financial circumstances into making intelligent mortgage decisions.

15-year or 30-year mortgage?

Unfortunately, you have thousands of mortgage options to choose from. Fixed-rate and adjustable-rate mortgages come with all sorts of bells and whistles. The number of permutations is mind-numbing.

From a tax perspective, one of the most important mortgage selection issues is whether to take a 15-year or 30-year mortgage. To afford the monthly payments, most homebuyers need to spread the loan payments over a longer period of time, and a 30-year mortgage is the only option. A 15-year mortgage requires higher monthly payments because you pay it off more quickly.

Even if you can afford these higher payments, taking the 15-year option may not be wise. The money for making extra payments doesn't come out of thin air. You may have better uses for your excess funds. What you're really asking, if you're considering whether you should take a 30-year or a 15-year mortgage, is whether you should pay off your mortgage slowly or quickly. The answer isn't as simple as some people think.

First, think about alternative uses for the extra money you're throwing into the mortgage payments. What's best for you depends on your overall financial situation and what else you can do with the money. When you elect the slow, 30-year mortgage payoff approach and you end up blowing the extra money on a new car, for example, you're better off paying down the mortgage more quickly. In that case, take the 15-year version. (If you want to buy a car in the future, saving in a money market fund so that you don't need to take out a high-cost car loan makes sound financial sense.)

But suppose that you aren't so frivolous with your extra money, and instead, you take the extra $100 or $200 per month and contribute it to a retirement account. That step may make financial sense. Why? Because additions to 401(k)s, SEP-IRAs, Keoghs, and other types of retirement accounts generally are tax-deductible (see Chapter 20).

When you dump that $200 into a retirement account, you get to subtract it from the income on which you pay taxes. If you're paying 35 percent in federal and state income taxes, you shave $70 (that's $200 multiplied by 35 percent) off your tax bill. (You're going to pay taxes when you withdraw the money from the retirement account someday, but in the meantime, the money that would have gone to taxes is growing on your behalf.) You get no tax benefits from that $200 when added to your mortgage payment when you elect a faster payoff mortgage (15-year mortgage).

With kids, you have an even greater reason to fund your retirement accounts before you consider paying down your mortgage faster. Under current rules for determining financial aid for college expenses, money in your retirement accounts isn't counted as an asset (see Chapter 24) that you must use toward college costs.

If you're uncomfortable investing and would otherwise leave the extra money sitting in a money market fund or savings account — or worse, if you would spend it — you're better off paying down the mortgage. Take the 15-year approach. If the investments in your retirement account plummet in value, the impact of the tax-deferred compounding of your capital may be negated. Paying off your mortgage quicker, on the other hand, is just like investing your money in a sure thing — but with a modest rate of return.

In most cases, you get to deduct your mortgage interest on your tax return. So if you're paying 7 percent interest, it really may cost you only around 4 percent to 5 percent after you factor in the tax benefits. If you think that you can do better by investing elsewhere, go for it. Remember, though, that you owe income tax from profits on your investments held outside retirement accounts. You aren't going to get decent investment returns unless you're willing to take risks. Investments such as stocks and real estate have generated better returns over the long haul. These investments carry risks, though, and aren't guaranteed to produce any return.

When you *don't* have a burning investment option, paying down your mortgage as your cash flow allows is usually wiser. If you have extra cash and have contributed the maximum allowed for retirement accounts, you may want to invest in real estate or perhaps a business. You have to decide if it's worth the extra risk in making a particular investment rather than paying down your mortgage.

We are concerned with the increasing promotion and popularity of interest-only and other low down payment mortgages. Not only do such loans carry higher interest rate and other costs (such as private mortgage insurance), but consumers may also be in for some rude surprises. For example, interest-only loans lure people with their relatively low initial payments. However, years into the mortgage, the payment leaps higher as you begin to finally work at paying down the principal. For more information regarding mortgage options and decisions, pick up a copy of *Mortgages For Dummies* by Eric Tyson and Ray Brown (Wiley).

How large a down payment?

What if you're in the enviable and fortunate position of having so much money that you can afford to put down more than a 20 percent down payment (which generally is the amount needed to qualify for better mortgage terms including not having to take out private mortgage insurance)? Perhaps you're one of those wise people who don't want to get stretched too thin financially, and you're buying a less expensive home than you can afford. How much should you put down?

Some people, particularly those in the real estate business (and even some tax and financial advisors), say that you should take as large a mortgage as you can for the tax deductions — that is, don't make a larger down payment than you have to. This is silly reasoning. Remember that you have to pay out money in interest charges to get the tax deductions.

Again, what makes sense for you depends on your alternative uses for the money. When you're considering other investment opportunities, determine whether you can reasonably expect to earn a higher rate of return than the interest rate you'll pay on the mortgage.

In the past century, stock market and real estate investors have enjoyed average annual returns of around 10 percent per year (just remember, the past doesn't guarantee the future). So if you borrow mortgage money at around 7 percent today, you may come out ahead by investing in these areas. Besides possibly generating a higher rate of return, other real estate and stock investing can help you diversify your investments.

Of course, you have no guarantee that you can earn 10 percent each year. And don't forget that all investments come with risk. The advantage of putting more money down for a home and borrowing less is that paying down a mortgage is essentially a risk-free investment (as long as you have emergency money you can tap).

If you prefer to limit the down payment to 20 percent and invest more elsewhere, that's fine. Just don't keep the extra money (beyond an emergency reserve) under the mattress, in a savings account, or in bonds that provide returns lower than the mortgage is costing you.

Refinancing decisions and taxes

When your mortgage has a higher rate of interest than loans currently available, you may save money by refinancing. Because refinancing requires money and time, you need to crunch a few numbers and factor in taxes to determine whether refinancing makes sense for you. Ask your mortgage lender or broker how soon you can recoup the refinancing costs, such as appraisal expenses, loan fees and points, title insurance, and so on.

For example, if completing the refinance costs you $2,000 and reduces your monthly payment by $100, the lender or broker typically says that you can save back the refinance costs in 20 months. This estimate isn't accurate, however, because you lose some tax write-offs when your mortgage interest rate and payments are reduced. You can't simply look at the reduced amount of your monthly payment (mortgage lenders like to look at that reduction, however, because lowering your payments makes refinancing more attractive).

To get a better estimate without spending hours crunching numbers, take your marginal tax rate as specified in Chapter 1 (for example, 28 percent) and reduce your monthly payment savings on the refinance by this amount. For example, if your monthly payment drops by $100, you really save only around $72 a month after factoring in the lost tax benefits. So you recoup the refinance costs in 28 months ($2,000 of refinance costs divided by $72) — not 20 months.

If you can recover the costs of the refinance within a few years or less, go for it. If it takes longer, refinancing may still make sense if you anticipate keeping the property and mortgage that long. If you estimate that you need more than five to seven years to break even, refinancing probably is too risky to justify the costs and hassles.

When you refinance, don't forget to adjust the amount of tax you pay during the year. See the section "Exploring the tax savings in home ownership," earlier in this chapter, for more information on how to change your tax withholding.

Besides getting a lower interest-rate loan, another reason people refinance is to pull out cash from the house for some other purpose. This strategy can make good financial sense, because under most circumstances, mortgage interest is tax-deductible. If you're starting a business or buying other real estate, you can usually borrow against your home at a lower cost than on a business or rental property loan. (If you're a high-income earner, you may lose some of the tax deductibility of your home mortgage interest deductions — read the explanation of the limitations on itemized deductions in Chapter 9.)

If you've run up high-interest consumer debt, you may be able to refinance your mortgage and pull out extra cash to pay off your credit cards, auto loans, or other costly credit lines, thus saving yourself money. You usually can borrow at a lower interest rate for a mortgage and get a tax deduction as a bonus, which lowers the effective borrowing cost further. Interest on consumer debt, such as auto loans and credit cards, isn't tax-deductible.

Borrowing against the equity in your home can be addictive and may contribute to poor spending habits. An appreciating home creates the illusion that excess spending isn't really costing you. Remember that debt is debt, and you have to repay all borrowed money. In the long run, you wind up with greater mortgage debt, and paying it off takes a bigger bite out of your monthly income. Refinancing and establishing home-equity lines also costs you more in loan application fees and other charges (points, appraisals, credit reports, and so on).

Selling Your House

As we discuss earlier in this chapter, a homeowner can realize large profits (capital gains) when selling his house. **Schedule D, Capital Gains and Losses,** is filed only when gains exceed the $250,000/$500,000 threshold. You file Schedule D with Form 1040 from the same tax year in which you sell your house.

Form 1099-S must be filed to report the sale or exchange of real estate unless the sale price is $250,000 or less ($500,000 or less for married couples) and all the sellers provide written certification that the full gain on the sale is excludable from the sellers' gross income. Neither you nor the IRS receives Form 1099-S from the firm handling the sale of your house unless the gross sale price exceeds $500,000 for married couples or $250,000 for an unmarried seller.

The following sections talk about the tax issues affecting house sales.

Not wanting to sell at a loss

Many homeowners are tempted to hold on to their properties when they need to move if the real estate market is soft or the property has a lower value than when they bought it, especially because the loss isn't tax-deductible. We don't recommend this strategy.

You may reason that in a few years, the real estate storm clouds will clear and you can sell your property at a higher price. Here are three risks associated with this way of thinking:

- ✔ You can't know what's going to happen to property prices in the next few years. They may rebound, but they also can stay the same or drop even further. A property generally needs to appreciate at least a few percentage points each year just to make up for all the costs of holding and maintaining it. So you're losing more money each year that you hold the property and it doesn't appreciate at least a few percentage points in value.

- ✔ If you haven't been a landlord, don't underestimate the hassle and headaches associated with the job. Being a long-distance landlord is even more of a challenge. You can always hire someone to manage your property, but that approach creates costs, too — usually about 6 to 10 percent of the monthly rental income.

- ✔ After you convert your home into a rental property, you need to pay capital gains tax on your profit when you sell (the only exception is if you temporarily rent your home while you're still actively trying to sell it). This tax wipes out much of the advantage of having held on to the property until prices recovered. If your desire is to become a long-term rental property owner, you can, under current tax laws, do a tax-free exchange into another rental property after you sell (we discuss this topic in the section, "Rollover of capital gains on rental or business real estate" later in this chapter).

We understand that selling a house that hasn't made you any money isn't much fun. But too many homeowners make a bad situation worse by holding on to their homes for the wrong reasons after they move. No one wants to believe that they're losing money. But remember, the money is already lost. Many people who hold on rub salt into their real estate wounds. If and when the value of the property you're waiting to sell finally increases, odds are that other properties you'd next buy also will have increased. Unless you have sufficient money for the down payment to buy your next home, or you want to keep such a property as a long-term investment, holding on to a home you move from usually isn't wise.

Converting a home into rental property

One advantage to keeping your current home as an investment property after you move is that you already own it. Locating and buying a property takes time and money. Also, you know what you have with your current home. When you go out and purchase a different property to rent, you're starting from scratch.

One of the tax benefits of rental real estate is the depreciation deduction. As your property ages, the IRS allows you to write off or deduct from your rental income for the "wearing out" of the building. Although this deduction helps reduce your income taxes, be aware that you may not be able to deduct as much for depreciation expenses when you convert your home to rental property as you can on a rental bought separately. If your home has appreciated since you bought it, the IRS forces you to use your original (lower) purchase price for purposes of calculating depreciation. To make tax matters worse, if your home has declined in value since you originally purchased it, you must use this lower value, at the time you convert the property, for purposes of depreciation.

Don't consider converting your home into a rental when you move unless this decision really is a long-term proposition. As we discuss in the preceding section, selling rental property has tax consequences.

If the idea of keeping the home you move from as a long-term investment appeals to you, take stock of your overall financial situation *before* you make the final call. Can you afford to purchase your next home given the money that's still tied up in the home you're considering keeping as a rental? Can you afford to contribute to tax-deductible retirement plans, or will the burden of carrying two properties use up too much of your cash flow? Will your overall investments be well diversified, or will you have too much of your money tied up in real estate (perhaps in one area of the country)?

House sales, taxes, and divorce

A divorce complicates many personal and financial issues. Real estate is no different. In the past, if ownership of a home that had appreciated in value were transferred between spouses because of a divorce, capital gains tax was owed. This is no longer one of the additional costs of divorce. Transfers of property between spouses aren't taxed if the transfers are made within one year of divorce (and both spouses are U.S. residents or citizens).

If you're selling your house because of a divorce, when you sell the house can have significant tax ramifications. If you agree to sell the house in the divorce settlement, each of you can make up to $250,000 in profit before any tax is levied.

Investing in Real Estate

For most people, the only real estate they own or consider owning is the home in which they live. If that's all you desire, we aren't going to push you into the business of investing in and managing rental property. It's a great deal of work, and other investments are certainly available, such as mutual funds (that own stocks), that are far more convenient and just as profitable.

But some people just have that itch to own something tangible. Real estate is, well, *real*, after all. You can fix it up, take pictures of it, and drive your friends by it!

Good versus bad real estate investments

You can invest in real estate in a number of ways. The traditional and best method is to purchase property in an area that you've researched and are familiar with. Single-family homes and multiunit buildings generally work best for most investors. Make sure that you do your "due diligence." Have the property professionally inspected and secure adequate insurance coverage.

If you want a stake in real estate but don't want the responsibilities and hassles that come with being a landlord, consider real estate investment trusts (REITs). REITs offer the benefits of property ownership without the headaches of being a landlord. REITs are a collection of real estate properties, such as shopping centers, apartments, and other rental buildings. REITs trade as securities on the major stock exchanges and can be bought through mutual funds such as Vanguard REIT Index, Fidelity Real Estate, and Cohen & Steers Realty Shares.

Be careful, though; some real estate investments rarely make sense because they're near-certain money losers. Many investors get sucked into these lousy investments because of the supposed high-expected returns and tax breaks. Limited partnerships, for example, which are sold through stockbrokers and financial planners who work on commission, are burdened by high sales commissions, ongoing management fees, and illiquidity (see Chapter 22).

Time-shares are another nearly certain money loser. With a time-share, you buy a week or two of ownership, or usage, of a particular unit, usually a condominium in a resort location. If you pay $8,000 for a week (in addition to ongoing maintenance fees), you're paying the equivalent of more than $400,000 for the whole unit year-round, but a comparable unit may sell for only $150,000. All that extra markup pays the salespeople's commissions, administrative expenses, and profits for the time-share development company.

Deciding whether real estate investing is for you

Whether you should invest in real estate versus other investments, such as stocks, bonds, or mutual funds, depends on many factors. The first and most important question to ask yourself is whether you're cut out to handle the responsibilities that come with being a landlord. Real estate is a time-intensive investment — it isn't for couch potatoes. Investing in stocks can be time-intensive as well, but it doesn't have to be if you use professionally managed mutual funds. Conversely, you can hire a property manager with real estate experience to reduce your workload. But the time required to own and oversee rental property can still be significant.

An often-overlooked drawback to investing in real estate is that you earn no tax benefits while you're accumulating your down payment. Rental property also is usually a cash drain in the early years of ownership. Retirement accounts, on the other hand, such as 401(k)s, SEP-IRAs, Keoghs, and so on (see Chapter 20), give you immediate tax deductions as you contribute money to them. Although real estate offers many tax deductions, as we discuss earlier in the chapter, the cost of real estate reflects the expected tax breaks. So don't invest in real estate because of the tax deductions.

A final consideration with regard to whether real estate investing is for you: Do you have a solid understanding of real estate and how to improve its value?

Enjoying rental property tax breaks

When you purchase property and rent it out, you're essentially running a business. You take in revenue — namely rent from your tenants — and incur expenses from the property. You hope that, over time, your revenue exceeds your expenses so that your real estate investment produces a profit (cash flow, in real estate lingo) for all the money and time you've sunk into it. You also hope that the market value of your investment property appreciates over time. The IRS helps you make a buck or two through a number of tax benefits. The major benefits follow.

Operating-expense write-offs

In addition to the deductions allowed for mortgage interest and property taxes, just as on a home in which you live, you can deduct on your tax return a variety of other expenses for rental property. Almost all these deductions come from money that you spend on the property, such as money for insurance, maintenance, repairs, and food for the Doberman you keep around to intimidate those tenants whose rent checks always are "in the mail."

But one expense — depreciation — doesn't involve your spending money. Depreciation is an accounting deduction that the IRS allows you to take for the overall wear and tear on your building. The idea behind this deduction is that, over time, your building will deteriorate and need upgrading, rebuilding, and so on. The IRS tables now say that for residential property, you can depreciate over 27½ years, and for nonresidential property, 39 years. Only the portion of a property's value that is attributable to the building(s) — and not the land — can be depreciated.

For example, suppose that you bought a residential rental property for $300,000 and the land is deemed to be worth $100,000. Thus the building is worth $200,000. If you can depreciate your $200,000 building over 27½ years, that works out to a $7,272 annual depreciation deduction.

If your rental property shows a loss for the year (when you figure your property's income and expenses), you may be able to deduct this loss on your tax return. If your adjusted gross income (AGI) is less than $100,000 and you actively participate in managing the property, you're allowed to deduct your losses on operating rental real estate — up to $25,000 per year. Limited partnerships and properties in which you own less than 10 percent are excluded. (See Chapter 13 for details.)

To deduct a loss on your tax return, you must *actively participate* in the management of the property. This rule doesn't necessarily mean that you perform the day-to-day management of the property. In fact, you can hire a property manager and still actively participate by doing such simple things as approving the terms of the lease contracts, tenants, and expenditures for maintenance and improvements on the building.

If you make more than $100,000 per year, you start to lose these write-offs. At an income of $150,000 or more, you can't deduct rental real estate losses from your other income. People in the real estate business (for example, agents and developers) who work more than 750 hours per year in the industry may not be subject to these rules. (Refer to Chapter 13 for more information.)

You start to lose the deductibility of rental property losses above the $100,000 limit, whether you're single or married filing jointly. You can carry the loss forward to future tax years and take the loss then, if eligible. This policy is a bit unfair to couples, because it's easier for them to break $100,000 with two incomes than for a single person with one income. Sorry — this is yet another part of the marriage tax penalties!

Rollover of capital gains on rental or business real estate

Suppose that you purchase a rental property and nurture it over the years. You find good tenants and keep the building repaired and looking sharp. You may just find that all that work pays off — the property may someday be worth much more than you originally paid for it.

Tax credits for low-income housing and old buildings

The IRS grants you special tax credits when you invest in low-income housing or particularly old commercial buildings. The credits represent a direct reduction in your tax bill because you're spending to rehabilitate and improve these properties. The IRS wants to encourage investors to invest in and fix up old or rundown buildings that likely would continue to deteriorate otherwise.

The amounts of the credits range from as little as 10 percent of the expenditures to as much as 90 percent,

depending on the property type. The IRS has strict rules governing what types of properties qualify. Tax credits may be earned for rehabilitating nonresidential buildings built in 1935 or before. "Certified historic structures," both residential and nonresidential, also qualify for tax credits. See IRS instructions for Form 3468 to find out more about these credits.

However, if you simply sell the property, you owe taxes on your gain or profit. Even worse is the way the government defines your gain. If you bought the property for $100,000 and sell it for $150,000, you not only owe tax on that difference, but you also owe tax on an additional amount, depending on the property's depreciation. The amount of depreciation that you deducted on your tax returns reduces the original $100,000 purchase price, making the taxable difference that much larger. For example, if you deducted $25,000 for depreciation over the years that you owned the property, you owe tax on the difference between the sale price of $150,000 and $75,000 ($100,000 purchase price minus $25,000 depreciation).

All this tax may just motivate you to hold on to your property. But you can avoid paying tax on your profit when you sell a rental property by "exchanging" it for a similar or like-kind *property,* thereby rolling over your gain. The section of the tax code that allows rollovers is a 1031 exchange. (You may not receive the proceeds — they must go into an escrow account.) The rules, however, are different for rolling over profits (called 1031 exchanges, for the section of the tax code that allows them) from the sale of rental property than the old rules for a primary residence.

Under current tax laws, the IRS continues to take a broad definition of what like-kind property is. For example, you can exchange undeveloped land for a multiunit rental building.

The rules for properly doing a 1031 exchange are complex. Third parties are usually involved. Make sure that you find an attorney and/or tax advisor who is expert at these transactions to ensure that you do it right.

Real estate corporations

When you invest in and manage real estate with at least one other partner, you can set up a company through which you own the property. The main reason you may want to consider this setup is liability protection. A corporation can reduce the chances of lenders or tenants suing you.

Read the discussion in Chapter 21 about incorporating, the different entities under which you may do business, and the pros and cons of each. For a crash course on rental property investing, pick up a copy of *Real Estate Investing For Dummies,* by Eric Tyson and Robert Griswold (Wiley).

Chapter 24

Children and Taxes

In This Chapter
▶ Taking advantage of child tax goodies
▶ Figuring out taxes, financial aid, and educational expenses
▶ Understanding the "kid" tax system

Raising children involves many decisions and trade-offs. Many new parents are surprised at the financial and tax consequences of having kids. We include this chapter so that you can spend more time enjoying the first smile, first step, first word, and first high-five, and save on your taxes.

Bringing Up Baby

Although kids can cost a bunch of money, the expenses, or the thousands of diaper changes during the infant years, rarely deter people from wanting a family. And for good reason — kids are wonderful, at least most of the time. They're the future. (If you don't have kids, who do you think is going to fund your Social Security and Medicare benefits during your retirement years?)

Raising a family can be the financial equivalent of doing a triathlon. It can stretch and break the budgets of even those who consider themselves financially well off and on top of things. Taxes are an important factor in a number of kid-related issues. This chapter includes our take on some of the important tax issues that you may confront before conception and during the many years you're raising a child.

Getting Junior a Social Security number

When a child is born, he or she may be a bundle of joy to you, but to the federal government and the IRS, Junior is just a number — more specifically, a Social Security number. The IRS allows you to claim your children as dependents on your tax return. For tax year 2006, each child is "worth" a $3,300 deduction as your dependent. So if you're in the 28 percent federal tax bracket, each child saves you a cool $924 in federal taxes ($3,300 × 0.28). Not bad, but the deduction isn't going to cover much more than the cost of diapers for the year. *Note:* As we discuss in Chapter 4, high-income earners have this wonderful deduction reduced or even eliminated.

For you to claim your child as a dependent on your tax return, he or she must have a Social Security number. You also need a Social Security number for your child whenever you want to establish investment accounts in his or her name (although you may not want to after you understand the drawbacks of doing so, which we discuss later in this chapter).

The IRS requires a Social Security number because people were *inventing* children — you know, telling the IRS they'd just had twins when the closest they actually came to becoming parents was babysitting their best friend's kid one evening!

If you need **Form SS-5, Application for a Social Security Card,** simply contact the Social Security Administration (800-772-1213; www.ssa.gov) and ask to have one mailed to you. Fill it out and mail it back ASAP. After all, how many times in your child's life do you get to save nearly $1,000 annually just by spending two minutes filling out a government form?

Childcare tax goodies

In addition to the extra personal deduction that you can take with each new child and the tax savings that come with that deduction, you also need to be aware of the tax perks (for childcare and related expenditures) that may save you thousands of dollars.

Dependent-care tax credit

When you hire childcare assistance for your youngster(s), you may be able to claim a tax credit on your annual return (which you claim on **Form 2441**). To be eligible for this credit, you (and your spouse, if you're married) must work at least part time, unless you're a full-time student or you're disabled. Your kid(s) must be younger than the age of 13 or physically or mentally disabled.

Because a credit is a dollar-for-dollar reduction in the taxes you owe, it can save you hundreds of tax dollars every year. And not only do you count childcare expenses toward calculation of the tax credit, but you may also be able to count the cost of a housekeeper, or even a cook, if the expense benefits your kids.

The dependent-care tax credit is a maximum of $3,000 per child with a $6,000 per family limit. The income threshold at which the credit begins to be reduced increases to $15,000, and the portion of qualifying employment-related expenses for which credits can be claimed is 35 percent.

As we discuss later in this section, tax and other considerations influence your desire as a parent to work outside the home. Working at least part-time makes you eligible for this tax credit. If you choose to be a full-time mom or dad, unfortunately you aren't eligible for the dependent-care tax credit.

Teaching kids about taxes and money

Show your kids your pay stub! Sharing information about what you earn and what you pay in taxes with your children can be highly educational for them. This information gets kids thinking about the realities of living within an income.

Your pay stub helps kids see not only what you earn each month, but also how much goes out for expenses, like taxes. You can then have discussions about the costs of rent and mortgages, utilities, food, and everything else. Your children may better understand your financial constraints, and, as a result, they'll be more responsible for earning money, paying taxes, and meeting monthly bills. You don't do them (or yourself) any favors by keeping them in the dark about financial matters.

In the absence of information, children have no concept of the amount their parents earn. Some have outrageously inflated ideas of how much their parents make — especially children whose parents eagerly fulfill their requests for purchases.

If your employer offers a dependent-care assistance plan (discussed in the following section), you may be able to reduce your taxes by taking advantage of that benefit rather than the dependent-care tax credit. Your tax credit is reduced or eliminated whenever you use your employer's dependent-care plan spending account. To find out more about how to claim this credit on your annual tax return, see Chapter 14.

Dependent-care spending accounts

Increasing numbers of employers offer flexible benefit or spending plans that enable you to choose from among a number of different benefits, such as health, life, and disability insurance; vacation days; and dependent-care expenses.

You can put away money from your paycheck to pay for childcare expenses on a pretax basis. Doing so saves you from paying federal, state, and even Social Security taxes on that money. These flexible benefits plans allow you to put away up to $5,000 per year ($2,500 if you're married filing separately). However, the exact amount that you can put away depends on the specifics of your employer's plan.

Dependent-care spending accounts are a use-it-or-lose-it benefit. If you don't spend the money for childcare expenses during the current tax year, the IRS forces you to forfeit all the unused money at the end of the year. So, be careful not to go overboard by contributing more than you're certain to use.

As we mention in the preceding section, participating in your employer's dependent-care assistance plan reduces your tax credit. You can't do both. When you're in the federal 25 percent tax bracket and higher, you should be able to save more in taxes by using your employer's plan than by taking the credit on your tax return. The only way to know for sure is to run the numbers.

You can also use the dependent-care tax credit and spending accounts that we discuss in this section to pay for the costs of taking care of other dependents, such as an ill or elderly parent. Please see Chapter 14 and your employer's employee benefits manual for more information.

Child tax credit

Every child you can claim as a dependent, who is a U.S. citizen and younger than the age of 17 on December 31, can reduce your tax bill by $1,000. If you have three or more kids and your total child tax credit exceeds your tax bill, part of the credit may be refundable. The credit is reduced by $50 for every $1,000 or fraction thereof of modified adjusted gross income above $75,000 for singles, $110,000 for married couples filing jointly, and $55,000 for married couples filing separately.

The same income ceilings apply as before for claiming this credit, and no future increases for inflation are planned for the income ceilings. The $1,000 credit will be adjusted for inflation after 2010.

The 2001 tax bill expanded the refundability of the child tax credit for low-income families with one or two children. The credit now is refundable to the extent of 10 percent of the amount that a taxpayer's earned income exceeds $11,300 (which increases with inflation). The credit will be refundable to the extent of 15 percent of the amount that earned income exceeds $15,000. Families with three or more dependent children face more complicated, although beneficial, calculations. See Chapter 14 for more information about how to claim this credit.

Adoption tax credit

Recent tax law changes have substantially increased the tax credits to parents who adopt children. Please see Chapter 14 for all the details.

Costs and benefits of a second income

One of the most challenging decisions that new parents face is whether to work full time, part time, or not at all. We mean work at a paying job, that is — parenting is the lowest-paid but potentially most rewarding job there is. The need or desire to work full time is obvious — doing so brings more money home.

In addition to less sleep at night and frequent diaper changes, children mean increased spending. At a minimum, expenditures for food and clothing increase. Although you may have less time to shop for yourself, causing your personal spending to decrease, you're likely to spend more on housing, insurance, childcare, and education. And don't forget the host of not-so-incidental incidentals. Toys, art classes, sports, field trips, and the like can rack up big bills, especially if you don't control what you spend on them.

You may rightfully feel that working full time prohibits you from playing as active a role in raising your children as you want. As you consider the additional expenses of raising children, you may also need to factor in a decrease in income.

Financially speaking, taxes can have a big impact on the value or benefit of working full time, especially for two-income couples. Remember that the tax brackets are set up so that the last dollars of earnings are taxed at a higher rate (refer to Chapter 1).

Deciding whether to work full time by counting the salary that your employer quotes you as the total value of that second income leaves you open to making a potentially big personal and financial mistake.

For example, take the case of Ron and Mary, a nice couple who struggled with how to handle their work schedules after the birth of their first child. They both worked full time. Mary, a marketing manager, earned $55,000 per year, and Ron, a schoolteacher, made $32,000 per year. Ron was considering working part time or not at all so that he could be at home with their daughter, but because of Ron and Mary's prior financial commitments, such as their mortgage, they believed that they couldn't afford for Ron to work less than full time.

Ron and Mary took a closer look at their finances and taxes and started to see things a little differently. Taxes took a whopping 40 percent of Ron's income, so his take-home pay was just $19,200 per year, or $1,600 per month. Then they added up all the additional costs of both parents working full time: daycare, a second car, more meals eaten out, and so on. When they totaled up all the extra costs (including taxes) that could be reduced or eliminated if Ron didn't work at all or worked on a greatly reduced basis, they figured that Ron was effectively contributing about $300 per month from his full-time job — or about $1.80 per hour!

Ultimately, because of his low after-tax effective hourly income, Ron decided to quit his job and work part time at home. This solution gave the family the best of both worlds — a more involved dad and husband and some income without most of the extra costs that come with a second job. And because Ron was able to work part time, he and his wife were able to earn some tax credits (see the "Dependent-care tax credit" section, earlier in this chapter) for part-time childcare for their daughter.

Of course, people enjoy other benefits from working, besides income. Be sure, however, to examine taxes and other expenses on that second income to ensure that you're making your financial decision to work based on complete and accurate information.

Education Tax Breaks and Pitfalls

What, you may ask, do taxes have to do with educational expenses? How you invest to pay for educating your children can have an enormous impact on your family's taxes, your children's ability to qualify for financial aid, and your overall financial well-being.

The (hidden) financial aid tax system

The financial aid system (to which parents apply so that their children are eligible for college scholarships, grants, and loans) treats assets differently when held outside rather than inside retirement accounts. Under the current financial aid system, the value of your retirement plans is *not* considered an asset. Thus the more of your money you stash in retirement accounts, the greater your chances of qualifying for financial aid and the more money you're generally eligible for.

Most new parents don't place their savings in retirement accounts. Many nonwealthy parents make the error of saving and investing money in a separate account for their child (perhaps even in the child's name) or through some other financial product, such as a life insurance policy. Doing so is a mistake because these products are taxed at a much higher level than other savings strategies.

Most important, parents need to save and invest through retirement accounts that give significant tax benefits. Contributions to a 401(k), 403(b), SEP-IRA, Keogh, and other retirement accounts (see Chapter 20) usually produce an upfront tax deduction. An additional and substantial benefit is that after the money is placed in these accounts, it grows and compounds without being taxed until you withdraw it.

Therefore, forgoing contributions to your retirement savings plans so you can save money in a taxable account for Junior's college fund doesn't make sense. When you do, you pay higher taxes both on your current income and on the interest and growth of this money. In addition to paying higher taxes, money that you save *outside* retirement accounts, including money in the child's name, is counted as an asset and reduces your child's eligibility for financial aid. Thus you're expected to contribute more to your child's educational expenses.

Note: As we discuss later in the chapter, if you're affluent enough that you expect to pay for your kid's entire educational costs, investing through custodial accounts, Education Savings Accounts, and Section 529 college savings plans can save on taxes.

College cost tax deductions

Unfortunately, the up-to-$4,000 deduction you used to be able to take on the front of your Form 1040 or 1040A in recent years for college costs disappeared at the end of 2005. Hope and Lifetime Learning Credits are still available, though, so you should check them out later in this chapter. (At the time this book goes to press, Congress is still considering extending this deduction which would be retroactive to the end of 2005. Stay tuned.)

Recent tax bills expanded tax breaks to allow for greater ability to deduct the interest paid on student loans. The interest write-off on student loans is no longer restricted to interest paid during the first five years of loan payback. Also, early repayment of interest is now deductible.

When a millionaire's kid gets more financial aid than a middle-class family's kid

What's truly amazing and sad about the way the current financial aid system works is that some affluent people who don't really need aid can get more than those who aren't nearly as financially well off. Here's a real case that, although somewhat extreme, is not that unusual. This story highlights the shortcomings of the current procedures used to determine financial need.

Kent, a doctor earning $200,000 per year, and his spouse Marian, a housewife, had a son who applied for and received financial aid. By the time their son was ready to apply to college, Kent had quit working as a physician and was earning little money while doing some part-time teaching. However, he had a seven-figure balance in his retirement savings plan, which he had accumulated over his years of work. Being savvy financial managers, Kent

and Marian had little money invested and available outside tax-sheltered retirement accounts. Because the financial aid system ignores retirement accounts in its analysis, and because Kent's income was modest at the time his son applied for aid, the family got significant aid.

On the other hand, Wendy, the daughter of Rick and Liz, full-time employees with a combined income of $60,000, received no financial aid. Why? Because Rick and Liz had been saving money in Wendy's name. By the time she was ready to apply to college, she had about $25,000 saved. Rick and Liz also accumulated some other modest investments outside retirement accounts, but only about $30,000 in retirement accounts. Because of the assets available outside retirement accounts and their current income, they were deemed not needy enough for aid.

The income thresholds for those who can take the student loan interest write-off are now between $50,000 and $65,000 for single taxpayers and between $105,000 and $135,000 for couples and increases annually for inflation.

Education Savings Accounts: Tread carefully

You can establish a Coverdell Education Savings Account (ESA) for each child and make contributions of up to $2,000 per child per year until the child reaches age 18. Contributions to an ESA, which can be made up until the due date of the income tax return, aren't tax-deductible. However, ESA investment earnings can compound and be withdrawn free of tax as long as the funds are used to pay for college costs. In the year of withdrawal, the new Hope Scholarship and Lifetime Learning Credits may not be claimed for the student, unless you elect to pay income tax on the earnings portion of your withdrawal — see the next section for more about these credits.

ESA balances can be used for pre-college educational costs (in other words, for schooling costs up through and including grade 12). Eligible educational expenses for primary and secondary students include tuition, fees, books, supplies, computers and other equipment, tutoring, uniforms, extended-day programs, transportation, Internet access, and so on, while expenses for college students include only tuition, fees, room and board, required books and supplies, and special-needs services qualify. (College room and board expenses qualify only if the student carries at least one-half the normal workload.) Contributions to the accounts of special-needs children are permitted past the age of 18 and balances can continue in those accounts past the age of 30.

Before running out to contribute to an ESA, be aware that college financial aid officers are generally going to treat this type of savings in such a way that it harms a child's financial aid award. Financial aid officers typically treat funds placed in an ESA either as a child's asset, which reduces financial aid by 35 percent for each dollar in the child's name, or as a prepaid tuition plan, which reduces aid dollar for dollar.

Unless you're affluent enough to pay for the full cost of your children's college education without any type of financial aid, hold off on contributing to an ESA until it's clearer how financial aid offices are going to treat them. If you're affluent, you may not be eligible to contribute to one anyway. The full $2,000 per child contribution to an ESA may be made only by couples with AGIs less than $190,000 and single taxpayers with AGIs less than $95,000. The $2,000 limit is reduced for married taxpayers with AGIs of more than $190,000 ($95,000 if single) and eliminated if the AGI is more than $220,000 ($110,000 for singles).

If you earn more than these thresholds and want your kids to have ESAs, there's a loophole. Simply have someone else who isn't earning more than the threshold amounts, such as a grandparent, make the ESA contribution on your behalf.

Here are some other ESA rules and regulations that you need to be aware of:

- ✔ The tax-free exclusion of the earnings isn't available on a distribution from the ESA in the same year you claim a Hope Scholarship or Lifetime Earning Credit.

- ✔ Contributions to the account must be made before the child reaches 18 unless the child is considered special needs, which is defined as "an individual who, because of a physical, mental, or emotional condition (including learning disability), requires additional time to complete his or her education."

- ✔ The money in the account can't be used to invest in a life insurance policy.

- ✔ When the beneficiary reaches age 30, any balance must be distributed to him or her, and he or she must include any earnings in his or her income (unless the account holder is considered special needs). However, prior to reaching 30, the beneficiary may transfer or roll over the balance to another beneficiary who is a member of his or her family. The distribution must be made within 30 days of the beneficiary's 30th birthday, or within 30 days of his or her death.

- ✔ Any part of a distribution that must be included in income because it wasn't used to pay college expenses is subject to a 10 percent penalty, unless the distribution is paid as a result of death or disability, or the amount distributed would have been used for educational expenses except for the fact that your student received a scholarship or some other sort of award.

Here's an example of how the earnings on an ESA get taxed: Grandma and Grandpa contributed $600 over the years to Chloe's account. It's now worth $1,000; thus the investment earnings total $400 ($1,000 − $600). Because Chloe withdraws the $1,000 but uses only $750 (75 percent) to pay college expenses, of the $400 in earnings, only 75 percent, or $300, is exempt from tax. Chloe must pay tax on the $100 balance. If she had used the entire $1,000 to pay her college expenses, the entire $400 of earnings would be exempt from tax. One additional point: The $100 on which Chloe had to pay tax is also subject to a 10 percent penalty.

Chloe can elect to waive the exclusion from tax on her withdrawal from her ESA if she claims the Hope Scholarship or Lifetime Learning Credits instead. In this case, the 10 percent penalty in the preceding example doesn't apply because Chloe includes the earnings from her ESA in her income.

Section 529 plans — state tuition plans

Section 529 plans (named after Internal Revenue Code section 529), also known as qualified state tuition plans, are among the newer tax-advantaged college savings plans around. And recent tax law changes made them even better.

A parent or grandparent can put more than $100,000 (in some states, the limits on accounts size are more than $250,000 per qualifying student!) into one of these plans for each child. You can put up to $60,000 into a child's college savings account immediately, and that counts for the next five years' worth of $12,000 tax-free gifts (actually, a couple can immediately contribute $120,000 per child) allowed under current gifting laws (see Chapter 25). Money contributed to the account isn't considered part of the donor's taxable estate (although if the donor dies before five years are up after gifting $60,000, a prorated amount of the gift is charged back to the donor's estate).

Section 529 plan investment earnings can be withdrawn tax-free (that's right — completely free of taxation) as long as the withdrawn funds are used to pay for qualifying higher educational costs. In addition to paying college costs (tuition, room and board, or other related expenses), you can use the money in Section 529 plans to pay for graduate school and for the enrollment and attendance expenses of special-needs students.

Some states provide tax benefits on contributions to their state-sanctioned plans, whereas other states induce you to invest at home by taxing profits from out-of-state plans.

Unlike contributing money to a custodial account with which a child may do as he or she pleases when he or she reaches the age of either 18 or 21 (it varies by state), these state tuition plans must be used for higher education expenses. Some state plans even allow you to change the beneficiary or take the money back if you change your mind. (If you do withdraw the money, however, you owe tax on the withdrawn earnings, plus a penalty — typically 10 percent.)

A big potential drawback — especially for families hoping for some financial aid — is that college financial aid offices may treat assets in these plans as the child's, which, as discussed earlier in the chapter, can greatly diminish financial aid eligibility.

Another potential drawback is that you have limited choices and control over how the money in state tuition plans is invested. The investment provider(s) for each state plan generally decides how to invest the money over time within given investment options. In most plans, the more years your child is away from college, the more aggressive the investment mix is. As your child approaches college age, the investment mix is tilted more to conservative investments. Most state plans have somewhat high investment management fees, and some plans don't allow transfers to other plans.

Please also be aware that a future Congress could change the tax laws affecting these plans and diminish the tax breaks or increase the penalties for nonqualified withdrawals.

Clearly, there are pros and cons to Section 529 plans. They generally make the most sense for affluent parents (or grandparents) of children who don't expect to qualify for financial aid.

Do a lot of research and homework before investing in any plan. Check out the investment track record, allocations, and fees for each plan, as well as restrictions on transferring to other plans or changing beneficiaries. These plans are relatively new, and the market for them is changing quickly, so take your time before committing to one of them.

The rules and regulations surrounding Section 529 and ESAs are complex. To find out more, check out Margaret's book *529 & Other College Savings Plans For Dummies* (Wiley).

Hope Scholarship and Lifetime Learning Credits

Tax credits assist some parents with the often high costs of education. We say some because the credits are phased out for single tax filers with AGIs between $45,000 and $55,000 and married couples filing jointly with AGIs between $90,000 and $110,000 (these phase-out ranges annually increase with inflation).

The first of the two credits — the Hope Scholarship Credit — allows up to a $1,500 tax credit toward tuition and fees in each of the first two years of college.

The second credit — the Lifetime Learning Credit — allows a credit for up to 20 percent of $10,000 in tuition and fee expenses (worth $2,000) per taxpayer. The Lifetime Learning Credit can be used toward undergraduate and graduate education and toward coursework that upgrades job skills.

If you, as a taxpayer, claim either of these credits in a tax year for a particular student, you aren't eligible to withdraw money without taxation from an ESA or a Section 529 plan account for that same student, nor can you take the new college cost tax deduction. Also, you can't take the Hope Scholarship Credit in the same year that you use the Lifetime Learning Credit for the same student; if you have more than one student who qualifies, though, you may be able to take the Hope credit for one, and the Lifetime Learning Credit for the other(s).

Minimizing your taxes and paying for college

Socking money away into your tax-sheltered retirement accounts helps you reduce your tax burden and may help your children qualify for more financial aid. However, accessing retirement accounts before age 59½ incurs tax penalties.

So how do you pay for your children's educational costs? There isn't one correct answer, because the decision depends on your overall financial situation. Here are some ideas that can help you meet expected educational expenses and minimize your taxes:

- **Don't try to do it all yourself.** Unless you're affluent, don't even try to pay for the full cost of a college education for your children. Few people can afford it. You and your children will, in all likelihood, have to borrow some money.

- **Apply for aid, regardless of your financial circumstances.** A number of loan programs, such as Unsubsidized Stafford Loans and Parent Loans for Undergraduate Students (PLUS), are available even if your family isn't deemed financially needy. Only Subsidized Stafford Loans, on which the federal government pays the interest that accumulates while the student is still in school, are limited to those students deemed financially needy.

  In addition to loans, a number of grant programs are available through schools, the government, and independent sources. Specific colleges and other private organizations (including employers, banks, credit unions, and community groups) also offer grants and scholarships. Some of these have nothing to do with financial need.

- **Save in your name, not in your children's.** If you've exhausted your retirement account contributions, saving money that you're earmarking to pay for college is okay. Just do it in your name. If your children's grandparents want to make a gift of money to them for college expenses, keep the money in your name; otherwise, have the grandparents keep the money until the kids are ready to enter college.

- **Get your kids to work.** Your child can work and save money to pay for college costs during junior high, high school, and college. In fact, if your child qualifies for financial aid, he or she is expected to contribute a certain amount to his or her educational costs from money earned from jobs held during the school year or summer breaks and from his or her own savings. Besides giving the student a stake in his or her own future, this training encourages sound personal financial management down the road.

- **Borrow against your home equity.** If you're a homeowner, you can borrow against the equity (market value less the outstanding mortgage loan) in your property. Doing so is usually wise because you can borrow against your home at a reasonable interest rate, and the interest is generally tax-deductible. (Refer to Chapter 9 for information about tax-deductibility rules.) Be careful to borrow an amount you can afford to repay and that won't cause you to default on your loan and lose your home. *Mortgages For Dummies,* which Eric Tyson co-wrote (Wiley), can help you with such borrowing decisions.

✔ **Borrow against your company retirement plans.** Many retirement savings plans, such as 401(k)s, allow borrowing. Just make sure that you're able to pay back the money. Otherwise, you'll owe big taxes for a premature distribution.

Taxes on Your Kids' Investments

Parents of all different financial means need to be aware of the financial aid implications of putting money into an account bearing a child's name. Read the section "Educational Tax Breaks and Pitfalls" earlier in this chapter before investing money in your children's names.

Double-what bonds?

Among the many forms of bonds (debt) that our fine government issues are Series EE (double "E") and Series I bonds. These are one of the many classes of Treasury bonds issued by that national organization with a penchant for borrowing money. You may hear about these bonds as a suggested investment for children's college expenses.

EE bonds purchased after 1989 and all I bonds have a unique tax twist if you use the proceeds to pay for educational tuition and fees. (Room and board and other education-related costs aren't covered.) The interest earned on the bonds is fully exempt from federal taxation (interest on the Treasury bonds is already state tax–free) as long as two other requirements are met:

✔ The purchaser of the bond must be at least 24 years of age.

✔ At the time the bonds were redeemed to pay for educational tuition and fees, the holder of the bond may not have an AGI in excess of $78,100 if single or $124,700 if married and filing a joint return. (For single filers with an AGI between $63,100 and $78,100 and married couples between $94,700 and $124,700, a partial interest–tax exemption applies.)

Even if you're somehow able to know years in advance what your income will be when your toddler has grown into a college-bound 18-year-old, you've gotta file yet another tax form, Form 8815, to claim the exclusion of the interest of EEs and Is from federal taxation. And don't forget that not a year goes by without Congress messing with the federal tax laws. So the income requirements for the tax exemptions can change.

You also need to know that EE and I Bonds often pay a lower rate of interest than other, simpler comparable bonds. The yield or interest rate on EE and I bonds is also a chore to understand. You must hold these bonds for at least five years in order to receive the return. The return is equal to 85 percent of the average yield payable on five-year Treasury notes during the period held, or 4 percent, whichever is higher.

Regardless of how you use the EE and I bond proceeds, you may defer taxation of the interest on them until you cash them, or you may choose to pay tax on each year's interest in the year it's earned. If you're planning on using these bonds to pay qualified higher education expenses, make sure you don't pay the tax on a yearly basis — after you've paid the tax, you can't get a refund even if you do eventually use these bonds to pay for Junior's college tuition.

Don't waste your time on these complicated bonds. They are testimony to the absurdly complex tax code and government rules. You're better off investing in mutual funds that offer some growth potential. But if we haven't dissuaded you, make sure that you buy these bonds from the Federal Reserve Bank in your area and hold them in an account with the Federal Reserve, or you can purchase them online at www.treasurydirect.gov. Doing so ensures that you'll always get a statement on your account and won't lose track of the bonds when you're no longer being paid interest!

Taxes for kids under 18

Prior to tax year 2006, prior to reaching the magical age of 14, kids had a special tax system that applied to them. Effective in 2006, kids can still be kids in the eyes of the IRS for tax purposes until they turn 18. Specifically, the first $850 of *unearned income* (income from interest and dividends on investments) that a child earns isn't taxed at all. It's tax-free! In contrast, earned income is considered income earned from work. Refer to Chapter 8 to find out when you need to file a tax return for your child.

The next $850 of unearned income for this age set is taxed at the federal level at 10 percent. Everything higher than $1,700 is taxed at the parents' income tax rate. The system is set up in this fashion to discourage parents from transferring a lot of assets into their children's names, hoping to pay lower taxes.

Because the first $1,700 of unearned income for the child is taxed at such a low rate, some parents are tempted to transfer money into the child's name to save on income taxes. Quite a number of financial books and advisors recommend this strategy. Consider this passage referring to transferring money to your children, from a tax book written by a large accounting firm: "Take advantage of these rules. It still makes sense to shift some income-producing assets to younger children." Wrong! As we discuss in "The (hidden) financial aid tax system," earlier in this chapter, this shortsighted desire to save a little in taxes today can lead to your losing out on significant financial aid later. And what about your limited discretionary income? You don't want to put money in your child's name if it means that you aren't fully taking advantage of your retirement accounts.

Consider putting money into an account bearing your child's name only if

✔ You expect to pay for the full cost of a college education and won't apply for or use any financial aid, including loans that aren't based on financial need.

✔ You're comfortable with the notion that your child will have legal access to the money at age 18 or 21 (depending on the state in which you live) if the money is in a custodial account in the child's name. At that age, the money is legally your child's, and he or she can blow it on something other than a college education.

After all the caveats and warnings, if you're still thinking about putting money into an account bearing your child's name, consider buying tax-friendly investments that won't generate significant tax liabilities until after the child turns 18. (See Chapter 22 for tax-friendly investment ideas.) As we discuss in the following section, after your kids turn 18, all income they earn is taxed at their rate, not yours.

You also can buy investments in your name and then transfer them to your child after Junior turns 18. (Each parent is limited to giving $12,000 to each child per year before you have to start worrying about preparing and filing a gift tax return.) That way, if the investment declines in value, you can take the tax loss; if the investment turns a profit, you can save on your taxes by transferring the investment to your child and having your child pay tax on it after turning 18. This strategy won't work if your child is a movie or kidband star and in a higher tax bracket than you are!

Tax-wise and not-so-wise investments for educational funds

You hear many sales pitches for "tax-wise" investments to use for college savings. Most aren't worthy of your consideration. Here's our take on the best, the mediocre, and the worst.

Mutual funds are ideal

Mutual funds, which offer investors of all financial means instant diversification and low-cost access to the nation's best money managers, are an ideal investment when you're saving money for educational expenses. See Chapter 22 for a discussion of the tax-wise ways to invest in funds.

Think twice about Treasury bonds

Many tax and financial books recommend investing college funds in *Treasury bonds issued by the federal government.* We aren't enthusiastic about some of these (see the sidebar "Double-what bonds?"). Zero-coupon Treasuries are particular tax headaches. They are sold at a discount to their value at maturity instead of paying you interest each year. Guess what? You still have to report the effective interest you're earning each year on your tax return. And just to give you a headache or pad your tax preparer's bill, you or your preparer have to calculate this implicit interest. Yuck!

Don't bother with cash-value life insurance

Life insurance policies that have cash values are some of the most oversold investments to fund college costs. The usual pitch is this: Because you need life insurance to protect your family, why not buy a policy that you can borrow against to pay for college? Makes sense, doesn't it? Insurance agents also emphasize that the cash value in the policy is growing without taxation over time. Although this part of their sales pitch is true, you have better alternatives.

The reason you shouldn't buy a cash-value life insurance policy is that, as we discuss earlier in this chapter, you're better off contributing to retirement accounts. These investments give you an immediate tax deduction that you don't receive when you save through life insurance. Because life insurance that comes with a cash value is more expensive, parents are more likely to make a second mistake — not buying enough life insurance coverage. When you need life insurance, you're better off buying lower-cost term life insurance.

Make sure your money grows

An investment that fails to keep you ahead of inflation, such as a savings or money market account, is another poor investment for college expenses. The interest on these accounts is also taxable, which doesn't make sense for many working parents. You need your money to grow so you can afford educational costs down the road.

Chapter 25

Estate Planning

In This Chapter

▶ Arriving at the ultimate and final insult — taxes for dying?!?

▶ Reviewing strategies for reducing estate taxes

▶ Utilizing trusts, wills, and more trusts

▶ Finding places where you can find help if you need it

Among the dreariest of tax and financial topics is the issue of what happens to your money when you die. Depending on how your finances are structured and when you pass on, you (actually, your estate) may get stuck paying estate taxes when you die.

Unfortunately, you can't predict when the grim reaper will pay you a visit. This scenario doesn't mean that we all need to participate in complicated estate planning. On the contrary, if your assets aren't substantial, a few simple moves may be all you need to get your affairs in order.

Estate planning takes time and money, which are precious commodities for most people. Whether spending your time and money on estate planning is worthwhile depends on your personal and financial circumstances, both now and in the near future.

Figuring Whether You May Owe Estate Taxes

With all the warnings about the enormous estate taxes that you may owe upon your death, you may think that owing estate taxes is a common problem. It isn't, and with recent tax law changes, paying estate taxes will become far less common in the years ahead. But some insurance agents, attorneys, and estate-planning "specialists" use scare tactics to attract prospective clients, often by luring them to free estate-planning seminars. What better way to find people with money to invest!

Understanding the federal estate tax exemption

In tax year 2006, an individual at his or her death can pass $2 million to beneficiaries without paying federal estate taxes. On the other hand, a couple, if they have their assets, wills, and trusts properly structured (as discussed later in this chapter), can pass $4 million to beneficiaries without paying federal estate taxes. Because most people still are trying to accumulate enough money to retire or take a trip around the world someday, most folks typically don't have this problem and have this much money around when they die.

In 2009, the amount that a deceased person may leave to his or her heirs increases to $3.5 million. Thus married couples making use of bypass trusts eventually will be able to shield $7 million from federal estate taxes. (See "Establishing a bypass trust" later in this chapter for more info.)

In 2010, your estate could be worth billions of dollars and be passed on to your heirs without any estate tax. In that year and that year alone, the estate tax vanishes. However, in the next year — 2011 — the allowable amount that can be passed on free of estate tax reverts back to $1 million. Does that sound ridiculous or what?

Although we can't and don't want to predict future tax laws, we believe that you can probably count on the higher exemption amounts in large part sticking around. However, we don't think that you should count on the complete repeal of estate taxes in 2010 being made permanent. (Ultimately, what happens with future changes in the estate tax laws will be driven by the composition of Congress and which party holds the presidency. The repeal will be more likely to stick if Republicans have firm control of these branches of government.) We discuss a variety of estate tax–reduction strategies later in this chapter, but first we talk about how the IRS figures your taxable estate.

Determining your taxable estate

Unless you die prematurely, whether your assets face estate taxes depends on the amount of your assets that you use up during your retirement, unless you already possess great wealth. How much of your assets you use up depends on how your assets grow over time and how rapidly you spend money.

To calculate the value of your estate upon your death, the IRS totals up your assets and subtracts your liabilities. Assets include your personal property, home and other real estate, savings and investments (such as bank accounts, stocks, bonds, and mutual funds held inside and outside of retirement accounts), and life insurance death benefits (unless properly placed in a trust, as we describe later in this chapter). Your liabilities include any outstanding loans (such as a mortgage), bills owed at the time of your death, legal and other expenses to handle your estate, and funeral expenses.

If you're married at the time of your death, all assets that you leave to your spouse are excluded from estate taxes, thanks to the unlimited marital deduction (which we discuss later in this chapter). The IRS also deducts any charitable contributions or bequests that you dictate in your will from your assets before calculating your taxable estate.

How High Are Estate Taxes?

Under current tax law, if your estate totals more than $2 million at your death, you may owe federal estate taxes. The top federal estate tax rate for 2006 is a hefty 46 percent.

In addition to raising the amounts that can be passed on free of federal estate taxes, as discussed in the prior section, tax law changes lower the tax rates that apply to estates large enough to be subject to estate taxes (see Table 25-1). As we discuss earlier in the chapter, the reason for the abrupt change in 2010 is the repeal of the estate tax that year, but the 2001 tax bill also includes a provision for its reinstatement in 2011. We think that some of the reduction in estate tax rates will stick around for the long term, but for planning purposes, don't count on the repeal of the estate tax.

Table 25-1	Top Federal Estate Tax Rate
Year	*Tax Rate*
2006	46%
2007–2009	45%
2010	None — estate tax repealed!
2011	55%

States also can levy additional estate (levied on the estate) and inheritance (charged to the recipient) taxes. With the elimination in 2005 of the provision that allowed states to share in federal estate taxes collected, more states are imposing their own estate or inheritance tax, or are choosing to calculate the tax due to the state on the basis of the share of federal estate taxes they would have received under the pre-2001 federal law.

Reducing Expected Estate Taxes (If You're Rich)

You have your work cut out for you as you try to educate yourself about estate planning. You can find many attorneys and non-attorneys selling estate-planning services, and you can encounter many insurance agents hawking life insurance. All are pleased to sell you their services. Most people don't need to do fancy-schmancy estate planning with high-cost attorneys. We give you the straight scoop on what, if anything, you need to be concerned with now and at other junctures in your life, and we tell you the conflicts of interest that these "experts" have in rendering advice.

Thanks to all the changes in the tax laws and the thousands of attorneys and tax advisors working to find new ways around paying estate taxes, a dizzying array of strategies exist to reduce estate taxes — including taking up residence in a foreign country! We start with the simpler stuff and work toward the more complex.

Remember, as we discuss earlier in this chapter, new tax laws substantially increase the amount of assets that you can pass on to your heirs free of estate taxes. Thus, far fewer people will need to engage in complicated or even any estate planning (beyond preparing a will).

Giving it away

Nothing is wrong with making, saving, and investing money. But someday, you have to look in the mirror and ask, "For what purpose?" You can easily rationalize hoarding money — you never know how long you'll live or what medical expenses you may incur. Besides, your kids still are paying off their credit cards and don't seem to know a mutual fund from an emergency fund. (Not that you'd want to be judgmental of your kids or anything!)

How much can you give?

Current tax law allows you to gift up to $12,000 per individual each year to as many people — such as your children, grandchildren, or best friends — as you desire without any gift tax consequences or tax forms required. If you're married, your spouse can do the same. The benefit of gifting is that it removes the money from your estate and therefore reduces your estate taxes. Even better is the fact that all future appreciation and income on the gifted money also is removed from your estate, because the money now belongs to the gift recipient. (The current annual tax-free gifting limit of $12,000 per recipient will increase in future years with inflation.)

Upon your death, your money has to go somewhere. By directing some of your money to people and organizations now, you can pass on far more now because you'll be saving nearly 50 percent in estate taxes. Plus, while you're alive, you can experience the satisfaction of seeing the good that your money can do.

You can use gifting to remove a substantial portion of your assets from your estate over time. Suppose that you have three children. You and your spouse each can give each of your children $12,000 per year for a total gift of $72,000 per year. If your kids are married, you can make additional $12,000 gifts to their spouses for another $72,000 per year. You also can gift an unlimited amount to pay for current educational tuition costs and medical expenses. Just be sure to make the payment directly to the institution charging the fees.

Yet another tax — the generation-skipping transfer tax — can be assessed on a gift. This tax applies if the gift giver is a grandparent making a gift to a grandchild (and the grandparent's son or daughter is still alive) or in the case of a gift made to an unrelated individual who is more than 37½ years younger. See the advice of a qualified tax advisor if this tax may apply.

What should you give?

You have options in terms of what money or assets you gift to others. Start with cash or assets that haven't appreciated since you purchased them. If you want to transfer an asset that has lost value, consider selling it first; then you can claim the tax loss on your tax return and transfer the cash.

Rather than giving away assets that have appreciated greatly in value, consider holding onto them. If you hold such assets until your death, your heirs receive what is called a stepped-up basis. That is, the IRS assumes that the effective price your heirs "paid" for an asset is the value on your date of death — which wipes out the capital gains tax that otherwise is owed when selling an asset that has appreciated in value. (Donating appreciated assets to your favorite charity can make sense because you get the tax deduction for the appreciated value and avoid realizing the taxable capital gain.)

Making gifts greater than $12,000 per year

You can make gifts of greater than $12,000 per year to an individual; however, you have to prepare and file **Form 709, United States Gift (and Generation-Skipping Transfer) Tax Return.** Chances are good that you won't have to pay any tax on the transfer, but when giving gifts that large, the IRS does want to have a record.

You're allowed to make gifts larger than $12,000 per year to pay for another person's tuition or medical expenses without filing a Form 709. If you decide you want to pay your beloved niece's tuition to her Ivy League college (how nice of you), just make sure that you write the check directly to the school. Likewise, in the case of paying someone else's medical expenses, send your check directly to the medical care provider or institution.

If you make a large gift of cash or property to charity, and you otherwise aren't required to file Form 709, you don't need to report this gift, even if its value is in excess of $12,000, provided that you gave up all interest in the property you transferred. Don't forget to include your gift on Schedule A of your Form 1040 — even though the property you're gifting may not be part of this year's income, you're still entitled to an income tax deduction. Check out Chapter 9 for all the rules.

Gifts to political organizations aren't really gifts at all. If you're so inclined and make large payments to political organizations, you don't trigger a requirement to file a Form 709, even if your gift is greater than $12,000. What a deal!

Because there won't be any estate tax in 2010, a so-called carry-over basis will apply to your assets if you die in that year, and you won't be able to wipe out capital gains on inherited assets. The inheritor's (heir's) tax basis is the lesser of the deceased's cost basis and the asset's fair market value at the date of death. At this time, an estate's executor will have the power to step up the basis of the estate's assets by up to $1.3 million ($3 million for assets left to a spouse).

One other little detail worth noting for year 2010 changes: An estate or heir still may sell the deceased's primary residence and qualify for the capital gains tax exclusion for sale of primary residence discussed in Chapter 23.

A more complicated way to gift money to your heirs and still retain some control over the money is to set up a Crummey Trust. (Its name has nothing to do with the quality of the trust!) Although the beneficiary has a short window of time (a month or two) to withdraw money that's contributed to the trust, you can verbally make clear to the beneficiary that, in your opinion, leaving the money in the trust is in his or her best interest. You also can specify in the trust document itself that the trust money be used for particular purposes, such as tuition. Some of the other trusts we discuss later in the "Setting up trusts" section may meet your needs if you want more control over the money you intend to pass to your heirs.

Leaving all your assets to your spouse

Tax laws wouldn't be tax laws without exceptions and loopholes. Here's another one: If you're married at the time of your death, any and all assets that you leave to your spouse are exempt from estate taxes normally due upon your death. In fact, you may leave an unlimited amount of money to your spouse, hence the name unlimited marital deduction. Assets that count are those willed to your spouse or for which he or she is named as beneficiary (such as retirement accounts).

Although leaving all your assets to your spouse is a tempting estate-planning strategy for married couples, this strategy can backfire. The surviving spouse may end up with an estate tax problem upon his or her death because he or she will have all the couple's assets. (See the following section for a legal way around this issue, appropriately called a bypass trust.) You face three other less likely but potential problems:

- ✔ You and your spouse could die simultaneously.
- ✔ The unlimited marital deduction isn't allowed if your spouse isn't a U.S. citizen.
- ✔ Some states don't allow the unlimited marital deduction, so be sure to find out about the situation in your state.

Establishing a bypass trust

A potential estate tax problem is created upon the death of a spouse if all of his or her assets pass to the surviving spouse. When the surviving spouse dies, $2 million (for tax year 2006) can be passed on free of federal estate taxes.

If you have substantial assets, both you and your spouse can take advantage of the $2 million estate-tax-free rule and pass to your heirs a total of $4 million estate-tax-free. By shielding an additional $2 million from estate taxes, you save your heirs more than $900,000 in estate taxes. Thanks to recent tax law changes, the value of this strategy mushrooms as the amount you can pass on free of estate taxes greatly increases. How? Each of you can, through instructions in your will, direct assets to be placed into a *bypass trust* (also known as credit shelter or exemption equivalent).

Upon the death of the first spouse, assets equal in value to the amount that can be passed tax-free (the exemption amount) held in that spouse's name go into a trust. The surviving spouse and/or other heirs still can use the income from those assets and even some of the principal. They can receive 5 percent of the value of the trust or $5,000, whichever is greater, each year. They also can draw additional principal if they need it for educational, health, or living expenses. Ultimately, the assets in the bypass trust pass to the designated beneficiaries (usually, but not limited to, children).

For a bypass trust to work, you likely will need to rework how you hold ownership of your assets (for example, jointly or individually). You may need to individually title your assets so that each spouse holds $2 million in assets and so that each can take full advantage of the $2 million estate tax–free limit.

Remember, in the years ahead, bypass trusts will become even more valuable. As the amount that an individual can pass on free of estate taxes rises to $3.5 million in 2009, a married couple will be able to pass on a total of $7 million free of estate taxes when they use a bypass trust.

Our attorney friends tell us that you need to be careful when setting up a bypass trust so that it's funded up to the full amount of the current federal tax–free exemption amount. The reason: The surviving spouse may otherwise end up with less than what would've been desired. Be sure to read the section "Getting advice and help," later in this chapter, for how to obtain good legal and tax advice.

Buying cash-value life insurance

Two major types of life insurance exist. Most people who need life insurance — and who have someone dependent on their income — need to buy term life insurance, which is pure life insurance: You pay an annual premium for which you receive a predetermined amount of life insurance protection. If the insured person passes away, the beneficiaries collect; otherwise, the premium is gone. In this way, term life insurance is similar to auto or home-owner's insurance.

The other kind of life insurance, called cash-value life insurance, is probably one of the most oversold financial products in the history of Western civilization. Cash-value policies (whole, universal, variable, and so on) combine life insurance with a supposed savings feature. Your premiums not only pay for life insurance, but some of your dollars also are credited to an account that grows in value over time, assuming that you keep paying your premiums. On the surface, a cash-value life policy sounds potentially attractive.

When bought and placed in an irrevocable life insurance trust (which we discuss later in this chapter), life insurance, it's true, receives special treatment with regard to estate taxes. Specifically, the death benefit or proceeds paid on the policy upon your death can pass to your designated heirs free of estate taxes. (Some states, however, don't allow this.)

People who sell cash-value insurance — that is, insurance salespeople and other life insurance brokers masquerading as estate-planning specialists and financial planners — too often advocate life insurance as the best, and only, way to reduce estate taxes. But the other methods we discuss in this chapter are superior in most cases.

Insurance companies aren't stupid. In fact, they're quite smart. If you purchase a cash-value life insurance policy that provides a death benefit of, say, $1 million, you have to pay substantial insurance premiums, although far less than $1 million. Is that a good deal for you? No, because the insurance company invests your premium dollars and earns a return the same way as you otherwise would have, had you invested the money instead of using it to buy the life insurance.

Don't get seduced into buying cash-value life insurance for the wrong reasons

Some insurance salespeople aggressively push cash-value policies because of the high commissions (50 percent to 100 percent of the first year's premium paid by you) that insurance companies pay their agents. These policies are expensive ways to purchase life insurance. Because of their high cost (about eight times the cost of the same amount of term life insurance), you're more likely to buy less life insurance coverage than you need, which, unfortunately, is the sad result of the insurance industry pushing this stuff. The vast majority of life insurance buyers need more protection than they can afford to buy in cash-value coverage.

Agents know which buttons to push to get you interested in buying the wrong kind of life insurance. Insurance agents show you all sorts of projections implying that after the first 10 or 20 years of paying your premiums, you won't need to pay more premiums to keep the life insurance in force. The only reason you may be able to stop paying premiums is that you've poured too much extra money into the policy in the early years of payment. Remember that cash-value life insurance costs eight times as much as term.

Insurance agents also argue that your cash value grows tax-deferred. But if you want tax-deferred retirement savings, you first need to take advantage of retirement savings plans such as 401(k)s, 403(b)s, SEP-IRAs, and Keoghs. These plans, which will have even greater contribution limits in the years ahead thanks to recent tax law changes, give you an immediate tax deduction for your current contributions in addition to growth without taxation until withdrawal. Money paid into a cash-value life policy gives you no upfront tax breaks. When you've exhausted the tax-deductible plans, then variable annuities or a nondeductible IRA can provide tax-deferred compounding of your investment dollars (see Chapter 22).

Life insurance tends to be a mediocre investment anyway. The insurance company quotes you an interest rate for the first year only. After that, the rate is at the company's discretion. If you don't like the future interest rates, you can be penalized for quitting the policy. Would you invest your money in a bank account that quoted an interest rate for the first year only and then penalized you for moving your money in the next seven to ten years?

Through the years, between the premiums you pay on your life policy and the returns the insurance company earns investing your premiums, the insurance company is able to come up with more than $1 million. Otherwise, how could it afford to pay out a death benefit of $1 million on your policy?

Using life insurance as an estate-planning tool is beneficial if your estate includes assets that you don't want to subject to a forced sale to pay estate taxes after you die. For example, small-business owners whose businesses are worth millions may want to consider cash-value life insurance under special circumstances. If your estate will lack the other necessary assets to pay expected estate taxes and you don't want your beneficiaries to be forced to sell the business, you can buy life insurance to pay expected estate taxes.

For advice on whether life insurance is an appropriate estate-planning strategy for you, don't expect to get objective information from anyone who sells life insurance. Please see the section "Getting advice and help," later in this chapter.

Among the best places to shop for cash-value life insurance policies are Ameritas Direct (800-552-3553; www.ameritasdirect.com) and USAA (800-531-8000).

Setting up trusts

If estate planning hasn't already given you a headache, understanding the different types of trusts should. A trust is a legal device used to pass to someone else the management responsibility and, ultimately, the ownership of some of your assets. We discuss some trusts, such as bypass, Crummey, and life insurance trusts, earlier in this chapter; in this section, we talk about other trusts you may hear about when planning your estate.

Wills

Wills — legal documents that detail your instructions for what you want done with your personal property and assets upon your death — won't save you on taxes or on probate. Wills are, however, an estate-planning basic that most people should have but don't. Most of the world doesn't bother with wills, because laws and customs divvy up a person's estate among the spouse and children or other close relatives.

The main benefit of a will is that it ensures that your wishes for the distribution of your assets are fulfilled. If you die without a will (known in legalese as intestate), your state decides how to distribute your money and other property, according to state law. Therefore, your friends, more-distant relatives, and favorite charities will probably receive nothing. For a fee, the state appoints an administrator to supervise the distribution of your assets.

If you have little in the way of personal assets and don't really care who gets your possessions and other assets (state law usually specifies the closest blood relatives), you can forget about creating a will. You can save yourself the time and depression that inevitably accompanies this gloomy exercise.

When you have minor (dependent) children, a will is necessary to name a guardian for them. In the event that you and your spouse both die without a will, the state (courts and social service agencies) decides who raises your children. Therefore, even if you can't decide at this time who would raise your children, you at least need to appoint a trusted guardian who can decide for you.

Living wills, medical powers of attorney, and durable powers of attorney are useful additions to a standard will. A living will tells your doctor what, if any, life-support measures you would accept. A medical power of attorney grants authority to someone you trust to make decisions with a physician regarding your medical options. A durable power of attorney gives someone else the authority to act for you in other legal transactions if you're away or incapacitated, including signing your tax returns. These additional documents usually are prepared when a will is drawn up.

Living trusts

A living trust effectively transfers assets into a trust. When you use a revocable living trust, you control those assets and can revoke the trust whenever you desire. The advantage of a living trust is that upon your death, assets can pass directly to your beneficiaries without going through probate, the legal process for administering and implementing the directions in a will.

Living trusts keep your assets out of probate but in and of themselves do nothing to help you deal with estate taxes. Living trusts can contain bypass trusts and other estate tax–saving provisions.

Property and assets that are owned by joint tenants with a right of survivorship (owned by two or more individuals, with the deceased owner's share passing upon death to the surviving owner(s)) or inside retirement accounts — such as IRAs or 401(k)s — and have designated beneficiaries generally pass to heirs without going through probate. (Many states also allow a special type of revocable trust for bank accounts called a Totten trust, which also insulates the bank accounts from probate. Such trusts are established for the benefit of another person, and the money in the trust is paid to that beneficiary upon the account holder's death.)

Probate can be a lengthy, expensive hassle for your heirs. Attorney probate fees may approach 5 percent to 7 percent of the estate's value. In addition, the details of your assets become public record because of probate. In addition to saving you on probate fees and maintaining your financial privacy, living trusts are useful in naming someone to administer your affairs in the event you become incapacitated.

You can't escape the undertaker or the lawyers. Setting up a trust and transferring property in and out costs money and time. Thus living trusts are likely to be of greatest value to people who are age 60 and older, are single, and own assets worth more than $100,000 that must pass through probate (including real estate, nonretirement accounts, and businesses). Small estates are often less expensive to probate in some states than the cost and hassle of setting up a living trust. (The key is to maintain an *independent administration,* which is when the probate court trusts the executor to make most of the decisions without the court's supervision.)

Charitable trusts

If you're feeling philanthropic, charitable trusts may be for you. With a charitable remainder trust, you or your designated beneficiary receives income from assets that you donate to a charity. At the time of your death, or after a certain number of years, the principal is donated to the charity and is thus removed from your taxable estate. A charitable remainder trust makes especially good sense in cases where a person holds an asset that he or she wants to donate that has greatly appreciated in value. By not selling the asset before the donation, a hefty tax on the profit is avoided.

In a charitable lead trust, the roles of the charity and beneficiaries are reversed. The charity receives the income from the assets for a set number of years or until you pass away, at which point the assets pass to your beneficiary. You get a current income tax deduction for the value of the expected payments to the charity.

Getting advice and help

The number of people who happily will charge you a fee for or sell you some legal advice or insurance far exceeds the number actually qualified to render objective estate-planning advice. Attorneys, accountants, financial planners, estate-planning specialists, investment companies, insurance agents, and even some nonprofit agencies stand ready to help you figure out how to dispense your wealth.

Estate planning from the grave

It goes without saying that not everyone does the right type of estate planning before passing on. Some people die before their time, and others just can't seem to get around to the planning part, even when they're in failing health.

Although further planning after you're dead and gone is impossible, your heirs may legally take steps that can, in some cases, dramatically reduce state taxes. Some legal folks call these steps postmortem planning. Here's an example of how it works.

Suppose that Peter Procrastinator never got around to planning for the distribution of his substantial estate. When he died, all of his estate was to go to his wife. No dummy, his wife hired legal help so that she could disclaim, or

reject, part of Peter's big estate. Why would she do that? Simple, so that part of the estate could immediately go to their children. If she hadn't disclaimed, Peter would have missed out on his $2 million estate tax exclusion. By disclaiming, she possibly saved her heirs more than $900,000 in estate taxes.

The person doing the disclaiming, in this case Peter's wife, may not direct to whom the disclaimed assets will go. Peter's will or other legal documents specify who is second in line. Disclaimers are also irrevocable, must be made in writing, and are subject to other IRS rules and regulations. A knowledgeable executor and attorney can help you with disclaiming.

Most of these people and organizations have conflicts of interest and lack the knowledge necessary to do sound estate planning for you. Attorneys are biased toward drafting legal documents and devices that are more complicated than may be needed. Insurance agents and financial planners who work on commission try to sell cash-value life insurance. Investment firms and banks encourage you to establish a trust account that requires them to manage the assets in the future. Although the cost of free estate-planning seminars is tempting, you get what you pay for — or worse.

Start the process of planning your estate by first looking at the big picture. Talk to your family members about your financial situation. Many people never take this basic but critical step. Your heirs likely have no idea what you're considering or what you're worried about. Conversely, how can you develop a solid action plan without understanding your heirs' needs and concerns? Be careful not to use money to control or manipulate other family members.

For professional advice, you need someone who can look objectively at the big picture. Attorneys and tax advisors who specialize in estate planning are a good starting point. Ask the people you're thinking of hiring whether they sell life insurance or manage money. If they do, they can't possibly be objective and likely aren't sufficiently educated about estate planning, given their focus.

For preparation of wills and living trusts, check out the high-quality software programs on the market. Legal software may save you from the often-difficult task of finding a competent and affordable attorney. Preparing documents with software also can save you money.

Using legal software is generally preferable to using fill-in-the-blank documents. Software has the built-in virtues of directing and limiting your choices and keeping you from making common mistakes. Quality software also incorporates the knowledge and insights of the legal eagles who developed the software. As for the legality of documents that you create with software, remember that you and your witnesses properly signing the document, for example, make a will, legal and valid. An attorney preparing a document isn't what makes it legal. If your situation isn't unusual, legal software may work well for you.

For will and living trust preparation, check out WillMaker Plus by Nolo Press. In addition to enabling you to prepare wills (in every state except Louisiana), WillMaker Plus can help you create a living will, medical power of attorney (as we discuss in the sidebar "Wills" earlier in the chapter), and a living trust. Living trusts are fairly standard legal documents that serve to keep property out of probate in the event of your death (remember that it doesn't address the issue of estate taxes). The software package advises you to seek professional guidance for your situation, if necessary.

If you want to do more reading on estate planning, pick up a copy of *Plan Your Estate* by attorneys Denis Clifford & Cora Jordan (Nolo Press). When you have a large estate that may be subject to estate taxes, consulting an attorney or tax advisor who specializes in estate planning may be worth your time and money. Get smarter first and figure out the lingo before you seek and pay for advice.

Part VI
The Part of Tens

The 5th Wave   By Rich Tennant

©RICHTENNANT

No, you're thinking of H & R Block. This is H & R Bluff. We help you concoct zany schemes and excuses for filing a late return, underreporting income, that sort of thing.

NOT REALLY US CITIZEN

ACCOUNTING ERROR 2+2=3?

H&R BLUFF TAX CONSULTANTS

AMNESIA

KIDNAPPED GOV'T COVERUP

In this part . . .

You can read these short chapters just about anytime you have a few spare minutes, and they're packed with information that needs to stand out. We highlight the ten best ways to avoid an audit, the top ten ways to reduce your taxes that you or your friends may overlook, ten tax tips for members of the military and their loved ones, and ten interview questions you should be sure to ask a tax advisor you're considering hiring.

Chapter 26

Ten Tips for Reducing Your Chances of Being Audited

. . . .

*I*f you've never been audited, you probably fall into one of these categories: You're still young, you haven't made gobs of money, or you're just plain lucky. The fact is that many taxpayers are audited during their adult lives. It's just a matter of time and probability.

You can take some common-sense steps (honesty being the star of the show) to reduce your chances of having to face an audit. So here are our top tips for lessening your chances of being audited and avoiding all the time and associated costs of an audit.

Double-check your return for accuracy

Review your own return before you send it in. If the IRS finds mistakes through its increasingly sophisticated computer-checking equipment, you're more likely to be audited. They figure that if they find obvious errors, some not-so-obvious ones lurk beneath the surface.

Have you included all your income? Think about the different accounts you had during the tax year. Do you have interest and dividend statements for all your accounts? Finding these statements is easier if you've been keeping your financial records in one place. Check your W-2s and 1099s against your tax form to make sure that you wrote the numbers down correctly.

Don't forget to check your math. Have you added, subtracted, multiplied, and divided correctly? Are your Social Security number and address correct on the return? Did you sign and date your return?

Such infractions won't, on their own, trigger an audit. In some cases, the IRS simply writes you a letter requesting your signature or the additional tax you owe (if the math mistake isn't too fishy or too big). In some rare instances, the IRS even sends a refund if the mistake it uncovers is in the taxpayer's favor — really! Regardless of how the IRS handles the mistake, it can be a headache for you to clear up, and, more important, it can cost you extra money.

Declare all your income

When you prepare your return, you may be tempted to shave off a little of that consulting income you received. Who will miss it, right? The IRS, that's who.

Thanks largely to computer cross-checking, the IRS has many ways of finding unreported income. Be particularly careful if you're self-employed; anyone who pays you more than $600 in a year is required to file a Form 1099, which basically tells the IRS how much you received.

When you knowingly hide income, you face substantial penalties and, depending on the amount, criminal prosecution. That wouldn't be a picnic, especially if you can't afford to hire a good defense attorney.

Don't itemize

People who itemize their deductions on Schedule A are far more likely to be audited because they have more opportunity and temptation to cheat. By all means, if you can legally claim more total deductions by using Schedule A than you can with the standard deduction (this deduction stuff is all spelled out in Chapter 9), we say "itemize, itemize, itemize." Just don't try to artificially inflate your deductions.

On the other hand, if it's basically a toss-up between Schedule A and your standard deduction, taking the standard deduction is safer, and the IRS can't challenge it.

Earn less money

At first glance, earning less money may seem like an odd suggestion, but there really are costs associated with affluence. One of the costs of a high income — besides higher taxes — is a dramatic increase in the probability of being audited. If your income is more than $100,000, you have about a 1 in 20 chance each year of being audited. But your chance is less than 1 in 100 if your income is less than $50,000. You see, there are advantages to earning less!

If you manage to pile up a lot of assets and don't enjoy them in retirement, your estate tax return — your final tax return — is at great risk of being audited. Do you think a 1 in 20 or 1 in 100 chance is bad in the audit lottery? Uncle Sam audits about 1 in 7 estate tax returns. Nearly half of estate tax returns for estates valued at more than $5 million are audited because big bucks are at stake. The IRS collects an average of more than $100,000 for each estate tax return it audits! So enjoy your money while you're alive or pass it along to your heirs in the here and now — otherwise, your heirs may have trouble getting it in the there and later!

Don't cheat

It may have taken the IRS a while to wise up, but now the government is methodically figuring out the different ways that people cheat. The next step for the IRS — after they figure out how people cheat — is to come up with ways to catch the cheaters. Cheaters beware!

The IRS also offers rewards for informants. If you're brazen enough to cheat and the IRS doesn't catch you, you may not be home-free yet. Someone else may turn you in. So be honest — not only because it's the right thing to do but also because you'll probably sleep better at night knowing that you aren't breaking the law.

Tax protesters, take note. The IRS may flag returns that are accompanied by protest notes. Threats are bad, too — even if they're meant in fun (humor isn't rife at the IRS, we suspect). The commandment to follow is: Thou shalt not draw attention to thyself. The protest issue is interesting. During congressional hearings, tax protesters stand up and tell members of Congress that the income tax is unconstitutional. They say they have proof. If we can get our hands on the proof, we'll include it in the next edition of this book. In the meantime, pay your taxes and resist the temptation to send along a cranky letter with your tax returns and payments. To read the IRS's take on the typical tax protester's arguments, point your Web browser to www.irs.gov/pub/irs-utl/friv_tax.pdf for 66 action-packed pages, including legal citations.

Stay away from back-street refund mills

Although this advice doesn't apply to the majority of tax-preparation firms, unfortunately, some firms out there fabricate deductions. Run away — as fast as you can — from tax preparers who tell you, after winking, that they have creative ways to reduce your tax bill, or those who base their fees on how many tax dollars they can save you.

Also beware of any preparer who promises you a refund without first thoroughly reviewing your situation. Please refer to Chapter 2 and Chapter 29 for how to find a top-quality tax preparer.

Be careful with hobby losses

Some people who have full-time jobs also have sideline businesses or hobbies with which they try to make a few bucks. But be careful if you report the avocation as showing a loss year after year on your tax forms. Filers of Schedule C, Profit or Loss from Business, are at greatest risk for audits.

Here's an example. You like to paint surreal pictures, and you even sold one in 2004 for $150. But since then, you haven't sold any paintings (the surreal market has faded). Nevertheless, you continue to write off your cost for canvas and paint. The IRS will take a close look at that record, and you may be a candidate for an audit.

Don't be a non-filer

The IRS has a special project with a mission to go after the millions of non-filers. Lest you think that the IRS does things in small ways, the IRS assigned hundreds of agents to this project. Again, when you get caught — which is just a matter of time — in addition to owing back taxes, interest, and big penalties, you may also face criminal prosecution and end up serving time in the slammer. So keep a clear conscience, continue to enjoy your freedom, and file your tax returns. And remember, better late than never!

Don't cut corners if you're self-employed

People who are self-employed have more opportunities to make mistakes on their taxes — or to creatively take deductions — than company-payroll wage earners. As a business owner, you're responsible for self-reporting not only your income but also your expenses. You have to be even more honest when dealing with the tax authorities, because the likelihood of being audited is higher than average.

Don't disguise employees as independent contractors. This maneuver is covered by another IRS project. Remember the old barb: You can't put a sign around the neck of a cow that says, "This is a horse." You don't have a horse — you have a cow with a sign around its neck. Just because you call someone an independent contractor doesn't mean that person isn't your employee. If you aren't sure about the relationship, refer to Chapter 21.

Nothing is wrong with being self-employed. But resist the temptation to cheat because you're far more likely to be scrutinized and caught as a self-employed worker.

Carry a rabbit's foot

Try as you may to be an obedient taxpayer, you can be audited simply because of bad luck. Every year, the IRS audits some taxpayers at random. Although such an undertaking may seem like a colossal waste of time to a tax neophyte like yourself, this effort provides the IRS with valuable information about the areas of tax returns where people make the most mistakes — and about the areas where people cheat!

So, if you do get an audit notice, don't assume that you did anything wrong. However, be prepared for your audit — see Part IV of this book.

Chapter 27

Ten (or So) Often-Overlooked Tax-Reduction Opportunities

● ●

This chapter presents the more commonly overlooked opportunities to reduce individual income taxes. The income tax you pay is based on your taxable income minus your deductions. We start first with overlooked ways to minimize your taxable income. Then we move on to often-ignored deductions. We don't want you to be like all those people who miss out on perfectly legal tax-reduction strategies simply because they don't know what they don't know.

Move extra savings out of the bank

Out of apathy or lack of knowledge of better options, far too many people keep extra cash dozing away in their neighborhood bank. Yes, the bank has a vault and sometimes-friendly tellers who may greet you by name, but banks also characteristically pay relatively low rates of interest. Keeping your household checking account at the local bank is fine, but you're generally throwing away free interest if you keep your extra savings money there.

The better money market mutual funds often pay substantially greater interest than bank savings accounts and offer equivalent safety. And if you're in a high tax bracket, money market funds come in tax-free flavors. Please see Chapter 22 to find out more about tax-friendly investments.

Invest in wealth-building assets

During your working years, while you're earning employment income, you probably don't need or want taxable income from your investments because it can significantly increase your income tax bill. Real estate, stocks, and small-business investments offer the best long-term growth potential, although you need to be able to withstand dips and sags in these markets.

Most of the return that you can earn with these wealth-building investments comes from appreciation in their value, making them tax-friendly because you're in control and can decide when to sell and realize your profit. Also, as long as you hold onto these investments for more than one year, your profit is taxed at the lower, long-term capital gains tax rate. (Stock dividends are also now subject to lower tax rates—see Chapter 22.)

Fund "tax-reduction" accounts

When you funnel your savings dollars into retirement accounts, such as a 401(k), 403(b), SEP-IRA, Keogh, or IRA, you can earn substantial upfront tax breaks on your contributions. If you think that saving for retirement is boring, consider the tens of thousands of tax dollars these accounts can save you during your working years.

If you don't use these accounts to save and invest, you may very well have to work many more years to accumulate the reserves necessary to retire. Refer to Chapter 20 to find out more, including how recent tax law changes significantly increased the benefits of these accounts.

Work overseas

You've always wanted to travel overseas. When you go to work in a foreign country with low income taxes, you may be able to save big-time on income taxes. For tax year 2006, you can exclude $82,400 of foreign-earned income (whether working for a company or on a self-employed basis) from U.S. income taxes. To qualify for this income tax exclusion, you must work at least 330 days (about 11 months) of the year overseas or be a foreign resident. You claim this income tax exclusion on IRS **Form 2555, Foreign Earned Income Exclusion.**

If you earn more than $82,400, don't worry about being double-taxed on the income above this amount. You get to claim credits for foreign taxes paid on your U.S. tax return on **Form 1116, Foreign Tax Credit.** Perhaps to give you more time to fill out this form and others, the IRS gives Americans working abroad two extra months (until June 15) to file their tax returns.

As with many things in life that sound too good to be true, this pot of overseas gold has some catches. First, many of the places you've romanticized about traveling to and perhaps living in — such as England, France, Italy, Sweden, Germany, and Spain — have higher income tax rates than the ones in the United States. Also, this tax break isn't available to U.S. government workers overseas.

Look at the whole package when deciding whether to work overseas. Some employers throw in a housing allowance and other benefits. Some companies understand the tax breaks and reduce your pay accordingly. Be sure to consider all costs of living overseas, both financial and emotional.

Check whether you can itemize

The IRS gives you two methods of determining your total deductions. Deductions are just what they sound like: You subtract them from your income before you calculate the tax you owe. So the more deductions you take, the smaller your taxable income — and the smaller your tax bill. You get to pick the method that leads to the largest total deductions — and thus a lower tax bill. But sometimes the choice isn't so clear, so be prepared to do some figuring.

Taking the *standard deduction* usually makes sense if you have a pretty simple financial life — a regular paycheck, a rented apartment, and no large expenses, such as medical bills, moving expenses, or loss due to theft or catastrophe. Single folks qualify for a $5,150 standard deduction, and married couples filing jointly get a $10,300 standard deduction for tax year 2006.

The other method of determining your allowable deductions is to itemize them on your tax return. This painstaking procedure is definitely more of a hassle, but if you can tally up more than the standard deduction amounts, itemizing saves you money. Schedule A of your 1040 is the page for summing up your itemized deductions, but you won't know whether you have enough itemized deductions unless you give this schedule a good examination (refer to Chapter 9).

If you currently don't itemize, you may be surprised to discover that your personal property and state income or sales taxes are itemizable. If you pay a fee to the state to register and license your car, you can itemize the expenditure as a deduction (line 8 "Other Taxes" on Schedule A). The IRS allows you to deduct only the part of the fee that relates to the value of your car, however. The state organization that collects the fee should be able to tell you what portion of the fee is deductible. If it's a user-friendly organization, it even shows this figure on your invoice. What service!

When you total your itemized deductions on Schedule A and that amount is equal to or less than the standard deduction, take the standard deduction without fail (unless you're married filing separately, and your spouse is itemizing — then you have to itemize). The total for your itemized deductions is worth checking every year, however, because you may have more deductions in some years than others, and you may occasionally be able to itemize.

Because you can control when you pay particular expenses for which you're eligible to itemize, you can shift or bunch more of them into selected years when you know that you'll have enough deductions to take full advantage of itemizing. For example, suppose that you're using the standard deduction this year because you just don't have many itemized deductions. Late in the tax year, though, you feel certain that you'll buy a home sometime during the next year. Thanks to the potential write-off of mortgage interest and property taxes, you also know that you'll be able to itemize next year. It makes sense, then, to shift as many deductible expenses as possible into the next year.

Trade consumer debt for mortgage debt

Suppose that you own real estate and haven't borrowed as much money as a mortgage lender currently allows (given the current market value of the property and your financial situation). And further suppose that you've run up high-interest consumer debt. Well, you may be able to trade one debt for another. You probably can refinance your mortgage and pull out extra cash to pay off your credit card, auto loan, or other expensive consumer credit lines. You usually can borrow at a lower interest rate for a mortgage, thus lowering your monthly interest bill. Plus, you may get a tax-deduction bonus, because consumer debt — auto loans, credit cards, credit lines — isn't tax-deductible, but mortgage debt generally is. Therefore, the effective borrowing rate on a mortgage is even lower than the quoted rate suggests.

Don't forget, however, that refinancing your mortgage and establishing home equity lines involve application fees and other charges (points, appraisals, credit reports, and so on). You must include these fees in the equation to see whether it makes sense to exchange consumer debt for more mortgage debt.

Swapping consumer debt for mortgage debt involves one big danger: Borrowing against the equity in your home can be an addictive habit. We've seen cases in which people run up significant consumer debt three or four distinct times and then refinance their homes the same number of times over the years so they can bail themselves out. At a minimum, continued expansion of your mortgage debt handicaps your ability to work toward other financial goals. In the worst case, easy access to borrowing encourages bad spending habits that can lead to bankruptcy or foreclosure on your debt-ridden home.

Consider charitable contributions and expenses

When you itemize your deductions on Schedule A, you can deduct contributions made to charities. For example, most people already know that when they write a check for $50 to their favorite church or college, they can deduct it. Yet many taxpayers overlook the fact that they can also deduct expenses on work done for charitable organizations. For example, when you go to a soup kitchen to help prepare and serve meals, you can deduct your transportation costs to get there. You just need to keep track of your bus fares or driving mileage.

You can also deduct the fair market value of donations of clothing, household appliances, furniture, and other goods to charities — many of these charities will even drive to your home to pick up the stuff. Just make sure to keep some documentation: Write a detailed list and get it signed by the charity. Please see Chapter 9 for more on writing off charitable contributions and expenses.

Maximize miscellaneous expenses

A number of so-called miscellaneous expenses are deductible on Schedule A. Most of these relate to your job or career and managing your finances. These expenses are deductible to the extent that, in sum, they exceed 2 percent of your adjusted gross income (see Chapter 9):

- **Educational expenses:** You may be able to deduct tuition, books, and travel costs to and from classes if your education is related to your career. Specifically, you can deduct these expenses if your coursework improves your work skills. Continuing education classes for professionals may be deductible. When the law or your employer requires you to take courses to maintain your position, these courses are also deductible. But educational expenses that enable you to change careers or to move into a new field or career aren't deductible.

- **Investment and tax-related expenses:** Investment and tax-advisor fees are deductible, and so are subscription costs for investment-related publications. Accounting fees for preparing your tax return or conducting tax planning during the year are deductible, as are legal fees related to your taxes. If you purchase a home computer to track your investments or prepare your taxes, you may be able to deduct part of that expense, too.

- **Job search and career counseling:** After you obtain your first job, you may deduct legitimate costs related to finding another job within your field. For example, suppose that you're a gym teacher in Boston, and you decide you want to become a health club fitness instructor in Philadelphia. You take a crash course in yoga and then fly to Philly a couple of times for interviews. You can deduct the cost of the course and your trips — even if you don't ultimately change jobs. If you hire a career counselor to help you figure everything out, you can deduct that cost, too. On the other hand, if you're burned out on cooking and decide that you want to become a professional volleyball player in L.A., that's a new career. You may get a better tan, but you won't generate deductions from changing jobs.

- **Unreimbursed expenses related to your job:** If you pay for your own subscriptions to trade journals to keep up-to-date in your field, or if you buy a new desk and chair to ease back pain, you can deduct these costs. If your job requires you to wear special clothes or a uniform, you can write off the cost of purchasing and cleaning them, as long as the clothes aren't suitable for wearing outside of work.

  If you buy a computer for use outside the office at your own expense, you may be able to deduct the cost of the computer if it's for the convenience of your employer, or if it's a condition of your employment (and is used more than half the time for business). Union dues and membership fees for professional organizations are also deductible.

Scour for self-employment expenses

If you're self-employed, you already deduct a variety of expenses from your income before calculating the tax that you owe. When you buy a computer or office furniture, you can deduct those expenses (sometimes they need to be gradually deducted or depreciated over time). Salaries for your employees, office supplies, rent or mortgage interest for your office space, and phone expenses are also generally deductible.

Although more than a few business owners cheat on their taxes, some self-employed folks don't take all the deductions they should. In some cases, people simply aren't aware of the wonderful world of deductions. For others, large deductions raise the concern of an audit. Taking advantage of deductions for which you're eligible makes sense and saves you money. Hiring tax help is worth the money — either by using a book like this one and/or by paying a tax professional to review your return one year.

Chapter 28

Ten (Plus One) Tax Tips for Military Members (and Their Families)

• •

Members of the military and their families have always received special consideration from all branches of the U.S. government, and tax relief is no exception. This chapter highlights important elements of the *Military Family Tax Relief Act,* together with some other factors you may want to consider if you or your spouse is a member of the armed forces (including the reserves).

This chapter only provides some of the basics. If you or your spouse is in the military, you need to explore further. You can find additional information regarding paying income tax while you're in the military in **IRS Publication 3, Armed Forces Tax Guide,** which is available online at www.irs.gov, or by phone by calling 800-829-3676.

Not all of your income from the military may be taxable

In fact, if you're serving in a combat zone or a qualified hazardous duty area, all your compensation from active duty while you're stationed there is exempt from taxation unless you're a commissioned officer. Commissioned officers' pay earned while in a combat zone or a qualified hazardous duty area may be partially taxed. In addition, if you're hospitalized due to an injury in a combat zone, or because of disease that you caught there, your pay continues to be tax-exempt.

Even if you're not stationed in a combat zone, much of your military compensation is tax-exempt. For example, living allowances, including the Basic Allowance for Housing and the Basic Allowance for Subsistence, the Overseas Housing Allowance, and other housing costs, whether paid by the U.S. government or a foreign government, are exempt. So are moving allowances and travel allowances, including an annual round-trip for dependent students and leave between consecutive overseas tours of duty.

Even though you can exclude some or all of the income you've earned while serving in a combat zone or qualified hazardous duty area, you may still use these nontaxable amounts when calculating your earned income credit (EIC), child tax credit, or additional child tax credit in order to give yourself a bigger credit. Remember, making the election to include nontaxable combat pay when calculating these credits doesn't mean you have to include this income when calculating your tax. This income remains nontaxable!

Rules surrounding the sale of your home have been modified

Chapter 12 covers in great detail the sale of your principal residence and the exclusion of $250,000 of capital gain if single and $500,000 if married filing joint. One of the requirements to obtain this capital gains break is that you must be living in that house for at least two of the previous five years. Fortunately, someone somewhere realized that this created a hardship for members of the military, and the *Military Family Tax Relief Act* has addressed this rule. Now (and retroactive to the sale of your principal residence after May 6, 1997) if you or your spouse serve on qualified official extended duty as a member of the armed forces during any part of the five-year qualifying period, you may choose to exclude your period of service from the five years.

The provisions here are quite extensive, but they're clearly laid out in Publication 3. Check it out if you think this rule may apply to you.

Payments to your family increase if you're killed in action

The *Military Family Relief Act* increased from $6,000 to $12,000 the amount of benefits paid to the family of any member of the armed forces in the case of that member's death. The full death benefit paid isn't taxed to anyone. If you previously received a $6,000 benefit for a family member's death after September 10, 2001, that was partially taxed, you may be entitled to a refund. You need to file a Form 1040X for the year in which you received the formerly taxable benefit to obtain that refund.

Tax is forgiven if you're killed in a combat zone or in any terrorist or military action

In addition to the $12,000 tax-free gratuity a family receives when a member of the military is killed in combat, any income tax liability due to that person's income for the year of death and for any earlier tax years that the member served in a combat zone is forgiven. This means that any unpaid tax liability no longer needs to be paid, and any liability for these periods that was already paid will be refunded.

In addition, if the decedent, whether a military or civilian U.S. employee, is killed or later dies from wounds received in a military or terrorist attack, even if it does not happen in a designated combat zone, income tax is forgiven for the year of the attack and the year immediately prior for that person's income tax liability. Refunds will be given for taxes already paid that are later forgiven.

For couples filing jointly, and surviving spouses, even though the decedent's tax liability is forgiven, yours isn't. For any income-producing assets that you held jointly with your spouse, only one-half of the income will be excluded, and only one-half of the deductions will be allowed.

IRS Publication 3920, Tax Relief for Victims of Terrorist Attacks, gives you clear examples of how to calculate the amount of tax forgiveness. It also tells you which income is included in the forgiveness, and which isn't. However, the rules are complex; you may wish to consult a professional tax preparer before filing the necessary documents to obtain your refunds.

Filing and payment deadlines are automatically extended during combat and qualifying service

If you're currently stationed in a combat zone or you have qualifying service outside a combat zone, the deadlines for filing your tax returns, paying your taxes, filing claims for refunds, or taking any other actions with the IRS are automatically extended. The deadline for the IRS to take action against you in an audit or in collections is also extended. Whew! What a relief.

Extensions are extensions only, not a forgiveness of any tax owed. After you're no longer on active duty in a qualifying area (or no longer hospitalized continuously because of an injury or illness that resulted from duty in one of those areas), the clock begins to run again. You have 180 days after you're no longer stationed in a combat zone or a qualifying hazardous duty area plus the number of days that were left for you to take action with the IRS before you were sent to that combat zone or other qualifying area. For example, if you were deployed to Iraq on January 5, 2005, and return on November 30, 2006, your 2004 and 2005 income tax returns are automatically extended by 280 days (182 days plus the 102 days from January 6 through April 17, 2005), or September 8, 2007. Your 2006 return is also extended.

Deferring income tax payments because of military service

Even if you're not serving in a combat zone or other qualifying area, you may elect to delay the payment of your income tax that is due either before or during your period of military service. In order to defer payments, though, you must be performing active military service (part-time reserve service doesn't qualify), and you must notify the IRS, in writing, that you can't pay because you're in the military.

This provision is clearly intended for reservists and National Guard members with higher-paying jobs who have been called up for a period of active duty. In order to qualify for this deferral, your period of active service must be longer than 30 consecutive days, and must be mandated by either the president or the secretary of defense.

After you're no longer on active duty, you have 180 days to pay the amount of tax you deferred. After that point, the IRS will begin to charge you interest and penalties on any unpaid balance you have.

Deducting overnight travel expenses for members of the National Guard and the Reserves

If you fall into this category and you had to travel more than 100 miles from home for a meeting or a drill, you're now allowed to deduct unreimbursed expenses for transportation, meals, and lodging as a deduction on your Form 1040. You'll need to complete Form 2106 to calculate this deduction, but you'll take it on line 24 of your 1040. Look in Chapter 7 for more about this deduction.

No 10 percent penalty for early distributions from IRA, 401-K and 403-B plans for reservists called to active duty

As a result of the Pension Protection Act of 2006, qualified military reservists may now take distributions from their IRA, 401k, or 403b plan without paying the 10 percent penalty for early distributions. All reservists qualify who were called to active duty for at least 180 days or for an indeterminate time between September 11, 2001 and December 31, 2007. If that describes you and your situation, while your distributions are still subject to income tax, you won't be charged the additional 10 percent tax for taking an early distribution from your IRA (whether traditional, non-deductible, or Roth), your 401k plan, or your 403b plan.

This relief is retroactive to September 11, 2001. So, if you took a distribution after that date, and have already paid the penalty, guess what? You need to file an amended Form 1040X and get a refund for the penalty amount. Just write "Active Duty Reservist" on the top of the form. In Part II, Explanation of Changes, give the date you were called to active duty, the amount of the distribution you took, and the amount of the penalty you were charged. It's that simple!

If you want to re-contribute all or part of any distribution you took back to an IRA, you can. Normally, you'd have to re-contribute the money within two years after your active duty ends. Because this law was made retroactive to September 11, 2001, though, Congress has stretched that rule a bit to include those who've already completed their service. If your active duty ended before August 17, 2006 (the day after the bill was enacted), you have until August 17, 2008 to put the money back. Remember, though, that a re-contribution is not tax-deductible.

No 10 percent penalty for nonqualifying distributions from Coverdell ESAs or Section 529 plans for military academy students

If you've been fortunate enough to obtain one of the coveted spots at West Point, the U.S. Naval Academy, the U.S. Air Force Academy, the U.S. Coast Guard Academy, or the Merchant Marine Academy, you're in luck. The taxpayer is paying for all of your tuition, room, board, books, and so on. But what happens to the money your parents or other friends and relatives scrimped and saved and put into either an ESA or a Section 529 plan? Are you, or they, now going to be penalized because you don't need that money for your education?

In a word, no. Although the income portion of distributions will still be taxed to you, there will be no 10 percent penalty on top of the ordinary income tax, provided that you don't take more in distributions each year than the amount that your qualified educational expenses would cost if you had to pay for them. These amounts should be readily available from the financial offices of the military academy. Trust us, you're not the only one in this boat.

Military base realignment and closure benefits are excludable from income

If you receive payment for moving and storage services due to a permanent change of station, you're entitled to exclude these amounts from your income to the extent that your expenses involved in that move don't exceed the amount of the payment. In addition, don't include in income any amounts you receive as a dislocation allowance, a temporary lodging expense, temporary lodging allowance, or a move-in housing allowance.

Obviously, allowances are never as accurate as reimbursements (but are much easier for the government to administer), so the amounts that you spend on your move may be more or less than the amounts you actually receive. If you receive more than you spent, you must report the excess on line 7 of your Form 1040 or 1040A. If you received less than the actual costs of your move, you are, of course, entitled to deduct the nonreimbursed portion of your moving costs. Complete **Form 3903, Moving Expenses,** to determine the total amount of your deduction.

Beware of tax scams aimed at members of the military and their families

The existence of con artists is as old as the wheel, and the emergence of new technologies just makes it easier for them to scam unsuspecting taxpayers into paying them money, releasing personal information, or both.

Be wary of two current scams targeting military members and their families:

- ✔ One offers refunds in exchange for a hefty "postage fee."
- ✔ The other asks for personal information such as Social Security numbers, dates of birth, and credit card information (which they then use to tap into all your financial dealings and steal your identity).

You may even find "tax collectors" at your door, demanding payment now!

The IRS doesn't ever ask you for any sensitive information, such as personal identifying information or credit card numbers, by e-mail. It never charges you to process a refund request, and any IRS agent who visits your home will carry a picture ID with him or her (plus the agent will normally contact you prior to visiting). If you run across one of these situations, run, don't walk, away. Contact your local IRS office as soon as possible to notify them of the situation. They'll let you know if what you're looking at is legitimate or a scam.

Chapter 29

Ten Interview Questions for Tax Advisors

• •

*W*hen you believe that your tax situation warrants outside help, be sure to educate yourself as much as possible beforehand. Why? The more you know, the better able you'll be to evaluate the competence of someone you may hire.

Make sure that you ask the right questions to find a competent tax practitioner whose skills match your tax needs. We recommend that you start with the questions discussed in the following sections.

What tax services do you offer?

Most tax advisors prepare tax returns. We use the term tax advisors because most tax folks do more than simply prepare returns. Many advisors can help you plan and file other important tax documents throughout the year. Some firms also assist your small business with bookkeeping and other financial reporting, such as income statements and balance sheets. These services can be useful when your business is in the market for a loan, or if you need to give clients or investors detailed information about your business.

Ask tax advisors to explain how they work with clients. You're hiring the tax advisor because you lack knowledge of the tax system. If your tax advisor doesn't prod and explore your situation, you may be walking into a situation where "the blind are leading the blind." A good tax advisor can help you make sure that you aren't overlooking deductions or making other costly mistakes that may lead to an audit, penalties, and interest. Beware of tax preparers who view their jobs as simply plugging into tax forms the information that you bring them.

Do you have areas that you focus on?

This question is important. For example, if a tax preparer works mainly with people who receive regular paychecks from an employer, that tax preparer probably has little expertise in helping small-business owners best complete the blizzard of paperwork that the IRS requires.

Find out what expertise the tax advisor has in handling whatever unusual financial events you're dealing with this year — or whatever events you expect in future years. For example, if you need help completing an estate tax return for a deceased relative, ask how many of these types of returns the tax preparer has completed in the past year. About 15 percent of estate tax returns are audited, so you don't want a novice preparing one for you.

What other services do you offer?

Ideally, you want to work with a professional who is 100 percent focused on taxes. We know it's difficult to imagine that some people choose to work at this full time, but they do — and lucky for you!

A multitude of problems and conflicts of interest crop up when a person tries to prepare tax returns, sell investments, and appraise real estate — all at the same time. That advisor may not be fully competent or current in any of these areas.

By virtue of their backgrounds and training, some tax preparers also offer consulting and financial planning services for business owners and other individuals. Because he or she already knows a great deal about your personal and tax situation, a competent tax professional may be able to help in these areas. Just make sure that this help is charged on an hourly consulting basis. Avoid tax advisors who sell financial products that pay them a commission — this situation inevitably creates conflicts of interest.

Who will prepare my return?

If you talk to a solo practitioner, the answer to this question should be simple — the person you're talking to should prepare your return. But if your tax advisor has assistants and other employees, make sure that you know what level of involvement these different people will have in the preparation of your return.

It isn't necessarily bad if a junior-level person does the preliminary tax return preparation that your tax advisor will review and finalize. In fact, this procedure can save you money in tax-preparation fees if the firm bills you at a lower hourly rate for a junior-level person. Be wary of firms that charge you a high hourly rate for a senior tax advisor who then delegates most of the work to a junior-level person.

How aggressive or conservative are you regarding the tax law?

Some tax preparers, unfortunately, view their role as enforcement agents for the IRS. This attitude often is a consequence of one too many seminars put on by local IRS folks, who admonish (and sometimes intimidate) preparers with threats of audits.

On the other hand, some preparers are too aggressive and try tax maneuvers that put their clients on thin ice — subjecting them to additional taxes, penalties, interest, and audits.

Assessing how aggressive a tax preparer is can be difficult. Start by asking what percentage of the tax preparer's clients gets audited (see the next question). You can also ask the tax advisor for references from clients for whom the advisor helped unearth overlooked opportunities to reduce tax bills.

What's your experience with audits?

As a benchmark, you need to know that about 1 percent of all taxpayer returns are audited. For tax advisors working with a more affluent client base or small-business owners, expect a higher audit rate — somewhere in the neighborhood of 2 percent to 4 percent.

If the tax preparer proudly claims no audited clients, be wary. Among the possible explanations, any of which should cause you to be uncomfortable in hiring such a preparer: He or she isn't telling you the truth, has prepared few returns, or is afraid of taking some legal deductions, so you'll probably overpay your taxes.

A tax preparer who has been in business for at least a couple of years will have gone through audits. Ask the preparer to explain his or her last two audits, what happened, and why. This explanation not only sheds light on a preparer's work with clients, but also on his or her ability to communicate in plain English.

How does your fee structure work?

Tax advisor fees, like attorney and financial planner fees, are all over the map — from $50 to $300 or more per hour. Many preparers simply quote you a total fee for preparation of your tax return.

Ultimately, the tax advisor charges you for time, so you should ask what the hourly billing rate is. If the advisor balks at answering this question, try asking what his or her fee is for a one-hour consultation. You may want a tax advisor to work on this basis if you've prepared your return yourself and want it reviewed as a quality-control check. You also may seek an hourly fee if you're on top of your tax preparation in general but have some very specific questions about an unusual or one-time event, such as the sale of your business.

Clarify whether the preparer's set fee includes follow-up questions that you may have during the year, or if this fee covers IRS audits on the return. Some accountants include these functions in their set fee, but others charge for everything on an as-needed basis. The advantage of the all-inclusive fee is that it removes the psychological obstacle of your feeling that the meter's running every time you call with a question. The drawback can be that you pay for additional services (time) that you may not need or use.

What qualifies you to be a tax advisor?

Tax advisors come with a variety of backgrounds. The more tax and business experience they have, the better. But don't be overly impressed with credentials. As we discuss in Chapter 2, tax advisors can earn certifications such as CPAs and EAs. Although gaining credentials takes time and work, these certifications are no guarantee that you get quality, cost-effective tax assistance or that you won't be overcharged.

Generally speaking, more years of experience are better than less, but don't rule out a newer advisor who lacks gray hair or who hasn't yet slogged through thousands of returns. Intelligence and training can easily make up for less experience.

Newer advisors also may charge less so they can build up their practices. Be sure, though, that you don't just focus on each preparer's hourly rate. Ask each practitioner that you interview how much total time he or she expects your tax return to take. Someone with a lower hourly fee can end up costing you more if he or she is slower than a more experienced and efficient preparer with a higher hourly rate.

Do you carry liability insurance?

If a tax advisor makes a major mistake or gives poor advice, you can lose thousands of dollars. The greater your income, assets, and the importance of your financial decisions, the more financial harm that can be done. We know that you aren't a litigious person, but your tax advisor needs to carry what's known as errors and omissions, or liability insurance. You can, of course, simply sue an uninsured advisor and hope the advisor has enough personal assets to cover a loss, but don't count on it. Besides, you'll have a much more difficult time getting due compensation that way!

You may also ask the advisor whether he or she has ever been sued and how the lawsuit turned out. It doesn't occur to most people to ask this type of question, so make sure that you tell your tax advisor that you're not out to strike it rich on a lawsuit! Another way to discover whether a tax advisor has gotten into hot water is by checking with appropriate professional organizations to which that preparer may belong. You can also check whether any complaints have been filed with your local Better Business Bureau (BBB), although this is far from a foolproof screening method. Most dissatisfied clients don't bother to register complaints with the BBB, and you should also know that the BBB is loath to retain complaints on file against companies who are members.

Can you provide references of clients similar to me?

You need to know that the tax advisor has handled cases and problems like yours. For example, if you're a small-business owner, ask to speak with other small-business owners. But don't be overly impressed by tax advisors who claim that they work mainly with one occupational group, such as physicians. Although there's value in understanding the nuances of a profession, tax advisors are ultimately generalists — as are the tax laws.

When all is said and done, make sure that you feel comfortable with a tax advisor. We're not suggesting that you evaluate an advisor the way you would a potential friend or spouse! But if you're feeling uneasy and can't understand what your tax advisor says to you in the early stages of your relationship, trust your instincts and continue your search. Remember that you can be your own best tax advisor — finding out the basics will pay you a lifetime of dividends and can save you tens of thousands of dollars in taxes and tax advisor fees!

Glossary

. . . .

*H*ere we provide a list of common tax-related terms that you'll find useful when preparing your taxes or speaking to a tax professional.

• *A* •

Accelerated Cost Recovery System (ACRS): A little tax history here. The ACRS method of depreciation lets you claim larger depreciation deductions for business property in the early years of ownership. It was replaced by the MACRS (Modified Accelerated Cost Recovery System), effective tax year 1987. (See *Modified ACRS.*)

accelerated depreciation: This depreciation method yields larger deduction amounts for you — as opposed to the straight-line depreciation method. Depreciation amounts are larger in the early years and lesser in the later years. (See *straight-line depreciation.*)

accrual method: This accounting method lets you report income in the year it has been earned, even if not yet received, and expenses when incurred, even if not yet paid. (See *cash method.*)

active participation: This term is used to indicate whether you're eligible to participate in your employer's retirement savings or pension plan. If you're eligible, then your ability to deduct a regular Individual Retirement Account (IRA) contribution is based on your income (actually, your adjusted gross income).

adjusted basis: The adjusted basis reflects your cost of property (see *basis*) plus the cost of improvements minus depreciation. You calculate your property's adjusted basis when you sell your property so that, for tax purposes, you can figure your profit or loss. If you acquire the property by inheritance, the property's adjusted basis is its fair market value on the deceased's date of death. If you acquire the property by gift, the property's adjusted basis is the donor's adjusted basis plus any gift tax paid by the donor on its transfer to the recipient.

adjusted gross income (AGI): AGI consists of all your income (including wages, salaries, tips, and taxable interest) minus allowable adjustments. You calculate your AGI before sub-tracting itemized deductions and personal exemptions. You arrive at this figure at the bottom of the front side of your Form 1040.

after-tax contributions: Some retirement plans allow you to contribute money that has already been taxed. Such contributions are known as after-tax contributions.

alimony: Payments to a divorced or separated spouse that meet a number of IRS require-ments and are then deductible by the payer and taxable to the recipient. Receiving alimony qualifies you to make an IRA contribution.

alternative minimum tax (AMT): AMT is a second federal tax system designed to prevent higher-income people from taking too many deductions and paying too little in taxes. Keep calculating!

amended return: Your chance to file another form — 1040X — within three years of the original return, correcting a mistake or making a change in your tax return for that year. Kind of like correcting an exam you've already turned in to the professor — neat, huh?

amortization: Similar to depreciation but relating to the deduction for using up intangible assets (such as goodwill). This is a way of writing off (depreciating) these assets over their projected lives.

annual gift tax exclusion: Each year, you may gift up to $12,000 per recipient to as many recipients as your heart desires. The gift isn't taxable to the recipient (also not tax-deductible to the donor, unless given to a qualifying charity).

annuity: An investment product that is essentially a contract backed by an insurance company, and is frequently purchased for retirement purposes. Its main benefit is that it allows your money to compound and grow until withdrawal without taxation. Selling annuities is a lucrative source of income for insurance agents and "financial planners" who work on commission, so don't buy one until you're sure that it makes sense for your situation.

assessment: An assessment of tax is a bill for additional tax made when a return is filed that shows a balance due or when the IRS determines, after reviewing your return, that you owe additional tax. Unless the collection of tax is in jeopardy (see *jeopardy assessment*) or a mathematical error has been made, the IRS can't collect an assessment until you have exhausted all your administrative and legal avenues. When the IRS assesses additional tax beyond the amount shown on the original return, it must send you a Statutory Notice of Deficiency. If you choose not to challenge this determination, the IRS may collect the amount of the assessment after 90 days (or 150 days if the notice is sent abroad).

asset: A property or investment, such as real estate, stock, mutual fund, equipment, and so on, that has monetary value that could be realized if sold.

at-risk rules: Rules that limit your loss deductions to the cash amount you have invested.

audit: IRS examination and inquisition, generally at the IRS offices, of your financial records that back up what you declare and claim on portions of, or your entire tax return. One of life's ten worst experiences.

Automated Collection System (ACS): The IRS's "collection agency." If, after receiving three notices generated by an IRS service center, you haven't paid what is owed, your delinquent account is sent to the ACS. The ACS has the authority to enter into an installment agreement, and its contact with you is exclusively by telephone (hence the automation portion of its name). If the ACS can't collect from you, a revenue officer at a district office takes over your account.

away from home: Specific IRS guidelines that determine your ability to deduct business travel expenses.

backup withholding: When you fail to give your Social Security or other Taxpayer Identification number to the person or organization that pays you interest, dividends, royalties, rents, or a consulting fee, or when you fail to furnish the payer with a statement that you aren't subject to backup withholding, the payer must withhold federal income tax at the rate of 20 percent of the income received. The IRS, for example, notifies the payers of interest and dividends to begin backup withholding when you fail to report and pay tax on interest and dividend income on your tax return.

bad debt: Money that you're owed that you probably won't get. May be tax-deductible.

bankruptcy: Legal action that stops IRS and other creditors' collection actions against you.

basis: The tax basis of property (such as stock and real estate) used for determining the gain or loss on its sale or for claiming a depreciation, casualty loss, or other tax deduction. The tax basis is usually the property's cost to you. (See also *adjusted basis.*)

below-market-rate loan: A loan generally made between family members or friends at an interest rate lower than comparable loans available from financial institutions. The party making the loan, if audited, may be forced to pay income tax on the extra loan income they should have been receiving.

beneficiaries: The people to whom you desire to leave your assets. For each retirement account, for example, you denote beneficiaries.

boot: A term used to describe the receipt of cash, or its equivalent, in the tax-free exchange of investment real estate (known as a 1031 or Starker exchange). A tax-free exchange of real estate allows you, subject to IRS guidelines, to avoid paying tax on your profit when selling a rental property by rolling over that profit into another rental property. Boot is taxable when you're doing such a tax-free exchange, so if you don't want to owe any tax from a tax-free exchange of real estate, don't receive any boot!

business interest: The tax deduction that businesses may take for interest paid on business loans.

business meal: The closest thing to a free lunch you'll get from the IRS. Fifty percent of the cost of IRS-allowable business meals is deductible.

business use (of an automobile): If you use your car for noncommuting business purposes, you may deduct the actual costs of usage or claim the standard mileage rate. If you work for an employer, you take this deduction on Schedule A (Itemized Deductions).

bypass trust: Also known as *credit shelter* or *exemption equivalent trust.* A trust designed to provide benefits to a surviving spouse, and increased shelter from estate taxes for more of your estate.

C Corporation: A business entity taxed according to the corporate, not individual, income tax rate schedule. Income, known as dividends, paid out to the corporation's shareholders is taxed on each shareholder's own tax return.

calendar year: A 12-month period ending on December 31. In contrast, some companies use a fiscal calendar that ends during another time of the year.

capital expenditures or expenses: Expenses that you may not immediately deduct but that you can depreciate over time by adding them to the basis of the property. For example, if you put a new roof on your investment real estate property, that expense is depreciated over time because the roof increases the usefulness/value of the property.

capital gain or loss: A taxable gain or loss effected through the sale of a property or financial asset, such as a stock, bond, or mutual fund held outside of a retirement account. The gain or loss is calculated by subtracting the adjusted basis from the sale price of the asset.

capital gains distribution: Taxable distribution by a mutual fund or a real estate investment trust (REIT) caused by securities that are sold at a profit. This distribution may be either short term (assets held a year or less) or long term (assets held more than 12 months).

capital loss carryover: If you sell stocks, bonds, or other securities with net losses totaling more than $3,000 in a year, for tax purposes you must "carry over" the losses in excess of $3,000 to the subsequent tax year(s). Only $3,000 may be taken as a tax loss on your tax return.

cash method: Business accounting method by which you report income when the income is actually received, and expenses when actually paid. This method gives you more control over when income and expenses are recognized for tax purposes than the accrual method. (See *accrual method.*)

casualty loss: A deductible loss resulting from an unexpected cause, such as an earthquake, fire, or flood. These losses on your personal income tax return are deductible on Schedule A to the extent that they exceed 10 percent of your AGI (after a $100 deductible).

charitable contribution: Allowable deduction taken on Schedule A for donation of cash or property to IRS-approved/qualified charities.

child and dependent care credit: Tax credit taken off Form 2441 for expenses you incur for the care of a dependent (a child under the age of 13, or someone who is physically or mentally handicapped) in order to allow you to work.

child support: Payment specifically designated under a divorce decree. Child support payments aren't tax-deductible.

The Code: The Internal Revenue Code, or IRC; the verbiage that makes up the wonderfully complex tax laws.

Cohan Rule: Based on an actual case that George M. Cohan won against the IRS in the 1920s, the Cohan Rule allows deductions based on estimates rather than receipts for certain, primarily smaller, expenses such as taxi fares, tips, and cleaning and maintenance costs.

Collection Information Statement (CIS): A detailed financial and income statement (Form 433-A and Form 433-B) required by individuals and businesses applying for an installment agreement to pay delinquent taxes over a period of time.

community property: Property equally owned by husband and wife for which each spouse must, for state income tax purposes, report one-half of the joint income. Community property states include Arizona, California, Idaho, Louisiana, Nevada, New Mexico, Texas, Washington, and Wisconsin.

consumer interest: The interest incurred on personal and consumer debt (such as credit cards and auto loans). This interest isn't tax-deductible.

correspondence audit: IRS audit conducted entirely by mail. (See *audit.*)

cost of goods sold: In businesses such as retailing and manufacturing, the term applies to the cost of products sold or manufactured. Cost of goods sold includes such items as raw materials, wholesale prices paid for finished goods, labor costs, and so on.

credit: A tax credit reduces your tax bill dollar-for-dollar.

credit for the elderly or the permanently and totally disabled: If you're 65 or older, or if you're disabled, you may be able to claim this credit, but don't count on it. This credit has stringent requirements.

credit shelter trust: See *bypass trust*.

declining-balance method: An aggressive depreciation method that allows faster writing off of business assets.

deduction: An expense you may subtract from your income so as to lower your taxable income. Examples include mortgage interest, property taxes (itemized deductions), and most retirement account contributions.

deficiency: The difference between the tax you originally reported as owing on your tax return and the amount of tax you actually owed as determined by the IRS. You may be notified by mail of additional tax that you owe, or this amount may be determined by an audit. (See *assessment*.)

defined-benefit plan: A company-based retirement plan that pays you a monthly income based on how long you worked (your years of service) for that company or nonprofit agency.

defined-contribution plan: Increasingly common type of company-based retirement plan, such as a 401(k) plan, whereby you contribute money into an individual account and the future value of that account depends on how well the investments you choose perform.

dependent: A person whom you support (such as a child) and whom you may claim as an exemption on your tax return, thus saving you tax dollars.

dependent-care credit: See child and dependent-care credit.

depletion: Deduction reflecting the decrease of a depletable natural resource, such as oil and gas, timber, minerals, and so on.

depreciation: Allowable tax deduction for writing off the cost of business assets, such as cars, computers, and cellular phones. Each type of property is depreciated over a certain, IRS-approved number of years. The term also applies to the allowable deduction for the wear and tear on investment real estate over time.

depreciation recapture: That portion of a capital gain attributable to depreciation taken during the years that the untaxed income sheltered by the depreciation deduction was taxed at ordinary income tax rates rather than the potentially more-favorable capital gains rates.

directly related meals and entertainment: Deductions you can take if you're entertaining clients immediately before, during, or after a business discussion.

dividend: Income from your stock and/or mutual fund holdings. For assets held outside retirement accounts or in tax-free money market and tax-free bond funds, dividends are taxable (although stock dividends are taxed at a lower rate than ordinary income).

dividend reinvestment plan: Plan by which you purchase additional shares of stock or mutual funds using dividends. Reinvestment doesn't impact whether or not these dividends are taxable.

double-declining-balance method: An aggressive depreciation method that allows for faster writing off of business assets.

earned income: Money that you receive for doing work. Earned income is taxable and qualifies you to make a retirement account contribution that may be tax-deductible.

earned income credit: If your income is in the lower income brackets (for example, federal 10 and 15 percent tax brackets), you may qualify for this special and not-so-small tax credit.

effective marginal tax rate: See *marginal tax rate.*

enrolled agent: Licensed tax preparer who can represent you before the IRS.

equity: The difference between the market value of an asset and the loan amount owed on that asset. For example, if you own real estate worth $225,000 and have a $100,000 mortgage outstanding on it, your equity is $125,000 ($225,000 − $100,000).

estate: The value, at the time of your death, of your assets minus your loans and liabilities. Estates in excess of certain amounts are taxable at the federal and state level (see Chapter 25).

estimated tax: Tax payments you make to the IRS either through regular payroll withholding or on a quarterly basis if you're self-employed or retired. For most people, these estimated tax payments must total at least 90 percent of their actual tax bill; otherwise, penalties and interest are incurred.

exemption: A personal deduction amount that you're allowed to deduct on your tax return for yourself and each of your dependents.

fair market value (FMV): The price at which an asset, such as stock or real estate, is being traded (that is, bought and sold) or is estimated to be worth by an independent, objective third party, such as an appraiser.

federal short-term rate: The interest rate that the IRS uses in computing interest owed on tax underpayments and overpayments. This rate is determined every calendar quarter by computing the average yield on U.S. Treasury bonds having a maturity of less than three years and adding 3 percent for tax underpayments and 2 percent for tax overpayments.

fiduciary: A person or organization (such as an executor, trustee, or administrator) responsible for managing assets for someone else.

field audit: An audit in which the IRS makes a house call, likely at your own business, to examine your records.

filing status: The applicable category, such as single, married filing jointly, married filing separately, head of household, and qualifying widow(er) with dependent child, that determines your tax rates.

fiscal year: Twelve-month accounting period for a business that may end on the last day of any month. Contrast with calendar year, which must end on December 31.

foreign tax credit: Put on your reading glasses to figure this credit. The instructions alone take the better part of a day to wade through. Applies to taxes paid to foreign countries. (This may apply to you — even if you didn't work overseas — if you own international mutual funds outside of a retirement account.)

401(k) plan: Type of retirement savings plan offered by many for-profit companies to their employees. Your contributions are exempt (yes!) from federal and state income taxes until you withdraw the funds, presumably in retirement.

403(b) plan: Similar to a 401(k) plan but for employees of nonprofit organizations.

GAO: General Accounting Office. Congress's auditing and investigation arm.

goodwill: Purchase price paid for a business in excess of the business's assets minus its liabilities (net worth). Goodwill is depreciated or amortized over the years.

gross income: Your total taxable income before subtracting deductions.

gross receipts: The total revenue received by a business before subtracting cost of goods sold, returns, and so on.

half-year convention: A tax law that specifies claiming half a year's worth of depreciation for assets the first year that those assets are used or placed in service in the business.

head of household: Filing status under which you're unmarried — or considered to be unmarried — and are paying for more than 50 percent of the household costs in the place where you live with a relative whom you can claim as a dependent. (Whew!)

hobby losses: Losses arising from enjoyable activities that aren't conducted for profit. These losses can't be used to offset or reduce other taxable income.

holding period: The period of time for which you hold an asset (from date purchased until date sold).

home equity loan: Mortgage loan that allows you to borrow against the equity in your home. Generally, interest on the amount borrowed, up to $100,000, is tax-deductible.

home office: Tax deductions are allowed if your home is your principal place of business. These deductions lead to a fair number of audits, so make sure that you're entitled to the deduction.

• I •

IDRS: Integrated Data Retrieval System. Computer system that allows IRS employees instantaneous visual access to a taxpayer's tax account information.

imputed interest: Interest amount considered to have been earned on certain debts whose interest rates are below the applicable federal rate — that is, the rate set by the law. For example, if you get a loan at, say, 3 percent, the IRS says, not surprisingly, this is a below-market interest rate.

incentive stock option: Option allows for key company employees to exercise the right to buy stock in the company, typically at an attractive price. As a company grows and prospers, these options can end up being a significant portion of an employee's total compensation. Tax on the profit on this stock isn't triggered until the stock is sold.

independent contractor: Status defined by (more!) IRS rules, allowing an employed person to be treated as self-employed. Among other criteria, self-employed people are expected to maintain their own work area, work for multiple employers, and have control over their work and hours. People who qualify are responsible for paying their own estimated taxes.

Individual Retirement Account (IRA): A retirement account into which anyone with sufficient employment income or alimony may contribute up to $4,000 per year. There are now two types of IRAs — regular and Roth. Contribution may or may not be tax-deductible on a regular IRA.

information release (IR): The IRS issues these releases to clarify a point of law or an IRS procedure.

information returns: IRS forms (such as 1099, W-2, 1065) that are required to be filed with the IRS by the payers of interest, dividends, pensions, and freelance income stating the amount of income that was paid to a taxpayer in a given year. The IRS uses this "information" to nail people who don't report all of their income.

installment agreement: An arrangement whereby an individual or business can pay delinquent taxes over a period of time. This agreement must be negotiated with the IRS.

installment sale: When property is sold and a portion of the sale price is paid in two different years, the profits from the sale may be taxable over a period of time as well.

intangible assets: Nonphysical property, such as patents and notes receivable. Compare to tangible assets.

Internal Revenue Service (IRS): A service or not, this is the U.S. Treasury agency that enforces the tax laws and collects taxes.

intestate: Means you die without a will. Dying intestate generally isn't a good idea because state law determines what happens to your worldly possessions and assets as well as who cares for your minor children.

investment interest: Yes, investments pay in more ways than one; among them is your ability to borrow against your securities in a (nonretirement) margin account and to claim the interest of that loan as a deduction. A margin account is simply a type of brokerage account in which you may borrow money from the brokerage firm against the value of your securities held in the brokerage account. These write-offs are limited to the amount of investment income you earn.

IRC: Internal Revenue Code of 1986.

IRM: Internal Revenue Manual. Procedural reference guide that IRS employees follow in administering the Internal Revenue Code.

IRS personnel: Revenue agents — that is, IRS employees assigned to the examination division of the IRS who are responsible for auditing tax returns. Revenue officers are responsible for collecting delinquent taxes.

itemized deductions: Expenditures such as mortgage interest, property taxes, state and local taxes, and so on that are deductible on Schedule A to the extent that they exceed your standard deduction.

• J •

jeopardy assessment: Has nothing to do with Alex Trebek or the game show. When the Commissioner of the Internal Revenue Service — or his or her delegate — believes that the collection of tax is in danger of not being collected at all, the IRS may bypass the normal assessment process as required by law and make an immediate assessment. A taxpayer may protest a jeopardy assessment administratively and by court action.

joint return: Filing status for legally married people. This is usually, but not always, cheaper than filing separate returns. In unusual cases where one spouse has high allowable deductions, filing as married-filing-separately may save the couple tax dollars. Filing individually may also make sense when marital problems cause a lack of trust in a spouse's keeping current with taxes.

joint tenants: A method of ownership of property. Each party is considered the co-owner of a one-half interest unless it is specifically stated otherwise. Creditors of one tenant may attach that tenant's interest. Either tenant or their creditors may petition a court to divide the property so it can be sold. (See also *tenants by the entirety.*)

• K •

Keogh plan: A retirement savings plan available to self-employed individuals, which allows for substantial tax-deductible contributions.

kiddie tax: The relatively low rate of tax on the first $1,700 of unearned income, such as interest and dividends from investments, for children under 18 years of age. Income higher than $1,700 for these children is taxed on the parent's income tax return.

• L •

levy (Notice of Levy): Means by which a delinquent taxpayer's employment income or property is seized in order to satisfy the amount of tax that is owed to the government. A levy isn't how you want to pay your back taxes.

lien for taxes: A legal claim attaching to property (including bank and other accounts) of an individual who is delinquent in tax payments. The filing of a lien prohibits the sale or transfer of the property without satisfying the amount of the lien.

like-kind exchange: A tax-free exchange of real estate. Normally when you sell an asset, such as stock and mutual funds, that has appreciated in value, you owe tax on the profits realized. As long as you comply with the specific IRS rules, you may defer paying tax on the profits from investment real estate if you purchase another property. These exchanges are called 1031 or Starker exchanges.

long-term capital gain or loss: Gain or loss on the sale or exchange of an asset held for more than 12 months. For your pleasure, the IRS makes you complete Schedule D to report these gains or losses.

lump-sum distribution: The entire amount in your employer's retirement plan that is paid to you within one tax year. Among the qualifications are reaching age 59½, having become disabled or passed away, having left the employer, and so on. Such distributions often may be rolled over into a retirement account so that tax owed on the distribution can be deferred.

• M •

marginal tax rate: Not all income is treated equally. In fact, the IRS tax laws treat your first dollars of taxable income differently than your last ones. Specifically, lower tax rates apply to lower income amounts. Your marginal tax rate is the combined federal and state tax rates that you paid on your highest or last dollars of earnings.

marital deduction: This deduction allows unlimited asset transfers from one spouse to another without having to pay any estate or gift taxes. If your spouse is a Scrooge or wants to leave someone else a lot of money, you're outta luck to take full advantage of this.

medical expense: A deduction you can take if you itemize your expenses on Schedule A, and your medical expenses exceed 7.5 percent of your AGI. You probably won't qualify, but checking it out may be worthwhile if you have a large amount of unreimbursed medical expenses.

miscellaneous itemized deduction: Expenses you can claim on Schedule A, such as job expenses, to the extent that they exceed 2 percent of your AGI.

Modified ACRS (MACRS): This term refers to the entire depreciation system, modified in 1986 by Congress. This depreciation is less favorable to businesses than the ACRS and stretches out the number of years during which business assets must be depreciated. (See *Accelerated Cost Recovery System.*)

money-purchase plan: A type of Keogh plan where your annual contribution is a fixed percentage of your self-employment income.

mortgage interest: A tax cut for you, unless the politicians in Congress take it away with a flat tax. Mortgage interest on your primary and secondary residence is deductible on the first $1 million of mortgage debt and $100,000 of home equity debt.

mutual fund: A professionally managed, diversified fund that enables you to pool your money with that of many other investors. The three major types of funds are money market (which are similar to savings accounts), bond, and stock.

• N •

negligence: Negligence is a failure to make a reasonable attempt to comply with the tax laws. That portion of a tax underpayment attributable to negligence is subject to the negligence penalty.

net income: Business income left over after all deductions and expenses.

net operating loss (NOL): A loss from your business that exceeds your other income for the year. NOLs may be carried back three years to offset prior years' taxable income and then, if losses still remain, may be forwarded for the next 15 years until they are used up. A taxpayer may elect to forgo the carryback and elect to carry the NOL forward to future years.

Nonresident alien: A person who is neither a U.S. citizen nor a permanent resident or green card holder. As far as the IRS is concerned, nonresident aliens usually must pay tax only on income from U.S. sources.

notice status: Reference to those taxpayers who are receiving tax notices demanding payment of unpaid taxes.

offer-in-compromise: A formal application that you, or your tax advisor acting on your behalf, make to the IRS requesting that it accept less than full payment for what you owe for taxes, interest, and penalties. Offers may be made if there is doubt as to either collectibility of the tax or liability for the tax.

office audit: This examination of your tax records takes place at a local IRS office. The most common type of audit.

ordinary income: Income, such as from employment or investment interest and dividends, that isn't derived from the sale or exchange of an asset. In other words, income other than that from capital gains.

original issue discount (OID): Debt instruments (that is, bonds) that don't pay interest but that should increase in value over time. The discounted price at which the bond is issued relative to its face value at maturity is considered taxable interest income to be reported on your tax return annually (if you hold the bond outside a retirement account).

partnership: An unincorporated business entity that isn't itself taxable. Instead, tax obligations lie with the individual partners to whom the business's net profit (revenue minus expenses) is distributed annually.

passive activity: A business deal or venture in which you're a silent partner (that is, not actively involved in the management of the venture). Losses from these passive activities are limited in their deductibility to offset income from other passive activities.

passive-activity interest: This interest isn't considered investment-interest expense. The cost of this interest for tax purposes can be deducted only from passive-activity income.

payroll withholding: Withholding of taxes from your paycheck that your employer should perform.

pension: See *defined-benefit plan*.

personal exemption: It's great to be alive! Even the IRS acknowledges that and allows you a deduction on your tax return for yourself and your dependents.

personal interest: See *consumer interest*.

personal property: Includes your boat, plane, and car, but not real estate. Taxes on personal property may be deductible if the assets are used for business purposes. Auto registration fees based on the value of your car and paid to your state are deductible on your personal tax return.

points: The generally deductible prepaid interest that a borrower pays to obtain a mortgage.

probate: The legal process for administering and implementing the directions in your will. Makes probate attorneys wealthy. Minimize their income and maximize your estate by investigating living trusts, which keep your nonretirement assets out of probate.

profit-sharing plan: Type of an employer Keogh plan where the annual contribution made to the plan for employees may vary from year to year as a percentage of the employer's profits or each individual employee's salary.

qualified plan: A government-approved retirement plan (such as a pension plan, Keogh plan, or employee stock ownership plan) that allows for the tax-deferred compounding of your investment dollars over the years until withdrawal.

qualifying widow(er): A special tax filing status that allows a surviving spouse with dependents to use the same tax rates applicable to joint filers in the two years following the year of the first spouse's death.

Real Estate Investment Trust (REIT): An investment similar to a mutual fund but that invests in real estate properties. Provides you the benefits of property ownership without the burden of landlording.

real property: Real estate, such as land and buildings.

refund: Great feeling to get money back, isn't it? In this case, though, the money was yours in the first place, and you gave the government too much of it and didn't figure it out until you filed your annual tax return! Take a look at adjusting your withholding (get a copy of Form W-4).

residential rental property: Investment real estate from which at least 80 percent of the total rental income comes from dwelling units. Such property that you own and purchased after May 12, 1993, is depreciated over 39 years.

revenue agents: IRS employees assigned to the Examination Division of the IRS who are responsible for auditing tax returns.

revenue officers: IRS collection agents in the IRS's Collection Division who are responsible for collecting delinquent taxes.

revocable trust: A trust you set up to keep your nonretirement assets out of probate. These trusts can be changed or ended if you so desire.

rollover: The term used to describe moving money from your employer's retirement plan, for example, into your own IRA. Just make sure that you never take personal possession of the money. If you do take possession of the money, your employer is required to withhold 20 percent for federal income tax.

royalty: You may not be a member of the nobility, but receiving income from the licensing or sale of intellectual and material property that you own, such as books, movies, patents, natural resources, and so on, is a nice way to make up for that. This income is taxable as ordinary income.

• S •

S Corporation: A business entity that enjoys the benefits, such as limited legal liability, of being incorporated, but the income from which is taxed on a person's individual income tax return.

salvage value: The estimated value of a depreciable asset at the end of its useful life.

Section 179 deduction: The IRS allows you to write off or deduct a certain amount a year for the cost of tangible business equipment (such as computers and office furniture) in the year it was placed in service.

self-employment tax: The Social Security and Medicare taxes paid by self-employed people. If you work for an employer, your employer pays half of these taxes. If you're self-employed, you get to deduct half of the total self-employment taxes you pay.

separate returns: Individual tax returns filed by married people who aren't filing jointly. Normally, filing separately when you're married doesn't make sense, because it leads to the payment of higher total taxes by the couple.

short-term capital gain or loss: The gain or loss that derives from selling or exchanging an asset, such as a stock, bond, mutual fund, or real estate, held for 12 months or less.

SIMPLE: A newer small-business retirement plan (see Chapter 20).

Simplified Employee Pension (SEP-IRA): An easily established retirement plan for self-employed individuals under which you can put away a significant portion of your income on a tax-deductible basis.

single: Required tax-filing status for a person with no dependents who is not legally married.

standard deduction: Rather than spelling out (itemizing) each individual deduction, the IRS offers you the option of taking a flat deduction amount that depends on your filing status. If you don't own real estate or pay a lot in state income taxes, odds are you'll take the standard deduction.

statute of limitations: The period beyond which the government may not assess or collect a tax. Unless waived in writing, no tax may be assessed after three years from the date a return was filed, nor may the tax be collected more than ten years after the assessment. From your perspective, no refund claims may be made after three years from the filing date or two years after the date the tax was paid, whichever is later.

straight-line depreciation: A method of depreciation in which the deduction is taken in equal amounts each year in the life of an asset.

surviving spouse: A special tax filing status that allows the widow or widower to file a joint income tax return in the year of his or her spouse's death.

• T •

tangible assets: Physical property or equipment such as computers, cars, manufacturing assembly-line equipment, and so on. Compare also to *intangible assets.*

tax account: Means by which the IRS records all tax information for a taxpayer. Every taxpayer is assigned a tax account under a Social Security or other Taxpayer Identification number.

tax deferral: The legally allowed delay in paying tax. For example, contributions to retirement accounts may grow and accumulate earnings, and the tax on these earnings is deferred until the money is withdrawn.

tax year: Usually a period of 12 months, beginning on January 1 and ending on December 31, for summarizing your income and expenses. Some businesses utilize tax years that start and end at some other time of the year, such as October 1 through September 30 or July 1 through June 30.

taxable income: The amount on which you actually pay tax. Not every dollar of your income is taxable. You are taxed on the amount left after having subtracted whatever deductions, exemptions, and credits apply from your AGI.

Taxpayer Bill of Rights: These may not be inalienable rights, but Congress rolled out this bill in 1988 to help you cope with the IRS.

Taxpayer Identification Number (TIN): For individuals, this number is their Social Security number; for businesses, it's the Employer Identification Number. A TIN is also issued to taxpayers who don't have or aren't qualified to have a Social Security number.

tax-sheltered annuity (TSA): Annuities (offered by insurance companies) that are specific to nonprofit organizations. TSAs offer tax incentives to save and invest for retirement; however, TSAs do carry higher fees than no-load (commission-free) mutual funds, which are a better alternative for nonprofit 403(b) programs.

tenants by the entirety: A method of recording the ownership of property where each party is considered to have an interest in the entire property. Only a husband and wife may hold property in this manner. Without the consent of both parties, a creditor of one can't attach or force the partitioning of the property so that a sale can be made. (See also *joint tenants.*)

tenants in common: Real estate ownership by two or more people; the share of property owned by one of the tenants goes into his or her estate upon his or her death.

Totten trust ("in trust for" account): Bank accounts you control during your lifetime but that, upon your death, go to a named beneficiary without having to go through probate.

trust: A legal arrangement that passes ownership of your assets to someone else. There are many types of trusts.

200 percent-declining-balance method: An aggressive, fast method of depreciating business assets.

• U •

unified estate and gift tax credit: A huge tax credit, worth hundreds of thousands of dollars in tax savings, that allows a person to pass substantial assets free of estate taxes on to others. Also known as the applicable credit.

useful life: The amount of time a depreciable asset is expected to be in business use.

• W •

waiver: A taxpayer's consent to give up a right possessed under the law. A taxpayer can waive or consent to extending the statute of limitations pertaining to when an assessment may be made and the time frame in which a tax may be collected. A taxpayer can also waive the right that a Statutory Notice of Deficiency be issued so that an immediate assessment may be made.

will: A legal document stating your wishes regarding your assets and care of your minor children and requiring that your wishes be heeded when you die.

withholding: Amount withheld during the tax year from your income as a prepayment of your tax liability.

• Z •

zero-coupon bond: This bond doesn't pay annual interest but is purchased at a discount to its face value, which is paid at maturity. This increased value over time represents income on which taxes must be paid for nonretirement account

Index

(continued)

liens and levies by IRS, 319, 323–326

life expectancy tables (IRS), 402

life insurance. *See also* insurance

advance payments made to terminally or chronically ill, 114

cash-value, 426, 468–469

certain payments as alimony, 125

dividends, 215

group premiums on Form W-2, 10, 89

as poor investment, 403, 462, 468, 469

taxability of death benefits, 107

taxable interest on dividends, 206

term, 468

Lifetime Learning Credit, 79, 148, 193, 210, 289–290, 455–459

LIFO method of inventory valuation, 222

limited liability companies (LLCs), 416

limited partnerships (LPs), 425–426, 447

Link2Gov Corp., 70

liquidation distributions, 214

listed property, 232–235

living trusts, 470–471

living wills, 470

load mutual funds, 427–428

loan brokers, 439

loan origination fees, 179

loans. *See also* debt

at below-market interest, 114, 211

calculating affordability of new home, 439

high cost for cars, 442

home equity, 178, 179, 439, 444, 459–460

home improvement, 178

interest-free, 211

refund anticipation, 61, 476–477

local income taxes, deductible, 175

lodging and meals. *See* travel expenses

long distance telephone calls, federal excise tax on, 69, 82, 157, 297

long-term capital gains and losses, 250–251, 256–259

long-term care insurance, 114, 124, 172

lottery winnings, 86, 114

Louis, Joe, 358

luxury car limits for depreciation deduction, 232–233, 236

• M •

machine work expenses (farms), 244

mailing returns, 323, 347–348

management fees, rental property-related, 275

marginal tax rate, 12–14

mark-to-market traders, capital gains and losses, 272

marriage penalty, 45–47, 50, 448

married—filing jointly

caution! choice as irreversible, 44, 48

AMT example, 145

brackets and rates for 2006, 13

choosing as filing status, 44–45

comparison to filing separately, 47

earned income credit, 155

earned income credit phaseout, 295

education credits, phaseouts, 289–290

exemptions and phaseout amounts, 140

income minimums by age, 59

Innocent Spouse Rule, 44, 324, 368–371, 372

IRA contribution deductibility limits and phaseouts, 129

marginal tax rates by state, 14–16

spouses who are aliens, 45

standard deduction amount, 163

standard deduction for over-65 or blind, 164

student loan interest deduction, 133

tax credit for IRA contributions, 386

tax rate schedules for 2006, 140

married—filing separately

AMT trigger amount, 146

choosing as filing status, 44–48

in community property states, 48

comparison to filing jointly, 47

exemptions and phase-out amounts, 140

income minimums by age, 59

IRA contribution deductibility limits and phaseouts, 129

spouses who are aliens, 45

standard deduction amount, 163–164

standard deduction for over-65 or blind, 164

tax rate schedules for 2006, 141

taxability of Social Security benefits, 113

Martindale-Hubbell attorney database, 359

material participation requirement, 219, 281

maximum loan charges, 179

meal and hotel allowance, 196–198

meals and lodging. *See* travel expenses

medical and dental expenses

deductibility as percent of AGI, 174

health insurance for self-employed, 120, 124

health insurance premiums, 172

home improvements, 174

list of deductible items, 167–168

not deductible, 170

nursing homes, 173–174

records or receipts for, 30

(continued)

BUSINESS, CAREERS & PERSONAL FINANCE

0-7645-5307-0

0-7645-5331-3 *†

Also available:

- Accounting For Dummies †
  0-7645-5314-3
- Business Plans Kit For Dummies †
  0-7645-5365-8
- Cover Letters For Dummies
  0-7645-5224-4
- Frugal Living For Dummies
  0-7645-5403-4
- Leadership For Dummies
  0-7645-5176-0
- Managing For Dummies
  0-7645-1771-6

- Marketing For Dummies
  0-7645-5600-2
- Personal Finance For Dummies *
  0-7645-2590-5
- Project Management For Dummies
  0-7645-5283-X
- Resumes For Dummies †
  0-7645-5471-9
- Selling For Dummies
  0-7645-5363-1
- Small Business Kit For Dummies *†
  0-7645-5093-4

HOME & BUSINESS COMPUTER BASICS

0-7645-4074-2

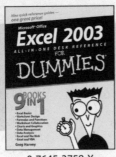

0-7645-3758-X

Also available:

- ACT! 6 For Dummies
  0-7645-2645-6
- iLife '04 All-in-One Desk Reference
  For Dummies
  0-7645-7347-0
- iPAQ For Dummies
  0-7645-6769-1
- Mac OS X Panther Timesaving
  Techniques For Dummies
  0-7645-5812-9
- Macs For Dummies
  0-7645-5656-8
- Microsoft Money 2004 For Dummies
  0-7645-4195-1

- Office 2003 All-in-One Desk Reference
  For Dummies
  0-7645-3883-7
- Outlook 2003 For Dummies
  0-7645-3759-8
- PCs For Dummies
  0-7645-4074-2
- TiVo For Dummies
  0-7645-6923-6
- Upgrading and Fixing PCs For Dummies
  0-7645-1665-5
- Windows XP Timesaving Techniques
  For Dummies
  0-7645-3748-2

FOOD, HOME, GARDEN, HOBBIES, MUSIC & PETS

0-7645-5295-3

0-7645-5232-5

Also available:

- Bass Guitar For Dummies
  0-7645-2487-9
- Diabetes Cookbook For Dummies
  0-7645-5230-9
- Gardening For Dummies *
  0-7645-5130-2
- Guitar For Dummies
  0-7645-5106-X
- Holiday Decorating For Dummies
  0-7645-2570-0
- Home Improvement All-in-One
  For Dummies
  0-7645-5680-0

- Knitting For Dummies
  0-7645-5395-X
- Piano For Dummies
  0-7645-5105-1
- Puppies For Dummies
  0-7645-5255-4
- Scrapbooking For Dummies
  0-7645-7208-3
- Senior Dogs For Dummies
  0-7645-5818-8
- Singing For Dummies
  0-7645-2475-5
- 30-Minute Meals For Dummies
  0-7645-2589-1

INTERNET & DIGITAL MEDIA

0-7645-1664-7

0-7645-6924-4

Also available:

- 2005 Online Shopping Directory
  For Dummies
  0-7645-7495-7
- CD & DVD Recording For Dummies
  0-7645-5956-7
- eBay For Dummies
  0-7645-5654-1
- Fighting Spam For Dummies
  0-7645-5965-6
- Genealogy Online For Dummies
  0-7645-5964-8
- Google For Dummies
  0-7645-4420-9

- Home Recording For Musicians
  For Dummies
  0-7645-1634-5
- The Internet For Dummies
  0-7645-4173-0
- iPod & iTunes For Dummies
  0-7645-7772-7
- Preventing Identity Theft For Dummies
  0-7645-7336-5
- Pro Tools All-in-One Desk Reference
  For Dummies
  0-7645-5714-9
- Roxio Easy Media Creator For Dummies
  0-7645-7131-1

* Separate Canadian edition also available

† Separate U.K. edition also available

Available wherever books are sold. For more information or to order direct: U.S. customers visit www.dummies.com or call 1-877-762-2974.
U.K. customers visit www.wileyeurope.com or call 0800 243407. Canadian customers visit www.wiley.ca or call 1-800-567-4797.

WILEY

SPORTS, FITNESS, PARENTING, RELIGION & SPIRITUALITY

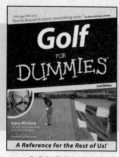

0-7645-5146-9

0-7645-5418-2

Also available:

- Adoption For Dummies
  0-7645-5488-3
- Basketball For Dummies
  0-7645-5248-1
- The Bible For Dummies
  0-7645-5296-1
- Buddhism For Dummies
  0-7645-5359-3
- Catholicism For Dummies
  0-7645-5391-7
- Hockey For Dummies
  0-7645-5228-7

- Judaism For Dummies
  0-7645-5299-6
- Martial Arts For Dummies
  0-7645-5358-5
- Pilates For Dummies
  0-7645-5397-6
- Religion For Dummies
  0-7645-5264-3
- Teaching Kids to Read For Dummies
  0-7645-4043-2
- Weight Training For Dummies
  0-7645-5168-X
- Yoga For Dummies
  0-7645-5117-5

TRAVEL

0-7645-5438-7

0-7645-5453-0

Also available:

- Alaska For Dummies
  0-7645-1761-9
- Arizona For Dummies
  0-7645-6938-4
- Cancún and the Yucatán For Dummies
  0-7645-2437-2
- Cruise Vacations For Dummies
  0-7645-6941-4
- Europe For Dummies
  0-7645-5456-5
- Ireland For Dummies
  0-7645-5455-7

- Las Vegas For Dummies
  0-7645-5448-4
- London For Dummies
  0-7645-4277-X
- New York City For Dummies
  0-7645-6945-7
- Paris For Dummies
  0-7645-5494-8
- RV Vacations For Dummies
  0-7645-5443-3
- Walt Disney World & Orlando For Dummies
  0-7645-6943-0

GRAPHICS, DESIGN & WEB DEVELOPMENT

0-7645-4345-8

0-7645-5589-8

Also available:

- Adobe Acrobat 6 PDF For Dummies
  0-7645-3760-1
- Building a Web Site For Dummies
  0-7645-7144-3
- Dreamweaver MX 2004 For Dummies
  0-7645-4342-3
- FrontPage 2003 For Dummies
  0-7645-3882-9
- HTML 4 For Dummies
  0-7645-1995-6
- Illustrator CS For Dummies
  0-7645-4084-X

- Macromedia Flash MX 2004 For Dummies
  0-7645-4358-X
- Photoshop 7 All-in-One Desk Reference
  For Dummies
  0-7645-1667-1
- Photoshop CS Timesaving Techniques
  For Dummies
  0-7645-6782-9
- PHP 5 For Dummies
  0-7645-4166-8
- PowerPoint 2003 For Dummies
  0-7645-3908-6
- QuarkXPress 6 For Dummies
  0-7645-2593-X

NETWORKING, SECURITY, PROGRAMMING & DATABASES

0-7645-6852-3

0-7645-5784-X

Also available:

- A+ Certification For Dummies
  0-7645-4187-0
- Access 2003 All-in-One Desk Reference
  For Dummies
  0-7645-3988-4
- Beginning Programming For Dummies
  0-7645-4997-9
- C For Dummies
  0-7645-7068-4
- Firewalls For Dummies
  0-7645-4048-3
- Home Networking For Dummies
  0-7645-42796

- Network Security For Dummies
  0-7645-1679-5
- Networking For Dummies
  0-7645-1677-9
- TCP/IP For Dummies
  0-7645-1760-0
- VBA For Dummies
  0-7645-3989-2
- Wireless All In-One Desk Reference
  For Dummies
  0-7645-7496-5
- Wireless Home Networking For Dummies
  0-7645-3910-8

HEALTH & SELF-HELP

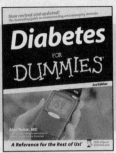

0-7645-6820-5 *†

0-7645-2566-2

Also available:
- Alzheimer's For Dummies
  0-7645-3899-3
- Asthma For Dummies
  0-7645-4233-8
- Controlling Cholesterol For Dummies
  0-7645-5440-9
- Depression For Dummies
  0-7645-3900-0
- Dieting For Dummies
  0-7645-4149-8
- Fertility For Dummies
  0-7645-2549-2
- Fibromyalgia For Dummies
  0-7645-5441-7

- Improving Your Memory For Dummies
  0-7645-5435-2
- Pregnancy For Dummies †
  0-7645-4483-7
- Quitting Smoking For Dummies
  0-7645-2629-4
- Relationships For Dummies
  0-7645-5384-4
- Thyroid For Dummies
  0-7645-5385-2

EDUCATION, HISTORY, REFERENCE & TEST PREPARATION

0-7645-5194-9

0-7645-4186-2

Also available:
- Algebra For Dummies
  0-7645-5325-9
- British History For Dummies
  0-7645-7021-8
- Calculus For Dummies
  0-7645-2498-4
- English Grammar For Dummies
  0-7645-5322-4
- Forensics For Dummies
  0-7645-5580-4
- The GMAT For Dummies
  0-7645-5251-1
- Inglés Para Dummies
  0-7645-5427-1

- Italian For Dummies
  0-7645-5196-5
- Latin For Dummies
  0-7645-5431-X
- Lewis & Clark For Dummies
  0-7645-2545-X
- Research Papers For Dummies
  0-7645-5426-3
- The SAT I For Dummies
  0-7645-7193-1
- Science Fair Projects For Dummies
  0-7645-5460-3
- U.S. History For Dummies
  0-7645-5249-X

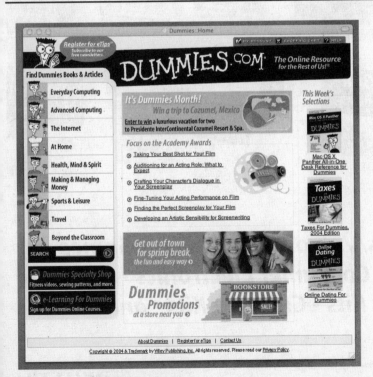

Get smart @ dummies.com®

- Find a full list of Dummies titles
- Look into loads of FREE on-site articles
- Sign up for FREE eTips e-mailed to you weekly
- See what other products carry the Dummies name
- Shop directly from the Dummies bookstore
- Enter to win new prizes every month!

* Separate Canadian edition also available

† Separate U.K. edition also available

Available wherever books are sold. For more information or to order direct: U.S. customers visit www.dummies.com or call 1-877-762-2974.
U.K. customers visit www.wileyeurope.com or call 0800 243407. Canadian customers visit www.wiley.ca or call 1-800-567-4797.